entertaining doesn't have to be stressful. It should be fun and fuss-free. Which is why Donna Hay has put together this collection of simple menus for truly instant entertaining. So no matter what the occasion, entertaining has just become a whole lot easier.

"If you are anything like me – almost always hungry, almost always pressed for time, in the market for a fresh idea and absolutely always put off by the daunting complexity of chefs' recipes – Donna Hay is for you ... she always saves time and never short-changes me on flavour."

R W APPLE, JR, FOOD CRITIC FOR *THE NEW YORK TIMES*

instant
entertaining

thank you

It seemed like such a great idea to turn my home kitchen into a test kitchen and the back deck of my house into a photography studio so I could stay at home with my newborn son Tom while doing this book. After all, what better way to tell if a recipe is truly instant than while juggling a baby, a three-year-old, calls from the magazine office and reviewing samples for my new home range? It took extra effort from all involved, whose job descriptions included some baby- and little-boy-care from time to time. For their extra effort, I will always be truly grateful. Very big thank yous to the following amazing people: Con Poulos, so talented, so passionate, so patient. You have that rare ability of being truly creative with beautiful eye for detail. I can't imagine what my working life would be with out you. Jane Collings, the most calm, even-tempered person I have ever met – if only I could be more like you. Thanks for your contribution to testing all the recipes, your ideas, shopping trips and playtime with my children – they are hoping you'll never leave. Ann Gordon, thanks for rocking baby Kit while scanning, designing and correcting proofs. Kylie Imeson, editor, champion food tester and source of much amusement. Thanks for cleaning up my recipes and for keeping our spirits light in times of high-stress deadlines. Amelia McFarlane for the gathering of props. Thank you also to the following people: Danielle Bighetti, our nanny, for surviving the crazy house. Jana Frawley and all the staff at *donna hay magazine*. Phil Barker, Chuck Smeeton and Fiona Nillson at News Magazines. Jane Friedman, Brian Murray, Shona Martyn, Jim Demetriou, Amruta Slee, Kylie Mason and Jill Donald from HarperCollins. Thank you to our produce suppliers – Farm Fresh Foods Paddington, Fratelli Fresh and Demcos Seafood – prop suppliers – The Bay Tree, beclau, T2, bodum, Provence, Design Mode International, Michael Greene Antiques, Tiffany & Co., F Mayer Imports, VnR Australia for The Love Plates range, Georg Jensen, hwi Homewares, Magis, Royal Doulton, rhubarb, Cranfields, Waterford Wedgwood, Francalia, Mud Australia – and kitchen suppliers – Smeg and Sunbeam. Love to friends and colleagues for their moments of inspiration and support: Jo from Babybliss, Nicky, Sibella, Brooke, Chris Jones, Marion Joyce and Roger. And also thank you to my wonderful, supportive mother, father and family. Finally, a huge thank you to my partner, Bill, and sons Angus and Tom.

Fourth Estate

An imprint of HarperCollins*Publishers*

First published in Great Britain in 2006
by Fourth Estate an imprint of HarperCollins*Publishers*

HarperCollins*Publishers*
25 Ryde Road, Pymble, Sydney, NSW 2073, Australia
31 View Road, Glenfield, Auckland 10, New Zealand
77–85 Fulham Palace Road, London W6 8JB, United Kingdom
2 Bloor Street East, 20th Floor, Toronto, Ontario M4W1A8, Canada
10 East 53rd Street, New York, NY 10022, USA

INSTANT ENTERTAINING copyright © Donna Hay 2006
Design copyright © Donna Hay 2006
Photographs copyright © Con Poulos 2006

Art direction: Ann Gordon
Editor: Kylie Imeson
Food editor: Jane Collings
The right of Donna Hay and Con Poulos to be identified as the author and photographer of this work has been asserted under the *Copyright Amendment (Moral Rights) Act 2000*.

Cover: Parmesan Wafer Salad, see page 14.

Reproduction by Graphic Print Group, Adelaide, Australia.
Produced in Hong Kong by Phoenix Offset on 157gsm Chinese Matt Art.
Printed in China.

ISBN 0007240945
ISBN 9780007240944

A catalogue record for this book is available from the British Library.

HarperCollins books may be purchased for educational, business or sales promotional use. For information in Great Britain, please write to the Special Markets Department of HarperCollins.

instant entertaining

donna hay

photography by con poulos

FOURTH ESTATE

contents

introduction 6

1 weeknights 8

2 saturday night 40

3 sunday lunch 72

4 special occasion 104

5 barbecues + brunch 148

glossary 180

conversion chart 187

index 188

introduction

One of my favourite things to do is sit around the table with family and friends, watching them enjoy great food, wine and conversation. It's what memories are made of. But we all lead busy lives and sometimes the thought of cooking for twelve, six or even two can be a little daunting. So that's why I've put together this collection of simple but special recipes that will make your lunch, dinner party or barbecue a memorable occasion for all the right reasons. With this book, entertaining is no longer stressful, it's a pleasure. Each menu, including starter, main, side and dessert, is clearly presented so you can choose which one suits. And it's not just the food, each chapter has simple style ideas that can be done in seconds – the perfect finishing touch for your table. So pick a menu, invite your guests and have fun entertaining.

weeknights

weeknights
Having people over for dinner during the week doesn't have to be a big production. With just a little effort, you'll have an impressive dinner to serve in no time. So invite your friends this week, life's too short to only entertain on the weekends.

EASY ITALIAN
starter parmesan wafer salad
main veal with olives and pine nuts
side crispy roast potatoes
dessert roasted peach bruschetta

ASIAN FEAST
starter sesame salt sugar snap peas
main wok-fried salt and pepper chicken
side peanut and coriander noodles
dessert coconut and lime ice-cream sandwiches

BISTRO BASICS
starter asparagus with simple lemon hollandaise
main garlic butter steaks
dessert molten chocolate cakes

LAST-MINUTE DINNER
starter haloumi in vine leaves
main chilli, garlic and lemon chicken
dessert ice-cream tiramisu

GREEK INSPIRED
starter seared fetta salad
main oregano roast lamb
side dill potatoes
dessert lemon yoghurt panna cotta

SUMMER NIGHT
starter peaches wrapped in prosciutto
main lemon, ricotta and pea pasta
dessert strawberry shortcakes

EASY ITALIAN

starter
parmesan wafer salad

main
veal with olives and pine nuts

side
crispy roast potatoes

dessert
roasted peach bruschetta

parmesan wafer salad

veal with olives and pine nuts + crispy roast potatoes

parmesan wafer salad

1 cup grated parmesan cheese
2 red apples, thinly sliced
80g (3 oz) rocket (arugula) leaves
1½ tablespoons balsamic vinegar*
1 tablespoon olive oil
sea salt and cracked black pepper
150g (5 oz) goat's cheese

Preheat the oven to 180°C (355°F). Arrange 8 x 1½
tablespoons of parmesan in circles on a baking tray lined
with non-stick baking paper and bake for 10 minutes or until
crispy. Set aside to cool. Toss the apple and rocket in the
combined vinegar, oil, salt and pepper. Arrange on serving
plates with the goat's cheese and parmesan wafers. Serves 4.

veal with olives and pine nuts

⅔ cup pine nuts, toasted
8 black olives, pitted and chopped
1 cup flat-leaf parsley leaves
2 tablespoons lemon juice
sea salt and cracked black pepper
plain (all-purpose) flour for dusting
8 x 100g (3½ oz) veal schnitzel steaks
80g (3 oz) butter

Combine the pine nuts, olives, parsley, lemon juice, salt and
pepper and set aside. Place the flour in a shallow dish. Press
the veal into the flour to coat and shake off excess. Place
the butter in a frying pan over high heat and melt. Add half
the veal and cook for 1 minute each side or until cooked to
your liking. Repeat with the remaining veal. Place the veal on
serving plates, top with the pine nut mixture and drizzle with
the pan juices. Serve with the crispy roast potatoes. Serves 4.

crispy roast potatoes

190g (6½ oz) roasting potatoes*, peeled and chopped
¼ cup (2 fl oz) olive oil
1 tablespoon rosemary leaves
1 tablespoon sage leaves
sea salt

Preheat the oven to 200°C (390°F). Pat the potatoes dry with
a tea towel, place in a baking dish lined with non-stick baking
paper and toss with the oil, rosemary, sage and salt. Roast
for 45–50 minutes or until cooked through and golden. Serve
with the veal with olives and pine nuts. Serves 4.

roasted peach bruschetta

4 slices wood-fired or crusty bread
soft butter for spreading
¼ cup caster (superfine) sugar
2–3 peaches, stones removed and thickly sliced

Preheat the oven to 200°C (390°F). Spread both sides of the
bread with the butter and place on a baking tray lined with
non-stick baking paper. Sprinkle each slice with half the sugar
and top generously with the peach. Sprinkle with the
remaining sugar and bake for 20 minutes or until the bread is
crisp and the peaches are lightly golden. Serve with thick
(double) cream or vanilla bean ice-cream. Serves 4.

roasted peach bruschetta

ASIAN FEAST

starter

sesame salt sugar snap peas

main

wok-fried salt and pepper chicken

side

peanut and coriander noodles

dessert

coconut and lime ice-cream sandwiches

sesame salt sugar snap peas

wok-fried salt and pepper chicken + peanut and coriander noodles

sesame salt sugar snap peas

500g (1 lb) sugar snap peas, trimmed
2 teaspoons sesame oil
¼ cup (2 fl oz) lemon juice
1 tablespoon sesame seeds, toasted
sea salt

Steam the sugar snap peas over boiling water for 1–2 minutes or until tender and bright green. Toss with the sesame oil, lemon juice, sesame seeds and salt and serve warm as a snack with drinks. Serves 4.

wok-fried salt and pepper chicken

1 tablespoon flaked sea salt
2 teaspoons finely cracked szechwan* or black peppercorns
2 large mild red chillies, seeded and chopped
1 teaspoon chinese five-spice powder*
4 chicken breast fillets, trimmed and quartered
1 tablespoon vegetable oil
400g (14 oz) broccolini*, trimmed and halved

Combine the salt, szechwan pepper, chilli and five-spice powder in a bowl. Toss the chicken in the spice mixture to coat. Heat half the oil in a wok or large frying pan over high heat. Add the half the chicken and cook, stirring occasionally, for 7 minutes or until cooked through. Remove from the pan and keep warm. Repeat with the remaining oil and chicken. Add the broccolini to the pan for the last 4–5 minutes. To serve, place the chicken and broccolini on a serving plate with the peanut and coriander noodles. Serves 4.

peanut and coriander noodles

375g (13 oz) dry rice noodles
2 tablespoons vegetable oil
1 cup chopped unsalted roasted peanuts
2 large red chillies, seeded and chopped
1 tablespoon grated ginger
6 green onions (scallions), sliced
1½ tablespoons fish sauce*
2 tablespoons lime juice
1 cup mint leaves
1 cup coriander (cilantro) leaves

Soak the noodles in boiling water for 5 minutes. Drain. Heat the oil in a frying pan or wok over high heat. Add the peanuts, chilli and ginger and cook for 2–3 minutes or until the peanuts are golden. Toss the peanut mixture with the noodles, green onions, fish sauce, lime juice, mint and coriander. Serve with the wok-fried salt and pepper chicken. Serves 4.

coconut and lime ice-cream sandwiches

4 scoops vanilla bean ice-cream
8 thin store-bought sweet biscuits or vanilla snap biscuits*
1 cup flaked coconut, toasted
1 tablespoon finely grated lime rind

Place the ice-cream on half of the biscuits. Combine the coconut and lime rind and sprinkle some of it on top of the ice-cream. Place the remaining coconut mixture on a flat plate. Top the ice-cream with the remaining biscuits and roll the sides in the coconut mixture. Serve immediately. Serves 4.

coconut and lime ice-cream sandwiches

BISTRO BASICS

starter

asparagus with simple
lemon hollandaise

main

garlic butter steaks

dessert

molten chocolate cakes

asparagus with simple lemon hollandaise

garlic butter steaks

asparagus with simple lemon hollandaise

500g (1 lb) asparagus, trimmed
rocket (arugula) to serve
cracked black pepper
simple lemon hollandaise
125g (4 oz) butter
1 tablespoon lemon juice
3 egg yolks
sea salt

Steam the asparagus until just tender, set aside and keep warm. To make the simple lemon hollandaise, place the butter and lemon juice in a saucepan over low–medium heat until bubbling. Place the egg yolks in a blender and with the motor running on high, slowly add the hot butter mixture and continue to blend until thick. Stir though the salt. To serve, place the asparagus on serving plates, spoon over the simple lemon hollandaise and serve with the rocket and pepper. Serves 4.

garlic butter steaks

80g (3 oz) butter
2 tablespoons olive oil
2 teaspoons dijon mustard
1 clove garlic, crushed
sea salt and cracked black pepper
4 flat (field) mushrooms
8 x 75g (3 oz) thin boneless sirloin or fillet steaks, fat removed
2 cups baby spinach leaves, wilted

Combine the butter, oil, mustard, garlic, salt and pepper in a bowl. Heat a large frying pan over high heat. Brush the mushrooms with the butter mixture and cook for 2 minutes each side or until cooked. Remove from the pan and keep warm. Brush the steaks with the butter mixture and cook for 2 minutes each side or until cooked to your liking. Remove from the pan and keep warm. Add the remaining butter mixture to the pan and heat for 30 seconds or until warm. Place the spinach on serving plates and top with the steaks and mushrooms and pour over the butter mixture. Serves 4.

molten chocolate cakes

¼ cup plain (all-purpose) flour, sifted
⅓ cup icing (confectioner's) sugar, sifted
¾ cup almond meal* (ground almonds)
2 egg whites, beaten
80g (3 oz) butter, melted
160g (6 oz) dark chocolate, melted
4 x 10g (⅓ oz) squares dark chocolate
raspberries to serve

Preheat the oven to 150°C (300°F). Place the flour, sugar, almond meal, egg whites, butter and chocolate in a bowl and mix well to combine. Spoon half the mixture into 4 x ½ cup (4 fl oz) capacity lightly greased ovenproof dishes. Place the chocolate squares on top of the mixture and top with remaining the mixture. Bake for 20 minutes or until cooked but gooey in the middle. Stand in the dish for 5 minutes before turning out. Serve with the raspberries. Serves 4.

An impressive dessert that is easy and quick to make – that's exactly what the molten chocolate cakes are. The chocolate centre stays soft for around an hour after baking. The cakes can still be made ahead of time, simply put them in the microwave for a few seconds on medium–high or place them on serving plates in a 150°C (300°F) oven for a few minutes to soften the centres again.

molten chocolate cakes

LAST-MINUTE DINNER

starter
haloumi in vine leaves

main
chilli, garlic and lemon chicken

dessert
ice-cream tiramisu

haloumi in vine leaves

chilli, garlic and lemon chicken

haloumi in vine leaves

4 large vine leaves* in brine, rinsed and dried
olive oil for brushing
250g (8 oz) haloumi cheese*, sliced into four
2 tablespoons oregano leaves
2 tablespoons finely grated lemon rind
cracked black pepper
2 oxheart (beef steak) tomatoes*, sliced
rocket (arugula) leaves to serve

Preheat the oven to 180°C (355°F). Brush the leaves with the oil. Place a slice of haloumi on each leaf, sprinkle with the oregano, lemon rind and pepper. Fold the leaf around the haloumi to enclose. Place on a baking tray lined with non-stick baking paper and bake for 10 minutes or until the haloumi is melted. Serve warm with the tomatoes and rocket. Serves 4.

chilli, garlic and lemon chicken

1 tablespoon olive oil
1 tablespoon sage leaves
2 tablespoons salted capers*, rinsed and dried
2 cloves garlic, sliced
1 large mild red chilli, chopped
1 tablespoon shredded lemon rind
1 tablespoon olive oil, extra
4 chicken breast fillets, cut into thirds
steamed green beans to serve
lemon wedges to serve

Heat the oil in a frying pan over medium–high heat. Add the sage, capers, garlic, chilli and lemon rind and cook for 2 minutes or until fragrant. Remove from the pan and set aside. Heat the extra oil in the pan. Add the chicken and cook for 3–4 minutes each side or until cooked through. Place on serving plates and top with the caper mixture. Serve with the green beans and lemon wedges. Serves 4.

ice-cream tiramisu

2 tablespoons espresso coffee
¼ cup (2 fl oz) coffee liqueur
8 small store-bought sponge finger (savoiardi) biscuits*
4 large scoops vanilla bean ice-cream
chocolate flakes to serve

Combine the espresso and liqueur. Place two biscuits on each serving plate, spoon over some of the espresso mixture and top with the ice-cream. Spoon over the remaining espresso mixture, sprinkle with the chocolate flakes and serve. Serves 4.

This is the ideal last-minute dinner menu as many of the ingredients can be swapped for whatever is in the fridge and pantry or available at the corner store. Use fetta or goat's cheese instead of the haloumi, and swap the chicken for firm white fish fillets*. For the dessert, use any flavour ice-cream available. If there's no coffee liqueur in the liquor cabinet, add a little sugar to the espresso instead.

ice-cream tiramisu

GREEK INSPIRED

starter

seared fetta salad

main

oregano roast lamb

side

dill potatoes

dessert

lemon yoghurt panna cotta

seared fetta salad

oregano roast lamb + dill potatoes

seared fetta salad

250g (8 oz) firm fetta cheese, quartered
olive oil for brushing
2 cucumbers, seeded and chopped lengthwise
2 tomatoes*, thickly sliced
½ cup chopped flat-leaf parsley leaves
cracked black pepper
olive oil, extra, for drizzling
lemon wedges to serve

Heat a non-stick frying pan over high heat. Pat the fetta dry
with absorbent paper, brush with the oil and place in the pan.
Cook for 1 minute each side or until golden. To serve, arrange
the cucumbers, tomato and parsley on serving plates. Top with
the fetta, sprinkle with the pepper and drizzle with the extra
oil. Serve with the lemon. Serves 4.

oregano roast lamb

650g (21 oz) boneless lamb backstrap, trimmed
sea salt and cracked black pepper
1 bunch oregano
olive oil to drizzle
¼ cup honey
¼ cup dijon mustard

Preheat the oven to 200°C (390°F). Rub the lamb with the
salt and pepper. Separate the oregano into small sprigs and tie
to the lamb with kitchen string. Place on a baking tray lined
with non-stick baking paper and drizzle with the oil. Roast for
10 minutes or until cooked to your liking. Mix the honey and
mustard and place in a small serving bowl. Serve with the
lamb and the dill potatoes. Serves 4.

dill potatoes

850g (28 oz) kipfler (fingerling) potatoes, sliced,
    cooked and cooled
½ red onion, finely sliced
¼ cup roughly chopped dill
½ cup flat-leaf parsley leaves
3 tablespoons white wine vinegar*
1 tablespoon sugar
2 tablespoons fruity olive oil
1 tablespoon dijon mustard
sea salt and cracked black pepper

Place the potato, onion, dill and parsley in a serving bowl
and toss to combine. Whisk together the vinegar, sugar,
oil, mustard, salt and pepper and pour over the salad and
toss to combine. Serve immediately with the oregano roast
lamb. Serves 4.

lemon yoghurt panna cotta

1 cup (8 fl oz) (single or pouring) cream*
½ cup (4 fl oz) milk
2 teaspoons powdered gelatine
2 tablespoons water
½ cup icing (confectioner's) sugar, sifted
1 teaspoon finely grated lemon rind
2 tablespoons lemon juice
¾ cup thick natural yoghurt
blueberries to serve

Place the cream and milk in small saucepan over low–medium
heat and simmer for 5–6 minutes. Combine the gelatine and
water and set aside for 5 minutes. Remove the cream mixture
from the heat, add the icing sugar and stir until dissolved. Add
the gelatine mixture, lemon rind and lemon juice and stir until
combined. Whisk in the yoghurt. Pour into 4 x ½ cup (4 fl oz)
capacity cups and refrigerate for 4 hours or until firm. Serve
with the blueberries. Serves 4.

lemon yoghurt panna cotta

SUMMER NIGHT

starter

peaches wrapped in prosciutto

main

lemon, ricotta and pea pasta

dessert

strawberry shortcakes

peaches wrapped in prosciutto

lemon, ricotta and pea pasta

peaches wrapped in prosciutto

2 peaches
6 slices prosciutto*, halved
80g (3 oz) rocket (arugula) or mixed lettuce or salad leaves
½ cup (4 fl oz) balsamic vinegar*
¼ cup brown sugar
cracked black pepper

Cut each peach into six wedges and wrap in the prosciutto.
Place on serving plates with the rocket. Place the vinegar and
sugar into a non-stick frying pan over high heat and boil until
thickened. Cool slightly, spoon over the peaches, sprinkle with
the pepper and serve. Serves 4.

lemon, ricotta and pea pasta

400g (14 oz) pappardelle or wide ribbon pasta
¼ cup (2 fl oz) lemon juice
3 tablespoons olive oil
1 cup cooked green peas
½ cup sliced mint leaves
sea salt and cracked black pepper
500g (1 lb) fresh ricotta cheese
grated parmesan cheese to serve

Place the pasta in a large saucepan of salted boiling water and
cook for 10–12 minutes or until al dente. Drain and return to
the pan. Toss the pasta with the lemon juice, oil, peas, mint,
salt and pepper. Add the ricotta and mix gently. Spoon onto
serving plates and top with the parmesan. Serves 4.

strawberry shortcakes

2 x 250g (8 oz) punnets strawberries, hulled and halved
¼ cup caster (superfine) sugar
1 teaspoon vanilla extract
8 store-bought shortbread biscuits
250g (8 oz) mascarpone*
¼ cup (2 fl oz) (single or pouring) cream*
1 tablespoon caster (superfine) sugar, extra

Place the strawberries, sugar and vanilla in a large non-stick
frying pan over high heat. Cook for 1–2 minutes or until the
sugar has melted and the strawberries have softened slightly.
Set aside to cool. Whisk together the mascarpone, cream and
extra sugar until smooth. Place half the biscuits in the base
of serving bowls or on serving plates. Spoon the mascarpone
mixture onto the biscuits and top with the strawberry mixture
and remaining biscuits. Serves 4.

Everyone needs a stand-by, done-in-minutes
dessert recipe and these strawberry shortcakes
are it. If strawberries aren't in season, use
sliced figs, nectarines, apricots or soft pears.
Otherwise use fresh raspberries.

strawberry shortcakes

style

affogato flavours

Affogato is a shot of espresso coffee poured over a scoop of vanilla ice-cream. For something different, serve it with chocolate, espresso, toffee or caramel ice-cream. Ask your guests which flavour they would prefer, scoop it into a serving glass, serve it with a small glass of espresso and a spoon. Serve affogato instead of or after dessert.

sweet centre

Dessert is made extra-simple and super-quick with these ice-cream filled brioches. Cut circles out of the tops of each brioche and remove some of the middle. Fill the hole with a scoop of your favourite ice-cream and serve immediately. They are an ideal dessert to serve at a cocktail or drinks party. If you can't find brioche, use plain, sweet buns.

ice-cream bar

Make a self-serve ice-cream bar for your guests. Purchase tubs of ice-cream in assorted flavours, then chop up different chocolates and sweets so everyone can add what they like to their favourite ice-cream. Use chocolate-covered honeycomb, malt balls and coconut. You can also put out chocolate fudge sauce and toasted, chopped nuts.

after-dinner mint

For a new take on traditional after-dinner mint chocolates, fill the bottom of each glass with chopped filled or plain chocolate biscuits and top with a scoop of vanilla bean ice-cream. Crush peppermint-flavoured boiled sweets and sprinkle over the top of the ice-cream. As the ice-cream softens your guests will get spoonfuls of all the flavours mixed together.

style

homemade placemats

Draw a plate, knife, fork and glass on paper and use them as disposable placemats to add a unique touch to your table. Use large sheets of paper in any colour you like and draw the shapes in charcoal or crayon to add colour. Go the extra step and write your guests' name above or on the plate if you want everyone to sit in a certain place.

chopstick rest

For a simple but stylish chopstick rest, use a smooth pebble. Put a pebble beside each guest's bowl and place the chopsticks on top. You may also want to lay out Chinese soup spoons if you're serving a noodle soup so your guests can eat the broth. Chopsticks and Chinese soup spoons are inexpensive and available from Asian food stores and supermarkets.

in the news

Use sheets of newspaper from foreign papers as a table runner. They are a great conversation starter, especially if you have invited a group of people who don't all know each other well, and add a focal point to the table. Buy international newpapers from major newsagencies. Start a collection so you can match the paper with the style of food you're serving.

to share

For a quick weeknight get together, place all the cutlery, chopsticks, napkins and glasses in the middle of the table. That way you can get on with the cooking and your guests will have everything they need as the food comes to the table. Buy pairs of disposable chopsticks that come wrapped in paper from Asian food stores.

saturday night

saturday night Forget the stresses of the working week and kick back by having a few friends over for dinner. Make a banquet to share or a more traditional three-course dinner. Whatever you choose, cooking is a breeze and the result will be a hit.

ASIAN FUSION
starter   thai chicken wonton stack
main   chilli-caramelised pork on cucumber salad
side   lemongrass greens
dessert   caramelised pineapple tarts

THE CLASSICS
starter   white asparagus with taleggio
main   bacon-wrapped beef with red wine glaze
side   porcini mash
dessert   caramelised crostini with figs

THAI BANQUET
mains   shredded duck and chilli noodle salad
crispy fish with chilli ginger glaze and thai herbs
chicken salad with coconut milk dressing
dessert   melon in lemongrass syrup

ITALIAN FEAST
starter   raw tuna, lemon and chilli linguini
main   roast garlic baked chicken
side   salsa verde potatoes
dessert   simple passionfruit soufflés

WINTER FAVOURITES
starter   figs with ricotta, prosciutto and caramelised balsamic
main   oregano and preserved lemon veal cutlets with garlic brown butter mash
side   breadcrumb zucchini
dessert   rich chocolate dessert cakes with raspberry cream

SUMMER SUPPER
starter   goat's cheese tarts
main   crispy peppered salmon
side   fennel and celeriac slaw
dessert   coconut plum crumbles

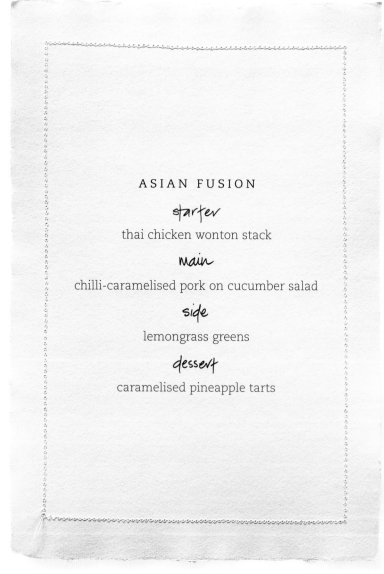

ASIAN FUSION

starter

thai chicken wonton stack

main

chilli-caramelised pork on cucumber salad

side

lemongrass greens

dessert

caramelised pineapple tarts

thai chicken wonton stack

chilli-caramelised pork on cucumber salad

thai chicken wonton stack

vegetable oil for shallow-frying
8 wonton wrappers*
2 cooked chicken breast fillets, shredded
1 cup basil leaves
1 cup mint leaves
1 cup coriander (cilantro) leaves
1 large mild red chilli, seeded and shredded
2 tablespoons lime juice
2 teaspoons fish sauce*
2 teaspoons brown sugar

Heat 1cm (⅓ in) of the oil in a frying pan or wok over high heat. Cook the wonton wrappers in batches until crisp. Drain on absorbent paper. Combine the chicken, basil, mint, coriander and chilli. Place two wontons on each serving plate and top with the chicken mixture. Combine the lime juice, fish sauce and sugar and pour over the wonton stack. Serves 4.

chilli-caramelised pork on cucumber salad

1 tablespoon sesame oil
650g (21 oz) pork fillet, trimmed and sliced
1 tablespoon grated ginger
1 large mild red chilli, seeded and chopped
¼ cup (2 fl oz) soy sauce
⅔ cup brown sugar
1 tablespoon fish sauce*
2 tablespoons lime juice
2 cucumbers, thinly sliced
½ cup bean sprouts
½ cup mint leaves
½ cup coriander (cilantro) leaves

Heat the oil in a large frying pan or wok over high heat. Add the pork and cook for 2 minutes each side or until just cooked through. Remove from the pan and set aside. Reduce the heat to low and add the ginger, chilli, soy sauce, sugar, fish sauce and lime juice to the pan. Stir to dissolve the sugar and then simmer for 8 minutes or until thickened. Add the pork to the pan and toss in the sauce to coat. Combine the cucumber, bean sprouts, mint and coriander and serve with the pork. Serves 4.

lemongrass greens

2 stalks lemongrass*, chopped
½ red onion, chopped
4 kaffir lime leaves*, shredded
1 tablespoon vegetable oil
200g (7 oz) baby bok choy*, trimmed+
200g (7 oz) broccolini*, trimmed
200g (7 oz) gai larn* (chinese broccoli), trimmed
sea salt

Place the lemongrass, onion and lime leaves in a food processor and process until a rough paste forms. Heat the oil in a large frying pan or wok over medium heat. Add the lemongrass paste and cook for 30 seconds or until fragrant. Add the bok choy, broccolini, gai larn and salt and toss to coat. Cover the pan with a lid and cook for 3 minutes or until the greens are tender. Serves 4.
+ Use any combination of crisp green vegetables you have on hand, such as snow peas (mange tout), broccoli, beans, asparagus and sugar snap peas.

caramelised pineapple tarts

250g (8 oz) ready-prepared puff pastry*
2 tablespoons desiccated coconut
8 thin slices pineapple, core removed
40g (1 oz) butter, melted
1 tablespoon brown sugar
coconut ice-cream or sorbet to serve

Preheat the oven to 200°C (390°F). Roll out the pastry on a lightly floured surface until 3mm (⅛ in) thick and cut into 4 x 13cm (5 in) circles. Sprinkle the pastry with the coconut and place two pineapple slices on each circle, leaving a 1cm (⅓ in) border. Brush the pineapple with the butter and sprinkle with the sugar. Place on baking trays lined with non-stick baking paper and bake for 15 minutes or until puffed and golden. Serve with the coconut ice-cream. Serves 4.

lemongrass greens   caramelised pineapple tarts

THE CLASSICS

starter

white asparagus with taleggio

main

bacon-wrapped beef with red wine glaze

side

porcini mash

dessert

caramelised crostini with figs

white asparagus with taleggio

bacon-wrapped beef with red wine glaze + porcini mash

white asparagus with taleggio

400g (14 oz) white asparagus, trimmed and peeled
80g (3 oz) butter
⅓ cup (2½ fl oz) white wine
1½ teaspoons lemon thyme leaves
sea salt and cracked black pepper
4 thick slices taleggio cheese*

Cook the asparagus in a saucepan of boiling water for
2–3 minutes or until just tender. Drain and keep warm.
Place the butter, wine, thyme, salt and pepper in a frying
pan over high heat and cook for 1 minute. Place the
asparagus and taleggio on serving plates and spoon over
the butter sauce. Serves 4.

bacon-wrapped beef with red wine glaze

30g (1 oz) butter
1 leek, sliced
1 tablespoon horseradish
4 x 250g (8 oz) fillet steaks
8 rashers bacon
sea salt and cracked black pepper
red wine glaze
50g (1½ oz) butter, extra
½ cup (4 fl oz) red wine
½ cup (4 fl oz) beef stock*
2 tablespoons red currant jelly*
sea salt and cracked black pepper

Preheat the oven to 180°C (355°F). Heat a frying pan over
high heat. Melt the butter in the pan, add the leek and cook,
stirring, for 3–4 minutes or until softened. Remove from the
heat and stir through the horseradish. For each piece of steak,
lay out two rashers of bacon, overlapping slightly, and top
with the leek. Sprinkle the steaks with the salt and pepper,
wrap in the bacon and secure with kitchen string. Heat a
frying pan over high heat. Cook the steaks for 1–2 minutes
each side. Place on a baking tray lined with non-stick baking
paper and cook for 10–15 minutes or until cooked to your
liking. While the beef is cooking, make the red wine glaze.
Place the extra butter, wine, stock, red currant jelly, salt and
pepper in the pan and boil for 8–10 minutes or until slightly
reduced. Spoon over the red wine glaze and serve with the
porcini mash. Serves 4.

porcini mash

150g (5 oz) mashing potatoes*, peeled and halved
2 tablespoons finely chopped dried porcini mushrooms*
80g (3 oz) butter
½ cup (4 fl oz) milk
sea salt and cracked black pepper

Cook the potatoes and mushrooms in boiling salted water
for 15 minutes or until the potatoes are soft. Drain and
mash with the butter, milk, salt and pepper. Serve with the
bacon-wrapped beef with red wine glaze. Serves 4.

caramelised crostini with figs

60g (2 oz) butter, melted
2 tablespoons icing (confectioner's) sugar
8 large slices of baguette
200g (7 oz) mascarpone*
¼ cup (2 fl oz) milk
2 tablespoons brown sugar
1 teaspoon vanilla extract
4 figs, sliced
brown sugar, extra, for sprinkling

Place the butter and icing sugar in a bowl and mix well to
combine. Brush both sides of the bread with the butter
mixture. Preheat a char-grill pan to medium–high. Toast the
bread on each side until golden brown. Place a slice of bread
on each serving plate. Whisk the mascarpone, milk, brown
sugar and vanilla until thick and smooth. Divide the
mascarpone mixture between the bread slices, top with the
figs and sprinkle with the extra brown sugar. Top with the
remaining bread slices and serve. Serves 4.

Seasonal ingredients that only have a short
availability don't have to ruin a dinner menu.
For the starter, swap the white asparagus for
green asparagus or green beans. Instead of
figs in the dessert, use red apples, firm pears,
peaches, apricots or nectarines.

caramelised crostini with figs

THAI BANQUET

mains

shredded duck and chilli noodle salad

crispy fish with chilli ginger glaze

and thai herbs

chicken salad with coconut milk dressing

dessert

melon in lemongrass syrup

shredded duck and chilli noodle salad

crispy fish with chilli ginger glaze and thai herbs

shredded duck and chilli noodle salad

150g (5 oz) cellophane noodles* (mung bean starch)
4 large mild red chillies, seeded and shredded
4 large mild green chillies, seeded and shredded
1/3 cup chopped roasted peanuts
1½ cups coriander (cilantro) leaves
1½ cups thai basil or basil leaves
1½ cups mint leaves
3 cooked duck breast fillets or 1 cooked chinese
    barbecue duck, shredded
3 tablespoons lime juice
3 tablespoons fish sauce*
2 tablespoons brown sugar

Place the noodles in a bowl and cover with boiling water.
Allow to stand for 2 minutes or until soft. Drain. Toss the
noodles with the red and green chillies, peanuts, coriander,
basil, mint and duck. To serve, combine the lime juice, fish
sauce and brown sugar and pour over the salad. Serves 4.

crispy fish with chilli ginger glaze and thai herbs

4 x 150g (5 oz) firm white fish fillets*, skin on
2 tablespoons rice flour*
vegetable oil for shallow-frying
1 cup coriander (cilantro) leaves
1 cup mint leaves
chilli ginger glaze
¼ cup finely grated ginger
4 large mild red chillies, seeded and shredded
½ cup caster (superfine) sugar
½ cup (4 fl oz) white vinegar
2 teaspoons fish sauce*

To make the chilli ginger glaze, place the ginger, chillies, sugar,
vinegar and fish sauce in a saucepan over medium–high heat
and boil for 3–4 minutes or until slightly thickened. Set aside.
Cut the fish into pieces and toss in the rice flour to coat. Heat
1cm (1/3 in) of the oil in a frying pan over high heat. Cook the
fish in batches, skin-side down, for 3 minutes, turn and cook
for 30 seconds or until cooked through and crisp. Drain on
absorbent paper. Place the fish on serving plates and spoon
over the chilli ginger glaze. Sprinkle with the coriander and
mint and serve. Serves 4.

chicken salad with coconut milk dressing

3 chicken breast fillets, trimmed
¾ cup (6 fl oz) coconut milk
½ teaspoon sea salt
200g (7 oz) baby spinach leaves
6 green onions (scallions), shredded
4 kaffir lime leaves*, very finely shredded
coconut milk dressing
¼ cup (2 fl oz) coconut milk, extra
1 tablespoon lime juice
2 teaspoons fish sauce*
2 teaspoons brown sugar

Place the chicken, coconut milk and salt in a frying pan over
low–medium heat and cook for 12–15 minutes each side or
until cooked through. Remove the chicken from the pan, allow
to cool and slice. Place the spinach, green onions, lime leaves
and chicken on serving plates. To make the coconut milk
dressing, combine the extra coconut milk, lime juice, fish
sauce and sugar. To serve, spoon over the dressing. Serves 4.

melon in lemongrass syrup

2 stalks lemongrass*, quartered
½ cup caster (superfine) sugar
1 cup (8 fl oz) water
¼ honeydew melon*, peeled, seeded and sliced
2 nashi pears*, sliced
store-bought coconut ice-cream or sorbet to serve

Place the lemongrass, sugar and water in a saucepan over
high heat. Bring to the boil and simmer for 3 minutes or
until slightly thickened. Place the melon and pears on serving
plates and spoon over the syrup. Serve with the coconut
ice-cream. Serves 4.

All the dishes on this menu complement each
other. Place the dishes in the middle of the
table to share. That way everyone gets to taste
a bit of everything.

chicken salad with coconut milk dressing

melon in lemongrass syrup

ITALIAN FEAST

starter
raw tuna, lemon and chilli linguini

main
roast garlic baked chicken

side
salsa verde potatoes

dessert
simple passionfruit soufflés

raw tuna, lemon and chilli linguini

roast garlic baked chicken + salsa verde potatoes

raw tuna, lemon and chilli linguini

300g (10 oz) linguini or spaghetti
2 tablespoons olive oil
½ teaspoon dried chilli flakes
2 cloves garlic, crushed
⅓ cup salted capers*, rinsed and dried
⅓ cup (2½ fl oz) lemon juice
sea salt and cracked black pepper
1½ cups shredded rocket (arugula) leaves
150g (5 oz) sashimi tuna*, finely chopped
shaved parmesan cheese to serve

Cook the pasta in a large saucepan of salted boiling water
for 10–12 minutes or until al dente. Drain and keep warm.
Return the pan to the heat, add the oil, chilli flakes, garlic and
capers and cook for 2 minutes. Return the pasta to the pan,
add the lemon juice, salt and pepper and toss to combine.
Divide the pasta between serving plates and top with the
rocket, tuna and parmesan. Serves 4.

roast garlic baked chicken

1 head garlic
1 teaspoon olive oil
80g (3 oz) butter, softened
4 chicken breasts with part wing bone, skin on
sea salt and cracked black pepper

Preheat the oven to 180°C (355°F). Cut the top off the garlic
and drizzle with the oil. Wrap the garlic in foil, place on a
baking tray and bake for 30 minutes or until the garlic is soft.
Allow to cool slightly then squeeze the garlic cloves from the
skin. Combine the garlic and butter. Make a small hole
between the skin and the flesh of the chicken and spoon the
garlic butter under the skin of each chicken breast. Use your
fingers to spread the butter over all the flesh. Sprinkle the
chicken with the salt and pepper. Heat a frying pan over high
heat. Add the chicken, skin-side down, and cook for 2 minutes
or until golden. Turn and cook for 1 minute or until golden.
Place the chicken on a baking tray lined with non-stick baking
paper and bake for 8–10 minutes or until cooked through.
Serve with the salsa verde potatoes. Serves 4.

salsa verde potatoes

12 baby new potatoes, halved
1 tablespoon dijon mustard
2 tablespoons lemon juice
2 cups flat-leaf parsley leaves
1 cup dill leaves
¼ cup (2 fl oz) olive oil
sea salt and cracked black pepper

Steam or boil the potatoes until tender. While the potatoes are
cooking, place the mustard, lemon juice, parsley, dill, oil, salt
and pepper in a food processor and process until finely chopped.
Toss the hot potatoes in the salsa verde and serve with the
roast garlic baked chicken. Serves 4.

simple passionfruit soufflés

melted butter for greasing
caster (superfine) sugar for dusting
150ml (5 fl oz) passionfruit pulp
¼ cup caster (superfine) sugar
2 tablespoons lemon juice
1 tablespoon cornflour (cornstarch)
3 teaspoons water
5 egg whites
⅓ cup caster (superfine) sugar, extra

Preheat the oven to 180°C (355°F). Brush 4 x 1 cup (8 fl oz)
capacity ramekins with the butter, dust with the sugar and
place on a baking tray. Place the passionfruit, sugar and
lemon juice in a small saucepan over low heat and stir until
the sugar is dissolved. Increase the heat and bring to the boil.
Combine the cornflour and water and mix to a smooth paste.
Remove the pan from the heat and whisk in cornflour paste.
Return the pan to the heat and cook, whisking continuously,
for 1 minute. Pour the passionfruit mixture into a large bowl
and refrigerate until cold. Place the egg whites in the bowl of
an electric mixer and beat until soft peaks form. Add the extra
sugar in a thin stream and beat until glossy. Gently fold the
egg white mixture through the passionfruit mixture, spoon into
the ramekins and bake for 12–15 minutes or until risen and
golden. Serve immediately. Serves 4.

simple passionfruit soufflés

WINTER FAVOURITES

starter

figs with ricotta, prosciutto and
caramelised balsamic

main

oregano and preserved lemon
veal cutlets with garlic brown butter mash

side

breadcrumb zucchini

dessert

rich chocolate dessert cakes with
raspberry cream

figs with ricotta, prosciutto and caramelised balsamic

oregano and preserved lemon veal cutlets with garlic brown butter mash

figs with ricotta, prosciutto and caramelised balsamic

4 very thin slices prosciutto*
1 radicchio*, leaves separated
4 figs, halved
150g (5 oz) fresh ricotta cheese
caramelised balsamic
½ cup (4 fl oz) balsamic vinegar*
¼ cup brown sugar

Place the prosciutto under a preheated hot grill (broiler) and cook for 2 minutes or until crisp. Break the prosciutto slices in half. Place the radicchio, figs, ricotta and prosciutto on serving plates. To make the caramelised balsamic, place the vinegar and sugar in a small frying pan over medium heat and cook for 3–4 minutes or until thickened. Cool slightly before spooning over the salad. Serves 4.

oregano and preserved lemon veal cutlets with garlic brown butter mash

2 tablespoons olive oil
¼ cup small sprigs oregano
¼ cup finely sliced preserved lemon rind
4 cloves garlic, sliced
4 veal cutlets
sea salt and cracked black pepper
mashed potatoes to serve
garlic brown butter
60g (2 oz) butter
2 cloves garlic, extra, crushed

Heat a large frying pan over medium heat. Add the oil, oregano, lemon rind and garlic and cook for 2 minutes or until fragrant. Remove the oregano, lemon rind and garlic from the pan leaving the oil. Sprinkle the veal with the salt and pepper and add to the pan. Cook for 3–4 minutes each side or until cooked to your liking. Return the oregano mixture to the pan and toss to coat. To make the garlic brown butter, place the butter in a medium frying pan over medium heat and cook for 1 minute or until browned. Take off the heat and add the garlic. To serve, place the mashed potatoes on serving plates and pour over the garlic brown butter. Top with the veal and spoon over the oregano mixture and pan juices. Serves 4.

breadcrumb zucchini

4 small zucchinis (courgettes), halved lengthwise
80g (3 oz) sliced parmesan cheese
1 cup fresh breadcrumbs
1 tablespoon chopped flat-leaf parsley leaves
sea salt and cracked black pepper
2 tablespoons olive oil

Preheat the oven to 180°C (355°F). Place the zucchini in a single layer in a baking dish and cover with the parmesan. Combine the breadcrumbs, parsley, salt and pepper and sprinkle over the parmesan. Drizzle with the oil and bake for 30 minutes or until golden. Serves 4.

rich chocolate dessert cakes with raspberry cream

100g (3½ oz) dark chocolate, chopped
50g (1½ oz) butter
½ cup brown sugar
½ teaspoon vanilla extract
2 eggs, beaten
⅓ cup plain (all-purpose) flour, sifted
2 tablespoons cocoa powder, sifted
100g (3½ oz) raspberries
½ cup (4 fl oz) thick (double) cream*
cocoa powder, extra, for dusting
raspberries, extra, for serving

Preheat the oven to 180°C (355°F). Place the chocolate and butter in a saucepan over low heat and stir until smooth. Set aside to cool. Add the sugar, vanilla and eggs and mix to combine. Add the flour and cocoa and mix to combine. Pour the mixture into 4 x ½ cup (4 fl oz) capacity non-stick greased muffin tins and bake for 12–15 minutes or until cooked when tested with a skewer. While the cakes are cooking, combine the raspberries and cream. When the cakes are cool, split in half, fill with the raspberry cream and dust with the extra cocoa. Serve with the extra raspberries. Serves 4.

breadcrumb zucchini

rich chocolate dessert cakes with raspberry cream

SUMMER SUPPER

starter
goat's cheese tarts

main
crispy peppered salmon

side
fennel and celeriac slaw

dessert
coconut plum crumbles

goat's cheese tarts

crispy peppered salmon + fennel and celeriac slaw

goat's cheese tarts

500g (1 lb) ready-prepared puff pastry*
150g (5 oz) goat's cheese, sliced
2 tablespoons oregano leaves
sea salt and cracked black pepper
2 tablespoons olive oil
2 cups watercress
balsamic vinegar*
extra virgin olive oil
caramelised onions
1 tablespoon olive oil, extra
1 red onion, sliced
1 tablespoon brown sugar
2 tablespoons balsamic vinegar*, extra
sea salt and cracked black pepper

Preheat the oven to 200°C (390°F). To make the caramelised onions, place the extra oil, onion, sugar, extra vinegar, salt and pepper in a frying pan over medium–high heat. Simmer for 3 minutes or until soft and caramelised. Set aside. Roll out the pastry on a lightly floured surface until 3mm (⅛ in) thick and cut into 8 x 10cm (4 in) circles. Place two pastry circles on top of each other and place on baking trays lined with non-stick baking paper. Spread with the caramelised onions leaving a 1cm (⅓ in) border. Top with the goat's cheese, oregano, salt and pepper. Drizzle with the oil and cook for 15–20 minutes or until puffed and golden. Serve with the watercress tossed in the vinegar and extra virgin olive oil. Serves 4.

crispy peppered salmon

4 x 300g (10 oz) salmon fillets
vegetable oil for brushing
1 tablespoon cracked black pepper
sea salt
1 lemon, cut into eight wedges

Heat a non-stick frying pan over high heat. Brush the salmon with the oil and sprinkle with the pepper and salt on both sides. Cook skin-side down for 4 minutes, turn and cook for a further minute or until cooked to your liking. Place the lemon in the pan and cook for 1 minute each side or until caramelised. Serve with the fennel and celeriac slaw. Serves 4.

fennel and celeriac slaw

500g (1 lb) celeriac* (celery root), peeled and finely sliced
2 x 200g (7 oz) fennel*, trimmed and finely sliced
dressing
½ cup whole-egg mayonnaise
1 tablespoon lemon juice
1 tablespoon horseradish cream
1 tablespoon water

To make the dressing, combine the mayonnaise, lemon juice, horseradish cream and water. Place the celeriac and fennel in a bowl and toss to combine. Pour over the dressing and toss to combine. Serve with the crispy peppered salmon. Serves 4.

coconut plum crumbles

4 large plums, halved and stones removed
¾ cup desiccated coconut
¼ cup caster (superfine) sugar
1 teaspoon vanilla extract
1 egg white
vanilla bean ice-cream to serve

Preheat the oven to 180°C (355°F). Place the plums, cut-side up, in a baking dish. Mix together the coconut, sugar, vanilla and egg white. Fill the plums with the coconut mixture and pile high. Bake for 15 minutes or until golden. Serve warm with the vanilla bean ice-cream. Serves 4.

This is the ideal make-ahead menu. Make the goat's cheese tarts and coconut plum crumbles ahead of time and reheat before serving. The fennel and celeriac slaw can also be made ahead. All that is left to do is cook the salmon.

coconut plum crumbles

style

fortune by name

Fortune cookies make easy, inexpensive and fun placesettings.
Write your guests' names on squares of hand-torn paper and
slot it into the gap in the cookie. After everyone has taken
their seat, they can break open the cookie and read their
fortune; it's a great way to get everyone talking at the table.
Buy them from Asian food stores or supermarkets.

cheese for one

Make a single-serve cheese platter for each of your guests.
That way there is no reaching across the table or waiting for
the cheese to be passed to you; everyone can nibble at their
leisure. Place a selection of cheeses, a stack of crackers or
lavash, and fruit, such as figs and miniature apples, on small
bread boards. And don't forget the cheese knives.

antipasto

Antipasto doesn't have to be placed in the middle of the table and shared. Serve dips, olives and prosciutto in small bowls on individual plates with lavash or slices of bread so all your guests have their own portions to eat, and everything you want is right in front of you. Single-serve antipasto is a quick, simple starter for a lunch or dinner.

apple a day

Miniature apples make cute, simple placesettings. Write your guests' names on pieces of paper cut into the shape of a leaf, punch a hole in one end, thread with ribbon and tie it to the apple stem. Place it on printed paper also cut into a leaf shape. You can buy miniature apples from greengrocers. If they are not available, use regular apples or small pears.

style

by candlelight

Give your tealight holders a new lease on life. Using holders of different shapes and sizes, wrap patterned and translucent paper around the outside and secure the paper with velvet and satin ribbons. Place tealight candles inside and light them to make sure the paper is not too close to the flame. And remember, never leave lit candles unattended.

rose cups

Use decorative coffee and tea cups as vases for roses. Cut the stems of the roses quite short and place as many blooms as possible in each cup. Place the cups on a platter or group them in the middle of the table to create a centrepiece. This is a good way to use your favourite cups that are chipped but are too precious to throw away.

liqueur coffee

Let your guests choose what flavour liqueur they would like in their coffee. Decant several different flavoured liqueurs into small carafes and bottles and serve with shots of espresso, milk or cream, and sugar. Everyone can then add the amounts they like. Collect patterned and plain carafes and bottles from antique and junk shops, and garage sales.

edible centrepiece

Stack store-bought meringues, cookies, amaretti or chocolates on plates and use them as a table centrepiece. You can wrap them in coloured tissue or wrapping paper to suit your theme. After dinner your guests can eat them or take them home. During the festive season, place bowls of treats around the house so there is always something for visitors to nibble on.

sunday lunch

sunday lunch
While away the afternoon with good friends and simple, delicious food. Settle in, open a bottle or two of wine and just enjoy each other's company. After all, Sunday is supposed to be the most leisurely day of the week.

INDULGENT AFTERNOON
starter   toasted bread salad
main   roast chicken with caramelised parsnips
side   steamed paper bag greens
dessert   simple lemon puddings

LAZY DAY
starter   tomato and capsicum soup
main   chicken and leek pot pies
side   mint and butter peas
dessert   rhubarb meringue mess

AUTUMN FEAST
starter   pancetta with blue cheese and pear
main   garlic roast lamb cutlets
side   lemon butter pan spinach
dessert   fig pie

ASIAN INSPIRED
starter   simple fish cakes
main   noodles in spicy coconut broth
side   spice-fried pork
dessert   green tea and mint granita

VEGETARIAN FARE
starter   garlic and sage marinated antipasto
main   simple leek and ricotta tarts
side   fennel and parsley salad
dessert   raspberry-spiked chocolate brownies

MEDITERRANEAN MEAL
starter   goat's cheese and sweet capsicum salad
main   schnitzel with black olive crust
side   garlic and tomato simmered beans
dessert   warm apple cinnamon crumb cakes

INDULGENT AFTERNOON

starter

toasted bread salad

main

roast chicken with
caramelised parsnips

side

steamed paper bag greens

dessert

simple lemon puddings

toasted bread salad

roast chicken with caramelised parsnips

toasted bread salad

175g (6 oz) piece crusty sourdough bread
3 tablespoons olive oil
2 cloves garlic, crushed
sea salt and cracked black pepper
70g (2½ oz) mixed salad leaves
4 small fresh mozzarella (bocconcini*) cheeses, torn
3 roma tomatoes, cut into wedges
½ cup flat-leaf parsley leaves
dressing
3 tablespoons red wine vinegar*
2 tablespoons olive oil, extra

Preheat the oven to 180°C (355°F). Tear the bread into bite-size pieces and toss with the oil, garlic, salt and pepper. Place on a baking tray and bake for 15 minutes or until golden and crisp. Set aside to cool. Place the bread, salad leaves, mozzarella, tomatoes and parsley in a serving bowl and toss to combine. To make the dressing, whisk together the vinegar and extra oil, pour over the salad, toss to combine and serve immediately. Serves 4.

roast chicken with caramelised parsnips

4 parsnips, trimmed and peeled
60g (2 oz) butter, melted
sea salt
2 tablespoons brown sugar
2 teaspoons sea salt, extra
2 teaspoons cracked black pepper
2 tablespoons chopped rosemary leaves
4 chicken breast fillets, trimmed
4 slices prosciutto*

Preheat the oven to 200°C (390°F). Cut the parsnips into long strips using a vegetable peeler. Place on a baking tray lined with non-stick baking paper and toss with the butter, salt and sugar. Roast for 10 minutes or until the parsnips are starting to brown. Push the parsnips to one side of the dish. Combine the extra salt, pepper and rosemary and sprinkle over both sides of the chicken. Wrap each chicken breast in a slice of prosciutto and place on the baking tray with the parsnips. Roast for 12 minutes or until the chicken is cooked through. Serve with the parsnips and steamed paper bag greens. Serves 4.

steamed paper bag greens

2 lemons, sliced
150g (5 oz) green beans
12 spears asparagus
1 tablespoon olive oil
sea salt and cracked black pepper

Preheat the oven to 200°C (390°F). Cut 4 x 30cm (12 in) squares of non-stick baking paper. Divide the lemon between the paper squares and top with the beans and asparagus. Drizzle with the oil and sprinkle with the salt and pepper. Fold the paper over the vegetables and fold over the ends to enclose. Place on baking trays and bake for 15 minutes or until the vegetables are just soft. Serves 4.

simple lemon puddings

100g (3½ oz) butter, softened
¾ cup caster (superfine) sugar
2 teaspoons finely grated lemon rind
2 eggs
2 tablespoons lemon juice
½ cup plain (all-purpose) flour
½ teaspoon baking powder
½ cup almond meal (ground almonds)*

Preheat the oven to 170°C (340°F). Place the butter, sugar and lemon rind in the bowl of an electric mixer and beat until light and creamy. Add the eggs and beat well. Add the lemon juice, flour, baking powder and almond meal and mix to combine. Pour mixture into 4 x ¾ cup (6 fl oz) capacity greased ovenproof ramekins and bake for 25–30 minutes or until cooked when tested with a skewer. Serve warm with thick (double) cream and vanilla bean ice-cream. Serves 4.

No time to bake the puddings? Combine 100g (3½ oz) mascarpone, ¼ cup (2 fl oz) cream*, 2 teaspoons sifted icing (confectioner's) sugar and 1 teaspoon finely grated lemon rind and sandwich between shortbread with blueberries.

steamed paper bag greens

simple lemon puddings

LAZY DAY

starter

tomato and capsicum soup

main

chicken and leek pot pies

side

mint and butter peas

dessert

rhubarb meringue mess

tomato and capsicum soup

mint and butter peas + chicken and leek pot pies

tomato and capsicum soup

2 x 400g (14 oz) cans peeled tomatoes
500g (1 lb) store-bought char-grilled
  capsicums (bell peppers)
2 tablespoons olive oil
4 cloves garlic, crushed
2 cups (16 fl oz) chicken stock*
1 tablespoon sugar
sea salt and cracked black pepper
2 tablespoons basil leaves
shaved parmesan cheese to serve

Place the tomatoes and capsicums in a food processor
and process until smooth. Heat the oil and garlic in a
saucepan over medium heat for 1 minute or until fragrant.
Add the tomato mixture, stock, sugar, salt and pepper
and cook for 4–6 minutes or until hot. Top with the basil
and parmesan. Serves 4.

chicken and leek pot pies

1 tablespoon olive oil
2 leeks, sliced
6 chicken thigh fillets, trimmed and chopped
1 tablespoon thyme leaves
2 potatoes, peeled and chopped
1¼ cups (10 fl oz) chicken stock*
½ cup (4 fl oz) (single or pouring) cream*
sea salt and cracked black pepper
300g (10 oz) ready-prepared puff pastry*
1 egg, lightly beaten

Preheat the oven to 200°C (390°F). Heat a large frying
pan over medium heat. Add the oil and leeks and cook for
4 minutes or until soft. Add the chicken, thyme, potatoes
and stock and simmer for 20 minutes or until the chicken
is tender and the potatoes are soft. Stir through the cream,
salt and pepper. Spoon the mixture into 4 x 1½ cup
(12 fl oz) capacity ovenproof dishes. Roll out the pastry
on a lightly floured surface until 3mm (⅛ in) thick. Top the
dishes with the pastry and trim the edges. Brush with the
egg and bake for 15 minutes or until the pastry is puffed
and golden. Serve with the mint and butter peas. Serves 4.

mint and butter peas

3 cups frozen peas
⅔ cup (5 fl oz) chicken stock*
40g (1½ oz) butter
sea salt and cracked black pepper
2 tablespoons chopped mint leaves
2 tablespoons grated parmesan cheese

Place the peas and stock in a saucepan over medium heat
and cook, covered, for 5 minutes or until the peas are soft.
Remove from the heat and roughly mash with the butter,
salt and pepper. Stir through the mint and parmesan and
serve with the chicken and leek pot pies. Serves 4.

rhubarb meringue mess

5 stalks rhubarb, chopped
¾ cup (6 fl oz) orange juice
1 teaspoon vanilla extract
¼ teaspoon ground cinnamon
2 tablespoons caster (superfine) sugar
1 cup (8 fl oz) (single or pouring) cream*
2 tablespoons icing (confectioner's) sugar
4 store-bought meringues

Place the rhubarb, orange juice, vanilla and cinnamon
in a saucepan over medium heat and cook, covered, for
8–10 minutes or until the rhubarb is soft. Stir through the
caster sugar, transfer to a bowl and refrigerate until cold.
Whisk together the cream and icing sugar until thick. To
serve, break the meringues into large pieces and place
in the bottom of serving bowls or glasses. Top with the
rhubarb and cream and serve immediately. Serves 4.

For do-ahead entertaining, make the soup, pies
and rhubarb mixture and freeze. Defrost them in
the fridge before heating. The pies can be heated
from frozen. Place them in a 200°C (390°F)
oven until the pastry is golden, then decrease to
140°C (285°F) so the filling heats through.

rhubarb meringue mess

AUTUMN FEAST

starter

pancetta with blue cheese and pear

main

garlic roast lamb cutlets

side

lemon butter pan spinach

dessert

fig pie

pancetta with blue cheese and pear

garlic roast lamb cutlets

pancetta with blue cheese and pear

8 slices pancetta*
60g (2 oz) rocket (arugula) leaves
1 tablespoon balsamic vinegar*
1 tablespoon olive oil
8 thin slices pear
8 slices blue cheese

Place the pancetta on a baking tray and cook under a hot grill (broiler) for 1–2 minutes or until golden and crisp. Toss the rocket in the vinegar and oil. To serve, place the rocket, pear, blue cheese and pancetta on serving plates. Serves 4.

garlic roast lamb cutlets

12 cloves garlic, peeled
6 x 170g (6 oz) king edward or roasting potatoes, sliced
4 small zucchinis (courgettes), halved lengthwise
1 tablespoon rosemary leaves
2 tablespoons olive oil
sea salt and cracked black pepper
8 double lamb cutlets, trimmed +
mustard mint sauce
1½ cups chopped mint leaves
1½ tablespoons seeded mustard
2½ tablespoons honey

Preheat the oven to 220°C (425°F). Place the garlic, potatoes, zucchinis, rosemary, oil, salt and pepper in a baking dish, toss to combine and roast for 25 minutes. While the vegetables are cooking, heat a frying pan over high heat and brown the lamb on all sides. To make the mustard mint sauce, place the mint, mustard and honey in a bowl and mix to combine. Place the lamb on top of the vegetables. Brush the lamb with some of the mint sauce and roast for a further 8–10 minutes or until the lamb is golden and the potatoes are soft. To serve, place the lamb and vegetables on serving plates and top with the remaining mint sauce. Serve with the lemon butter pan spinach. Serves 4.
+ Your butcher will be able to cut double cutlets for you. They stay moist and tender when roasted. Use only four double cutlets if they are large.

lemon butter pan spinach

60g (2 oz) butter
1 tablespoon finely grated lemon rind
2 cloves garlic, crushed
400g (14 oz) baby spinach leaves
2 tablespoons lemon juice
sea salt and cracked black pepper

Place the butter in a frying pan over high heat. Add the lemon rind and garlic and cook for 1 minute or until the garlic is lightly golden. Add the spinach and turn with tongs until soft and wilted. Pour over the lemon juice and sprinkle with the salt and pepper. Serve immediately with the garlic roast lamb cutlets. Serves 4.

fig pie

280g (10 oz) ready-prepared shortcrust pastry*
½ cup almond meal (ground almonds)*
2 tablespoons plain (all-purpose) flour
¼ cup caster (superfine) sugar
40g (1½ oz) butter, melted
½ teaspoon vanilla extract
2 large figs, sliced +
caster (superfine) sugar, extra, for sprinkling

Preheat the oven to 180°C (355°F). Roll out the pastry on a lightly floured surface until 3mm (⅛ in) thick. Combine the almond meal, flour, sugar, butter and vanilla and spread over the pastry leaving a 3cm (1 in) border. Top with the fig and sprinkle with the extra sugar. Fold the pastry edges to enclose and bake for 25–30 minutes or until the pastry is golden. Serve with thick (double) cream or vanilla bean ice-cream. Serves 4.
+ Depending on the season, replace the figs with peaches, necatrines, apricots, apples or pears.

lemon butter pan spinach   fig pie

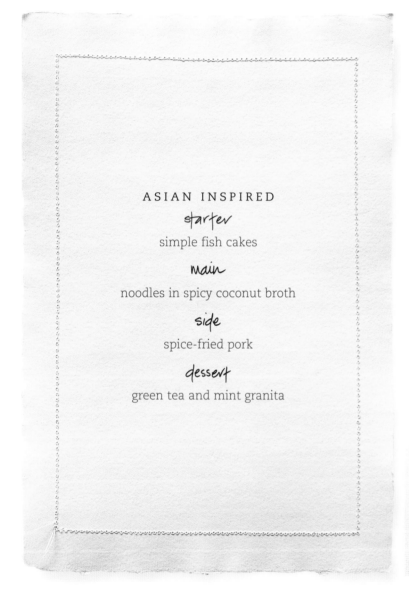

ASIAN INSPIRED

starter

simple fish cakes

main

noodles in spicy coconut broth

side

spice-fried pork

dessert

green tea and mint granita

simple fish cakes

noodles in spicy coconut broth + spice-fried pork

simple fish cakes

350g (12⅓ oz) firm white fish fillets*
2 egg whites
2 teaspoons grated ginger
2 tablespoons chopped coriander (cilantro) leaves
3 tablespoons rice flour*
sea salt and cracked black pepper
vegetable oil to shallow fry
lemon wedges to serve
mixed salad leaves to serve

Cut the fish into rough 5mm (¼ in) squares. Place the fish, egg whites, ginger, coriander, rice flour, salt and pepper in a bowl and mix to combine. Heat 1cm (⅓ in) of the oil in a frying pan over medium–high heat. Add heaped tablespoons of the mixture, flatten slightly and cook for 1 minute each side or until lightly golden. Drain on absorbent paper and serve hot with the lemon wedges and salad leaves. Serves 4.

noodles in spicy coconut broth

200g (7 oz) dry rice noodles*
1½ tablespoons red curry paste*
1 stalk lemongrass*, finely chopped
3 kaffir lime leaves*, shredded
2 teaspoons grated ginger
2½ cups (1 pint) coconut milk
1 cup (8 fl oz) chicken stock*
½ cup (4 fl oz) water
200g (7 oz) green beans, trimmed
1 tablespoon fish sauce*
lime wedges to serve

Place the noodles in a bowl, cover with boiling water and stand for 2 minutes or until soft. Drain. Heat a saucepan over high heat. Add the curry paste, lemongrass, lime leaves and ginger and cook for 1 minute or until fragrant. Add the coconut milk, stock and water, bring to the boil and simmer for 3 minutes. Add the beans and cook for a further 3 minutes or until just tender. Stir through the fish sauce. Divide the noodles between serving bowls and pour over the coconut broth. Serve with the lime wedges and top with the spice-fried pork. Serves 4.

spice-fried pork

500g (1 lb) pork fillet, trimmed
1 teaspoon chilli powder
1 teaspoon cracked black pepper
sea salt
1 teaspoon chinese five-spice powder*
1 tablespoon rice flour*
2 tablespoons vegetable oil

Slice the pork into thin rounds. Place in a bowl with the chilli powder, pepper, salt, five-spice powder and rice flour and toss to combine. Heat half the oil in a wok or large frying pan over high heat. Add half the pork and cook for 1 minute each side or until golden. Remove and repeat with the remaining oil and pork. Serve with the noodles in spicy coconut broth. Serves 4.

green tea and mint granita

3 cups (24 fl oz) boiling water
3 quality green tea bags
¾ cup caster (superfine) sugar
⅓ cup (2½ fl oz) lemon juice
1 tablespoon finely chopped mint leaves

Place the water and tea bags in a medium saucepan and stand for 5 minutes for the tea to steep. Remove the tea bags and add the sugar and lemon juice. Place over low heat and stir until the sugar has dissolved. Remove from the heat and cool. Add the mint and pour into a 20 x 30cm (7¾ x 12 in) metal tin and freeze for 1 hour. Rake the top with a fork to break up the ice crystals and return to the freezer. Repeat the process three times or until the granita is snow-like. Serve in small chilled bowls. Serves 4.

Run out of time to make and freeze the granita? Purchase ready-made lemon or lime sorbet and serve scoops in chilled bowls with slices of melon, such as honeydew melon or rockmelon (cantaloupe). Sprinkle with finely chopped fresh mint leaves to serve.

green tea and mint granita

VEGETARIAN FARE

starter

garlic and sage marinated antipasto

main

simple leek and ricotta tarts

side

fennel and parsley salad

dessert

raspberry-spiked chocolate brownies

garlic and sage marinated antipasto

simple leek and ricotta tarts

garlic and sage marinated antipasto

6 artichoke hearts, halved and well drained
200g (7 oz) mixed green and black olives
200g (7 oz) cherry tomatoes, halved
4 tablespoons fruity olive oil
15 sage leaves
3 cloves garlic, sliced
cracked black pepper
2 tablespoons white wine vinegar*
150g (5 oz) fetta cheese, sliced

Combine the artichokes, olives and tomatoes. Place the oil
and sage in a small saucepan over medium heat and cook
for 1 minute. Add the garlic and pepper and cook for a further
2 minutes or until the sage is crisp. Remove from the heat
and stir through the vinegar. Pour over the artichoke mixture
and stand for 5 minutes before serving. Serve with the fetta
and crispbread biscuits or slices of crusty bread. Serves 4.

simple leek and ricotta tarts

500g (1 lb) fresh ricotta cheese
¼ cup grated parmesan cheese
2 eggs
600g (20 oz) ready-prepared puff pastry*
1 leek, trimmed and finely sliced
45g (1½ oz) butter, melted
2 teaspoons thyme leaves
sea salt and cracked black pepper

Preheat the oven to 180°C (355°F). Place the ricotta,
parmesan and eggs in a bowl and whisk until smooth.
Roll out the pastry on a lightly floured surface until 3mm
(⅛ in) thick. Cut into 4 x 15cm (6 in) squares and place on
baking trays lined with non-stick baking paper. Spread the
ricotta mixture over the pastry squares leaving a 2cm (¾ in)
border. Place the leek on top of the ricotta mixture and
brush with the butter. Sprinkle with the thyme, salt and
pepper and bake for 25–30 minutes or until the leek is
golden. Serve with the fennel and parsley salad. Serves 4.

fennel and parsley salad

4 baby fennel, trimmed and thinly sliced
2 cups flat-leaf parsley leaves
¼ cup (2 fl oz) orange juice
2 tablespoons olive oil
1 tablespoon seeded mustard
sea salt and cracked black pepper

Place the fennel and parsley in a serving bowl and toss to
combine. Place the orange juice, oil, mustard, salt and pepper
in a bowl and whisk to combine. Pour over the salad and
serve with the simple leek and ricotta tarts. Serves 4.

raspberry-spiked chocolate brownies

200g (7 oz) dark chocolate, chopped
250g (8 oz) butter
1¾ cups brown sugar
4 eggs
1⅓ cups plain (all-purpose) flour
¼ teaspoon baking powder
⅓ cup cocoa, sifted
1½ cups raspberries, fresh or frozen+

Preheat the oven to 180°C (355°F). Place the chocolate and
butter in a small saucepan over low heat and stir until melted
and smooth. Place in a bowl with the sugar and eggs. Sift
over the flour, baking powder and cocoa and mix to combine.
Pour into a 23cm (9 in) greased square cake tin lined with
non-stick baking paper. Top the mixture with the raspberries
and bake for 30–35 minutes or until set. Serve warm or cold
with thick (double) cream or vanilla bean ice-cream. Makes 16.
+ If using frozen raspberries there is no need to defrost them
first. You can also use fresh or frozen blueberries.

fennel and parsley salad

raspberry-spiked chocolate brownies

MEDITERRANEAN MEAL

starter

goat's cheese and sweet capsicum salad

main

schnitzel with black olive crust

side

garlic and tomato simmered beans

dessert

warm apple cinnamon crumb cakes

goat's cheese and sweet capsicum salad

schnitzel with black olive crust with garlic and tomato simmered beans

goat's cheese and sweet capsicum salad

½ cup (4 fl oz) white vinegar
½ cup sugar
½ cup (4 fl oz) water
1 red capsicum (bell pepper), seeded and cut into strips
1 yellow capsicum (bell pepper), seeded and cut into strips
80g (3 oz) rocket (arugula) leaves
150g (5 oz) soft goat's cheese, sliced
2 teaspoons olive oil
sea salt and cracked black pepper

Place the vinegar, sugar and water in a saucepan over medium heat and cook, stirring, for 2 minutes or until the sugar has dissolved. Add the red and yellow capsicum and cook for 5 minutes or until just soft. Drain and reserve liquid. Place the rocket, capsicum and goat's cheese on serving plates. Combine ¼ cup (2 fl oz) of the reserved liquid with the oil, salt and pepper. Pour over the salad and serve. Serves 4.

schnitzel with black olive crust

3 cups fresh breadcrumbs
⅓ cup finely chopped black olives
1 tablespoon chopped oregano leaves
sea salt and cracked black pepper
2 eggs
4 pork, chicken or veal schnitzel steaks
vegetable oil for shallow-frying

Combine the breadcrumbs, olives, oregano, salt and pepper in a large bowl. Place the eggs in a shallow dish and whisk to combine. Dip both sides of each schnitzel in the egg and then press both sides firmly in the breadcrumb mixture. Heat 5mm (¼ in) of the oil in a large frying pan over medium–high heat until hot. Cook the schnitzels two at a time for 2–3 minutes each side or until golden, drain on absorbent paper and keep warm in the oven. Serve with the garlic and tomato simmered beans. Serves 4.

garlic and tomato simmered beans

1 tablespoon olive oil
3 cloves garlic, sliced
4 roma tomatoes, cut into wedges
½ cup (4 fl oz) dry white wine or chicken stock*
300g (10 oz) green or flat beans, trimmed
¼ cup torn basil leaves
sea salt and cracked black pepper

Heat a frying pan over medium heat. Add the oil and garlic and cook for 1 minute or until fragrant. Add the tomatoes and wine and cook for 5 minutes. Add the beans and cook for a further 5 minutes or until just tender. Stir through the basil, salt and pepper and serve with the schnitzel with black olive crust. Serves 4.

warm apple cinnamon crumb cakes

60g (2 oz) butter, softened
⅔ cup caster (superfine) sugar
1 teaspoon ground cinnamon
1 egg
⅓ cup sour cream
1 cup plain (all-purpose) flour
1 teaspoon baking powder
topping
1½ tablespoons plain (all-purpose) flour, extra
1 tablespoon brown sugar
¼ teaspoon ground cinnamon, extra
15g (½ oz) butter, extra, melted
½ green apple, cored and thinly sliced

Preheat the oven to 160°C (320°F). Place the butter, caster sugar, cinnamon, egg, sour cream, flour and baking powder in a food processor and process until smooth. Spoon the mixture into 4 x 1 cup (8 fl oz) capacity greased non-stick muffin tins. To make the topping, combine the extra flour, brown sugar, extra cinnamon and extra butter. Toss the apple in the flour mixture and place on top of the cakes. Sprinkle with any remaining flour mixture. Bake for 25–30 minutes or until the cakes are cooked when tested with a skewer. Serve warm with vanilla bean ice-cream. Serves 4.

warm apple cinnamon crumb cakes

style

time for tea

Fresh mint tea makes a refreshing change from coffee and the usual black teas at the end of a meal. Tie a small bunch of mint together with kitchen string and serve with a glass of boiling water and sugar cubes. Use patterned Moroccan-style glasses or ceramic mugs. Your guests can jiggle the mint in their glass for as little or as long as they like.

buttoned up

Dress up your table with simple homemade napkin rings. Make them using fabric-covered buttons of different sizes in colours to suit your napery. Thread ribbon or elastic through the backs of the buttons, tie to form a loop and slip around rolled or folded napkins. Place one on each plate or stack them at one end of the table if you're entertaining buffet-style.

a touch of glass

Old wine glasses of different heights and shapes make great vases. Group them together for a low, tiered centrepiece. Collect glasses from junk shops and garage sales. Look for ones with etching and scalloped patterns to add extra interest. Glasses are ideal for hibiscus, magnolias, gardenias, camellias and other flowers that don't have very long stems.

take your place

For a more formal meal, make a placesetting for each person using wooden pegs. Place a square of hand-torn, textured cardboard or paper between the teeth of a peg with your guest's name written on it. For extra decoration, put other pegs on the napkin. Buy old and new pegs of different shapes from antique, junk and craft shops, and supermarkets.

style

diy mocha

Instead of cooking dessert, have some fun and serve do-it-yourself mocha. Give everyone a shot of espresso, a bowl of dark chocolate shavings, a cup of steamed milk and a spoon so they can add just the right amounts to suit their taste. To create little curls of chocolate, use a vegetable peeler and shave extra so your guests can nibble while they stir.

flavoured waters

Give plain water a lift by delicately flavouring it. Place slices of green apple and mint leaves, raspberries or lemongrass and pieces of ginger in the water an hour before your guests are due to arrive so it will have just a hint of flavour. Put bottles and carafes filled with the flavoured water and ice along the table so everyone can help themselves.

packed lunch

Pack your guests' lunch in billy cans or pails with lids and head off to the park or beach for a picnic. Line the cans with inexpensive scarves to keep the food secure and place napkins between drink bottles and cutlery to prevent breakages. You can also paint dots or stripes on the outside of the cans so your guests will know which one is theirs.

table runner

For a simple table runner, sew together tea towels. Collect antique tea towels or buy inexpensive ones from kitchen shops and supermarkets. Use all the same pattern or mix and match for a patchwork effect. After you're finished using the runner, soak away the wine stains and throw it in the washing machine. You can also make tablecloths.

special
occasion

special occasion

Cooking for special times doesn't have to be complicated or stressful. Whether it's an intimate dinner for two, a buffet to feed a crowd or an afternoon tea with friends, with these menus any occasion becomes memorable.

DINNER FOR TWO

nibble   seared scallops on crispy wontons

starter   buffalo mozzarella and zucchini salad

main   grilled lobster with pistachio and preserved lemon butter

side   crispy potato cakes

dessert   peaches and raspberries with toasted cream

DINNER PARTY FOR EIGHT

nibble   prawn cocktails

starter   roast tomatoes with goat's cheese croutons

main   pork cutlets with beetroots and onions

dessert   rosewater semifreddo with nougat liqueur mocha

BUFFET FOR TWELVE

starter   salmon carpaccio with campari dressing

main   veal roasted in cherry tomato sauce

sides   baked parmesan risotto

spinach, green bean and almond salad

dessert   chocolate hazelnut celebration cake

DRINKS PARTY

nibbles   salt and pepper squid

chilli and lemongrass chicken

spiced coconut prawns

sesame pork rice-paper rolls

prosciutto melts

COCKTAIL PARTY

bites   smoked salmon on herb frittatas

chicken dumplings with chilli glaze

rare roast beef with horseradish cream

carrot and parsnip fritters with marinated fetta

crispy four cheese puffs

AFTERNOON TEA

nibbles   almond macaroons with chocolate truffle filling

vanilla bean panna cotta cups with raspberries

chicken sandwiches

little apple tarte tatins

lemon curd cupcakes

DINNER FOR TWO

nibble

seared scallops on crispy wontons

starter

buffalo mozzarella and zucchini salad

main

grilled lobster with pistachio

and preserved lemon butter

side

crispy potato cakes

dessert

peaches and raspberries

with toasted cream

seared scallops on crispy wontons

buffalo mozzarella and zucchini salad

seared scallops on crispy wontons

20g (¾ oz) butter
½ teaspoon finely grated lemon rind
4 scallops, trimmed and cleaned
sea salt and cracked black pepper
1 green onion (scallion), finely sliced
crispy wontons
4 wonton wrappers*
vegetable oil for shallow-frying

To make the crispy wontons, cut a circle from each wonton using a round 5cm (2 in) cookie cutter. Discard the trimmings. Heat 1cm (⅓ in) of the oil in a saucepan over high heat. Cook the wontons two at a time until golden and crisp. Drain on absorbent paper and set aside. Heat a frying pan over high heat. Add the butter and melt. Add the lemon rind and stir. Sprinkle the scallops with the salt and pepper, add to the pan and cook for 20–30 seconds each side or until golden and just cooked through. Place a little of the green onion on each wonton and top with a scallop. Spoon over a little of the pan juices and serve with pre-dinner drinks. Serves 2.

buffalo mozzarella and zucchini salad

1 small green zucchini (courgette), thinly sliced
1 small yellow zucchini (courgette), thinly sliced
3 tablespoons small mint leaves
1½ tablespoons olive oil
1½ tablespoons lemon juice
½ teaspoon caster (superfine) sugar
sea salt and cracked black pepper
1 x 130g (4½ oz) buffalo mozzarella*, halved

Place the zucchinis and mint in a bowl. Combine the oil, lemon juice, sugar, salt and pepper, pour over the salad and toss to combine. Place on serving plates and top with the mozzarella. Serves 2.

grilled lobster with pistachio and preserved lemon butter

2 x 250g (8 oz) raw lobster tails, halved and cleaned
1 lemon, halved
pistachio and preserved lemon butter
80g (3 oz) butter, softened
¼ cup finely chopped raw unsalted pistachio nuts
1½ tablespoons finely chopped preserved lemon rind*
1 tablespoon chopped flat-leaf parsley leaves
sea salt and cracked black pepper

To make the pistachio and preserved lemon butter, place the butter, pistachios, lemon rind, parsley, salt and pepper in a bowl and mix to combine. Spread the butter over the lobster flesh and place on a baking tray. Cook the lobster under a medium preheated grill (broiler) for 8 minutes or until the lobster is cooked through. Serve with the lemon and crispy potato cakes. Serves 2.

Fresh is most definitely best when it comes to seafood. Buy scallops and lobster tails from the fishmonger or fish market as close to the day of serving as possible. At the fishmongers, seafood should be displayed or stored on ice, not in water. The flesh should be white and firm, and have a sweet sea smell. Also, check the lobsters' legs, which shouldn't be discoloured at the joints. If you prefer, use prawns instead of scallops and replace the lobster with firm white fish fillets*.

grilled lobster with pistachio and preserved lemon butter

crispy potato cakes

2 starchy potatoes*, peeled
2 teaspoons rice flour
sea salt
vegetable oil for shallow frying

Cut the potato into long threads using a zester. Place on absorbent paper and squeeze gently to remove any excess liquid. Toss the potato in the combined rice flour and salt. Heat 1cm (⅓ in) of the oil in a frying pan over medium–high heat. Add tablespoonfuls of the potato mixture to the oil, flatten with a spatula and cook for 3–4 minutes each side or until golden and crisp. Drain on absorbent paper. Serves 2.

peaches and raspberries with toasted cream

4 egg yolks
⅓ cup caster (superfine) sugar
2 tablespoons sweet dessert wine
1 peach, halved
100g (3½ oz) raspberries
1 tablespoon icing (confectioner's) sugar

Preheat the oven to 160°C (320°F). Place the egg yolks, sugar and wine in a bowl and beat with an electric mixer for 6–8 minutes or until thick and pale. Divide the peach and raspberries between two small ovenproof dishes. Pour over the egg mixture and dust with the icing sugar. Bake for 12–15 minutes or until golden. Serve warm. Serves 2.

crispy potato cakes

peaches and raspberries with toasted cream

DINNER PARTY FOR EIGHT

nibble
prawn cocktails

starter
roast tomatoes with goat's cheese croutons

main
pork cutlets with beetroots and onions

dessert
rosewater semifreddo with nougat

liqueur mocha

prawn cocktails

roast tomatoes with goat's cheese croutons

prawn cocktails

½ cup whole-egg mayonnaise
2 tablespoons lime juice
1 teaspoon finely grated lime rind
8 baby cos (romaine) lettuce leaves
16 sprigs chervil
16 cooked prawns, peeled
lime wedges to serve

Combine the mayonnaise, lime juice and lime rind. Place the lettuce, chervil and prawns in serving bowls and spoon over the mayonnaise. Serve with the lime. Serves 8.

roast tomatoes with goat's cheese croutons

200g (7 oz) punnet yellow teardrop tomatoes*, halved
250g (8 oz) punnet cherry tomatoes*, halved
250g (8 oz) small tomatoes on the vine*
350g (12 oz) green tomatoes*, halved
3 roma tomatoes*, quartered
⅓ cup oregano leaves
¼ cup (2 fl oz) olive oil
8 slices crusty bread
300g (10 oz) soft goat's cheese
2 tablespoons red wine vinegar*
sea salt and cracked black pepper

Preheat the oven to 180°C (355°F). Place the tomatoes in a baking dish, sprinkle with the oregano and half the oil and cook for 30–40 minutes or until soft. Place the bread under a preheated hot grill (broiler) and toast one side until golden. Spread the untoasted side with the goat's cheese and grill until the cheese is just starting to brown. Place the goat's cheese croutons and tomatoes on serving plates and top with the combined vinegar, salt, pepper and remaining oil. Serves 8.

pork cutlets with beetroots and onions

1½ tablespoons fennel seeds
3 tablespoons roughly chopped sage leaves
3 tablespoons rosemary leaves
½ cup flaked sea salt
8 double pork cutlets, trimmed and scored
8 beetroots, trimmed, cleaned and quartered
24 spring onions, trimmed
¼ cup (2 fl oz) olive oil
2 tablespoons rosemary leaves, extra
2 teaspoons sugar
sea salt and cracked black pepper

Preheat the oven to 220°C (425°F). Place the fennel, sage, rosemary and salt in a small food processor and process to a rough powder. Rub the pork with the fennel mixture and place on a baking tray. In a baking dish, toss the beetroots and spring onions in the combined oil, extra rosemary, sugar, salt and pepper. Place the pork in the oven. After 10 minutes, place the beetroots and spring onions in the oven and roast for a further 20 minutes or until the pork is cooked to your liking. Serves 8.

Crackling is the making of a good pork cutlet. To make sure the crackling goes crisp and crunchy when cooking, ensure that the skin is quite dry. Don't store the pork with the skin of one cutlet resting against the flesh of another or it will absorb the moisture from the meat. The best way to dry out the skin is to leave it uncovered in the fridge for an hour or so.

pork cutlets with beetroots and onions

rosewater semifreddo with nougat

3 eggs
2 egg yolks, extra
1 teaspoon vanilla extract
1 teaspoon rosewater*
1 cup caster (superfine) sugar
1¾ cups (14 fl oz) (single or pouring) cream*
100g (3½ oz) store-bought almond or pistachio nougat,
    sliced or finely chopped

Place the eggs, extra yolks, vanilla, rosewater and sugar in a
heatproof bowl. Place the bowl over a saucepan of simmering
water and whisk for 4–5 minutes or until heated and frothy.
Remove from the heat and beat with an electric mixer for
5–6 minutes or until pale and thick. Place the cream in the
bowl of an electric mixer and beat until very soft peaks form.
Gently fold the egg mixture through the cream until just
combined. Spoon the mixture into 8 x ¾ cup (6 fl oz) capacity
ramekins or freezerproof cups. Cover and freeze for 4–6 hours
or until firm. Serve with the nougat slices on the side or
topped with the chopped nougat. Serves 8.

liqueur mocha

100g (3½ oz) dark chocolate, roughly chopped
½ cup (4 fl oz) (single or pouring) cream*
⅔ cup (5 fl oz) hazelnut liqueur
2 tablespoons icing (confectioner's) sugar
8 shots espresso coffee

Place the chocolate and cream in a small saucepan over
medium heat until melted and smooth. Remove from the
heat, add the hazelnut liqueur and sugar and stir. Pour
into serving glasses and add the coffee. Serves 8.

rosewater semifreddo with nougat

liqueur mocha

BUFFET FOR TWELVE

starter

salmon carpaccio with campari dressing

main

veal roasted in cherry tomato sauce

sides

baked parmesan risotto

spinach, green bean and almond salad

dessert

chocolate hazelnut celebration cake

salmon carpaccio with campari dressing

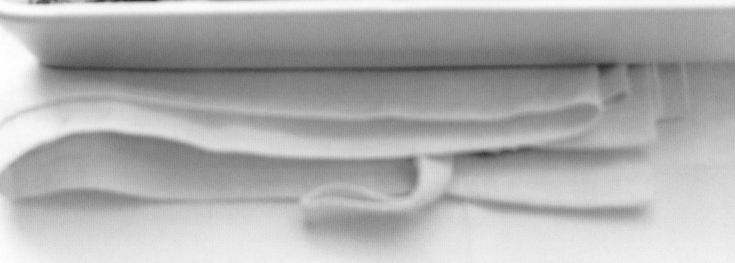

veal roasted in cherry tomato sauce

baked parmesan risotto

3 cups arborio rice*
8 cups (64 fl oz) chicken stock*
2 cups finely grated parmesan cheese
80g (3 oz) butter
sea salt and cracked black pepper

Preheat the oven to 180°C (355°F). Place the rice and stock in a large baking dish and stir to combine. Cover tightly with foil or a lid and bake for 45 minutes or until most of the stock is absorbed and the rice is al dente. Add the parmesan, butter, salt and pepper and stir for 3–4 minutes or until the risotto is thick and creamy. Serves 12.

spinach, green bean and almond salad

1½ cups slivered almonds
⅓ cup (2½ fl oz) lemon juice
½ cup (4 fl oz) olive oil
⅓ cup (2½ fl oz) chicken stock*
1½ tablespoons dijon mustard
1½ tablespoons finely grated lemon rind
½ teaspoon caster (superfine) sugar
sea salt and cracked black pepper
250g (8 oz) baby spinach leaves
1kg (2 lb) green beans, trimmed and blanched

Toast the almonds in a frying pan over medium heat for 1 minute or until golden. Remove from the pan. Add the lemon juice, oil, stock, mustard, lemon rind, sugar, salt and pepper to the pan and simmer for 1 minute. Place the spinach and beans on a serving plate, top with the almonds, pour over the dressing and serve immediately. Serves 12.

baked parmesan risotto

spinach, green bean and almond salad

salmon carpaccio with campari dressing

2 tablespoons olive oil
½ cup salted capers*, rinsed and dried
1 x 700g (23 oz) sashimi salmon*
120g (4 oz) baby rocket (arugula) leaves
campari dressing
¼ cup (2 fl oz) Campari
¼ cup (2 fl oz) lemon juice
¼ cup (2 fl oz) olive oil, extra
1½ teaspoons sugar
sea salt

Heat a frying pan over medium–high heat. Add the oil and capers and cook for 2 minutes or until crisp. Set aside. With a sharp knife very thinly slice the salmon and place on serving plates. Top with the capers and rocket. To make the Campari dressing, mix together the Campari, lemon juice, oil, sugar and salt. Drizzle the Campari dressing over the salmon. Serves 12.

veal roasted in cherry tomato sauce

12 slices provolone cheese*
24 basil leaves
12 veal schnitzel steaks
sea salt and cracked black pepper
olive oil for frying
cherry tomato sauce
3 x 250g (8 oz) punnets cherry tomatoes*, halved
4 cloves garlic, sliced
3 tablespoons oregano leaves
200g (7 oz) black olives
2 tablespoons finely grated lemon rind
3 tablespoons olive oil, extra

Preheat the oven to 180°C (355°F). To make the cherry tomato sauce, place the tomatoes, garlic, oregano, olives, lemon rind and extra oil in a large baking dish and toss to combine. Bake for 40 minutes or until the tomatoes are soft. Place a slice of provolone and two basil leaves on one half of each slice of veal and fold to enclose. Sprinkle with the salt and pepper. Heat a large frying pan over high heat. Add the oil and cook the veal in batches for 30 seconds each side or until brown. Place the veal on the tomatoes and spoon over some of the sauce to coat. Return to the oven and cook for 5 minutes or until the veal is just cooked through. Serves 12.

chocolate hazelnut celebration cake

300g (10 oz) butter, chopped
3 cups brown sugar
4 eggs
1 cup hazelnut meal (ground hazelnuts)* or almond meal (ground almonds)*
1 cup (8 fl oz) milk
2 cups plain (all-purpose) flour
2 teaspoons baking powder
1 cup cocoa powder
fresh berries to serve
chocolate icing
1 cup (8 fl oz) (single or pouring) cream*
½ cup cocoa powder, extra, sifted
400g (14 oz) dark chocolate, chopped
150g (5 oz) butter

Preheat the oven to 160°C (320°F). Place the butter and sugar in the bowl of an electric mixer and beat until light and creamy. Add the eggs and beat well. Add the hazelnut meal and milk, sift over the flour, baking powder and cocoa and mix until combined. Spoon the mixture into 2 x 20cm (8 in) round greased and lined cake tins and bake for 55 minutes or until cooked when tested with a skewer. Allow cakes to cool.
To make the chocolate icing, place the cream and extra cocoa in a saucepan over low heat and stir until smooth. Add the chocolate and butter and stir until smooth. Place the mixture in a bowl and refrigerate until cold. Beat the icing with an electric mixer until light and fluffy. Spread the icing over the tops of both cakes and place one cake on top of the other. Keep cool until serving. Serve with the berries. Serves 12.

A filled, double-layer cake is an impressive dessert to serve, and it's simple too. Make the cakes up to two days ahead of time and store them in an airtight container. Spread the cakes with the icing on the day of serving so dessert will be ready and waiting even before anyone arrives.

chocolate hazelnut celebration cake

DRINKS PARTY

nibbles

salt and pepper squid

chilli and lemongrass chicken

spiced coconut prawns

sesame pork rice-paper rolls

prosciutto melts

salt and pepper squid

chilli and lemongrass chicken

salt and pepper squid

1 tablespoon szechwan peppercorns*
½ teaspoon chilli flakes
1½ teaspoons chinese five-spice powder*
2 teaspoons sea salt
½ cup rice flour*
12 small squid hoods, cleaned, quartered and scored
2 egg whites, lightly beaten
vegetable oil for deep frying
lemon wedges to serve

Heat a frying pan over medium heat. Add the peppercorns, chilli flakes, five-spice powder and salt and cook, stirring, for 1 minute or until fragrant. Place the spice mixture in a small food processor and process to a rough powder. Mix half the spice mixture with the rice flour. Dip the squid in the egg whites and toss in the spice mixture to coat. Heat the oil in a large frying pan or wok over high heat. Cook the squid in batches for 1 minute or until crisp. Drain on absorbent paper and toss with the remaining spice mixture. Serve with the lemon. Serves 6–8.

chilli and lemongrass chicken

2 teaspoons sesame oil
2 stalks lemongrass*, very finely chopped
2 large mild red chillies, seeded and chopped
1 tablespoon finely grated ginger
500g (1 lb) chicken mince
3 tablespoons lime juice
3 tablespoons fish sauce*
2 teaspoons brown sugar
¼ cup shredded mint leaves
16 witlof* (belgian endive) or baby cos (romaine) leaves

Heat a frying pan over high heat. Add the oil, lemongrass, chillies and ginger and cook for 1 minute. Add the mince and cook, stirring, for 5 minutes or until the chicken is cooked through. Stir through the lime juice, fish sauce, sugar and mint. Spoon the lemongrass chicken into the witlof and serve. Makes 16.

spiced coconut prawns

1 stalk lemongrass*, very finely chopped
1 tablespoon grated ginger
2 large mild red chillies, finely chopped
2 cloves garlic, crushed
1 tablespoon vegetable oil
3 tablespoons desiccated coconut
1kg (2 lb) green (raw) prawns, peeled and
   cleaned, tails left intact
salt and pepper
lime wedges to serve

Heat a non-stick frying pan over medium heat. Add the lemongrass, ginger, chillies, garlic and oil and cook, stirring, for 2 minutes or until fragrant. Add the coconut and cook for 1 minute or until toasted. Remove from the pan and set aside. Add the prawns, salt and pepper to the pan and cook for 2–3 minutes or until cooked through. Return the coconut spice mixture to the pan and toss with the prawns. Serve warm with the lime. Serves 6–8.

Don't be tied to the kitchen at a drinks party. Have food circulating around at intervals, not continuously, and ask friends to help by passing around the food. Prepare as much as possible before guests arrive so all that is left to do is the assembly and cooking those dishes that need to be served hot. For the salt and pepper squid, clean, quarter and score the squid and store in the fridge. Make the spice mixture in advance, too. The chilli and lemongrass chicken mixture can also be made ahead of time, reheated and spooned into the witlof* (belgian endive) leaves. Also peel and clean the prawns. Make the sesame pork rice-paper rolls and keep them in the fridge, covered with a damp tea towel, so they don't dry out.

spiced coconut prawns

sesame pork rice-paper rolls

1 tablespoon vegetable oil
2 tablespoons sesame seeds
2 tablespoons grated ginger
300g (10 oz) pork fillet, trimmed and sliced
24 rice paper* rounds
½ cup hoisin sauce*
4 cups grated carrot
6 green onions (scallions), sliced
2 cups coriander (cilantro) leaves
2 cups mint leaves
2 cups basil leaves

Heat a frying pan over high heat. Add the oil, sesame seeds and ginger and cook, stirring, for 2 minutes or until the sesame seeds are golden. Remove from the pan and set aside. Add the pork to the pan in batches and cook for 1–2 minutes or until browned and cooked through. Remove from the heat. Add to the sesame mixture, mix to combine and set aside. Soften each round of rice paper in warm water for 1 minute and pat dry with absorbent paper. To assemble, divide the pork, hoisin sauce, carrot, green onions, coriander, mint and basil between the rice papers. Fold over the base and then roll to enclose the filling. Keep covered with a damp, clean cloth until ready to serve. Makes 24.

prosciutto melts

12 slices goat's cheese
3 teaspoons thyme leaves
6 slices prosciutto*, halved
12 thick slices baguette
olive oil for brushing

Preheat the oven to 180°C (355°F). Sprinkle the goat's cheese with the thyme. Wrap a piece of prosciutto around each slice of the goat's cheese and place on a slice of baguette. Place on a baking tray and brush with the oil. Cook for 10–12 minutes or until the goat's cheese has melted and the baguette is crisp. Makes 12.

Get the drinks party started with an icy mint cocktail. Place 1½ cups (12 fl oz) cranberry juice, 10 large scoops ice and ½ cup (4 fl oz) vodka, gin or campari in a blender and blend until the ice is well crushed. Add 5 large mint leaves and blend until the mint is chopped. Serve in tall glasses with a straw. Make the drinks in batches as people arrive so the ice doesn't melt. Serves 4.

sesame pork rice-paper rolls

prosciutto melts

COCKTAIL PARTY

bites

smoked salmon on herb frittatas

chicken dumplings with chilli glaze

rare roast beef with horseradish cream

carrot and parsnip fritters with

marinated fetta

crispy four cheese puffs

smoked salmon on herb frittatas

chicken dumplings with chilli glaze

smoked salmon on herb frittatas

2 eggs, lightly beaten
2 tablespoons (single or pouring) cream*
1 tablespoon finely chopped dill leaves
1 teaspoon finely grated lemon rind
sea salt and cracked black pepper
60g (2 oz) cream cheese, softened
1 tablespoon lemon juice
2 teaspoons salted capers*, rinsed, dried and chopped
4 slices smoked salmon, cut into thirds
¼ red onion, finely sliced

Preheat the oven to 150°C (300°F). Place the eggs, cream, dill, lemon rind, salt and pepper in a bowl and whisk to combine. Pour the egg mixture into 12 x 2 tablespoon capacity greased non-stick mini muffin tins. Cook for 6–8 minutes or until just set. Cool in the tins for 3 minutes before removing. Combine the cream cheese, lemon juice and capers. Top the frittatas with the cream cheese mixture, a piece of smoked salmon and the onion and serve. Makes 12.

chicken dumplings with chilli glaze

300g (10 oz) chicken mince
¼ cup chopped canned water chestnuts*
2 tablespoons chopped coriander (cilantro) leaves
2 teaspoons finely grated ginger
2 tablespoons soy sauce
20 wonton wrappers*
vegetable oil for greasing
chilli glaze
4 large mild red chillies, seeded and sliced
½ cup (4 fl oz) white vinegar
½ cup sugar

Combine the mince, water chestnuts, coriander, ginger and soy sauce. Place tablespoonfuls of the mixture on the wonton wrappers. Brush the edges with water, bring the corners together and press to seal. Place the dumplings in an oiled steamer over a saucepan of boiling water and steam for 8 minutes or until the dumplings are cooked through. To make the chilli glaze, place the chillies, vinegar and sugar in a saucepan over high heat and boil for 8 minutes or until syrupy. To serve, place the dumplings on chinese soup spoons and spoon over the chilli glaze. Makes 20.

rare roast beef with horseradish cream

12 slices baguette
olive oil for brushing
¼ cup sour cream
2 teaspoons horseradish cream
watercress sprigs to serve
250g (8 oz) piece rare roast beef, finely sliced

Brush the bread with a little of the oil and cook on a preheated hot char-grill until golden and crisp on both sides. Combine the sour cream and horseradish cream. To serve, place sprigs of watercress, a slice of beef and a dollop of the sour cream mixture on the bread. Makes 12.

Planning to make lots of different cocktails will only overload the to-do list for a party. Champagne cocktails are simple, so make bellinis, Kir Royales or classic champagne cocktails. For the bellinis, push a ripe, soft peach through a sieve with the back of a wooden spoon and fill a champagne flute a quarter full with the juice. Top with chilled champagne and serve. If peaches aren't in season, use store-bought peach juice. For the Kir Royales, add a dash of crème de cassis to each glass and fill with champagne. To make the classic champagne cocktails, put a few drops of bitters on white sugar cubes and place one in the bottom of each glass. Fill to a quarter full with orange liqueur, then top with champagne and serve. There's no need to buy expensive champagne when making these cocktails (sparkling wine will do), as other flavours will be added to it.

rare roast beef with horseradish cream

carrot and parsnip fritters with marinated fetta

60g (2 oz) rice flour
½ cup (4 fl oz) iced water
2 teaspoons baking powder
1 egg
½ teaspoon ground cumin
1½ cups grated carrot
1½ cups grated parsnip
¼ cup chopped flat-leaf parsley leaves
sea salt and cracked black pepper
¼ cup (2 fl oz) vegetable oil
350g (12⅓ oz) marinated goat's cheese*
wild rocket (arugula) leaves to serve
cracked black pepper to serve

Place the rice flour, water, baking powder, egg, cumin, carrot, parsnip, parsley, salt and pepper in a large bowl and mix to combine. Heat the oil in a large frying pan. Place tablespoons of the carrot mixture in the pan, flatten slightly and cook in batches for 1–2 minutes each side or until golden. Serve warm topped with the goat's cheese, rocket and pepper. Makes 35.

crispy four cheese puffs

½ cup grated cheddar cheese
¼ cup finely grated parmesan cheese
50g (1½ oz) blue cheese, chopped
100g (3½ oz) fresh ricotta cheese
sea salt and cracked black pepper
16 wonton wrappers*
vegetable oil for shallow frying

Combine the cheddar, parmesan, blue cheese, ricotta, salt and pepper. Place 2 tablespoons of the mixture onto each wonton wrapper and wet the edges with a little water. Fold in half and press to seal. Heat 1cm (⅓ in) of the oil in a frying pan over medium–high heat until hot. Fry the wontons in batches until puffed and golden. Drain on absorbent paper. Makes 16.

carrot and parsnip fritters with marinated fetta   crispy four cheese puffs

AFTERNOON TEA

nibbles

almond macaroons with

chocolate truffle filling

vanilla bean panna cotta cups with raspberries

chicken sandwiches

little apple tarte tatins

lemon curd cupcakes

almond macaroons with chocolate truffle filling

vanilla bean panna cotta cups with raspberries

almond macaroons with chocolate truffle filling

⅔ cup blanched almonds
1 cup icing (confectioner's) sugar
2 egg whites
1 tablespoon caster (superfine) sugar
chocolate truffle filling
200g (7 oz) dark chocolate
⅓ cup (2½ fl oz) (single or pouring) cream*

Preheat the oven to 180°C (355°F). Place the almonds and icing sugar in a food processor and process until very finely chopped. Place the egg whites in a bowl and whisk until soft peaks form. Add the caster sugar and beat well. Fold through the almond mixture. Place 2 teaspoonfuls of the mixture on baking trays lined with non-stick baking paper and bake for 8–10 minutes or until crisp on the outside. Allow to cool on the trays. To make the chocolate truffle filling, place the chocolate and cream in a saucepan over low heat and stir until smooth. Refrigerate until thick. Sandwich together the biscuits with a generous spoonful of the chocolate truffle filling. Makes 16.

vanilla bean panna cotta cups with raspberries

¼ cup (2 fl oz) water
3½ teaspoons powdered gelatine
3¼ cups (26 fl oz) (single or pouring) cream*
¾ cup icing (confectioner's) sugar
1 vanilla bean*, split and scraped
1 piece lemon rind
150g (5 oz) raspberries
2 teaspoons icing (confectioner's) sugar, extra

Place the water in a bowl and sprinkle over the gelatine. Set aside for 5 minutes. Place the cream, sugar, vanilla bean and lemon rind in a saucepan over medium–low heat and simmer, stirring occasionally, for 5 minutes. Add the gelatine mixture and stir for 2 minutes. Remove the vanilla bean and lemon rind. Pour into 12 small glasses or cups and refrigerate for 4 hours or until set. To serve, toss the raspberries in the extra icing sugar and place on top of the panna cotta. Makes 12.

chicken sandwiches

12 slices white bread
butter for spreading
2 cups chopped cooked chicken breast fillet
¾ cup whole-egg mayonnaise
2 tablespoons lemon juice
2 tablespoons chopped basil leaves
2 tablespoons shredded mint leaves
sea salt and cracked black pepper
whole-egg mayonnaise, extra, for spreading
⅓ cup finely chopped chives

Spread one side of the bread with the butter. Combine the chicken, mayonnaise, lemon juice, basil, mint, salt and pepper. Divide between half the bread slices and top with remaining bread. Cut into small triangles and brush one side with the extra mayonnaise. Press the mayonnaise into the chives and serve. Makes 24.

Throwing an afternoon tea party is a lot of fun, especially if some of the cooking is done in advance. The lemon curd for the cupcakes will keep in a jar in the fridge for up to two weeks. Bake the macaroons and cupcakes two days ahead of time and after they've cooled, store them in an airtight container. Fill them just before serving. The vanilla bean panna cotta cups can be made two days in advance. Keep them covered in the fridge. The little apple tarte tatins can be made on the morning before the party. Leave them in the tins, then reheat them in the oven just before serving. Make the chicken sandwiches a few hours ahead of time and cover them with a just damp tea towel to stop the bread from drying out.

chicken sandwiches

little apple tarte tatins

butter, melted, for greasing
60g (2 oz) butter, extra
¾ cup caster (superfine) sugar
2 tablespoons water
2 green apples, peeled, cored and sliced
300g (10 oz) ready-prepared puff pastry*

Preheat the oven to 180°C (355°F). Lightly grease 12 x ½ cup (4 fl oz) capacity non-stick muffin tins with the melted butter. Heat a frying pan over medium heat. Add the extra butter and melt. Add the sugar and water and cook, stirring, until the sugar has dissolved. Continue to cook for 5 minutes or until the mixture is a light golden colour. Add the apples and cook for 5 minutes. Arrange the apples in the base of each tin and top with the caramel mixture. Roll out the pastry on a lightly floured surface until 3mm (⅛ in) thick. Cut out rounds of the pastry to fit inside the tins. Bake for 10 minutes or until the pastry is puffed and golden. Allow to stand for 2 minutes then invert onto serving plates. Serve warm or cool with thick (double) cream. Makes 12.

lemon curd cupcakes

125g (4 oz) butter, softened
½ cup caster (superfine) sugar
1 teaspoon vanilla extract
2 eggs
1 cup plain (all-purpose) flour
2 teaspoons baking powder
¼ cup (2 fl oz) milk
icing (confectioner's) sugar for dusting
lemon curd
½ cup (4 fl oz) lemon juice
125g (4 oz) butter, extra, chopped
1 cup caster (superfine) sugar, extra
3 eggs, extra, beaten

Preheat the oven to 180°C (355°F). To make the lemon curd, place the lemon juice, extra butter, extra sugar and extra eggs in a heatproof bowl over a saucepan of rapidly simmering water for 6–8 minutes, stirring continuously, or until the mixture has thickened. Refrigerate until cool. Place the butter, sugar and vanilla in the bowl of an electric mixer and beat until light and creamy. Gradually add the eggs and beat well after each addition. Add the flour, baking powder and milk and beat well. Spoon the mixture into 12 x ½ cup (4 fl oz) capacity muffin tins lined with paper patty cases and bake for 15 minutes or until cooked when tested with a skewer. Set aside to cool. Cut a circle out of each cupcake and fill with the lemon curd. Top with the cupcake circle and dust with the icing sugar. Makes 12.

little apple tarte tatins

lemon curd cupcakes

style

single stem

A single flower in a small juice or nectar bottle is an elegant, done-in-a-minute table decoration. Use open lisianthus or rose bloom, remove all the leaves and buds from the stems, and place in a bottle filled with water. Group the bottles on a plate, place them in a line down the middle of the table or put one in front of each guest's plate.

icy treats

An ice-cream and sorbet tasting plate is a simple dessert for lots of guests. Place eggcups in the freezer to chill, fill them with different types of ice-cream and sorbet and place on stacked cake stands. Everyone can pick the flavour they want, but make sure you scoop enough so there's more than one for each person. Collect eggcups from antique and junk stores.

stitched up

Give traditional doilies a new lease on life by making them into a table runner. Stitch doilies of different shapes, sizes and colours onto a length of cotton or linen fabric. If you don't have enough to make a runner, make a large placemat to put in the middle of the table. Take care when washing doilies, especially if they are old or family heirlooms, as they can be fragile.

take away

Put together grown-up party favours by filling cellophane bags with store-bought filled macaroons. Make a bag for each guest or couple and tie them up with ribbon. Give them out as guests leave so they can be nibbled on the way home or enjoyed the next day with coffee. You could also use shortbread biscuits, small filled cookies or chocolate truffles.

style

fragrant fruit

Instead of a vase of flowers or a perfumed candle, use fragrant fruit to scent the dining room. Fill a large, decorative bowl with one type of fruit, such as quinces, guavas, persimmons or mangos, and place it on a sideboard or table. They will fill the room with a subtle fragrance that won't clash with food. Choose fruits in season as they will have stronger scent.

cover up

There's no need to have lots of vases of different shapes and sizes to make the perfect floral centrepiece, you can use jars. Place them in white paper sweet bags to hide labels that haven't come off completely or jars that don't match. Start a collection by washing out jam and condiment jars after you've finished eating their contents.

autumn leaves

Bring autumn to the table by using coloured leaves as a table decoration. Cover the table with a white tablecloth, position the leaves on the cloth and top with a piece of sheer fabric. Also put a leaf on each guest's plate. These can be made into quick and easy placesettings by writing each person's name on the leaf with a felt-tip pen.

chocolate block

A delicious and lazy dessert, especially if you're catering for a crowd, is a block of couverture chocolate. Couverture is a bittersweet chocolate high in cocoa butter that goes well with dessert wine, port, muscat or coffee liqueur. After the meal, place the block of chocolate on a platter and let everyone chip away chunks with a small, sharp knife as they sip.

barbecues
+ brunch

barbecues + brunch
Think beyond the usual entertaining times and invite people over for brunch or a mid-afternoon barbecue. They're more laid-back, more relaxed times to get together, so heat up the grill or set the table for brunch.

CLASSIC BBQ
starter — chilli and lime grilled corn
main — steak sandwiches with lemon aioli
side — char-grilled asparagus salad
dessert — peach and passionfruit trifle

SUMMER LUNCH
starter — mushroom and ricotta bruschetta
main — balsamic and lemon chicken
side — summer potato salad
dessert — seared nectarines with caramelised yoghurt

SOUTHERN-STYLE GRILL
starter — chicken, lime and coriander quesadillas
main — crispy fish with green chilli salsa
side — avocado and chickpea salad
dessert — almond wafers with lime sorbet and tequila

SPICED GRILL
starter — grilled eggplant and white bean salad
main — spiced lamb with tahini dressing
side — mint and fetta tabbouli
dessert — date and almond cakes with orange syrup

LATE BREAKFAST
main — three cheese frittata
sides — crispy bacon rosemary ties
herb-roasted tomatoes
dessert — apple and strawberry galettes

BRUNCH DATE
mains — lemon and sugar puff pancakes
berry bircher
raspberry and mango in rosewater syrup
side — almond and maple yoghurt

CLASSIC BBQ

starter

chilli and lime grilled corn

main

steak sandwiches with lemon aioli

side

char-grilled asparagus salad

dessert

peach and passionfruit trifle

chilli and lime grilled corn

steak sandwiches with lemon aioli

chilli and lime grilled corn

80g (3 oz) butter, melted
2 tablespoons finely grated lime rind
½ teaspoon chilli powder
sea salt and cracked black pepper
4 cobs corn, silk removed

Preheat a barbecue or char-grill to medium. Combine the butter, lime rind, chilli powder, salt and pepper. Brush over the corn and cook for 10 minutes turning occasionally and brushing with the butter mixture. Serve topped with any remaining butter mixture. Serves 4.

steak sandwiches with lemon aioli

8 x 100g (3½ oz) sirloin or fillet steaks
sea salt and cracked black pepper
4 slices wood-fired bread, toasted
80g (3 oz) wild rocket (arugula) leaves
lemon aioli
¾ cup whole-egg mayonnaise
2 cloves garlic, crushed
2 tablespoons lemon juice

To make the lemon aioli, combine the mayonnaise, garlic and lemon juice. Preheat a barbecue or char-grill to high. Sprinkle the steak with the salt and pepper and cook for 2 minutes each side or until cooked to your liking. To serve, place the bread on plates and top with the steaks, lemon aioli and rocket. Serves 4.

char-grilled asparagus salad

400g (14 oz) asparagus, trimmed
80g (3 oz) curly endive (frisée)
parmesan cheese shavings to serve
2 tablespoons wholegrain mustard
2 tablespoons honey
2 tablespoons olive oil
sea salt and cracked black pepper

Preheat a barbecue or char-grill to medium. Cook the asparagus for 2 minutes each side or until just tender. Place on a serving plate and top with the endive and parmesan. Whisk together the mustard, honey, oil, salt and pepper, spoon over the salad and serve. Serves 4.

peach and passionfruit trifle

½ cup (4 fl oz) sweet dessert wine
2 tablespoons caster (superfine) sugar
3 passionfruit, pulp only
4 large slices sponge cake* or 8 sponge finger (savoiardi) biscuits*
2 peaches, sliced
¾ cup (6 fl oz) (single or pouring) cream*
1 tablespoon icing (confectioner's) sugar

Place the dessert wine, sugar and passionfruit in a frying pan and simmer for 4 minutes or until slightly thickened. Place the cake on serving plates, top with the peaches and spoon over the dessert wine mixture. Place the cream and sugar in a bowl and whisk until soft peaks form. Serve with the trifle. Serves 4.

char-grilled asparagus salad

peach and passionfruit trifle

SUMMER LUNCH

starter

mushroom and ricotta bruschetta

main

balsamic and lemon chicken

side

summer potato salad

dessert

seared nectarines

with caramelised yoghurt

mushroom and ricotta bruschetta

balsamic and lemon chicken + summer potato salad

mushroom and ricotta bruschetta

4 large slices wood-fired bread
8 small flat (field) mushrooms
olive oil for brushing
1 clove garlic, halved
sea salt and cracked black pepper
100g (3½ oz) fresh ricotta cheese
2 teaspoons thyme leaves
finely grated parmesan cheese to serve
lemon wedges to serve

Preheat a barbecue or char-grill to medium–high. Brush the bread and mushrooms with the oil and cook for 2 minutes each side or until the bread is toasted and the mushrooms are soft. To serve, rub the bread with the garlic and place on serving plates. Top with the mushrooms and sprinkle with the salt, pepper, ricotta, thyme and parmesan. Serve with the lemon wedges. Serves 4.

balsamic and lemon chicken

4 chicken breast fillets, trimmed
4 large sprigs sage
½ cup (4 fl oz) balsamic vinegar*
¼ cup (2 fl oz) lemon juice
2 tablespoons brown sugar
sea salt and cracked black pepper

Place the chicken in a large, shallow dish with the sage. Combine the vinegar, lemon juice, sugar, salt and pepper and pour over the chicken. Refrigerate for 15 minutes to marinate. Preheat a barbecue or char-grill to medium–high. Drain the chicken and sage from the marinade and reserve. Cook the chicken and sage for 4–5 minutes each side or until the chicken is cooked through. While the chicken is cooking, place the marinade in a small saucepan over high heat and cook for 2–3 minutes or until slightly thickened. To serve, slice the chicken into large pieces and place on serving plates with the sage. Spoon over the sauce and serve with the summer potato salad. Serves 4.

summer potato salad

600g (20 oz) kipfler (fingerling) potatoes, sliced
50g (1½ oz) shredded rocket (arugula) leaves
dressing
2 tablespoons chopped preserved lemon rind*
1 tablespoon wholegrain mustard
½ cup whole-egg mayonnaise
2 tablespoons lemon juice
sea salt and cracked black pepper

Place the potatoes in a saucepan of boiling water and cook until tender. Drain and rinse under running water. Toss the potato with the rocket. To make the dressing, place the preserved lemon rind, mustard, mayonnaise, lemon juice, salt and pepper in a bowl and whisk to combine. To serve, pour the dressing over the potatoes and rocket and toss gently. Serve with the balsamic and lemon chicken. Serves 4.

seared nectarines with caramelised yoghurt

½ cup brown sugar
4 nectarines, halved and stones removed
caramelised yoghurt
1½ cups thick natural yoghurt
2 teaspoons vanilla extract
2 tablespoons brown sugar

Place the sugar on a plate and press the cut side of the nectarines into the sugar. Heat a non-stick frying pan over medium–high heat. Place the nectarines in the pan, sugar-side down, and cook for 1 minute or until golden. Remove from the pan. To make the caramelised yoghurt, combine the yoghurt and vanilla. Sprinkle with the sugar and stand for 1 minute so the sugar melts. Serves 4.

seared nectarines with caramelised yoghurt

SOUTHERN-STYLE GRILL

starter

chicken, lime and coriander quesadillas

main

crispy fish with green chilli salsa

side

avocado and chickpea salad

dessert

almond wafers with lime sorbet

and tequila

chicken, lime and coriander quesadillas

crispy fish with green chilli salsa

chicken, lime and coriander quesadillas

2 chicken breast fillets, cooked and thinly sliced
½ tablespoon lime juice
½ cup coriander (cilantro) leaves
1 large mild red chilli, seeded and chopped
2 green onions (scallions), finely sliced
1⅓ cups grated cheddar cheese
sea salt and cracked black pepper
8 small flour or corn tortillas
vegetable oil for brushing
lime wedges to serve
sour cream to serve

Preheat a barbecue or char-grill to medium. Combine the chicken, lime juice, coriander, chilli, green onions, cheddar, salt and pepper. Divide the mixture between half the tortillas and top with the remaining tortillas. Brush both sides with the oil and cook for 2–3 minutes each side or until crisp. Cut in half and serve warm with the lime wedges and sour cream. Serves 4.

crispy fish with green chilli salsa

2 cups coriander (cilantro) leaves
2 tablespoons finely grated lemon rind
2 tablespoons olive oil
sea salt and cracked black pepper
8 x 70g (2½ oz) firm white fish fillets*, skin on
mixed salad leaves to serve
green chilli salsa
5 large mild green chillies
½ red onion, sliced
1 lemon, peeled and chopped
2 teaspoons sugar
sea salt and cracked black pepper

Preheat a barbecue or char-grill to high. To make the green chilli salsa, cook the chillies for 3–4 minutes or until blackened. Halve the chillies, deseed and chop. Combine with the onion, lemon, sugar, salt and pepper. Set aside. Place the coriander, lemon rind, oil, salt and pepper in a food processor and process until smooth. Brush the coriander mixture on the skin of the fish and cook for 3 minutes each side or until cooked through. Place on serving plates, top with the green chilli salsa and serve with the salad leaves. Serves 4.

avocado and chickpea salad

400g (14 oz) can chickpeas (garbanzos), drained and rinsed
1 avocado, peeled and quartered
½ cup mint leaves
4 slices iceberg lettuce
¼ cup (2 fl oz) lime juice
1 tablespoon olive oil
½ teaspoon sugar
sea salt and cracked black pepper

Roughly chop the chickpeas and combine with the avocado and mint. Place the chickpea mixture on the lettuce. Combine the lime juice, oil, sugar, salt and pepper and drizzle over the salad. Serves 4.

almond wafers with lime sorbet and tequila

2 egg whites
½ cup caster (superfine) sugar
¼ cup plain (all-purpose) flour
½ cup almond meal* (ground almonds)
70g (2½ oz) butter, melted and cooled
⅓ cup flaked almonds
store-bought lime sorbet to serve
4 shots tequila, well chilled, to serve
2 passionfruits, halved, to serve

Preheat the oven to 190°C (375°F). Mix the egg whites and sugar. Add the flour, almond meal and butter and mix to combine. Spread the mixture into 4 x 14cm (5½ in) circles on a tray lined with non-stick baking paper. Press the almonds into the mixture and bake for 15 minutes or until golden. Place scoops of lime sorbet in serving bowls, pour the tequila into cold shot glasses and serve with the passionfruit halves and wafers. Makes 4.

On a hot day, salad leaves can wilt. Make sure they stay crisp by refreshing them in iced water. Dry them well and don't dress the leaves until just before serving or they'll lose their crunch.

avocado and chickpea salad   almond wafers with lime sorbet and tequila

163

SPICED GRILL

starter

grilled eggplant and white bean salad

main

spiced lamb with tahini dressing

side

mint and fetta tabbouli

dessert

date and almond cakes with orange syrup

grilled eggplant and white bean salad

spiced lamb with tahini dressing + mint and fetta tabbouli

grilled eggplant and white bean salad

2 eggplants (aubergines), sliced
4 tablespoons olive oil
sea salt
90g (3 oz) baby spinach leaves
440g (15½ oz) can white beans*, drained and rinsed
250g (8 oz) cherry tomatoes*, sliced
parsley dressing
2 tablespoons sherry vinegar*
1 tablespoon pine nuts
2 cloves garlic, crushed
1½ cups flat-leaf parsley leaves
3 tablespoons olive oil, extra
sea salt and cracked black pepper

Preheat a barbecue or char-grill to hot. Brush the eggplant with the combined oil and salt and cook for 1 minute each side or until soft. To make the parsley dressing, place the vinegar, pine nuts, garlic, parsley, extra oil, salt and pepper in a food processor and process until finely chopped. To serve, arrange the spinach, white beans, tomatoes and eggplant on a serving platter and spoon over the parsley dressing. Serves 4.

spiced lamb with tahini dressing

2 teaspoons ground cumin
½ teaspoon chilli powder
sea salt and cracked black pepper
750g (1⅔ lb) boneless lamb loin, trimmed
flat or turkish bread, toasted, to serve
rocket (arugula) leaves to serve
tahini dressing
½ cup tahini*
⅓ cup (2½ fl oz) water
⅓ cup (2½ fl oz) lemon juice
2 cloves garlic, crushed
1 tablespoon sugar

Combine the cumin, chilli powder, salt and pepper and sprinkle over the lamb. Preheat a barbecue or char-grill to medium–high. Cook the lamb for 4–5 minutes each side or until cooked to your liking. To make the tahini dressing, place the tahini, water, lemon juice, garlic and sugar in a bowl and whisk to combine. To serve, slice the lamb and serve with the tahini dressing, bread, rocket and mint and fetta tabbouli. Serves 4.

mint and fetta tabbouli

1 cup cracked wheat* (burghul/bulghur)
1 cup (8 fl oz) boiling water
1 cup chopped mint leaves
1 cup chopped flat-leaf parsley leaves
6 green onions (scallions), sliced
150g (5 oz) fetta cheese, crumbled
¼ cup (2 fl oz) lemon juice
1 tablespoon olive oil
sea salt and cracked black pepper

Place the wheat and water in a bowl, cover with plastic wrap and stand for 5 minutes or until the water has been absorbed. Mix the wheat with the mint, parsley, green onions, fetta, lemon juice, oil, salt and pepper and toss to combine. Serve with the spiced lamb with tahini dressing. Serves 4.

date and almond cakes with orange syrup

½ cup plain (all-purpose) flour
¾ cup almond meal* (ground almonds)
½ teaspoon baking powder
½ cup caster (superfine) sugar
½ cup roughly chopped pitted dates
75g (2½ oz) butter, melted
2 tablespoons milk
1 egg
orange syrup
½ cup caster (superfine) sugar, extra
½ cup (4 fl oz) orange juice
2 tablespoons finely grated orange rind

Preheat the oven to 160°C (320°F). Place the flour, almond meal, baking powder, sugar and dates in a bowl and mix to combine. Add the butter, milk and egg and mix to combine. Spoon the mixture into greased 1 cup (8 fl oz) capacity muffin tins and bake for 25 minutes or until cooked when tested with a skewer. While the cakes are cooking, make the orange syrup. Place the extra sugar, orange juice and orange rind in a saucepan and stir over low heat until the sugar has dissolved. Simmer for 5–7 minutes or until slightly thickened. Spoon the warm syrup over the warm cakes and serve with thick (double) cream. Serves 4.

date and almond cakes with orange syrup

LATE BREAKFAST

main

three cheese frittata

sides

crispy bacon rosemary ties

herb-roasted tomatoes

dessert

apple and strawberry galettes

crispy bacon rosemary ties

three cheese frittata

crispy bacon rosemary ties

8 rashers smoked bacon, rind removed
8 large sprigs rosemary

Preheat the oven to 180°C (355°F). Wrap each rasher of the bacon around a sprig of rosemary and place in a baking dish. Bake for 20 minutes or until the bacon is crisp. Serve with the three cheese frittata and herb-roasted tomatoes. Serves 4.

three cheese frittata

8 eggs
¾ cup (6 fl oz) milk
sea salt and cracked black pepper
30g (1 oz) butter
¼ cup shredded basil leaves
250g (8 oz) fresh ricotta cheese, drained
1 cup grated aged cheddar cheese
½ cup grated gruyère cheese*
buttered toast to serve

Heat a non-stick frying pan with an ovenproof handle over medium heat. Whisk together the eggs, milk, salt and pepper. Place the butter in the pan and melt. Pour in the egg mixture and sprinkle over the basil, ricotta, cheddar and gruyère. Cook for 3–4 minutes or until the frittata is starting to set around the edges. Place the pan under a preheated hot grill (broiler) and cook for 8–10 minutes or until the frittata is set. Serve warm cut into wedges with the toast, crispy bacon rosemary ties and herb-roasted tomatoes. Serves 4.

herb-roasted tomatoes

4 tomatoes*, halved
24 basil leaves
8 small sprigs thyme
olive oil for drizzling
sea salt and cracked black pepper

Preheat the oven to 180°C (355°F). Cut three slashes in each tomato and push in three basil leaves. Push a sprig of thyme into one slash in each tomato. Place on a baking tray lined with non-stick baking paper, drizzle with the oil and sprinkle with the salt and pepper. Bake for 30 minutes. Serve with the three cheese frittata and crispy bacon rosemary ties. Serves 4.

apple and strawberry galettes

360g (12½ oz) ready-prepared puff pastry*
4 tablespoons strawberry jam (jelly)
¼ cup almond meal* (ground almonds)
1 apple, thinly sliced
100g (3½ oz) strawberries, thinly sliced
1 tablespoon sugar

Preheat the oven to 190°C (375°F). Roll out the pastry on a lightly floured surface to 3mm (⅛ in) thick, cut into 4 x 14cm (5½ in) circles and place on a baking tray lined with non-stick baking paper. Spread each pastry circle with the jam, sprinkle with the almond meal and top with the apple and strawberries. Sprinkle with the sugar and bake for 15–20 minutes or until the pastry is puffed and golden. Serves 4.

herb-roasted tomatoes

apple and strawberry galettes

BRUNCH DATE

mains

lemon and sugar puff pancakes

berry bircher

raspberry and mango in rosewater syrup

side

almond and maple yoghurt

lemon and sugar puff pancakes

berry bircher

lemon and sugar puff pancakes

1 cup plain (all-purpose) flour
2½ teaspoons baking powder
⅓ cup caster (superfine) sugar
200g (7 oz) fresh ricotta cheese
⅔ cup (5 fl oz) milk
2 teaspoons finely grated lemon rind
60g (2 oz) butter, melted
2 eggs, separated
butter, extra, for greasing
1 cup caster (superfine) sugar, extra
lemon wedges to serve

Sift the flour, baking powder and sugar into a bowl. Add the ricotta, milk, lemon rind, butter and egg yolks and mix to combine. In a separate clean bowl, whisk the egg whites until soft peaks form. Fold the egg whites through the flour mixture. Heat a non-stick frying pan over medium–low heat. Add a little of the extra butter to the pan and then add spoonfuls of the mixture and cook for 2–3 minutes each side or until golden and puffed. Remove from the pan and roll in the extra sugar to coat. Repeat with the remaining mixture. Serve with the lemon wedges. Makes 20.

berry bircher

1½ cups rolled oats
1 cup (8 fl oz) apple juice, warmed
½ cup chopped raw unsalted pistachio nuts
½ teaspoon ground cinnamon
1 cup thick natural yoghurt
2 cups mixed berries
maple syrup to serve

Place the oats and apple juice in a bowl, cover with plastic wrap and allow to stand for 30 minutes or until the oats are soft. Mix through the pistachios, cinnamon and yoghurt and half the berries. To serve, top with the remaining berries and maple syrup. Serves 4.

almond and maple yoghurt

½ cup chopped blanched almonds
½ cup (4 fl oz) maple syrup
2 teaspoons vanilla extract
2 cups thick natural yoghurt

Place the almonds in a frying pan over medium heat and stir until golden. Add the maple syrup and vanilla and simmer for 1 minute. Set aside to cool. Divide the yoghurt between four glasses and pour over the almond mixture. Serve with the raspberry and mango in rosewater syrup. Serves 4.

raspberry and mango in rosewater syrup

½ cup sugar
1 cup (8 fl oz) water
½ teaspoon rosewater*
1½ cups raspberries+
2 mangoes, peeled and thickly sliced

Place the sugar and water in a saucepan over low heat and stir until the sugar has dissolved. Simmer for 5 minutes, remove from the heat and stir through the rosewater. Refrigerate until cold. To serve, place the raspberries and mango in a bowl and pour over the rosewater syrup. Serve with the almond and maple yoghurt. Serves 4.
+ Use frozen raspberries and mangoes if fresh aren't available.

Having people over for breakfast or brunch can seem overwhelming. Some of these recipes can be made the day before. Place the bircher in the serving glasses, cover and store in the fridge. Top with the berries and maple syrup just before serving. Make the almond and maple mixture and rosewater syrup and put them both in the fridge until your guests arrive.

raspberry and mango in rosewater syrup + almond and maple yoghurt

style

it's a wrap

To make a glass vase of flowers look especially neat, wrap leaves around the inside to hide the stems. Using banana leaves, wet one side of each leaf so they will stick to the glass, then add the water and flowers. Trim the stems of the flowers before arranging them in the vase so they will last for several days after purchasing.

single serve

Make up individual serves of condiments to match your menu. Buy a small bamboo steamer for each guest from an Asian food store and tie ribbon around the outside. Decant condiments like mayonnaise, tomato sauce and mustard into small jars and bottles, then pack them into the steamers. Place one in front of each guest's plate.

table scent

Instead of flowers, place bunches of herbs in several small jugs along the dining table. Put a combination of different herbs in each jug. Choose varieties that have a strong fragrance, such as mint, thyme, rosemary and basil, or that are included in the dishes you've cooked. After you've finished using them on the table, store them in the fridge for cooking.

you're set

Sushi mats make great placemats. Buy one for each guest and thread ribbon between the gaps in the mat and attach a knife, fork and napkin. You can then roll them up and take them outdoors or on a picnic. Sushi mats are inexpensive and easy to clean – just brush the crumbs out. They are available from Asian food stores and supermarkets.

style

freshen up

After a barbecue pass around a bowl of warm refresher towels so everyone can clean their hands. Fold up a square of muslin or baby face washer for each person and place them in a microwave-proof, lidded bowl. Wet the muslin with water, add a strip of lemon rind and microwave for about 30 seconds. The lemon rind will give the towels a fresh scent.

in bloom

Eggcups make great vases for single blooms. Group them together on a plate with a frangipani, daisy or rose in each one as a centrepiece or put an eggcup in front of every placesetting. To make them into placecards, write the name of each guest on a luggage tag and tie it around the base of each eggcup with kitchen string or ribbon.

iced coffee

On a warm day, skip the hot coffee at brunch and serve iced coffee the way the Italians do. Just before serving, fill a tall glass for each person with shaved ice and pour over a shot of cooled, strong espresso. Top with a dollop of softly whipped, unsweetend cream. Serve icing (confectioner's) sugar on the side for those who like it sweet.

centre stage

Use a tealight holder as a floral centrepiece. Take out the tealight candles, fill the glass holders with water and place small flowers, such as hydrangeas, inside. For flowers with longer stems, like lisianthus and miniature roses, place small glass nectar or juice bottles in the holders. You can buy tealight holders from junk and antique shops.

glossary

almond meal
Also known as ground almonds, it is available from most supermarkets. Used instead of, or as well as, flour in cakes and desserts. Make your own by processing whole skinned almonds to a fine meal in a food processor or blender (130g/4 oz almonds will give 1 cup almond meal). To remove the skins from almonds, wrap in a tea towel and rub vigorously.

arborio rice
Has a short, plump-looking grain with surface starch which creates a cream with the stock when cooked to al dente in risotto. Substitute with carnaroli rice.

baby bok choy
A mild-flavoured green vegetable, also known as chinese chard or chinese white cabbage. It can be cooked whole after washing. If using the larger type, separate the leaves and trim the white stalks. Limit the cooking time so that it stays green and slightly crisp.

balsamic vinegar
This Italian vinegar, although tart like other varieties, has a less astringent taste and more of a rich, red wine flavour. Like some wines, the older a balsamic vinegar is, the better it tastes.

bocconcini
Fresh mozzarella balls, that are small in size and usually made from cow's milk. Sold in a whey liquid at supermarkets and delicatessens.

broccolini
A cross between gai larn (chinese broccoli) and broccoli, this green vegetable has long, thin stems and small florets. Sold in bunches at supermarkets and greengrocers, it can be substituted for broccoli.

buffalo mozzarella
Made from water buffalo's milk, this is considered to be the best mozzarella. It is sold in whey in balls at specialty food stores and delicatessens.

capers
The small, deep green flower buds of the caper bush. Available packed either in brine or salt. Use salt-packed capers when possible, as the texture is firmer and the flavour superior. Rinse thoroughly before use.

celeriac
A root vegetable (also called celery root) with white flesh and a mild celery flavour. It is available in winter from supermarkets and greengrocers. Use in salads and soups or roast it with meats.

cellophane noodles
See noodles.

cherry tomatoes
See tomatoes.

chinese five-spice powder
This combination of cinnamon, anise pepper, star anise, clove and fennel is excellent with chicken, meats and seafood. It is sold in Asian food stores and most supermarkets.

cracked wheat
Also known as burghul and bulghur, whole wheat is par-boiled, then cracked and dried. It is used in the salad tabbouli. Available from supermarkets.

cream
Pouring or single cream is also called medium cream. It has a butterfat content of 20–30 per cent. Thick or double cream, which is thick enough to be dolloped, has a butterfat content of 45–55 per cent.

fennel
With its mild aniseed flavour and crisp texture, fennel bulbs are ideal for salads or roasted with meats or fish. Available from supermarkets and greengrocers, it is best in spring.

fish sauce
An amber-coloured liquid drained from salted, fermented fish and used in Thai dishes. Available from supermarkets and Asian food stores, where it is often labelled 'nam pla'.

firm white fish fillets
In this book, snapper, barramundi or blue-eye cod fillets have been used where firm white fish fillets are listed in the ingredients. Use any other white fish that has a firm texture, holds it shape when cooked and is quite 'meaty'.

gai larn
A leafy, dark green vegetable, also known as chinese broccoli. Steam, blanch or stir-fry and serve with soy sauce as a simple side dish. Buy from the greengrocers.

green tomatoes
See tomatoes.

gruyère cheese
Originating in Switzerland, this firm cheese is made from cow's milk and is light yellow in colour. Gruyère melts well and is ideal in cooking. Also use it in sandwiches or serve at the end of a meal as part of a cheese plate. Buy from specialty food stores.

haloumi
Firm white Middle Eastern cheese made from sheep's milk. It has a stringy texture and is usually sold in brine. Available from delicatessens and some supermarkets.

hazelnut meal
Available at many supermarkets, it is also called ground hazelnuts. Make your own by processing whole skinned hazelnuts to a fine meal in a food processor or blender (130g/4 oz hazelnuts will give 1 cup hazelnut meal). To remove the skins from hazelnuts, wrap in a tea towel and rub vigorously.

hoisin sauce
A thick, sweet Chinese sauce made from fermented soybeans, sugar, salt and red rice. Used as a dipping sauce or marinade and as the sauce with Peking duck. Available from Asian food stores and most supermarkets.

honeydew melon
A medium-sized melon with yellow skin and green flesh. Buy from supermarkets and greengrocers.

kaffir lime leaves
Fragrant leaves used crushed or shredded in Thai-style dishes. Available fresh or dried in packets from Asian food stores and some greengrocers.

lemongrass
Aromatic grass that is popular in Thai cooking as it gives a spicy, lemony flavour. Sold fresh in Asian food stores and greengrocers.

marinated goat's cheese
Marinated in olive oil, herbs and peppercorns, it is sold in jars at supermarkets and delicatessens.

mascarpone
A fresh Italian triple-cream curd-style cheese. It has a similar consistency to thick (double) cream and is often used in the same way. Available from specialty food stores and many delicatessens and supermarkets.

mashing potatoes
There are so many varieties of potatoes available and some are better for mashing than others. To get creamy, smooth mash use the sebago, pontiac, exton, king edward, nicola or bison. Do not buy if they have a green tinge.

nashi pears
Shaped like an apple but with a pear flavour, this Asian pear has a yellow skin and crisp, white flesh. Buy in summer from greengrocers and supermarkets.

noodles
Like pasta, keep a supply of dried noodles in the pantry for last-minute meals. Fresh noodles will keep in the fridge for a week if you prefer to use those. Available from Asian food stores and most supermarkets.

cellophane noodles
Also called mung bean starch, these noodles are very thin and almost transparent. Soak them in boiling water, drain and add them to other ingredients.

rice noodles
Fine, dry noodles that need to be soaked in boiling water for a short time, then drained, before use.

pancetta
A cured and rolled Italian bacon similiar to prosciutto but softer in texture and less salty. It is sold in slices at delicatessens and can be cooked or eaten raw in antipasto.

porcini mushrooms
Available fresh in the UK and Europe but sold dried in Australia and the US. They have a meaty texture and earthy flavour. Soak them before using and keep the liquid for cooking. Buy from delicatessens and specialty food stores.

preserved lemon rind
Preserved lemons are rubbed with salt, packed in jars, covered with lemon juice and left for about 4 weeks. Remove the flesh and chop the rind for use in cooking. Available from delicatessens and specialty food stores.

prosciutto
Italian ham that has been salted and air-dried for up to 2 years. Paper-thin slices are eaten raw or used to flavour cooked dishes. Also known as parma ham. Substitute with thinly sliced smoked bacon.

provolone cheese
An Italian cheese available from delicatessens and specialty food stores. Made from cow's milk, it has a firm, waxy texture, is pale yellow in colour and has a mild flavour.

puff pastry
This pastry is so time-consuming and quite difficult to make, many cooks choose to use ready-prepared puff pastry. It can be ordered in advance in blocks from patisseries or bought in both block and sheet forms from the supermarket. If buying sheets of puff pastry you may need to layer several to get the desired thickness.

radicchio
A type of chicory that has red leaves and a slightly bitter, peppery flavour. Buy it from the greengrocers and use it in salads. If it isn't available, use rocket or witlof instead.

red currant jelly
This condiment has a slightly tart flavour. It is made from red currants, sugar and lemon juice. Available from specialty food stores and delicatessens, use it to flavour sauces for meat.

red curry paste

Buy good-quality pastes in jars from Asian food stores or the supermarket. When trying a new brand, it is a good idea to add a little at a time to test the heat. Otherwise, make your own.

red curry paste

3 small red chillies
3 cloves garlic, peeled
1 stalk lemongrass*, chopped
4 green onions (scallions), chopped
1 teaspoon shrimp paste*
2 teaspoons brown sugar
3 kaffir lime leaves*, sliced
1 teaspoon finely grated lemon rind
1 teaspoon grated ginger
½ teaspoon tamarind concentrate*
2–3 tablespoons peanut oil

Place all the ingredients except the oil in the bowl of a small food processor or spice grinder. With the motor running, slowly add the oil and process until you have a smooth paste. Refrigerate in an airtight container for up to 2 weeks. Makes ½ cup.

red wine vinegar

Containing red wine, this vinegar is used in salad dressings and sauces for meats. Buy from supermarkets.

rice noodles

See noodles.

rice flour

A fine flour made from ground white rice. Used as a thickening agent, in baking and to coat foods when cooking Asian dishes. Buy from supermarkets.

rice paper

Vietnamese sheets made from rice flour and water, then dried. Dampen them with warm water and use them to make fresh spring rolls. Available from Asian food stores and some supermarkets.

roasting potatoes

For crunchy, golden roast potatoes, use desiree, pontiac, spunta, russet burbank (idaho), sebago. Ensure potatoes do not have any soft spots or a green tinge. They will keep in a cool, dry place for several weeks.

roma tomatoes

See tomatoes.

rosewater

Made from the diluted essence of distilled rose petals, this natural flavouring is traditionally used in Turkish delight as well as puddings, drinks, jellies and syrups. Available from most supermarkets.

salted capers

See capers.

sashimi salmon

Top-grade salmon that can be eaten raw. It is sold with no skin or bones and is available from fishmongers. Buy it as close to serving as possible.

sashimi tuna

Top-grade tuna that can be eaten raw. It is sold with no skin or bones and is available from fishmongers. Buy it as close to serving as possible.

sherry vinegar

The sherry gives this vinegar its mellow, full-bodied flavour. It is ideal for salad dressings and sauces. Available from delicatessens and specialty food stores.

shortcrust pastry

A savoury or sweet pastry that is available ready-made in the frozen section of supermarkets. It is sold in blocks and sheets. Keep a supply for last minute pies and desserts or if you have time, make your own.

shortcrust pastry

2 cups plain (all-purpose) flour
185g (6 oz) cold butter, chopped
2–3 tablespoons iced water

Place the flour and butter in a food processor and process until it resembles fine breadcrumbs. With the motor running, add enough iced water to form a smooth dough and process until just combined. Knead the dough lightly, wrap in plastic wrap and refrigerate for 30 minutes. Preheat the oven to 180°C (355°F). Roll out the pastry on a lightly floured surface or between sheets of non-stick baking paper until 2–3mm (⅛ in) thick and line the tin. Place a piece of non-stick baking paper over the pastry and fill with uncooked rice or beans, or baking weights. Bake for 10 minutes or until the pastry is golden. Add the filling and bake again as the recipe states. Makes 350g (12 oz), which is enough to line a 26cm (10 in) pie dish or tart tin.

sweet shortcrust pastry

2 cups plain (all-purpose) flour
3 tablespoons caster (superfine) sugar
185g (6 oz) cold butter, chopped
2–3 tablespoons iced water

Place the flour, sugar and butter in a food processor and process until it resembles fine breadcrumbs. With the motor running, add enough iced water to form a smooth dough and process until just combined. Knead the dough lightly, wrap in plastic wrap and refrigerate for 30 minutes. Preheat the oven to 180°C (355°F). Roll out the pastry on a lightly floured surface or between sheets of non-stick baking paper until 2–3mm (⅛ in) thick and line the tin. Place a piece of non-stick baking paper over the pastry and fill with uncooked rice or beans, or baking weights. Bake for 10 minutes or until the pastry is golden. Add the filling and bake again as the recipe states. Makes 350g (12 oz), which is enough to line a 26cm (10 in) pie dish or tart tin.

shrimp paste
Also called blachan, this strong-smelling paste is made from salted and fermented dried shrimps pounded with salt. Used in South-East Asian dishes, fry it before using and keep sealed in the fridge. Available from Asian food stores.

star anise
Small, brown seed-cluster that is shaped like a star. It has a strong aniseed flavour that can be used whole or ground in sweet and savoury dishes. Available from supermarkets and specialty food stores.

starchy potatoes
Use starchy potatoes for frying, such as spunta, sebago, russet burbank (idaho), kennebec, colican or patrones.

sponge cake
The basis for many instant desserts, sponge can be bought ready-made from supermarkets or bakeries. You can also make your own.

sponge cake
1¼ cups plain (all-purpose) flour
6 eggs
¾ cup caster (superfine) sugar
60g (2 oz) butter, melted
Preheat the oven to 180°C (355°F). Sift the flour three times. Set aside. Place the eggs and sugar in the bowl of an electric mixer and beat for 8–10 minutes or until thick, pale and tripled in volume. Sift the flour over the egg mixture and gently fold it through. Fold through the butter. Grease two shallow 20cm (8 in) round cake tins or one deep 18cm (7 in) square cake tin. Pour the mixture into the tins and bake for 25 minutes or until

the cakes are springy to touch and come away from the sides of the tins. Cool on wire racks. Serves 8–10.

sponge finger biscuits
Sweet, light, finger-shaped Italian biscuits, also known as savoiardi. Great for desserts, such as tiramisu, because they absorb other flavours and soften while maintaining their shape. Available from delicatessens and supermarkets.

stock
Flavoured, strained liquid obtained by simmering bones with vegetables and herbs. Quality stocks are avilable in supermarkets or make your own. Use them in soups, stocks and sauces.

beef stock
1.5kg (3 lb) beef bones, cut into pieces
2 onions, quartered
2 carrots, quartered
2 stalks celery, cut into large pieces
assorted fresh herbs
2 bay leaves
10 peppercorns
4 litres (8 pints) water
Preheat the oven to 220°C (425°F). Place the bones on a baking tray and roast for 30 minutes. Add the onions and carrots and cook for 20 minutes. Transfer the bones, onions and carrots to a stockpot or large saucepan. Add the remaining ingredients. Bring to the boil and simmer for 4–5 hours, skimming regularly. Strain the stock and use, refrigerate for up to 3 days or freeze for up to 3 months. Makes 2½–3 litres (5–6 pints).

chicken stock
1.5kg (3 lb) chicken bones, cut into pieces
2 onions, quartered
2 carrots, quartered
2 stalks celery, cut into large pieces
assorted fresh herbs

2 bay leaves
10 peppercorns
4 litres (8 pints) water
Place all the ingredients in a stockpot or large saucepan. Simmer for 3–4 hours, skimming regularly. Strain and use, refrigerate for up to 3 days or freeze for up to 3 months. Makes 2½–3 litres (5–6 pints).

vegetable stock
4 litres (8 pints) water
1 parsnip
2 onions, quartered
1 clove garlic, peeled
2 carrots, quartered
300g (10 oz) cabbage, roughly chopped
3 stalks celery, cut into large pieces
small bunch mixed fresh herbs
2 bay leaves
1 tablespoon peppercorns
Place all the ingredients in a stockpot or large saucepan and simmer for 2 hours, skimming regularly. Strain and use, or refrigerate for up to 4 days or freeze for up to 8 months. Makes 2½–3 litres (5–6 pints).

szechwan peppercorns
Dried berries with a spicy flavour that are sold whole. Toast in a hot, dry frying pan until fragrant, before crushing or grinding. Available from supermarkets and specialty food stores.

taleggio cheese
This white, washed rind cheese from Italy has a creamy, soft texture and mellow flavour. Made from cow's milk, it can be bought from specialty food stores and delicatessens.

tahini
A thick, smooth, oily paste made from toasted and ground sesame seeds. Available in jars from health food stores and most supermarkets.

tamarind concentrate
Also known as tamarind paste, it is made from the fruit of a tropical tree. It is used in Thai and Indian cooking. Available from Asian food stores and some supermarkets.

teardrop tomatoes
See tomatoes.

tomatoes on the vine
See tomatoes.

tomatoes
At their best in summer and spring, there are many different types of tomatoes. Store them in the fridge but allow them to return to room temperature before eating.

cherry tomatoes
Sweet and bite-sized, they are popular in salads or fried to make a sauce for meats and fish. They are sold in punnets and are deep red or bright yellow in colour.

green tomatoes
There is a variety of tomatoes that are green when ripe but it is fine to use under-ripe regular tomatoes. They have a slightly tart flavour and are ideal for frying and roasting as they hold their shape and don't lose their juices.

roma tomatoes
Also known as egg, plum or Italian tomatoes, these have a mild flavour and firm texture. This is the variety most often sold in cans.

oxheart tomatoes
Large pumpkin-shaped tomatoes, this variety is also called the beefsteak tomato. Ranging in colour from pink and red to black, they can be eaten as is or cooked.

teardrop tomatoes
These small, yellow tomatoes are shaped like tears. They are sold in punnets.

tomatoes on the vine
Small or large tomatoes sold on the vine to give them more flavour and fragrance. They are delicious roasted.

vanilla bean
The pod of an orchid native to Central America. It is added, whole or split, to hot milk or cream to allow the flavour to infuse. Available from specialty food stores, delicatessens and some supermarkets.

vanilla snap biscuits
185g (6 oz) butter
1 cup caster (superfine) sugar
1½ teaspoons vanilla extract
2½ cups plain (all-purpose) flour
1 egg
1 egg yolk, extra
Place the butter, sugar and vanilla in a food processor and process until smooth. Add the flour, egg and extra egg yolk and process until a smooth dough forms. Knead the dough lightly, wrap in plastic and refrigerate for 30 minutes. Preheat the oven to 180°C (355°F). Roll out the dough between two sheets of non-stick baking paper until 5mm (¼ in) thick. Cut the dough into circles using a 5cm (2 in) round cookie cutter. Place on baking trays lined with non-stick paper. Bake for 10–12 minutes or until golden. Cool on wire racks. Makes 45.

vine leaves
Also called grape leaves, as they come from the grape vine, they are used as an edible wrapping for foods, such as cheese. They are an essential ingredient in dolmades/dolmas. They are sold in brine at specialty food stores and delicatessens.

water chestnuts
Available in cans from supermarkets and Asian food stores, these chestnuts are grown in water. They have white flesh and a sweet, nutty flavour and subtle crunch. Chop or slice and use in Asian-style dishes, such as stir-fries and wonton dumplings.

white beans
These small, kidney-shaped beans are also often called cannellini beans. Available from delicatessens and supermarkets either canned or in dried form, which needs to be soaked overnight before using. Use them in salads or to make white bean hummus.

white wine vinegar
Containing white wine, this is more mellow in flavour than regular white vinegar. It is used in salad dressings and sauces or marinades for fish. Buy from supermarkets.

witlof
A slightly bitter salad leaf that can be eaten raw or baked. The tightly packed, small leaves are white with pale green tips. Available from greengrocers and some supermarkets, it is also called belgian endive or chicory.

wonton wrappers
Chinese in origin, these square, thin sheets of dough are avilable fresh or frozen. They can be steamed or fried. Fill them with meat and vegetables to make dumplings for soup or use as a crunchy base for pre-dinner nibbles.

conversion chart

1 teaspoon = 5ml
1 Australian tablespoon = 20ml
  (4 teaspoons)
1 UK & US tablespoon = 15ml
  (3 teaspoons/½ fl oz)
1 cup = 250ml (8 fl oz)

liquid conversions

metric	imperial	US cups
30ml	1 fl oz	⅛ cup
60ml	2 fl oz	¼ cup
80ml	2¾ fl oz	⅓ cup
125ml	4 fl oz	½ cup
185ml	6 fl oz	¾ cup
250ml	8 fl oz	1 cup
375ml	12 fl oz	1½ cups
500ml	16 fl oz	2 cups
600ml	20 fl oz	2½ cups
750ml	24 fl oz	3 cups
1 litre	32 fl oz	4 cups

cup measures

1 cup almond meal (ground almonds)	110g	3½ oz
1 cup breadcrumbs, fresh	50g	2 oz
1 cup sugar, brown	200g	6½ oz
1 cup sugar, white	225g	7 oz
1 cup caster (superfine) sugar	225g	7 oz
1 cup icing (confectioner's) sugar	125g	4 oz
1 cup flour, plain (all-purpose)	125g	4 oz
1 cup rice flour	100g	3½ oz
1 cup rice, cooked	165g	5½ oz
1 cup arborio rice, uncooked	220g	7 oz
1 cup basmati rice, uncooked	220g	7 oz
1 cup couscous, uncooked	180g	6 oz
1 cup lentils, red, uncooked	200g	6½ oz
1 cup polenta, fine, uncooked	180g	6 oz
1 cup basil leaves	45g	1½ oz
1 cup coriander (cilantro) leaves	40g	1¼ oz
1 cup mint leaves	35g	1¼ oz
1 cup flat-leaf parsley leaves	40g	1¼ oz
1 cup cashews, whole	150g	5 oz
1 cup cooked chicken, shredded	150g	5 oz
1 cup olives	175g	6 oz
1 cup parmesan cheese, finely grated	100g	3½ oz
1 cup green peas, frozen	170g	5½ oz

index

a

almond
and date cakes with orange
syrup 166
macaroons with chocolate
truffle filling 140
and maple yoghurt 174
wafers with lime sorbet and
tequila 162
antipasto, garlic and sage
marinated 94
apple
cinnamon crumb cakes,
warm 98
and strawberry
galettes 170
tarte tatins, little 142
asparagus
char-grilled salad 154
with simple lemon
hollandaise 22
white, with taleggio 50
avocado and chickpea
salad 162

b

bacon, crispy rosemary
ties 170
bacon-wrapped beef with red
wine glaze 50
baked parmesan risotto 122
balsamic and lemon
chicken 158
beans, garlic and tomato
simmered 98
beef
bacon-wrapped with red
wine glaze 50
garlic butter steaks 22
rare roast with horseradish
cream 134
steak sandwich with
lemon aioli 154
berry bircher 174
biscuits
almond macaroons with
chocolate truffle
filling 140
strawberry shortcakes 34
bread salad, toasted 78
breadcrumb zucchini 62
brownie, raspberry-spiked
chocolate 94
bruschetta
roast peach 14
mushroom and ricotta 158

c

cake
chocolate hazelnut
celebration cake 124
date and almond cakes
with orange syrup 166
lemon curd
cupcakes 142
molten chocolate cakes 22
rich chocolate dessert
cakes with raspberry
cream 62
warm apple cinnamon
crumb cakes 98
capsicum and tomato
soup 82
caramelised crostini with
figs 50
caramelised pineapple
tarts 46
caramelised yoghurt 158
carrot and parsnip fritters
with marinated
fetta 136
celeriac and fennel slaw 66
char-grilled asparagus
salad 154
cheese puffs, crispy four 136
chicken
balsamic and lemon 158
chilli, garlic and lemon 26
dumplings with chilli
glaze 134
and leek pot pies 82
lemongrass 128
lime and coriander
quesadillas 162
roast garlic baked 58
roasted with caramelised
parsnips 78
salad with coconut milk
dressing 54
sandwiches 140
schnitzel with black
olive crust 98
thai wonton stack 46
wok-fried salt and
pepper 18
chickpea and avocado
salad 162
chilli and lime grilled
corn 154
chilli, garlic and lemon
chicken 26
chilli-caramelised pork on
cucumber salad 46

chocolate
brownie, raspberry
spiked 94
cakes, molten 22
dessert cakes, rich, with
raspberry cream 62
hazelnut celebration
cake 124
cocktails 130, 134
coconut
and lime ice-cream
sandwiches 18
plum crumbles 66
corn, chilli and lime
grilled 154
crispy bacon rosemary
ties 170
crispy fish with chilli-ginger
glaze and thai herbs 54
crispy four cheese puffs 136
crispy peppered salmon 66
crispy potato cakes 112
crispy roast potatoes 14
crostini, caramelised, with
figs 50

d

date and almond cakes with
orange syrup 166
dill potatoes 30
dressings – see sauces and
dressings
duck, shredded, and chilli
noodle salad 54

e

eggplant, grilled and white
bean salad 166

f

fennel
and celeriac slaw 66
and parsley salad 94
fetta salad, seared 30
figs
on caramelised crostini 50
pie 86
with ricotta, prosciutto and
caramelised balsamic 62
fish
crispy, with chilli-ginger
glaze and thai herbs 54
cakes, simple 90
crispy, with green chilli
salsa 162
see also seafood

frittata, three cheese 170
fritters, carrot and parsnip
with marinated fetta 136

g

garlic
butter steaks 22
roast lamb cutlets 86
and sage marinated
antipasto 94
and tomato simmered
beans 98
glaze – see sauces and
dressings
goat's cheese
and sweet capsicum
salad 98
tarts 66
granita, green tea and
mint 90
green bean, spinach and
almond salad 122
green tea and mint granita 90
greens, lemongrass 46
greens, steamed paper
bag 78
grilled eggplant and white
bean salad 166
grilled lobster with pistachio
and preserved lemon
butter 110

h

haloumi in vine leaves 26
herb-roasted tomatoes 170
hollandaise, simple lemon 22

i

ice-cream
sandwiches, coconut and
lime 18
tiramisu 26
see also 36–37
iced coffee 179

l

lamb
garlic roast cutlets 86
oregano roast lamb 30
spiced, with tahini
dressing 166
leek and ricotta tarts,
simple 94
lemon
butter pan spinach 86
curd cupcakes 142

lemon (*cont*)
puddings, simple 78
ricotta and pea pasta 34
and sugar puff
pancakes 174
yoghurt panna cotta 30
lemongrass greens 46
lime and coconut ice-cream
sandwiches 18
little apple tarte tatins 142
liqueur mocha 118
lobster, grilled, with pistachio
and preserved lemon
butter 110

m

macaroons, almond, with
chocolate truffle filling 140
mango and raspberry in
rosewater syrup 174
mash, porcini 50
melon in lemongrass
syrup 54
mint and butter peas 82
mint and fetta tabbouli 166
molten chocolate cakes 22
mozzarella, buffalo and
zucchini salad 110
mushroom and ricotta
bruschetta 158

n

nectarines, seared with
caramelised yoghurt 158
noodles
peanut and coriander 18
shredded duck and chilli
salad 54
in spicy coconut broth 90

o

oregano roast lamb 30

p

pancakes, lemon and
sugar puff 174
pancetta with blue cheese
and pear 86
panna cotta,
lemon yoghurt 30
vanilla bean with
raspberries 140
parmesan wafer salad 14
parsley and fennel salad 94
parsnip and carrot fritters
with marinated fetta 136

passionfruit and peach
trifle 154
passionfruit soufflés,
simple 58
pasta
lemon ricotta and pea 34
tuna, lemon and chilli
linguine 58
pea lemon and ricotta
pasta 34
peach
bruschetta, roast14
and passionfruit trifle 154
and raspberries with toasted
cream 112
wrapped in prosciutto 34
peanut and coriander
noodles 18
peas
mint and butter 82
sesame salt sugar snap 18
pies and tarts
apple and strawberry
galettes 170
caramelised pineapple
tarts 46
chicken and leek
pot pies 82
fig pie 86
goat's cheese tarts 66
little apple tarte tatins 142
simple leek and ricotta
tarts 94
pineapple tarts,
caramelised 46
plum coconut crumbles 66
porcini mash 50
pork
chilli-caramelised pork on
cucumber and bean
sprouts 46
crispy bacon rosemary
ties 170
cutlets with beetroots
and onions 116
prosciutto melts 130
sesame pork rice
paper rolls 130
spice-fried 90
potato
cakes, crispy 112
crispy roast 14
dill 30
porcini mash 50
salad, summer 158
poultry – *see* chicken; duck

prawn cocktails 116
prawns, spiced coconut 128
prosciutto melts 130
puddings
simple lemon puddings 78
rhubarb meringue mess 82
peach and passionfruit
trifle 154
peaches and raspberries
with toasted cream 112
vanilla bean panna cotta
cups with raspberries 140
simple passionfruit
soufflés 58
lemon yoghurt panna
cotta 30

r

rare roast beef with
horseradish cream 174
raspberry
and mango in rosewater
syrup 174
and peaches with toasted
cream 112
-spiked chocolate
brownie 94
raw tuna, lemon and chilli
linguine 58
rhubarb meringue mess 82
rich chocolate dessert
cake 62
ricotta and leek tarts,
simple 94
risotto, baked
parmesan 122
roast beef, rare, with
horseradish cream 134
roast garlic baked
chicken 58
roast oregano lamb 30
roast tomatoes with goat's
cheese croutons 116
roast peach bruschetta 14
rosewater semifreddo with
nougat 118

s

salad
avocado and chickpea 162
buffalo mozzarella and
zucchini 110
char-grilled asparagus 154
chicken with coconut milk
dressing 54
fennel and parsley 94

salad (*cont*)
goat's cheese and sweet
capsicum 98
grilled eggplant and white
bean 166
pancetta with blue cheese
and pear 86
parmesan wafer 14
peanut and coriander
noodles 18
seared fetta 30
shredded duck and chilli
noodle 54
spinach, green bean and
almond 122
summer potato 158
toasted bread 78
salmon
carpaccio with campari
dressing 124
crispy peppered 66
smoked salmon on herb
frittatas 134
salt and pepper squid 128
sauces and dressings
campari dressing 124
caramelised balsamic 62
cherry tomato sauce 124
chili-ginger glaze 54
chilli glaze 134
coconut milk dressing 54
garlic butter 22
green chilli salsa 162
horseradish cream 134
lemon aioli 154
lemon curd 142
lemongrass syrup 54
orange syrup 166
raspberry cream 62
red wine glaze 50
simple lemon hollandaise 22
tahini dressing 166
seafood
crispy fish with chilli-ginger
glaze and thai herbs 54
crispy peppered salmon 66
crispy fish with green chilli
salsa 162
grilled lobster with pistachio
and preserved lemon
butter 110
prawn cocktails 116
raw tuna, lemon and chilli
linguini 58
salmon carpaccio with
campari dressing 124

salt and pepper squid 128
seared scallops on crispy
  wontons 110
simple fish cakes 90
smoked salmon on herb
  frittatas 134
spiced coconut
  prawns 128
scallops on crispy
  wontons, seared 110
schnitzel with black olive
  crust 98
semifreddo, rosewater with
  nougat 118
seared fetta salad 30
seared nectarines with
  caramelised yoghurt 158
seared scallops on crispy
  wontons 110
sesame pork rice paper
  rolls 130
sesame salt sugar
  snap peas 18
shortcakes, strawberry 34
shredded duck and chilli
  noodle salad 54
simple lemon puddings 78
simple fish cakes 90
simple leek and ricotta
  tarts 94
smoked salmon on herb
  frittatas 134
soufflés, simple
  passionfruit 58
soup
  noodles in spicy coconut
    broth 90
  tomato and capsicum 82
spice-fried pork 90
spiced coconut prawns 128
spiced lamb with tahini
  dressing 166
spinach
  green bean and almond
    salad 122
  lemon butter pan 86
squid, salt and pepper 128
steak sandwiches with lemon
  aioli 154
steaks, garlic butter 22
steamed paper bag greens 78
strawberry
  and apple galettes 170
  shortcakes 34
sweet capsicum and goat's
  cheese salad 98

t
tabbouli, mint and fetta 166
tarts – see pies and tarts
thai chicken wonton stack 46
three cheese frittata 170
toasted bread salad 78
tomato
  and capsicum soup 82
  and garlic simmered
    beans 98
  herb-roasted 170
trifle, peach and
  passionfruit 154
tuna, raw, lemon and chilli
  linguini 58

V
vanilla bean panna cotta
  with raspberries 140
veal
  cutlets, oregano and
    preserved lemon, with
    garlic brown butter
    mash 62
  with olives and pine
    nuts 14
  roasted in cherry tomato
    sauce 124

W
warm apple cinnamon crumb
  cakes 98
white asparagus with
  taleggio 50
white bean and grilled
  eggplant salad 166
wok-fried salt and pepper
  chicken 18

y
yoghurt
  almond and maple 174
  caramelised 158

Z
zucchini
  and buffalo mozzarella
    salad 110
  breadcrumb 62

donna hay is an Australian-based food stylist, author and magazine editor and one of the best-known names in cookbook and magazine publishing in the world. Her previous eight books have sold more than 2.2 million copies internationally and are renowned for their fresh style, easy-to-follow recipes and inspirational photography. These best-selling, award-winning titles – including *the instant cook, modern classics book* 1 and 2, and *off the shelf* – together with *donna hay magazine*, have captured the imagination of cooks worldwide and set a new benchmark in modern food styling and publishing. She has recently released the extremely popular *donna hay home* range of servingware, kitchenware and foods.

Tourism Planning

An Integrated and Sustainable
Development Approach

Tourism Planning

An Integrated and Sustainable Development Approach

Edward Inskeep

JOHN WILEY & SONS, INC.

New York   Chichester   Weinheim   Brisbane   Singapore   Toronto

14   13

Library of Congress Cataloging-in-Publication Data

Inskeep, Edward.
    Tourism planning : an integrated and sustainable development
approach / Edward Inskeep.
        p.   cm.
    Includes bibliographical references and index.
    ISBN 0-471-29392-X
    1. Tourist trade.   I. Title.
G155.A1147   1991
338.4'791—dc20   90-23096
                                                                         CIP

Contents

Series Foreword   xi

Foreword   xv

Preface   xvii

Part One   **Understanding Tourism Planning**   **1**

Chapter 1   **Background for Tourism Planning**   3

The Historical Development of Tourism   3
Contemporary Tourism Trends   12
Evolution of Tourism Planning   15
The Tourist and the Tourism System   18

Chapter 2   **Approach to Tourism Planning**   **25**

General Concepts of Planning   25
Tourism Planning Concepts   28
Levels and Types of Tourism Planning   34
Components of Tourism Development   38
Organizing the Tourism Project   40

Part Two   National and Regional Tourism Planning   47

Chapter 3   The Planning Process and General Surveys   49

The National and Regional Tourism Planning
    Process   49
General Surveys of the Area Characteristics   55
Survey of Institutional Elements   62
Case Studies   65

Chapter 4   Tourist Attractions and Activities   75

Approach to Survey and Evaluation   75
Types of Tourist Attractions and Activities   76
Other Attraction Considerations   91
Survey and Evaluation Techniques   93
Case Studies   95

**Chapter 5   Tourist Markets, Facilities, Services, and
                Infrastructure   107**

Tourist Market Survey   107
Survey of Tourist Facilities and Services   111
Survey of Transportation and Other
    Infrastructure   119
Case Studies   124

Chapter 6   Planning Analysis and Synthesis   131

General Analysis Approach   131
Market Analysis   132
Determining Tourist Facility and Infrastructure
    Needs   135
Integrated Analysis and Synthesis   141
Establishing Carrying Capacities   144
Case Studies   151

Chapter 7   Tourism Policy and Plan Formulation   161

Forms of Tourism Development   161
Formulating Tourism Policy   169
Techniques of Plan Formulation   174
National and Regional Planning Principles   180
Case Studies   185

Part Three Community Level of Tourism Planning   197

Chapter 8 Planning Tourist Resorts   199

Types of Resort Planning   199
Resort Planning Approach   201
Resort Planning Principles   211
Formulating the Resort Plan   214
Planning for Improvements to Existing
    Resorts   218
Case Studies   220

Chapter 9 Planning Urban and Other Forms of Tourism   235

Planning Approach   235
Urban Tourism Planning   236
Planning for Special Interest, Adventure, and
    Alternative Forms of Tourism   245
Planning for Other Forms of Tourism   253
Case Studies   259

Chapter 10 Planning Tourist Attractions   269

Planning Approach   269
Planning and Managing Natural Attraction
    Resources   272
Planning and Managing Cultural Attraction
    Resources   278
Planning Considerations for Special Types of
    Attractions   287
Some Special Considerations for Visitor Use   290
Case Studies   293

Chapter 11 Development and Design Standards   303

Importance of Establishing Standards   303
Some Site Planning Considerations   304
Site Development Standards   309
Design Considerations   318
Tourist Facility Quality Standards   326
Application of Standards   328
Case Studies   329

**Part Four   Environmental and Socioeconomic
                Considerations   337**

Chapter 12   Environmental Impacts   339

Relationship Between Tourism and the
        Environment   339
Types of Environmental Impacts   342
Environmental Quality   347
Environmental Policies and Impact Control
        Measures   348
Environmental Impact Assessment   351
Case Studies   355

Chapter 13   Socioeconomic Impacts   365

Approach to Evaluating Socioeconomic
        Impacts   365
Types of Socioeconomic Impacts   368
Socioeconomic Policies and Impact Control
        Measures   374
Measuring Economic Costs and Benefits   384
Case Studies   390

**Part Five   Institutional Elements and Plan
                Implementation   401**

Chapter 14   Planning the Institutional Elements of Tourism   403

Tourism Manpower Planning   403
Organizational Structures for Tourism   411
Tourism-Related Legislation   419
Tourism Investment Incentives   420
Case Studies   424

Chapter 15   Tourism Plan Implementation   429

Approach to Implementation   429
Roles and Coordination of the Public and Private
        Sectors   430
Implementation of Physical Plans, Projects, and
        Programs   431
Market Planning   442

Some Other Considerations   445
Implementation and Monitoring Process   448
Case Studies   451

Appendixes   457

A   An Action Strategy for Sustainable Tourism
Development   459

Acknowledgements   459
The Context   460
Introduction   460
1. Definitions   461
2. Implications for Policy   461
3. Implementation   463

B   Model Terms of Reference for Preparation of a
National Tourism Development Plan   469

General Development Objective   470
Special Considerations   470
Specific Objectives, Outputs, and Activities   471

C   Contents of the Zanzibar Tourism Development
Plan Report   487

Selected Bibliography   493

Index   499

Foreword

Edward Inskeep's comprehensive approach to tourism planning is an essential professional reference text for government officials, design professionals, and tourism developers. This book provides a valid and practical means of planning tourism to meet the collective needs of travelers, host communities, government, nongovernmental organizations, and the private sector.

This book provides a framework for linking tourism planning activities with contemporary policy concerns. For example, the guidelines promulgated by the author are directly responsive to an assessment framework for international tourism policy analysis developed by The George Washington University Tourism Policy Forum at its International Assembly held October 30–November 2, 1990 in Washington, DC. Participants from 21 countries identified the following policy issues, which are substantively addressed in this book.

Major Issues

Major issues addressed include the following:
- The physical environment is taking "center stage" in tourism development and management.
- There is a recognition that there are finite limitations to tourism development, both in terms of physical and social carrying capacity of destinations.
- Resident responsive tourism is the watchword for tomorrow: Community demands for active participation in the setting of the tourism agenda and its priorities for tourism development and management cannot be ignored.
- Tourism must strive to develop as a socially responsible industry; more specif-

ically, it must move proactively rather than simply responding to various pressures as they arise.
- Cultural diversity should be recognized within the context of a global society.
- Demographic shifts are occurring that will dramatically transform the level and nature of tourism.
- Patterns of tourism are being transformed by increasingly diverse life-styles.
- The political shift to market-driven economies is bringing about a global restructuring in which market forces rather than ideology are used to guide decisions and develop policy.
- The trend toward market economies and shrinking government budgets is creating strong pressures for privatization and deregulation of tourism facilities and services.

Emerging Issues

Emerging issues addressed include:
- Regional political and economic integration/cooperation will predominate.
- The growing demands of the high cost of capital for developing tourism infrastructure and rising taxation/fees will maintain and increase financial pressures on the tourism industry.
- The rise in influence of the global/transnational firm will accelerate.
- The widening gap between the north/south (developed/developing) nations continues to cause frictions and to be a constant source of concern for harmonious tourism development.
- Continued regional conflicts and terrorist activities are impediments to the development and prosperity of tourism.
- Health and security concerns could become a major deterrent to tourism travel.
- Technological advances are giving rise to both opportunities and pressures for improved productivity, human resource development, and restructuring the tourism industry.
- The human resource problem: There is a continuing and growing need to increase the supply of personnel and to enhance their professionalism.
- Despite recent progress, recognition by governments of the tourism industry and its importance to social and economic development and well-being of regions is still far from satisfactory; one part of the reason is a lack of credibility of tourism data.
- Growing dissatisfaction with current governing systems and process may lead to a new framework (paradigm) for tourism.

It should be noted that the book also includes (as an appendix) an Action Strategy for Sustainable Tourism Development, which was prepared at the Globe 90 Conference on Sustainable Development, held in Vancouver, March 1990.

Tourism Planning: An Integrated and Sustainable Development Approach is the first comprehensive planning text to respond to the challenges and opportunities facing tourism in the 1990s. The planning approach advanced by the author views the environment—which includes political, physical, social, and economic elements—as interrelated and interdependent components, which all need to be considered in the development process.

There is an increasing realization that market-driven development and private sector initiatives need to take into account social and environmental factors as key elements of sustainable tourism development. The author's extensive experience in tourism planning in developed and developing countries provides guidelines, case examples, and important lessons for contemporary planners, entrepreneurs, and policy makers.

Donald E. Hawkins, Professor and Director
International Institute of Tourism Studies
The George Washington University

Foreword

Tourism is still a new activity for many countries that have little or no experience in developing this sector of the economy. In the context of the phenomenal growth of tourism over the last decades and the forecast that it will become the world's largest export industry by the year 2000, countries are bound to give increasing importance to the development of tourism. However, because this is still a relatively new activity, there are quite a few examples of how the unplanned and haphazard growth of tourism can produce harmful results with often irreparable damage to the environment and negative consequences for the sociocultural values of a society. Integrated tourism planning, therefore, assumes considerable importance with proper emphasis on a comprehensive, long-term approach to achieve sustainable development in harmony with the country's overall development objectives. For these reasons, I welcome the appearance of a book that provides a comprehensive, integrated approach oriented toward environmental conservation and optimizing the sociocultural and economic benefits of tourism.

Divided into five parts, this book strives to be universal in its approach and application and includes case studies from both more and less developed countries. The book is designed for, and can be profitably used by, government tourism officials, university tourism and urban/regional planning departments, international agency staff dealing with tourism development, tourism consultants, and all those interested in the process of developing tourism through integrated planning.

Tourism Planning, by Edward Inskeep, is a book written by a knowledgeable and experienced expert whose services have been frequently used by the World Tourism Organization in the field of tourism development planning. There is no doubt that it will make a very useful contribution to the documentation already available on the subject and will enrich the libraries of all those who are interested or involved in tourism planning.

Antonio Enríquez Savignac
Secretary-General
World Tourism Organization

Preface

Tourism is becoming one of the most important social and economic activities of today's world. The number of domestic and international travelers is steadily increasing, and many countries in the world are now seeking to develop tourism for its many benefits. There is also justifiable concern about the possible negative effects of tourism and a growing desire to develop this sector in a planned and controlled manner that optimizes benefits while preventing any serious problems. In addition to newly developing tourism areas, those places that already have substantial tourism development are now reexamining their tourism sectors and, in many places, desiring to make improvements where necessary to meet contemporary standards and environmental objectives. Recognition is gradually being given to the urgency of developing tourism, as well as other sectors, in an integrated manner that sustains its resources for perpetual use, and helps conserve and not deteriorate an area's natural and cultural heritage.

This book is designed to fill a need in providing planning approaches and guidelines for the integrated and sustainable development of tourism that is responsive to community desires and needs. Considerable experience has been gained in recent years in the planning of tourism development, often based on mistakes made in the past, and there is now some basis for more effective planning, although planning should be viewed as a continuous process with approaches, principles, and techniques constantly evolving and being refined. The book examines tourism planning at all levels from the macro to micro and includes approaches that are applicable to both the more and less developed countries with case studies from many places in the world. For convenience of use, the book is divided into five parts. Part One covers the general background of and approaches to tourism planning, and the remainder of the book then examines specific aspects of this subject. Part Two is about the process, principles, and techniques of preparing national and regional tourism plans; Part Three looks at the community or more detailed levels of planning resorts, urban and other forms of tourism, and tourist attractions and the application of development and design standards; Part Four focuses on environmental and socio-economic considerations; and Part Five reviews those institutional elements that are important in developing tourism and the various approaches to plan implementation.

The book evolved from lecture notes used in teaching short courses on tourism planning, many years experience in formulating tourism plans and advising governments on tourism development in various countries of the world, and reviewing plans prepared by others. The approach used is intended to be a practical one of adapting basic planning processes, principles, and techniques to tourism, and presenting these within the framework of the rather limited amount of research that has been published on this subject in recent years. The orientation of the book is strongly toward incorporating environmental and sociocultural considerations in tourism planning, balanced with achieving the economic benefits desired, comprehensively examining all of the many facets of tourism in the planning process, involving the community in tourism planning and development, and integrating tourism into the total development policies and plans of areas. The book maintains that the sustainable development approach can be applied to any scale of tourism development from large resorts to limited size special interest tourism, and that sustainability depends on how well the planning is formulated relative to the specific characteristics of an area's environment, economy, and society and on the effectiveness of plan implementation and continuous management of tourism.

The contents of the book are directed to various groups, including tourism officials and government planners who must prepare, review, and implement tourism plans, university tourism, planning and other departments that are teaching tourism planning and their students wishing to learn about the field, consultants who are increasingly being contracted to prepare tourism plans, and others concerned with the controlled development of tourism. Because of the complicated and multidisciplinary nature of tourism planning, no one book can encompass in detail all the approaches and techniques available. Some users of the book will also need to consult other reference sources for further ideas and information.

Various persons and organizations provided valuable assistance in preparing this book. Special appreciation is extended to the World Tourism Organization and its staff for permission to use WTO material in the book and, more generally, for supporting the author in his many consulting activities for the WTO, utilizing the approaches set forth in this book. The several consulting firms and their principal staff who kindly provided case study and other material include: Tom Papandrew of Belt, Collins & Associates, Ltd. in Honolulu, Hawaii; Jim Branch of Sno-Engineering, Inc. in Littleton, New Hampshire; Peter Krippl of International Resort Developers in La Jolla, California; James MacGregor of MacLaren Plansearch in Vancouver, British Columbia; Chris

Balch of Pieda in Reading, England; Robert Cleverdon of Cleverdon Steer in Surrey, England; and others. The material provided by the planning department of the Resort Municipality of Whistler is appreciated. Thanks are extended to Donald Hawkins of The George Washington University and editor of this series and Pamela Chirls of Van Nostrand Reinhold for their assistance and particularly their patience with the author's delays in finishing the book, and to Camilla Stenavich of San Diego, California for her efficient production of the graphic illustrations.

Part One

Understanding Tourism Planning

Part One provides the background for understanding tourism planning. First it briefly describes the historical development of tourism and recent global trends in this sector, traces the evolution of modern tourism planning, specifies the reasons for planning tourism, presents the contemporary definition of tourists, and introduces the concept of the integrated tourism system. The importance now being given to tourism by many countries in formulating their socioeconomic development plans is pointed out.

Part One then explains the approach to tourism planning used in this book:

- Application of the general concept of planning and the basic planning process;
- The comprehensive, integrated, sustainable development and community approach to planning tourism and the important relationship between tourism and the environment; and
- The tourism components that need to be considered.

Planning tourism so that its natural and cultural resources are indefinitely maintained and even enhanced by tourism is an underlying concept of the approach applied throughout this book. This part concludes with the practical considerations of how to effectively organize the tourism planning project, including techniques for obtaining community involvement in tourism.

1

Background for Tourism Planning

The Historical Development of Tourism

It is important to appreciate the historical development of tourism, including the motivations for travel and the various forms of tourism that existed in the past, in order to better understand contemporary tourism and how best to plan for it.

Early Travel and Tourism

During prehistoric times of early man, people traveled for essential reasons of seeking food, escaping from enemies, obtaining relief from the pressures of over-population, achieving territorial expansion, engaging in bartering type of trade and perhaps, even then, satisfying curiosity about unknown lands. Early migrations of people seem to have taken place in all the habitable continents and regions, including successively over long distances, such as from Northeast Asia to the Americas.

Commencing some 5,000 years ago, with the development of intensive agriculture, cities, sea-going ships, and money as a medium of exchange, travel became more commonly motivated by trade, military activities, and government administration of large empires such as the Sumerian, Persian, Egyptian, Assyrian, Greek, and Roman empires in the Mediterranean and Middle Eastern regions. The Phoenicians developed commerce to a particularly high level in the Mediterranean region by going from place to place as traders. Commercial travel was also well developed in the Indian Ocean, initially by the Indus Valley civilization, then by the Gujaratis, and later by the Muscat and Omani traders who regularly sailed to India and as far away as China, giving rise to Sinbad the Sailor stories. Two thousand years ago, Indian traders were traveling to Southeast Asia, conveying their culture and religion as well as trade goods.

Alexander the Great's invasion of Asia in 334 B.C. provided the basis for the exchange of ideas and trade between Asia and the Mediterranean. East-West trade linkages between China and Europe were established from the second century B.C. along the arduous and dangerous routes now known as the famous Silk Roads, although more than Chinese silk was traded along these routes. The trading routes through central Asia are now becoming an important attraction for special interest tourists.

As empires developed, government administration was also a major reason for travel. By the second century A.D., the Romans, in particular had developed an extensive and well-constructed road system that provided administrative and commercial communications throughout their empire from Hadrian's Wall in Britain to the Euphrates in the Middle East. Inns were located about every 30 miles along this road network and hotels were situated in most of the towns. The inns were identified with pictographs indicating their level of facilities and services (Coltman 1989). Although the Romans developed the most extensive, relatively comfortable, and safest travel infrastructure of this period, road networks were also established in China during the Chou and Han Dynasties, in India during the Mauryan Dynasty, and in other eastern and western Asian states. In somewhat later periods, footpath networks were developed in the Mayan and other empires in the Americas that did not possess wheeled transportation.

Not all early travel was for trading, administrative, or military purposes. In Greece, people traveled to the Olympic Games, organized in 776 B.C., the first of the major international sports events currently so popular. In Asia Minor, Ephesus (in what is now Turkey), after being conquered and democratized by Alexander the Great, became a major trading center that also attracted many pleasure travelers to enjoy the city's varied features. The Romans particularly developed pleasure tourism, with the more affluent traveling to visit major attractions such as the Pyramids and other monuments in Egypt and historical places in Greece. These sites are still important attractions for contemporary tourists. The highly cosmopolitan city of Alexandria attracted many Romans and other tourists. Seaside resorts and health spas in Egypt, Greece, and as far away as Britain, where baths were constructed in what is now Bath, England, were popular with the Romans. Closer to home, they developed vacation villas in the Bay of Naples and elsewhere. During the latter part of the Roman Empire, the spread of Christianity led to religious travel to the cities of Jerusalem and Bethlehem.

The Middle Ages

With the fall of the Roman Empire in the fifth century A.D., economic activities and trade declined in Europe, the middle class population mostly disappeared, the transportation network disintegrated, banditry was common and trips were dangerous, all resulting in much diminished travel within Europe and the Mediterranean region and to places elsewhere. Religion became a dominant factor in people's lives and gradually the churches acquired considerable wealth giving rise, commencing in the eleventh century, to the construction of imposing new cathedrals, churches, and monasteries in the now-well known Romanesque, Gothic, and other styles, and associated religious pilgrimages. By the fourteenth century, religious pilgrimages in Europe were an important type of travel to such places as Rome in Italy and Santiago de Compostela in Spain, further extended with the opening up of Jerusalem and the Palestinean area by the Crusades (which also were a major type of travel venture during this period).

Reflecting the hardship of travel during the Middle Ages, the origin of the English word travel is the Old French word *travallier* from which is derived travail, meaning to labor hard. Although religiously based, pilgrimages were also social and recreational events, as evidenced by the accounts of Geoffrey Chaucer in the *Canterbury Tales*. To serve the pilgrims, a network of charitable hospices was established and commercial inns developed. Package tours were organized from Venice to the Holy Land, which included the cost of passage, meals, wine, accommodation, donkey rides, and bribe money to prevent confiscation of baggage, bureaucratic delays, or mischief from camel drivers (Feifer 1985). Even if people did not travel on an organized tour, they tended to travel together in groups for safety reasons. By the fifteenth century, Rome had more than a thousand hostelries, and tour guide books were available in various languages.

Although not as well documented, but referred to by Marco Polo and Chinese travelers, religious pilgrimages were an important type of travel in Asia during this (and earlier and later) period with both Hindus and Buddhists visiting important shrines, temples, and religious educational centers for study and staying in specially provided accommodation. Marco Polo's book recording his adventures and observations on his journey between Europe and Asia during the latter part of the thirteenth century was an important source of information for Europeans about Asia during this period. With the advent of Islam in the sixth century, Mecca and other Islamic centers became major destinations for Moslem pilgrims. Religious pilgrimages are still a significant travel motivation today, including to some of the same places such as Rome, Jerusalem, Mecca, and various Hindu and Buddhist sacred sites in Asia.

The Renaissance to World War II

The European Renaissance, extending from about the fourteenth to seventeenth centuries, reflected the improved productivity of agriculture and revival of cities, expanded trade and commerce, extensive global exploration and European discoveries (although anticipated several centuries earlier by trans-Atlantic Viking travels), the flowering of arts and literature, and the beginnings of modern science. It represented a break with the dominance of religion and encouraged individual fulfillment and a desire to explore and understand the world. From the standpoint of tourism development, the Renaissance led to travel for educational and experiential purposes as well as trade. The wealthy Elizabethan travelers from England went especially to Italy, considered to be the most culturally developed and progressive place of the time, often with stopovers in Frankfurt to attend its internationally-oriented trade fair (the forerunner of present-day trade fairs), as well as to Paris and across the frightening Alps on the way to Rome. Diplomatic travel increased as did university-related tours. During this period, the European voyages of exploration were made to the Americas, Africa, and Asia, active trade commenced with those lands, and migration of Europeans to overseas colonies was underway.

During the seventeenth and eighteenth centuries, the famous Grand Tour developed. This initially involved young English aristocrats, being educated for government administrative and diplomatic services and future political leadership, traveling for two to three years on the Continent. The main destination was still Italy to appreciate its culture, but as the Grand Tour evolved, it typically also included Germany, France, sometimes Vienna, and, later on, Switzerland and the Low Countries. For the very wealthy, travel was often done in considerable style with an entourage of tutors, valets, coachmen, footmen, and painters to copy monuments, statues, and landscapes. Travel was by means of sailing ship, stagecoach, and horseback. The Grand Tour became very popular and at its peak in the eighteenth century, many Britons were traveling on the Continent, as well as a few Americans, including Thomas Jefferson. Being on the journey to Italy, the Alps in addition to being rather feared for their danger became admired for their scenic beauty and included on the tour, which laid the foundation for Switzerland's development of tourism and of nature tourism in general. In 1778, the first guide book for this type of travel was published: Thomas Nugent's *The Grand Tour*. The French Revolution in 1789, followed by the Napoleonic Wars, disrupted British travel to the Continent and led to the demise of the Grand Tour as a distinctive but rather elitist type of pleasure travel.

The Industrial Revolution, commencing in the late eighteenth century in Europe, slightly later in North America, and still later elsewhere (the Meiji Revolution of the 1870s in Japan, for example), created the basis for modern tourism development. This economic and concomitant social revolution greatly increased labor productivity, leading to larger-scale urbanization, rapid growth of the middle class, better education levels, more leisure time and demand for recreational opportunities, and greatly improved means of transportation by railway and steamship. Along with the increased travel demand came development of accommodation, resorts, and related travel facilities and services.

Spas and seaside resorts were, as mentioned, first developed by the Romans, and again became fashionable among the affluent in the eighteenth century and popular with large numbers of people in the nineteenth century. The pattern of

St. Moritz, Switzerland—This well-known European resort was developed in the nineteenth century for winter sports and has since also expanded into a summer resort. It has maintained its popularity and quality level to the present. (Courtesy of the Swiss National Tourist Office)

resort development that often took place was discovery and early development by the wealthy, followed by middle class mass tourism with the wealthy then moving on to new places. Some of the better known European spas were Bath in England, Baden-Baden in Germany, Baden in Austria, and Bain-les-Bain in France. In North America, Saratoga Springs and White Sulphur Springs were well known, and later, Hot Springs, Arkansas and Glenwood Springs, Colorado became popular. Spas, although still existing today, including some of the early ones such as Baden-Baden, are now less popular than formerly except in Eastern Europe, where spa tourism is very important and expanding.

Seaside resorts commenced development in the early nineteenth century at such places as Brighton, Scarborough, and Margate in Britain and Nice and Cannes on the Mediterranean coast of France, originally as health resorts, but soon salt water bathing as a form of recreation became common. Brighton, with its long amusement pier (to be emulated in other resorts) became especially popular with day trippers coming by railway. Seaside resorts have, of course, evolved into a major form of tourism.

The railway, first used for passenger traffic in England in 1830, developed rapidly in both Europe and North America, as well as in Asia, Africa, and South America, during the mid and late nineteenth centuries. Rail provided a relatively fast and inexpensive means of transportation and was much utilized by tourists to reach seaside and mountain resorts and elsewhere. In 1841, Thomas Cook in Britain was the first travel agent to take advantage of rail by organizing the first train excursion, and package tours soon became common. The Thomas Cook travel agency is one of largest in the world today.

In addition to spa and resort hotels, large city hotels commenced development in the early nineteenth century in North America and Europe. In many ways, the prototypes of the Grand Hotels of Europe were developed in the USA and, in both areas, hotels became important multi-functional centers offering not only accommodation, but excellent restaurants, bars, and places for meetings, receptions, and socializing in general (Gomes 1985). The word hotel was deliberately adopted by early American hoteliers from the French term 'hotel,' which referred to a substantial city residence or large public building. This tradition of multi-functional hotels, especially in cities and resorts, is still being maintained today.

Mass production and widespread use of the automobile along with improvement of road networks in the early twentieth century further revolutionized travel, especially in the USA where the automobile became the chief means of domestic touring. Travel by automobile led to the development of tourist or motor courts alongside roads in the 1920s and 1930s, which have since evolved into the ubiquitous peripheral city motels and motor hotels of today. The motor coach or bus also became an important means of road transportation.

Although roads and railways and, in some areas, lake and river boats provided relatively convenient and inexpensive access within continental regions, transoceanic travel was by large passenger ships. The development of trans-Atlantic steamships, for example, during the mid-nineteenth century brought North America and Europe within two weeks travel, and the screw propeller ships developed in the 1860s eventually reduced travel time to six days. Ship services were also developed to Asia, South America, and Australia. The passenger liners of the early 1900s,1920s, and 1930s were known for their luxury but, for cost reasons, were restricted in their use to a relatively small number of affluent tourists who could afford to travel.

Commercial air travel commenced in the late 1920s but, because of cost and limited passenger carrying capacities, did not have much impact on tourism until later. World War II brought substantial changes that greatly affected future tourism including an end to the depression, increased prosperity and an expanded middle class, significant improvements in communications and air transportation, and exposure of military personnel, especially Americans, to other cultures and environments in both Europe and the Asia-Pacific region.

Recent Development of Tourism

Since World War II, tourism has grown to become a major socioeconomic activity of the world due to several influencing factors:
• Greater disposable income available for travel;

- Less working hours and a large number of employees who receive paid holidays and annual vacations, thus providing the leisure time for travel;
- Higher education levels and greater awareness of other areas of the world, leading to a desire of more persons to travel;
- Rapid and dispersed economic development leading to greatly increased business travel; and
- Major improvements in transportation including in air travel services and highway networks.

Development of commercial jet aircraft in particular has encouraged long-distance, economic travel of large numbers of people. The first commercial jet was the Boeing 707, introduced in 1958, followed by the jumbo or wide-bodied commercial jet in 1970 and various configurations of fuel efficient jet aircraft in the 1980s. Use of the automobile became even more common, and networks of high speed roads were developed in the USA, Europe, and elsewhere. In some countries, train networks and speeds were considerably enhanced. Along with the increased travel demand and improved means of traveling came rapid development of accommodation and other tourist facilities and services, and especially of new destinations and types of tourist attractions. The group and inclusive tour type of vacation travel has become common.

The number of international tourist arrivals has increased rapidly since the 1950s, from slightly over 25 million in 1950, 69 million in 1960, and 160 million in 1970 to 405 million in 1989, as shown in Figure 1.1. During the 1980–89 decade, growth has averaged almost 4 percent annually, despite the slow-down resulting from the international recession of the early 1980s. According to the WTO (WTO 1988), about 60 percent of international travel is related to holiday and leisure activities, approximately 30 percent is for business purposes, and the remainder is obligatory travel for family affairs, religious pilgrimage, study, and so forth. Much international tourism is comprised of intraregional travel (for example, among countries within Europe and North America) as well as interregional travel (for example, between North America, Europe, and Asia).

As shown in Table 1.1, of the major world regions, Europe attracts the largest number and percentage of international tourist arrivals, but it has received a gradually declining share of the total arrivals during the past several years. Although Europe is a dynamic tourism region with much development of tourist attractions, facilities, and services and a high market demand, it must also be remembered that Europe is comprised of several small and medium size countries where there is much crossing by tourists of international boundaries within relatively short distances from their homes and so, statistically, there is a large number of intraregional tourist arrivals. The most rapidly developing tourism region globally is East Asia and the Pacific area, which has experienced an average annual growth rate of about 12 percent during the 1980s decade, and received some 11 percent of all international arrivals in 1989.

Although international tourism is often much emphasized because of its generation of foreign exchange, domestic tourism is much more important. Taking nights spent in commercial tourist accommodation as a category of measurement, domestic tourism globally exceeds international tourism by a factor of 2.7

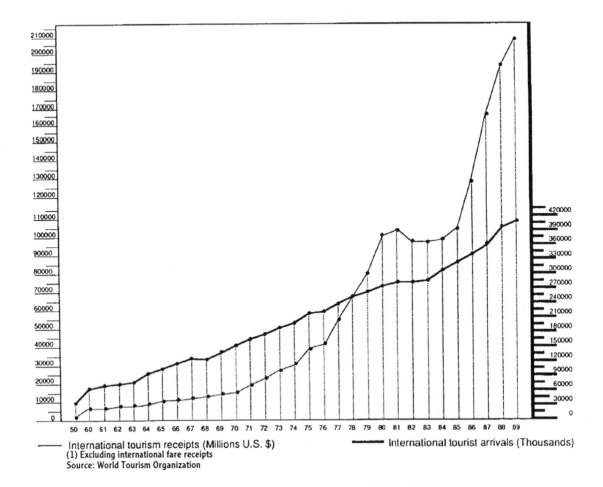

Figure 1.1. Development of World Tourism (1950–1989).

to 1, according to WTO figures, while total domestic tourist arrivals are about 10 times the number of international arrivals. Much of domestic travel is also for business and other obligatory purposes as well as for holiday. As indicated in Table 1.2, domestic tourism is particularly highly developed in North America, Europe including social tourism in Eastern Europe, Japan, and other more economically developed countries. But domestic tourism is also becoming important in less developed countries, especially for visiting friends and relatives and religious pilgrimages, and is receiving emphasis in the tourism programs of some developing countries.

The economic impact of tourism is globally significant. According to WTO figures (WTO 1989), total receipts from international tourism, not including international air fares, amounted to approximately $209 billion in 1989, having grown at an average annual rate of 9 percent during the 1980s. International tourism receipts (excluding transportation) represented about 7 percent of world

Table 1.1 International tourist arrivals by region—1989 (in thousands)

Region	Number of Arrivals	Percentage of Total
Africa	15,363	3.8
Americas	79,714	19.6
East Asian & Pacific	44,857	11.1
Europe	250,776	61.9
Middle East	11,677	2.9
South Asia	2,919	.7
Total	405,306	100.0

Source: World Tourism Organization
Note: Based on WTO regional commission areas

trade and 25 to 30 percent of the international exchange of services in 1989; it is one of the three leading categories of international trade along with oil and motor vehicles. For both international and domestic tourism, travel and tourism accounted for nearly $2 trillion in sales in 1987, equivalent to 12 percent of the world's gross national product, 5 percent of all goods and services produced, and 15 percent of the global services sector sales (WEFA 1988). The WTO estimates that tourism generates, directly and indirectly, some 74 million jobs in the world. For some places, particularly small island nations and territories, tourism accounts for a major source of cash income and foreign exchange.

In larger countries, the combination of domestic and international tourism can constitute a substantial economic activity. In the USA, for example, travel receipts from foreign and domestic tourism were estimated over $350 billion in 1989, of which domestic tourists spent $307 billion (U.S. Department of Commerce 1990). In that year, tourism contributed 6.7 percent of the gross domestic product and generated more than 5 million jobs. In Spain, one of the major tourist destination countries in the world, the revenues generated from international tourism in the 1950s to 1970s greatly helped finance the modern industrialization

Table 1.2 Domestic tourist arrivals by region—1988 (in millions)

Region	Number of Arrivals	Percentage of Total
Africa	5.3	.1
Americas	1,591.0	38.5
East Asian & Pacific	414.0	10.0
South Asia	57.8	1.4
Middle East	5.2	.1
Europe	2,060.0	49.9
Total	4,133.3	100.0

Source: World Tourism Organization
Note: Based on WTO regional commission areas

Le Bastion des Pêchurs, Budapest, Hungary—During the early 1990s, the East European countries are planning to rapidly expand tourism for its economic benefits. (Courtesy of the Hungarian tourism office)

of that country. Although tourism is sometimes questioned as a valid development sector because it seems to be dependent on economic prosperity, experience has shown that it is rather resilient to economic fluctuations and, in recent years, has been more stable than many commodity prices.

Because of the increasing socioeconomic importance of tourism and the fact that it has become a permanent element of contemporary life, more countries are including tourism as a major element in their development programs. The private sector is responding, and sometimes taking the initiative, by investing in tourism development projects.

Contemporary Tourism Trends

Although making predictions about the future is always risky, it is essential to consider trends in planning for future development. These trends can be monitored as time progresses and any necessary adjustments made to the plan if some of the circumstances change. Several tourism trends are discernible in the late 1980s, which will affect tourism planning in the 1990s. A basic trend is the continuing motivation for people to travel generally. Travel is now becoming a normal part of the life-styles of an increasing number of people who give this activity high priority in their household budgets. Even during periods of economic recession, often the impact on discretionary travel is not so much a marked decrease of total trips but a reduction in the amount of budget allocated to vacations, with people taking trips closer to home and seeking more travel bargains. Along with the desire of more people to travel is the rise of disposable incomes necessary for travel, both from expanded economic development in general and more two income families with both husbands and wives working.

The number of tourist market generating countries is increasing. In addition to the existing well-established market countries of Western Europe, North America, Japan, and Australia, the newly industrialized countries of East Asia, Latin America, Eastern Europe, and the Middle East may provide important markets in the near future. Even in lower income countries, the emerging middle class is commencing to travel more domestically and internationally.

Based on the growth rate during the 1980s, the WTO estimates that international tourist arrivals could increase at about 4 percent annually during the 1990s and could reach 515 million arrivals by 1995 and 637 million arrivals by the year 2000, with international tourism receipts rising at close to 9 percent annually to reach $527 billion in 2000. The regional percentage distribution of international arrivals will likely show somewhat of a decrease in Europe, remain about the same in the Americas, and increase in the other regions. Domestic tourism will also continue growing rapidly, especially in those developing countries that are experiencing rapid economic development and adopting policies for encouraging domestic tourism. Overall, tourism should expand in all the world's regions, but growth will be greatly dependent on the extent of political stability in some places. The Asia and Pacific region will probably continue being the fastest growing one based on its many types of attractions, its overall rapid economic development, which will stimulate expanded business travel and increased domestic and intraregional holiday travel, and the aggressive tourism development and promotion programs of many of the countries in the region. In terms of changing tourist profiles, the populations of many of the major market countries are aging, and the senior citizen and retired persons tourist market is becoming a substantial one. At the same time, youth tourism is being encouraged in many countries. Tourists are becoming more experienced and sophisticated and expecting good value of the tourism product for their money expenditures at whatever budget level they are traveling. Instead of a single long vacation annually, more tourists are taking shorter but more frequent holiday trips, often one during the summer and the other during the winter, combined with weekend trips.

A major trend is the increasing fragmentation of tourist markets with more tourists wanting to actively engage in recreational and sporting activities, learn about and participate in local cultures, seek new destinations, and develop special interests through traveling. The proliferation of special interest tours on al-

most every imaginable theme related to nature, culture, and professional and avocational interests is one of today's tourism phenomena. Also, there is increasing
interest in, and some areas are by policy developing, forms of alternative, soft and
eco-tourism such as village, rural, and nature tourism. Adventure tourism is becoming popular. Although the large passenger liner has been largely replaced by
air travel to specific destinations, cruise ship tourism is expanding rapidly and the
combination air-sea cruise is becoming common. Recognizing the emergence of
more specific types of tourist markets, there is increasing emphasis on matching
the tourist markets and products.

Meeting, conference, and convention tourism is already an important specialized form of tourism and is expected to continue growing, including new destinations being developed for convention tourism. Business travel can be expected
to increase as business activities expand; teleconferencing has not yet
supplanted face-to-face business meetings as previously expected. Combination
business and pleasure travel is already commonly practiced and will probably increase. The incentive tourism market, currently well developed, may expand in
the future based especially on new products and destinations. Small integrated
health resorts are becoming popular, including for business meetings.

New types of tourist products being developed include various forms of cultural, historic, and nature heritage tourism sites, water parks, theme parks, new
resort and special interest destinations, unusual types of accommodation including recycled historic buildings, use of interesting and historic forms of transportation as tourist attractions, and development of small but exclusive retreat resorts in remote locations. Generally, two major and contrasting types of holiday
accommodation may emerge: the integrated resort offering a wide range of recreation and leisure facilities and activities, and clean and comfortable but basic
lower-priced accommodation. Despite the expansion of smaller-scale and special
interest forms of tourism, conventional forms of mass tourism such as large beach
and mountain resorts and sight-seeing group tourism catering to general interest
markets will probably still be a dominant type of tourism development. In general, whatever the form of tourism, tourists are increasingly demanding high quality and well-planned—but not necessarily more expensive—destinations, and will
bypass those places known to have environmental problems such as air, water,
and noise pollution, congestion, poorly designed buildings, and unattractive
views.

Transportation technology of airplanes, trains, and automobiles has been rapidly improved in recent years and will continue to be improved. However, because of the lead time required to commercially develop substantially advanced
technology, which is already being designed, it is not likely that there will be
many major changes during the 1990s, but significant advances will probably
take place in the early twenty-first century. Increased use of computerization of
travel facility and service operations will continue.

The planned approach to tourism development is being widely adopted although implementation is not always fully effective. In the planning of tourism,
more governments now want to apply a policy of controlled development so that
benefits can be gained from tourism without it generating any serious environ-

mental or social problems. Based on experience gained during the past few decades there is now much more emphasis being placed on environmental and social considerations and on the sustainable development approach.

Evolution of Tourism Planning

In the past, and still a prevailing attitude in a few places, tourism planning was seen as a simplistic process of encouraging new hotels to open, making sure that there was transportation access to the area, and organizing a tourist promotion campaign. The only systematic planning that might be done was to select a suitable hotel or resort site and apply site planning, landscaping, and engineering design standards to the development. This approach was often successful for development of individual hotels or small resorts in the era before mass tourism. However, during the post-World War II period, as explained previously, tourism developed rapidly, and several areas, especially in the Mediterranean region as well as in the early tourism areas of the Caribbean and some other places, encouraged mass tourism without planning it. These places have since paid the social and environmental consequences of unplanned tourism development and regret not having taken the planned and controlled approach to development. As will be pointed out subsequently in this book, some of those unplanned tourism places are now having to take remedial actions to upgrade their environments and development patterns.

The Importance of Planning Tourism

Tourism is developed for various reasons. A main purpose is to generate economic benefits of foreign exchange earnings (for international tourism), income, employment, and government revenues, to serve as a catalyst for development of other economic sectors such as agriculture, fisheries, forestry, and manufacturing, and to help pay for and justify infrastructure that also serves general community and economic needs. Tourism can also justify applying measures for environmental and cultural heritage conservation for which resources otherwise might not be available. Socially, tourism in its best form provides recreational, cultural, and commercial facilities and services for use both by tourists and also by residents that may not have been developed without tourism. It provides the opportunity for education of people about other cultures and environments as well as their own national heritage, often circumventing ideological and political differences and reducing prejudicial attitudes, that is, achieving cross-cultural exchange.

However, tourism can also generate various problems such as the loss of potential economic benefits and local economic distortions, environmental degradation, the loss of cultural identity and integrity, and cross-cultural misunderstandings, reinforcing existing prejudices. These benefits and problems will all be examined in more depth in subsequent chapters of this book.

In order to optimize the benefits of tourism and prevent or at least mitigate any problems that might be generated, good planning and careful management of tourism are essential. More generally, planning for tourism is as important as is planning for any type of development in order for it to be successful and not create problems. The tourism sector objectives can be achieved more effectively if carefully planned and integrated into the country's total development plan and program. Specifically, tourism planning is necessary for the following reasons:

- Modern tourism is still a relatively new type of activity in many areas, and some governments and the private sector have little or no experience in how to properly develop it. A tourism plan and development program can provide guidelines in those areas for developing this sector.
- Tourism is a complicated, multi-sectoral, and fragmented activity, involving other sectors such as agriculture, fisheries and manufacturing, historic, park and recreation features, various community facilities and services, and transportation and other infrastructure. Planning and project development coordination are particularly necessary to ensure that all these elements are developed in an integrated manner to serve tourism as well as general needs.
- Much of tourism is essentially selling a product of an experience comprised of visitor use of certain facilities and services. There must be careful matching of the tourist markets and products through the planning process, but without compromising environmental and sociocultural objectives in meeting market demands.
- Tourism can bring various direct and indirect economic benefits that can best be optimized through careful and integrated planning. Without planning, these benefits may not be fully realized and economic problems can arise.
- Tourism can generate various sociocultural benefits and problems. Planning can be used as a process for optimizing the benefits and preventing or lessening the problems, and especially for determining what is the best tourism development policy to preclude sociocultural problems and to utilize tourism as a means to achieve cultural conservation objectives.
- The development of tourists attractions, facilities, and infrastructure and tourist movements generally have positive and negative impacts on the physical environment. Careful planning is required to determine the optimum type and level of tourism that will not result in environmental degradation and to utilize tourism as a means to achieve environmental conservation objectives.
- There is much justifiable concern expressed today about development of any type, including tourism being sustainable. The right type of planning can ensure that the natural and cultural resources for tourism are indefinitely maintained and not destroyed or degraded in the process of development.
- Like any type of modern development, forms of tourism change somewhat through time, based on changing market trends and other circumstances. Planning can be used to upgrade and revitalize existing outmoded or badly developed tourism areas, and, through the planning process, new tourism areas can be planned to allow for future flexibility of development.

- Tourism development requires particular manpower skills and capabilities for which there must be appropriate education and training. Satisfying these manpower needs requires careful planning and programming and, in many cases, developing specialized training facilities.
- Achieving controlled tourism development requires special organizational structures, marketing strategies and promotion programs, legislation and regulations, and fiscal measures that through the comprehensive and integrated planning process can be related closely to tourism policy and development.
- Planning provides a rational basis for development staging and project programming, which are important for both the public and private sectors to utilize in their investment planning.

One of the reasons for the tourism planning cited above is that new areas can be planned to allow for future flexibility of development and older tourism areas can be planned for revitalization. During the earlier development of tourism during the post-World War II period, it was proposed by Plog (1973) that tourist destination areas go through cycles based on the types of tourists they tend to attract, suggesting that all destination areas eventually decline. However, this has not always been the case and, with planning and imagination, older tourist destinations have been maintained and in some cases revived, and the planning approaches now being applied are aimed at maintaining the continued vitality of newly developed destinations. In fact, the evolution of tourist destinations can perhaps be anticipated and through planning, marketing, and management techniques not necessarily decline (Haywood 1986).

Experience has shown that communities, regions, and countries do benefit substantially from the proper planning of tourism and will do so more in the future. In an increasingly competitive tourism world that is also concerned about maintaining the resources for tourism, the places with the best planned tourism development are likely to be the most successful tourist destinations from the standpoints of both achieving high tourist satisfaction levels and bringing substantial benefits, with minimal disruptions, to the local economy, environment, and society.

Preparation of Tourism Plans

National, regional, community, and resort tourism planning commenced in the late 1950s when it became apparent that tourism was going to become a significant socioeconomic activity that could bring both benefits and problems. In the Asia–Pacific region, for example, the 1959 State Plan of Hawaii, now one of the most developed and successful island tourist destinations, included tourism as a major component and was quite progressive for its time in integrating tourism planning into the total regional development plan. Planning continued in this region through the 1960s and 1970s, with plans prepared for places such as Sri Lanka, Pakistan, Nepal, Taiwan, Malaysia, Bali, Fiji, French Polynesia and the Great Barrier Reef and central regions of Australia. Planning in Hawaii proceeded with the preparation of more detailed land use plans for resort areas. In Europe, during this period, major tourism plans included those prepared for Yugoslavia, Cyprus, Corsica, and the Languedoc–Roussillon coastal region of France. Tourism planning was also accomplished for some of the Caribbean Islands. For example, the National Physical Plan for Jamaica for 1970–1990 contained a major element on tourism development.

During the 1980s, tourism planning has been undertaken for many places of the more and less developed world. This has included revision and updating of some of the plans prepared previously. Tourism planning is now being pursued in many countries and regions that wish to develop tourism on a controlled basis. Indicative of the international recognition being given to the importance of both tourism as a development sector and the need for planning tourism, international agencies including the United Nations Development Programme (UNDP), the European Economic Community, and several of the bilateral aid agencies are financing tourism planning projects of various types in developing countries. The WTO has strongly supported the importance of planning tourism as evidenced in various WTO documents published commencing in the early 1970s, and further elaborated in its publication on integrated planning for tourism in the mid-1970s (WTO 1977). The WTO, as executing agency for the UNDP, has prepared tourism planning studies for many countries and regions in the world.

These recent tourism plans give much more emphasis than previously to the environmental and sociocultural factors of tourism development and to the concept of sustainable development based on careful resource analysis and development controls. Surveying and analytical techniques have been much improved, and planning principles and development standards are now better understood. More focus is now given to effective ways of implementing the plans. However, current tourism planning does not ignore existing development, some of which may date back to the nineteenth century, but often incorporates these features into the modern plan. In fact, some of the earlier developments, such as classic hotels and resorts, interesting means of transportation, and major historic sites, can form significant elements of the present-day plans.

The Tourist and the Tourism System

In order to plan for tourism, it is important to understand the definition of tourist and the concept of the tourism system, and furthermore to consistently utilize these definitions throughout the planning process so that there is a rational and common basis for research, analysis, and plan formulation.

Definition of Tourist

The commonly although not universally accepted definition of international tourist is that recommended by the United Nations Conference on International

Travel and Tourism held in 1963, which stated that a visitor is "any person visiting a country other than that in which he has his usual place of residence, for any reason other than following an occupation remunerated from within the country visited" (WTO 1981). The term visitor includes two distinct types of travelers:

1. Tourists—Temporary visitor staying at least 24 hours in the country visited and the purpose of whose journey can be classified as:
   a. leisure (i.e., recreation, holiday, health, religion, or sport);
   b. business;
   c. family;
   d. mission; and
   e. meeting.
2. Excursionists—Temporary visitors staying less than 24 hours in the destination visited and not making an overnight stay (including travelers on cruises).

The WTO has refined this definition and adopted the classification of travelers as depicted in Figure 1.2. It is important to note that tourists include not only holiday travelers but also visitors to a country for business, meetings, conferences and conventions, visiting friends and relatives (VFR), study, religion, and other more obligatory type purposes. This definition is very consistent with the concept of comprehensive tourism planning and development, because tourist facilities and services must also be provided for the non-holiday travelers and, in many cases, the same facilities and services are used by both non-holiday and holiday tourists. Also, as mentioned, business and other types of obligatory tourists frequently function as holiday tourists, including visiting tourist attractions and engaging in recreational activities, that is, combination business and pleasure travel.

The distinction between tourists (visitors staying at least 24 hours) and excursionists (visitors staying less than 24 hours and typically not overnight) is an important one for planning tourist facilities and services. Day excursionists (for example, cruise ship passengers or border crossing shoppers) will make use of restaurants, bars, specialized types of retail shops, local ground transportation, and perhaps some entertainment and recreation services, but not overnight accommodation or some other facilities and services.

As indicated in Figure 1.2, certain categories of travelers such as members of armed forces and diplomats traveling to duty stations and migrants traveling to work in the country are not considered visitors or tourists. However, some of these groups, especially foreign citizens who may stay in the country for several months or years and bring their families, become an important category of domestic tourists who utilize in-country tourist facilities and services. This specialized type of domestic tourist market can be significant in developing countries that often have large numbers of international agency, aid, and mission related foreign residents who can potentially spend part of their holiday time traveling in

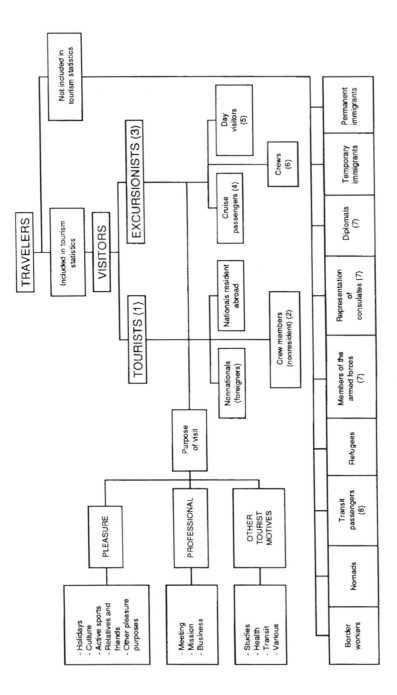

Figure 1.2. Classification of Travelers.

1. Visitors who spend at least one night in the country visited.
2. Foreign air or ship crews docked or in layover and who use the accommodation establishments of the country visited.
3. Visitors who do not spend the night in the country visited, although they may visit the country during one day or more and return to their ship or train to sleep.
4. Normally included in excursionists. Separate classification of these visitors is nevertheless recommended.
5. Visitors who come and leave the same day.
6. Crews who are not residents of the country visited and who stay in the country for the day.
7. When they travel from their country of origin to the duty station and vice-versa (including household servants and dependents accompanying or joining them).
8. Who do not leave the transit area of the airport or the port. In certain countries, transit may involve a stay of one day or more. In this case, they should be included in the visitors statistics.

Source: World Tourism Organization

the country or, from the standpoint of international tourist markets, vacation in nearby countries. Such foreign residents may also do considerable travel for business purposes in the countries where they live and work.

In tourism planning and marketing, especially in developing countries, the category of nationals resident abroad (under tourists in Figure 1.2) may be a significant one in cases where there has been large-scale migration overseas. Most of these migrants still maintain close contact with their families and friends at home and, besides sending back remittances, may visit their home countries and, in some cases, utilize local commercial accommodation and restaurants and purchase handicrafts and souvenirs.

Because of the large numbers of persons now living outside of their country of nationality, the tourists' place of residence may be a more important consideration than their nationality. The classic case of this situation is Hong Kong where there are many British passport holders among the residents. For marketing and planning purposes, place of residence as well as nationality should be statistically recorded and analyzed.

There is not a widely accepted definition of domestic tourists. These are defined in different ways by various countries and even differently among states or provinces within a single country. The National Tourism Resources Review Commission in the United States developed a definition of domestic tourists as follows (1973, 5): "A tourist is one who travels from his home for a distance of at least 50 miles (one way) for business, pleasure, personal affairs, or any other purpose except to commute to work, whether he stays overnight or returns the same day."

The U.S. Census Bureau, which conducts national travel surveys, defines a trip as "each time a person goes to a place at least 100 miles away from home and returns", and excludes trips for 1) travel as part of an operating crew on a train, airplane, truck, bus, or ship, 2) commuting to a place of work, and 3) student trips to and from school. The U.S. Travel Data Center, an independent, nonprofit research center on travel and tourism located in Washington, DC, uses the same definition as the Census Bureau (1984). The government of Canada classifies a tourist as one who travels at least 25 miles from the boundaries of his home community. The WTO's proposed definition of domestic tourists and domestic excursionists is largely based on length of stay, as is its definition of international tourists.

Until there is a universally accepted definition of domestic tourist, the tourism planner will need to use the one applied to the country or local area for which he is planning or, in the absence of an existing acceptable definition, devise one that is the most appropriate. In developing a suitable definition, consideration should be given to the dimensions of travel proposed by Gee, Makens, and Choy as follows (1989, p. 14): "Four basic dimensions are included in the criteria used for defining travelers in relation to the travel industry: distance, length of stay at the destination, residence of the traveler, and purpose of travel." They further state: "Frequently, a fifth dimension—mode of transport—is included as well. From an economic perspective, mode of transport can be a useful qualifier in analysis of tourism statistics."

The Tourism System

Although complicated, cutting across sectoral categories, and fragmented, tourism is and should be viewed as a single system comprised of interrelated parts. As a system, it can be defined, analyzed, planned, and managed in an integrated manner. Although sometimes referred to as an industry, the approach taken in this book is that tourism is a socioeconomic activity or sector. This concept reflects the importance of tourism's social and environmental as well as economic dimensions, and the fact that it makes use of facilities and services that are part of various existing standard industrial classifications. Viewing tourism as a socioeconomic activity recognizes that tourism is sometimes developed for noneconomic purposes, and its benefits are often social ones (for example, educational and recreational activities and tourists learning about different historical and geographic environments). At the same time, the tourism system can be described in economic terms of demand and supply.

Various tourism references, for example, Gunn (1988) and Mill and Morrison (1985), describe the tourism system in terms of demand and supply. Gunn identifies the 'population' with an interest in, and ability to travel, that is, the tourists as the demand, and the supply side comprised of the various modes of transportation, the attractions, facilities and services for tourists, and the tourist information and promotion provided. Gunn further specifies the influencing factors on the functioning of the tourism system as: natural resources, cultural resources, entrepreneurship, finance, labor, competition, community, government policies, and organization/leadership. Mill and Morrison identify the four major parts of the tourism system as being: 1) the market (tourists), 2) travel (transportation), 3) destination (attractions, facilities, and services), and 4) marketing (information and promotion), with each part closely linked in sequence with the other, including No. 4 (marketing) being linked with No. 1 (the markets).

In the planning for tourism development, the concept of tourism as an integrated system based on demand and supply factors is basic to its effective planning and management. The components of tourism, as related to the demand and supply factors, to be considered in its planning are elaborated in the next chapter. However, as is emphasized in the next chapter, in the sustainable development approach to tourism planning, the demand or market side should not be allowed to determine the supply side to the extent that sociocultural and environmental integrities are compromised and tourism resources degraded. The demand and supply sides must be balanced within the framework of maintaining social and environmental objectives.

References

Feifer, Maxine. 1985. *Going Places: The Ways of the Tourist from Imperial Rome to the Present Day.* London: Macmillan.

Gee, Chuck Y., James C. Makens, and Dexter J. L. Choy. 1989. *The Travel Industry*. New York: Van Nostrand Reinhold.

Gomes, Albert J. 1985. *Hospitality in Transition*. Houston: Pannell Kerr Forster.

Gunn, Clare A. 2nd ed. 1988. *Tourism Planning*. New York: Taylor & Francis.

Haywood, Michael K. 1986. "Can the Tourist-Area Life Cycle Be Made Operational?" *Tourism Management*. 7(3):154–167.

Mill, Robert Christie, and Alastair M. Morrison. 1985. *The Tourism System: An Introductory Text*. Englewood Cliffs, N. J.: Prentice Hall, Inc.

National Tourism Resources Review Commission. 1973. *Destination, U. S. A. Vol. 2*. Washington, DC: U.S. Government Printing Office.

Plog, Stanley G. 1973. "Why Destination Areas Rise and Fall in Popularity." *Cornell Hotel and Restaurant Administration Quarterly*: 12(1): 13–16.

U.S. Department of Commerce. 1990. "Travel Service" *U.S. Industrial Outlook 1990*. Washington, DC: U.S. Department of Commerce.

U.S. Travel Data Center. 1984. *National Travel Survey*. Washington, DC: U.S. Travel Data Center.

Wharton Econometric Forecasting Associates. 1988. *The Contribution of the World Travel and Tourism Industry to the Global Economy*. New York: American Express Travel Related Services Company, Inc.

World Tourism Organization. 1977. *Integrated Planning*. Madrid: World Tourism Organization.

——. 1981. *Technical Handbook on the Collection and Presentation of Domestic and International Tourist Statistics, Introduction*. Madrid: World Tourism Organization.

——. 1988. *Tourism Development Report — Policy and Trends*. Madrid: World Tourism Organization

——. 1989. *Yearbook of Tourism Statistics. Vol. 1*. Madrid: World Tourism Organization.

2

Approach to Tourism Planning

General Concepts of Planning

Tourism planning applies the same basic concepts and approaches of general planning, but adapted to the particular characteristics of the tourism system.

What is Planning?

In its broadest definition, planning is organizing the future to achieve certain objectives. There is a strong element of predictability in planning because it attempts to envision the future, although often now only in a general manner because it is realized that many factors cannot be very precisely predicted. Planning is carried out at all levels from individuals planning their everyday activities and personal lives to formalized comprehensive national and regional planning undertaken by some governments. Building layout and town planning goes back to the earliest days of human settlements. Modern town planning has its genesis in Britain in the late eighteenth century in response to the rapid urbanization and industrialization and their associated problems then commencing to take place.

Major types of planning practiced today include:
- Economic development planning;
- Physical land use planning;
- Infrastructure planning for transportation facilities and services, water supply, electric power, sewage and solid waste disposal, and telecommunications;
- Social facility planning for educational, medical, and recreation facilities and services;
- Park and conservation planning;

- Corporate planning; and
- Urban and regional planning, which now typically applies the comprehensive planning approach integrating economic, land use, infrastructure, social facility and park and conservation planning.

Most types of formal planning are done by government agencies except for corporate planning, which by definition is accomplished by private sector companies and corporations. The detailed level of planning such as for shopping centers, residential areas, and tourist resorts may be undertaken by the private sector, but these plans must meet the locational criteria and development standards of the local government and be approved by it. Because planning is a specialized kind of activity, it is often carried out by consultants contracted by the government or private sector, or by experienced and qualified specialists working in the planning departments of government agencies or private company offices.

Although there may be resistance to the concept of planning in some places, it is generally accepted as being a valid approach to guiding future development, rather than 'just letting things happen.' The conflicts that often arise in planning are relative to differing community interests on general issues of deciding the most desirable future type and level of development for an area and on specific development project proposals. In less developed countries and regions where entrepreneurial skills are weak and capital resources are limited, experience has shown that development, at least of the desired type, will not take place without being planned.

Contemporary Planning Approaches and Techniques

Planning concepts and approaches have somewhat changed during the last few decades based on experience gained in earlier years. Previously, there was much emphasis placed on preparation of the end state 'master plan,' which was assumed to be sufficient for guiding and controlling future development patterns. It was found that such plans were too rigid, not taking into account changing lifestyles, technology, and other circumstances, and were not feasible to implement over a long-term period. Now, the general approach being applied is that planning is a continuous process and must be flexible, depending on changing circumstances, but still achieve the basic development objectives.

As part of the flexibility approach, planning should be done incrementally with continuous monitoring and feedback on effects of previous development and evaluation of new trends, both of which may influence decision making on the next stage of development. This incremental planning can be done successively from the general to the more specific levels. For example, an area will be designated for residential and community facility use or a new town development on the long-range plan, with the detailed land use planning done at a later time when there is need for the development. At that time, contemporary living patterns can be considered in the final planning.

Also, it has been recognized that preparation of plans does not automatically guarantee that the recommendations will or can feasibly be implemented, and now much more focus is being placed on realistic and imaginative means to achieve implementation. The techniques and feasibility of implementation must be considered throughout the planning process, and the procedures and techniques for implementation clearly specified.

Furthermore, planning now applies the comprehensive and integrated approach, which recognizes that all development sectors and supporting facilities and services are interrelated with one another and with the natural environment and society of the area. In order to achieve effective development patterns and not generate serious environmental or social problems, all aspects of the area or development sector being planned must be understood and carefully integrated, and the environmental and social implications of development taken into account. Thus, the systems approach is currently being applied in many planning situations, including urban, regional, national, and development sector plans.

The systems approach to planning requires that sufficient information be available about the system in order to understand and analyze it. In order to collect and analyze this data, computer technology is important and where there are vast amounts of data, it is essential. Computer technology and information systems have virtually revolutionized modern planning. For basic surveys and analysis, geographic information systems (GIS) are available, and computers can be utilized for preparing map overlays of different types of information to determine relationships of various geographic characteristics used, for example, in resource evaluation and site selection analysis. Computer technology can be used for many planning functions: preparation of demand analyses; evaluation of alternative development scenarios; analysis of economic, environmental, and social impacts of proposed development projects; preparation of economic and financial analyses of projects; preparation of architectural and landscape design perspectives; and other functions. However, if basic data are limited and computer technology not available for a particular tourism planning project, it still can be carried out, albeit perhaps not as effectively, utilizing more traditional planning techniques if the systematic planning process and sound planning principles are still applied.

An important aspect of planning that has been emphasized for some time is community involvement in the planning process and decision making. This is based on the concept that planning is for the residents of an area, and they should be given the opportunity to participate in the planning of its future development and express their views on the type of future community they want to live in. Community involvement requires that more time be allocated to the planning process and may result in considerable debate over the implications of various types of development futures or scenarios that are available to the community, often including much discussion about the relative trade-offs of costs and benefits.

Because of the justifiably increasing concern about environmental and cultural degradation resulting from many types of development practices, an approach being greatly discussed in the late 1980s is what is being termed sustainable development. This actually refers to sustaining the resources of development from depletion so that they are available for continuing and permanent use in the future. This is a logical extension of the concept of incorporating environmental and social impact considerations and analyses in the planning process that has been underway for the past two decades. The sustainable development approach is receiving much attention by governments and international agencies and commencing to be accepted by the private sector.

Basic Planning Process

The basic planning process that applies to the preparation of any type of plan can be represented in various ways, but the conceptual approach is the same. The basic planning process follows successive steps that are expressed in this book as follows:

1. Study preparation—Decision to proceed with the study, writing of the study project terms of reference, and organization of the project.
2. Determination of development goals and objectives—The goals and objectives of development are first decided in a preliminary manner subject to modifications resulting from feedback during the plan formulation and impact evaluation stage.
3. Surveys—Surveys and inventory of the existing situation and characteristics of the development area.
4. Analysis and synthesis—Analysis of the survey information and synthesis of the analyses, which provides much of the basis for the plan formulation and recommendations.
5. Plan formulation—Formulation of the development policy and physical plan, typically based on preparation and evaluation of alternative policies and plans.
6. Recommendations—Formulation of the recommendations on plan-related project elements.
7. Implementation—Implementation of the plan and related recommendations, utilizing various techniques that have been identified in the plan.
8. Monitoring—Continuous monitoring and feedback on the plan's recommendations and implementation with any necessary adjustments made.

Tourism Planning Concepts

Effective tourism planning utilizes those general planning concepts that have proven to be effective in meeting the challenges facing modern development processes, but adapted to the particular characteristics of tourism.

Tourism Planning Approach

The basic tourism planning approach set forth in this book is aimed at practical application in the formulation of tourism development policies and plans. The basic planning process explained previously provides the general planning framework, and emphasis is placed on the concepts of planning being continuous and incremental, systems-oriented, comprehensive, integrated, and environmental, with the focus on achieving sustainable development and community involvement. These elements of this approach are described as follows:

- Continuous, incremental, and flexible approach—Although still based on an adopted policy and plan, tourism planning is seen as a continuous process with adjustments made as needed based on monitoring and feedback, but within the framework of maintaining the basic objectives and policies of tourism development.
- Systems approach—Tourism is viewed as an interrelated system and should be planned as such, utilizing systems analysis techniques.
- Comprehensive approach—Related to the systems approach, all aspects of tourism development including its institutional elements and environmental and socioeconomic implications are analyzed and planned comprehensively, that is, a holistic approach.
- Integrated approach—Related to the systems and comprehensive approach, tourism is planned and developed as an integrated system within itself and also is integrated into the overall plan and total development patterns of the area.
- Environmental and sustainable development approach—Tourism is planned, developed, and managed in such a manner that its natural and cultural resources are not depleted or degraded, but maintained as viable resources on a permanent basis for continuous future use. Carrying capacity analysis is an important technique used in the environmental and sustainable development approach.
- Community approach—There is maximum involvement of the local community in the planning and decision-making process of tourism and, to the extent feasible and desirable, there is maximum community participation in the actual development and management of tourism and its socioeconomic benefits.
- Implementable approach—The tourism development policy, plan, and recommendations are formulated to be realistic and implementable, and the techniques of implementation are considered throughout the policy and plan formulation with the implementation techniques, including a development and action program or strategy, specifically identified and adopted.
- Application of a systematic planning process—The systematic planning process is applied in tourism planning based on a logical sequence of activities.

  This approach is applied conceptually to all levels and types of tourism planning, but the specific form of application will, of course, vary depending on the type of planning being undertaken. The planning process will be further specified for each of the major levels of tourism planning being undertaken in the relevant subsequent chapters of this book. Even though a systematic approach is used, it must also be remembered that planning is both an art and a science, and a sense of imagination and creativity must be applied in tourism planning at all levels. Such creativity need not abrogate nor be contrary to the systematic approach and can in fact complement it to produce more successful tourism development.

Some Special Considerations in Planning Tourism

Although there is much emphasis today placed on matching the tourist products and markets, this should be done within the framework of maintaining sustainable development and not generating serious environmental or sociocultural problems. A completely market-led approach to tourism development that provides whatever attractions, facilities, and services the tourist market may demand could result in environmental degradation and loss of sociocultural integrity of the tourism area, even though it brings short-term economic benefits. To preclude this situation arising, some places such as Bhutan and Oman have adopted a product-led approach. This approach implies that only those types of attractions, facilities, and services that the area believes can best be integrated with minimum impacts into the local development patterns and society are provided, and marketing is done to attract only those tourists who find this product of interest to them. In many cases, the approach of balancing economic, environmental, and social objectives within the framework of maintaining sustainable development is the most appropriate one, but it depends very much on the overall national, regional, and community objectives.

Although tourism is expanding rapidly in many places and becoming one of the world's major socioeconomic activities, a particular country, region, or community should be cautious about developing an over-dependence on tourism. For both economic and social reasons, diversification of an economy is usually desirable, although not always possible. Economically, diversification provides a sounder basis for development in that any periodic economic fluctuations in one sector can likely be counterbalanced by strengths in other sectors. Socially, diversification encourages a greater mix of types of people and activities in an area. Wherever possible, all the potential economic sectors, based on the resources of the area, should be considered for development with tourism integrated into the multi-sectoral economy. It is sometimes too easy for an area to rely on tourism, as a growing sector, to the neglect of its other potential. However, for some places that possess limited resources except for tourism, there may be few other options open, and tourism must be given priority to achieve economic objectives. This situation often is the case of small island economies with fast-growing populations and, consequently, particular emphasis must be placed on maintaining the viability of the tourism sector.

Also, with the rapid growth of tourism, some communities, especially in North America and Europe, that are losing their historical economic base and seeking new types of economic development, are viewing tourism as a possible economic salvation. If their resources for tourism are very limited, they may consider rather artificial and tenuously based attractions to develop tourism, and proceed to develop these at substantial expense. Often these can be successful, but not always so, especially because there is increasing competition among communities to attract tourists. Tourism should not be seen categorically as a panacea to solve a community's economic problems. Each place must be carefully evaluated in terms of its tourism attraction potential, based on both its own resources and the possible domestic and external markets.

Tourism Planning Terminology and References

There is sometimes confusion about the terminology used in tourism planning, and it is important to define terms used in any planning reference. As used here, 'objective' refers to what is expected to be achieved from the planning of tourism development; 'policy' refers to the development approach applied to guide and determine decision-making; 'plan' refers to an orderly arrangement of parts of an overall system that reflects the policy; and 'strategy' refers to the means of accomplishing the policy and plan recommendations. Policy is expressed in terms of a set of statements and relates directly to the development objectives; a plan is usually termed here as a development plan and consists of maps, other graphic representations, and explanatory text including statements on recommendations; and strategy refers to a development or action program and other action-oriented means to accomplish the policy and plan. However, the terminology varies from one reference to another, including its use in some of the case studies presented in this book.

Another term that is widely used in connection with the environmental and sustainable development approach is 'conservation.' As used in this book, conservation refers to the planned management of specific sites and places and natural and cultural resources in general, and not necessarily categorical preservation, which is used to mean no change of the site, place, or resource, and sometimes includes restoration to its original condition. Conservation implies that some use and controlled change can take place if the basic integrity of the site, place, or resource is maintained.

A limited number of published references are available on techniques, principles, and models of comprehensive tourism planning, and shorter presentations on tourism planning are made in some recent general reference books on tourism—these are cited in the bibliography. Some park and recreation references include tourism components, for example, Pigram (1983). Inskeep (1987) has emphasized the importance of applying the environmental approach in planning tourism. Getz (1986) has made a comparative review of models in tourism planning and concludes that they all have certain deficiencies in integrating tourism systems theory and the planning process. However, this fact does not lessen the importance of applying the planned approach to tourism development based on present knowledge and experience.

Tourism and the Environment

One of the major tourism planning themes of this book is application of the environmental and sustainable development approach. The close relationship between tourism and the environment and the importance of environmental planning and sustainable tourism development planning are becoming increasingly recognized. The Manila Declaration of the World Tourism Organization, the most comprehensive international statement adopted on the goals of modern tourism, emphasizes the importance of both natural and cultural resources in tourism and the need for conservation of these resources for the benefit of both tourism and residents of the tourism area (WTO 1980). Following on from the Manila Declaration, the Joint Declaration of the World Tourism Organization and United Nations Environment Programme (UNEP), which formalized interagency coordination on tourism and the environment, states (WTO and UNEP 1982):

> The protection, enhancement and improvement of the various components of man's environment are among the fundamental conditions for the harmonious development of tourism. Similarly, rational management of tourism may contribute to a large extent to protecting and developing the physical environment and the cultural heritage, as well as improving the quality of life...

The importance of national and regional tourism planning as a conservation and sustainable development technique was expressed at a WTO and UNEP environmental workshop in 1983 as follows (WTO and UNEP 1983):

> Regional planning provides probably the best opportunity for achieving environmental protection goals through the use of zoning strategies. Thus zoning strategies and regulations can be used to encourage the concentration in some areas and/or dispersion in other areas of tourist activity so the extreme pressures are restricted to resilient environments and fragile environments can be given the most rigid protection measures, e.g. Coto Donana, in Spain. In this manner, nature conservation interests can be accorded their appropriate priority where it is the prime land use designation...

Appropriate relationships between tourism and the natural and sociocultural environments, which places responsibilities on both the tourist-receiving countries and the tourists themselves, were further specified by the WTO in 1985 during its Sixth General Assembly through its adoption of the Tourism Bill of Rights and Tourist Code (WTO 1985). This statement contained the following provisions:

- In the interest of present and future generations (States should) protect the tourism environment which, being at once human, natural, social and cultural, is the legacy of all mankind...
- The populations constituting the host communities in places of transit and stay are entitled to free access to their own tourism resources...
- They are also entitled to expect from tourists understanding of and respect for their customs, religions and other elements of their cultures which are part of human heritage.
- To facilitate such understanding and respect, the dissemination of appropriate information should be encouraged on:
    1. the customs of host communities, their traditional and religious practices, local taboos and sacred sites and shrines, which must be respected;
    2. their artistic, archaeological and cultural treasures, which must be preserved; and
    3. wildlife and other natural resources, which must be protected.
- Tourists should, by their behavior, foster understanding and friendly relations among peoples, at both the national and international levels, and thus contribute to lasting peace.
- At places of transit and stay, tourists must respect the established political, social, moral and religious order and comply with legislation and regulations in force. In these places, tourists must also:
    1. show the greatest understanding for the customs, beliefs and behavior of the host communities and the greatest respect for their natural and cultural heritage...; and
    2. refrain from exploiting others...

The Hague Declaration on Tourism, adopted at the Inter-Parliamentary Conference on Tourism (organized jointly by the Inter-Parliamentary Union and the World Tourism Organization) in 1989 set forth several principles for development of tourism, including emphasizing the importance of integrated planning of tourism. This declaration also pointed the essential relationship of the environment and tourism, as follows (WTO 1989):

> An unspoilt natural, cultural and human environment is a fundamental condition for the development of tourism. Moreover, rational management of tourism may contribute significantly to the protection and development of the physical environment and the cultural heritage, as well as to improving the quality of life.

The concept of planning for sustainable tourism development, as well as for sustainable development in general for all types of man's activities, is being given increasing emphasis internationally. Appendix A presents An Action Strategy for Sustainable Tourism Development, which was formulated by the Tourism Stream of Globe '90, a sustainable development conference held in Vancouver, Canada in 1990.

Levels and Types of Tourism Planning

Ideally, tourism should be planned as one element of and, at the same time, as the comprehensive planning that is done for an area. Sometimes this can be accomplished. More commonly, however, tourism planning must be done separately, but utmost efforts must be made to ensure that it is planned in such a manner that it can be integrated as a sector into the overall development policy, plan, and program. Tourism planning is prepared at various levels, with each level focusing on a different degree of specificity. Although not always possible to achieve, the planning should be prepared in sequence from the general to the specific, because general levels provide the framework and guidance for preparing specific plans. The various levels of tourism planning and design are described in the following sections.

International Level

This level of planning is concerned mostly with international transportation services, the flow and tour programming of tourists among different countries, complementary development of major attraction features and facilities in nearby countries, and multi-country marketing strategies and promotion programs. Some limited tourism planning, marketing, and cooperative activities generally take place at the international level through organizations such as the WTO and its regional commissions, the International Civil Aviation Organization (ICAO), some other United Nations agencies and their regional commissions, the International Air Transport Association (IATA), the Pacific Asia Travel Association (PATA), the Caribbean Tourism Organization (CTO), the Tourism Council of the South Pacific (TCSP), the Sub-Committee on Tourism (SCOT) of the Association of Southeast Asian Nations (ASEAN), the Tourism Coordination Unit (TCU) of the Southern Africa Development Coordination Conference (SADCC), and the tourism committee of the Organization for Economic Cooperation and Development (OECD). The major general purpose global tourism organization is the WTO, which in 1990 had 106 member countries and many affiliated members. An intergovernmental organization, the WTO has been designated by the United Nations as the executing agency for United Nations–sponsored tourism-related projects.

The international planning level is rather weak because it depends on the cooperation of individual countries, but it is nonetheless important for special function activities and is receiving encouragement from international agencies through their sponsorship of regional tourism projects. A highly interesting example of cooperation on regional tourism development is that of the Mayan

Road, which involves a 1,500-mile route connecting Mayan archaeological sites in the five Middle American countries of Mexico, Belize, Guatemala, Honduras, and El Salvador.

National Planning

The national level of tourism planning is focused on several elements:
- Tourism policy;
- A physical structure plan including identification of major tourist attractions, designation of tourism development regions, international access points and the internal transportation network of facilities and services;
- Other major infrastructure considerations;
- The general amount, types, and quality level of accommodation and other tourist facilities and services required;
- The major tour routes in the country and their regional connections;
- Tourism organizational structures, legislation and investment policies;
- Overall tourism marketing strategies and promotion programs;
- Education and training programs;
- Facility development and design standards;
- Sociocultural, environmental, and economic considerations and impact analyses; and
- National level implementation techniques, including staging of development and short-term development strategy and project programming.

Regional Planning

The regional level of tourism planning is for one region of a country, often a state or province, or perhaps an island group, and formulated within the framework of the national tourism policy and plan if such exists. Regional planning focuses on the elements of:
- Regional policy;
- Regional access and the internal transportation network of facilities and services;
- Type and location of tourist attractions;
- Location of tourism development areas including resorts areas;
- Amount, type, and location of tourist accommodation and other tourist facilities and services;
- Regional level environmental, sociocultural, and economic considerations and impacts analyses;
- Regional level education and training programs;
- Marketing strategies and promotion programs;
- Organizational structures, legislation, regulations, and investment policies; and

- Implementation techniques including staging of development, project programming, and regional zoning regulations.

Tourist facility development and design standards may also be prepared for this level of planning.

The regional level of tourism planning is, of course, more specific than the national level, although the degree of specificity at both levels depends on the size of the country or region. For a small country, the national plan may be at the same level of detail as a regional plan in a larger country, and small countries may not need both national and regional planning. Although much regional planning is done for administrative regions, it should be based, where possible, on logical tourism development regions regardless of whether these coincide with administrative boundaries. However, the tourism regions still require some type of organizational structure for coordinated implementation.

Subregional Planning

In some countries or regions, there is need for subregional planning, which is more specific than the regional level, but not as detailed as development area or resort land use planning. The components of the subregional plan will depend on

Cruise ship at St. George, Grenada, West Indies—Cruise ship tourism, already well developed in the Caribbean and Mediterranean, is rapidly expanding in those regions and becoming increasingly popular in several other places of the world. (Courtesy of the Grenada tourism office and taken by James R. Rudin)

the situation of the subregion, but typically would include tourist attraction features, general location of accommodation and other tourist facilities and services, access to the subregion, its internal transportation network and other infrastructure considerations, and relevant institutional factors.

Development Area Land Use Planning

Tourism development areas designated for integrated tourist resorts, resort towns, urban tourism, and tourist attractions require land use plans. This more detailed level of planning indicates the specific areas for hotels and other types of accommodation, retail shops and other tourist facilities, recreation, parks and conservation areas, the transportation system of roads, walkways and other elements such as a local airport or railway line and station, and the planning for other infrastructure of water supply, electric power, sewage and solid waste disposal, and telecommunications. These plans typically include prefeasibility and feasibility studies, evaluation of environmental and sociocultural impacts, staging of development and perhaps development programming, and organizational and financial means for effective implementation. Zoning regulations and specific architectural, landscaping, and engineering design standards are often prepared for this level of planning. Planning for tourist attractions may include visitor use and flow analysis and related recommendations.

Urban tourism development requires land use planning and sometimes improvement or beautification programs for towns and cities that are also important tourist destinations. There can be special tourism plans prepared for urban places or, more appropriately, tourism is included as one element of the comprehensive urban general plan.

Facility Site Planning

Site planning is very specific planning for individual buildings or complexes of buildings such as hotels, commercial centers, and visitor facilities. The actual location of buildings and other structures, recreation facilities, streets and walkways, parking, landscaping areas, and other land uses and their interrelationships are shown in map form.

Facility Design

Architectural, landscaping, and infrastructure designs and engineering specifications must be prepared for resorts, hotels, restaurants, attractions features such as visitor facilities at national parks, archaeological and historic sites, information and cultural centers, and other tourist facilities. These designs may be based on concepts and standards that have been adopted at the more general level of planning, adopted for the area or good international standards.

Special Studies

In addition to the levels of tourism planning and design described above, various types of special studies on tourism are often conducted, depending on the needs of the area. These studies include such diverse topics as economic impact analysis, sociocultural and environmental impact evaluation, marketing analyses and promotion programs, and development programs that are done independently of comprehensive plans. There can also be special planning studies on specific types of tourism development such as health, mountain, or youth tourism, prepared as part of the comprehensive plans or separately. Tourism product improvement studies for particular areas are a common type of special studies.

Often, a comprehensive national tourism planning project will also include regional and development area plans and development standards, architectural, landscaping, and infrastructure engineering design guidelines for tourist facilities, and perhaps some special studies, depending on the terms of reference for the project. The advantage of combining various levels of planning in one project is maintaining consistency of the planning approach and integration of the recommendations.

Components of Tourism Development

Basic to understanding the planning of tourism is knowledge of the components of tourism development and their interrelationships. Various categories of these components are presented in literature on tourism, but the same basic types of components are always included. For the purpose of the planning approach used in this book, the components are classified and described as follows:
- Tourist attractions and activities—All those natural, cultural, and special features and related activities of an area that attract tourists to visit it.
- Accommodation—Hotels and other types of facilities and their related services where tourists stay overnight during their travels.
- Other tourist facilities and services—Other facilities and services necessary for tourism development, including tour and travel operations (also called receptive services), restaurants and other types of eating establishments, retail outlets for handicraft, souvenir, specialty, and convenience goods, banks, money exchange, and other financial facilities and services, tourist information offices, personal services such as barbers and beauticians, medical facilities and services, public safety facilities and services of police and fire protection, and entry and exit travel facilitation of customs and immigration.
- Transportation facilities and services—Transportation access into the country,

region, or development area, the internal transportation system linking the attractions and development areas and transportation within the development areas, including all types of facilities and services related to land, water, and air transportation.

- Other infrastructure—In addition to transportation, the other necessary infrastructure, including water supply, electric power, sewage and solid waste disposal, telecommunications of telephone, telegraph, telex, and telefax,. and sometimes radio; at the development area level, drainage is also an important infrastructure consideration.
- Institutional elements—The institutional elements necessary to develop and manage tourism, including manpower planning and education and training programs, marketing strategies and promotion programs, public and private sector tourism organizational structures, tourism-related legislation and regulations, public and private sector investment policies, and economic, environmental, and sociocultural programs and impact controls.

Figure 2.1 shows these components within the framework of the total natu-

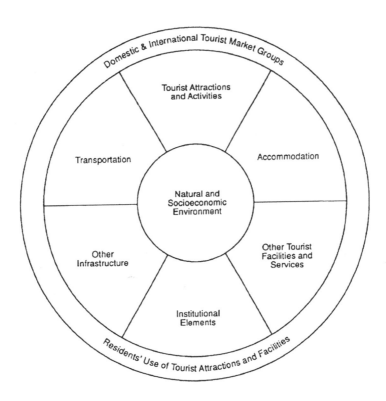

Source: Inskeep 1988

Figure 2.1. Components of a Tourism Plan.

ral and socioeconomic environment from which they derive, the markets of international and domestic tourists that they serve, and the area residents' use of the attractions, facilities, services, and infrastructure. These components will be examined in more depth in subsequent chapters of this book.

Organizing the Tourism Project

If a tourism planning project is to be successful, careful organization and management of the project is essential. A prefeasibility study sometimes needs to be conducted. The study terms of reference must be carefully formulated, the project team well selected and coordinated, and the project activities properly programmed.

Tourism Potential and Prefeasibility Assessment

Not all places have equal potential for developing tourism. If there are any doubts whether the area has sufficient resources and market sources for tourism development and whether the benefits of tourism will outweigh the costs involved, then a prefeasibility assessment of the overall potential and relative benefits and costs should be carried out before proceeding with organizing the project. At the national or regional levels, this study, which should be conducted before the terms of reference for the project are written, examines the resources available for tourism, the potential tourist markets of the area, and the likely economic, environmental, and social costs and benefits of developing tourism. It then determines whether the costs will justify the benefits. At the development area or project level, the prefeasibility study more specifically analyzes the costs and benefits of alternative types and levels of development.

Based on the prefeasibility assessment, it may be decided that tourism development is not feasible, at least in the near future, and that investment resources should be allocated to other economic sectors or projects; or it may be determined that tourism development would be economically justified, but the environmental or social costs would be unacceptably high. However, if tourism in the country or region (or the specific project in question) is generally considered to have potential and be worth developing, then the terms of reference can be formulated, giving consideration to the prefeasibility assessment made and of the likely costs and benefits of tourism.

Project Terms of Reference

The project terms of reference (TOR) should be thoughtfully and carefully prepared so that it is known exactly what the desired results and expected outputs of the project are and the activities required to accomplish these outputs. The TOR also usually include a definition of the kinds of team members or specializations necessary to undertake the study, the time required to accomplish the project activities, and an estimate of the total cost of preparing the study. Although the TOR should be specific as to the types of outputs desired, such as a national or resort plan, it should be sufficiently flexible to allow for and encourage use of imagination and creativity by the planning team.

Assessing the specific type of tourism planning needed and formulating appropriate terms of reference for the project is a rather specialized kind of activity, especially at the more general national and regional planning levels. Therefore, it is common practice for the government to bring in a short-term consultant experienced in formulating tourism planning studies to carry out this task in close cooperation with the government agencies involved. At the more detailed planning levels, a private sector company may write the TOR for the planning of its property. Appendix B sets forth model terms of reference for a comprehensive national tourism planning project that includes several levels and types of tourism plans in a single project.

Project Team and Coordination

To prepare a comprehensive tourism plan, a team of various specialists is required. The exact composition of the team will depend on the specific project requirements and the extent to which some team members can perform more than one function. For a national and regional planning project, the core team members are typically as follows:

- Tourism development planner;
- Tourism marketing specialist;
- Tourism economist; and
- Tourism transportation/infrastructure planner.

The additional specialists who are often required include:

- Tourism development ecologist or environmental planner;
- Tourism development sociologist or anthropologist;
- Air transportation planner;
- Tourism manpower planning and training specialist;
- Tourism organization specialist;
- Tourism legislation and regulations specialist; and
- Hotel and tourist facility specialist.

If more detailed levels of planning are included in the project or the study is primarily for resort or other type of land use planning and design, the specialists required typically may include:

- Resort land use and site planners;
- Hotel and resort market analyst;
- Hotel and resort financial feasibility analyst;
- Hotel/resort facility architect;

- Hotel/resort landscape architect; and
- Various types of infrastructure engineers, such as road, water, electrical, sanitary, soils, and telecommunications engineers.

If tourist attraction planning is required, then park planning, wildlife conservation, archaeological, historic and cultural heritage site planning, marine conservation and sports, golf course design, marina design, or other specialists may need to be included on the team. Some of the team members may only be required for short time periods while others will have greater involvement.

When the types of planning team functions have been decided, the project team can be selected, utilizing local staff, international or domestic consultants, or a combination of these. All team member should, of course, be qualified in their respective fields, and at least some of the key team members should, if possible, be familiar with the country, region, or area being planned, especially if it represents an unusual political, cultural, or environmental situation. If the plan is being prepared by consultants, the government agency involved or the client company for private sector projects should appoint one or more staff members to work with the project team as counterparts, in order to both assist them with their knowledge of local conditions and to gain experience in planning practice. If there will be need for follow-through by local staff with implementation of the plan, which is often the case, it is especially important that some counterparts be appointed so that they understand the rationale behind the plan's recommendations as a basis for more effectively implementing them.

It is essential that the team be well organized with one person designated as the team leader, responsible for team coordination and the project outputs. A liaison officer should be appointed from the government staff (or private client staff), maintaining close coordination with the relevant government agencies and private sector organizations.

For formal direction of a government type of project, a project steering committee, comprised of representatives of tourism-related government agencies and the involved private sector organizations, such as the hotel association or chamber of commerce, and chaired by a high-level official, should be appointed. This committee meets with the planning team periodically to offer guidance to the project and review its work, especially the project's draft reports on analyses, conclusions, and recommendations. Alternatively, a tourism board or advisory committee, if one exists, can serve as the project steering committee. At the community or local level of tourism planning, organization of workshops with participants from both the community and the commercial sector on tourism in the local area—its opportunities, problems, alternative future type and extent of development, and how residents can be involved in tourism—is a very useful technique to encourage community involvement in tourism and its planning. This approach has been successfully utilized in British Columbia, Canada (Murphy 1988) and on various WTO planning projects and has general application in many developing tourism areas.

Project Work Program

Preparation of a project work program is essential in organizing project activities and their interrelationships, so that activities are undertaken in logical sequence and the outputs are completed on schedule. A work program also indicates the team members who are responsible for the specific activities. Figure 2.2 sets forth a sample preliminary work program for a comprehensive national tourism planning project that is usually prepared as part of the project terms of reference to provide initial guidance to the team and client agency. This work program is then refined and further specified upon commencement of the project when the actual field conditions are better known.

Project Reports

Upon arrival in the project area and after discussions with the client staff and preliminary assessment of field conditions, the project team leader prepares the In-

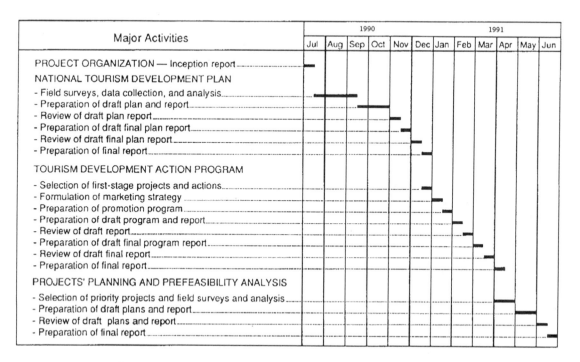

Note: The more detailed final work program is prepared at the commencement of the project and included in the inception report.

Figure 2.2. Sample Preliminary Work Program.

ception Report, which includes the detailed work program and schedule and any other pertinent information. Draft reports are always prepared during the project to set forth the findings, conclusions, and preliminary recommendations for review by the government and project steering committee (or private client company). In some cases of complex projects, it is desirable to prepare an interim report, before the draft report is prepared, of the survey and analysis findings and conclusions for review by the committee. Draft reports are usually prepared for each of the major components or outputs of the project, such as for the national plan, regional plans, resort plans, tourist attractions plans, and development program. If there are many modifications to be made to the first draft report, it may be necessary to prepare a second draft for review. When the planning project is being undertaken by the private sector, the draft reports or at least some of the most likely alternative plans can also be presented to the government at public hearings to obtain public responses to the proposals.

When there is agreement on the analyses, findings, conclusions, and recommendations contained in the draft reports, the study team finalizes its background work and recommendations and prepares a draft final report (or reports) for review by the steering committee and, upon approval or agreement on modifications to be made, produces the final report (or reports). This reporting sequence is summarized as follows:

1. Inception report
2. Interim report (possibly)
3. Draft report
4. Draft final report
5. Final report

The planning reports should be detailed with all the essential survey results, analyses, findings, conclusions, and recommendations clearly set forth. The reasons for the recommendations made should be carefully explained so that they are understandable to the average reader. Appendixes can be used for detailed supporting information and analyses. The reports will be organized based on the specific terms of reference of the project and the types of surveys, analyses, and recommendations being made. But planning reports tend to follow a generally similar and logical pattern derived in large part from the sequence of the steps in the planning process. Judicious use of readable maps, photographs, and other graphic material can greatly help make the reports more understandable and interesting.

If the final report is long and bulky, a summary report with the relevant graphic material should be prepared for distribution to key decision makers and the general public. It must be remembered that many of the report users are very busy and do not have the time to read the detailed reports, at least in their entirety. Even if the main report is not particularly long, it is a very useful technique to prepare and include a short summary section at the beginning of the main report.

Project Funding

In more developed countries, funding for tourism planning projects and feasibility studies at the national and regional levels is provided by the governments concerned or, in the case of detailed planning of specific privately developed project such as resorts, by the private company involved. In less developed countries with limited financial resources, planning project funding can be available internationally from agencies such the UNDP and other global agencies, the European Community and various other regional or special purpose international organizations, and from bilateral aid agencies. If the planning project is well justified, funding from some source can usually be found.

References

Getz, Donald. 1986. "Models in Tourism Planning: Towards Integration of Theory and Practice." *Tourism Management.* 7(1): 21-32.

Inskeep, Edward. 1987. "Environmental Planning for Tourism."*Annals of Tourism Research.* 14 (1): 118-135.

——— . 1988. "Tourism Planning: An Emerging Specialization." *Journal of the American Planning Association.* 54 (3): 360-372. Reprinted by permission of the *Journal of the American Planning Association.*

Murphy, Peter E. 1988. "Community Driven Tourism Planning." *Tourism Management.* 9(2): 96-104.

Pigram, John. 1983. *Outdoor Recreation and Resource Management.* Beckenham, England: Croon Helm.

World Tourism Organization. 1980. *Manila Declaration.* Madrid: World Tourism Organization.

———. 1985. *Tourism Bill of Rights and Tourist Code.* Madrid: World Tourism Organization.

———. 1989. *The Hague Declaration on Tourism.* Madrid: World Tourism Organization.

World Tourism Organization and United Nations Environment Programme.1982. *Joint Declaration Between World Tourism Organization and United Nations Environment Programme.* Madrid: World Tourism Organization.

———. 1983. *Workshop on Environmental Aspects of Tourism.* Madrid: World Tourism Organization.

Part Two

National and Regional Tourism Planning

Part Two focuses on the national and regional levels of tourism planning, and application to these levels of the planning approaches set forth in Part One: the systems-oriented, comprehensive, integrated, environmental, and sustainable development approaches, with emphasis on community involvement and participation in tourism planning and development. First, the general planning process explained in Part One is elaborated here for the national and regional levels of tourism planning, and determination of the plan content is reviewed. Then, each of the planning steps of surveys and evaluation of tourism resources and other elements of the existing tourism situation, the integrated analyses and synthesis, and formulation of the tourism policy and plan formulation are examined. Carrying capacity analysis is reviewed in some detail. Case studies are presented at the end of each chapter to demonstrate the actual application of various techniques and principles.

Part Two carries the planning process at the national and regional levels up to the policy and plan formulation steps. Later in the book, Part Four picks up on specific environmental and socioeconomic considerations and Part Five deals with the institutional elements and plan implementation.

3

The Planning Process and General Surveys

The National and Regional Tourism Planning Process

Figure 3.1 indicates application of the basic planning process described in Chapter 2 to national and regional tourism planning. This chart sequentially shows the detailed activities required to prepare the plan in an integrated manner. Each of the steps is briefly described in the following sections to provide an overview of the planning process and are further elaborated later in this and subsequent chapters.

Study Preparation

Under this step, a decision has been made by the government, in consultation with the private sector and general public through its institutional process, to develop tourism, or expand or improve its present development, in a planned manner. As explained in Chapter 2 under project organization, if there is any doubt about the relative economic, environmental, and social costs and benefits of developing or expanding tourism, then a prefeasibiltiy assessment should be carried out to make certain that there is potential for developing tourism and that its benefits will outweigh its likely costs in the foreseeable future. If this assessment is positive, then the terms of reference for the planning study are prepared, based in part on the prefeasibility assessment.

As emphasized in Chapter 2, the project terms of reference should be care-

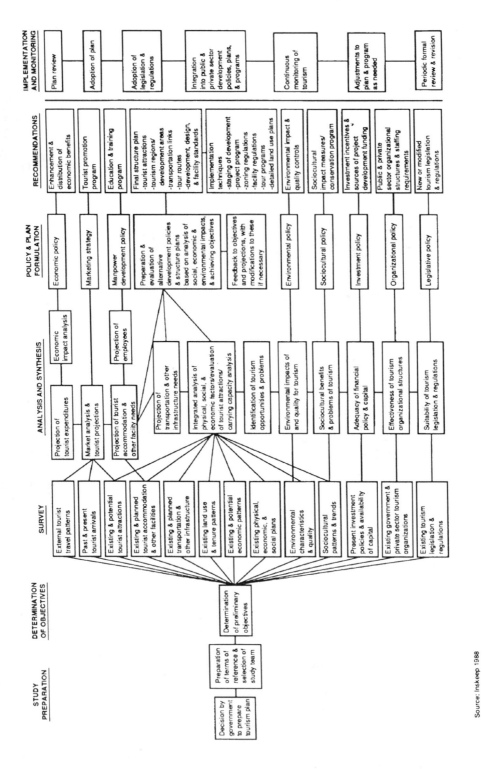

Figure 3.1. Process for Preparing the Comprensive Tourism Development Plan at the National and Regional Levels.

Source: Inskeep 1988

50

fully written so that the study achieves its desired results and outputs. Plans should have a horizon year indicating when the plan and its targets and recommendations are to be realized, within the framework of understanding that development may well continue beyond that date based on new planning, which will have taken place near the end of the present planning period. Establishing a horizon year provides a time framework for making projections, setting targets, and staging development. Long-range national and regional tourism plans involving policy considerations are usually prepared for a 15 to 20 year period although, in some cases, a 10-year period may be considered more relevant, especially in newly developing tourism areas where future conditions are less predictable.

Even though time periods are established for convenience of programming, they should be considered flexible based on changing circumstances. The overall planning recommendations are not necessarily invalid just because certain time periods set (for example, of tourist arrival targets) are not met. Because of unpredictable influences on meeting time-based targets, often the more important considerations are maintaining a balance between the development levels of tourist facilities and services and actual tourist use during the short-term period, so that there is not a waste of resources, while still striving to meet the market targets over the long term.

As explained in Chapter 2, effective organization of the project with a carefully selected and coordinated team, involvement of a steering committee or advisory board, and preparation of a realistic and detailed work program is essential during the study preparation stage.

Determination of Objectives

Goals and objectives indicate the desired results of developing tourism, usually of various types of socioeconomic benefits, and the special considerations that must be made, such as minimizing environmental and sociocultural impacts. As typically used by planners, goals refer to the more general aims of development and objectives to the more specific ones. Because the distinction between goals and objectives can be confusing to many users of planning studies, the approach used in this book (and in many actual planning studies) is to refer only to development objectives and not use the term goals.

The objectives of developing tourism in the planning area are obviously very important considerations because they are basic determinants of the tourism policy and plan. Consequently, they should be carefully determined in close consultation with the government and steering committee. Objectives should be decided at the commencement of the study because they will influence the types of surveys and analyses and formulation of the policy, plan, and recommendations. However, at this point, they are stated in a tentative fashion because the results of the analyses and plan formulation may indicate that some objectives are in conflict with one another or that certain objectives cannot realistically be achieved. For example, if one objective states that the economic benefits of tourism should be maximized and another objective stipulates that environmental and sociocultural impacts should be minimized, it may not be possible to prepare a policy and plan that simultaneously achieves both these objectives, or an objective of a rapid increase in tourist arrivals may not be possible to achieve because of market or facility constraints.

After the analysis has been completed and during the formulation of the policy, plan, and other recommendations, there is feedback to the objectives, as indicated in Figure 3.1, to determine whether the objectives are being achieved. At this point, any conflicts among the objectives can be ascertained. If it is found that some objectives are incompatible, alternative plans to reach the different objectives can be prepared and presented to the policy makers before a decision is made on which plan and related objectives to finalize. If some objectives are unrealistic to achieve, then they will need to be modified or the intention to develop tourism reassessed.

Tourism objectives should, of course, reinforce any general development objectives already adopted for the country or region. However, in some cases, it may be decided to modify the general objectives, based on those tourism objectives deemed necessary to achieve the overall development results.

Surveys

As the term implies, the survey stage of the planning process involves collecting data, both quantitative and qualitative, on all relevant aspects of the tourism considerations as listed on the planning process chart. This survey activity needs to be carefully organized to be efficiently conducted and will include field surveys of tourist attractions, facilities and services, and transportation and other infrastructure; discussions with the relevant government officials, private sector representatives, and community spokesmen; review of existing documents, maps and data, and any other means to obtain the information required. Often, an aerial overview survey of the country or region is an excellent way of becoming geographically oriented and observing environmental relationships that are not always obvious on the ground.

Sometimes, ingenuity and persistence must be applied to obtain the information required, and often, important ideas can be gained through discussions with local persons, including those in the private sector and community organizations. There is no substitute for making actual field inspections of tourist attractions, facilities, services, and infrastructure to make certain that accurate information is obtained and realistic evaluations are made. It is useful, although not always feasible, for the study team to travel together during the field survey so they can exchange ideas and become aware of the relationships of the various survey information to their respective disciplines. Because of the close relationship between the tourist products and markets, it is important for the market analyst to field inspect the tourist attractions, facilities, and services.

In addition to field surveys and document research, special surveys may need to be conducted, for example, of tourists to determine their characteristics, expenditure patterns, tour activities, attitudes, and satisfaction levels of the local tourism product. As part of the market survey, it may be necessary to interview tour operators and airlines in the overseas market countries to obtain their and their clients' perceptions of, and experiences with, the tourism area. If important information is not already available, this situation should be anticipated and the information collected, perhaps through special surveys or mapping projects, before the planning study commences, so that expensive project time is not wasted.

Depending on the size and type of planning area, a considerable amount of time and several team members, plus good logistical support, may need to be programmed for conducting the surveys, especially to visit places that are not easily accessible.

Analysis and Synthesis

Both quantitative and qualitative analysis and synthesis (combination and integration of the various components of the analyses) of the survey information must be carefully done. Synthesizing the analysis will, for example, include relating the types of tourist attractions to the types and extent of tourist markets as shown in Figure 3.1. The integrated analysis of physical, social, and economic factors will include, for example, establishing general visitor carrying capacities to help determine the overall optimum level of tourism development in the country or region (carrying capacity analysis is done more specifically at the community planning level).

An important type of synthesis is the identification of the major opportunities and problems or constraints for developing tourism in the area. These opportunities and constraints provide much of the foundation for determining future tourism development, and give a focus for formulating the major recommendations on developing or expanding and improving tourism.

The analysis and synthesis phase is a major activity, which usually requires considerable time and specialized capabilities, but the quality and extent of analysis very much depend on the availability of adequate and accurate survey data. As mentioned in Chapter 2, information systems technology and computer techniques of analysis, evaluation, and representation can greatly aid in analysis and synthesis.

Policy and Plan Formulation

As shown in Figure 3.1, this step refers to formulation of tourism policy on all the plan components and preparation of the physical structure plan and its related elements. The best approach to formulation is to first prepare and evaluate alternative policies and outline plans (or scenarios). There is seldom a single ideal plan for any area that achieves all the desired objectives but, rather, the optimum plan that achieves most of the objectives without generating serious problems evolves through evaluation of alternative policies and plans. After this evaluation, the policy and plan (or often a combination of various elements from different alternatives) that best meet the objectives, optimize economic benefits, reinforce positive and minimize negative environmental and sociocultural impacts are selected for finalization.

During this stage, there should be much involvement of the government, steering committee, and any other interested parties in review of the analyses and conclusions and evaluation of the alternatives policies and plans leading up to selection of the optimum ones.

Recommendations

Based on the analysis and synthesis prepared and optimum policy and plan selected, the structure plan can be finalized in detail and all the relevant recommendations made as shown in Figure 3.1. For some types of recommendations, alternatives must also be evaluated before the most suitable ones can be determined. For some elements of the plan, no changes to the existing situation may be necessary, but that fact must be stated. In some cases, alternative recommendations, all of which are acceptable, can be presented in the final plan document, with the government or private sector deciding which recommendations to pursue, depending on future circumstances. It is essential to also involve the government, steering committee, and other interested parties in review of all the recommendations.

Implementation and Monitoring

The final step in the planning process is implementation and monitoring the implementation and tourism is general. However, as referred to in Chapter 2, the means of implementation should be considered throughout the plan preparation and especially during the policy and plan formulation and recommendations stages, so that the final plan is realistic to achieve and implementable. Specific techniques of implementation, such as preparation of the project development program (sometimes referred to as the action program or development or action strategy), are shown on the chart under recommendations. Under the implementation step, the sequence of activities required for implementation is listed.

During and after implementation, tourism development must be monitored to ensure that it is accomplishing the objectives, following the development schedule, and not generating any economic, environmental, or sociocultural problems. If problems are detected, remedial measures must be taken to bring the development back on track. Sometimes, resulting from changing circumstances such as new market trends, adjustments should be made to the plan, but always making certain that any policy or plan modifications do not abrogate the agreed upon basic objectives of tourism development.

The Planning Report Content

For a complex planning project, it is a useful technique near the commencement of the project to outline the anticipated contents of the planning report with detailed chapter and section headings, based on the project terms of reference and the project team's planning approach. Organizing the report contents in a preliminary manner will assist the team in making certain that it considers all the important points of the survey and analysis conclusions, policy and plan recommendations, economic, environmental, and sociocultural impacts, institutional factors, and implementation techniques. This preliminary report outline can later be modified as needed to incorporate any changes or different approaches decided upon during the course of the study.

It can also be worthwhile to examine the reports of similar planning projects that have been completed to ascertain planning approaches and types of considerations and recommendations that have been made elsewhere. Because tourism planning is such a broad field and new development concepts are constantly being tried, much can often be learned from examining other project reports, as well as visiting other tourism areas and discussing tourism development concepts with tourism personnel. To demonstrate the types of plan elements to be considered in a comprehensive regional tourism plan and their report organization, the contents of the Zanzibar tourism development plan report are reproduced in Appendix C.

General Surveys of the Area Characteristics

The general geographic characteristics of the country or region should be surveyed to provide the background for overall understanding of the area and to provide the basis for specific research and analysis of particular relevant aspects of the environment. A complete planning report will contain an introductory chapter summarizing these characteristics as general background information for users of the plan.

This general survey requires both document and map research and field visits that can often be combined with the specific surveys carried out for various components of the plan such as for tourist attractions, facilities, and infrastructure. Except for the type of information observed on field visits, much of the basic survey data required will already be available in map or report form from the government, universities, and other special studies already completed and published. However, the availability of data varies appreciably among countries and regions, and, in some cases, estimates will need to be made based on observation. It is useful to make the effort to read general geography and history books about the country or region.

Location

The location of the country or region should be specified and mapped, relative to its regional and global situation. Location becomes an important consideration with respect to distances from major tourist market countries at the national planning level and from other regions in the country at the regional planning level as input to the market analysis. For tour programming, locational analysis may reveal the opportunity to include the planning area on multi-destination tours, and there may be possibilities for complementary tourism product development with nearby countries or regions.

Natural Environment

Several characteristics of the natural environment must be surveyed as explained in the follow sections.

Climate

Climatic patterns include rainfall, temperatures, humidity, extent of sunshine (or cloudiness), fog, wind speeds and directions, and the seasonal variations of these factors. Climatic seasonality can be particularly important considerations where climate is a major type of tourist attraction. Also, intensity and frequency of climatic hazards such as high winds and rainfall (hurricanes, tornados, typhoons, cyclones, intense monsoon rains, and so forth) resulting in loss of life and property damage should be recorded. At the national or regional levels, climatic patterns only need to be indicated for the different climatic zones, not for all specific places. Climatic characteristics should be plotted on maps as well as described.

Topography

Topography refers to the surface features of the land, particularly the land configurations and slope, such as flat, hilly, and mountainous areas, and the hydrography of lakes, rivers, and wetlands (swamps, and so forth). At the the national and regional planning levels, detailed mapping is not required, but topographic characteristics can be generalized into, for example, lands of less and more than 20 percent slopes, which is often used as the dividing line between developable and nondevelopable land, and the major water features. Areas prone to flooding, erosion, and landslides should be identified.

Wildlife and Vegetation

Wildlife is indicated by type, extent, and general location. For most wildlife, their habitat range must be considered, not only their present location. Any conservation problems of wildlife, such as existence of endangered species should be researched. Vegetation can be generalized into categories such as large-tree forest cover, scrub forest, grassland, barren, and so forth, but with the general types of common species and specific unusual species identified; any conservation problems of the vegetation should be researched.

Coastal and Marine Areas

Coastal and marine characteristics to be surveyed include types of coastline with the location and characteristics of beaches, reefs, and offshore islands identified, tidal ranges and high and low tide lines along the shore, any erosion or deposition taking place noted, and underwater sea life of coral formations, fishes, and so forth, described. Any existing conservation problems such as reef damage and endangered species should be investigated. In some marines areas, for example, reefs have been seriously damaged by mining of the coral for use in construction, dynamiting of the reef areas by fishermen to kill fish, pollution from on-shore fertilizer and waste discharges, and sedimentation resulting from on-shore erosion problems; or there may have been reef damage resulting from uncontrolled tourist use. Underwater topography also may be important to know. The marine areas should be examined for any hazards they present, such as strong currents and undertows that are dangerous for water recreation.

Geology

Aspects of geological characteristics that are important to consider include locations and extent of underground water and mineral resources and suitability of areas for development in terms of stable foundation material. Any earthquake hazard areas and degree of hazard should be researched.

Ecological Systems

Important ecological systems, usually comprising a combination of climate, topography, vegetation, and wildlife and ecological systems of both land and water areas, should be identified and their scientific and conservation value evaluated. Mangrove swamps, for example, are important ecosystems providing sea life and plant habitats, slowing water runoff, and preventing coastal erosion.

Natural Resource Areas

Natural resource areas to be identified include, for example, lands that are highly suitable for agriculture or encompass exploitable minerals and water areas con-

Ironbridge, England—Constructed in the late eighteenth century, this structure, along with other well-preserved examples of the early period of the Industrial Revolution in this same area, represent the increasingly practiced activity of industrial archaeology. As is the case of Ironbridge, these places also constitute an important type of tourist attraction in several countries. (Courtesy of the British Travel Authority)

taining commercial fisheries potential that should perhaps be reserved for those uses. Based on analysis and recommendations of the tourism planning study, tourism resource areas will also be identified.

Historical Influences

Knowledge of the history of an area is important in tourism planning because many aspects of the history are visually expressed as tourist attractions such as archaeological and historic sites and places of historic events, and have influenced contemporary life-styles, customs, arts, and handicrafts. The history of an area also has influenced social value systems and attitudes that are significant sociocultural considerations in tourism. The history of the planning area need not be presented in complete detail but should highlight the background needed for understanding relevant elements of the tourism planning analysis and plan formulation.

Sociocultural and Economic Patterns

Sociocultural and economic factors to be considered are described in the following sections.

Population Characteristics

The number and geographic distribution of population, which are important considerations in any type of development, can be shown in tabular or chart form for the past and present population figures with the population distribution shown on maps. Migration patterns of the population might also be relevant (for example, migration from rural to urban places and from low to high employment areas because they indicate where employment is needed). Out- and in-migration patterns also are indicative of employment patterns. Any population projections that have been prepared should be researched.

Age-sex profiles of the population and their geographic distribution can be indicated by general age categories. The distribution of age-sex groups may be a consideration in determining the availability of labor supply in certain areas. Education levels, also important to know for manpower planning, can be shown in major categories such as completion of primary school, secondary school, and university and technical college. Indication of literacy levels may be relevant in some areas. Employment categories and level of unemployment and underemployment should be researched, including employment in tourism-related activities, as related to the manpower planning component of the tourism study.

Cultural Patterns

Cultural patterns including social structure, value systems, customs, life-styles, and attitudes as related to development of tourism and residents working in tourism should be identified. In some large countries and regions, there may be various different cultural groups, each with their own cultural systems and different sets of cultural values and attitudes, depending on the geographic area and socioeconomic characteristics of the residents. For example, urban dwellers may have quite different attitudes and values than rural residents in the same region.

In strongly traditional or tribal areas, an in-depth study may be required to understand local cultural patterns and how best to develop tourism in those areas. Religious values such as constraints on consumption of alcoholic beverages and dress and behavioral codes must be understood. Local life-styles, music, dance, drama, ceremonies, dress, arts, and handicrafts should be observed both as possible attraction features for tourists and for consideration in the sociocultural impact evaluation of tourism.

Economic Patterns

The economic profile of the country or region should be researched, including the major components of the economy, gross national product, income levels and distribution, type and value of exports and imports and the balance of payments, and other economic factors that relate to the economic analysis of tourism and establishing linkages between tourism and other economic sectors. Some countries have compiled and analyzed a substantial amount of economic data, including preparing input-output tables, while economic data are less available in other areas. Historical growth and changes in economic patterns and the prospects for future economic development are important to understand with respect to prevailing trends. Economically depressed areas should be identified. Unusual (to the potential tourists) economic activities, which can range from traditional agricultural and fishing techniques to modern plantations and factories, may offer interesting types of tourist attraction features and should be noted.

Land Use, Settlement, and Tenure Patterns

At the national and regional planning levels, the general land use patterns such as agriculture by type, industry, designated park, recreation and conservation areas, and the settlement patterns of rural, village, town, and city along with the transportation network (described in Chapter 5) should be mapped. Land use and settlement patterns are important to know relative to selection of tourism development areas. Any existing regional land use zoning and related development regulations should be mapped and the regulations researched relative to those applicable to tourism development.

Land tenure (the type of land ownership or use rights) may be a very important consideration in determining the availability of land for tourism development. Land tenure categories may include private and government or public lands, fee ownership or leasehold, communal or individual ownership, and so on. In some Pacific Islands, for example, land may be communally owned with the various owners now living in many different places and, in some islands, the economically productive trees may be in different ownership than the land; this situation obviously presents some difficulties in assembling land for development purposes.

Environmental Quality

The overall level of environmental quality of the country or region and especially of the existing and potential tourism development areas is an important consideration in attracting tourists, as well as being important for residents, and should be surveyed and evaluated. Environmental quality factors to be considered during the survey include the following:

- Air quality—Extent of air cleanliness or pollution and the types and sources of pollution.
- Quality of domestic water supply—Potability, taste, and the types, extent, and sources of any pollution.
- Quality of surface waters—Appearance, cleanliness, and the types, extent, and sources of any pollution of rivers, lakes, wetlands, coastal waters, and offshore underwater areas.
- Quality of underground water—Potability, mineralization, and the types, extent, and sources of any pollution of underground water resources, as these factors affect provision of water supply and the quality of surface waters.
- Noise levels—Extent of quietness or excessive noise levels, particularly in accommodation, residential, park, recreation, conservation, and tourist attraction areas.
- Cleanliness of public places—Extent of cleanliness or dirtiness including littering of public places such as streets and walkways, public building grounds, parks and recreation areas, and roadsides; extent of cleanliness of commercial areas also should be considered.
- Landscaping—Extent, types, and maintenance levels of landscaping, especially along streets, on building grounds, and in park and recreation areas.
- Building design and maintenance—Appropriateness and attractiveness of building design styles, and the adequacy of building maintenance of public and commercial buildings.
- Urban design—The land use and building interrelationships, provision of parks, plazas, and landscaping and overall appearance of the urban environment.
- Signs—Types, sizes, location, lighting, extent of use, and general design appearance of advertising and other types of signs.
- Functional land use and transportation patterns—Extent that land use patterns are functional, well interrelated, and efficiently served with transportation facilities and services in both urban and rural areas.
- Congestion levels—Ease of mobility and extent of pedestrian and vehicular congestion.
- Open space, parks, and conservation areas—Extent that there are sufficient open space and park areas and conservation of important ecological areas and archaeological and historic places.
- Scenic views—Extent that scenic views have been retained through preservation of view planes and corridors in developed areas (for example, of mountain and coastal scenery and important buildings).
- Environmental diseases—Types, prevalence, and geographic distribution of environmentally-related diseases such as cholera, malaria, typhoid, and dysentery.

There may also be other environmental quality factors in a particular planning area that should be surveyed and evaluated. Chapter 12 on environmental considerations further explains how to evaluate these environmental factors.

Survey of Institutional Elements

The institutional elements to be surveyed and evaluated in the planning process include present development policies and plans, government and tourism organizational structures, political ideology and influences on the development process, investment policies and availability of capital, tourism-related legislation and regulations, and tourism employee training programs and institutions. These are researched generally at this point for subsequent input into the planning analysis, policy and plan formulation, and the recommended implementation approaches. Survey of the institutional elements requires both document research and discussions with government agencies and the private sector.

Present Development Policies and Plans

Most countries and many regions of countries, especially states or provinces, have some form of adopted development policies and plans. These may be long-term or medium-term, commonly for five-year periods, and sometimes include a tourism sector. Especially important to consider are the basic economic, physical, and social development policies and strategies of the country or region. These should be carefully reviewed to determine any overall policies that may influence the formulation of tourism policy. It may well be the case that, based on its findings, the tourism planning study will recommend changes or refinements of these policies and development, but the present policies and plans must first be understood.

There may be existing physical development plans and project programs for the country, region, and urban areas that should be reviewed for any possible relevant inputs into the tourism planning study. Plans for new or improved roads and airports, and new or expanded urban or industrial areas will influence decision-making on the tourism plan. Any transportation plans should particularly be examined. In some places, there may have been tourism plans prepared in the past but now are outdated (the current tourism study may be a revision of a previous tourism plan), which should be carefully reviewed for useful background information and recommendations that are still valid.

Government and Tourism Organizational Structures

The overall system of government and its organizational structure should be understood as one of the considerations for determining the most suitable organizational role of government in tourism development. For example, tourism would be somewhat differently organized in a country with a highly centralized government structure than in one with a more decentralized government. The organization of government agencies whose functions relate to tourism such as transportation and communications, environmental protection and cultural development, and immigration and customs, as well as any central planning departments should particularly be examined, including their interagency coordination arrangements.

The structures, functions, and staffing of any existing tourism department, bureau, development corporation, advisory board, or committee should be surveyed and evaluated relative to their appropriateness and effectiveness for managing tourism and implementing the tourism policy and plan. Charts can be prepared to graphically represent these organizational structures and their relationships to other government agencies. Private sector tourism-related organizations such as hotel, tour and travel, and restaurant associations should be examined relative to their functions, organizational structures, staffing, and effectiveness, including their relationships to government agencies.

Political ideologies and influences can greatly affect the type and extent of tourism development and how it is developed and managed, and these factors must be considered in the planning process. Emphasizing this point, Gunn (1988, 62–63) states:

> A review of tourism politics generally suggests that the dimensions and results of tourism planning will be influenced most by the nation's ideology and its interpretation for overall social, political and economic goals (DeKadt, 1979, 33). Policies and practices for tourism will follow the overall policies and practices of the nation as a whole. This is reflected in the relative roles of government and private enterprise, how profits are divided, the sectors most likely to benefit, domestic versus foreign travel influence, and relative dependence on tourism.

Independent of basic differences in political ideologies, the government policies toward tourism development, often influenced by sociocultural and environmental considerations, can vary greatly. Some countries may want to greatly control tourism for reasons of limiting outside influences on their religious and cultural systems, while others desire to develop tourism rapidly for economic reasons. Major international events such as the Olympics, trade fairs, and important conferences may, for example, be hosted at great expense by countries for reasons primarily of enhancing national prestige and gaining international exposure, although they may also bring direct and indirect economic benefits. The tourism planner must be aware of the political influences on the tourism development planning that he is undertaking for the country or region, and the tourism manager cognizant of these factors in implementation of the tourism policies and plans.

At the beginning of the 1990s decade, the political ideologies of several countries in the world are undergoing rapid changes of which the outcome is not yet known. However, the trend seems to be toward varying degrees of mixed economic systems, with somewhat decentralized government structures and decision making and generally moderate involvement by government in the development planning process. Consequently, the tourism planner and manager must be particularly sensitive to any political changes taking place that may affect his recommendations. At the same time, it should be recognized that, based on analysis of relatively stable international tourist markets and application of sound planning principles, many forms of tourism are valid no matter what the current political ideology is, and often the main political consideration is deciding the most effective means of implementing the tourism plan.

Investment Policies and Availability of Capital

The present investment policies for investment in development projects, including for tourism projects, should be researched. Investment policies refer particularly to provision for joint venture development between outside and local capital resources or between the government and private sectors, and incentives allowed to encourage private sector investments. As will be examined in Chapter 14, the planning study may well recommend changes in investment policies, but the existing situation must first be understood.

Related to determination of investment policies, investigation must be made of the availability of local and outside capital for tourism project investment, including for both tourist facilities and tourism-related infrastructure. Availability of capital resources may need to be investigated internationally as well as locally. Hotels and resorts in particular can require major capital outlays for some types of infrastructure such as water supply, roads, and airports. Researching the availability of capital also includes the investigation of loan availability for the planning area, locally or from elsewhere, and the costs of obtaining and servicing loans.

Tourism Legislation and Regulations

If tourism already exists in the country or region, some tourism-related legislation and regulations may have been adopted and should be researched. There may be a basic tourism law and specific regulations, such as on hotel standards and classification systems, tour and travel agency operations, and tour guide services. Also, some general regulations such as on land use zoning, building construction, and hygienic standards of restaurants are applicable to tourism development. All these need to be investigated and evaluated as input to determining the future legislation and regulations required for the successful implementation of the tourism plan and continuing management of tourism, including any modifications needed to present legislation and regulations.

Tourism Education and Training Programs and Institutions

If there is already some tourism development, there may be existing tourism education and training programs and perhaps training institutions that should be surveyed and evaluated, as input into the manpower planning and development component of the planning study. These programs may include hotel, catering, tour and travel operations, and tourism management subjects such as on planning, marketing, and research techniques.

Case Studies

The case studies selected represent several aspects of the initial steps in the national and regional planning process. An example of detailed tourism development objectives reflecting a balanced development approach is taken from the regional plan for two provinces in eastern Indonesia in Southeast Asia. As an example of an approach to a general land use survey for tourism planning, the existing land use survey from the national tourism plan for Malta in the Mediterranean region is explained. To show the comprehensiveness of background surveys required in a national tourism plan, the types of area surveys conducted for the national tourism plan of Fiji in the South Pacific are reviewed. Finally, the survey of the unusual climatic regime of Sri Lanka in South Asia and the relationship of that climatic pattern to the seasonality of tourism is examined.

Tourism Development Objectives of Nusa Tenggara, Indonesia

The Nusa Tenggara, Indonesia regional tourism development plan (UNDP/WTO 1981) was prepared by the WTO as a United Nations Development Programme assisted project in 1981. This plan was part of a continuing program by the Indonesian government to prepare regional tourism plans for the various provinces of the country. The Nusa Tenggara region includes the two related provinces of Nusa Tenggara Barat and Nusa Tenggara Timur, which are comprised of several islands extending over some 900 kilometers in the eastern part of the country. These islands had limited general development and a diverse mixture of cultural groups, some of which are still highly traditional outside the main urban areas; the islands are particularly known among connoisseurs for their unique hand-woven tie-dye textiles. The resources for tourism include features related to both the natural land and water environment, including some good beaches and marine diving areas and the traditional cultural patterns. Concurrent with preparation of the tourism plan, a previously designated major national park, Komodo National Park, and other conservation areas in the region were also being planned, and the tourism and park planning teams coordinated closely together in conducting field surveys and formulating their respective plans.

Because it was considered essential that tourism be carefully developed to bring some economic benefits without requiring high investment costs or generating any local sociocultural or environmental problems, the objectives of the plan were formulated to be quite specific. They were directed to achieve several aims:

- Developing domestic and international tourism for both economic and social benefits, including expanding the national and international awareness and understanding of this little known region;
- Minimizing investment of scarce government development resources;
- Maximizing distribution of economic benefits throughout the society, including creating local employment and establishing strong linkages with other economic sectors;
- Promoting conservation of traditional cultural patterns and minimizing negative sociocultural impacts;
- Promoting conservation of the natural environment and minimizing negative environmental impacts;
- Developing attractions that residents as well as domestic and international tourists can use;
- Utilizing existing infrastructure for tourism to the extent possible and developing new infrastructure that is multi-purpose for both general and tourism use;
- Training local persons to work effectively in tourism; and
- Establishing tourism development patterns that can be logically phased in over a long period of time.

When it was completed, the tourism plan was adopted by the government and followed through with development programming and some implementation. The national park plan was also adopted, and development of the first stage visitor facilities in the park has been completed.

Listed below are the major objectives of developing tourism in Nusa Tenggara; these reflect the adopted national tourism objectives as well as regional tourism policy.

- Encourage foreign tourism in order to increase the country's foreign exchange, improve regional economic development, and expand international understanding of Indonesia and Nusa Tenggara, but with promotion of selective tourist markets that will provide optimum benefits without creating undue social, economic, and environmental problems.
- Encourage domestic tourism, including youth tourism and both budget and affluent domestic travelers in order to help redistribute income within Indonesia and, through increasing the understanding of different Indonesian cultures and environments, contribute to sociocultural integration of the country and development of a sense of national unity.
- Integrate tourism development into total local, regional, and national development patterns and programs, including Pelita III, without placing a burden on the government's development resources, and encourage private sector investment in tourist facilities.
- Improve the general income level and economic and social welfare of people in Nusa Tenggara, and encourage the distribution of economic benefits of tourism as widely as possible throughout society, including development of activities related to tourism such as handicraft production, agriculture, and industry.

- Provide additional employment opportunities for people in Nusa Tenggara in all aspects of tourism and related activities with emphasis on employment, to the extent possible, of persons from within Nusa Tenggara and from the local areas where tourism is developed.
- Promote the conservation of traditional cultural patterns and their artistic expressions and places of specific historic and cultural importance that represent the heritage of Nusa Tenggara, and minimize any adverse impact of tourism on traditional cultures and the general society through carefully controlled development.
- Promote conservation of the natural environment, especially the resources of natural landscape beauty, flora and fauna, and the marine environment of beaches, sea gardens, and sea life, and specific outstanding natural features, and minimize any adverse environmental impact of tourism, particularly air, water, visual, and noise pollution and preemption of public use areas, through carefully controlled development.
- Provide tourist attractions, facilities, and services that can be used by both domestic and foreign pleasure tourists and by business and government travelers, with these attractions, facilities, and services also being available for use by local residents.
- Utilize, to the extent possible, existing and already programmed infrastructure, especially the expensive components of land, air, and sea communications, and integrate new tourism infrastructure needed into total development programming, so that the infrastructure necessary for tourism is multi-purpose and serves general needs as well as tourism requirements; tourism can help justify and pay for development of multi-purpose infrastructure.
- Develop the attitudes, managerial, and technical skills of local people to effectively participate in tourism and provide efficient tourism services, while still maintaining the natural friendliness of local people toward tourists.
- Establish a tourism development pattern and program that provides logical and phased development over the next 5-, 10-, and 20-year periods in consonance with the national, regional, and local areas' capabilities of socially absorbing the impact of tourism, of economically providing the necessary infrastructure, and of training local people to work in tourism.

Survey of Existing Land Use in the Tourism Plan for Malta

The Maltese Islands Tourism Development Plan (Horwath and Horwath 1989) was prepared in 1989 as a UNDP/WTO assisted project. Malta, an independent country located in the Mediterranean Sea south of Sicily and comprised of the islands of Malta, Gozo, and Comino, is already substantially developed as a tourist destination, having received 785,000 foreign tourist arrivals in 1989. As its attractions, Malta offers a mild Mediterranean climate combined with good beaches and highly interesting historic places; the country is very accessible to the major northern European tourist markets. The government of Malta wished to expand tourism for its economic benefits, but on a carefully planned and controlled basis with a long-term objective of improving the quality of and diversifying the tourism product, somewhat shifting the types of tourist markets, and maintaining and upgrading the overall environmental quality and functional efficiency of the existing tourism areas specifically and the islands in general.

Figure 3.2, which shows the existing land use survey map of the Malta planning study, indicates some of the major types of existing land uses that were considered in the planning, as follows:

- Development zone boundaries—Those areas zoned for development (in 1989) and mostly already developed with urban uses; their location therefore becomes a consideration in determining where new tourism development can be situated.
- Industrial areas—Those areas that have been industrially developed and therefore would not likely be compatible with tourism development.
- Airport—The airport location is an important consideration because tourism development should not be located too near the airport where it would be affected by aircraft movements and noise, but there should still be good access between the airport and tourism development areas for the convenience of tourist arrivals and departures.

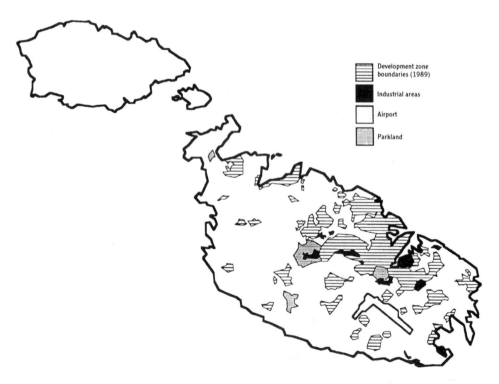

Figure 3.2. Maltese Islands Tourism Development Plan—Existing Land Use and Zoning Boundaries.

- Parkland—The existing parklands can be an attraction for tourists but are also lands that should not be developed with tourist facilities because their public park use is more important.

The tourism plan for Malta will be further presented in case studies in subsequent chapters. Other countries with a similar situation of having substantial and economically successful existing tourism but that have had tourism plans prepared in the late 1980s and early 1990s to better control future development include Cyprus in the eastern Mediterranean Sea and the Cayman Islands in the Caribbean Sea.

Background Surveys in the Fiji Tourism Plan

The national tourism development plan for Fiji (Belt, Collins & Assoc. et al 1973) was prepared by a consortium of consulting firms as a UNDP/World Bank assisted project in 1973. This planning project was a comprehensive one that examined and made recommendations on all aspects of tourism and, in addition to the national plan, included several regional and urban tourism plans and detailed planning for a proposed large beach resort. The planning team of more than 20 persons, including some short-term specialists, spent several months in Fiji conducting the surveys and analyses and preparing the draft plans. Close coordination was maintained throughout the project with the relevant government agencies and private tourism sector, and some government planners and tourism officials were assigned to work with the international team members.

Located in the central South Pacific, Fiji is comprised of several hundred islands and islets of which about one hundred are inhabited. The two major islands of Viti Levu and Vanua Levu constitute some 87 percent of the total land area of the country. Fiji has the second largest reef complex, after the Great Barrier Reef in Australia, in the world. The attractions of the country include primarily natural ones of beach and marine areas in a subtropical climatic setting, complemented by scenic beauty, the interesting cultural patterns of the Fijian people, indigenous and colonial architectural styles, and duty-free shopping. The background surveys for the Fiji tourism plan included a description of the location of the country, characteristics of the natural environment of geology, topography, hydrography, vegetation, indigenous animal life, the reef system and climatic patterns, historical influences, demographic and settlement patterns, cultural characteristics, economic patterns, and land tenure considerations.

Several of these characteristics as they relate to tourism are summarized in this case study. A major consideration was the topography of the country, which is typically rugged in the island interiors with most of the agricultural activities and settlements concentrated in the coastal plains and river valleys. Much of the land is steep-sloped (over 18 percent slope as mapped in the planning analysis) and, although offering attractive views, is unsuitable for intensive development. It was estimated that approximately one-sixth of the total land is flat or undulating, one-sixth is rolling and hilly, and the remainder is steep. In many places the steep slopes come to or very near the shoreline, thus limiting the amount of developable land adjacent to the shore and beaches.

The plan pointed out that many beaches exist on both the larger and smaller islands, but there are also long stretches of coastline without any beaches and that some of the beaches that do exist are of mediocre quality or flanked by steep slopes and coral reefs exposed at low tide. Overall, the number of high quality beaches in developable and accessible locations is limited, especially given the need for recreation and fisheries use by residents, as well as demand for beach hotel sites. Thus, topographic characteristics of the country are an important consideration in locating tourism development. However, although a locational constraint, a sufficient number of suitable beach hotel and resort sites were found to provide a viable basis for substantial tourism development.

Related to topography and location of good quality beaches, a factor also was the existence of mangrove swamps along many sections of the coast. Some of these mangrove areas are located near beaches and had been considered for removal and land fill to provide land for resorts and other types of development. The plan emphasized that mangrove areas are important ecologically (for example, in natural land formation, as a sea life habitat with the possibility for seafood production, and for control of flooding), but that in selected areas it could be considered for reclamation for tourism, urban, and agricultural uses. An experimental technique being applied in some places in Fiji was maintaining the shoreward portions of mangrove in their natural state but reclaiming inland portions for agricultural use.

With its subtropical climate and beach environments, Fiji's major tourism potential was targeted for beach and water related recreation and relaxation. Therefore, micro-climatic patterns were a very important consideration in the planning for tourism in the islands. Being in the southeast trade wind belt of the South Pacific and possessing mountainous topography, there are extreme variations of climate, particularly in the rainfall, which ranges from 250 inches on the southeastern or windward sides of the mountainous islands to 70 inches on the northwestern or leeward sides, with considerable variation in the extent of seasonality of rainfall. Climatic patterns were categorized into four zones based on temperatures, total rainfall, and seasonality of rainfall as follows (temperatures are in Fahrenheit):

- Strong to moderate dry season with a mean annual temperature of 78 degrees and an annual rainfall of 55 to 100 inches;
- Very weak dry season—moderate rainfall with a mean annual temperature of 77 degrees and an annual rainfall of 80 to 130 inches;
- Very weak dry season—high rainfall with a mean annual temperature of 77 degrees and an annual rainfall of 100 to 200 inches; and
- Moderate to no dry season with a mean annual temperature of 67 degrees and an annual rainfall of 80 to over 200 inches.

The plan pointed out that, from a climatic standpoint, the drier, warmer areas are more suitable for tourism with respect to having pleasant weather conditions for visitors. A specific aspect of climate that the plan analyzed was the hazards to development presented by hurricanes. Fiji lies within the hurricane zone of the

Pacific region and has experienced periodic severe hurricanes that inevitably will continue occurring, but the precise paths and frequency of hurricanes are unpredictable. The plan emphasized that the specific siting and construction standards of tourism facility development must take into account the likely possibility of hurricane damage.

Where there is definite seasonality, the rainy season occurs from January to March and the dry season from June to September. The dry season period is of particular importance to the North American tourist markets because this is the traditional northern hemisphere vacation period (although it does not correspond to the northern hemisphere winter season), and the southern hemisphere's winter season (Australia in the southern hemisphere is an important tourist market for Fiji).

A major consideration in planning tourism in Fiji was also the land tenure situation. As the plan indicated, the land must be available in otherwise suitable locations for tourism development, and the availability must be at a price (either through purchase or lease) that is equitable to both the owners and the developers. In Fiji, nearly 84 percent of the total land area is held by indigenous Fijians under customary tenure and cannot be alienated by sale to private individuals. This tenure is characterized by extended family communal ownership of specific parcels of land. However, leasing of Fijian land can be effected through the administration of the Native Land Trust Board, which reviews lease terms to ensure that proper land use is proposed and equitable lease fees are obtained. Freehold land that can be bought and sold occupies about 10 percent of the land area although much of this is in developable and accessible areas. Sale of freehold land is becoming common. The remaining 6 percent of the land is Crown or public lands, which are mostly mangrove and rugged interior areas, some of which are suitable for public park use. The plan mentioned that some existing tourism development in Fiji seems to have been located based only on land availability regardless of other locational criteria. A land tenure consideration was also the aim of distributing tourism development on the various different types of land ownership in order to achieve a reasonable distribution of the equity benefits of development.

As can be seen, the background survey of topography, climate, and land tenure, along with location of good quality beaches and infrastructure development (especially accessibility) provided essential input into the Fiji planning analysis and plan formulation. Population distribution was also examined with respect to availability of a nearby labor supply to work in the tourism areas. Because of the wide distribution of population throughout the developable coastal areas of the country, this factor was not a major constraint in location of tourism areas. General economic patterns were reviewed as background for the economic impact analysis of the plan and other development considerations. The country's overall development policies and plans, as well as existing urban plans, were examined as they might affect tourism policy and planning. Sociocultural patterns were also surveyed and evaluated as they relate to tourist attraction features and the sociocultural impacts of tourism and how to cope with these.

Climatic Patterns Survey for the Sri Lanka Tourism Plan

The tourism plan for Sri Lanka (Harris Kerr Forster et al 1967) was prepared in the late 1960s and considered to be a model of the tourism planning approach used and application of sound planning principles. Located south of India in the Indian Ocean, Sri Lanka offers varied attractions of rich cultural patterns, some outstanding archaeological and historic sites, scenic mountain landscapes and tea plantations, many good beaches and marine areas, exotic wildlife, and a tropical climate with an unusual regime. Tourism has substantially developed since preparation of the tourism plan with many of the plan's recommendations having been followed, although during the mid to late 1980s, tourism was somewhat affected by internal political disturbances.

As shown in Figure 3.3, the approach to showing climatic patterns in a manner suitable for tourism planning analysis was to indicate areas of different rainfall levels, because this is a highly variable climatic factor both seasonally and throughout the island. Average rainfall ranges from 25 to 50 inches in some of the coastal areas to over 200 inches in the highest elevations. However, much of the rainfall takes place during two distinct monsoonal periods as shown on the map.

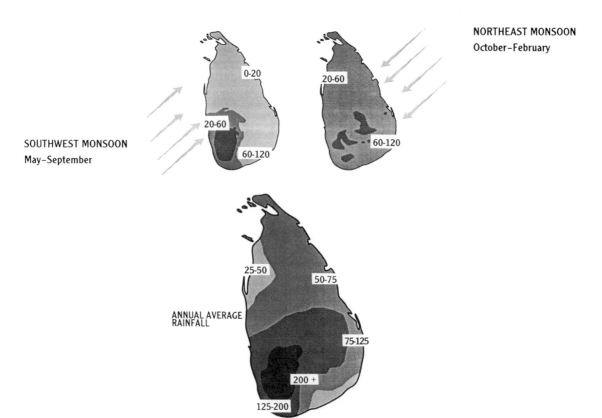

Figure 3.3. Sri Lanka Tourism Plan—Climatic Patterns (numbers refer to inches of rainfall).

Rains occur in the western part of the island during the southwest monsoon from May to September, when the eastern areas are drier; and rainfall is highest in the eastern part of the island during the northeast monsoon period lasting from October to February, when the western areas are drier. This double monsoon regime offers a major advantage to the country of having drier periods at various places along the coastline throughout the year. Good beaches for resort development exist along both the east and west coasts. Thus, seasonality of beach-oriented tourism based on rainfall patterns is greatly reduced at the national level, although, of course, seasonality of rainfall still affects each of the coastal areas. As a tropical country, temperatures are mild throughout the year, with a decrease in temperatures at the higher elevations where some mountain resorts have developed.

References

Belt, Collins & Associates, Ltd. et al. 1973. *Tourism Development Programme for Fiji.* Honolulu, Hawaii.

De Kadt, Emanuel, Editor. 1979. *Tourism: Passport to Development?* New York: Oxford University Press.

Gunn, Clare A. 2nd ed. 1988. *Tourism Planning.* New York: Taylor & Francis.

Harris Kerr Forster, et al. 1967. *Ceylon Tourism Plan.* Honolulu, Hawaii.

Horwath and Horwath, Inc. 1989. *Maltese Islands Tourism Development Plan.* London.

Inskeep, Edward. 1988. "Tourism Planning: An Emerging Specialization." *Journal of the American Planning Association.* 54 (3): 360-372. Reprinted by permission of the *Journal of the American Planning Association.*

United Nations Development Programme and World Tourism Organization. 1981. *Tourism Development Plan for Nusa Tenggara, Indonesia.* Madrid: World Tourism Organization.

4

Tourist Attractions and Activities

Approach to Survey and Evaluation

The attraction features of a country or region provide the basis for developing tourism; they form the most essential element of the tourism product. Without substantial attraction features, pleasure-oriented tourism would not be possible to develop, although facilities and services are still required for business, government/mission, conference, religious, and other types of obligatory travel. Tourist attractions and activities can encompass a very wide variety, especially because of the great diversity of interests of today's tourist markets. At the same time, some features that local residents believe are of great interest are not so to most visitors. Therefore, imagination, perspective, and objectivity are essential in identifying, evaluating, and developing attractions.

Usually, attractions should be sought that reflect an area's inherent, distinctive, and unique natural and cultural character, and be authentically developed to reinforce that character. As emphasized in the planning approach of this book, tourism can be one of the techniques used to accomplish environmental and cultural conservation and maintain an area's unique sense of place. However, there are situations where development of special types of features, such as theme parks and gambling casinos, not directly related to the character of the local area, is justified and profitable if they are not socially or environmentally disruptive. Each tourism area must be individually assessed to determine whether special types of attractions are warranted.

Typically, selection and evaluation of tourist attractions and activities should be made relative to the existing and potential tourist markets, that is, the tourist attractions and activities and the tourist markets must be matched together if tourism is to be successful. Thus, although evaluation of tourist attractions and the market analysis are presented separately in this book, they are in fact actually applied in conjunction with one another. The types of attractions available will largely determine the types of markets to aim for and the tourism promotional approach used, and the demands of the available tourist markets are a major factor in deciding on the type of attraction development (as well as tourist facility development) that is needed.

But as noted in Chapter 2, a policy adopted in some places is to apply strict controls on the type and extent of tourism development and tourist markets to be attracted, applying a product-led approach. This approach implies that the inherent attractions and tourist facilities of the area are developed (or conserved) in the manner that the country believes is the most appropriate for its own environmental and sociocultural benefit, and tourist markets are found that are attracted to that particular product. Often, the approach applied in many places is a combination of market-led and product-led tourism within the framework of balancing economic development and conservation. Whatever policy is adopted, it is a consideration in evaluating the tourist attractions of an area.

An important approach is to relate tourist attraction features with tourist activities. A feature by itself may have some interest, but it can be much more interesting if related activities are developed or organized. This is an especially important principle today because, as mentioned in Chapter 1, one of the trends in tourism is the increasing activity or participatory orientation of tourists who want, for example, to engage in sports and active recreation and learn about the local environment and culture. Therefore, tourist attractions should also be identified and evaluated with respect to the opportunities they offer for development of related tourist activities and involvement.

Types of Tourist Attractions and Activities

In order to survey and evaluate tourist attractions, it is important to understand the types of tourist attractions and activities that should be considered in planning tourism and how these can be categorized for analysis purposes. Some types of attractions were recognized many years ago, especially evidenced by the Roman tourist excursions to the monuments of Egypt and elsewhere in the Mediterranean region, and their development of coastal resorts and mineral water spas. A warm, sunny climate was also recognized as being desirable at that time. Although landscape gardens were appreciated, wild natural areas were considered dangerous and ugly in the Western countries until romanticized by poets and landscape painters in the nineteenth century when natural areas commenced becoming major attraction features. This concept of natural beauty as an attraction for tourists was further reinforced by the designation and development of national parks in the USA in the mid-nineteenth century (the first national park was Yellowstone, established in 1872). With the advent of mass tourism, especially since World War II, the different types and number of attractions have greatly increased, and this proliferation of attractions and related activities is still underway. Attractions development has now become one of the exciting areas of tourism.

Tourist attractions can be categorized in various ways, all of which are logically based. Gunn (1988), for example, organizes them into touring circuit attractions (short-stay) and longer-stay (focused) attractions, based on two types of tourism: those that satisfy touring markets for travelers on tours involving many separate locational stops and those at or near longer-stay destinations. Lew (1987) reviewed the research methods used in the study of tourist attractions and the tourist attractiveness of places and concluded that most studies can be classified into one or more of three general perspectives: the ideographic listing, the organization, and the tourist cognition of attractions. However, all these approaches make comparisons of attractions based on their historical, locational, and valuational aspects. A common system of classification and one used in this book is to establish the major categories of:

- Natural attractions that are based on features of the natural environment;
- Cultural attractions that are based on man's activities; and
- Special types of attractions that are artificially created.

These three major categories can then be divided into more specific subcategories as explained in the following sections. These general divisions can be applied in virtually any tourism planning area with the subdivisions created for the specific area being planned based on its particular characteristics.

Natural Attractions

Major categories of natural attractions include the types described in the following sections.

Climate

A warm, sunny, dry climate is typically considered desirable by most tourists, especially those from cold winter areas, and particularly when associated with other attractions such as beach, marine, and mountain areas that provide opportunities for recreation activities. Certain kinds of health resorts are also often located in warm, sunny, and dry climatic areas. But some types of popular tourist activities such as snow skiing and tobogganing require cold weather and snow but preferably still clear skies. "Conservation" of a desirable climate through control of air pollution is essential for tourism.

Climatic seasonality must be considered in evaluating climate as an attraction. A long climatically desirable season is obviously an advantage for development of tourism so that the investment made in facilities, services, and infrastructure is maximized. In evaluating seasonality, consideration must be given to resource opportunities and markets available that lengthen the tourist season, create a double season, or extend a high level of visitor use throughout the year. However, a certain amount of seasonality may have to be accepted in many places.

Scenic Beauty

The overall natural scenic beauty of an area may be a major motivation to visit there, especially if conservation measures have been applied to maintain the cleanliness and natural character of the environment. Attractive and interesting agricultural landscapes such as the rolling green fields of Britain and the terraced rice fields of Southeast Asia can also be considered as places of scenic beauty.

Associated with areas of scenic beauty are activities such as pleasure driving with stops at scenic view points, hiking, picnicking, camping, and wildlife viewing. Remote scenic areas may offer opportunities for adventure-oriented tourists engaging in such activities as river rafting, rock climbing, and long-distance trekking. Outstanding scenic areas should be designated as national or regional parks, and other scenic areas should have development controls applied to them even though some development is allowed.

Beaches and Marine Areas

Beaches and associated marine areas for sunbathing, swimming, boating, wind and board surfing, water skiing, parasailing, snorkeling and scuba diving, sport fishing, and other water recreation activities are major attractions in many places in the world. These features attract both general interest tourists who are seeking relaxation and recreation as well as special interest tourists who engage in such activities as scuba diving and sport fishing. Much of the tourism developed in the Caribbean, Mediterranean, Pacific Islands, and Indian Ocean Islands regions is based on beach and marine tourism combined with a warm, sunny climate. Beach and marine areas should also have conservation measures applied in the form of parks, reserves, and development controls.

Flora and Fauna

Unusual and interesting flora and fauna can be very important attractions, especially when combined with scenic landscapes. Outstanding examples of flora and fauna as attractions are the game parks of East Africa and South Asia and the redwood parks of California, which attract tourists from throughout the world. In addition to general interest tourists visiting these places are those with special interests, such as bird watchers and amateur botanists. Controlled hunting of wildlife can be an attraction in some places.

Animal and plant life conservation is a major issue in many parts of the world because of various problems, especially reduction of wildlife habitat by encroachment of agricultural and urban uses and poaching of protected animals. Because wildlife may constitute major attraction features, tourism can often be used as the rationale for wildlife conservation, as is the case in several East African countries where there is much concern about the diminishing numbers of several species of animals, and major conservation efforts are underway. In South Asia, Project Tiger, in part sponsored by the World Wildlife Fund, has been so far successful in rejuvenating the tiger population in that region.

Zoos, aquariums, and botanic gardens are specialized flora and fauna features and, if well developed and maintained, can be major international attractions, such as the San Diego Zoo and Wild Animal Park in California and botanic gardens at Kew near London, Kandy in Sri Lanka and Bogor in Java, Indonesia. These can also be important in assisting the conservation of endangered species and conducting biological research; for example, many zoos have breeding programs for endangered species and some have even reintroduced species such as the Arabian oryx back into their native habitats where they had disappeared. A modern concept of zoo development is providing naturalistic environments for the animals and the safari park, where animals can roam in a natural habitat and visitors view them from vehicles.

Special Environmental Features

Special environmental features such as high mountains, unusual geological formations, caves, geysers, hot springs, and mild forms of volcanic activity are important attractions for both general sight-seeing and special interest tourists. Activities associated with special environmental features include, for example, mountain and rock climbing, spelunking (cave exploration), and development of health spas focused on mineral hot springs. Large caves such as Mammoth Cave and Carlsbad Caverns in the USA attract millions of visitors each year. Mountain climbing in the Himalayas is a major specialized attraction and important source of income for the countries involved.

Parks and Conservation Areas

As mentioned, important natural areas and their flora and fauna should be designated for some type of conservation status, such as national or regional parks, nature reserves, and wildlife refuges. Any existing designated major parks or other types of conservation areas should, of course, be included in the survey and evaluation of tourist attractions. If such features in the planning area appear to warrant consideration for park or conservation status but have not been so designated, then the tourism planning team should note this in their survey. In some tourism studies, park planning may be one of the components of the planning project. The International Union for Conservation of Nature and Natural Resources (IUCN) has specified categories and criteria for establishment of parks and conservation areas. However, the concept of national parks varies among countries depending on the local situation; for example, in the USA and Canada, national parks must be in public ownership with little or no development allowed except for visitor facilities, while in the U.K., parks may include private lands, agricultural activities, and villages, but with development controlled and public access allowed. The planning team should review any existing park criteria and standards that are applied in their planning area within the framework of internationally accepted standards.

Evaluation of parks and their facility development as tourist attractions should include the consideration that an important concept of park development and operation now is to educate the visitors about what they are viewing with emphasis on ecology and conservation. This approach is very compatible with the trend that tourists want to learn about the environments that they are visiting. Park concepts and visitor facility planning will be further examined in Chapter 10, "Planning Tourist Attractions."

Health Tourism

Usually, but not always, related to the natural environment are various types of health tourism. As mentioned, spas based on hot mineral waters were were first developed some two thousand years ago by the Romans, and many spa resorts were developed during the nineteenth century. Some of these still exist in Europe, North America, Asia, and elsewhere and are particularly popular in Eastern Europe where spas are a major form of tourism, attracting tourists mostly from that region. The evaluation of any existing mineral waters for possible development as spas must take into account the potential markets that can be attracted to the spa resort, as well as the resource itself.

Another type of health tourism developed more recently is the "diet" resort, a place where people go to lose weight and regain physical vitality. These can be located anywhere but are often situated in desirable climatic areas. Some centers for treatment of drug addiction and alcoholism function in certain ways as resorts and may be considered as a type of health tourism as are the few remaining sanitoria for tuberculosis patients.

Cultural Attractions

Major types of cultural attractions, based on man's activities, include those described in the following sections.

Archaeological, Historical, and Cultural Sites

Archaeological, historical, and cultural sites, including cultural and national monuments, historic buildings, districts, and towns, important religious buildings such as churches, synagogues, temples, mosques, and monasteries, and places of historic events such as battlefields constitute a major type of attraction feature in most parts of the world. Important archaeological and historic sites exist in virtually all parts of the world. Major examles are: Stonehenge, Westminster Abbey, and the Tower of London in the U.K.; the many classical

Great Zimbabwe Ruins in Zimbabwe (top) and Emperor Fassil's Castle at Gondar in Ethiopia (bottom)—Although sub-Saharan Africa is best known for its natural features of wildlife, scenic places, and beaches, archaeological and historic features are also significant attractions for tourists and important expressions of national cultural heritage. (Courtesy of the Zimbabwean and Ethiopian tourism offices)

81

Egyptian, Greek, Roman, and other monuments in the Mediterranean region; the Alhambra in Spain and Versailles Palace near Paris; Zimbabwe ruins in southern Africa; Petra and many other sites in the Middle East; Moenjodaro and Harrapa of the Indus Valley civilization; the Taj Mahal and many other archaeological and historic sites in South Asia; Angkor Wat in Cambodia; the Imperial Palace in Beijing; Nara and Kyoto in Japan; Cuzco and Machu Picchu in Peru; Uzmal and Chichen Itza in Mexcio and other Mayan sites in Central America; and Mesa Verde Indian ruins, colonial and frontier towns, and Gettysburg Battlefield of the USA. The United Nations Educational, Scientific and Cultural Organization (UNESCO) has begun the process of designating, based on certain criteria, the most important archaeological and historic sites throughout the world as world cultural heritage sites.

Some interesting recent developments in archaeology include:

- Underwater research of sunken ships and towns that can provide unusual museum exhibits, such as the Varsa ship in Sweden and artifacts of the earthquake-sunken city of Port Royal in Jamaica;
- Opportunities, under controlled conditions, for recreation divers (for example, diving to explore the many Japanese ships sunk in the Truk Lagoon in Micronesia during World War II);
- Industrial archaeology of the late eighteenth and nineteenth centuries early industrial development, which has been interpreted in a very interesting manner for tourists in places such as at Ironbridge in England and Lowell, Massachusetts in the USA;
- Restoration of historic ornamental gardens being undertaken at various places in Europe, North America, and Asia; and
- Use of advanced technology to determine the contents of sites without actual excavation.

Archaeological sites are, of course, important for viewing by tourists and, reflecting tourism trends in recent years, participation by tourist laymen in archaeological excavations, on a supervised basis, has become popular.

Archaeological, historical, and cultural sites are designated for conservation, and major sites may be declared as national archaeological or historic parks or monuments. An approach now being applied to some cultural sites is that of cultural heritage site development involving not only conservation of the site but an integrated presentation and explanation of the site through exhibit, demonstration, and animation techniques. Colonial Williamsburg in Virginia, USA and the Viking Village in York, England are good examples of heritage site development. Development and visitor use of archaeological, historic, and cultural sites will be examined further in Chapter 10.

Distinctive Cultural Patterns

Cultural patterns, traditions, and life-styles that are unusual (different from those of the tourists) and, in some cases, unique to one place can be of much interest to many tourists. These cultural patterns include customs, dress, ceremonies, life-styles, and religious beliefs and practices and are often associated with rural and village life but may be prevalent in some urban places. Although of much potential interest to tourists, care must be taken in the presentation of cultural patterns and the interface between residents and tourists so that social problems are not generated, as will be examined in Chapters 10 and 13.

Arts and Handicrafts

The performing art forms, including dance, music, and drama, and the fine arts of painting and sculpting can be important attractions, especially if effectively presented. Art forms can be those associated with small-scale traditional cultures or those related to the major Western, Middle Eastern, or Asian cultures. Performing arts centers and theaters are often developed at considerable cost for presentation of the performing arts, primarily for the benefit of residents but often substantially supported by tourists. Handicrafts of an area can be both an interesting attraction for tourists and a source of income for local artisans. Related to arts and handicrafts are the traditional or distinctive architectural styles of an area that can be of much interest to tourists (for example, the traditional architectural styles in Southeast Asia, which can still be seen in some places, and the Islamic and Arab styles found in the Middle East). Well-executed contemporary architectural styles are also of general interest.

Interesting Economic Activities

An often successful type of specialized cultural attraction is observation, description, and sometimes demonstration of interesting economic activities such as operation of tea and rubber plantations and processing plants, use of working elephants in a tropical forest, traditional fishing and agricultural techniques in many areas, and the operations of modern manufacturing plants. Traditional market places are also widely popular with tourists. It requires very little investment to effectively present these activities to tourists, but knowledgeable tour guides are essential.

Interesting Urban Areas

In contrast to rural and village life, large urban areas with their varied architectural styles, historic buildings and districts, civic centers, shopping facilities, restaurants, parks, and street life are of interest to many tourists who enjoy general urban sightseeing and absorbing the ambience of a city's character, as well as visiting specific attraction features such as museums and public buildings. In addition to organized city tours, opportunities should be examined for establishing "urban trails" that lead visitors through interesting parts of the city, with stops at major features on the existing pedestrian and public transportation system, as a way of encouraging self-guided exploration.

In some cities, theater performances, including plays, operas, concerts, and

Folk dancing in Europe (top) and Southeast Asia (bottom)—Local traditional dances comprise an important cultural attraction for tourists, and tourism helps justify and support preservation and, in some places, revitalization of these dance forms. (Courtesy of the World Tourism Organization)

dance presentations are major attractions for tourists as well as residents. Theater is an important attraction and source of local revenue in such cities as London, Paris, New York, Moscow, Leningrad, Sydney, and Tokyo. Tourist attendance at theater performances often provides an important and much-needed source of revenue to maintain the theater operations.

Museums and Other Cultural Facilities

Related to various aspects of both natural and cultural features of an area are different types of museums on such themes as archaeology, history, ethnology, natural history, arts and crafts, science, technology and industry, and many specialized subjects. These are usually developed primarily for residents to enjoy but, if well done, can also be important attractions for domestic and international tourists. Museums such as the Metropolitan Museum in New York, the Smithsonian complex of museums in Washington, DC, the British Museum in London, the Louvre in Paris, the Hermitage in Leningrad, and the Museum of Anthropology in Mexico City are internationally famous. In addition to national and regional museums, there are also site museums associated with specific archaeological, historical, or natural features. The contemporary museum presentation approach is not only to display artifacts but also to educate the visitors through interpretative exhibits and special programs.

Other cultural facilities such as cultural centers, important commercial art galleries, and antique shops or, in some places, whole districts of galleries, and antique shops should be considered as tourist attractions. Some towns that have attracted artists and a concentration of commercial art galleries, such as Laguna Beach, California and Santa Fe, New Mexico in the USA, are popular stopping places for tourists.

Cultural Festivals

Various types of cultural festivals related to the local traditions and arts can be major attractions. Large religious festivals and pageants such as the Carnival in Rio de Janeiro, Mardi Gras in New Orleans, and the Pera Hera in Kandy, Sri Lanka attract many tourists as well as residents. The various types of music festivals held annually in Europe and North America are very popular. The Aloha Week festival in Hawaii was organized several years ago in order to both develop a Hawaiian cultural festival that did not previously exist and to attract tourists during a historically low tourist season. The annual arts festival in Bali, Indonesia, organized to support Balinese performing and visual arts, attracts many residents and international tourists.

Friendliness of Residents

Although not quantifiable, a very real attraction for many tourists can be the friendly, hospitable character of local residents and, more generally, their tolerance and acceptance of tourists visiting their environment. The honesty and reliability of residents in their dealings with tourists are also important factors.

Special Types of Attractions

Special types of attractions not particularly related to either natural or cultural features, but that are artificially created, are described in the following sections.

Theme Parks, Amusement Parks, and Circuses

Theme parks are oriented to particular themes, such as history, adventure, unusual geographic places, fantasy and futurism, or a combination of these in one park, and offer simulated experiences, shows, thrill rides, shopping, and a variety of restaurants and snack bars in a clean and controlled environment. Best known of the theme parks and their prototypes are Disneyland in Anaheim, California, opened in 1955, and Disney World in Orlando, Florida. A Disneyland has been constructed in Tokyo, and Euro Disneyland, located near Paris and scheduled to open in 1992, will be the largest theme park in Europe. Jakarta, Indonesia, has developed a smaller theme park based on Disney concepts and technology. Many other theme parks have been developed in North America (for example, the various Six Flags parks in the USA and Wonderland near Toronto, Canada). During the 1980s and expected to continue into the 1990s, theme parks have become increasingly popular in Europe (Brown and Church 1987).

Theme parks can be very successful; in the late 1980s, Disney World was annually attracting some 25 million visitors who spent about two billion dollars. However, they may also be failures, and their market and economic feasibility must be carefully analyzed before development is undertaken. Both Disneyland and Disney World keep expanding and renewing their features, which helps maintain their continuing vitality; for example, Disney World added the major attraction of the Experimental Prototype Community of Tomorrow (EPCOT), which has proven to be very popular. Large theme parks can greatly affect the economy and land use and transportation patterns of a region, and integrated planning of the park with its surrounding area is essential.

Theme parks evolved from amusement parks, which developed from the entertainment provided at fairs, carnivals, and circuses of Medieval Europe and Asia. In the USA, Coney Island is one of the famous amusement parks on the East Coast. Traveling amusement parks are still common, especially those touring smaller towns, and amusement park facilities are now being integrated into some large shopping centers. As major attractions in tourism, theme parks have replaced amusement parks, although some urban amusement parks in Europe, such as Tivoli Gardens in Copenhagen and the Prater in Vienna attract tourists as well as residents.

Traveling circuses have long been popular, catering primarily to residents of the area where the circus stops over, and are not typically major attractions for tourists. However, some permanent circuses are famous, such as the Russian circus in Moscow and Leningrad and acrobatic circuses in China and Korea, and attract many tourists who are visiting those places.

Shopping

Shopping is a significant activity and type of expenditure of many tourists and must be considered in tourism planning as a possible attraction as well as service. The Japanese tourist market, for example, is well known for its high expenditures on shopping for goods to take home. In urban tourism, large department stores that are internationally well known such as Bloomingdale's in New York, Neiman Marcus in Dallas, and Harrod's in London attract many tourists visiting those cities. Large, well-known shopping centers such as the Ala Moana Center in Honolulu, Hawaii and West Edmonton Mall in Edmonton, Canada attract much shopping activity by tourists visiting those places. Specialty shops handling such items as fashion clothing and jewelry in many types of tourist destinations are popular. As mentioned previously, the distinctive arts and crafts of some areas such as India and Thailand can be a major attraction and an important source of local income. Souvenir items are also popular with many tourists even though they may be considered rather kitsch by others. Even if they do not spend large amounts on shopping, tourists often want to take home some mementos of their travels.

Duty-free (which actually may refer to low duty but not free of duty) shopping for consumer goods, especially liquor, tobacco, jewelry, luggage, watches, perfume, and electronic and optical items, has been developed as a major attraction in cities such as Hong Kong and Singapore and is an important source of tourist income in many other places. More generally, most international airports have duty-free shops that can provide a minor source of revenue from tourists. In consideration of developing duty-free shopping as a major attraction, its feasibility should be carefully assessed because low-cost consumer items are now available in some of the tourist market origin countries, and there is less incentive for tourists to buy those goods while traveling.

Meetings, Conferences, and Conventions

Domestic and international conference and convention tourism, including small meetings, training courses, seminars, and workshops as well as large conferences and conventions, is a significant type of tourism throughout the world and steadily expanding in all countries. Many countries, regions, cities, resorts, and individual hotels have developed various types of meeting facilities and some conference facilities, such as the Trade and Convention Center in Vancouver, Canada and the conference center in Manila, Philippines, are major investment projects. As is examined in Chapter 9, conference tourism seems to function best in locations that offer a range of nearby attractions and activities for conference-goers and their spouses, who are often brought along, to engage in during their leisure time, including opportunities for sightseeing, shopping, eating out, entertainment, and recreation. There should be good accessibility to the city for large-scale conferences and conventions and to the country for international conferences. Also, it is an advantage for the conference facilities to be located in a country or region that can generally provide a range of interesting attractions and facilities for pre- and post-conference tours.

Although expanding, conference tourism is highly competitive and should be carefully evaluated for each area to determine its overall market and economic feasibility and the most appropriate type of facilities to be developed. If determined feasible and developed, competent operation and aggressive marketing are required on a continuing basis. At any scale of development, conference centers must meet certain standards and often need to include specialized facilities and services such as for simultaneous language translation and exhibit space in order to be acceptable to conference organizers.

Special Events

Special events, such as sports contests, fairs, and expositions, can be major tourist attractions for short time periods. These are organized for the purpose of attracting tourists and also for reasons such as national or regional prestige and gaining new facility complexes for permanent use, perhaps along with concomitant redevelopment of urban districts. International sports events, such as the Olympic, Commonwealth, and Asian games, may draw global interest while others are of widespread national importance. Such events are held regularly but in different locations each time. International fairs and expositions can attract both international and domestic tourists; an example is the series of Expos organized at different places throughout the world during the past few decades.

Although prestigious and sometimes profitable, large events can also be environmentally disruptive to the areas where they are held, and some places have expressed concern about the overall costs and benefits of sponsoring such events. Each local situation must be specifically evaluated before a decision is made by the government to host or offer to host major events.

Gambling Casinos

Gambling casinos have been developed in certain places as major attractions, but usually in areas that have limited natural and cultural attraction features and where there is little negative social impact from gambling on the local residents. Nevada, especially the cities of Las Vegas and Reno, in the USA, has become a major tourism destination based on gambling casinos supplemented by entertainment, and these cities are now developing into important general leisure resort areas that attract large conferences and conventions. Atlantic City in New Jersey on the east coast of the USA was a dying nineteenth century beach resort that is now attempting to revitalize itself through development of gambling, legalized there in 1978, and based particularly on the nearby New York metropolitan market. However, perhaps because of the lack of other activities, Atlantic City did not attract as many overnight tourists as expected. The economic, environmental, and social impacts and overall success of this endeavor in Atlantic City are still being observed and studied. Casinos are also often developed to supplement the basic attractions of an area such as has been done in New Caledonia in the Pacific Islands, Aruba and other island destinations in the Caribbean, and London, Monaco, and Baden Baden in Europe. These casinos typically include restaurants and entertainment as part of their attraction. Many cruise ships also offer gambling facilities.

Evaluation of whether gambling should be developed as a primary or secondary attraction in either a newly developing or already developed tourism area must take into account several factors: the type of clientele the area wishes to attract; the marketability of gambling to the potential tourist markets; the extent to which gambling is necessary to develop or expand tourism; its compatibility with other attractions of the area; any problems that might arise related to gambling such as organized crime, drugs, and prostitution; and its possible social impact on the local population. In places where local income levels are low and residents are not accustomed to the concept of controlled gambling, the social impact considerations become important. If for social reasons, residents are not allowed into the casinos and these are reserved only for tourist use, local resentment of tourism may develop.

Entertainment

Entertainment is a broad category and has already been referred to relative to the traditional and contemporary performing arts and its association with gambling casinos and their resort environments. Nightclubs, discos, and some restaurants in tourism areas provide evening entertainment that is popular with many tourists and considered essential for successful operation of some hotels and resorts. In the inventory and evaluation of tourist attractions, account should be taken of the type and quality of any existing entertainment facilities and services.

For the planning of attractions, consideration needs to be given to whether entertainment should be encouraged and what the suitable types are for the area. In some places the focus is placed on providing entertainment that has some basis in the local culture, such as folk dancing and singing, while in other areas the "international" type of contemporary music and dance is considered quite appropriate, or perhaps a combination of these will be the best approach.

Recreation and Sports

Most recreation facilities are of a local scale catering to residents of an area. But some types can be important primary or secondary attractions for tourists, such as championship golf courses and tennis centers, polo grounds, horse and other types of race tracks (which may also include betting on the races), and stadiums for major spectator sports events such as football, soccer, baseball, basketball, rugby, and bull fights. Some major sports events such as the annual Rose Bowl in Southern California attract national and international interest. In some areas, recreation and sports facilities may be expressly developed to attract tourists; in other places, they are developed primarily for local use but also attract tourists for major events; and some are developed as secondary or complementary attractions, such as golf courses and tennis centers in beach resorts.

As previously mentioned in relation to natural features, recreation and sports facilities may be developed as the primary attraction, as for example, in ski resorts. Sport hunting and fishing are popular sports in North America and Europe and comprise a high value type of tourism in other places, especially in those countries in Africa that still allow controlled big game hunting, Mongolia, and the Soviet Union. Game fishing is well developed in the Caribbean and off the west coast of Mexico and Southern California and is commencing in some of the Pacific Island areas, along the East African coast, and elsewhere. Hunting and fishing possibilities must be carefully evaluated with respect to their impact on wildlife conservation and compatibility with other types of tourist activities.

Tourist Facilities and Services as Attractions

Although usually seen as serving tourists, outstanding or unusual tourist facilities and services can be attractions in themselves and induce tourists to visit an area, or be important complementary attractions to the major ones. These include the types of facilities and services described in the following sections.

Hotels and Resorts

Particularly well-designed, historic, or unusual hotels and resorts can be attractions in themselves (for example, the palace hotels in India that are converted maharajas' palaces, the paradors of Spain that are historic buildings, such as monasteries and palaces, converted to hotels, the yurt style tented camp resorts in Central Asia, some of the luxurious nineteenth century resort hotels in Europe and North America, and the contemporary large-scale "fantasyland" resorts in Hawaii). Usually high quality service is associated with these types of hotels and resorts. In surveying and evaluating tourist attractions in an area, opportunities should be noted for conversion of historic and interesting buildings into accommodation, or complexes of such buildings into holiday villages.

Transportation

Interesting, historic, and unusual forms of transportation can be made into attractions such as the Palace on Wheels tour in northern India, which utilizes railway coaches previously owned by wealthy princes, the revived 1920s Orient Express rail trip in Europe, the nineteenth century steamboat tours on the Mississippi River in the USA, the Nile River cruises in Egypt, and camel trekking in the Sahara. Typically, but not always, these types of tours offer high quality service.

Cuisine

The food of an area, in addition to being an important service for tourists, can be a significant secondary tourist attraction, especially if the area offers a special type of cuisine that is well prepared and presented. For special-interest gourmet tours, such as organized in Europe, cuisine is the primary attraction.

Other Attraction Considerations

In addition to tourist attraction features, there are several other considerations that must be made in evaluating the attractiveness of the tourism area, as described in the following sections.

Ethnic, Religious, and Nostalgic Associations

Ethnic, religious, or nostalgic associations of some tourists to particular places can be the reason for travel to those destinations and should be recognized as a type of attraction associated with specific tourist markets. Ethnic associations often relate to the ancestral origin of the tourists (for example, Irish-Americans visiting Ireland and seeking their ancestral homes, or overseas ethnic Chinese visiting their ancestral villages in China). There is much regional tourist movement in South Asia of Indians, Pakistanis, and Bangladeshis visiting their friends and relatives in the areas where they lived before partition. An example of promotion of ethnic tourism is the Balikbayans program of the Philippines, which encourages Filipinos living abroad to visit their home country.

Religious pilgrimages comprise a major type of travel in many places of the world, and very important sacred places generate much long-distance travel. Mecca, Medina, Jerusalem, Varanasi and other places in India, and the Vatican in Rome are long-established religious destinations that are attracting many modern pilgrims. As an example of recognizing the potential market for religious travel, the birthplace of Buddha at Lumbini in southern Nepal is being developed as a major destination for Buddhist pilgrims, as are places in northern India where Buddha traveled (Buddha's Trail). These places are particularly attracting Japanese Buddhists who wish to visit the geographical origin of their religion. Religious tourism can require substantial development of tourist facilities, services, and infrastructure, and can generate considerable socioeconomic benefits to an area. It can also result in problems of congestion and overdevelopment if not carefully planned and organized.

Examples of historic associations as attractions are the visits made by Japanese and Americans to places in the Pacific Islands and by Americans to Europe where they fought during World War II, and of retired colonial administrators visiting former colonies where they were previously stationed and may have lived for many years. This is sometimes referred to as nostalgic tourism. In the case of the World War II battlegrounds, war memorials have been constructed, which provides a physical focus for the tourists to visit. The importance of nostalgic tourism should be recognized and can be promoted, but after one or two generations have passed, these specialized markets are much diminished.

Political Stability, Public Health and Safety, and Other Considerations

Although not an attraction as such, the extent of political stability of an area and the popular perception of political stability, whether realistic or not, by the potential tourist markets is a significant factor in attracting tourists. Several areas experienced much reduced tourism during the 1970s and 1980s because of political disturbances, and other places had decreased tourist travel because of concern by potential tourists about being affected by political disturbances even though there were not any problems at those particular destinations. A pattern of terrorist actions in particular areas can also be a deterrent to tourist travel in those places, or tourists may be reluctant to use particular types of transportation that have experienced terrorism. Therefore, the extent of political stability and likely future stability must be realistically assessed in a tourism area.

Another important consideration is the extent of public safety of the country or region and especially in the tourism areas. A high level of crime such as murder, rape, and theft will be a deterrent to attracting tourists, while an area that is known to be safe and maintain an efficient and honest police force will have an advantage in promoting itself. A high incidence of prostitution and use of drugs will also be a deterrent to some tourists.

The extent to which prostitution is legally allowed or illegally exists in a tourism area must be individually decided by the government of each area, taking into consideration various factors: the social implications of prostitution based on the local value system, which varies from one to another place; the impact of their profession on the prostitutes themselves (Cohen 1982); the fact that this activity will be an attraction to some tourists but disliked by others; the overall general and tourism image of the area; and the control measures required if prostitution is allowed, or the feasibility of prevention if it is not legally permitted.

Public health and the degree of possibility of tourists contracting health problems is a consideration in evaluating tourism areas as is examined in Chapter 15.

Destination Travel Costs

A major factor in the attractability to tourists may be the cost of travel to the destination and the cost of using tourist facilities and services at the destination, compared to the costs of travel to and within similar destinations elsewhere. This consideration is especially important if the aim is to attract a large number of general interest resort and sight-seeing tourists who often have destination alternatives. Special interest tourism markets are more specific and include tourists who are more willing to pay a higher cost to pursue their travel interests. Cost is, of course, less of a concern to affluent tourists who can afford to travel where they want, although they will still expect "good value for their money."

If there is existing tourism development, the present costs of the destination should be reviewed, or, if there is little existing tourism, the projected future cost must be considered within the framework of the present and projected future costs of visiting competing destinations. If the destination costs are relatively high, then investigation should be made on ways to reduce the costs, or perhaps reconsider the type of tourism development and related markets to aim for.

Survey and Evaluation Techniques

The existing and potential attractions of an area should be systematically and objectively identified and evaluated as part of the survey and analysis step of the planning process. The actual selection of attractions for development and the planning concepts for conservation/development of specific attractions will be done during the plan formulation stage.

Identification and Description of Attractions

The first step in the survey of tourist attractions is document research and interviews of government officials and other local resource persons to determine the general types and locations of attractions available. Then a preliminary list of attraction categories, types of characteristics for which information is to be obtained, and the evaluation criteria are prepared; these may be modified as the survey proceeds.

Next, a field survey is undertaken to visit the attraction features. For some types of attractions, the survey may need to be conducted during more than one season to determine seasonal differences of the sites' characteristics (for example, of a potential ski resort that also may offer possibilities for summer season tourism, or of a high altitude scenic or historic site to determine whether it can be open to visitors during the winter, or of a tropical beach environment to ascertain how much it is affected during the trade winds or monsoon season). For some types of cultural attractions, such as music and dance, special performances may need to be arranged for the survey team.

The identification of the attractions should be done systematically, indicating name, type, location, accessibility, special characteristics, type of any existing development and any advantages or problems of the existing development, including a photograph if relevant, and a written summary description about the feature. Usually, a separate page or index card is prepared for each attraction.

If the feature is likely to be the focus of development, or several attractions of the same type need to be compared, the description should be specific indicating all pertinent characteristics. For example, for beach areas:

- Length and width of the sand area;
- Angle of slope of the beach;
- Extent of tidal action (high and low tide lines);
- Type of beach vegetation and sand dune ecology;
- Type of topography adjacent to the beach;
- Water characteristics of depth, type of bottom material, clarity of water, any pollution of water and source of pollution, water currents and undertows and any danger presented to swimmers, wave conditions and suitability for body and board surfing;
- Underwater characteristics of topography, reef and coral formations and quality of coral and other sea life for diving, any damage to or pollution of the coral and any sunken ships or other objects that may present hazards or be interesting to divers;
- Direction and extent of wind and suitability for sailing and wind surfing;
- Suitable locations for development of piers if necessary; and
- History of erosion or deposition of the beach.

Potential ski resorts and some other types of features need to have a comparably detailed environmental survey. In surveying the characteristics of attractions, the information needed to determine carrying capacities (explained in Chapter 6) should be included.

The place-specific attractions should be plotted on a map of the overall planning area so that they can later be analyzed with respect to the transportation system and potential tourism development areas. Other types of attractions such as climate can be described and mapped, and non-place specific cultural attractions such as music, dance, and handicrafts should be described.

The evaluation of attractions should be made relative to their respective importance at the regional, national, and international levels. Evaluation must take into account the potential tourist markets for the attraction features, use of the attractions by residents of the area, national, regional, and local accessibility, relative costs of conservation and development, carrying capacity of the attractions' environments, and the environmental and sociocultural implications of development. Accessibility may be a particularly important consideration. The attractions can usually be best evaluated by using a numerical evaluation matrix technique such as explained in the next section. However, judgment and experience must also be applied in the evaluation.

An important result of the evaluation will be deciding which are the primary attractions, that is, those that would induce tourists to visit the area, and which are secondary, that is, those that are not sufficiently important to induce tourists to visit but that would serve as complementary features to provide more activities and interest features for tourists and increase their length of stay. Also, the evaluation will indicate which are the predominant types of attractions, such as nature or culturally oriented, an important consideration in the market analysis. It is often a combination of attractions that provides the best basis for tourism development.

If, after the evaluation, it is determined that the natural and cultural attractions are not sufficiently important to successfully market tourism, or if additional attractions are needed to meet the development objectives, then consideration can be given to development of special types of attractions such as theme parks, gambling casinos, entertainment, duty-free shopping, or specialized recreation and sports facilities. Or it may be decided that the limitation of attractions or their high cost of development may preclude the feasibility of developing tourism and expansion of other economic sectors should be examined instead, although this should have been determined during the prefeasibility analysis.

Matrix Evaluation Technique

The matrix evaluation technique is commonly used in planning analysis in order to apply a systematic and objective approach to evaluation and decision making. However, this technique is only as effective as its input of quantitative and qualitative information, and its results should be reviewed within the framework of the overall experience and judgment of the planning team. Figure 4.1 presents a sample matrix evaluation chart that can be applied to evaluating the relative importance and development feasibility of tourist attraction features in a country or region. Additional criteria can be added to this matrix based on any other considerations applicable to the planning area or project.

Case Studies

Case studies of survey and evaluation of tourist attractions are presented for four different types of tourism areas. In the tourism plan for Burma, situated in southern Asia, attractions were identified very specifically into many different categories. In the tourism plan for Malta, in the Mediterranean region, five categories of attractions were identified, and comprehensive evaluation was made of tourism development areas that include attraction features. The survey and evaluation of attractions in the tourism plan for Mongolia, located in central Asia, was divided into the major categories of natural and cultural types of features with an overall evaluation. In the tourism plan for the South Pacific country of Fiji, the criteria for identifying and evaluating attractions were specified, and the attractions were inventoried and evaluated with recommendations for future conservation and development.

Identification of Tourist Attractions in Burma

Identification and evaluation of tourist attractions in Burma (renamed Myanmar in the late 1980s) were conducted as part of a national tourism development planning project (UNDP and WTO 1983) that was undertaken in two phases. The first phase, completed in 1983, was preparation of the national tourism plan and prefeasibility analysis for both international and domestic tourism; the second

Attraction Feature	Evaluation Factor							
	Accessibility	Economic Feasibility of Development	Environmental Impact of Development	Sociocultural Impact of Development	National/ Regional Importance	International Importance	Total Value	Comments
NATURAL FEATURES								
National Park A								
National Park B								
Trekking/Scenic Area A								
Trekking/Scenic Area B								
Beach/Marine Area A								
Beach/Marine Area B								
Beach/Marine Area C								
Cave Complex								
Geysers Complex								
Hot Springs A								
Hot Springs B								
Botanic Garden								
Zoological Safari Park								
CULTURAL FEATURES								
Archaeological Site A								
Archaeological Site B								
Historic Site A								
Historic Site B								
Historic Site C								
Museum A								
Museum B								
Traditional Dance and Music								
Handicrafts								
Traditional Village A								
Traditional Village B								
Cultural Festival								
SPECIAL FEATURES								
Casinos								
Theme Park A								
Theme Park B								
Duty-Free Shopping								
Convention Center A								
Convention Center B								

Notes:

1. This list of attraction features is only an example; the actual list will depend on the specific existing and potential attractions in the area. The evaluation factors can be modified depending on the situation in the study area.

2. The evaluation ranking can be done on a scale of 1 to 5 or 1 to 10, with the upper end of the scale indicating the positiveness of the factor (for example, good accessibility, acceptable economic feasibility of development, limited negative environmental and sociocultural impacts, and high level of regional, national, or international importance in terms of attracting tourists). The more important factors can be given a higher numerical weighting.

Figure 4.1. Sample Evaluation Matrix for Tourist Attractions.

phase, completed in 1988, involved preparing a detailed plan for the Pagan archaeological site and village in central Burma, as well as detailed design, final feasibility analysis, and development programming for three major hotels, one each in Rangoon, Mandalay, and Pagan. The plans and related recommendations for both these phases have been adopted by the government and implementation is underway.

Burma is a relatively large country with a wide range of attractions, and tourism is in its beginning stage with limited development of tourist facilities and services and a modest level of tourist arrivals. The attractions were identified for the planning of both international and domestic tourism. Based on background research and extensive field surveys, a large number of major and secondary attractions were identified and categorized as follows:

- Proposed national parks. (There were no existing national parks, but a park planning project, assisted by the United Nations, was underway during the tourism plan preparation period, and that project provided information to the tourism planning team.)
- Natural areas with conservation and recreation value.
- Major outdoor recreation areas.
- Hot springs with resort development potential.
- Beaches with recreation and resort development potential.
- Underwater coral gardens.
- Caves and waterfalls.
- Outstanding scenic views.
- Youth camps (existing).
- Archaeological and historic sites.
- Outstanding religious places (Buddhist temples, shrines, etc.).
- Interesting urban and village environments.
- Major festivals and special events.
- Museums.
- Handicraft production centers.
- Cultural performance facilities.
- Special features (for example, memorials, botanic and zoological gardens, aquariums, and war cemeteries).
- Golf courses.

In addition to the place-specific types of attractions listed above, which were plotted on maps, other types of attractions were identified as follows:

- Unusual, interesting, and diverse cultural patterns;
- Music, dance, drama, and puppetry;
- Unusual and diverse cuisine; and
- Interesting handicrafts.

Although not attractions as such, other advantages of the country in attracting tourists that were identified included: the relatively low cost of traveling within the country in terms of transportation, accommodation, and other services; low crime rate in the urban and village areas and good public safety for tourists within the prescribed tourism areas; and relatively few problems of drugs and prostitution compared to some other Asian destinations. Security problems existed in some parts of the country and tourists were not permitted to enter those areas.

After evaluation, the major and secondary attractions were determined, and recommendations were made for improvements needed to those attractions. Because of the importance of Pagan, one of the major archaeological sites in Asia, in representing the country's cultural heritage and as a tourist attraction, it was recommended that a special detailed plan be prepared for the Pagan area in Phase 2 as noted above. That plan included land use zoning, environmental improvements, recommendations for controlled visitor use of the site, and ways in which the nearby village could benefit from tourism. Pagan was already receiving assistance from the government and UNESCO for archaeological conservation.

Survey and Evaluation of Tourist Attractions in Malta

The background of the Maltese Islands Tourism Development Plan (Horwath and Horwath 1989) was described in Chapter 3. The survey and evaluation of tourist attractions in that project were based on five place-specific categories, which are shown in Figure 4.2 and described as follows:

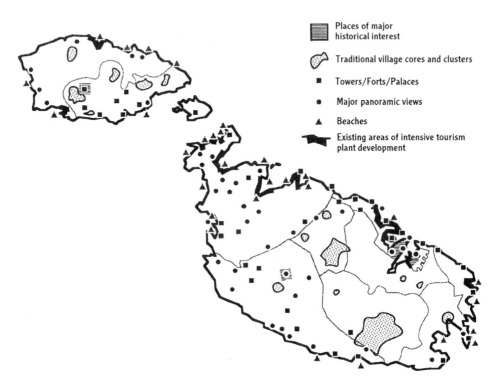

Figure 4.2. Maltese Islands Tourism Development Plan—Tourist Attractions.

- Places of major historic interest—These particularly include entire historic urban districts and also archaeological sites.
- Traditional village cores and clusters—These are village areas of traditional architectural character and life-styles.
- Towers, forts, and palaces—These are specific historic features of touristic interest.
- Major panoramic views—The Maltese Islands are small-scale but hilly, and an interesting feature of island tours are the many views offered.
- Beaches—These are specifically located and named, and are classified into rocky and sandy types.

The existing areas of intensive tourism development are also depicted in order to graphically show the relationships of existing development to the various attraction features. In the plan report text, the major attractions are described and evaluated by tourism zones. In addition to the place-specific attractions, the plan identified general features such as the warm, sunny, equable climate and the friendly people.

The tourist attractions survey approach included field inspections with identification and evaluation of the coastal bay resources for tourism, including any existing development. The survey team utilized a very useful technique by preparing both a field survey map, showing the environmental assets and problems of the bays, and a data card, evaluating any existing accommodation development. Figure 4.3 shows an example of this approach for a bay that has some existing development. As can be seen on the survey map, the access road and parking, a hotel, other development, view points and view planes, and other visual assets and problems are identified and evaluated. The data card describes the general hotel characteristics, contextual compatibility (how well the development fits into the natural environment), contextual characteristics of layout, ancillary development and accessibility, whether the site capacity is overdeveloped, appropriate, or underdeveloped, and a policy statement on the extent of improvement needed to the hotel.

Survey and Evaluation of Tourist Attractions in Mongolia

Located in central Asia, Mongolia had limited development of tourism in the late 1980s based on general sight-seeing and high value hunting. Wishing to expand tourism on a planned basis, the government undertook a tourism planning program with UNDP and WTO assistance, resulting in the National Tourism Plan for Mongolia (Shankland Cox 1989). The planning project was comprised of four parts: 1) a national tourism plan for 1990 to 2005; 2) policies and strategy for implementing the plan; 3) a development or action program for 1990 to 1995; and 4) detailed planning and conceptual design of three tourism demonstration projects (expansion of an existing Gobi Desert tourist camp, planning of a new tourist camp, and planning of visitor facilities at an historic site).

The objectives of developing tourism were specified in the plan as follows:

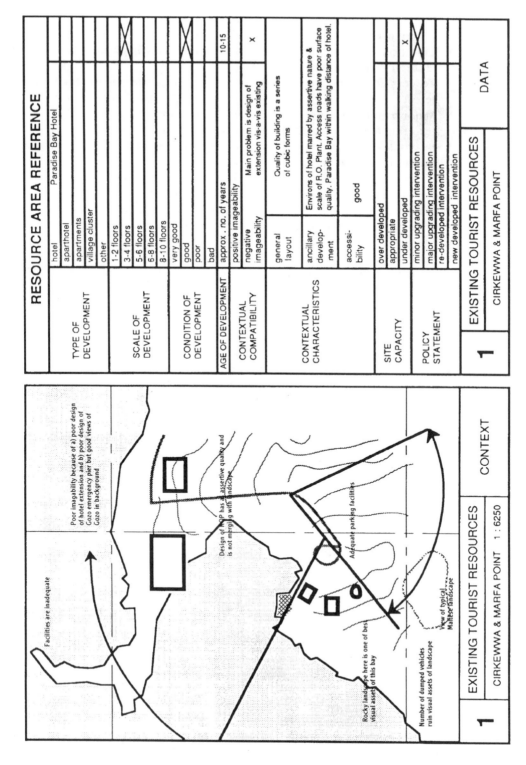

RESOURCE AREA REFERENCE

TYPE OF DEVELOPMENT	hotel	Paradise Bay Hotel	
	aparthotel		
	apartments		⊠
	village cluster		
	other		⊠
SCALE OF DEVELOPMENT	1-2 floors		
	3-4 floors		
	5-6 floors		
	6-8 floors		
	8-10 floors		
CONDITION OF DEVELOPMENT	very good		
	good		
	poor		
	bad		
AGE OF DEVELOPMENT	approx. no. of years		10-15
CONTEXTUAL COMPATIBILITY	positive imageability		
	negative imageability	Main problem is design of extension vis-a-vis existing	x
CONTEXTUAL CHARACTERISTICS	general layout	Quality of building is a series of cubic forms	
	ancillary develop-ment	Environs of hotel marred by assertive nature & scale of R.O. Plant. Access roads have poor surface quality. Paradise Bay within walking distance of hotel.	
	accessi-bility	good	
SITE CAPACITY	over developed		
	appropriate		
	under developed		⊠
POLICY STATEMENT	minor upgrading intervention		
	major upgrading intervention		x
	re-developed intervention		
	new developed intervention		

1	EXISTING TOURIST RESOURCES	DATA
	CIRKEWWA & MARFA POINT	

1	EXISTING TOURIST RESOURCES	CONTEXT
	CIRKEWWA & MARFA POINT 1 : 6250	

Map annotations:
- Facilities are inadequate
- Poor imagability because of a) poor design of hotel extension and b) poor design of Gozo emergency pier but good views of Gozo in background
- Design of R.O.P has assertive quality and is not merging with landscape
- Adequate parking facilities
- View of typical Maltese landscape
- Rocky landscape here is one of best visual assets of this bay
- Number of dumped vehicles ruin visual assets of landscape

Figure 4.3. Maltese Islands Tourism Development Plan—Field Survey Map and Data Card.

- To identify a concept for tourism that reflects the particular characteristics of Mongolia in relation to international market opportunities;
- To increase the scale of international tourism with a view to earning more foreign currency;
- To develop tourist centers in parts of the country with different characteristics to widen visitors' choice and to assist in the dispersal of economic activity;
- To devise forms of tourism development that are most cost-effective in terms of the level of investment required in relation to the length of the season, and to minimize foreign exchange leakage;
- To improve existing services and facilities for tourists and establish future standards appropriate to the identified market;
- To provide opportunities for the diversification and restructuring of the economy and for the creation of cooperatives and small business enterprises; and
- To minimize in the process any adverse social, cultural, or environmental impacts.

In the plan, tourist attraction features were field surveyed and evaluated to the extent that they were accessible to the planning team. Attractions were categorized into natural and cultural type features. The natural features, shown in Figure 4.4, were designated as follows:

- Areas of outstanding environmental quality—This was identified as being the most important aspect of Mongolia's attraction based on the diversity of landscape steppe, craggy mountains, dense forests, and desert, and the unspoiled, vast, open character and overall tranquility of the environment. Areas possessing high environmental quality value were selected based on the following criteria:
  1. General character;
  2. Variety of visual incident;
  3. Mixture of landscape form;
  4. Range of flora and fauna;
  5. Sense of intimacy and enclosure;
  6. Absence of urban development;
  7. Density of population; and
  8. Proximity of national parks, reserves, and protected area.
- Existing national parks.
- Existing nature reserves.
- Proposed national parks.
- Exceptional natural features—One outstanding natural feature, a waterfall, was identified.
- Wildlife—Mongolia possesses abundant and some unusual wildlife, including various types of deer, elk, boar, bear, sable, wolf, lynx, Angali sheep, ibex, gazelles, wild ass, wild camel, snow leopard, fox, and wild cat. Strict conservation measures are applied to wildlife with controlled hunting allowed to the extent of maintaining an ecological balance between the animal populations and their habitats; wildlife viewing is an attraction, although not yet developed.

The cultural attraction features relate to historical, architectural, and archaeological sites, shown in Figure 4.4, and include important monasteries, temples,

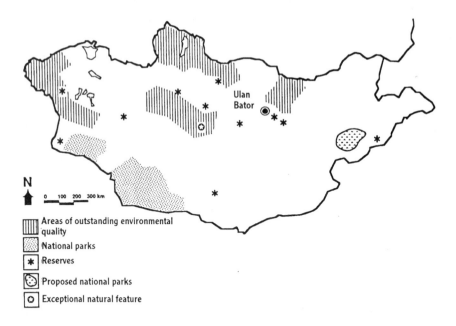

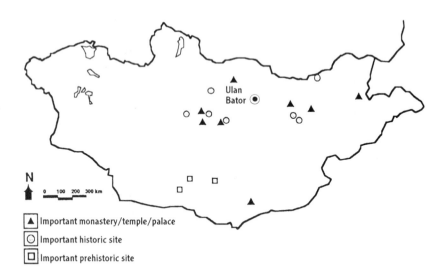

Figure 4.4. Tourism Plan for Mongolia—(top) Natural Tourist Attractions, (bottom) Cultural Tourist Attractions.

and palaces, other important historic sites, and significant prehistoric sites. Several of the historic places have been restored and others are planned for restoration, and some of the archaeological sites have been or are scheduled to be excavated. Several Buddhist temples and monasteries of the sixteenth and seventeenth centuries were identified and evaluated with respect to their general touristic interest, and historic sites including Karakorum, the capital of Genghis Khan, designated. The 'mystic' of Genghis Khan associated with Mongolia and its former historical influences in Western Asia/Eastern Europe and China were described as a general attraction for many tourists. Cultural facilities, especially museums, are described as important complementary features of tours in the country. Other important features identified are the still existing nomadic traditions and life-styles, with herdsmen and their families living in timber-framed tents (ghers), fine horsemanship, archery and Mongolian wrestling, folk art traditions that are being revived, and local festivals.

Overall, the plan concluded that the major attractions of Mongolia are the scenic, open, unspoiled landscapes with a profusion of flora and fauna and scattered nomadic encampments, combined with the association of the country with Genghis Khan. Specific attraction features are of secondary importance and should be used to provide diversity in tour itineraries.

Tourist Attraction Recommendations in the Fiji Tourism Plan

The background of the national tourism plan for Fiji (Belt, Collins & Associates et al 1973) was described in a case study in Chapter 3. Fiji possesses both natural and cultural attraction features, some that are existing and others that require conservation and/or development measures for effective presentation to visitors. The attractions examined were those considered to be of national importance; those of local interest within the tourism development regions were shown on the regional plans. The criteria used in the national plan for selection of the attractions are as indicated below, although, as stated in the plan, not every attraction necessarily meets all the criteria nor is intended to do so.

- Outstanding enough to attract and satisfy the varied interests of both overseas visitors and local people;
- Authentic in nature and representative of the specific characteristics of Fiji;
- Archaeologically, historically, and ecologically unique, representative, or important;
- Feasible to develop for use by both residents and visitors;
- Readily accessible to accommodation areas, population centers, and to different age groups;
- Diverse as to types of areas and activities throughout the country;
- Opportunity for the revival and conservation of significant traditional activities, customs, and artifacts; and
- Encouraging cross-cultural exchange and international understanding.

Based on document research, interviews of local resource persons, and field surveys, an inventory of attractions was prepared and, with application of the criteria, existing and recommended attractions were selected, categorized, and described as indicated below. The place-specific attractions were plotted on maps under the two major divisions of: 1) scenic, natural, and recreational, and 2) cultural, historical, and archaeological.

- Friendly and hospitable people—The people of Fiji are known for their vitality, friendliness, outgoing and humorous nature, and sense of hospitality to friends and strangers. The plan points out that this is a vulnerable characteristic subject to misunderstandings and that visitors must be taught to understand and respect Fijian traditions and the people of Fiji educated about the customs of foreigners.
- Traditional customs, artifacts, and legends—As a multi-cultural society, Fiji offers different types of life-styles, customs, and traditions, including music, dance, ceremonies, handicrafts, and festivals associated with legends, offering tourists the opportunity to experience wide cultural exposure.
- Museums and model villages—There is one good quality national museum in the capital city of Suva, and the plan recommends that smaller museums be established in tourism areas elsewhere in the country. The traditional Fijian village with its standard layout around a central open area used for community activities and the traditional, distinctively styled buildings are of much interest to tourists. In order for large numbers of tourists to experience a Fijian village without undue disturbance of existing villages, the plan recommends that model villages be developed in tourism areas (some model villages already exist), either as interpretative museum exhibits or functioning villages with resident populations but open to tourists on a controlled basis. The plan emphasizes that competent guide services are essential for tourists to appreciate the model villages. More generally, the plan recommends that all traditional villages should be encouraged to maintain their customary layouts, design, and landscaping even though contemporary house types may be introduced, because of the functional and aesthetic advantages inherent in the traditional village patterns. The plan emphasizes the importance of the villages being well maintained and clean, and endorses the existing annual competition organized to determine the best maintained villages on the main island, recommending that this type of competition also be held in the other islands of the country.
- Cultural institute—A Fijian cultural institute was recommended to be developed as a focal point for conservation of music, dance, ceremonies, handicrafts, traditional house and canoe construction techniques, legends, and customs. This institute would include research and training activities and performance and demonstration areas. It would be open to tourists as a major attraction and admission fees would help support the institute.
- Archaeological and historical features—There are numerous important archaeological and historic sites representing the different historical periods and cultures of Fiji, which are recommended to be preserved and developed with facilities where necessary and opened to tourists. These include some entire historic villages, petroglyphs, fortifications, and colonial buildings and town districts.
- Beaches, natural features, parks, and nature reserves—White, sandy beaches, coral reef formations and associated sea life, specific natural features such as waterfalls, river rapids, mountains and gorges, general scenic beauty, and wildlife (especially a wide variety of birds) were identified for conservation and, where relevant, development with visitor facilities. The existing nature re-

serves were evaluated and designated on the attractions plan. Because Fiji had not yet established any national parks, several outstanding scenic areas were recommended for consideration as future national parks, and some proposed marine parks and reserves were endorsed by the plan.

- Water-related activities—The plan indicated that there was much potential for further development of water-related recreation and sports activities, including swimming, reef walking, snorkeling, scuba diving, and fishing, with possibilities for deep sea game fishing. The importance of observing water safety measures with training in water safety and provision of life guards was emphasized. The plan stated that the islands also have much potential for continued development of local ship cruises with shore stops at various islands.
- Sports—Organized sports, both spectator and participatory, including cricket, soccer, rugby, hockey, track, volleyball, softball, and lawn tennis, are popular in Fiji and can be an attraction for tourists.
- Scenic roads and viewpoints and riding and hiking trails—In keeping with the principle in Fiji of multi-use of infrastructure, no new scenic roads were recommended to be developed only for recreational purposes, but existing and proposed roads that traverse scenic areas (which includes most of the country's roads) were recommended to be improved or constructed to take advantage of scenic views, developed with scenic viewpoints at appropriate locations, and suitably landscaped with road-oriented advertising signs strictly controlled. Fiji already has a system of trails used by residents, and the plan recommended that these be improved where necessary and made available for hiking and horse riding by tourists, as well as for continued use by residents. Many of these trails are situated in scenic areas and lead to some interesting attraction features such as waterfalls.
- Festivals and special events—The plan pointed out that for residents festivals and special events are an important means of developing local interest and identity, encouraging conservation and improvement of local art forms, and focusing attention on particular activities, and are a source of entertainment and fun; and they are also of much interest to tourists. The plan listed the existing festivals and special events and identified possibilities for new events, including annual arts, traditional games and horsemanship festivals, an early days (colonial period) pageant, a deep sea fishing tournament, boat racing events, including an Australia to Fiji yacht race, traditional canoe racing, and modern boat regattas.
- Handicraft and duty-free shopping—The plan stated that locally produced handicrafts are already available but could be improved in variety and quality, with emphasis on maintaining authenticity. It was recommended that the government establish minimum standards for handicrafts and label all handicrafts meeting these standards to inform tourists which items meet the quality standards. Duty-free shopping is already a major attraction for both cruise ship and overnight visitors, and the plan recommended that a fair pricing structure be maintained, merchandising techniques be improved, and the appearance of the duty-free shopping areas be enhanced to provide an interesting and attractive shopping environment.

- Dining and entertainment—The plan pointed out the importance of restaurants and interesting cuisine as attractions to tourists, and recommended that the number and diversity of independent restaurants (outside of hotels) be increased to provide more choice to tourists. Entertainment, mostly of traditional dance, music, and certain ceremonies, already exists and the plan emphasized the importance of maintaining quality control of these performances. The plan endorsed the proposal that had been already made for the development of national dance and arts theaters.

In formulating the Fiji tourism plan, the locations of place-specific tourist attractions were an important consideration in determining the locations of tourism development regions and specific development areas.

References

Belt, Collins & Associates, Ltd. et al. 1973. *Tourism Development Programme for Fiji*. Honolulu, Hawaii.

Brown, John and Ann Church. 1987. "Theme Parks in Europe." *Travel and Tourism Analyst*. February 1987.

Cohen, Erik. 1982. "Thai Girls and Farang Men: The Edge of Ambiguity." *Annals of Tourism Research*. 9(3): 403–428.

Gunn, Clare A. 2nd ed. 1988. *Tourism Planning*. New York: Taylor & Francis.

Horwath and Horwath, Inc. 1989. *Maltese Islands Tourism Development Plan*. London.

Lew, Alan A. 1987. "A Framework of Tourist Attraction Research." *Annals of Tourism Research*. 14(4): 553–575.

Shankland Cox. 1989. *National Tourism Plan for Mongolia*. London and Hong Kong.

United Nations Development Programme and World Tourism Organization. 1983. *National Tourism Development Plan and Prefeasibility Analysis for the Socialist Republic of the Union of Burma*. Madrid: World Tourism Organization.

5

Tourist Markets, Facilities, Services, and Infrastructure

Tourist Market Survey

If some tourism exists in a country or region, the survey of past and present tourist arrivals provides important input to the market analysis and can offer insight to tourist perceptions of the area. This survey should be made of both international and domestic tourists and, where relevant, residents' present and likely future use of tourist attractions, facilities, and services. Complete data may not be available from existing records, and best estimates will need to be made or special field surveys conducted. The market survey also typically includes interviews of tour operators in the tourist market countries or regions, regardless of whether any tourism exists in the planning area. A review of general travel patterns internationally, within the global region and nationally (for subnational regional plans) should be conducted and an assessment made of general travel and tourism trends to provide the framework for the market analysis.

Tourist Arrivals and Characteristics

The past and present annual number of tourist arrivals should be determined as an indicator of the general growth and level of tourism, and monthly figures obtained to calculate the seasonal fluctuations of arrivals. The characteristics and attitudes of tourist arrivals, including by different seasons, should be ascertained to the extent possible as described in the following sections.

- Place of origin—The nationality and country of residence for international tourists and region or city of residence for domestic tourists are essential data required for marketing purposes. The country of residence in addition to nationality is important to record because there are many people living permanently in countries different than their passport nationalities and significant numbers of expatriates living outside their countries of nationality for long periods of time throughout the world. Some of these, such as foreigners working overseas, are of fairly high socioeconomic levels and tend to travel extensively in the countries and regions where they are currently living.
- Purpose of visit—Purpose of visit includes the categories of holiday, business, study, official mission/diplomatic, visiting friends and relatives, and sometimes other categories depending on the local situation. Returning residents (for expatriates) should also be included so that this category can be separated from short-stay tourists. The purpose of visit characteristic obviously is important as marketing and facility planning inputs.
- Length of stay—Length of stay, based on the number of nights spent in the area, is an important factor that relates to the extent of facility use and total expenditures of tourists.
- Age, sex, and number of family members traveling together—These are important characteristics to know in determining the tourist profile for marketing and tourist facility planning purposes. Age can be grouped into general categories (many tourists do not want to give their exact age).
- Type of employment and income levels—Type of employment can be generalized into such categories as managerial, professional, skilled worker, housewife, student, and retired. Income levels can also be grouped into broad categories (many persons do not like to indicate their exact incomes). These are useful factors to know for marketing and facility planning purposes.
- Where traveled and stayed during visit—Places visited in the country and the type or name of accommodation used is important information for planning purposes.
- Number of times visited—Whether this is a first or successive visit to the country is desirable to record especially for holiday tourists, because return visits indicate a sustained interest in the destination.
- Individual or group travel—Whether the tourist is traveling independently or is with a group tour is important to know for marketing purposes, and also often relates to facility use and expenditure patterns.
- Expenditure patterns—The total amount spent by each tourist and the distribution of spending, based typically on the categories of accommodation, food and drink, shopping, local transportation and tours, and miscellaneous, is essential information in order to determine the economic impact of tourism and provides input to recommending ways to increase visitor spending. Expenditure patterns can best be determined through a special tourist survey, although estimates can be made from hotel, restaurant, tour agency, and retail shop receipts and, for foreign tourists, possibly from foreign exchange currency figures to obtain gross expenditures.
- Visitor attitudes and satisfaction levels—Determining visitor attitudes and satis-

faction levels about the country or region generally, and its tourist attractions, facilities, and services specifically, can provide valuable information for improving tourism (or not making any changes, depending on the results of this survey), at least based on present market desires. This information can best be obtained through a special survey that usually also includes the tourists' expenditure patterns and characteristics so that all these factors can be correlated in the analysis. This survey can additionally include questions relative to improvements that the tourists would like to have made and whether they would consider returning for future visits.

The basic information for international tourists can be obtained from the Embarkation/Disembarkation (ED) immigration cards if they are properly designed and tabulated. However, visitor expenditures and attitudes and some of the other characteristics require special tourist surveys, as referred to previously. These surveys are usually organized at the points of departure of tourists such as the airports and can be conducted on a sampling basis, but should be carefully designed to take into account seasonal differences of tourist profiles. It may be necessary to conduct the survey during different tourist seasons of the year. Information on domestic tourists is more difficult to obtain because they do not pass through immigration, and special surveys are required of them. Domestic tourists may be surveyed at the accommodation where they are staying or at major attraction sites that they are visiting. Also, survey questions on travel patterns may be included in a national or regional population census. In some places, a household survey needs to be undertaken to determine travel patterns of domestic tourists and residents utilizing tourist attractions and facilities. It may be necessary to include provision for special international and domestic tourist surveys in organization and budgeting of the planning study.

Cruise Ship Tourists

In many island and coastal areas, cruise ship tourism may be existing or have potential for development and should be analyzed as a type of tourist market. Cruise ship tourism, even though it does not typically involve overnight use of accommodation, can be important in terms of expenditures that these tourists make onshore for tours, shopping, meals, and sometimes entertainment. Cruise ship passengers are technically not tourists but are excursionists because their stay usually is less than 24 hours in the country. However, in some areas, cruise ship tourism includes land travel and overnight stays to visit major attraction features, with tourists disembarking at one port, traveling overland for a few days, and embarking on the ship at another port further along the cruise itinerary.

If there are existing cruise ship stopovers, the market survey should include cruise ship passengers. Basic information on the passenger characteristics can be obtained from the cruise ship operators, and special surveys can be conducted of the passengers to determine their specific characteristics, expenditure patterns, and attitudes toward the local area they have visited. In terms of market analysis, this survey provides a basis for assessing any improvements needed in the provision of facilities and services and the overall expansion potential for cruise ship tourism in the area.

In places where yachting tourism has developed, the yachtsmen should also be surveyed periodically to determine their characteristics, length of stay, expenditure patterns, and any improvements of yachting facilities and services they would like to have made.

Tour Operators

It is very useful and typically included in a major planning project to arrange for interviews of tour operators in the existing and potential market origin countries and, for domestic tourism, regions of the country if many of the domestic tourists make use of tour operators. Operators included in this survey are those who currently handle tours to the area or may be interested in handling such tours in the future. They are familiar with any problems that they may have had in arranging tours to the area, are conscious of pricing structures and attractions of competing destinations, have received feedback from tourists who have visited the area, and will have their own perceptions of the desirability of the tourism area as a destination. Tour operators represent the travel trade's viewpoint on the relative tourism merits of the area and any improvements that may be needed. Personal interviews of the tour operators is the most effective approach, but telephone interviews or mail questionnaires can also be utilized. Tour operators can be surveyed on a sampling basis, but the major operators involved should be included.

General Travel Patterns and Tourism Trends

For the national level of tourism planning, general travel patterns to other countries in the region and global travel patterns and tourism trends should be reviewed, as should travel patterns within the country for regional tourism planning. A survey of these general travel patterns should include consideration of the number, origin and types of tourists, and location and types of destinations that are popular. These general travel patterns are especially important to understand in order to analyze long-range tourist markets that visit more than one place on multi-destination tours. General travel patterns are surveyed even if there is not any existing tourism in the study area.

Tourism trends to be aware of include, for example, emerging new market countries and market segments, new types of attractions and destinations, and improved means of transportation. If relevant to the area, cruise ship travel patterns and cruise tourism trends should also be reviewed.

General travel patterns and tourism trends can be obtained from the WTO, regional tourism associations such as the PATA and the CTO for some parts of the world, general tourism literature including tourism and related professional journals, and some of the tourism trade association publications. It can be very useful to discuss trends with major hotel and tour operators. Also, tourism conferences often focus on trends taking place in the field.

Survey of Tourist Facilities and Services

General Approach

As part of of the survey and evaluation stage of the planning process, any existing tourist facilities and services should be surveyed and evaluated with respect to their type, extent, and suitability for the present and future level and type of tourism development. This survey and evaluation provides the basis for recommending improvements needed to existing facilities and services. Also, the present pattern may well influence the locational considerations in formulation of the physical plan.

Standards for survey and evaluation need to be established, based both on accepted international standards and the tourist markets being aimed for. An important factor in the evaluation is that most tourists expect reasonable "good value for money" at any quality level of facility and service, that is, that the cost of facilities and services available is properly correlated to the quality level and not overpriced. It is especially important that minimum standards of hygiene and safety be carefully evaluated.

The inventory and evaluation of facilities and services require field surveys, sometimes tourist attitude surveys (referred to in the previous section on market surveys) and a systematic approach. This survey should include personal interviews of hotel, tour and travel agency, major restaurant, and other tourism enterprise managers and of any existing private sector tourism organizations such as a hotel association in order to obtain the trade's views on how tourism and their component of it could be improved. These interviews can also provide general information on the existing tourist markets as input to the market analysis. Any proposed new or expanded facilities and services already approved for development and likely to be developed should be included in the survey because they will be part of the existing pattern in the near future. The location of facilities and their major characteristics should be indicated in tabular form and, where relevant, plotted on maps, with a description and evaluation made in the plan text.

Accommodation

There is a wide variety of types of accommodation that may exist or can be planned for an area. Although terminology exists for different types of accommodation, the distinction among the terms is increasingly blurred, and the terms are often not now used according to their original connotations. Also, the terminol-

Hotel del Coronado in San Diego, California—This late nineteenth century beach resort hotel, one of the largest wooden structures in North America, has been carefully maintained and restored and provides high quality accommodation and a major attraction for visitors to the city. (Courtesy of the Hotel del Coronado)

ogy varies somewhat among the different countries of the world. In addition to physical form, accommodation can be defined based on its type of clientele, pricing, quality level and ownership. For the purposes of survey, analysis, and planning, the terminology used in each area should be based on a combination of the generally accepted international definitions and any locally accepted usage.

The most common type of accommodation is hotels, which include:

- City or downtown hotels usually catering to both business and holiday travelers;
- Convention hotels catering to large conferences and conventions and often also general business and holiday travelers;
- Airport hotels located near large airports designed for use by transient travelers, but also now often including meeting facilities for use by business travelers flying in to hold meetings with local persons;

- Hotels oriented to major railway or bus stations in cities and catering to transient travelers; and
- Resort hotels, which offer a wide range of facilities and services including recreation and amenity features in an attractive environment and oriented to holiday tourist markets.

The larger urban hotels contain restaurants and other commercial facilities and services and commonly some recreation and health facilities. Hotels may have configurations ranging from high-rise to medium- and low-rise or be comprised of individual cottage units or, in some cases, a combination of these different forms. Types of rooms may range from standard to various categories of suites.

Motels, motor hotels, or motor lodges are oriented to automobile travelers, include self-parking facilities (although many city hotels now also provide some parking facilities) and typically are located along major highways in rural and urban areas. A common locational pattern is a concentration of motels situated alongside highways in the urban periphery and at major highway intersections, often in association with restaurants and other facilities related to automobile travel. Some motels do not include restaurants facilities while others now contain restaurants, and some motels now offer meeting facilities. The traditional terms of inn and lodge typically refer to small-scale establishments and connote a feeling of coziness and friendliness, although some large hotels now call themselves inns.

Other types of accommodation include:

- Guest houses and "bed and breakfast" establishments, long popular in Britain and becoming common in the USA, Canada, and elsewhere (Indonesia, for example, has many guest houses called 'homestays'), which are private homes or places of a residential character offering rooms;
- Pensions, a term used in France to refer to small family owned and operated hotels, typically not including a restaurant;
- Youth hostels, inexpensive dormitory type accommodation designed for young travelers found throughout the world;
- Ashrams for religious pilgrims in Asia;
- Campgrounds, which provide camping sites and sometimes rental tents and cabins with provision of toilet, washing, and sometimes recreational facilities, very common in North American and Europe and becoming popular elsewhere;
- Caravan parks, often called recreational vehicle (RV) parks in the USA, which provide spaces and facilities for mobile accommodation of trailers and motorized campers; and
- Floating accomodations such as houseboats developed, for example, by the hundreds on the lakes at Srinagar in Kashmir, India, and the currently experimental permanently floating hotels; cruise ships and lake and riverboats also provide floating accommodation.

In Europe, the term of "holiday village" is commonly used to refer to low-rise accommodation units with eating and recreation facilities and designed with a village-like environment, perhaps even with a central open square bounded with small retail shops. Highly self-contained resort hotels that offer a wide range of organized activities for guests have been developed by Club Mediterrane'e in many places in the world; this concept has more recently been emulated by other companies, such as Club Robinson. Some specialized type accomodations are developed in historic buildings such as the paradors in Spain, palace hotels in India, and in old village complexes in Yugoslavia and Korea. Traditional type accommodation, such as the ryokans in Japan, are popular with some tourists. Although not usually part of the accommodation inventory, accommodation is also provided through exchange programs of persons from one area exchanging use of their home with persons from another area for a specified vacation period.

An increasingly important type of accommodation are self-catering units that contain kitchen facilities and often a separate sitting room and one or more bedrooms. These units usually have the configuration of apartments, townhouses, or single-family houses, often termed villas, and are popular with families or couples sharing a vacation who want to have the opportunity to prepare their own meals and enjoy more living space than available in hotel rooms. Self-catering units are a common form of accommodation in the Mediterranean region, the Caribbean, Hawaii, New Zealand, Australia, and elsewhere. Such units meet a certain market demand, although there is typically less expenditure by the tourist occupants who cook some of their own meals (but will usually buy the meal ingredients locally). It is now common practice to include some self-catering units in large resorts in addition to the hotel accommodation.

A holiday village in Turkey—Holiday villages are a popular type of resort in the Mediterranean region. They offer a low-profile, village-like environment, with provision of integrated commercial and recreational amenity features. (Courtesy of the World Tourism Organization)

Usually associated with self-catering units but also applicable to hotels is the condominium type of ownership whereby each unit is individually owned in fee simple with the landscaped areas and recreation and other facilities owned in common by all the unit owners. Condominium units can either be retained for full-time use by the owners, who are sometimes retired persons who want to live in a resort environment, or contracted to a property management company who rents them on a short-term basis to tourists. Under this arrangement, it is common for the owner to retain use rights for a short period each year for his or her own vacation or be allowed to rent any unit in the complex at a discount for vacation use.

A specialized form of condominium ownership is time-sharing, whereby the unit is owned by several different persons, each of whom has the right to use it during a specified period or the right to contract it for rental to other tourists during that period. A person, for example, may buy a specified two weeks ownership during which he or she has exclusive use of the unit. Under both the condominium and time-sharing systems, the owners pay monthly fees for maintenance of the common facilities and services in the complex. Condominium ownership and time-sharing takes various legal formats, and it is important that areas that allow condominiums and time-sharing adopt relevant legislation in order to properly regulate this type of ownership.

Some countries have applied classification systems for accommodation, especially hotels and motels, that classify establishments into quality categories ranging from the luxury to basic levels according to specific criteria. A common system is a five-star level classification with the four- and five-star levels representing high quality accommodation that provides a broad range of facilities and services, the three-star level indicating medium quality, and one- and two-star denoting the basic levels. Other systems use different categories such as deluxe, superior, and good or A, B, C, D, and E. Room rate structures are typically correlated to the star levels, although there may be considerable variation of room pricing. Some countries also apply special classifications to other types of accommodation such as pensions and guest houses. Minimum standards of safety and hygiene are applicable to all classification levels and, of course, to any accommodation in an area.

The survey of accommodation will include the type of each establishment, location, number of rooms or units, quality level, special characteristics or facilities and services offered, room rates, and average annual occupancy rates, including any seasonal variations in occupancies. The evaluation must include both the physical plant and the kind of facilities and services offered by the establishments and the quality level of services. A hotel, for example, may have excellent physical facilities but offer very poor quality service, and this should be noted. If a hotel classification system is already being applied in the country or region and is considered by the planning team to be realistic, it can be used to establish quality levels of the hotels. Otherwise, an internationally accepted system of measurement should be applied, but taking into account that there are regional differences in quality levels. The WTO, for example, has published basic hotel classification system criteria for each of the major regions of the world.

Other Tourist Facilities and Services

Several other types of tourist facilities and services must be surveyed and evaluated if any tourism exists in the country or region. Even if tourism has not yet developed, some of the basic community facilities and services must still be considered with respect to their capability of serving tourism in the future. These various facilities and services are reviewed in the following sections.

Tour and Travel Operations

Tour and travel operations include agencies offering local tour programs and tourist handling services of transportation ticketing, such as airline, rail, and bus ticketing and hotel reservations, that is, inbound and outbound travel services. Any existing rental car, motorcycle, and bicycle operations should also be included in this survey and evaluation. Particularly important in some tourism areas, especially those offering sightseeing, cultural, and special interest tourism, is the availability and competence level of tour guide services, including language capabilities in places attracting tourists of different language backgrounds. Local tours offered should be reviewed with respect to tour costing levels and itinerary programming to determine how realistic and effective they are, and the quality, reliability, and safety of tour cars and buses examined. Any specialized types of tours such hunting and photographic safaris, hiking and trekking, mountain climbing, river rafting, and boating should be included in the survey and evaluation. It is useful for the planning team to take some of the local tours as tourists to observe their approaches.

Any existing regulations applicable to tour and travel agencies and tour guides should be examined, including licensing and bonding requirements for agencies and examination procedures for tour guides to ascertain if they meet appropriate standards. The extent to which local tour agencies handle inbound tours should be carefully examined. In some places, especially in newly developing tourism areas, inbound tours may be controlled by foreign operators to the detriment of local business; however, the local agencies must also possess the capability of handling tours efficiently.

Eating and Drinking Establishments

Restaurants, bars, and other types of eating and drinking outlets, both hotel associated and independent, that are designed for or could be patronized by a tourist clientele must be inventoried and evaluated. Considerations to be made include:
* Type and variety of cuisine offered;
* Quality level of food, drink, and service;
* Pricing levels of food and drink;
* Levels of hygiene maintained;
* Physical attractiveness and comfort level of the establishments; and

- Locations of the establishments relative to tourist accommodation locations and travel itineraries.

Depending on the type of tourist markets, the availability of alcoholic beverages may be a consideration in some places, especially where there are local religious restrictions (or prohibition) on consumption of alcoholic drink.

As mentioned in Chapter 4, in addition to satisfying normal tourists' demand for good quality meals, unusual or distinctive cuisine can be an important secondary attraction. Many tourists like to try the local cuisine, if different than that to which they are accustomed, at least once and often several times. Western tourists, for example, have discovered that many exotic cuisines, such as those of Asia and the Middle East, which have been developed over the centuries and utilize locally produced ingredients, have much to offer in the way of taste, smell, texture, and appearance. Also, unusual foods, such as the various wild game meats (usually raised on game farms) served in some East African restaurants in naturalistic surroundings, have wide appeal to tourists. An important consideration is that, because local cuisine utilizes locally produced ingredients, its use precludes the need to import expensive food items, thus bringing greater economic benefits to the area. Therefore, the survey should include the present availability and possibility of future development of local cuisine, including the feasibility, where necessary, of adapting it to the typical tourists palate but still retaining its distinctive character and use of local ingredients.

Tourist Information

Usually provided by the government tourism office but also by some hotels and tour and travel agencies, tourist information facilities and services must be surveyed and evaluated with respect to suitability of location, convenience of access, competence, knowledge, courtesy, and often foreign language capabilities of the personnel, and the type and suitability of printed material available. The availability of general background information and guide books about the area and their cost levels should also be investigated.

Shopping and Personal Services

Shopping facilities and services were referred to in Chapter 4 with reference to shopping as an attraction for tourists who want to purchase arts, handicrafts and souvenirs, specialty items such as fashion clothes and jewelry, and duty-free items such as liquor, tobacco, perfume, electronic, and optical items. Additionally important as a service to tourists is the availability of convenience items such as film, newspapers, magazines, books, and toiletries in shops that are easily accessible. Personal services such as barber and beautician shops and massage services should also be available. Evaluation should be made of the types of facilities, goods and services available, their location and convenience of access, and pricing levels.

Money Exchange and Other Financial Services

For international tourism, money exchange facilities and services should be evaluated with respect to convenience of location and type and quality of services offered, including at airports, railway stations, and other points of entry of tourists. Especially important is the speed and ease of money exchange services at airports where tourists are often in a hurry and have transportation waiting for them. Any special considerations to be made, such as convenience and ease of completing the foreign currency forms required by some countries and reconversion of currency on the tourists' departure from the country, should also be evaluated.

The acceptability by local hotels and other tourism enterprises of major credit cards, now used by many tourists, and of traveler's checks should be investigated to determine that, with proper identification presented by the tourists, these can be easily utilized. More generally, banking services need to be examined in terms of tourists being able to transfer money and, of course, for use by business travelers.

Medical Facilities and Services

Some tourists have endemic health problems, and accidents and other emergency medical problems can always arise; therefore it is essential that adequate medical facilities and services be available in the tourism area. The availability of qualified doctors and other medical personnel, properly equipped hospitals and clinics, and at least the common types of over-the-counter and prescription drugs must be surveyed and evaluated. For tourism in remote areas, there may be the need for permanent standby medical evacuation services. For some kinds of adventure tourism such as mountain climbing or river rafting, there is need for helicopter evacuation services, and scuba diving areas should have decompression chambers readily available. If existing medical facilities and services are not adequate for future tourism development, it is common for the tourism area government and often large hotels and resorts to provide these as part of their facilitation for tourists. Adequate medical care is also necessary for employees working in tourism, often a consideration when tourism is developed in remote areas.

Public Safety

As emphasized in Chapter 4, a reasonable level of public safety is a highly desirable precondition for tourism. Public safety facilities and services that should be considered include the extent, reliability, effectiveness, and honesty of the police force in tourism areas, security measures exercised at hotels and other accommodation establishments, fire protection services available for tourist facilities, and general capabilities of the tourism areas to maintain political stability and control terrorist actions. At the same time, tourists should be informed of any local security or crime problems and to exercise precautions when and where necessary, and the survey should include review of whether tourists are so informed as a routine procedure, such as in tourist information and hotel room brochures.

Postal Services

Adequate postal service is essential for tourism, both for tourists' use and the efficient operation of tourist facilities. Postal services should be evaluated with respect to their locational convenience, including provision of postal services in hotels, reliability of delivery time, protection against loss, and the efficiency and friendliness of postal clerks.

Entry and Exit Facilitation

For international tourism, the entry and exit facilitation procedures of immigration and customs should be evaluated with respect to adequacy of physical facilities, convenience and logical sequence of procedures, and honesty, friendliness, and efficiency of the personnel involved. The time required to pass through immigration and customs, often very long at some airports during peak travel periods, should especially be considered. Tourists' experiences at the point of entry is their first impression of the country, and it ideally should be a pleasant one. However, in evaluating facilitation procedures, it should also be realized that some regulations are essential, and the immigration and customs personnel must be strict in applying these.

Other Facilities and Services

For certain forms of tourism, other types of facilities and services may be required such as gasoline service stations, self-service laundries, and food stores for auto travelers and campers. For each area and type of tourism planned, the specific facility and service needs will need to be identified.

Survey of Transportation and Other Infrastructure

Importance of Infrastructure

The term 'infrastructure' in planning refers to those forms of construction on or below the ground that provide the basic framework for effective functioning of development systems such as urban areas, industry, and tourism. Adequate infrastructure is essential for the successful development of tourism and can be a particularly critical factor in less developed countries and regions, which often have limited infrastructure (Heraty 1989). Transportation facilities and services, water supply, electric power, sewage and solid waste disposal, drainage, and telecommunications are all components of the infrastructure typically required for development of tourism at its various levels. Proper development of infrastructure is also very important to maintain environmental protection from air and water pollution, congestion, and other types of environmental problems, and in achieving resource conservation such as recycling of sewage effluent to provide a supply of irrigation water for landscaping.

The basic infrastructure of an area that serves general community and economic development needs can often serve tourism with only moderate expansion and, in turn, infrastructure built or improved to serve tourism can serve general community needs. In fact, this multiple use of infrastructure with tourism helping to pay for infrastructure costs can be one of the socioeconomic benefits of tourism. However, in some cases such as for isolated resorts, it may be necessary to construct new infrastructure just for tourist facilities.

All types of infrastructure are surveyed and evaluated as part of the planning process in order to provide a basis for making recommendations on any improvements needed to bring the infrastructure up to standard for present use and to satisfy the future projected tourism patterns. Often there are existing plans for improvement and expansion of transportation and other infrastructure, and these plans must be evaluated with respect to present and future tourism needs. Any new facilities and services that are already approved and likely to be developed should be included in the survey and evaluation.

Transportation Facilities and Services

The major transportation considerations are access to the country or region and the internal transportation system, and the various modes of transportation to be considered by air, land, and water. Access to the country or region can be by various means. For long-haul travel and travel to remote locations and island destinations, air is typically the primary means of access. The survey and evaluation of air access facilities and services include:

- Adequacy of the airports, including the size, layout, efficiency of operations, passenger handling capacities, and capabilities and maintenance levels of terminal facilities;
- Number, lengths, bearing load capabilities, and maintenance levels of the runways;
- Existing origin, type, and frequency of air flights handled and total passenger capacities of present service with any particular problems such as undue delays or cancellation of flights noted; and
- Any plans for improvements of the facilities and changes or expansion (or reduction) of passenger flight origins, schedules, and passenger capacities. The safety records of flights destined for or originating from the airports and of the airlines serving the country or region should be examined.

Road automobile and bus, rail, and water access is also surveyed in terms of capacities, frequency of scheduled services, efficiency and maintenance levels of bus and rail stations and ship docking facilities, particular problems, and future plans. For any mode of transportation, evaluation of access must be related to the location of the major existing and potential tourist markets and capabilities to handle the numbers of tourists from those origin areas. For public transportation, it is important to evaluate the quality levels of comfort and service provided. Travel costs such as air fares must also be surveyed and evaluated within the context of comparable distance fares to other tourist destinations. Relative to access to the country or region, the cost, efficiency, and convenience of ground transportation services from the access points, particularly the airports that are often located some distance from the tourists' immediate destinations, should be evaluated.

The country or region's internal transportation system of airports and air services, roads and bus services, railways and rail services, water transportation, and any other types must be surveyed and evaluated with respect to its capability to serve present and possible future levels of tourism. Especially important to evaluate is access from the tourists' entry points to the tourism development areas, tourist attractions, and urban places. This evaluation should include quality and comfort levels and pricing as well as the types of facilities and services. The extent of integration of the internal transportation network including the different modes of transportation should be analyzed.

Locational mapping of the transportation network and its characteristics is necessary, and this mapping can include a system of grading the quality level of the network components. The transportation map can then be related to the mapping of tourism development areas and tourist attractions.

Other Infrastructure

Survey and evaluation of other infrastructure is generally done at the national and regional levels as a basis for determining overall availability and constraints and suitable policy recommendations for infrastructure development. However, even at the national and regional levels of planning, potential tourism development areas such as resorts and major attraction features need to be more closely examined with respect to the availability of local infrastructure in order to help determine their feasibility for development. It would be pointless, for example, to recommend a large resort in a desert area where there is no possibility of economically providing a water supply. The various components of other infrastructure are reviewed in the following sections.

Water Supply

Of the various components of infrastructure, after transportation access, water supply is the most critical because it depends on availability of a basic supply resource. Tourist facilities, especially accommodation and related landscaping and swimming pools, require large amounts for their effective operation. Both the extent and the quality of water supply or the resources for supplying water must be considered generally at the national and regional levels and more specifically for the tourism development areas.

If the present water supply systems are not adequate to serve projected future tourism development, then the water resources must be evaluated. The potential resources may include underground water, surface water from lakes, rivers, and catchment surfaces such as building roofs and airport runways, and desalination of ocean, sea, or brackish underground water. The development costs of alternative water resources will need to be evaluated. These costs may vary over time. For example, desalination techniques such as reverse osmosis are being rapidly improved and have been found to be cost effective for use in resorts if no other sources are available and is now being used in some Caribbean Island resorts. In some areas, a combination of water resources is the most efficient. In the Maldive Islands, for example, many of the small island resorts use a combination of the limited amount of available groundwater with roof catchment and storage of rainwater, supplemented during dry periods by desalination.

In addition to availability of water, the water quality levels and any need for treatment must be considered. If local water quality standards are not adequate, then international standards adopted by the World Health Organization (WHO) should be applied. Investigation should also be made of any water conservation and recycling techniques that currently are or potentially could be utilized in the planning area. For example, it is now common practice in resorts to recycle treated sewage effluent for use as landscaping and golf course irrigation water, and it is possible at greater cost to recycle effluent with tertiary treatment techniques for use as potable water. Other conservation techniques are sometimes applied, such as utilizing salt water for toilet flushing in water-deficient coastal or island resorts through installation of two separate water systems, although these may present their own special problems.

Electric Power

Electric power is also essential for most types of tourism development, but this component of infrastructure is more flexible than water supply because, if necessary, electric power can be generated on-site for tourist facilities and resorts, albeit sometimes at high cost. The overall electric power system of the country or region should first be surveyed and then more specifically analyzed for the existing and potential tourism development areas. In addition to the availability of electric power, the reliability of service, including voltage consistency, should be reviewed. Even with a reliable external source, most good quality hotels and resorts maintain their own on-site emergency power generation with sufficient output to supply at least the essential services.

The feasibility of utilizing energy conservation measures such as solar power for water heating should be investigated. Several hotels in the Pacific Islands, for example, use solar panels to supply the majority of their water heating energy needs. Also, as will be reviewed in Chapter 11, environmentally sensitive building design, such as open sided hotel lobbies (not requiring air conditioning) in tropical environments can be applied to conserve energy.

Sewage Disposal

Adequate disposal of sewage is essential in any area, including tourism areas, in order to prevent pollution of underground and surface waters and unpleasant odors. It was not uncommon, especially before environmental problems became an issue in many places, for beach hotels to discharge their sewage effluent into the immediate offshore water, often resulting in pollution of the water area in which their guests went swimming. The service area capacities, and quality of centralized sewage collection and treatment systems, if they exist in the tourism areas, should be evaluated with respect to their capability of serving present and projected future tourism development. If central systems have not been developed, the local disposal systems of existing facilities such as septic tanks should be examined to determine whether they are adequate or creating any pollution problems. If they are inadequate, then recommendations must be made on improvements needed.

Determination of appropriate sewage disposal techniques must be related to the scale and environmental situation of the development. Often, small-scale tourist facilities can utilize relatively simple septic tank and leaching bed disposal techniques, if soil conditions are suitable. Larger scale hotels and resorts require central sewage collection systems and treatment plants. Techniques for installation of satisfactory sewage disposal systems for hotels and resorts are well refined and available but become a cost factor that must be considered in tourist facility development.

Solid Waste Disposal

In order to prevent environmental problems, proper solid waste disposal must always be considered in the planning of tourist facilities. A survey should be made whether government operated solid waste collection and disposal systems exist, and their effectiveness evaluated. If no centralized system is available in the tourism areas, then the hotels and resorts will need to establish their own systems. Various techniques of solid waste disposal can be utilized depending on the local situation (for example, sanitary land fill if sites are available, and incineration or compaction, which still require, however, some place for disposal of the remaining material). Burning of solid waste is used as a source of heating and energy in some places, and recycling of at least some of the solid waste, which obviates the need for disposal and provides raw materials for a variety of uses, is becoming common practice. Often a combination of techniques is the most practical.

Telecommunications

Telecommunications are also essential for tourism, both for the operation of accommodation, touring services, and other tourist facilities and for tourists, especially business travelers, to use. Even very basic and remote resorts need some form of telecommunications for operational purposes and for any emergencies that might arise such as serious accidents by tourists or staff requiring medical treatment. Telecommunications include telephone, telegraph, telex, and recently, telefax (which uses the telephone system). In remote areas such as the Australian Outback, interior of Papua New Guinea and some Pacific Islands radio or radio telephone is utilized. The survey and evaluation should review the availability and reliability of telecommunications in tourism areas, with recommendations made on any improvements needed for present and future use.

Drainage

Proper drainage of the land is an important component of infrastructure, although usually a consideration only at the community level of tourism planning. Effective drainage precludes flooding during periods of heavy rainfall or when nearby rivers or lakes are flooding from rainfall elsewhere. Even in desert environments, the occasional rain can be very intense, leading to serious and sometimes destructive flooding. Drainage works are usually associated with roadways but in low-lying areas may require canals and special floodways.

Employee Housing and Community Services

Although not infrastructure in the usual sense, tourism employee housing and related community facilities and services such as schools, libraries, medical clinics, religious buildings, post offices, community centers, and retail shops must be considered in the survey and evaluation for tourism planning. If the tourism development is located in or near well-developed urban and town areas, there may be sufficient housing and community facilities for the tourism employees. But in remote areas or where the tourism development is large-scale, requiring many employees, new housing with adequate and integrated community facilities and services, as well as the basic infrastructure, will need to be planned and developed, whether by the public or private sectors.

Case Studies

The first case study is of the transportation survey and analysis for tourism development in Mongolia, a particularly important consideration because of the remoteness of that country in central Asia from its major tourist markets. The second study is of the accommodation survey and analysis for Cyprus, located in the eastern Mediterranean region, where tourism is already substantially developed, and accommodation was an important element of the background survey and analysis for the Cyprus tourism plan.

Transportation Analysis in the National Tourism Plan for Mongolia

The background of the Mongolia Tourism Plan (Shankland Cox 1989) was described in a case study in Chapter 4. Located in central Asia, Mongolia is an example of a newly developing tourism country that is situated at relatively long distances from its major market countries and has a large thinly populated land area and widely dispersed tourist attractions and destinations. Consequently, both external access and internal transportation facilities and services are key elements in the development of tourism. Important considerations in the transportation analysis were multi-use of facilities and services to serve both tourism and general needs, and incorporation of already planned expansion and improvement programs into the tourism planning process.

The plan first analyzed air access to and within the country. Figure 5.1 shows the existing and planned air routes. The single international airport is located near the capital city of Ulan Bator and was planned for improvement in 1990 to be capable of handling the largest civilian aircraft currently flying. International air access, crucial to developing international tourism, was available only from Moscow, Irkutsk, and Beijing in 1989, but new routes were planned to Warsaw or Berlin by 1990–91, Tokyo via Beijing by 1993, Singapore by 1995, and tentatively to one of the major Western European cities in the near future. The tourism plan endorsed the opening of these new international entry points in order to provide more direct service from potential tourist market regions and reduce reliance on the existing routes.

The flight frequencies and passenger capacities of the existing international air service were reviewed and determined to be deficient for the expansion of tourism, with the recommendation made that capacities be expanded either by increased flight frequencies or use of charter flights. Only two airlines—Aeroflot and MIAT (Mongolian Civil Air Transportation Corporation) served Mongolia in 1989, and MIAT is open for discussion of negotiating landing rights at the international airport to other airlines. This would be another approach to expanding the air passenger capacity needed.

Because of the long distances involved to reach some of the existing and proposed tourist attractions and destinations in Mongolia, including the Gobi Desert tourist camps, and the generally poor condition of the existing road system, internal air transportation is also very important for tourism development. As shown in Figure 5.1, MIAT operates internal flights from the international airport to domestic airports at all 18 provincial centers and to some other local airports. There are daily flights to these centers with additional flights scheduled during the summer tourism season. Helicopters serve otherwise inaccessible mountain areas. Plans are underway for improvements to the provincial airports where needed.

International rail service connects Ulan Bator to Moscow (via the Trans-Siberian Railway) and Beijing, with frequent (generally daily) service to Moscow during the summer (somewhat less frequent service during the winter) and weekly service to Beijing. Moderate use of rail access to Mongolia is made by foreign hol-

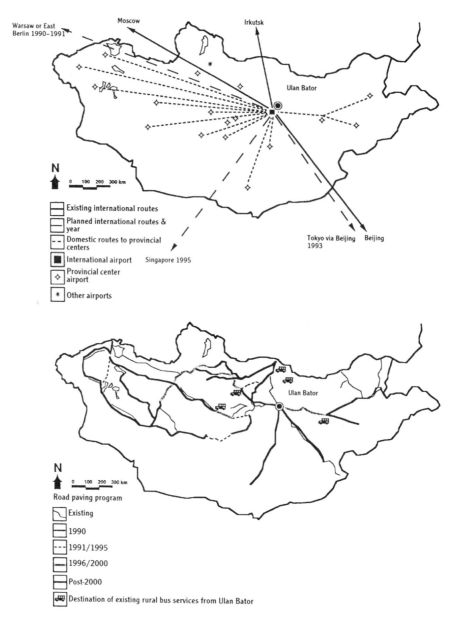

Figure 5.1. Tourism Plan for Mongolia—(top) Air Communications, (bottom) Road Communications.

iday tourists and most of the rail passenger traffic is comprised of Mongolians and foreign business travelers. Additional rail service could be provided should the demand increase, including arranging for tourist groups to charter complete trains.

The road system of the country is classified into a hierarchy of three levels:

1. Trunk or main roads linking the provincial and larger urban centers to one another and the capital of Ulan Bator;
2. Provincial roads distributing traffic from the provincial centers to the district centers of each province; and
3. Local roads providing a network of tracks connecting farms, collectives, and herding camps to the district and provincial centers.

Outside of the Ulan Bator region, the quality of roads is generally poor and difficult for use by tourists, which, as mentioned, forces reliance on the domestic air transportation system. The planning report indicates that, even in the case of using air transport, there are still problems in transferring to land-based transportation at some destinations. However, major road improvements are programmed, as shown in Figure 5.1, and these improvements are a major consideration in the planning and programming of tourism development projects.

The plan analyzed the long distance bus services where they were available and indicated that the government policy was to continue developing bus services where distances are generally not more than 200 to 300 kilometers and the road quality of acceptable standard. The plan suggested that, as roads are improved and bus services expanded, there will be the opportunity for more casual touring by tourists although journeys will still be long because of the distances involved. The plan also analyzed local transportation facilities and services of urban buses and taxis, mostly available only in Ulan Bator, pointing out the improvements needed to these for tourism, and emphasized the need for self-drive rental cars, at least in the Ulan Bator area, for use by tourists as tourism becomes less formalized.

Water transportation on the country's lakes and rivers was also analyzed in the plan, which indicated that there were virtually no facilities available for tourists to use this mode of transportation. However, a hydrofoil planned to be placed in operation on one of the lakes in the early 1990s will offer both high-speed access and sight-seeing opportunities for tourists in that area. The plan points out that, where future tourist facilities have ready access to rivers and lakes, boating for various purposes could become an important supporting activity to tourism.

Accommodation Analysis in the Cyprus Tourism Development Plan

Tourism planning in Cyprus offers an example of accommodation analysis in a developed destination that wishes to continue expanding tourism but on a more controlled basis. The Comprehensive Tourism Development Plan for Cyprus (UNDP and WTO 1988) was prepared in 1988 by international consultants in coordination with local subcontractors. Situated in the eastern Mediterranean, Cyprus is substantially developed with tourism and received 1,112,000 foreign tourist arrivals in 1988, based on the European and Middle Eastern tourist markets.

The primary attractions are the good beaches combined with the warm, sunny Mediterranean climate, with important secondary features of archaeological and historic sites representing a long and varied history. The interior mountains offer cooler temperatures, scenic forested landscapes, and interesting traditional villages. Most tourism development is concentrated in several places along the coast with some accommodation in the capital city of Nicosia.

The plan identified three major strategic objectives: 1) growth of tourism's contribution to the Gross Domestic Product (GDP), based on targets set by the national planning bureau; 2) protection of the environmental and cultural qualities of Cyprus; and 3) attraction of higher expenditure tourists. As indicated in the plan, the fast growth of tourism since 1974 has made Cyprus a mass tourism destination, causing severe environmental degradation of the coastal areas and some loss of cultural identity, and, recognizing the country is small with limited resources, steps should be taken to control the future growth of tourist accommodation and tourist arrivals. An integral part of the study involved conducting a carrying capacity analysis for tourism of the coastal region and recommending ways in which some existing tourism areas could be improved. It was seen that the third objective of attracting higher spending tourists would make it possible to increase tourism's contribution to GDP without excessive increases in accommodation and tourist arrivals that would further jeopardize the environmental and cultural qualities of the island.

Because of the existing major development of accommodation and its particular characteristics and influence on present and future tourism patterns, analysis of accommodation was an important component of the study. Various types of accommodation have been developed in Cyprus. At the end of 1986, there were 31,658 Cyprus Tourism Organization (CTO) registered tourist beds classified into hotels and hotel apartments and 10,270 beds in new classifications comprising type "C" hotel apartments, tourist villas, tourist apartments and furnished apartments originally in the unlicensed sector but that were recognized by the CTO at the end of 1986—a total of 41,928 registered tourist beds. In addition, there is an informal accommodation sector resulting from the considerable growth of the retirement and second home market, and it was evident that much of this is available for rental by tourists. It was estimated that in 1986, some 208,000 tourists, 24 percent of the total that year, stayed in this type of non-registered accommodation. Of these, 75,000 stayed in their own apartments or villas. The economics of renting this informal accommodation to tourists is not as critical as in the formal sector, because retirement and second home development is not normally based only on commercial viability.

Accommodation was analyzed in several respects. Hotels in Cyprus are classified into star categories from one to five, and hotel apartments are classified into the three categories of A, B, and C plus the categories of tourist villas, tourist apartments, and furnished apartments. The percentage of distribution of all the registered accommodation into the various categories was calculated by year from 1981 to 1986 in order to determine the trends in distribution mix as well as the overall growth and present distribution. Because of the approximate doubling of accommodation available between those years, this trends analysis was an important indicator of investor perception of market demand and, of course, the actual market demand. The growth and distribution of accommodation by type and category was calculated for each of the eight main tourism zones in the planning area of the island, which indicated the general types of tourist markets in each zone and the recent growth trends by zone. Accommodation size (that is, number of units such as number of hotels and blocks of apartments and average number of beds by type of unit and location by tourism zone) was calculated. The report indicated that the limited amount of five-star hotel development over the last five years (1981–86) and the small size of hotels in general are important indicators of the extent of local investment, with most hotel projects probably operating less efficiently than their counterparts in competing destinations where there would be greater economies of scale.

The form and layout of hotel development was analyzed by star category in terms of total area of sites and number of units to arrive at an average site area, and the total number of beds and average beds per unit to arrive at the average number of beds per hectare. This calculation was applied to each of the tourism zones. The results of the density analysis showed a traditional pattern with the higher category or quality of accommodation having the lower density of development for the hotels. Also, as would be expected, the more luxurious hotel developments occupied the larger sites. It was concluded that hotel development generally optimizes site areas more efficiently than hotel apartments. Densities are also influenced by the zoning regulations and other legal requirements. These density and other calculations were important indicators to determine future accommodation land use requirements and appropriate development standards.

The forms of accommodation development were evaluated: the higher class hotels generally occupy key sites adjacent to some of the best beaches in monolithic structures rising to eight stories and, in most cases, the lower category hotels and hotel apartments occupy the less desirable sites often rising to no more than two or three stories and in many cases with poor views and access to beaches. Development tends to be small in scale and not well integrated. Attempts have been made at adopting the traditional village types of layout concepts, but this has been difficult to implement due to the small sites involved, and often the nearby conventional accommodation detracts from these more innovative design approaches.

Land values for tourism development were evaluated and determined to be high due to speculation, especially in prime locations and in coastal areas and established tourism centers. Land values were determined for different types of sites—coastal prime, coastal average, hinterland, and downtown—for various tourism zones. The financial constraints of trying to develop high value land for hotels was reviewed, indicating the problems involved, especially for local investors with limited financial resources.

All the planned and committed accommodation development projects were determined, and the estimated increase in beds for each accommodation type for 1988 and 1991 in the formal sector was calculated. An evaluation was made of the extent of additional proposals that would likely be made during the late 1980s.

Other calculations that were made or that already existed and were incorporated into the accommodation analysis included the number of tourist arrivals staying in each type of accommodation, the average length of stay and number of bed nights for each type of accommodation, occupancy rates by type of accommodation, and bed to staff ratios by type of accommodation. The bed to staff ratios ranged from 1.86 for five-star hotels to 6.13 for one-star hotels, and from 4.49 for A class hotel apartments to 8.98 for C class hotel apartments. This calculation is important in determining future employment and training needs and the economic impact of employment. Occupancy rates were somewhat lower in hotel apartments than hotels, and much lower in tourist apartments.

The report indicated that much of the accommodation and tourism development generally is undertaken by many small investors and operators who tend to overdevelop in places, causing the natural amenities to become saturated during the high season. Furthermore, these types of investors are unable to cope financially with a fall in occupancy rates and handle cyclical market mechanisms as well as in other places. Therefore, allowing complete market freedom for development in Cyprus would be unwise. The plan report stated that it will be increasingly necessary in the future not only to construct more accommodation to meet growth but also to ensure that it concentrates on the needs of the higher-expenditure segments of the market and does not encourage the proliferation of narrow-based, traditional small to medium-size projects. The report concluded that a strategy based on controlled growth with stronger links forged between the private and public sectors is the most appropriate course of action for the future.

References

Heraty, Margaret J. 1989. "Tourism Transport—Implications for Developing Countries." *Tourism Management.* 10(4): 272–274.

Shankland Cox. 1989. *National Tourism Plan for Mongolia.* London and Hong Kong.

United Nations Development Programme and World Tourism Organization. 1988. *Comprehensive Tourism Development Plan for Cyprus.* Madrid: World Tourism Organization.

6

Planning Analysis and Synthesis

General Analysis Approach

As indicated in the planning process chart in Chapter 3, the three main aspects of the planning analysis are:

- Market analysis and projections of accommodation and other tourist facility needs and determination of the transportation and other infrastructure requirements. These factors then feed into the integrated analysis and synthesis.
- Integrated analysis and synthesis of physical (natural and built environment), social and economic factors, including tourist attractions and activities and present policies and plans, and establishment of general tourist carrying capacities at the national and regional levels. From this can be derived a summary of the major opportunities and constraints for developing tourism.
- Analysis of the institutional elements (which will be reviewed in subsequent chapters of this book).

As emphasized in Chapter 2, a basic approach applied in this book is integrated planning of all the components of tourism and of tourism into the total development patterns and plan of the country or region. Also important is environmental planning for sustainable development, which means that tourism, in the process of its development and operation, will not generate any serious environmental or social problems and that the resources for tourism will not be deteriorated or destroyed but permanently available for continuous use. The environmental approach implies that utmost consideration is given to conservation of the natural and built environment and to sociocultural patterns in the process of planning new development. It is at this stage of the planning process on planning analysis and synthesis that the integrated and environmental approach is particularly applied, in order to provide the necessary input to plan formulation.

The environmental planning approach is planning with nature and society and not against them. As emphasized in Chapter 2, this approach is particularly important because of the close relationship between tourism and the environment. The environmental approach requires that the planning team has a thorough understanding of the environment and society and the interrelationships of all their elements. Without this knowledge, it will not be possible to properly conduct the analysis and formulate the plan. However, even though the environmental planning approach is applied, it is still necessary to assess the environmental and sociocultural impacts of proposed tourism development and continuously monitor the impacts of tourism after development. This will make certain that any possible negatives impacts are minimized and the positive ones are reinforced, with remedial action taken to correct any problems that might arise.

Market Analysis

The market analysis defines the type and extent of tourist markets that can potentially and realistically be induced to visit the area and that the government, in setting its tourism objectives, desires to attract. With respect to the latter point, for example, it may be considered that certain types of tourists are not desirable. The so-called "hippie" tourists of the 1960s and 1970s were for various reasons deemed by some governments not to be the type of tourists they wanted and consequently that market was discouraged in those areas. Also, some governments do not want to develop gambling tourism because they feel that it may attract undesirable market segments as well as be socially detrimental to the local residents. In a highly product-led tourism development approach, the market analysis will be based only on those market segments that are attracted to the inherent natural and cultural attractions of the area.

From the standpoint of planning tourism development, the market analysis results in tourist arrival projections or establishment of market targets in terms of the number, type, length of stay, and other characteristics of tourists by time periods. This is essential input to planning the tourist attractions and activities, facilities, services, transportation, and other infrastructure required. The market analysis also provides the basis for formulating the marketing strategy and promotion program. Market analysis techniques are not treated in-depth in this book because marketing is a major subject treated in other references, but the tourism planner should be aware of the basic approaches to market analysis.

Projection Techniques

Various tourist projection techniques are used:
- Time series or straight-line projection of past growth trends if there is some tourism already developed in the area;
- The experience of tourism growth elsewhere in similar tourism situations;
- Market segmentation and catchment analysis;
- Global and regional trends; and
- Tourist destination capacity or receptivity analysis.

The most effective approach and one commonly used is market segmentation, which refers to the process of grouping together people of similar characteristics, origins, and desires for travel experiences. However, historical growth trends in the planning area (for a partially-developed tourist destination), global and regional trends, experience of similar destinations, and capacity analysis must also be considered. Capacity or receptivity analysis is very important in determining the maximum number of tourists that can be adequately handled without serious environmental or social problems resulting or the tourist destination being perceived as less desirable by the tourists. A later section of this chapter explains carrying capacity analysis.

Market segmentation analysis is typically based on the four factors of:
- Socioeconomic or demographic segmentation, which categorizes tourists based on their socioeconomic characteristics such as age, education, and income levels.
- Product-led segmentation, which relates the types of tourists to the particular tourism products such as attractions and facilities that the area has to offer or can potentially offer.
- Psychographic segmentation, which involves grouping tourists by their attitudes, interests, life-styles, and travel motivations.
- Geographic segmentation, which groups tourists by location of origin as related to the time-distance and cost of traveling to the tourist destinations, and also considers the environmental and cultural contrasts and similarities between the origin and destination. Obviously, the accessibility factor is of utmost importance, but it also must be considered in relation to the first three types of market segmentation. For example, affluent adventure or special interest tourists may travel a long distance at high cost to reach their desired destinations.

Consideration must also be given to special factors such as cultural affinities that motivate some tourists to visit places where they or their ancestors originated or places of similar cultural values (this perhaps can be placed under product-led segmentation). Competitor analysis (that is, relative merits of the tourism product and its cost in competing destinations) is also an important element of the market analysis. The market analysis provides the basis for making the projection of tourist arrivals by number, characteristics, types of travel interests, and length of stay. The projections are usually made for specified time periods, usually for each five years of the life of the plan.

Special Considerations in the Market Analysis

A common approach used by the WTO and other agencies is to establish market targets, which refers to the number and types of tourists that the area can realistically attract if certain actions are undertaken (for example, provision of more frequent air service from the market countries, improvement of some major tourist attractions, organization of interesting tour programs, development of new accommodation, and implementation of a market promotion program). This approach is particularly relevant to newly developing tourism areas where such actions are essential to attract and handle tourists. The targets, if adopted officially, give the government and private sector a specific objective to aim for and an incentive to undertake the necessary actions and investment.

Market projections or targets depend on many variables that are only partially predictable, including international economic conditions and their impact on travel. Consequently, it is common practice to establish a range of high and low projections or targets, based on different growth assumptions, that will still satisfy the objectives of tourism development and provide a sufficiently accurate basis for preparing a program of facility development. Often the mid-range projection is used for planning purposes. The high and low ranges can be adjusted through periodic review of market trends.

Experience has shown that market projections or targets may be valid during the long term, but the time period of realizing the demand level of tourists may need to be adjusted. For example, a market target for 1995 may actually be reached in 1998 but otherwise be valid. With this relatively minor type of deviation, the important task for the tourism planner is to adjust the development program to maintain a balance between the facility development and the market demand levels, so that there is not a waste of investment resources resulting from underutilized facilities or a constraint imposed on satisfying market demands by limited facilities. However, this balance is not always easy to maintain as evidenced in even mature destinations such as Hawaii and Singapore, which frequently experience either an oversupply or undersupply of hotel rooms.

For long-term changes in market trends, planning should allow for future adjustments through staging of development. At the national level, for example, development of a new tourism region can be delayed until there is sufficient market demand; at the regional level, a new resort need not be developed until justified by increased market demand; and at the resort level, a proposed new hotel or hotel expansion need not be constructed until demand warrants.

The focus of market analysis here is an input to the preparation of the tourism plan. However, because of the rapid development of tourism and new tourism products and the competitiveness of this sector, continuing market research can be an important element in product development for an area (Hodgson 1990), as well as for any adjustments necessary to the promotion program.

Determining Tourist Facility and Infrastructure Needs

Based on the market analysis and determination of the projected or targeted number and types of tourist arrivals and their estimated average length of stay, the number and type of accommodation and other tourist facilities, services, and the infrastructure needed in the future can be calculated.

Accommodation Projections and Land Area Requirements

The formula for projecting accommodation and an example for average annual and high season demand are set forth below. This example is only for one type of tourist market and accommodation; the formula should, of course, be applied to each of the market segments and related types of accommodation to arrive at a total accommodation demand for the country or region.

Demand for beds
The formula is:

$$\frac{\text{No. of tourists (per time period)} \times \text{average length of stay (in nights)}}{\text{No. of nights (per time period)} \times \text{accommodation occupancy factor}}$$

For example, to calculate annual demand:

$$\frac{100{,}000 \text{ tourists per year} \times 7 \text{ nights}}{365 \text{ nights} \times 75\% \text{ occupancy}} = \frac{700{,}000}{274} = 2{,}555 \text{ beds}$$

For example, to calculate high season demand:

$$\frac{50{,}000 \text{ tourists per 4 months} \times 7 \text{ nights}}{120 \text{ nights} \times 95\% \text{ occupancy}} = \frac{350{,}000}{114} = 3{,}070 \text{ beds}$$

Demand for rooms
The formula is:

$$\frac{\text{No. of beds demand}}{\text{Average room occupancy (persons per room)}}$$

For example, to calculate annual demand:

$$\frac{2{,}555 \text{ beds}}{1.7} = 1{,}503 \text{ rooms}$$

For example, to calculate high season demand:

$$\frac{3{,}070 \text{ beds}}{1.7} = 1{,}805 \text{ rooms}$$

Allowance should be made for the percentage of tourists staying in noncommercial accommodation such as with friends and relatives. If this factor is, for example, 5 percent, then 95 percent of 100,000 tourists in the above example would be used as the number of tourists for calculating accommodation needed. Any existing accommodation can be subtracted from the total demand figures to arrive at additional accommodation required, but realize that all or some of the existing rooms stock may need to be upgraded or otherwise modified to meet future project demand. New accommodation requirements are projected by time periods, based on the tourist market projections, to provide the basis for development programming.

The assumed factors for average annual and high season accommodation occupancies will vary from place to place depending on the profitability break-even points in different areas and types of accommodation and the amount of profitability above the break-even points to be assumed. Obviously, a higher occupancy factor implies greater profitability; it has been said that a vacant hotel room is a wasted resource forever. The 1.7 factor for average room occupancy is one that often applies to resort holiday oriented accommodation in which most rooms are occupied by two or more persons. For business oriented hotels with many single room occupancies, this factor would be lower, perhaps about 1.2.

As shown in the example, the seasonality factor must be taken into account and the beds/rooms demand calculated for the high season months. It may be considered uneconomic to develop a sufficient number of rooms for the short-term peak period, perhaps only a few weeks or a month each year, which would result in a lower year-round occupancy factor. The demand will be calculated to achieve an acceptable annual average occupancy rate realizing that tourist demand cannot be totally met during the high season. In the example given above, a rather extreme case of seasonality, provision of a sufficient number of rooms to meet peak season demand would result in an average annual occupancy of about 62 percent, which would be marginally financially acceptable to many hotel investors on long-term basis.

A tourism area with an inherent seasonality of its primary attraction, such as a beach resort with a cold winter season or a rainy monsoon period or a ski resort with a warm summer season, should also be selected for its opportunities for off-season activities such as conferences, special events, and different types of recreation. The ski resort of Aspen, Colorado in the USA, for example, has developed a very strong summer season with numerous meeting, seminar, and summer activities. Other techniques such as offering discounts on transportation fares and accommodation rates are commonly employed to attract tourists during a the low season. For very high peak periods that happen only very occasionally, such as when a special major event is being held, an approach for providing additional accommodation is allowing and encouraging private householders to take guests in their homes.

Although both beds and rooms are used as a unit measure in different countries, the accommodation room seems to be a preferable type of unit to use because the number of beds per room can vary from time to time whereas the number of rooms is more fixed. Also, from an economic standpoint, the rate difference between single and double room occupancy is not greatly different nowadays, and most rooms are of a standard size designed either for single or double occupancy with little difference in construction and operating costs between the two.

The accommodation projection is used as a basis for projecting general land area requirements because, except for the place-specific tourist attractions, accommodation is the component of tourism that requires the most land. Land area requirements are first projected in a preliminary manner and should be carried out in conjunction with the carrying capacity analysis. The market analysis, accommodation projection, and determination of land area requirements may need to be modified based on the carrying capacity analysis, evaluation of economic, environmental, and sociocultural impact evaluation, the tourism policy adopted, and other considerations. At this analysis and plan formulation stage of the planning process, there is continuous feedback taking place before reaching the optimum balance of development and market patterns.

The total amount of accommodation projected is translated into total land area requirements by applying density standards based on the type of tourism to be developed, as indicated in the tourism objectives and policy. The total land area requirements are then allocated to the various selected tourism development areas based on the results of the integrated analysis and carrying capacity studies. For example, if there is a calculated need for 10,000 accommodation units of various types during the life of the plan, and it is determined, based on the market analysis, that 1,000 of these should be situated in urban areas to primarily serve business travelers, 500 should be allocated to mountain lodges for wildlife and nature tourism, and the remaining 8,500 units should be located in medium to low density beach resorts at an average density of 20 units per hectare (including provision of extensive recreation facilities), then 425 hectares of suitable beach resort land will be required, at one or several locations. By applying appropriate density standards to the urban and mountain lodge units required, the land area requirements can be calculated for those types of development. These figures then become inputs to the policy and plan formulation.

Other Tourist Facility and Service Requirements

The projection of other tourist facilities and services needed such as tour and travel agencies, restaurants, medical facilities and services, and postal services is not as straight-forward to calculate as are accommodation and land area requirements. This projection will depend to a great extent on the type of tourism being developed. For example, sight-seeing tourism will need more tour handling facilities and guide services than resort-based tourism, while resort tourism will require development of more local recreational facilities such as golf courses. The existing level of facility and service development, much of which serves general community needs as well as tourism, is also an important consideration. Standards for projecting other tourist facility and service requirements can best be derived by the planners from similar types of mature destination areas. However, the projections must be flexible to allow for changing circumstances of the expected tourist flows.

If only a modest level of tourism development is being planned and the existing community and commercial facilities and services are well developed, only limited additional development of them will be required, and the government and private sector can respond to these needs without undue stress. If these facilities and services are not well developed or major tourism growth is projected, then the plan and development program must make provision for their future development. Some of these facilities and services can be provided within the hotels and resorts and are considered at the detailed level of planning. A major requirement at the national and regional level is to establish standards, adopt necessary regulations, and sometimes provide incentives for their development at the community level, and to plan for the skilled manpower to perform the services needed. These factors are examined in later chapters of this book.

Transportation Requirements

As explained in Chapter 5, the two aspects of transportation facilities and services to be planned are access to the country or region from the major market areas and the internal transportation system that connects the access points to the tourism development and attraction areas, along with consideration of the various possible modes of transportation. Based on the market analysis and projection of tourist arrivals, length of stay and seasonal distribution, likely tourist activities and travel movements within the planning area, and recommended transportation modes to be used, it is possible for the transportation planner to estimate future tourist traffic demands on the transportation system.

With respect to analyzing access requirements to the country or region, the market analysis will have indicated the present and expected future volume of tourist flows from the various market origin countries or regions. The number of tourists coming on multi-destination tours and therefore perhaps from a different point of origin than their own countries will also need to be considered. If there is only one type and point of access, such as an airport, the transportation planner's primary concern will be the air passenger capacities and frequencies of flights from the tourists' points of origin. From some places, there will be transfers involved between the points of origin and destination that must be taken into account, although these should be kept to a minimum as much as possible. Frequency of flights must be considered in addition to total capacities because tourists obviously want to have maximum convenience of arrival and departure times. Also, the seasonality factor must be calculated to determine the demand during the high and low seasons. Often, additional scheduled flights must be added during the peak period, or charter flights may be required to supplement the scheduled ones.

Based on these calculations of tourist demand and considering normal non-tourist traffic demands, total future passenger demand can be projected. Also, with knowledge of the air service policy adopted by the government of the area, policies of airlines serving the area, types of airplanes and their capacities being used at present and likely to be available in the future, and air routes and other relevant factors, future requirements for air service can be determined. That determination and the projected passenger flows in turn provide the input needed to decide on airport facility requirements. It may well be that, based on this analysis, the planning team will recommend changes to air and other transportation policies if tourism is to be effectively developed.

If there is more than one access point (for example, two airports, or also seaports and land or rail access), the market analysis of origin and destination will provide the basis for determining tourist flows and their seasonality through the different access points, always allowing for flexibility to account for changing market trends. Then the analysis is the same as for a single access: giving consideration to passenger capacities on various transportation modes, frequency of service, and seasonal variations to arrive at the future transportation needed. For land travel, capacities of bus and rail service can be calculated and projected, and tourist flows by automobile can be translated into road capacity needs. If cruise ship tourism is envisaged, passenger flows are projected, and the types and capacities of ships are assumed as a basis for determining port facility requirements. Non-tourist demand must, of course, be included in this analysis.

Internal transportation analysis considers both the network of the transportation system, including roads, rail, regional and local airports, and sea, river, and lake ports, and the system's passenger or tourist carrying capacities. The network is reviewed with respect to connection of the tourist access points to the tourism development regions or areas where the attraction features, accommodation, and other facilities and services are located. In consultation with the tourism planner, the transportation planner will need to project the tourist movements through the country or region and relate that to the network and its present capacities in order to determine future improvements that may be required, either in the basic network or the capacities of the network. General traffic demand must, of course, be considered, and in fact, on major routes of the network, general traffic may be much greater than tourist traffic.

For all aspects of the transportation system, utmost consideration in the analysis must be given to the quality of transportation facilities and services as well as the quantitative factors. The analysis should include evaluation of whether any improvements are needed in safety standards, schedule reliability, comfort levels, efficiency, convenience, and the competence and quality of customer relations of personnel involved, in order to meet tourists' needs and expectations.

As indicated previously, many areas already have had transportation plans prepared, including traffic demand projections, and these should be reviewed with respect to the tourist traffic projected in the tourism plan. If tourism has not been taken into account in the preparation of these transportation plans, they will need to be modified accordingly. In long-range planning, new and improved forms of transportation and changes in transportation network system approaches will need to be considered. For example, the relatively recent development of long-range jumbo jet airplanes that can overfly places where air flights previously had to stop for refueling, such as Anchorage, Alaska and some Middle Eastern cities, have changed the tourism patterns of those places. Also, deregulation of airlines, commencing in the USA in the 1980s, has affected routes and fares. The current use of the hub and spoke system approach to air routes, which involves major airports serving as hubs receiving long-distance, high-volume traffic and distribution of passengers on the spoke routes by smaller planes to regional and local destinations, may be more widely adopted in newly developing tourism areas and affect transportation patterns.

Other Infrastructure Considerations

As examined in Chapter 5, other infrastructure for tourism includes water supply, electric power, sewage and solid waste disposal, drainage, and telecommunications. At the national and regional planning levels, precise calculation of other infrastructure requirements is typically not necessary, but it is an important consideration with respect to determining the overall availability of existing or feasibility of providing future infrastructure, selecting tourism development regions and areas, including resort sites, and establishing the standards of infrastructure planning and engineering design at the more detailed level. The planning team's infrastructure planner will prepare the general analysis required as input to the overall plan preparation.

Water supply is typically the most critical component in terms of availability. The other infrastructure can usually be provided through adequate investment in facilities and services. The demand for water supply to serve tourism development varies greatly depending on the type of development and environmental situation. A large beach resort with swimming pools, extensive landscaping, and a golf course located in a hot desert environment will have a much higher demand than a single hotel in a wetter, cooler area, or a campground. Individual daily tourist consumption of water will range from 50 liters for camping sites to 800 liters and sometimes more in a large desert resort.

In the selection analysis of tourism development areas such as resorts, the number of accommodation rooms projected along with the type of resort envisaged will indicate the water demand. The analysis then proceeds with an investigation of whether a sufficient water supply can be provided at an economically justifiable cost. If an adequate water supply is not feasible to develop, then another resort site will need to be found. If a limited water supply is available, the type and size of resort to be developed will need to be modified.

For other infrastructure requirements, demand analysis is prepared in the same manner, utilizing international standards, as the water demand projections. The analysis should include investigation of whether existing systems' capacities are sufficient to absorb the additional demand generated by tourism, to what extent and at what cost the capacities will need to be increased, or whether new systems (for example, of electric power generation and distribution or centralized sewage collection and treatment) will be required and whether the costs will be justified.

The cost analysis must consider both the initial installation and operational costs. The cost benefit analysis should include both the economic costs and benefits (that is, costs and benefits to the society and economy in general from the investment made in infrastructure) and the financial costs and benefits directly related to the infrastructure project itself if the financial costs are to be recovered from payment of user fees. Some major infrastructure such as airports, highways, and water supply systems may be economically beneficial to tourism and society in general and therefore is often provided by the government as an incentive for private sector investment in facility development, but it may not be financially feasible based on its own direct revenues.

The analysis should also investigate the possibilities for conservation of infrastructure and resources, for example:

- Alternative energy sources such as solar, wind, geothermal, ocean thermal, and wave and tidal action;
- Desalination of salty water for potable use;
- Recycling of sewage effluent to produce water for landscaping and golf course irrigation and potable use;
- Use of surface catchment and storage of rainwater;
- Various water use conservation techniques to reduce consumption demand;
- Recycling of solid waste material for reuse and burning of the material for heating and power; and
- Use of fiber optics for telecommunications and satellite communication techniques.

Integrated Analysis and Synthesis

Analysis of physical, social, and economic factors and evaluation and existing development policies and plans are conducted with reference to their relationships to tourism. Along with the survey and evaluation of tourist attractions, activities, facilities, services, and infrastructure, they are basic inputs to formulation of the tourism plan. This analysis should be integrated and synthesized so that the analysis of each factor is related to the analysis of all the other factors and their interrelationships are understood. The word synthesis means "the putting together of parts or elements so as to form a whole" and is an important concept in planning analysis.

Analysis Approach

The physical elements to be analyzed include:
- Characteristics of the natural environment such as climate, topography, hydrography, vegetation and wildlife, and important ecological systems;
- Significant resource areas such as lands of high agricultural capability and economically viable mineral deposits;
- Land use and settlement patterns;
- Existing and already planned accommodation, tourist facilities and services; and
- Existing and already planned transportation facilities and services, and other major infrastructure.

These, with the location-based tourist attraction features, are shown on maps, often together on one or a few maps in order to see and analyze their interrelationships. The map overlay technique can be used manually or, if the technology is available, computer map analysis can be applied. Thus it can be seen, for example, whether existing or planned roads will provide effective access to the attractions and potential tourism development areas, whether there will be compatibility between possible tourism development or attraction areas and important agricultural or mineral resource areas, and whether there will be any problems presented by the existing or planned location of urban or industrial areas with possible attraction features or tourist resort sites. These will, of course, be major considerations in formulating the tourism plan to ensure that tourism development is integrated into and compatible with overall development patterns.

The integrated analysis will indicate, for example, the climatically desirable areas for tourism development and places that are environmentally developable as related to location of major tourist attraction features and transportation network. An important aspect of the analysis is establishing carrying capacities that, because of its importance, is reviewed separately in the next section of this chapter. Analysis of land tenure patterns will identify any particular problems of tenure that may arise in making sites available for tourism development, and will provide the basis for determining the best approach to securing the availability of development sites or conserving certain types of attractions. Sometimes, the land tenure analysis will provide the basis for recommending more equitable distribution of land ownership among development sites so that no one owner receives most of the benefits of appreciated land values.

The analysis of economic patterns will indicate the type and distribution of economic activities and the types, levels, and location of employment and unemployment. It will also identify areas that are economically depressed and therefore need new development such as tourism. Social patterns are analyzed with respect to population distribution, age-sex profiles, education levels, and population projections in total and by area that, along with the economic patterns analysis, will indicate the type and location of where future labor supply will likely be available or deficient. Some of this economic and population data can also be placed on the map overlays.

The sociocultural analysis will also identify any particular patterns or attitudes that may influence the type and location of tourism development, as well as be input into formulating the sociocultural program. For example, the prevailing attitude in some areas may be for rapid growth of tourism while, in other places, the residents may not want to have any tourism or desire only limited development. There may also be the danger of tourism disturbing social systems in some traditional cultural areas. Consideration should be given to not developing tourism in those places or developing only certain types of very limited scale tourism during the foreseeable future.

The existing physical, social, and economic policies and plans need to be reviewed for policies that may influence tourism planning, and for proposed development projects such as new roads, urban expansion, and industrial areas. Both compatible and possible conflicting aspects of the policies and plans should be identified and, where relevant, included on the analysis maps.

There has been some, although not a great amount, of research done on regional analysis of tourism resources. For example, Smith (1987), based on research in Canada, describes a procedure for defining tourism regions on the basis of country-level resource patterns and identifies four basic structures: urban tourism, outdoor recreation, cottaging/boating, and urban fringe tourism. His conclusion is that actual tourism regions are more complex and somewhat different than the simplified regions that had been defined by the government.

Identification of Opportunities and Constraints

A useful technique often applied at this stage of the planning process is to identify the major opportunities and problems or constraints for developing tourism, based on the integrated analysis, including the market analysis and carrying capacity studies. There is sometimes the danger of becoming so involved in the details of the survey and analysis that the perspective on important issues is lost if it is not built into the planning process. Identification of the major opportunities and constraints can help the planners focus attention on those matters that should be emphasized in the policy and plan formulation. However, identification of opportunities and constraints should still give utmost consideration to achieving balanced development, meeting environmental and social as well as economic objectives.

Major opportunities may, for example, include:

- An outstanding or unique type of tourist attraction that should be given priority in development and marketing;
- Some highly successful existing tourism development that should be retained and reinforced;
- A particular market segment with much potential that should be promoted as a marketing advantage;
- A well-developed infrastructure component that can be utilized for tourism; or
- A highly motivated service-oriented labor supply that can be tapped for tourism.

Major constraints to be overcome may, for example, include:

- Difficult access to the area requiring air routing, capacity, and airport improvements;
- Cumbersome visa and travel facilitation procedures requiring a change in government immigration procedures;
- Possible negative environmental or social impacts resulting from certain types of tourism development, necessitating careful environmental planning and controls;
- A poor market image of the area, requiring a special marketing campaign;
- A limited number of existing tourist attractions that need to be augmented by special types of attractions; or
- Poor quality existing accommodation that requires upgrading.

Establishing Carrying Capacities

Carrying capacity analysis is a basic technique now commencing to be widely used in tourism and recreation planning to systematically determine the upper limits of development and visitor use and optimum utilization of tourism resources. As defined by Mathieson and Wall (1982, 21), carrying capacity "is the maximum number of people who can use a site without an unacceptable alteration in the physical environment and without an unacceptable decline in the quality of experience gained by visitors." To this definition should be added, "without an unacceptable adverse impact on the society, economy, and culture of the tourism area." Establishing carrying capacities is based on the concept of maintaining a level of development and use that will not result in environmental or sociocultural deterioration or be perceived by tourists as depreciating their enjoyment and appreciation of the area. There are numerous examples of carrying capacities being exceeded in tourism areas in the Mediterranean region and elsewhere, especially those places that were developed some years ago without the benefit of good planning, with consequent environmental degradation and loss of some tourist markets. The importance of incorporating carrying capacity analysis into the tourism planning process has been emphasized, for example, by McCool (1978), Getz (1983), O'Reilly (1986), and Romeril (1989) despite some difficulties in establishing precise means of measurement and standards. The approach taken in this book is that, even though there is always some impreciseness involved in determining carrying capacities and variable assumptions must be made, the basic concept is a sound one. Carrying capacity analysis provides an essential guideline to be used in formulating the tourism plan at any level.

At the national and regional planning levels, carrying capacities need to be established generally for the planning area (usually based on analysis of the specific major attraction features, development sites, and sometimes tourist transit points) and calculated more precisely for each development site at the community planning level. As mentioned, by establishing upper limits on development and therefore the number of tourist arrivals (or more accurately the number of tourist days), the carrying capacity analysis will provide feedback to the market analysis, so that any necessary adjustments can be made to the market projections or targets. It may be found, for example, that the area cannot reasonably absorb all the tourists who potentially could be attracted. As indicated in the market analysis section, tourist destination capacity or receptivity analysis is one of the considerations in projecting tourist markets.

Carrying capacities can be established for both undeveloped tourism places and those that are already developed and perhaps even reaching or exceeding their saturation levels. In fact, it is often the existing tourist destinations, which are commencing to suffer some environmental or social problems of overdevelopment or unsuitable development, that have become concerned about establishing carrying capacities through the planning process and want to apply some controls on and often redirect their tourism development. It obviously is much better to anticipate and plan for optimum development levels than allow saturation to be reached and then take difficult and often expensive remedial measures.

It should not be assumed that carrying capacity constraints are confined to the more developed countries and areas. A popular but remote destination may experience various types of capacity constraints. Visitor use at Machu Picchu, a major Inca archaeological site in the Andean region of Peru, is constrained by the passenger capacity of the rail access, and the limited amount of accommodation at the site and the ruins themselves cannot absorb vast number of visitors without suffering congestion and perhaps environmental damage. In the case of the Galapagos Islands, located in the Pacific Ocean 600 miles west of Ecuador and known for its unique species of wildlife, the Ecuadorean government established highly controlled tourism based on the carrying capacities of cruise ships, boats, and the small island hotels. This maintained visitor use at safe levels to protect the irreplaceable wildlife and, at the same time, visitor expenditures were utilized to support conservation for scientific research purposes (Gee, Makens, and Choy 1989, 165–166).

It is not uncommon that countries or regions will relate the number of tourist arrivals to the number of inhabitants in the area, using this as a simple type of carrying capacity analysis. Because determination of realistic carrying capacities depends on analysis of the many elements of the physical and sociocultural environment and the type, activities, and length of stay of the tourists, the actual capacity levels may be more or less than the population level of the area depending on these other factors. Trying to establish ratios between resident population and number of tourists is simplistic and naive but, after proper research to arrive at reasonable capacity levels, translation of the results into population/tourist ratios can be a useful technique for publicizing the reasonable capacity levels and gaining political and public acceptance of this concept.

Measurement Criteria of Carrying Capacity

The measurement criteria presented here are for establishing carrying capacities primarily for tourist destination areas although the capacities of the transit zones,

zones, that is, the transportation facilities and services used by tourists traveling from the generating areas to their destinations, are also important to analyze in the transportation component of tourism planning. The approach explained here is a basic one and taken from WTO literature (WTO 1983).

In determining carrying capacity, the two aspects to be considered are:

- The indigenous physical and socioeconomic environment—This refers to the capacity that can be achieved without resulting in damage to the physical (natural and man-made) environment and generating sociocultural and economic problems to the local community, and maintaining the proper balance between development and conservation. Exceeding saturation levels may lead to either permanent damage to the physical environment or socioeconomic and cultural problems, or both.
- The tourism image and tourist product—This refers to the capacity or number of visitors that are compatible with the image of the tourist product and the types of environmental and cultural experiences that the visitors are seeking. If the tourism development area becomes saturated, the very attractions that visitors come to experience may be destroyed or degraded, and the destination will decline in quality and popularity.

With respect to the indigenous environment, the criteria for determining optimum capacity levels include the following:

- Physical:
  1. Acceptable levels of visual impact and congestion;
  2. Point at which ecological systems are maintained before damage occurs;
  3. Conservation of wildlife and natural vegetation of both the land and marine environments; and
  4. Acceptable levels of air, water, and noise pollution.
- Economic:
  1. Extent of tourism that provides optimum overall economic benefits; and
  2. Level of tourism employment suited to the local community.
- Sociocultural:
  1. Extent of tourism development that can be absorbed without detriment to the sociocultural life styles and activities of the community; and
  2. Level of tourism that will help maintain cultural monuments, arts, crafts, belief systems, customs, and traditions without detrimental effects.
- Infrastructure:
  1. Adequate availability of transportation facilities and services;
  2. Adequate availability of utility services of water supply, electric power, sewage and solid waste disposal and telecommunications; and
  3. Adequate availability of other community facilities and services such as those related to health and public safety.

The criteria that can be applied in determining carrying capacities relative to tourism image or visitor satisfaction levels include the following:

- Physical:
  1. Overall cleanliness and lack of pollution of the destination environment;
  2. Lack of undue congestion of the destination environment, including of tourist attraction features;

   3. Attractiveness of the landscape or townscape, including quality and character of architectural design; and
   4. Maintenance of the ecological systems and flora and fauna of natural attraction features.
- Economic:
   1. Cost of the holiday and 'value for money.'
- Sociocultural:
   1. Intrinsic interest of the indigenous community and culture;
   2. Quality of local arts, handicrafts, cuisine, and cultural performances; and
   3. Friendliness of residents.
- Infrastructure:
   1. Acceptable standards of transportation facilities and services;
   2. Acceptable standards of utility services; and
   3. Acceptable standards of other facilities and services.

Each area and its type of tourism is unique, and the criteria for measuring carrying capacity must be specifically defined for the area. The evaluation of carrying capacity based on the criteria selected will in some cases be measurable (for example, levels of environmental pollution and employment benefits) and in certain cases they will establish maximum levels (for example, limited water supply), but many criteria such as impact on cultural traditions can only be assessed qualitatively.

The analysis of the final carrying capacity levels must establish a balance among positive and negative factors and hence the volume of tourism that will bring optimum benefits to the country or region, the local population, and the tourists themselves to maintain their satisfaction levels. Decisions may need to be made on trade-offs of various costs and benefits. Some areas will give greater weight to physical factors while others will place priority on socioeconomic ones, but at least the decision will be made based on systematic analysis. However, certain of the criteria, such as water supply or availability of developable land, may set a maximum level of development even though the maximum capacities based on other criteria are not reached.

Seasonality is an overriding consideration in the concept of carrying capacity. The threshold or saturation level of visitor use of a destination usually is reached only during the peak periods of use and not during the low season or on an average annual basis. Therefore, the peak tourist demand period must be considered in calculating carrying capacities. Related to this factor, as referred to in a previous section, is the decision whether to develop sufficient accommodation and other facilities and services and infrastructure to satisfy the peak demand period even though much of this capacity may lie idle during the remainder of the year. The peak period use level of development may also impose burdens on the environment even when it is not being utilized during parts of the year. As pointed out previously, there are techniques that can be applied to reduce the peak demand period and even-out seasonality, thus also reducing peak environmental impacts as well as being economically beneficial.

Complicating the analysis of carrying capacity for some of the criteria is that the physical level of damage and the residents' and tourists' perceptions of satu-

The Alhambra in Grenada, Spain (above) and Place of the Lions in the Alhambra (right)—This Moorish-built thirteenth century fortress and palace is one of the most visited historic sites in Spain by both international and domestic tourists. Careful control of visitor flows through the complex must be exercised so that its site carrying capacity is not exceeded at any particular time. (Courtesy of the Spanish Ministry of Information and Tourism)

ration levels may all be different. Tourists may accept a higher saturation level in terms of crowding, for example, than do residents, or the actual level of environmental damage may exceed both the residents' and tourists' perceptions of environmental problems. Also, perceptions of congestion vary among cultural areas of the world. As a generalization, Southern Europeans will tolerate more congestion and closer interpersonal spaces than do Northern Europeans and most North Americans, and some Asian societies accept higher congestion levels than do Europeans and North Americans.

Carrying capacity analysis does not replace environmental and socioeconomic impact assessment of destination areas or continuous monitoring of the impacts of tourism. Impact assessment should still be done as a complementary action to carrying capacity analysis, providing another technique of ensuring that capacities are not exceeded and especially to detect specific impact problems that may have been overlooked in the capacity analysis. With the application of any technique, none of which is infallible, monitoring of impacts with any necessary remedial action taken is essential.

Capacity Standards

Some carrying capacity standards are expressed statistically in terms of number of visitors using the various tourist attractions, facilities, and services. These standards vary from one place to another, depending on the type of tourism being developed, the local environmental characteristics, the types of tourist markets aimed for, and the local community perceptions of saturation levels. It is impossible here to indicate all the carrying capacity standards that might be applicable in tourism planning. However, the parameters of some of the commonly used standards for visitor usage are reviewed here.

The capacity of beaches is probably the most studied of all tourism capacity standards, in part because they are one of the most important types of tourism resources and have too often been overdeveloped. Beaches are easily measured in relation to the length of sea frontage and the depth. In some countries, techniques have been used to take into account other factors such as accessibility, the quality of beach, underwater features, and hinterland topography by a graded evaluation. Various standards apply to beach capacity, depending on the local situation. For example, in the Mediterranean region, there is high beach usage whereas in tropical beach resorts, tourists spend much of their time around swimming pools in shaded areas rather than on the beach itself. Beach capacity can vary from 1.7 square meters per person in the Netherlands and 3 square meters per person in Spanish resorts to densities lower than 30 square meters in tropical resorts (WTO 1983). A common capacity standard utilized for good quality resorts is 10 square meters of beach area and 1 meter of beach frontage per person using the beach. Beach turnover is approximately 1.5 to 3 persons per day with fewer than 25 percent of users swimming and the rest lying on the beach. Based on the assumed usage and capacity standards, the total number of tourists that can be absorbed by a beach-oriented resort can be calculated.

Some standards for rural and recreation activities are cited by the WTO (1983) as follows, expressed in visitors per day per hectare except where noted:

- Forest park: up to 15.
- Suburban nature park: 15–70.
- High-density picnicking: 300–600.
- Low-density picnicking: 60–200.
- Sports/team games: 100–200.
- Golf: 10–15.
- For water-based activities:
    1. Fishing/sailing: 5–30;
    2. Speed boating: 5–10; and
    3. Water skiing: 5–15.
- For nature trails in persons per day per kilometer
    1. Hiking: 40; and
    2. Horse riding: 25–80.
- For ski resorts, a general guide is 100 skiers per hectare of trailways.

For measuring air, water, and noise pollution and infrastructure development thresholds, specific standards are available and can be calculated based on the number of tourists using the facilities and the assumed tourist usage of the facilities and services. Conservation of ecological systems and flora and fauna is quantifiable based on the conservation objectives established. Economic impact measures can be quantified while social impact measures and congestion levels are more qualitative and must be established based on the characteristics and desired threshold levels in each particular tourism area. Visitor use of tourist attractions is examined in more detail in Chapter 10, and tourist facility development and design standards are reviewed in Chapter 11.

In formulating the tourism plan, the study team will need to establish capacity standards applicable to the particular planning area, considering its environmental, sociocultural, and economic characteristics, the existing and planned infrastructure, the type of tourism being proposed, attitudes of residents, types of tourist markets, the experience of similar tourism destinations elsewhere, and its own best judgment. Based on monitoring of the first stage of development, the standards can be adjusted later if necessary.

Case Studies

Case studies of various kinds of planning analyses are presented. The environmental analysis in the tourism plan for Malta examines characteristics of the natural environment and resource areas. In the regional planning analysis of Bali, Indonesia, environmental, resource, and accessibility factors were the critical elements. For thermal spa selection analysis in Hungary, several criteria were applied. In the carrying capacity study of Goa, India, beach capacity was the primary criterion with consideration also given to other factors.

Environmental Analysis in the Malta Tourism Plan

The background of the Maltese Islands Tourism Development Plan (Horwath and Horwath 1989) was described in Chapter 3. An aspect of the environmental analysis of the Malta plan was the preparation of a composite map showing the environmentally sensitive areas and development constraints, as indicated in Figure 6.1. This analysis is important not only for helping determine the suitable types and locations for tourism development and use so that tourism does not generate ecological problems, but also forms the basis for preparing and adopting an envi-

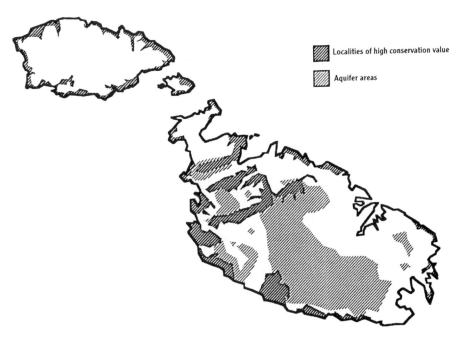

Localities of high conservation value

Aquifer areas

Figure 6.1. Maltese Islands Tourism Development Plan—Environmentally Sensitive Zones and Development Constraints.

ronmental law for the country, applicable to all types of development. Because of Malta's small size and limited remaining natural areas, environmental conservation is particularly urgent.

The environmentally sensitive areas were delineated based on several criteria:

- Agricultural classification—Lands of good agricultural capability that should be retained for agricultural use;
- Ecological (flora and fauna)—Lands that contain important flora and fauna that should be preserved;
- Geological—Areas of important geological features that should be preserved;
- Entomological—Areas important as insect habitats; and
- Ornithological—Areas important as bird habitats, including stopping points for migratory birds.

The map also shows the location of underground water aquifers where any development permitted should have strict controls applied so that groundwater recharging capability is not impaired nor the groundwater polluted. Because of limited water supply in the islands, maintenance of groundwater resources is essential.

Resort Area Selection Analysis in the Bali Tourism Plan

Based on its rich cultural traditions, scenic beauty, and good beaches, Bali, Indonesia has become one of the major tourist destinations in Southeast Asia. Recognizing the potential for developing tourism in Bali and also the importance of carefully planning this sector to control environmental and cultural impacts, a major tourism study was undertaken in the early 1970s. The Bali tourism planning project, assisted by the UNDP/World Bank, was conducted in phases, with the first phase being preparation of a comprehensive regional tourism development plan (SCETO 1970), including selection of a site for development of a large new resort. Later phases related to detailed planning and implementation of the resort, as well as implementation of several other aspects of the regional plan. Utmost consideration in all the planning phases was given to environmental and cultural conservation. The later planning phases and the implementation process were carried out through the 1970s and 1980s and will continue into the 1990s.

The regional analysis shown on Figure 6.2 was directed to determining suitable areas for the proposed resort development. At the regional level, three criteria were applied as shown on the maps:

- Map No. 1—Areas of major economic activity. These are areas of intensive irrigated rice cultivation based on highly fertile volcanic soils, major urban areas, and other land uses that should not be preempted for tourism development.
- Map No. 2—Areas not physically suitable for tourism development. These are hilly and mountainous areas and volcanic lava fields, which would be expensive and environmentally damaging to develop.

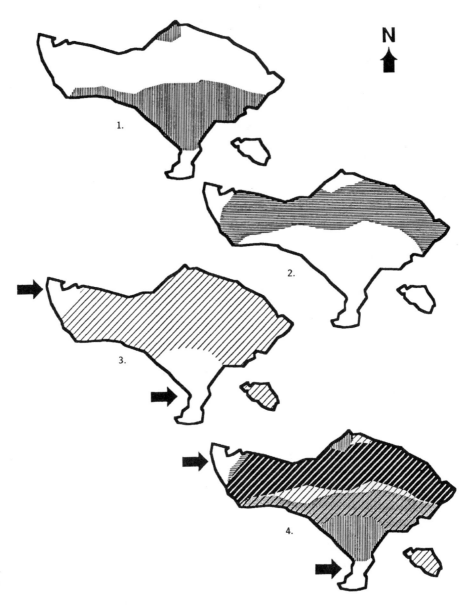

Figure 6.2 Bali Tourism Plan—Resort Area Selection Analysis.

- Map No. 3—Areas distant from the tourist entry points. The two entry points to the island are the ferry terminal connection with Java (and linking the road networks of Java and Bali) at the west end of the island and the international and domestic airport in south-central Bali. Areas that are too distant from these entry points (about one hour's driving time) for convenience of tourist access were designated as not suitable for major tourism development.

Map No. 4 is a composite of the first three maps and shows the areas that, according to the criteria, are suitable for resort development—only the western and south-central parts of the islands. The area actually selected was the south-central tip, the Bukit Peninsula, which is near the international airport where most of the international tourists arrive and is also easily accessible to the main urban center and provincial capital of Denpasar and the the various tourist attraction features concentrated in this part of Bali. The Bukit Peninsula is comprised of rather rough limestone topography with no surface drainage and is not suitable for intensive agriculture. The exact resort site was selected at Nusa Dua Beach on the east side of the peninsula.

Thermal Spa Locational Analysis for Hungary

A detailed comprehensive study of planning for the use of thermal water in recreation and tourism was prepared as a United Nations/Government of Hungary project in the mid-1970s and described in a subsequent publication (Grove 1977). Although already somewhat developed, thermal spa tourism had potential for considerable improvement and expansion in the country but required a systematic planning approach to achieve this expansion. One of the the challenges of the project was to determine the most suitable places for development out of the thousands of potential spa sites in the country. Along with this task was the need to integrate spa development into the overall regional and local development patterns and establish land use and design guidelines for suitable development of the spas. This case study focuses on the nature of the project—its objectives, the planning process and levels of planning applied, and the approach used to select the most suitable sites for development as a national network of spas. The project was viewed as being investment-oriented for the first-stage proposals made, with recommendations made on suitable guidelines for the detailed planning, implementation, and management of the thermal spas and associated facilities.

The principal objectives of planning for the development of spas were specified in the study as follows:

- Enrich Hungary's general tourist attraction by providing widespread opportunities for thermal bathing;
- Increase the volume of domestic and international tourists and their contribution to the national economy;
- Further develop therapeutical tourism as a distinct sector of thermal tourism;
- Achieve a better geographical distribution of tourist activities;
- Lengthen the tourism season;
- Induce a large number of transit tourists to spend some time in the country; and
- Stimulate economic and social development in less advanced regions.

The project was national in scope but focused on a single resource—thermal water—and on only one type of uses of that resource—in tourism and recreation.

The general aim of the project (as distinct from the objectives of development set forth above) was to give the government and district authorities a decision-making framework for planning the use of thermal water in tourism and recreation. The planning process applied by the team to accomplish the project was:

- Assess the nature and extent of the given resource and its potential for the stated use;
- Identify the likely demand for thermal water facilities in tourism and recreation;
- Establish the conditions under which the resource could be successfully exploited to meet the demand;
- Prepare broad guidelines for the use of thermal water in tourism and recreation—its planning, development, and management;
- Prepare physical proposals in differing degrees of detail for different time horizons; and
- Explore the socioeconomic results and impact of the proposed development.

The above list of tasks was embodied in three levels of planning used for the programming of the project activities and its major outputs:

- Strategic planning with a long-range perspective;
- Proposals for the first stage of development; and
- Model plans for four thermal resorts and a design manual for all future developments.

Hungary uses planning horizons of one year for short-term plans, five years for medium-term plans, and fifteen years for long-term planning, with the most important planning period being the medium-term, which corresponds to the national five-year development plans. The recommended first-stage development projects in this planning were related to the national five-year planning period (as is usually the case in tourism planning projects).

In the approach to spa site selection, a comprehensive survey and analysis of thermal resources and associated attractions, infrastructure, settlement patterns, and other factors was initially conducted. Out of the some 3,200 thermal sites in the country, 2,240 sites were first identified based on their being accessible. The next task was to choose from among the accessible 2,240 places those worthy of detailed study. The crucial selection criteria were decided based on the concept that the potential of thermal water in recreation and tourism will mostly be realized through its association with other attractions. The most important attractions were considered to be a pleasant general setting with a desirable microclimate and specific nearby features such as historical monuments, views, opportunities for sports, and so on.

Utilizing the analysis of the survey information and application of these criteria, 352 places (of the accessible 2,240 thermal water sites) were selected. However, these were still considered to be too many for formulating a comprehensive but realistic network of thermal spas covering the whole country. Therefore, a second stage of selection was required. This was applied based on the following criteria:

- Characteristics of thermal water supply and existing bath facilities;
- Environmental quality of the area;

- Capacity and use of existing tourist facilities;
- Infrastructure, urban services and housing conditions; and
- Population characteristics.

Because of the large volume of data involved, a computer program designed to rank the places in order of suitability for designation or further development as thermal resorts was used. Before applying the computer analysis, the project team eliminated those places where thermal water was understood to be too deep for economical drilling. This reduced the number of places from 352 to 300. The ranking by computer showed that the 300 settlements lay on a fairly smooth curve, with no distinct thresholds at which suitability for development increased sharply. So the project team determined that, based on the team's general understanding of the nature of an appropriate network and its estimation of the resources likely to be available, about 120 spa sites would be required, the top two-fifths of the computer print-out. Based on further investigation of the actual sites, 118 places were selected. These were divided into three categories according their potential range of attraction: 1) international and national; 2) regional; and 3) district. The 118 selected spas were then further analyzed for selection of 31 first-stage development sites, and finally 4 places were selected for model detailed planning. Figure 6.3 illustrates this process of selecting the thermal site settlements.

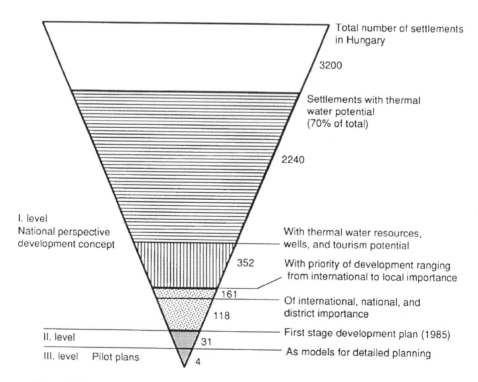

Figure 6.3. Process of Selecting Settlements for Three Levels of Planning in Hungary.

Further analysis of the geographic distribution of these 118 places with more than local significance revealed a number of fairly distinct clusters, which led the project team to group and map the thermal resorts into a number of zones. The establishment of planning zones facilitated organizing relationships among the different places in the national network. These zones were not proposed to become units for statutory planning or development control but, rather, were convenient areas for deciding at the strategic level the distribution of various facilities required for thermal tourism. The zones were then utilized for regional level planning of the thermal resorts.

Tourism Carrying Capacity Study of Goa, India

The regional tourism carrying capacity study for the state of Goa, located on the west-central coast of India facing the Indian Ocean, was conducted in 1989 (WTO 1989) along with assessment of the social and environmental impacts of tourism and preparation of guidelines for control and planning of further development of this sector in the region. This study provided immediate guidelines for tourism development and was important input into the proposed preparation of a comprehensive regional tourism plan to be carried out for the state in the early 1990s. Occupying some 3,700 square kilometers, with a coastline of 106 kilometers of which about 65 kilometers consists of sandy beaches, the state of Goa is home to about 1.1 million inhabitants. The metropolitan access to Goa is via road and air from Bombay in the north, although the local airport also handles international air traffic including charter flights organized for international tour groups.

The state already has substantial tourism development and attracted more than 850,000 tourists in 1988, the majority of whom are domestic travelers. Most of the existing accommodation is beach oriented and concentrated in the central area of the region, with some new beach resort development taking place in the southern area. The tourism resources in Goa are comprised of extensive beaches and a scenic natural environment of lush vegetation of palm groves along the coast and forested inland hills and mountains and some wildlife combined with the distinctive cultural patterns of arts, crafts, and music and highly interesting religious and historic buildings. Goa was a Portuguese colony for several centuries and left a cultural heritage that is unique in the country. Old Goa with its sixteenth century European styled buildings and ruins is a major attraction feature, and a more general attraction is the Goan architectural style of churches, houses, and other buildings found throughout the state. Important Hindu temples and Islamic monuments are also significant attractions. With the exception of a few limited areas of underwater currents, the sea is safe for swimming and other water recreation activities. Also, a major water sports facility and national training complex was being planned for development in the early 1990s. The government policy is for the controlled expansion of tourism for both domestic and international tourists.

The climate is coastal tropical with warm year-round temperatures, a distinct monsoon season of high rainfall from June to September, relatively high humidity, and about 250 days of sunshine annually. Domestic tourists visit Goa throughout the year with some decrease during the monsoon season, whereas there is a definite seasonality of foreign tourist arrivals with the low arrival season during the monsoon period and the peak season during November through January.

In formulating the carrying capacity study, first it was determined that the major attraction of Goa for holiday tourists is the quality and extent of beaches, as reflected in the fact that, except for some small mountain lodges, virtually all new tourism development is taking place along the coast. Although tourists visit the natural and cultural attractions located in the inland areas, they stay in beach-oriented accommodation, all of which are situated within day tour time-distance from the beach hotels. Therefore, the beaches and their adjacent lands along with labor supply capabilities, infrastructure capacities, and social impact evaluation were the primary considerations in this carrying capacity analysis.

Based on the seasonal distribution of tourist arrivals and the fact that the majority of domestic tourists do not make intensive use of the beach for swimming but prefer shopping and visiting other areas, it was estimated that an average density of 40 square meters of beach area per tourist bed would be an appropriate standard in assessing beach carrying capacity. Assuming an average width of sandy beach of 40 meters, application of that standard means that not more than one bed per running meter of beach should be developed. Additionally, it was decided that not more than 70 percent of the beach or 46 out of the 65 kilometers should be developed, in order to:

- Protect the general landscape character of the area, with particular reference to the vegetation of coconut trees, as well as other aspects of distinguished coastal configuration;
- Protect the coastal villages and their surrounding areas, so that villagers can continue their customary daily activities without disturbances;
- Avoid ribbon or continuous development along the coastline, but instead encourage development to take place in groupings with adequate natural vegetation in between;
- Avoid disfigurement of the coastal character because of building activities; and
- Cater also for the recreational and other needs of the local inhabitants.

Application of the standard of one meter of beach frontage per tourist bed to the 46 kilometers results in an overall regional maximum development level of 46,000 tourist beds.

As 30 percent of beds of lower rate levels are expected to be constructed in places not directly facing the beach and sea, not more than 35 kilometers of beach frontage are expected to be actually utilized for development. This pattern will result in a density of about 57 meters of beach area per tourist bed in accommodation fronting the beach although tourists stay in non-beach oriented accommodation will still make some use of the beaches. As mentioned, because many domestic tourists as well as local residents do not use the beach intensively, it is unlikely that the number of people on particular beaches on any day will exceed the above densities. Even when a concentration of users occurs at the popular beaches on peak use days, the densities will not likely drop below 10 square meters per person, a level that is considered acceptable both in this region and internationally.

Based on assumptions made of future accommodation occupancy rates (75 percent for domestic tourists and 50 percent for foreign tourists) and average length of stay (4 to 5 days for for domestic tourists and 15 days for foreigners) and a ratio of 80 percent domestic and 20 percent foreign tourists (aimed at increasing the proportion of foreign tourists through marketing and product development strategies), the 46,000 beds allowed would imply a level of approximately 4.1 million tourist arrivals annually, almost five times the 1988 level of tourists visiting the region.

Based on assumptions of direct employee requirements of 1.0 employees per bed (about 2.0 employees per room) in the upper classes of hotels and .4 employees per bed in other classes of accommodation (slightly less than 1.0 employees per room) and an assumed distribution of types of accommodation based on the types of tourists attracted, the direct tourism sector employee requirement was calculated to be 60,000 persons, and the indirect employee requirement was calculated to be 300,000 (only twice the present number because of assumed greater productivity of workers in this sector in the future). Based on the present level of underemployment and unemployment and projected growth of population and employment in other sectors of the economy, it was determined that an adequate labor supply will exist to serve the projected level of tourism development. In fact, one of the major reasons for developing tourism is to provide this substantial amount of employment.

With respect to the social impact evaluation of tourism, the approach used in this study was to calculate the ratio of the average and peak daily number of tourists to the resident population within the tourism development (that is, coastal) areas. This was found to be within the range of major tourism areas elsewhere in the world. Another important consideration was the fact that the great majority of tourists in Goa are currently and will continue being domestic vistors of people of similar cultural backgrounds and customs to the Goans. The future demand for water supply for the projected level of tourism was calculated, based on an average consumption of .8 cubic meters per day per bed for a total 36,800 cubic meters maximum demand. It was determined that an adequate water supply would be available in the state to serve both tourism and general community needs, based on existing and proposed water development schemes. However, the report recommended that water conservation techniques be applied, including recycling of sewage effluent for use as irrigation water. Similarly, other infrastructure requirements of electricity, sewage and solid waste disposal, telecommunications, and the transportation system were determined to be adequate for tourism in the future if infrastructure development and improvement programs are undertaken as needed, but current deficiencies, such as in the telephone system, were noted in the report.

The other sections of the report on environmental and social impact assessment and development controls examined those areas in detail and made recommendations for specific actions and controls needed.

References

Gee, Chuck Y., James C. Makens, and Dexter J. L. Choy. 2nd ed. 1989. *The Travel Industry*. New York: Van Nostrand Reinhold.

Getz, Donald. 1983. "Capacity to Absorb Tourism: Concepts and Implications for Strategic Planning." *Annals of Tourism Research*. 10(2): 239–263.

Grove, David. 1977. *Hungary's Unrivalled Leisure Resource—Planning the Use of Thermal Water in Recreation and Tourism: An Account of a United Nations/Hungarian Regional Development Project*. Budapest: Bureau of the Regional Development Planning Project.

Hodgson, Peter. 1990. "New Tourism Product Development: Market Research's Role." *Tourism Management*. 11(1): 2–5.

Horwath and Horwath, Inc. 1989. *Maltese Islands Tourism Development Plan*. London.

Mathieson, Alister, and Geoffrey Wall. 1982. *Tourism: Economic, Physical and Social Impacts*. New York: Longman.

McCool, Stephen R. 1978. "Recreation Use Limits: Issues for the Tourism Industry." *Journal of Travel Research*. 17(2): 2–7.

O'Reilly, A. M. 1986. "Tourism Carrying Capacity: Concepts and Issues." *Tourism Management*. 7(4): 254–258.

Romeril, Michael. 1989. Tourism and the Environment—Accord or Discord? *Tourism Management*. 10(3): 204–208.

Smith, Stephen L. J. 1987. "Regional Analysis of Tourism Resources." *Annals of Tourism Research*. 14(2): 254–273.

SCETO. 1970. *Bali Tourism Plan*. Paris.

World Tourism Organization. 1983. *Risks of Saturation or Tourist Carrying Capacity Overload in Holiday Destinations*. Madrid: World Tourism Organization.

———. 1989. *Tourism Carrying Capacity Study—Goa, India*. Madrid: World Tourism Organization.

7

Tourism Policy and Plan Formulation

Forms of Tourism Development

In formulating the tourism development policy and plan, it is important to understand the different forms and physical types of tourism development that can be considered for the country or region. Although there is a wide variety of tourism development forms throughout the world, these can be categorized for convenience of explanation and planning. The forms considered here are those that represent the planned development approach although they often also have developed spontaneously (but usually with problems resulting from lack of planning and development controls). In many cases, various different forms are appropriate in a single country or region, depending on the specific resources, locations, tourist markets, tourism policies adopted, and other factors involved.

Resort-based Tourism

One of the most common forms of modern holiday tourism is some type of resort-based development. A tourist resort can be defined as a destination area that is relatively self-contained and typically provides a wide range of tourist facilities and services including those designed for recreation and relaxation. Because of the present trend of tourists increasingly wanting to participate in recreation, sports, and cultural activities, resorts are expanding the variety of facilities and services that they provide. Resort-based tourism does not preclude tourists from taking tours of the local area and spending some time outside the resort. The two principal forms of resorts are integrated resorts and town resorts.

Integrated Resorts

Integrated resorts, including holiday villages, are planned developments for virtually exclusive use by tourists, although employees may live in or near the resorts, and are oriented to particular features such as a beach, lake and marine recreation areas, ski slopes, mountain scenery, national parks or major natural features, major archaeological or historic sites, a healthful climate (for health resorts), championship golf courses or other important sports facilities, and sometimes a combination of these. Integrated resorts may vary in size from one hotel to several hotels and other types of accommodation totaling thousands of rooms, and typically are self-contained, including various tourist facilities and services of a commercial center or facilities, recreation and sports facilities, sometimes cultural facilities, and perhaps a conference center or major meeting facilities in the hotels.

Some integrated resorts contain a wide range of accommodation from various types of hotels and cottages to self-catering apartments, townhouses, and villas. The self-catering units may be lived in by retirees, be second vacation homes, or be available for rent to short-term visitors. Resort configurations can vary from intensive high-density development with tall buildings to medium and low density, low profile types. Extensive open space and landscaping are typically an important element of planned resorts. Although planned at one time as integrated developments, actual construction may take in stages over a long period of time depending on market and other conditions. Hawaii, for example, is well known for the several large integrated resorts on its various islands, some that are still undergoing staged development. Planned resorts are being developed in many areas of the world.

Town Resorts

A town resort combines the usual land uses and activities of a town community but is economically focused on resort activities and contains hotels and other types of accommodation and tourist facilities and services. This type of resort is also typically oriented to a specific attraction feature such as snow skiing, a beach, lake and marine recreation, spa facilities, mountain scenery, a desert climate, important archaeological and historic sites, and religious pilgrimages. There are, for example, many ski, beach, and spa resort towns in Europe and North America, beach resort towns in Australia, and spa resort towns in Japan. The hill stations developed during the colonial period in South and Southeast Asia also function as town resorts.

Retreat Resorts

Although a form of integrated resort, the so-called retreat resorts that are becoming popular in various parts of the world, such as the Caribbean and Pacific Islands, warrant special consideration. These are small-scale, perhaps only 25–50 rooms, but often high quality planned resorts located in remote areas such as on small islands or in the mountains. The only access may be by boat, small airplane, or narrow, winding road. Retreat resorts cater to guests who wish a quiet, isolated vacation environment but usually with some recreation activities available. Remote hunting and fishing lodges often function as retreat resorts. Because of their specialized character and often high development and operational costs, retreat resorts require careful feasibility analysis before they are developed and selective marketing after development.

Urban Tourism

This very common form of tourism takes place in large cities where tourism may be important but is not a primary activity of the urban area. Hotels and other tourist facilities and services are an integral part of the urban fabric and serve both holiday and business travelers. However, location of hotels and other tourist facilities is still an important consideration in planning urban tourism, especially as they relate to the transportation system and major attraction features. The tourist attractions are typically ones that are visited and used by residents as well as tourists. It is now common practice to develop or redevelop certain urban areas, such as historic districts, oriented particularly to tourism and residents' leisure use. Conference and convention facilities are often developed in cities to attract more tourists.

Special Interest and Adventure Tourism

Special interest tourism refers to tourists, usually in small group tours, who are traveling to learn about and experience particular specific features related to an area. These special interest themes are often associated with the tourists' long-term avocational or vocational interests. Special interest tourism can focus on a wide range of features from cultural manifestations of dance, music, fine arts, handicrafts, architecture, traditional ways of life, unusual economic activities, archaeology and history, aspects of nature such as flora, fauna, geology, national parks, and marine environments to those related to the tourists' professional interests. Being resource based, the conceivable types of special interests is virtually infinite.

Related to special interest tourism is adventure tourism whereby the tourists engage in physically, personally challenging and sometimes dangerous (or perceived to be dangerous) activities such as safaris in remote areas, trekking and hiking, mountain climbing, river rafting, and white water boating through river rapids. Hunting and fishing may be considered as an aspect of special interest and adventure tourism.

Special interest and adventure tourism does not require large-scale or even greatly expensive development of facilities and infrastructure. However, careful organization, knowledgeable guide services, some integrated transportation facilities and services, and at least basic accommodation and catering facilities are essential. If they are available, some types of special interest tourists may utilize high quality facilities and services. Special interest and adventure tourism is one of the rapidly expanding types of tourist markets and tourism development.

Water Transport Tourism

Water transportation-based tourism has considerable potential in some places and is generally a rapidly expanding form of specialized tourism. Water transport tourism is very much resource based and depends on availability of navigable waterways and imaginative development.

Cruise Ship Tourism

Cruise ship tourism, important for many years, is now taking some new configurations and can be significant in some coastal areas. It is also a technique of opening up new tourism areas that do not yet have onshore tourist facilities and infrastructure. As mentioned previously, a popular form of cruise ship tourism today is the "fly-sea cruise" tour whereby the tourists fly to a major city in the region that they intend cruising, embark on a cruise ship, often a medium-size one, cruise the region for several days or weeks, and then disembark and return home by air. Medium size cruises, with shore stops at various islands are well developed in the Caribbean and Mediterranean seas and elsewhere. It is also common practice, as mentioned, for cruise passengers, at their option, to include some overland travel to visit major attraction features, as part of the cruise tour. Large round-the-world type cruises also still operate.

Specialized 'adventure' cruises are popular with certain market segments. These were initially developed by the Linblad organization and now are being emulated by other companies. These are relatively high cost cruises to such exotic places as the Antarctica and the Galapagos Islands. Small ship adventure cruises are being developed in such places as the Southeast Asian islands. These small ships accommodate about 30–50 passengers and specific cruises may be oriented to a particular theme related to the culture or natural environment of the area they are cruising, that is, special interest tourism.

Lake cruises also have potential in some areas such as the lakes of eastern and southern Africa, the Great Lakes of North America, Lake Titicaca in South America, and the Black and Caspian seas of Eurasia.

River and Canal Tourism

River boat tourism involves tourists taking river boat cruises with accommodation and meals provided on board the boat. River boat tourism has been developed, for example, on the Mississippi River using historic type paddle boats, as a type of nostalgic tourism, and the Nile River. The tourism experience is related to both the cruise itself with scenic views along the river course and shore stops at interesting places. River tourism also offers the possibility of opening up remote areas to tourism with appeal to adventure and special interest tourists. Bangladesh, for example, as a riverine country is considering developing river boat tourism. Old canal systems offer the potential for houseboat vacation travel such as been developed recently in the northeastern USA and northern Europe. River rafting and canoeing, often with overnight camping alongside the river, can be considered a special form of river transport tourism as well as recreation.

Yachting Tourism

In some coastal and island ports that are located in interesting sailing areas and possess protected anchorages, yachting tourism may have potential for development. Although limited in scale, yachting is becoming more popular and yachtsmen may spend weeks or months on their cruises with frequent and often long shore stopovers. Also becoming common is fly-sea yachting arrangements that involve the yachtsmen flying to a seaport, renting a yacht for one or two weeks for local cruising, and then flying home. Yachting is well developed in the Mediterranean and Caribbean regions and is starting to become popular in the Pacific Islands region.

Residential Tourism

Residential tourism refers to cabins, houses, villas, townhouses, and apartments that are developed expressly as vacation or retirement homes, and often include a combination of these in one development. (As mentioned, vacation and retirement homes are commonly major components of large integrated resorts.) Although not strictly a type of tourist, retirees who have purchased or rent homes in a retirement community or resort away from their original homes, function somewhat as tourists through their expenditures and activities and bring economic benefits to the area. Some countries, for example, in the Mediterranean region, promote the retirement of foreigners in their areas for economic reasons. Some of the states in the USA that have warm, sunny climates and recreation opportunities have encouraged development of large retirement or senior citizen communities.

Vacation or holiday second homes have become a common form of tourism development in North America and Europe and is commencing elsewhere. Although staying in their own accommodation, vacation home tourists still make some local expenditures and pay property taxes, and their homes may be rented to other tourists during part of the year. Described in Chapter 5, condominium ownership is common for vacation and retirement homes in some areas.

Alternative Forms of Tourism

The term alternative tourism, also called responsible, appropriate, or, as recently suggested at a conference on alternative tourism (Nash and Butler 1990), sustainable tourism, is used to refer to small-scale, non-conventional, non-mass specialized forms of tourism that are socially and environmentally sensitive and respectful, as opposed to conventional forms of mass tourism such as large resorts. Although the forms of tourism typically identified as 'alternative,' 'responsible,' or 'appropriate' are important and should be considered in many tourism development planning studies, the terminological meanings are rather ambiguous (although no more suitable term has yet been found) and are used in this book to reflect popular usage by tourism specialists to refer to particular types of tourism.

As repeatedly emphasized, the approach of this book is that, with proper planning and controlled development, all forms of tourism can and should be socially and environmentally sensitive and responsible, aiming toward sustainable development, and that the types of tourism selected for an area depend on many environmental, social, and economic factors that must be analyzed. As mentioned, at the national and regional planning levels, several forms of tourism might all be appropriate in the country or region. Alternative forms of tourism in particular can be considered where there is concern about the sociocultural and environmental impacts of mass tourism, especially in areas with traditional cultures and ecologically sensitive environments.

Although exact definitions vary, it is commonly accepted that forms of alternative tourism relate to facilities and activities that allow tourists to directly experience the host culture and/or environment in non-exploitive ways that respect the society and environment. But even though small-scale, social and environmental safeguards must still be planned into development of alternative tourism. One of the economic advantages of alternative tourism is that most of the economic benefits of employment and income are received directly by the resident population who own and operate the tourist facilities and services. Another advantage is that these small-scale forms of tourism do not require major infrastructure development or high capital investment costs.

Examples of alternative forms of tourism include:

- Village tourism, where small groups of tourists stay in or near traditional, often remote villages and learn about village life and the local environment;
- Rural, farm, or agro-tourism, where tourists stay with farm families and learn about farming activities or stay on tropical plantations, learning about plantation life and activities;
- Walking and cycling tours, with the tourists staying in hostels, private homes, or bed and breakfast establishments, meeting local people, and learning about the local culture and environment;

- Fishing tourism, with tourists staying in coastal villages with fishermen's families and going on joint fishing trips;
- Nature eco-tourism of hiking, trekking, and canoeing in natural areas, with local guides to explain the environmental characteristics; and
- Urban eco-tourism, with the tourists learning about urban social groups, language, or special craft skills.

As another possible form of alternative tourism, it is now becoming common for small groups, often community organizations, to travel to and stay in an area assisting local people with a particular project such as building low-cost houses or developing a village water supply.

Other Forms of Tourism

There are several other forms of tourism that which may be appropriate for the country or region and should be considered in formulating the tourism policy and plan.

Transportation-Oriented Tourism

Hotels and other tourist facilities and services are commonly developed near major transportation centers, especially international airports, some of which now incorporate a hotel within the airport terminal or have direct pedestrian connection to a hotel, to serve passengers in transit for several hours or overnight for the convenience of taking early morning flights. These are generically termed airport hotels. Many of these hotels now provide facilities for meetings between local and traveling business persons to save the time of travelers going into the city, and conference facilities may be developed in association with airport-related accommodation. Some tourist facilities are also often located near major train and bus stations in large cities to serve arriving and departing passengers.

Associated with road travel is the development of motels and motor hotels along roads. On major highways and especially near intersections of major highways and in urban fringe areas, it is now common for large complexes of motels, restaurants, shops, and perhaps recreation and entertainment facilities to be developed for road travelers, including truck drivers. On a smaller scale, rest stops that provide sanitary facilities, picnicking, and lounging areas are located at selected places alongside heavily traveled roads.

Camping and Caravan Tourism

Camping is popular in many countries and regions, especially in association with scenic areas or specific natural and cultural attractions. Usually, camping facilities are developed for domestic tourists, but in some places they are also utilized by international tourists traveling by automobile or bus. Specialized camping parks are developed by group organizations such as the Boy and Girl Scouts and religious groups for their own organizational use.

Caravan or RV parks serve tourists traveling by campers, either trailers pulled by cars or self-contained motorized camper vehicles. Caravan parks have been developed in Europe, especially in the U.K., and RV parks, usually privately operated, are very common in the USA. Both camping and caravan parks contain sanitary facilities and, for caravans, utility hook-ups, and some provide retail shops for the sale of food and other supplies and may include recreation facilities.

Youth Tourism

Travel for education, recreation, and sports by youth, either independently or in organized groups, has long been an established type of tourism and is now also being encouraged in many developing countries. Youth tourism is often but not always subsidized by the government in the form of providing youth hostels and other types of inexpensive but clean dormitory type accommodation, discounts on transportation fares, and sometimes the provision of tour buses. Many youth hostels are oriented to domestic young travelers, but some also cater to international youth. Youth hostel directories are available for young people traveling internationally.

Safari, Trekking, and Mountain Tourism

As a specialized type of camping tourism, safari tourism typically involves small groups traveling and camping at different places along the way, usually but not always at designated camping sites. Safari tourism is particularly associated with hunting and photographic tours in wildlife areas such as eastern and southern Africa, but also can be related to botanical, cultural, or sight-seeing tourism in remote areas. In East Africa, hotels or lodges, many of which are of quite high quality, have been developed in or near the game parks oriented to game viewing by the guests. Several of these lodges are designed to overlook waterholes and salt licks that attract game, usually in the late afternoons, that can be viewed by the guests from their rooms, special viewing areas on terraces, underground bunkers, and the hotel rooftops. These lodges additionally provide game viewing day tours in special vehicles that travel through the parks. Lodges have also been developed in or near the game parks in South Asia, with arrangements for touring the parks by vehicle.

Trekking and hiking, involving long walks with camping along the way and usually in remote scenic areas, are popular, for example, in the Himalayan region of northern Pakistan and India, Nepal, and Bhutan, and in the mountain regions of North America and Europe. Trekking can also be done by horse, pony, donkey, and camel. Mountain climbing expeditions are a very specialized form of tourism, popular in various mountain regions of the world.

Even where there is not often much in-place facility development needed, except at the access points, for safari, trekking, and mountain climbing tourism, it does require organization, specially trained and experienced guides, and provision of equipment and supplies. It can be a high value type of tourism because of the fees paid to guides and porters, for government permits to visit the area, and for hunting permits to have the right to hunt certain animals. A particular planning concern of this type of tourism is the environmental impact of the tourist activities in natural environments and, in some places, the cultural impact on traditional societies.

Social Tourism

Social tourism has been developed in some countries, particularly but not only in the more politically socialized countries, as an approach to provide vacations for lower income people and those who would otherwise not take the initiative to travel or understand how to make vacation arrangements. Often, social tourism takes place within the same country or in nearby ones, with subsidized facilities provided by the government and employers or trade unions, clubs, and other associations to which the people belong. Also, provision of subsidized camping and caravan parks, transportation fares, and accommodation rate discounts for national citizens or state residents and other techniques are utilized by many countries and regions to encourage travel by persons who otherwise would not be able to afford it.

Another technique practiced by some countries to encourage and subsidize domestic travel is to give travel bonuses each year to employees, typically government civil servants, along with providing inexpensive tourist facilities, either developed by the government or with the government providing incentives to the private sector for their development, at desirable domestic destinations. Provision by the government or a religious organization of basic facilities for religious pilgrims at important sacred sites is a common practice.

In a particular tourism area, there may also be other possible forms of tourism such as ethnic, nostalgic, and religious tourism that the planning team should consider in their formulation of the tourism plan.

Formulating Tourism Policy

Coherent and realistic tourism development policy establishes the basis for developing and maintaining tourism and is an essential element of the national or regional tourism plan. Applying decision making within the framework of adopted policy is much more beneficial than taking *ad hoc* responses to opportunities and problems as they arise. The types of tourism development policies examined in this section refer to the type and extent of tourism that should be developed in an area and any special factors to be considered in its development, including those for sustaining the natural and cultural resources of tourism.

Approach to Policy Formulation

Tourism development policy is determined in the plan formulation stage of the planning process. It is first formulated on a preliminary basis, with evaluation of alternative policies, and then finalized after it has been tested for its suitability in achieving the objectives of developing tourism and its feasibility of implementation. In a large country or region, different policies may be adopted for different areas, but these together comprise an overall policy statement for the area.

Policy is determined based on several considerations. The objectives of developing tourism provide the most important basis for establishing policy because policy is the expression of how the objectives can be achieved. For example, if the objective is for minimization of sociocultural impact, then the policy may be for highly controlled, limited tourism development. More generally, tourism policy must reflect the overall development policy and plan of the country or region so that tourism is an integrated sector. The background review of existing policy and planning will have provided the basis for this integration. For example, a general policy may call for increased economic development in a particular region of the country, and therefore the tourism policy will give priority to development in that region if it has tourism potential. The political and economic ideology of the country or region also affects policy as related to the respective roles of the public and private sectors in developing tourism.

Policy also evolves from the survey, analysis, and synthesis of any present tourism development patterns and infrastructure, tourist attractions, and tourist markets. Socioeconomic and environmental factors are very important considerations in policy determination, especially the social and environmental absorptive or carrying capacity of the area. Although international tourism and often some aspects of domestic tourism are developed primarily for their economic benefits, tourism policy must be based on all considerations so that it is developed in a balanced manner.

The government should assume the lead role in determining tourism policy because policy affects the entire country and its communities and must balance economic, environmental, and social concerns. National and community objectives should prevail over individual, group, or sector interests, while still recognizing the right of those interests to be considered. However, the private sector should be involved in the policy decision-making process, and the resulting policy should provide a framework within which the private sector can effectively function. Just as importantly, the government should also involve the community or its spokesmen in this policy decision making and not impose policy on the people.

Policy Considerations

Tourism policy can take many forms depending on the objectives of developing tourism, the resources for tourism, national development policy, and other considerations. Some of the basic issues that need to be resolved in deciding policy are reviewed in the following sections.

Role of Government

A basic policy decision that must be made is whether the government assumes a passive, active, or somewhat intermediate role in the development of tourism. A passive involvement is when the government neither discourages nor encourages tourism, and adopts measures for the general development process, such as on air traffic agreements and investment incentives, which may assist tourism but are not specifically designed for this sector. An active involvement is when the government has adopted a general policy for developing tourism and a tourism plan setting forth the objectives, specific policies, and development structure for tourism development, provides an adequate budget for tourism marketing and actively promotes tourism, offers tourism-related training programs, makes investment incentives available for hotel and other facility development, adopts tourism-related legislation and regulations, improves airports and encourages air traffic agreements aimed at increasing tourist flows, and other measures. The government may also pursue a more specific developmental role by providing some or all of the infrastructure for tourism developments, such as resorts, develops tourist attraction features, and constructs hotels and other tourist facilities and services if the private sector cannot be induced to do this.

In any country or region that wants to develop or expand tourism, the government needs to perform an active role in terms of adopting tourism policy, plans, and regulations, making certain that basic infrastructure, including access to the area, is adequate, and other measures. In newly developing tourism areas and especially in developing countries (which typically have weakly developed private sectors with no experience in developing tourism, underdeveloped infrastructure, limited development of domestic tourism, and little international knowledge of the attractions of the country and other constraints), the government usually must perform a very active role to get tourism started. This often includes initially developing and managing major hotel, tour, and travel operations and other facilities and services (Jenkins and Henry 1982). After tourism has become established, the government can assume a more normal active role, including divesting itself of actual ownership and management of tourist facilities and services.

It has sometimes been stated that first domestic tourism must be established in a developing country before international tourism can be developed. However, this thesis is questionable and has not always been successful in actual practice. In some cases, there is little domestic tourism demand or local affordability to travel and what travel exists is based on facilities and services that are not suitable for a broad international market, although it may be adequate for some special interest and 'alternative' forms of tourism. If the country wants to develop international tourism, particularly for its foreign exchange and other economic benefits, which is usually the case, it needs to develop attractions, facilities, services, and infrastructure for the international markets. Then it often happens that, as the country's economy expands based in part on international tourism, the domestic tourism sector also develops. In more developed countries, domestic tourism can help provide the basis for commencing international tourism. In some developing countries, domestic and international tourism may develop concurrently. For example, India, which has a low average per capita income level but a large and rapidly growing middle class and some upper middle class, is by national and regional policy actively developing both domestic and international tourism with virtually all quality levels of facilities being used by both types of tourists, although some facilities have a greater orientation to one or the other.

Environment Protection, Cultural Conservation, and Sustainable Development

Applying contemporary concepts of tourism development, there are usually one or more policy statements relative to tourism being planned and developed so that the natural environment is not degraded, archaeological and historical sites are conserved, sociocultural impacts are minimized, and desirable aspects of cultural patterns are maintained and, if necessary, revitalized. More generally, a policy may be stated about tourism being developed in a controlled manner in order to achieve sustainability of its resources.

Reasons for Developing Tourism

The reasons for developing tourism should be stated in the policy. These may include:
- Economic reasons such as earning foreign exchange, providing employment, income and government revenue, using tourism as a catalyst for development or expansion of other sectors such as agriculture and fisheries (cross-sectoral linkage effects), and using tourism to help pay for infrastructure development;
- Social reasons of encouraging cross-cultural exchange among different groups of people and introducing a country or region and its cultures and environments and sometimes its recent socioeconomic progress to people from elsewhere in the country or world (regional and national prestige reasons);
- For domestic tourism, social reasons of providing opportunities for recreation, relaxation, and education to citizens away from their homes and political reasons of educating citizens about their country and its diversity in order to develop a sense of national pride and identity (important in some newly developing countries); and
- Using tourism to help achieve environmental and cultural conservation objectives for which resources would not otherwise be available.

Often, there is a combination of reasons for developing tourism, all of which can be beneficial to the country or region.

Type of Tourism To Be Developed

Deciding the types of domestic and international tourism and the types of tourist markets to aim for is a basic policy consideration. The types of tourism can range from general interest sight-seeing or large-scale beach or mountain resort-oriented tourism to small-scale special interest tourism related to nature or culture, alternative types of tourism of social and environmental activities, special feature tourism based on theme parks, gambling casinos, or sports facilities, or a combination of these in different parts of the country or region. The quality level of tourism needs to be decided. For example, some potential destinations are now opting for what is often termed "quality" tourism, which relates to controlled development aiming for high expenditure tourist markets. In some island and coastal areas, the type of tourism will include cruise ship and yachting tourism.

Extent of Tourism Development

Related to the type of tourism development, as well as socioeconomic and environmental considerations, is the extent of tourism that is appropriate for the country or region. This can also range from a very limited small-scale level of a few thousand tourists annually to mass tourism involving millions of visitors (assuming that the attractions are available and other conditions suitable to attract a large number of tourists). A large country or region may decide to develop different levels of tourism in different areas, and at different times.

Growth Rate of Tourism

The growth rate of tourism to be aimed for—slow, medium, or fast—is often a policy consideration. It may be desirable to control the growth rate for several reasons, for example:
* Social reasons of allowing residents adequate time to adjust to tourism and participate in its planning and socioeconomic benefits;
* Development reasons of balancing tourism with infrastructure development and the various other demands on limited capital resources;
* Manpower planning reasons of allowing sufficient time for training persons to work effectively in tourism; and
* Economic reasons of integrating development of various economic sectors, not creating economic distortions in the economy nor generating undue land speculation.

Location and Staging of Development

General geographic location and staging of tourism development can also be a policy decision that is further defined in the development structure plan. For example, it may be decided that certain areas and not others will be developed during the time frame of the plan, or that development should be staged in a particular manner to be compatible with overall development objectives, or sometimes that development be staged in a particular manner for political reasons.

Other Types of Policies

Other types of tourism development policies may relate to multi-use of tourism infrastructure, relation between domestic and international tourism, education and training, social integration of tourism, and investment and employment policies. The latter, for example, may involve the consideration of whether only national or regional capital may be used in tourism investment or if joint venture with outside investors is allowed, and whether only national citizens are permitted to work in tourism or if nationals of other countries can also be employed.

Some policies should be flexible to respond to changing circumstances and so stated in the policy. For example, the extent of investment incentives that will be permitted should usually be flexible, depending on the current situation. Also, policy may need to be modified over time, based on changing circumstances of market trends and development patterns within the tourism area, but not to the extent of abrogating the objectives of developing tourism.

Techniques of Plan Formulation

In formulating the structure plan it is essential to apply a systematic approach to provide a rational basis for planning, but the planner must also be imaginative in finding new and different solutions to problems when necessary. The experience of similar tourism areas or particular aspects of tourism development that are similar in other places can often provide useful ideas in formulating the plan. Mapping is essential and, as is the case with the planning analysis, the overlay mapping technique (or use of computer mapping), which shows relationships of the plan inputs and components is very useful. The various inputs to, and approaches applied in, formulating the plan are reviewed in the following sections.

Consideration of Development Objectives and Policies

The objective and policies set forth the overall parameters for the type of development to be planned and provide a guide for formulating the plan. For example, if the objective is to minimize sociocultural impact and the policy is to greatly control and limit development, then retreat resort, special interest, and alternative forms of tourism can be considered; if the objective is to minimize environmental impact and the policy is to maximize integration of facilities with the natural environment, then low-density, low-rise accommodation can be considered; or if the objective is to optimize economic benefits and the policy is to develop substantial tourism but still with environmental and social controls, then large,

Valletta, Malta's historic capital (top) and Hagar Qim, one of Malta's late Neolithic period temples (bottom)—Tourism planning in Malta is based on development of archaeological and historic places as well as beach-oriented resort activities in order to diversify the tourism product and tourist markets. (Courtesy of the Malta Ministry of Tourism)

well-planned, integrated resorts may be the suitable development form. As indicated previously, the objectives and policies at this stage are often preliminary and feedback from evaluation of the alternative structure plans may result in modification of the objectives and policies.

Survey and Analysis Inputs

Survey and analysis inputs, examined in Chapter 6, are very important in the systematic formulation of the plan and must be considered in both the quantitative and qualitative sense. As shown on the planning process chart in Figure 3.1, there are various inputs from the survey, analysis, and synthesis to make in the plan formulation.

Tourist Attractions

The survey and evaluation of existing and potential tourist attractions and related activities indicate the type and location of major attractions, which is a basic input to the plan. If the major attractions are location-based, such as national parks or archaeological or historic sites, they will obviously be a major consideration in determining other recommendations such as the location of transportation facilities and tourism development regions or areas. The type and location of tourist attractions also largely determine the tour routes and tour programming for sight-seeing tourist activities. If it has been decided to develop special types of attractions such as a large convention center, theme park, gambling casino (as a primary attraction), or major sports facility, a location analysis study for these features will need to be conducted.

Tourist Facilities and Land Area Requirements

The projected types and amounts of accommodation and other tourist facilities and their land area requirements, explained in Chapter 6, are important inputs for the plan formulation. The tourist facility land area requirements are distributed in the plan, based on several considerations:
- The forms of tourism development to be applied;
- The integrated analysis and synthesis of physical, economic, and social factors (including carrying capacities of potential tourism development areas);
- Type and location of tourist attraction features;
- Location of existing and already planned tourist facilities;
- Location of existing and already planned transportation and other infrastructure development;
- Present overall development policies and plans; and
- Availability of land in the potential development areas.

Transportation Facilities and Services

Existing and already planned transportation facilities and services become an important input to the plan because, in order to minimize capital investment requirements, the existing major transportation system should be used to the greatest extent possible for tourism. The transportation analysis will have indicated improvements required to the existing system, as well as new transportation facilities and services necessary to develop the projected level of tourism.

Other Infrastructure

The analysis of the availability of other existing infrastructure in terms of type, extent, and location may be an influencing factor in the plan formulation, especially if the principle is applied to tourism of utilizing existing infrastructure to the greatest extent possible. As emphasized in Chapter 6, the capacity and location of water supply systems and of water resources, such as underground water resources, may be an especially important consideration.

Integrated Analysis and Synthesis

The integrated analysis and synthesis of environmental, social, and economic factors along with the tourist attractions, facilities, and infrastructure, which shows the interrelationships of the various elements in composite map form, as explained in Chapter 6, is basic input to the plan formulation in order to decide where tourism development can be appropriately located. Considerations deriving from the integrated analysis and synthesis may include, for example:

- The location of existing and planned urban areas, resource areas such as for agriculture and mining, airport zones and significant conservation areas to be preserved will generally preclude those places from being considered for major tourism development;
- The environmental analysis and especially the determination of carrying capacities will indicate optimum levels of tourism development that can take place in potential tourism areas and identify those places that should not be developed for environmental hazard reasons;
- The climatic and topographic patterns will identify places more and less suitable for tourism;
- The sociocultural patterns will indicate the present and projected population distribution and areas where labor supply will be available and places where attitudes or traditions of residents may be an influencing factor in deciding on the type and extent of tourism; and
- The analysis of economic patterns will show where economically depressed areas are located that require development such as tourism.

Land Availability

The availability of land for tourism development in particular areas, even though they are not currently developed with other uses or represent an important resource, must be considered with respect to land tenure, that is, will its owner make it available for development and, if so, will its cost be at a level to make the proposed development economically feasible. In some cases of multiple ownerships of a major development site, a consideration is determining how feasible it will be to assemble the separately owned parcels into a single unit necessary for integrated planning and development.

Major Opportunities and Constraints

The determination of major opportunities and problems or constraints for tourism, as explained in chapter 6, will provide a focus in the plan preparation for taking advantage of the opportunities and trying to resolve the constraints. For example, if there is an outstanding type of tourist attraction unique to the country or region, it should be given much emphasis in the plan formulation, or if a significant constraint is accessibility to and within the area, transportation would be given major emphasis in the plan's recommendations.

Preparation and Evaluation of Alternative Plans

An important plan formulation technique is to prepare alternative plans in outline format. Each alternative shows a different approach and different types of recommendations. The alternatives are then evaluated with respect to how well each one satisfies the plan objectives, reflects the development policies, generates the desired economic benefits at acceptable costs, minimizes negative environmental and sociocultural impacts and reinforces positive ones, and is realistic to implement. Part Four of this book examines environmental and socioeconomic considerations as inputs for the plan formulation. It is important to involve the government and project steering committee, if one is organized, in the evaluation of alternatives because this is a crucial decision-making step in the planning process. Often, trade-offs between the relative benefits and costs of alternative plans must be made which should involve mutual discussion by the government, private sector, and community leaders.

In order to systematically evaluate the alternative plans, the matrix technique is often employed. Figure 7.1 presents a sample matrix evaluation approach, which can be adapted to specific planning situations. Although some data such as economic costs and benefits may be available, much of the evaluation will need to be made in qualitative terms but can be expressed numerically.

Evaluation Factor	Evaluation Ranking			
	Alternative 1	Alternative 2	Alternative 3	Comments
Satisfies overall tourism development objectives				
Reflects overall national/ regional development policy				
Reflects tourism development policy				
Optimizes overall economic benefits at reasonable cost				
Provides substantial employment and increased income				
Provides substantial net foreign exchange earnings				
Helps develop economically depressed areas				
Does not preempt other important resource areas				
Minimizes negative sociocultural impacts				
Helps achieve archaeological/ historic site preservation				
Helps revitalyze traditional arts and handicrafts				
Is not disruptive to present land use and settlement patterns				
Minimizes negative environmental impacts				
Reinforces environmental conservation & park development				
Makes maximum use of existing infrastructure				
Makes maximum multi-purpose use of new infrastructure				
Provides opportunity for staging development				

Notes:
1. This list of evaluation factors is only indicative of the type which could be used, and the evaluation factors actually used will depend on the specific planning situation. If the plan objectives are complete and specific, they can sometimes be used directly as the factors.

2. The evaluation ranking can be done on a scale of 1 to 5 or 1 to 10 with the upper end of the scale indicating the higher achievement level. The more important factors can be given a greater numerical weighting. The comments column is important for noting special situations, for example, substantial employment may be provided by the plan but considerable migration of workers may be required to provide the employment.

Figure 7.1. Sample Evaluation Matrix for Alternative Plans.

Finalizing the Plan

The best alternative plan, or often a combination of alternatives, is selected based on the evaluation and then prepared in final form. The final national or regional structure plan will indicate the major elements of:

- Major and secondary tourist attraction features;
- Tourism development regions for a national plan and tourism development areas such as for resorts in a regional plan and tourism centers;
- Transportation access points or gateways to the country or region;
- Internal transportation network connecting the access points with the major attractions and development regions or areas;
- Where relevant, the tourist excursion routes; and
- Staging of development, usually by approximate five-year periods.

The final plan should then be evaluated in detail in terms of economic benefits and costs and environmental and sociocultural impacts to make certain that is the optimum plan and best meets the tourism development objectives and expresses the development policies, or whether some adjustments to the plan should be made. In the course of formulating the plan, it may be determined that some of the objectives or policies or perhaps the market projections or targets are impossible to achieve. These will need to be modified. After the final plan is decided upon and evaluated, the recommendations on institutional elements and implementation techniques are determined as is examined in Part Five.

National and Regional Planning Principles

Each country or region must be planned according to its particular characteristics and development objectives and policies. But there are certain basic concepts and principles that are generally applicable based on what has proven to be functional and successful in already developed tourism areas. Conversely, certain other approaches have been shown not to be very effective or have generated serious problems. These concepts and principles are reviewed in the following sections.

Gateway and Staging Area Concept

A suitable international access point (or points) to a country and a regional access point (or points) is essential for developing tourism. The access points are often termed the national or regional gateways. International airports are often the access points to countries, especially for long-haul tourists, although land border crossings and seaports also function as gateways for international travelers to some countries. Regional access may be by air, land, or sea. These gateways usually have already been established before tourism was planned and developed, and so they become a given factor around which tourism must be planned, although often the access facilities and services must be upgraded and expanded to handle tourism.

In a small country or region, a single gateway is usually sufficient, but larger countries may have more than one international access and larger regions more than one gateway. This situation offers the advantage of tourists entering at one point, making a tour of the country, and exiting at another point, thus saving backtracking to the entry point and often encouraging tourists to see more of the country. Also, more than one gateway provides a choice to tourists in planning their itineraries. In a larger, diverse country or region with only one existing gateway, it may be worth considering developing a second one in a strategic location to encourage greater tourist flows and increase their length of stay, especially if the second access can serve general as well as tourism needs. Multiple gateways also offer the advantage of distributing passenger demands and not overloading facilities at any single access point.

A principle that has worked well in tourism development is the concept of establishing a staging area, which is at or near the point (or points) of entry of tourists and from which tourists travel to other parts of the country and also, of course, the point of exit by tourists from the area. The staging area provides tourist facilities and services for at least overnight stays and often contains various attraction features, or can be developed with some attractions that tourists can enjoy while they are waiting for their onward transportation or tour to commence or waiting for departure from the area. When the national or regional gateway is located in or near a major city, the city performs the staging area function.

Clustering of Attractions Development

As emphasized previously, the attractions of an area, whether natural, cultural, or special type, are the reasons for holiday tourists to visit an area and also are often visited by business travelers. Major attractions such as national parks, significant archaeological and historic sites, and good beaches or ski slopes on which resort development is based are so important that their location determines much of the planning for tourism development. In other situations, attractions such as cultural performances are of the type that can be located in various places. Attractions of secondary importance may or may not need to be developed depending on whether they can help attract tourists, or they may be developed for other reasons such as for conservation of environmental and cultural features used primarily for scientific purposes or to be local recreation facilities designed primarily for use by residents.

In order to attract more tourists to an area and induce them to stay longer, as well as making it more convenient for organizing tours and providing infrastructure, an important principle is to cluster attractions in particular areas. An approach often used is to develop several secondary, mobile, or special types of attractions near a major attraction so that the area is of greater overall interest to tourists. For example, a secondary attraction of a cultural center for dance and music performances and demonstration and sale of handicrafts of a local ethnic group can be located near a national park or in an historic town that is the major attraction, and a city destination can develop attractions in the outlying rural and village areas for day and overnight tours from the city.

Establishment of Tourism Regions and Development Areas

At the national level, an important planning concept is designation and establishment of tourism development regions that contain one or more clusters of tourist attractions and accommodation and other tourist facility areas, all well served by the regional transportation network. Designation of tourism regions provides the basis for integrated regional planning of the region so that they function effectively and are relatively self-contained. It also allows for logical staging of tourism development from one region to another over a period of time, as well as staging within the regions. For example, Nepal is reaching the saturation level of tourism development in the Kathmandu Valley and Pokhara regions, and the government is planning to open up new tourism regions in the eastern and western parts of the country.

Tourism regions are logical geographic and planning entities that are selected based on their containing significant tourist attractions and related activities, existing good access or potential for developing a regional gateway, an integrated internal transportation network, and suitable areas for development of tourist facilities. Administratively, it should be possible to plan the regions on an integrated basis, although this may need to be done at a cooperative level. Tourism regions may extend across state, provincial, or even international boundaries.

Within the development regions, it is often desirable to establish a tourism center (this may also be the staging area for the region) that has good access from outside the region and to other parts of the region and offers a concentration of facilities and services for tourists. The tourism center or staging area provides a convenience for tourists and makes it easier for the government and private sector to develop infrastructure, facilities, and services. However, if there are cities, towns, or several large resorts in a tourism region that provide a wide range of facilities and services, there may not be a need for a tourism center to also be established.

At the regional level, with the exception of certain types of small-scale tourism development, a basic principle is the concentration of tourist facilities and services in specific areas, typically in the form of integrated resorts, resort towns, or urban tourism centers. As opposed to dispersed development, concentration offers several advantages:

- Opportunity for integrated planning and application of development, design, and environmental controls;
- More efficient provision of transportation access and other infrastructure;

- Convenience to tourists of facilities and services being in proximity;
- Capability of concentrated development to support more specialized facilities and services; and
- Containment of any negative environmental and sociocultural impacts in specific areas.

Based on accumulated experience, the concentration principle is now being widely applied in tourism areas throughout the world with dispersed development being discouraged in many places because of problems generated by a scatteration of facilities.

The criteria for selecting resort or other development area sites include the following:

- Tourist attraction feature (or features), such as a beach, lake, ski slope, major archaeological or historic site, or major natural feature, at or relatively near the site, keeping in mind that facility development should not impinge upon, but be set away from, the immediate setting of natural and archaeological/historic features.
- Desirable micro-climatic conditions as related to the type of development.
- Attractive physical environment of the site and nearby area.
- Sufficient amount of available and developable land, which is economically feasible to develop and does not have a more important economic, conservation, or other resource use.
- Good existing or potential access from the tourist gateway to the area and from the area to other attraction features in the region.
- Availability of, or feasibility of developing, infrastructure of adequate water supply, electric power, sewage and solid waste disposal, and telecommunications at an acceptable cost.
- Suitable general area for the resort with compatible nearby land uses or the opportunity for establishing buffer zones around the site and no excessive air, water, or noise pollution of the site environment.
- Positive attitude of any nearby residents to developing tourism and no likelihood of the tourism development generating any serious sociocultural or economic problems for residents of the general area if appropriate socioeconomic measures are implemented.
- Availability of nearby labor supply to work in the resort or possibility of attracting employees from elsewhere and feasibility of providing any migrant employees with housing and community facilities.

There might be additional criteria depending on the local circumstances and type of resort being planned. However, a single site may not meet all the criteria, and it may be necessary to compromise on some of them. Some types of resorts have specific requirements. For example, ski resorts, need a sufficient vertical difference in elevation (1,000–1,500 to 4,000–5,000 feet) and ski slope gradients of 25 to 75 percent, adequate snow fall coming at frequent intervals, sufficient cold to maintain the snow but preferably with much sunshine, protection from prevailing winds, and a base area large enough to accommodate lift equipment terminals and various tourist facilities, usually including accommodation.

Transportation and Other Infrastructure Principles

In addition to suitable access points to the country or region, an efficient and interesting internal transportation facilities network and services system is important in order to provide access to the regions at the national level and to the tourism development areas at the regional level. If possible, the internal tourist excursion route network should avoid backtracking as much as possible with loop tour routes developed, especially for sight-seeing tourism. An effective way to plan the internal transportation network is to apply tour programming techniques to alternative routes to determine the most effective ones for development of tourist routes. A routing that offers scenic views, optimizes the opportunity to visit various attractions, meets time-distance parameters, and provides comfortable and safe transportation facilities is preferable.

A principle that applies at both the national/regional and resort planning levels is to, wherever possible, develop tourism so that it makes maximum use of existing and already planned infrastructure without overloading it (or improving it so that it does not become overloaded). If new infrastructure is required, it should be developed to be as multi-purpose as possible so that is serves general community as well as tourism needs. Multi-use of infrastructure is typically more economical and has the advantage that tourism is helping to pay for infrastructure that also benefits other sectors of the economy and society. Infrastructure improvements justified by tourism can be a catalyst for general economic and social development. If infrastructure is developed only for tourism or if major improvements are required for tourism development, which can often be the case, its costs and revenues should be calculated in the economic costs and benefits analysis of tourism to make certain that the infrastructure development is economically justified.

Seasonality Considerations

If the area is likely to experience seasonal differences in tourist arrivals, as is often the case resulting from either the types of attractions or the character of the tourist markets or both of these factors, the national and regional plan should incorporate ways to reduce seasonality, realizing that it is often impossible to entirely eliminate seasonal variations. Various techniques can be applied to reduce seasonality. Types of tourist attractions can be selected or developed that will attract visitors at different times of the year and especially during the low season. By policy, tourism developments such as resorts or urban tourism areas can develop low-season activities such as festivals and special events, conferences, and special types of recreation facilities. For example, it is common practice now for resorts to develop conference tourism during the low season and for ski resorts to develop summer mountain hiking, riding, and other recreational activities. An imaginative recent concept for golf courses in places with cold winters is to develop 'cross-country' skiing on the fairways during the winter season. As mentioned previously, marketing techniques can be applied, such as offering discounted transportation fares and accommodation rates during the low season and encouraging domestic use at discounted rates of facilities during the low season. More fundamentally, changing and staggering the traditional schedules of vacation periods of the tourist markets would greatly help, although this is more difficult to accomplish.

Staging of Development

The tourism plan should be formulated so that it is easy to stage tourism development over a period of time. This will require that the various tourism regions at the national level and development areas at the regional level are selected and their related infrastructure planned in such a manner that each region or area can be developed economically and efficiently as a separate unit when needed. The importance of staging is further examined in Chapter 15 "Tourism Plan Implementation."

Case Studies

The four case studies presented on national and regional tourism development policies and plans represent different environmental situations and approaches within the framework of applying basic planning principles. The national tourism plan for Burma applies the tourism region and center principle with staging of development by region. The strategic policy plan for Malta is designed to integrate tourism development policy into the overall development plan of the country. The tourism development policy for Zanzibar reflects an approach to a newly developing tourism region. The subregional tourism plan for the northeast area of Northern Ireland is based on rejuvenation and expansion of tourism in an already developed destination.

Burma Tourism Structure Plan

A case study in Chapter 4 described the background of the Tourism Development Plan for Burma (UNDP and WTO 1983). This plan represents planning for a country with limited existing tourism development, but having a variety of highly interesting cultural and natural attractions that give it considerable potential for tourism. The policy approach to planning was for relatively gradual expansion of tourism, keeping it in balance with development of facilities and services, with utmost consideration given to environmental and sociocultural factors.

The tourism structure plan shown in Figure 7.2 indicates the tourism development regions (called development areas on map), tourism centers within the

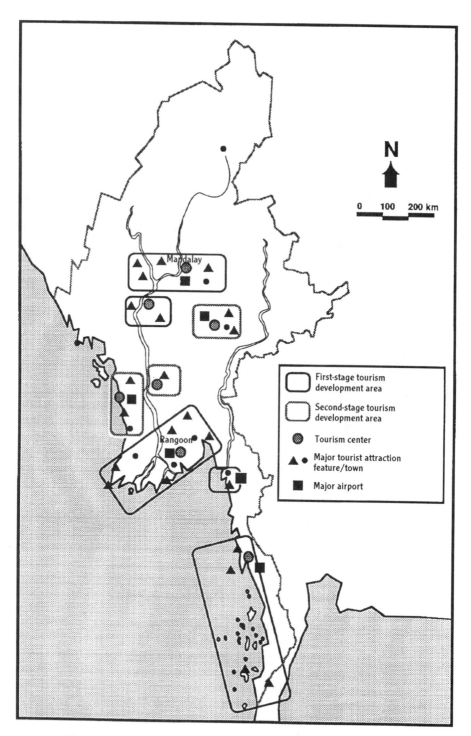

Figure 7.2. Burma Tourism Development Plan—Development Regions.

regions, the major place-specific tourist attraction features, the transportation network, and the major cities and towns. The regions were determined based on being logical geographic units with each containing significant attractions, accessibility to and within the region by road, rail, or air or a combination of access modes, and having a city or town that can function as a gateway and tourism center and distribution point within the region. The capital city of Rangoon and its international airport functions as the gateway and staging area to the country. The internal transportation network connects all the regional tourism centers to Rangoon.

As indicated on the map, the eight tourism regions are designated for first or second stage development, which provides a basis for development programming. More detailed regional level tourism plans were prepared for each of the regions, with development staging also indicated within the regions.

Based on the structure plan, prototypical general sight-seeing tour programs were recommended for 5–6 day, 8–9 day and 12–13 day tours of the country. Also, several special interest type tours were suggested, including:

- Archaeological and historical tours in the central regions of the country;
- National parks and wildlife tours when the parks and nature sanctuaries are developed with visitor facilities;
- Marine (diving) tours in the coastal regions; and
- Cultural tours of traditional hill tribe villages.

Malta Strategic Policy Plan

The background of the Maltese Islands Tourism Development Plan (Horwath and Horwath 1989) was described in a case study in Chapter 3. Malta is an example of a country that already has substantial tourism development. The principal plan objective was to improve and diversify the tourism product and shift to higher quality and more diversified tourist markets, within the framework of expansion of tourism as a major economic sector of the country.

In the plan formulation, the two main islands were divided into 12 zones, 10 on Malta Island and 2 on Gozo Island, to provide for the systematic analysis of relatively homogeneous areas for which policy recommendations can be made. Figure 7.3 shows these zones. Within each zone, policies were formulated for the actions required to improve the areas as related to tourism development as shown in Figure 7.4. TPUs (tourism planning units) were designated as specific "no go" tourism areas within which no new development should be allowed until detailed plans have been prepared and adopted to guide future development. The tourism planning policies are closely related to overall development policy and planning for the islands, and the policy recommendations were to be integrated into the comprehensive physical plan then being prepared for the country.

Two of the tourism zones were designated as priority areas for detailed planning and development improvements. In the planning project, detailed planning and some urban design were prepared for these priority areas and also for visitor

1 The Capital
2 The Historical Port Core
3 The New Tourism Areas
4 The Capital Area
5 North Central Area
6 South Central Area
7 East Coast Area
8 Marsaxlokk Bay Area
9 Mdina Basin
10 The Northern Area
11 North and West Area—Gozo
12 Southern Area—Gozo

Figure 7.3. Maltese Islands Tourism Development Plan—Tourism Zones.

facilities and conservation programming of selected major archaeological and historic sites. The plan recommends an effective institutional approach for reviewing and taking action on future tourism development projects such as hotels and resorts proposed by the private sector.

Zanzibar Tourism Development Policy

The Zanzibar regional tourism development plan (UNDP and WTO 1983) was prepared in 1983. Zanzibar is comprised of the islands of Zanzibar and Pemba, off the coast of Tanzania in East Africa, and has a population of approximately one-half million. Zanzibar is a semi-autonomous entity of Tanzania. The islands are well known for their production and export of cloves, which provide the major source of cash income. Historically, Zanzibar was an important Arab trading center for East Africa and was a focus of Swahili cultural development. The Stone Town area of Zanzibar city is the largest and best example of Southern Arabian-

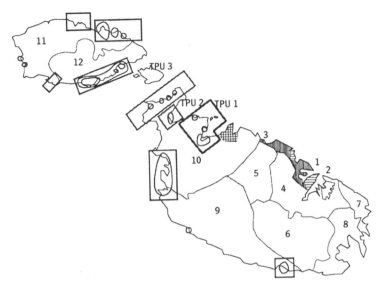

Zone 1: See detailed plan.
Zone 2: Formulation of program of affordable upgrading of residential areas, twinned with complementary set of tourist and cultural projects.
Zone 3: See detailed plan.
Zone 4: Implementation of corridor improvement programs and formulation/promotion of tourist circuits/policy of urban containment.
Zone 5: Village core conservation and improvement programs linked to environmental corridor studies and promotion of tourist circuits at the interface with Zone 3. A strict policy or urban containment should be enforced.
Zone 6: Again, corridor improvement programs and promotion of tourist circuits are the key elements in conjunction with village core conservation and improvement actions.
Zone 7: Launching a rolling program of public works initiatives targeted on popular local resort areas and accompanied by local media public awareness campaigns aimed at improving built environment/public health, safety, and fire standards through a "bottom-up" local initiative to complement the broader international market interventions.
Zone 8: Preventive or remedial action programs to minimize the direct or indirect negative environmental impact created by the industrial development around Marsoxlokk Bay and surrounding areas.
Zone 9: Program of secondary and tertiary route improvements to facilitate inter- and intrazonal assets. Promotion of Rabat as a country holiday staging post. Complete upgrading of Ta'Qali crafts center, integrated with development of Ta'Qali national park.
Zone 10: Determine policy for coastal resources:
- Potential for additional exploitation.
- Policy of phasing out existing activities and redeveloping or reclaiming as unexploited resource.
- Policy of ameliorative action or general environmental upgrading.
- Short-term policy aimed at increasing coastal capacity through low capital investment measures, particularly the limitation of beach concessions and ban on issuing new concessions.
- Special "Tourism Planning Unit (TPUs)" should be delineated and designated as "no go" development areas. Planning task forces should then be deployed to formulate best use plans for the units. Only when these policy plans are complete should the processing applications be reinstigated.
Zone 11: Policies may be grouped under two categories:
TPU 6 & 7/A1 & A2
Designated as special tourism planning units, they should, like the units in Zone 10 on Malta, be the subject of special task force study. The two areas identified have already been intensively exploited.
Policies recommended are:
- Enforcement of strict development controls and guidelines.
- Launching of pilot public works projects geared, like Paceville and Bugibbe, at Leverina private sector participation.
- A follow-on rolling program of public and private sector programs would then be replicated elsewhere.
TPU 8/B1, B2, & B3
- Policy of best use plan formulation for areas where essentially the resources have not been exploited but where significant potential exists.
Zone 12: TPU 9, B4, B5, & B6
- Includes the controversial area of Ta'cence. The major historical asset of Fort Chambrey and the port and harbor area of Mgarr.
- Ideally, this whole coastal stretch should be the subject of a detailed planning study. As an interim, a clear set of development conditions and performance criteria should be established for the three component areas and their contiguous areas.
- Particular emphasis should be placed on determining the scale and rate/phasing of development in respect to other interdependent resource constraints.

Figure 7.4. Maltese Islands Tourism Development Plan—Strategic Policy Plan.

Swahili architectural styles and urban layout in East Africa, and has had a development and conservation plan prepared by the United Nations Centre for Human Settlements (Habitat). These historical features along with a pleasant tropical climate, good beaches, marine areas for diving and sport fishing, the islands' scenic beauty, and clove farms comprise the tourism resources of Zanzibar.

Tourism was very limited with only a modest level of facilities and services available to tourists and attraction features that required conservation and development. The planning project was designed to prepare a comprehensive regional plan with detailed planning for specific sites of various types of accommodation and tourism use of historic buildings. The tourism development policy recommended in the plan, extracted from the plan report, is as follows:

> Formulation and adoption of appropriate tourism policy is the essential first step in developing tourism. Tourism policy indicates the type and direction which the area wishes to take on tourism development and provides the general basis for planning tourism and making decisions on its continuing development. Adoption of tourism policy indicates that the area has made an official commitment to develop tourism, and the policy provides the legal basis for guiding the general type and extent of tourism to be developed.
>
> ...the major elements of a suitable tourism policy statement for Zanzibar are recommended as follows:
>
> - International tourism should be developed as an important means of achieving greater understanding and appreciation of Zanzibar's history, culture and natural environment by foreigners, and of residents' developing some understanding of other people's customs and cultures.
> - International tourism also should be developed to provide additional employment, income and foreign exchange for Zanzibar, and to help diversify the islands' economy.
> - Domestic tourism should be developed as an important means of recreation, increasing understanding by Zanzibaris of their own historical, cultural and environmental heritage and by mainland Tanzanians of Zanzibar's rich historical and cultural heritage.
> - Domestic tourism also should be developed as a means of redistributing income within Zanzibar, especially from urban to rural areas and from mainland Tanzania to Zanzibar.
> - Tourism development should be integrated into the overall development policy, planning and strategy of Zanzibar and receive appropriate priority and its necessary share of development resources.
> - Tourism should be developed and operated so that it pro-

motes conservation and revitalization of the desirable aspects
of traditional cultural patterns, arts and handicrafts, and maintenance of the essence of religious beliefs and practices, all of
which represent the historic and and cultural heritage of Zanzibar; tourism should be planned, developed and organized so
that it does not result in serious social problems or cultural disruptions.

- Tourism should be developed in a carefully planned, controlled and organized manner so that it promotes conservation
of the natural environment, especially places of scenic beauty,
indigenous flora and fauna, important natural ecological systems, outdoor recreation potential, beaches and underwater
environments; tourism development should not result in any
type of serious air, water, noise and visual pollution.

- Tourism development should proceed on a controlled, systematic basis, according to a staged program of allocating development resources to specified places; the pace of tourism
development should be kept in balance with the number and
type of tourist arrivals, the development of infrastructure and
with Zanzibar's economic and social capability of absorbing
tourism growth.

- Tourism should be developed so that it will serve as a catalyst
for increased development of related economic activities such
as handicraft production, agriculture and fisheries and other
related industries and help in supporting improvements of
transportation facilities and services and other infrastructure.

- Tourism should be planned and developed so that it makes
maximum use of existing infrastructure and that improved
and new infrastructure should serve general purpose needs as
well as tourism.

- Tourist accommodation and other facilities should be designed to reflect and represent Zanzibar's distinctive architectural styles, the islands' tropical environment and utilize local
building materials to the extent possible; maximum use
should be made of renovated existing buildings which have architectural and historical significance for tourist facilities.

- All aspects of tourism development and operations should be
organized so that tourism functions in an efficient and integrated manner to meet the needs of international and domestic tourists and achieve the objectives of tourism development; especially important is the coordination of tourism
development among the various government agencies and
parastatals.

- Tourist facilities and services should be designed to meet the
range of needs of various tourist market segments, including
international and local standards, without being unduly

expensive to develop on the one hand and always meeting minimum requirements of sanitation, safety and on the other.

- Emphasis should be placed on employment of local persons in tourism; and persons working in all aspects of tourism should be properly trained to function effectively in their employment, and be given maximum opportunity for career development and job satisfaction.
- The general public should be educated to understand tourism and its role in Zanzibar's development policy and be given all possible opportunities to use and enjoy tourist facilities and attractions while still respecting and maintaining suitable standards of these facilities and services.

Tourism Development Plan for the Northeast Area of Northern Ireland

The subregional tourism plan for the northeast area of Northern Ireland in the U.K. was prepared for the Department of the Environment for Northern Ireland by a consortium of consultants in the late 1980s (Pieda Tourism and Leisure et al 1989). This case study is an example of a substantially developed tourism area that was somewhat declining in popularity and required rejuvenation through the planning process. The planning area, comprised of three local authorities, encompasses about 1,400 square kilometers and a population approaching 88,000. The center of the area is 72 kilometers by road from Belfast, the major city of Northern Ireland. At the time of plan preparation, tourism directly provided 7 percent of the area's employment and is considered to be a very significant sector in the future subregional economy.

This area is Northern Ireland's major coastal destination for overnight visitors and a leading destination for leisure day trips. In volume, the area received 1.7 million tourist nights in 1987 and 1.6 million day trippers in 1986. The majority of visitors are domestic with a much smaller number of overseas vacationers, including from Britain. Despite its extent of tourism development, the area was experiencing a declining market share of visitors, with its dominance as a major tourist destination severely eroded in recent years.

The approach to plan preparation was generally as follows:

- Analyze the historical and present tourism situation and any prevailing trends.
- Conduct a survey of visitors to provide information on the activities, perceptions, and attitudes of persons currently visiting the area.
- Survey and evaluate the tourism resources.
- Identify the major strengths and weaknesses of these resources.
- Prepare a locational analysis including entry points, destination/activity areas, touring bases, and tourism zones.
- Formulate an overall tourism strategy with aims (or objectives) and target markets.

- Formulate a locational strategy within the framework of the tourism strategy.
- Determine priority actions and projects and key projects.
- Specify steps for implementation of the plan.

In evaluating tourism resources, detailed discussions were held with numerous persons and organizations involved in the area's tourism. A descriptive inventory was prepared of these resources, and the seven most popular specific attractions, based on recorded visits, were identified. Evaluation of the area's provision of accommodation was emphasized as this was considered an important issue. Based on this evaluation, the major strengths and weaknesses of tourism were determined as follows:

- Strengths:
    1. Established tourism area—It is already a popular destination for overnight and day visitors.
    2. Key attractions—It already has important and unique visitor attractions.
    3. Accommodation—It has a substantial base of accommodation.
    4. Natural resources—It has a wealth of outstanding scenery and other natural resources, including the coast, sea, rivers, forest parks, and rural countryside.
    5. Accessibility—It enjoys excellent and direct road access, good rail links, and easy access to airport and sea ports.
    6. Leisure facilities—It is well served by existing indoor and outdoor leisure and recreation facilities.
    7. Shopping—Its main urban center has popular shopping facilities that attract tourists.
    8. Investment commitments—It has benefited from recent public and private sector investments, and interest has been indicated in pursuing future investment.
- Weaknesses:
    1. Northern Ireland—It has avoided the worst of civil unrest in the province, but it is still tarnished with the same image in the eyes of many tourists.
    2. Peripherality—It is a peripheral part of the U.K. and remote from European markets.
    3. Limited attractions—It appears to have a good range of places to visit, but the survey indicated a feeling that there is insufficient provision of wet weather attractions.
    4. Underdeveloped assets—It has specific areas and assets that are not being adequately promoted and developed as tourism assets.
    5. Lack of integration—It has no recognized tourist trails (or roads) that link together attractions, features, and stopping places.
    6. Population base—Its local population is not large enough to generate substantial VFR tourism or to give all-year-round support to particular facilities.
    7. Overseas market share—It does not attract a high proportion of overseas overnight visitors, in spite of its undoubted attractions.
    8. Business base—Its local industry and commerce are not large enough to encourage a great deal of business tourism.

9. Signposting—Its directional signposting and general interpretation (of attractions) are totally inadequate.

10. Areas of deficiency—Its main destination and accommodation bases are in the west, while eastern parts are underused and undervisited.

11. Built environment—It has a number of settlements that require environmental improvement.

The overall aims of the proposed development strategy were to:

- Attract more people to the area;
- Make people stay longer in the area; and
- Make them come back more often.

The proposed strategy was formulated with these specific target markets in mind:

- Home (domestic) holidaymakers;
- Day trippers;
- Nondomestic holidaymakers;
- Activity-oriented holidaymakers; and
- Small conferences and business meetings.

The plan pointed out that all of these five target markets will require an enhancement of the area's tourist facilities and services, and these market-led priorities were identified and incorporated into the strategy for specific locations and areas.

The locational analysis of the existing situation and the recommended locational strategy are depicted in Figure 7.5. As can be seen on the map, the main strategic features are destinations/activity areas, touring bases, entry points, and tourism zones. In summary, the locational strategy recommendations are:

- Continued enhancement of destination/activity areas and their integration within a system of tourist roads;
- Continued enhancement of touring bases, including development of better hotel and self-catering accommodation;
- Emphasis on enhancement of existing, and development of new, touring bases;
- Extension of tourism zone 1 and its attributes westwards;
- Encouragement of tourism development to create two new tourism zones;
- Establishment of formal entry point facilities at four places;
- Promotion of zone 5 as a tourism resource; and
- Encouragement of measures that actively support tourism as an economic activity in other rural areas (zone 6).

The plan included specific recommendations on location and development of two vehicular trail systems and stopover points at a variety of attraction features, some of which are recommended to be newly developed and others, which are existing, to be improved.

The priority actions and projects recommended are organized by the categories of:

- Enhancement of destination areas;
- Integration by tourist trails (roads);

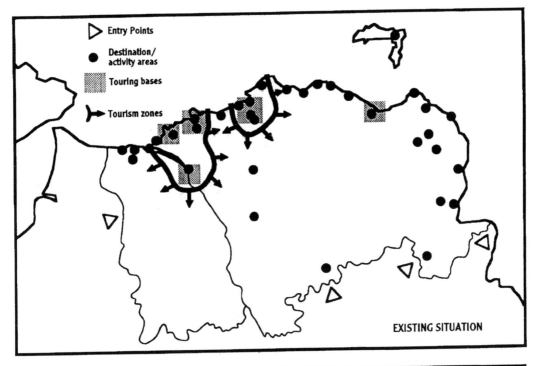

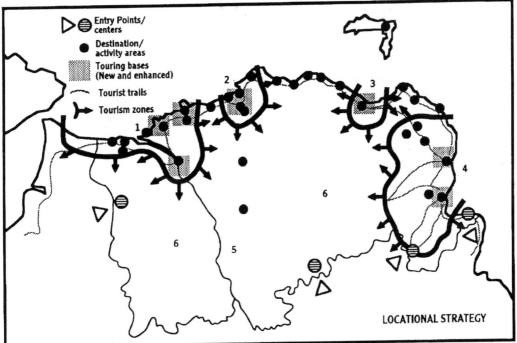

Figure 7.5. Tourism Study—Northeast area of Northern Ireland.

- Improvement of touring bases;
- Development of entry points;
- Managing the River Bann Corridor; and
- Promoting tourism in rural areas.

Actions and projects are individually identified and improvements specified with detailed conceptual planning prepared for some of the projects. In addition, the most important or key projects are recommended for priority development. The economic benefits of the plan were calculated, and they indicated that 3,100 additional jobs could be generated by the expansion of tourism during the 15-year plan period.

References

Jenkins, C. L., and B. M. Henry. 1982. "Government Involvement in Tourism in Developing Countries." *Annals of Tourism Research.* 9(4): 499–521.

Horwath and Horwath, Inc. 1989. *Maltese Islands Tourism Development Plan.* London.

Nash, Dennison and Richard Butler. 1990. "Alternative Forms of Tourism." *Annals of Tourism Research.* 17 (2): 302–305.

Pieda Tourism and Leisure, Ulster Marketing Surveys, and Shirley Millar, Tourism Consultant. 1989. *Tourism Study—North East Area (Northern Ireland).* (Commissioned by the Department of the Environment for Northern Ireland.) Belfast: Department of the Environment.

United Nations Development Programme and World Tourism Organization. 1983. *National Tourism Development Plan and Prefeasibility Analysis for the Socialist Republic of the Union of Burma.* Madrid: World Tourism Organization.

———. 1983. *Zanzibar Tourism Development Plan.* Madrid: World Tourism Organization.

Part Three

Community Level of
Tourism Planning

Part Two examined the national and regional levels of tourism planning while Part Three reviews the community, or more detailed, level of planning. The community level of tourism planning, as organized in this part, first sets forth some resort planning approaches, procedures and principles, next examines planning for urban and other more specialized forms of tourism, and then reviews the planning of tourist attractions and the organization of visitor activities related to the attractions. The final chapter in this part looks at some of the basic development and design standards that should be considered in the site planning and design of tourist facilities.

Because the community level of tourism planning adapts mostly the same approach, process, and techniques applied at the national and regional levels as described in Part Two, Part Three does not repeat explanation of much of that material, such as site carrying capacity analysis and selection criteria, in detail. Basically, the comprehensive, integrated, environmental, sustainable development and community involvement approach is applied the same at the community level of tourism planning as it is at the national and regional levels, but is now adapted to this more specific level. As in Part Two, case studies are presented at the end of each chapter to illustrate the actual application of some successful approaches, techniques, and principles.

8

Planning Tourist Resorts

Types of Resort Planning

As described in Chapter 7, a tourist resort is a destination area that is relatively self-contained and typically provides a wide range of tourist facilities and services, especially those designed for recreation and relaxation, learning experiences, or health. Resorts can be highly integrated, initially planned as cohesive entities, or, as evidenced by some older resorts, may have evolved over time without initial integrated planning but still function as self-contained destinations offering a range of facilities and services. Often, the latter type of traditional resort has received some planning after its initial development in order to improve its integration and be more functional and attractive to tourists. This post-development planning for improvement and sometimes expansion of traditional resorts has become especially common in recent years so that they can maintain their economic viability and compete effectively with the newer planned resorts. Any environmental and sometimes social problems that have resulted from their lack of initial planning will be mitigated and meet contemporary environmental standards.

The approach applied in this chapter on resort planning is aimed at both the planning of new resorts and the improvement, integration, expansion where possible, and revitalization of existing, more traditional type resorts. Although resorts may go through cycles often described as the four stages of discovery, growth, maturity, and decline (Coltman 1989), resulting from various factors, including changing life-styles, travel motivations, and new technology (especially in transportation), traditional resorts need not necessarily reach a plateau of popularity and then decline. Through the planning process, resorts can often be rejuvenated with environmental improvements and development of new markets and products. Also, with proper and imaginative planning, new integrated resorts need not eventually experience the decline stage but can remain viable through the continuing planning process.

The example of the development of gambling in Atlantic City, referred to previously, is an on-going attempt to rejuvenate that traditional American East Coast beach resort. Another example of beach resort revitalization is Brighton, which was a very popular nineteenth century beach resort in southern Britain, based on convenient rail access from a large population area, and which experienced a sharp decline of visitors during the post-World War II period with the advent of inexpensive air package tours from the U.K. to the Mediterranean beach resort areas. Resulting from planning and marketing efforts and some redevelopment in recent years, Brighton is undergoing revitalization now, based in part on convention and conference tourism. Waikiki, an unplanned and often criticized large beach resort area in the urban area of Honolulu, Hawaii, has maintained its vitality through continuing environmental and commercial improvements and development of new high quality hotels as well as rehabilitation of some of the older historic hotels. Waikiki serves a target market desiring a dynamic urban tourism environment combined with beach and marine activities and sight-seeing tours, while the more recent integrated planned resorts on the neighbor islands of Hawaii, which are also exceedingly popular, cater to a different tourist market desiring more recreation- and relaxation-oriented activities.

Not all resorts being developed today go through the discovery and growth stages of development, but are initially developed on a large-scale and, through intensive marketing activities, achieve immediate popularity and a substantial clientele. An example of this development approach is Cancun on the east coast of the Yucatan Peninsula of Mexico, which, through the cooperation of the World Bank and the government of Mexico's tourism agency, FONATUR (Fondo Nacional de Turismo), was initially planned and developed as a large integrated beach resort in the 1970s and was still expanding in the 1980s. This resort was sited on a largely deserted offshore beach island, which allowed for easier land acquisition than if a developed area had been selected that required resettlement of many people. Separately, on the mainland, a new town was constructed for the resort employees and their families.

The types of resorts to be considered in planning are beach and seaside resorts, mountain and ski resorts, holiday villages, spas and health resorts, and more specialized types, such as those oriented to marine diving, sport fishing, retreat relaxation, unusual and outstanding environmental features, and archaeological and historic sites. Resorts are now commonly based on a combination of attraction features catering to a diverse and activity-oriented tourist market mix. Because of contemporary market trends toward greater activity orientation of tourists, recreation and learning facilities and services are an increasingly important component of resort planning and operational management.

An example of a planned resort development based on both historic and scenic/recreational lake attractions is Kyongju in the Republic of Korea. This country has adopted a policy for developing domestic and international tourism that recognizes the need for a planned balance between resource protection and development. The Kyongju project, which involved various central government agencies and the Kyongju tourism agency, with some World Bank involvement, includes the city of Kyongju, Bomun Lake, and ruins of 14 historic sites, including some royal tombs. The development objectives were to enhance the country's cultural heritage through protection, conservation, and development of historic resources, build an international resort city based on the ancient Korean culture, and increase resident incomes by developing tourism-related facilities and activities in the area. Prepared in the early 1970s and now largely implemented, the Kyongju plan projects included road development, preserving historic monuments, constructing hotels, catering facilities, an amenity core, apartments, and parks, and maintaining forests and open space according to an integrated plan. The hotels and other facilities are focused on Bomun Lake, which is located only a short distance from the historic sites.

Resort Planning Approach

Figure 8.1 graphically illustrates the general resort planning process, which is described in the following sections. Although this planning process is presented in a neatly sequential manner, it should be noted that the actual planning, especially for large projects, is often in fact more complicated in the sense that revisions of the plan for later stages of development may be made over a long period of time with the plan evolving based on changing market conditions, experimentation with actual development of certain aspects of the plan, local response to the initial first stage development, and other influencing factors. The step shown at the bottom of the planning process chart for plan refinement of later phases of resort attempts to convey this continuing planning activity. However, even though plan revisions are made, they should be done within the framework of the plan objectives, site carrying capacity levels, and environmental and social impact parameters. Public review should take place at the crucial steps of the planning process to ensure that the plan meets government and community objectives.

Basic Approach

Ideally, the resort site will have been selected, its general type, size, and character determined, a conceptual plan prepared, and a prefeasibility analysis conducted to indicate its likely viability in the national, regional, or subregional plan, as explained in Chapter 7. The regional plan will have included the survey and evaluation of tourists attractions in the area, the environmental, economic, and sociocultural considerations, the market analysis and general projection of type and number of accommodation units and other tourist facilities, services and infrastructure required, including transportation access to the resort area, and selection of the site according to the criteria listed in Chapter 7. However, the market and product assessment conducted in the national or regional plan will

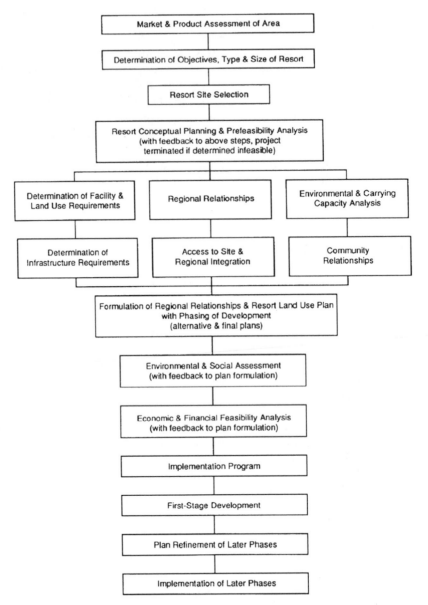

Figure 8.1. Resort Planning Process.

usually require further specification and often updating for the specific resort area as a more definitive basis for its planning.

In the absence of a regional tourism plan or if that plan is outdated, the resort planning project will need to commence with the basic considerations of market and product assessment, determination of the resort development objectives, type and size, the site selection, conceptual planning, and prefeasibility analysis to first make certain that the proposed resort is likely to be economically viable and environmentally and socially acceptable and to determine its general characteristics. The market analysis will determine the types and extent of market demand that can be anticipated or generated and should include consideration of both domestic and international markets, based on the tourism product available, accessibility, competition from similar resorts, and any other relevant factors. The product assessment needs to include the attractions of the immediate resort site and the general resort area, accessibility to the general area and resort site, and the social and physical infrastructure. At this stage, it is important to formulate the objectives of the resort development and its basic concept or "image" of the resort, that is, what is the desired type, character, and size of the proposed resort, including what general socioeconomic market level and quality of development it is aiming for, and its approach to protecting the environment and involving the local community.

If there is no regional plan, then regional planning considerations must be made in the resort planning process to ensure that the proposed resort is integrated into regional patterns of resource development and infrastructure and will have adequate access, is well related to any other tourist attraction features in the region, and has the coordinated support of the various local government agencies involved in the planning process and community organizations that will be affected by the resort. Local government and community involvement can be achieved through establishing a project steering committee, holding public hearings on the proposed project at various stages of its planning, and arranging informal meetings between the planning team and government agency staff and community organizations.

After determination of the type, size, and location of the resort, its regional relationships and access, the facility, land use, and other infrastructure requirements and site environmental analysis, and its community relationships, outline plans are formulated and evaluated with respect to meeting the resort development objectives, achieving economic and financial viability, and limiting any negative environmental and socioeconomic impacts. Based on this evaluation, the optimum plan is selected and refined as the final plan. Local government and community involvement and feedback is especially important to maintain during this plan formulation stage. Then the final environmental and social impact assessment and the final economic and financial feasibility analysis are prepared with feedback to the plan and any necessary adjustments made. A map scale of 1:2,000 to 1:5,000 is suitable for the draft plans and a scale of 1:1,000 to 1:2,000 is appropriate for the final plan drawings.

Because large resorts typically require many years to complete and there are always unpredictable and changing factors in market and product characteristics, phasing of resort development is essential. The first phase, expected to be developed in the near future, will be precisely planned, while subsequent phases will be more generally planned in order to allow flexibility for later more precise planning based on circumstances prevailing at that time. However, development concepts for later phases should be initially described and shown on the plan in order to maintain the integrity and consistency of the resort character or 'image' and

Mauna Lani Resort on the Island of Hawaii in the State of Hawaii—This recently developed resort represents integrated planning for various hotels, condominium self-catering units, a commercial center, golf courses and other recreational facilities, public parks, historic areas, and a utility service complex. The environmental approach was applied throughout the resort planning process. (Courtesy of Belt, Collins & Associates)

make certain that the proposed development stays within environmental and social impact parameters.

As with national and regional planning, a multi-disciplinary team approach is required for resort planning, including:

- Resort land use and site planners;
- Hotel and resort market analysts;
- Hotel and resort economic and financial feasibility analysts;
- Various types of transportation and other infrastructure engineers;
- Perhaps hotel architects and resort landscape architects; and
- Often environmental specialists and sociologists.

Other specialists may be required depending on the type of resort, such as golf course, marina, and ski lift and slope designers, and historic preservation specialists.

Regional Relationships

Consideration of regional relationships to the resort is especially necessary to determine if adequate access is available to satisfy the projected or targeted market demand and size of resort being planned. It will also help decide the type of access, whether by air, road, water, or a combination of these transportation modes. Also important is the relationship and access of the resort to other attraction features in the area and nearby towns that may provide shopping and entertainment facilities for tourists and where resort employees may live. The availability of water and electric power supply, sewage and solid waste disposal, and telecommunications in the region must be investigated. The regional settlement and demographic patterns should be examined with respect to determining the potential labor supply to work in the resort and the availability of housing and community services for resort employees who may migrate from outside the area. Any sociocultural impact implications of the resort development at the regional level should also be examined.

Existing regional plans and development programs should be examined to determine whether any proposed changes in land uses, transportation, and other infrastructure will affect the resort and, more generally, if these plans and programs provide the basis for integrating the proposed resort into the regional development patterns. The presence of other resorts in the same vicinity or region should be considered in terms of whether the proposed resort will compete with or be complementary to existing resorts. The regional relationships review may well indicate that some improvement of regional infrastructure such as the transportation or water supply system is required in order to satisfactorily serve the resort. The cost of any regional level improvements necessary for the resort development will need to be included in the economic feasibility analysis of the resort development.

Site Environmental Analysis and Community Relationships

In applying the environmental and sustainable development planning approach, a careful and detailed environmental survey and analysis of the site and its immediate environs is essential. The elements to be considered in this survey and analysis, and which are plotted on maps, include the following:
- Location and size of the site.
- Natural environmental characteristics including:
    1. Detailed topography of the land, which is shown on contour maps and

usually divided into slope categories, such as 0 to 5 percent, 6 to 10 percent, and so on, related to developability; often special topographic surveys are required to obtain this information.

2. Climate, including temperatures, rainfall, wind patterns, humidity, fog,
   and amount of sunshine, indicated by seasons; micro-climatic conditions
   within the resort site may be important to record.

3. Water features and characteristics, including any streams or rivers and
   their water flow characteristics, ponds and lakes, the offshore current patterns, tidal ranges and underwater topography in seaside locations, and
   the quality of surface waters, including type and extent of any pollution.

4. Extent and quality of natural attraction features and their need for conservation, including, for example, the width, length, type, and quality of
   beach sand (or other type of shoreline) in seaside areas; the length, elevation differences, gradients, and area of ski slopes in skiing areas; the type
   and extent of scenic views and opportunities for hiking and riding in
   mountain areas; and the type, extent, and quality of mineral springs in
   health resorts. The attraction features will have been previously surveyed
   to help determine the location, type, and size of resort, but are surveyed
   and analyzed in more detail at this stage to provide a basis for determining
   their integration into the resort plan and the conservation and development measures that should be applied.

5. Geology, including any interesting geological formations that should be
   preserved, underground water resources, and the quality level of underground water.

6. Vegetative cover, including types and location of important trees and
   other vegetation that possibly should be preserved.

7. Indigenous animal life and their conservation value.

8. Soils, including type and depth of soils as related to landscaping, grading,
   and building foundation considerations.

9. Environmental hazards, including any proneness of the site or parts of the
   site to high winds and rainfall, earthquakes, landslides, erosion, and
   flooding.

10. Important ecological systems and their conservation value.

11. Scenic view sites and planes, especially those that give the site a particular
    environmental character and should be preserved.

- Land use, tenure, and infrastructure patterns, including:

  1. Existing land use and settlement patterns, including any existing tourism
     development and any proposed changes of land uses on the site.

  2. Historical land uses of previous land use patterns that may provide useful
     information about the site.

  3. Any existing archaeological and historical sites by type and location that
     should be researched for scientific purposes and considered for preserva-
     tion and integration into the resort plan.

  4. Land tenure patterns if the site is not yet acquired and available for devel-
     opment.

  5. Transportation facilities and services of any existing or proposed roads,

railway, footpaths, or other type of transportation facilities and and their characteristics and extent of use.

6. Other infrastructure facilities and services and their characteristics.

- Socioeconomic characteristics, including:
    1. Characteristics and distribution of any existing population living on the site.
    2. Any existing economic activities on the site.
    3. Land values of the the site if it is not yet acquired and available for development.
- Nearby site characteristics, including:
    1. Environmental characteristics of adjacent and nearby lands as they may relate to or be affected by the resort development, including areas within view of the site that may affect its visual quality.
    2. Land uses, transportation facilities, and other infrastructure of adjacent and nearby lands as they relate to or may be affected by the resort development, including any existing or proposed land uses and infrastructure that may generate air, water, noise, or visual pollution affecting the site.
    3. Socioeconomic characteristics of nearby areas, especially related to providing employees to work in the resort and availability of housing and community facilities and services for resort employees, as well as any possible social impacts generated by the resort development.

As an example of the importance of a land use survey of even apparently undeveloped sites, it is a requirement in Hawaii that all resort and other development sites be surveyed by a competent archaeological team before the plan is prepared so that any archaeological sites are located, excavated, and documented with important sites preserved. Otherwise, obscure but scientifically important archaeological sites may be destroyed in the process of the resort development.

Analysis of the resort site characteristics can best be done using the map overlay technique to show relationships of the various characteristics. As explained, this analysis may now be accomplished using computer technology. The composite map will indicate developable areas, places that should be conserved as important attraction features and for environmental reasons and, on hilly sites, where view corridors and planes should be maintained. Any existing development will be shown on the composite map. The environs of the site should be included in this analysis so that the resort development can be planned as an integrated area in the regional setting. Based on this analysis, the major opportunities and problems of the site and its environs can be ascertained, including identification of those site features that will give the resort its special and unique character.

An essential aspect of the environmental analysis is the determination of the carrying capacity of the site, as explained in Chapter 6. If a regional plan has been properly prepared, the general carrying capacity of the area will have been calculated, but a more detailed carrying capacity analysis should be carried out as part of the resort planning analysis. Carrying capacity standards will need to be determined based, in large part, on the type of resort being planned, the general character of the regional setting (for example, whether it is already intensively developed or is mostly agricultural or open space), the environmental sensitivity of the site itself, and the standards that are applicable in similar resorts elsewhere. Carrying capacity standards applied in a high quality, low-density type resort in a remote undeveloped area would be higher than the standards used for a higher density resort in an urban type of setting.

As emphasized, carrying capacity analysis provides only guidelines for establishing development thresholds or saturation levels. These levels will vary somewhat depending on how well the resort is planned, developed, and managed. The carrying capacity levels should, of course, be calculated for peak period use as well as average use, and a decision made as to what extent, if any, the saturation levels are allowed to be exceeded for the very short peak period.

If there is a resident population living on or near the site, community relationships will need to be carefully considered. The resident population should, through their local government agencies or community organizations, be informed about the proposed resort, involved in reviewing the draft planning proposals, and met with to discuss about how they can be involved in and benefit from the new development. If at all possible, the site should be selected and planned so that relocation of residents is not required, but this is not always feasible. If relocation is necessary, particular attention must be given to equitable compensation being paid to the residents for their land and housing, and assistance provided in effecting relocation to a suitable new area, situated if possible near the resort site so that residents can still maintain their former community relationships. Relocation is not always an easy task, especially in places where people are traditionally attached to the land for social and economic reasons. A fair compensation and relocation program should be carefully prepared in consultation with the residents, with adequate time and budget allocated to accomplish this program. Efforts should be made for residents of the site and its environs to directly benefit from the resort development if they want, through provision of employment in the resort construction and operations and higher quality housing and community services than they previously had available.

Determining Facility, Land Use, and Infrastructure Requirements

Based on the general type and size of the resort initially established in the regional plan or as part of the resort planning study, and with input from the site environmental analysis and regional and community relationships, the resort facility, land use, and infrastructure requirements can be determined. Typical resort facilities and land uses that should be considered include the following:

- Accommodation, including hotels and other types of accommodation such as apartments, townhouses, villas, and camping and caravan parks.
- Commercial facilities, including restaurants, retail shops selling convenience, specialty, and handicraft items, barbering, and beautician services, and so forth.
- Recreation and cultural facilities such as golf courses, tennis and other game

courts, swimming pools, beach, diving or ski facilities, children's playgrounds, cultural centers and performance stages, and small museums.

- Health facilities such as mineral water baths, massage and exercise facilities, and sauna rooms.
- Convention and meeting facilities of various types and sizes.
- Specialized entertainment facilities such as night clubs, casinos, cinemas, and performing theaters.
- Resort administration, utility and maintenance facilities for development and operation of on-site infrastructure, resort management operations, and maintenance of the resort common areas, including roads, recreation facilities, landscaping, and perhaps a resort commercial center.
- Land and water conservation areas of specific environmental features, which may also be important attraction features of the resort; sometimes special environmental features such as botanic gardens or aviaries are specially developed in resorts as attractions.
- Archaeological and historic sites that may be on the site and serve as major or minor attraction features.
- Resort nurseries, which are often developed on-site in large resorts to provide the resort landscaping material; these nurseries may sometimes be developed to also serve as small botanic gardens in the resort.
- Landscaped areas and buffer zones to give the resort a sense of openness, define its boundary, and buffer it from adjacent land uses and lands not suitable for development, such as steep sloped areas, to be retained as open space.
- Hotel, catering, and tourism training schools, which are not often but may be included in a large resort.
- Employee housing areas and related community facilities for some or all of the resort employees, which may be located on or near the site.

Determination of the types of resort facilities will, of course, depend on the type of resort being planned and, to some extent, its size. A large resort, for example, will typically include more specialized commercial, recreation, and cultural facilities, often concentrated in a resort or recreation center because of the greater number of clientele to support these facilities, than a smaller one-hotel resort where facilities will necessarily be of smaller scale and variety. A large integrated beach or ski resort may include a variety of types of accommodation ranging from medium and low-rise hotels, cottages, self-catering apartments, townhouses and villas, a resort center with restaurants, retail shops, nightclubs and discos, a small museum and performance stage, a recreation complex of a golf course and tennis and other game courts, and a separate convention center, plus the major attraction of the beach and perhaps a marina or ski slopes and lift equipment.

A difficult decision affecting land use requirements that often must be made is to what extent some facilities such as restaurants, retail shops, conference and meeting facilities, performance stages, and recreation facilities are located in the hotels or outside the hotels in centralized complexes. Often the hotels want to retain many of these facilities in their own establishments as a source of revenue, but if all such facilities are located in the hotels, there is not the opportunity to develop a viable resort center that provides an interesting place for visitors to go and offers them a choice of facilities. Usually, the best approach is to allow the hotels to provide some small-scale facilities on-site as a convenience to tourists and source of some hotel revenue, but to concentrate the major ancillary facilities in a central complex outside the hotel. Experience with resort development has indicated that tourists want to spend some of their time outside the hotels, especially to try different restaurants, shops, and recreation activities, for a change of environments and experiences.

Whether conference and meeting facilities are located within the hotels or in a separate complex must be decided and depends to a considerable extent on the size of conventions, conferences, and meetings, and consequent size of facilities required, which the resort wishes to attract. Minor recreation facilities such as swimming pools are justifiably located on the hotel grounds, but major ones such as golf courses and large tennis complexes are best located where they can conveniently serve all the resort guests.

Determination of the land use space requirements will depend on the type of resort and especially its intensity of development being planned. For example, in a medium-density, low-rise beach resort, in which an average density of 50 hotel rooms per hectare of hotel site area may be appropriate, a projection of market demand for 2,000 rooms would require 40 hectares of land area for the hotel sites, and a demand for 500 apartment and townhouse units at an average density of 10 units per hectare would require 50 hectares of land area for this type of land use. A resort center will vary in size depending on the number of facilities of restaurants and shops and other activities planned to be in the center. An 18-hole golf course, depending on its specific characteristics, will require 50 to 60 hectares of land area. The land area requirements of each development site is calculated to include internal roadways and parking, landscaping and open space, and on-site recreation facilities such as swimming pools and tennis courts. The area requirements of other land use categories for the resort common use areas such as the attraction features, conservation areas, major resort roads and other transportation elements, resort commercial and convention centers, and utility and maintenance service areas are calculated based on the specific characteristics of those uses with allowance made for sufficient landscaping and open space to buffer the uses and give them suitable environmental settings.

Based on the type and extent of facility development, the infrastructure requirements of access to the resort and the internal transportation system, water supply, electric power, sewage and solid waste disposal, and telecommunications can be calculated, utilizing accepted infrastructure development standards. As emphasized in Part Two, access and water supply are often the most crucial elements of infrastructure and the availability of these, as well as the other types of infrastructure, will have been considered in the regional planning of the resort area and the resort prefeasibility analysis. The resort utility and maintenance facility and land use requirements may be substantial if the resort includes extensive common area landscaping and recreation facilities, as well as water and sewage treatment plants and their distribution systems.

As mentioned, the determination of facility, land use, and infrastructure re-

Poste de Flacq Island near St. Géran Hotel, Mauritius—As part of the resort hotel development, this nearby small island was designated for day-use activities, with very limited permanent structures permitted and the natural enviromental character retained. Poste de Flacq is open to any visitors, including residents, on a fee basis (for transportation to the island), in addition to the hotel guests, and is a very popular day tour destination. (Courtesy of the Mauritius Government Tourist Office)

quirements will also depend on the site environmental analysis and especially the determination of the carrying capacity, which will have established the acceptable maximum level of development. There must be feedback between the environmental analysis and the determination of the facility, land use, and infrastructure requirements.

Resort Planning Principles

Each resort and its site are unique, and the planning must be adapted to the local situation; categorical application of a formula approach may result in a stereotyped and uninteresting resort plan. However, some basic principles are applicable in most resort planning and should be considered in the plan formulation.

Some Fundamental Concepts

A basic principle is to emphasize what is unique about the type of resort and its environment in order to give the resort a distinctive 'image' and character that provides a contrast to the tourists' home environment. If the resort environment is an interesting one (such as on the seaside or in the mountains), which is the case for many resorts, the specific environmental setting should be the dominant theme with the resort facilities reinforcing and complementing the environmental features and not dominating them. If the immediate environment is not especially interesting, as may be the case, for example, near an archaeological or historic site or at an artificial type of man-made attraction, then the planning, design, and landscaping of the resort should in itself create a definite theme, perhaps one related to the attraction feature or a distinctive architectural style that gives it a sense of uniqueness. In either situation, it is essential to establish a compatible relationship and proper scale between the resort facility development and the natural environment.

In environmentally-oriented resorts, providing the opportunity for tourists to have contact with nature, through views or closer physical contact by walking and using the environmental features or often a combination of these, is important in emphasizing the tourists' experience of being in a different environmental setting. This contact with nature can be reinforced with development of landscaping and gardens within the resort, as well as maintaining the natural environmental features of the site and environs as the dominant ones. In many cases, the resort should be considered as a nature park within which tourist facilities are carefully located and designed.

In some resort situations, the opportunity for contact with local residents is also important to plan for so that the resort is not an isolated enclave and tourists can learn about the local culture and society. This contact can take place in the nearby towns and villages by developing some interesting attractions such as shopping and museums, and by encouraging residents to visit the resort attractions and use its recreation and commercial facilities.

Some Specific Principles

Some more specific principles that have general application include the following:

- Conservation of special environmental features—These include major attraction features such as beaches and marine areas, ponds, lakes, lagoons, archaeological and historic sites, ski slopes, large trees and groups of trees, unusual geological formations, and hilltops that should be preserved to maintain the resort character. Places unsuitable for development, such as swamps and steep slopes, need to conserved. These can often be made into interesting environmental features of the resort by, for example, landscaping and developing footpaths and scenic viewpoints on steep slopes and boat rides through wetland areas.

- Maintenance of view planes and corridors—Maintaining both nearby and distant views of important environmental features such as mountains, beaches, oceans and lakes, and prominent archaeological and historic structures through careful siting and height limit controls of the resort buildings is essential to maintain and reinforce the resort character.
- Grouping of resort facilities and activities—Functional grouping of the different types of accommodation, recreation, and commercial facilities provides for efficient use by visitors and servicing by infrastructure and offers contrasting activity areas including some that are quiet and tranquil and others that are busy and dynamic.
- Proper relationship of the major accommodation areas to the main resort attractions—This principle involves siting of the hotels and other accommodation areas near to, for convenience of access, but not impinging upon and depreciating the environmental setting of the major attraction features such as beaches, water areas, and golf courses. In mountain and ski areas, siting of facilities should be places offering good views, but not obstructing the views, and should be conveniently located for access to the attraction features.
- Central and convenient location of commercial and recreation facilities—Commercial, cultural, and related facilities are typically located in a resort center (in a large resort) with convenient access from the major accommodation areas. Although not necessarily in a central location, the major recreation facilities should have convenient access.
- Controlled access to the resort—Controlled access limits the amount of traffic in the resort and reduces the possibility for traffic problems. Usually, one or two major access points to the resort are sufficient, and a separate access point for service vehicles is often provided.
- Efficient and interesting internal circulation network—The internal circulation network should be efficiently laid out, with adequate off-street parking and good landscaping, and designed to be interesting and safe for users by offering attractive views and discouraging high-speed driving. Emphasis should be placed on development and use of an internal walkway system and a non-polluting public type of internal transportation system.
- Buffer zone around the resort—A landscaped area along the resort boundaries provides a buffer between the resort and adjacent land uses that is especially important if the resort will create any disturbances to adjacent land uses or those uses are not completely in harmony with the resort (realizing that the resort site has been selected in part based on compatible nearby land uses).
- Provision of general public access to the resort and major attraction features—The resort and major attraction features should be open and easily accessible to the general public and residents of the area on a controlled basis (to prevent crime, vandalism, and nuisances) and not reserved exclusively for tourist use.
- Provision of adequate infrastructure—In addition to good access and internal circulation system, the resort should have an adequate water supply, electric

- power, sewage and solid waste disposal, drainage, and telecommunications systems in order to prevent environmental problems. This should be economically efficient to operate.
- Appropriate facility design and landscaping—Suitable siting, architectural design, and landscaping are essential to reinforce the resort's environment, give it a special character, and provide an interesting and attractive setting for tourists.
- Staying within the environmental capacity of the resort site—As emphasized previously, not exceeding carrying capacity levels is essential in order to maintain the resort's continuing viability and market attractiveness and not to generate environmental or social problems.
- Provision of adequate housing and community facilities and services for resort employees—If the resort is located near existing villages, towns, or cities, resort employees will probably live in those places. However in remote areas or if the number of resort employees is very high requiring in-migration of people, provision will need to be made on or near the resort site for housing and related community facilities and services for some or all of the employees. Often, the best approach is development of a new planned and integrated community located near the resort.
- Phasing of development—The resort should be planned in such a manner that its development can be phased over a period of time. Planning for phasing implies that each stage is somewhat self-contained and can function effectively before the remaining stages are developed.

As will be explained in more detail in Chapter 13, "Socioeconomic Impacts," there are various techniques that can be applied to socially and economically integrate the resort into the local community so that residents of the area can directly benefit from the resort development. Chapter 11 examines the development and design standards applicable to tourist facility development in resorts and Chapter 12 explores environmental considerations in more depth.

Formulating the Resort Plan

Formulation of the resort plan requires both the systematic approach set forth here and, equally important, a sense of imagination and creativity on the part of the planning team. The basic approach used is the same as for national and regional planning: formulating alternative outline plans, evaluating these, and then selecting and refining the final plan.

Steps in Plan Formulation

The basic steps in formulating the resort plan are as follows:

1. Consideration of the development objectives and the desired type and character of the resort.

2. Determination and mapping of regional relationships and access to the resort, including consideration of any proposed regional land use and transportation changes that may affect the resort planning.

3. Consideration of any community feedback on the resort development and local government policies and regulations that affect the resort, and maintenance of close coordination with the local government agencies and community organizations.

4. Consideration of relationships with adjacent and nearby land uses.

5. Consideration of socioeconomic and infrastructure relationships with the local community, including the local labor supply, as well as housing and community facilities and services for future resort employees and their families.

6. Using the environmental analysis maps, determination of the resort areas suitable for development, conservation, and other uses.

7. Allocation of the facility and land use area requirements to the environmental maps, application of the resort planning principles reviewed previously and any additional ones decided upon, and allocation of the number and type of accommodation units to the various designated accommodation sites. Simultaneously, plan the main and service vehicle access points and internal circulation system as related to the land use areas, considering all the possible means of circulation with emphasis on pedestrian-oriented and nonpolluting type transportation system.

8. Preparation of plans for the other infrastructure required.

9. Preparation of alternative outline composite land use and infrastructure plans and evaluation of these using the matrix technique with respect to various criteria, including:

   - Meeting the development objectives and achieving the desired type and character of the resort; meeting regional development objectives may also be an important criterion;
   - Providing the types and number of accommodation units required to meet the targeted market demand;
   - Extent of positive and negative environmental impact and staying within the carrying capacity parameters;
   - Extent of positive and negative sociocultural impact;
   - Feasibility of providing infrastructure;
   - Extent of economic and financial feasibility; and
   - Other factors, for example, feasibility of phasing development.

10. Selection of the optimum plan and refining it, including specification of development staging. The first stage development area is typically planned in more detail than the subsequent stages.

11. Preparation of development standards and architectural and landscaping guidelines. Conceptual site plans and architectural and landscape design concepts may be prepared for the first stage development area.

12. Preparation of the final environmental and social impact assessment of the resort with feedback and any necessary adjustments made to the plan.

13. Preparation of the final economic and financial analysis with feedback and any necessary adjustments made to the plan.
14. Preparation of the implementation program, including:
    - Zoning regulations and design review procedure;
    - Respective public and private investment policy;
    - Financial plan, setting forth estimates of costs, revenues, cash flows, and financial arrangements, including sources of financing;
    - Administrative procedures for development and operation of the resort. This may include consideration of establishing a development and management authority or corporation;
    - Development program for first stage development of the resort; and
    - Investment brochures and promotion of the resort.

Special Considerations

A practical consideration to be made in the planning process is determining to what extent local construction capability exists to develop the resort and whether the necessary construction materials are available locally. If local construction capability to handle both the resort development and other general construction demands in the area is limited, this may be a factor in deciding the phasing of development or may result in increased costs if outside construction firms are brought in. While local building materials should be used to the greatest extent possible, it may also be necessary to import materials at higher cost. If it is necessary to bring in construction workers from outside the area, housing and community facilities will need to be provided for them. Importing construction workers as well as permanent resort employees, especially if from a different national, cultural, or language background, to the local area may create social conflicts with residents that must be considered and anticipated.

Some of the basic decisions to be made in resort development implementation are the respective investment roles of the public and private sectors, particularly in the financing of infrastructure, the most suitable type of resort development and management organizational structure, the best means to ensure that the desired development and design standards of tourist facilities are maintained, and the development program. These and other implementation considerations are reviewed in Chapter 15 on implementation.

The financial plan will need to consider the factors of:
- Capital costs for land acquisition, off-site and on-site infrastructure, common area landscaping, accommodation, commercial, cultural and recreational facilities (including site preparation and landscaping), research, plan preparation, and facility and engineering design;
- Operational costs of resort administration, maintenance of common areas, security and infrastructure, operation of the infrastructure, and other resort services;
- Estimates of revenues from sale or lease of the development sites, any commer-

Golf course and condominiums at Kapalua Bay Resort on the Island of Maui in Hawaii—A commonly applied planning principle in integrated resports is to locate townhouse or apartment units adjacent to the golf course fairways in order to provide attractive landscape views from the units and gain increased land values alongside the fairways. (Courtesy of the Kapalua Bay Resort)

cial operations carried out by the resort administration, and any infrastructure user fees;

- Sources of financing and financial arrangements;
- Projections of total costs and revenues;
- The cash flows required, considering any subsidies, taxes, and development incentives involved; and
- The final net benefits accruing to the developer, whether a public or private entity, including appreciation of assets.

If the infrastructure of water supply, electric power, sewage and solid waste disposal, and telecommunications are provided from the general community systems of the area, the user fees are paid to those companies. If this infrastructure is provided by the resort, the user fees are paid to the resort development company or authority.

Throughout the planning and implementation process, close liaison should be maintained with the government agencies involved to keep them informed and obtain their feedback on the plan. Typically, public hearings are held to officially review the draft and final plans. Also, a close relationship should be maintained by the developer and his planning team, whether a public or private entity, with local community organizations to receive their feedback on the development proposals and ascertain how the resort can best be integrated into the local community. If the public agencies and community organizations have been involved in the planning process and are in agreement with the proposed resort plan, they will more likely support it.

Planning for Improvements to Existing Resorts

The procedure for planning improvements to and often the expansion of existing resorts is much the same as for new resorts, except that there are usually more constraints, both those presented by the existing development and in implementation. Constraints of the existing development may include, for example in a worst case scenario, insufficient landscaping, park and open space areas, limited vehicular parking, traffic congestion resulting from an inadequate circulation and underdeveloped walkway and public transportation system, other substandard infrastructure, poorly designed and functionally inefficient buildings, proliferation of advertising signs and overhead utility lines that mar the landscape, and scenic views obstructed by unsuitable siting of buildings. In more serious cases, the environmental carrying capacity may have been exceeded, resulting in severe environmental problems, and social problems may exist. For implementation of improvements, there may be problems of financial constraints, outdated regulations, and various local vested groups who have difficulty agreeing on the changes needed. In some traditional resort areas, the government and tourism enterprises may want to shift the tourist markets, usually to a higher spending market segment profile.

In planning for improvements and expansion, the planning procedure shown in Figure 8.1 can be followed, except, of course, that the site already exists, although there may be some choice available to select the expansion area. The tourist markets are assessed with consideration given to any changes desired in the market mix. Because there is existing tourism, the present market can be surveyed to determine both the tourists' characteristics and their perception of the present quality of the resort development and how they feel it should be improved. The tourist product of the existing development should be evaluated, especially the quality of the attraction features and the facility development as related to the existing and targeted tourist markets. The redevelopment objectives and desired type and size of the renovated resort are established, and a conceptual plan and prefeasibility analysis are prepared.

The determination of facility, land use, and infrastructure requirements includes both the existing development and any redevelopment and upgrading needed, as well as possible expansion based on the targeted markets. The site environmental analysis, of course, includes the existing land use and development patterns with identification of specific problems, and the carrying capacity analysis of the overall site is prepared, including the existing developed areas and any proposed expansion areas. If the carrying capacities are reaching saturation or being exceeded, the facility and land use requirements may need to be adjusted accordingly, although some capacity constraints may be resolved through infrastructure and other types of improvements. Community relationships may be an especially important factor to research because development already exists and may be creating some social problems. Regional relationships should be reviewed to determine whether the existing access to the area requires improvement and if other regional factors are well related to the resort.

With application of the planning principles and consideration given to the special characteristics and problems of the area, alternative plans are formulated and evaluated and a final plan selected and refined, an environmental and social impact assessment is carried out, and the final economic and financial feasibility analysis is conducted. Phasing of improvements and new development is indicated in the plan, and an implementation program is prepared. Important aspects of plan implementation are:

- Review of present regulations and design guidelines and identifications of aspects that may be obsolete, with any necessary changes made to update them;
- Preparing a viable financial plan, including realistic sources of financing and any development incentives needed; and
- Deciding on the most appropriate administrative structure, whether public or private or a combination of these, and legal mechanism to achieve the recommended improvements and expansion.

Often a major planning consideration is whether new development should take place as in-fill of the present developed area if there is that possibility, be a contiguous extension of present development, or be located on a new nearby site with a connection to the existing resort. If the existing resort has a special character and historic association, one approach is to retain that character as it is (with any necessary upgrading done) and develop the expansion on a new nearby site. The existing resort, if well known, can help market the expansion and the new development can, in turn, help finance retention of the existing development character.

It is particularly important that the planning be conducted in close coordination with the local government agencies, private sector tourism associations, and general community organizations because of the complexity typically associated with improving existing tourist resorts and the need to resolve the many vested interests represented in the existing development. This approach also helps to encourage the support and involvement of these groups in implementation of the plan.

Case Studies

The case studies presented are of large-scale resort plans, all of which are being implemented in different types of environments, with two being beach-oriented and the third a ski and mountain resort. The Nusa Dua resort in Bali represents an integrated resort plan providing a wide range of facilities developed by a public corporation. The Mauna Lani resort in Hawaii is somewhat smaller-size but highly integrated and contains may self-catering and residential units as well as hotels. The Whistler ski resort in British Columbia represents integrated planning and controlled development of a resort community and village center with ski slopes developed for year-round use. Case studies of smaller-scale resorts are presented in Chapters 11 and 12 as they relate to development and design standards and environmental considerations.

Nusa Dua Resort, Bali

The Nusa Dua resort in Bali, Indonesia is an example of a large-scale beach resort developed within the framework of a regional plan and planned as an integrated resort to be implemented over a long period of time. A case study in Chapter 6 presented the planning analysis that resulted in selection of the resort site in an area of southern Bali. That site met the location criteria of having potentially good access to the airport, the provincial capital city of Denpasar, and the island's excursion road network to the major tourist attraction areas, provided a large developable site area with little existing land use development or important value for other resource use, and offered attractive beaches and ocean/island views. Although in private ownership, the land was available at a reasonable cost. Bali's primary attractions are its rich and diverse cultural patterns and scenic beauty, but it was found from experience with tourism areas elsewhere in Bali and the world that, given the opportunity, most tourists prefer to stay in a beach resort as a base for taking cultural and sightseeing day tours, so that they can spend some of their time engaging in beach relaxation and marine activities, that is, combining touristic experiences.

In addition to identifying the Nusa Dua resort site as the place where the majority of new accommodation would be developed on the island during the foreseeable future, the Bali regional tourism plan (SCETO 1970) also recommended that, on a controlled basis, there be continued improvement and tourist use of the existing major tourism centers at Sanur and Kuta (also beach-oriented) and small-scale tourist facilities located elsewhere on the island, so that a wide variety of types, locations, and price ranges of accommodation and their environments are available to tourists and the benefits of tourism are widely spread geographically. The regional plan showed several tourism centers, including Nusa Dua, Sanur, and Kuta, various areas of touristic interest (where tourists visit on day tours), and a network of excursion or sight-seeing roads all linked with the tourism centers. In addition to selecting the Nusa Dua resort site, the regional plan included a conceptual land use plan and prefeasibility analysis of Nusa Dua to make certain that it would be an environmentally and economically feasible development. The Nusa Dua project was a joint effort of the government of Indonesia and the World Bank.

The planning approach of the Nusa Dua resort development plan (Pacific Consultants 1973) was to review and refine the regional relationships of the resort access road, regional infrastructure relationships of water supply and electric power, the service town relationships (to Denpasar and nearby villages), and the need for subregional development planning and controls of the peninsula where the resort is situated. In preparation of the resort plan, first the development objectives were established. These focused on the planning of Nusa Dua to be a high quality international resort with emphasis on providing very good standard infrastructure, achieving a high aesthetic quality of the resort through extensive landscaping, and reflecting the unique cultural and environmental character of Bali. Then the planning methodology was defined, the site environmental analysis (including use of aerial photographs) was conducted, and the facility and land use requirements were determined based on the market analysis of demand and density standards, which were consistent with the desired type of the resort.

Based on the facility requirements, the infrastructure needs were determined and planned. In terms of accommodation, 2,500 guest rooms were planned for the first stage and 2,000 rooms were scheduled for the second stage, with a possible longer-term demand for an additional 2,000 rooms in subsequent stages. Alternative plans were prepared and evaluated, and the final plan was selected and refined. An interesting aspect of the plan formulation was to establish a project image of the different activity areas of the resort environment.

Figure 8.2 depicts the Nusa Dua plan. For the first two stages of 4,500 rooms on 12 hotel sites, which comprised the main portion of the project (detailed plan in Figure 8.2), a centralized concept was applied, and for the possible later stages of 2,000 more rooms, a decentralized, lower density approach was assumed. For the centralized resort area, several important resort planning principles were applied as follows:

- Grouping of the facilities by different types such as the hotel sites, commercial and cultural facilities, some sports and recreation facilities, and service and utility facilities.
- Orientation of the hotel sites to the beach, but set back from the shoreline so that the beach retains its natural appearance, and there is sufficient space along the beach for recreation use by the resort guests and general public.
- Development of a substantial 'amenity core' or resort center in a central location with convenient access from the hotels and other resort facilities. This resort center is designed to contain retail shops, restaurants, airline and travel agency offices, a tourist information center, post office, banks, insurance and other offices, and to function as the social activity focus of the resort. The original plan included two commercial sub-centers, but these were deleted as not being justified.
- Development of a 'festival park' or cultural center with an outdoor stage theater for Balinese dance, music, and drama performances, located adjacent to

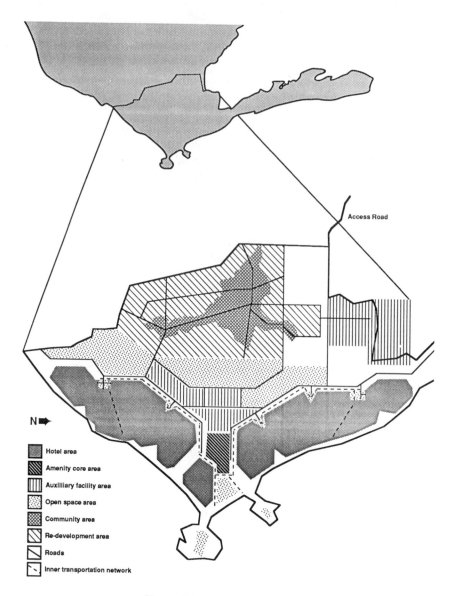

Figure 8.2. Nusa Dua Resort Plan.

the amenity core on one side and next to a landscaped park and adjacent lagoon with water views on the other side.

• Provision of an integrated landscaped park and open space system comprised of the two offshore land-tied islands, developed with walkways and viewing areas; continuous open space developed with a walkway and shelters along the entire resort shoreline and connected to the island parks; and internal landscaped areas and beach access corridors linked with the shoreline parks.

- Provision for public access corridors between groups of hotels to the beach, open for use by both Balinese residents and resort guests. One of these corridors is designed to be sufficiently wide to allow access by local fishermen to their traditional boat landing beach, which is now incorporated into the resort and being encouraged to continue operation.
- Location of a convention center and community service facility area in a central location inland from the resort center and with convenient access from the hotels and resort center.
- A sports center (for tennis and other sport facilities) sited in a central location but not on a prime site.
- Location of the utility plants for water treatment and distribution and sewage collection and treatment on one side of the resort, on a site not particularly suitable for other purposes but with good access and close enough to the resort facilities to economically service them.
- Location of a resort landscaping nursery on an accessible, centrally situated, but inland site. With labeling, this nursery will also be of interest to resort guests for them to identify local vegetation, and it can function as a botanic garden.
- Location of a hotel and tourism training center on one side of the resort, not occupying a prime site but with convenient access to the resort facilities for the students' practical training and to the neighboring village where some students will live.
- Not shown on the plan, but added later, is a large golf course situated adjacent to the resort on the southwest side and occupying an attractive hilly site with ocean views. After the resort plan was approved, land was purchased for this golf course area as a contingency in case the need for a golf course would be determined later, as it in fact was.
- An existing Hindu temple on the site was preserved because of its religious importance and for use by resort employees.
- An integrated circulation system of the single main access road, major and minor internal resort roads, a traffic terminal, an internal shuttle bus network with its own roadway, and a walkway network. Parking is all off-street in parking lots associated with the individual hotel sites and other facility areas.
- The resort was planned to be efficiently developed in stages, with the first stage containing the resort center and other centralized facilities so that it could function effectively in itself, and with these central facilities and the basic overall infrastructure developed large enough (or designed to be developed in increments), to serve the initial and later stages.
  For the infrastructure, the plan recommended:
- Development of a new water supply source, based on a separate water resource study, from deep wells located several kilometers from the resort, which, in addition to serving the resort would be integrated into the Denpasar water system, as well as the installation of a water treatment plant and distribution system in the resort;
- Extension of the island's electric power grid to serve Nusa Dua;
- Development of a separate sewage collection and treatment plant system to serve the resort;

- Extension of the island's telecommunications system to serve the resort; and
- Development of a drainage system utilizing various types of drainage ways, including the swale type, which is environmentally attractive and can be landscaped.

The later stage decentralized resort areas, one of which is beach-oriented and the other of which is hillside- and ocean view–oriented, were also planned according to sound principles such as setback of hotels from the shoreline. The three nearby existing villages and their relationships to the resort are shown on the plan, and infrastructure improvements to these villages of water supply, electric power, and road upgrading were recommended so that they would benefit from the resort infrastructure development.

Several techniques were recommended and employed for implementation of the resort plan. As described, the resort was planned to be developed in logical stages. Zoning regulations, which were prepared as part of the resort plan and later refined, recommended various development standards including:

- A maximum building height of 15 meters (a height limit adopted for all of Bali);
- A net land use density not to exceed 85 guest rooms per hectare on all the hotel sites; and a floor area ratio not to exceed 0.5;
- Setbacks of buildings from lot lines of 25 meters;
- Reservation for public use of all areas within 30 meters of the shoreline;
- A distance of at least 30 meters between main buildings;
- Prohibition of removal of large trees except by permit for construction purposes; and
- Strict control of exterior advertising signs.

Architectural design guidelines were also included in the plan. These were later refined by an architectural design review committee specifically established for the resort development, which had the responsibility for reviewing all development proposals and requesting developers to make any modifications to their designs that were deemed necessary for the facilities to fit well architecturally into the resort environment. The design guidelines emphasized use of Balinese architectural motifs and traditional type building materials to the greatest extent possible, as well as design features, such as open-sided hotel lobbies, suitable for a tropical climate.

Organizationally, implementation was achieved through the establishment of a public development corporation, called the Bali Tourism Development Corporation (BTDC), which developed and operates the resort. The BTDC was initially financed by the government (in part through a World Bank loan and the remainder from government funds), with the long-term goal of the resort being financially self-sustainable. The land was acquired by the government through purchase at market value of private ownerships. The BTDC contracted the final infrastructure engineering and architectural design of the common facilities such as the resort center. It also constructed the basic resort infrastructure, as well as the access road to and beyond the airport, the recommended nearby village infrastructure, the resort center, the resort nursery, other common-use facilities, and the park and open space facilities and landscaping, all of which comprised a major task requiring a few years to complete. The individual hotel sites were leased to the private sector (or other public corporations) for development, with the lease rent based on the number of hotel rooms allocated to each site.

The lease rent was calculated to amortize, over a period of time, the initial cost of resort development and its continuing operation, with the user fees paid by the hotel operators for water, electric power, sewage disposal, and other services paying for those infrastructure operational costs. The resort center commercial properties were leased to private entrepreneurs. The hotel and tourism training center, opened in the late 1970s, was developed by the central government as a separate operation.

In order to encourage hotel developers to locate in Nusa Dua, a decree was passed that no large-scale hotels would be approved elsewhere in Bali for a certain period of time. However, small and medium-size hotels were allowed and, in fact, many of these were developed in various areas of the island, which maintained the viability of other tourism areas. Various hotel investment incentives provided by the government were available to the developers in Nusa Dua as they were to developers elsewhere in the country.

Although there were some delays in developing the infrastructure and inducing the first, 'pioneer' developers to lease hotel sites, the resort has become successful, attracting several good hotel developers, and is popular with tourists. By the end of the 1980s, all of the seven first stage hotel sites of 2,500 rooms had been leased and virtually all developed, and the second stage development of 2,000 rooms was commencing. The intended quality of the resort has been maintained, and the hotels are generally very well designed and reflect the distinctive Balinese environment. The development of the later stages of the additional 2,000 rooms will be decided based on circumstances.

A case study in Chapter 13 further examines some of the various socioeconomic approaches applied in Nusa Dua and elsewhere in Bali to integrate tourism into the local society.

Mauna Lani Resort, Hawaii

The Mauna Lani resort is an excellent example of a large-scale, mixed-use beach and recreation resort that has been planned within the regional context and in an environmentally sensitive manner, with planning adapted to changing market demands. The resort is situated in the South Kohala area on the northwest coast of the island of Hawaii in the state of Hawaii between West Hawaii's major port facility at Kawaihae and the Keahole Airport, and is about 12 miles from Waimea, the region's main urban commercial center. This stretch of coast has long been recognized as a desirable location for developing large-scale resorts and has been shown for some years by the state of Hawaii and the county of Hawaii as a major resort region on their various plans. The Hawaii County General Plan, adopted in 1971 and updated twice since then, designates South Kohala as a "Major Resort Area," described as a "self-contained resort destination area which provides basic and support facilities for the needs of the entire development."

In order to encourage and support resort development in the region, the government made substantial investments in public infrastructure, including the construction of a coast highway, the Keahole Airport, a regional water system, and improvements to Kawaihae Harbor. In addition to Mauna Lani, two other large resorts have developed in the region, the Mauna Kea Beach Resort and the Waikaloa Beach Resort. Within a day touring distance from Mauna Lani is Volcanoes National Park, various archaeological and historic places, and other attractions. The Kohala Coast region is in the rain shadow side of the island and experiences a consistent warm, dry, and sunny climate.

The Mauna Lani resort was privately developed within the framework of strict government land use and environmental controls. The land was purchased for resort development in 1972 and received the appropriate land use rezonings and initial plan approval for the proposed resort development during the mid- to late 1970s. The plan approved in 1980 for the 778-acre project site set a maximum number of 3,000 hotel rooms and 3,182 residential units. An environmental impact assessment was prepared and approved as part of the planning procedure. The 3,000 hotel room limit is in accordance with the county's general plan limit for a major resort. In the 1980s, the first stage of the resort, including the Mauni Lani Bay Hotel and Bungalows, the Ritz-Carlton Mauna Lani Hotel, some condominiums, an 18-hole golf course, shopping and entertainment facilities, an historic park and network of trails, was completed and the resort opened. In the late 1980s, a revision of the plan was prepared and approved for expansion of the overall site area to 1,432 acres in order to provide for a second 18-hole golf course and a lower density level of development of the hotels and residential zones as well as more park, open space, commercial, and support facility areas. The maximum number of hotel rooms and residential units was still maintained at, respectively, the 3,000 and 3,182 limits.

This revision resulted from a special study that indicated a market demand for more golf facilities, the wish of the developer to somewhat lower the hotel and residential densities to achieve the design goals and standards of a luxury resort, the desire to provide for a new shoreline park, and the need to expand some of the other facility areas.

The resort development objectives are to provide a full range of facilities and amenities within a resort/residential community and integrate a compatible mix of uses in an overall design that meets "world class" standards. Development is planned to proceed at a rate that is responsive to changing market demand for resort hotel and residential facilities. The resort company will remain flexible in providing these facilities so that they satisfy current and projected needs, keeping within the context of a luxury resort development. Environmentally, the resort concept is to retain open space areas and historic and scenic resources that reinforce the unique character of the site. The plan preserves scenic views as well as natural and established features, including the shoreline, the historic fish ponds and other historic sites, and the existing trail system.

Figure 8.3 shows the revised resort plan (Belt, Collins & Associates 1989). Several features of this plan are important to note:

• Orientation of the hotel sites to the beach and shoreline or other interesting

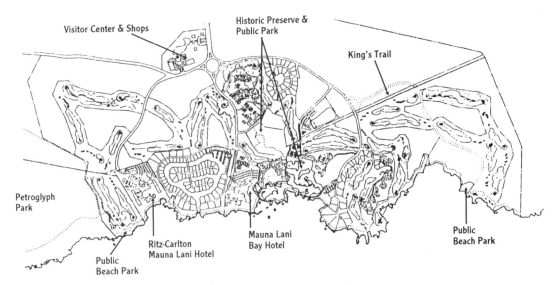

Figure 8.3. Mauna Lani Resort Plan.

features such as the historic fish ponds, with maintenance of views to the ocean and mountains.

- Maintenance of an historic preserve and related public park of the Polynesian fish ponds in the center of the resort, which are important to preserve as an historic site and also provide a highly interesting environmental feature of the resort, and preservation of an historic trail (King's Trail) that extends through the south part of the site to the historic preserve.
- Provision of a beach park at the south end of the resort and a shoreline park at the north end, which also complements the adjacent Puako Archaeological Petroglyph Park. The resort developer by contract with the state government has agreed to maintain this archaeological park and develop suitable visitor facilities in it.
- Provision of general public access and parking to the the two shoreline/ beach parks and the fish ponds historic preserve and public park, and a walking trail along the entire shoreline.
- Development of a boat marina and related lagoon-oriented residential units.
- Design of the golf fairways to offer a variety of environmental settings and views, including some fairways located along the shoreline, and to provide open space corridors and views between the development areas (which also enhances the value of properties adjacent to the fairways).
- Development of a single access road from the main coastal highway, with an internal street system of cul de sacs that prevents through-traffic flows.
- Development of integrated recreation facility centers of the tennis and racquet club, beach club, marina facilities complex, and golf clubhouse.
- Location of the major commercial facilities along with the visitor arrival center

in a single integrated complex at the entrance to the resort (but not in a central location).

- Location of the resort support facilities of the sewage treatment plan, the resort offices, warehousing and storage, and contractor's yard and light industrial uses associated with the resort expansion activities off to one side of the resort, but with convenient access to it and the main coastal road.

The overall rugged natural character of the volcanic landscape of the site has been retained to the greatest extent possible and enhanced with native plants.

Resort Municipality of Whistler

The Resort Municipality of Whistler is located about 75 miles north of Vancouver in British Columbia, Canada and offers the most developed ski area in the country with a variety of year-round resort facilities and activities. The resort village is at an elevation of 2,190 feet and the two nearby mountains where the ski slopes are situated are Blackcomb Mountain at 7,494 feet and Whistler Mountain at 7,160 feet. Climatically, the winters are moderate with substantial snowfall and the summers are relatively dry and warm. These two areas represent the longest lift serviced vertical drops (more than 5,000 feet) and ski runs (seven miles at Blackcomb and five miles at Whistler) in North America, with a combined capacity of approximately 20,000 skiers at one time. More than 170 ski runs are serviced by 27 lifts with about 3,500 acres of skiable terrain, and cross-country skiing is available on some ten miles of groomed trails and numerous ungroomed trails; skiers are able to ski throughout the summer in certain areas. During the 1987–88 winter ski season, more than one million skier visits (or skier days) were recorded at the resort (Planning Department 1989), and 100,000 skier visits were recorded during the 1988 summer season. During the 1986–87 winter season, about one-half of the visitors were from Canada, about one-third from the USA (mostly the western states), and some from Japan, Australia, and elsewhere. During this period, the average length of visitor stay was three to five nights for 33 percent of the visitors and six to seven nights for 44 percent of the visitors.

The municipal area encompasses about 31,200 acres and, in 1988, had approximately 2,400 permanent residents with additional population of some 1,425 during the winter tourist season. In 1988, there were about 1,600 hotel and other types of accommodation rooms, some recreational vehicle and campground sites, more than 2,500 condominiums, and over 2,300 houses and duplexes, some of which are rental units. There is a variety of restaurants, bars, and retail shops in the village. In addition to skiing, resort facilities include a championship golf course, swimming facilities at seven lakeside beaches, several swimming pools and two covered water slides, a conference center with 35,000 square feet of meeting space and 14,000 square feet of trade show area, tennis courts, various parks, and cycling and walking trails. The several lakes also offer canoeing, fishing, picnicking, and other activities. Special events and festivals are scheduled throughout the year.

The entire history of the Whistler resort development is too complex to repeat in detail here, but several aspects of the evolution of the resort are important to note because they represent excellent approches to the planning mountain resort development. Whistler was originally known as Alta Lake, a wilderness area accessible by train or horsback. Its early economy was based on summer recreation, mining, and logging. Summer lodges were built on Alta Lake for holiday and honeymoon retreats with one of these, Rainbow Lodge, built in 1915, being a well-known fishing lodge in North America. Hawkins (1987) divided the development history of Whistler into five time frames:

- 1900–1960—rural lake community;
- 1961–1974—suburban sprawl and speculation;
- 1975–1978—skiing and town center policies;
- 1979–1982—urban winter resort; and
- 1983–1987—resort with year-round destination potential.

The last period has continued into the late 1980s and early 1990s.

With the development of ski slopes on Whistler Mountain in 1965 and the paving of the road from Vancouver to Whistler in 1969, growth accelerated and the Whistler Valley evolved from a summer to a winter recreation area. The Squamish–Lillooet Regional District, which was responsible for the administration of Whistler, tried to remedy the lack of much needed planning controls, but resource use conflicts and uncontrolled growth characterized Whistler in the early 1970s. There was much negative visual impact resulting from logging operations and wildfire scars with slow regeneration of the forest cover. In 1974, the government commissioned a study to evaluate the ski potential in this general area, which concluded that (Sno-engineering 1975, 10):

> If developed in a proper and timely manner, the Blackcomb/
> Whistler complex could become a major destination resort capa-
> ble of attracting skiers not only from all sections of North Amer-
> ica but from international markets as well.

Figure 8.4 reproduces the concept plan of that study, which indicates the relationship of the two mountain skiing areas to the proposed resort village at their base, which would be well situated to serve both recreation areas.

During the same period, it was recommended that a local government and townsite be established for Whistler, and a community development study be prepared. In 1975, the Resort Municipality of Whistler Act was passed, and a sewage collection and treatment system was installed. Adequate sewage disposal was essential to maintain the water quality in the developed area. The first community plan was completed in 1976 (Resort Municipality of Whistler 1976). The policy objectives of this plan, which are resource based and controlled development–oriented, were in summary form as follows:

- To protect and enhance the natural environment of the resort municipality (by enforcing restrictive use of sensitive areas, writing predevelopment impact studies, building swage and garbage disposal facilities, and implementing reforestation and reclamation projects);

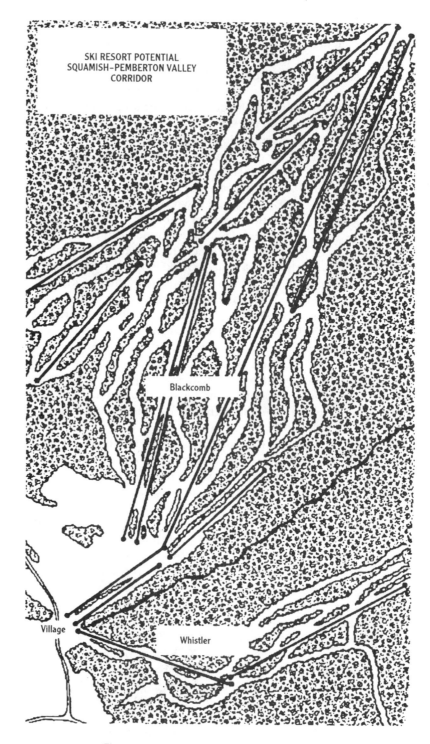

Figure 8.4. Whistler Ski Resort—Concept Plan.

- To provide for the year-round recreational needs of the residents and visitors (by promoting camping facilities, encouraging year-round facilities, and implementing waterfront and trail rights-of-way);
- To provide a stable year-round economy;
- To encourage commercial and residential facilities ancillary to recreational activity up to but not exceeding a level suitable to serve the recreation resource by encouraging a range of accommodation types and limiting development to ski facility capacities;
- To ensure that development in the municipality preserves the view and is in keeping with the natural landscape by encouraging harmonious landscape design and restricting development above the 2,400-foot contour;
- To limit the development of the recreation resource and the provision of ancillary services to a level that will not overload the access highway and rail link, through controlled growth;
- To provide a transportation system for the efficient movement of people and goods within the municipality and between the municipality and other parts of the province (by minimizing winter vehicular traffic through controlled development and providing public transportation and other techniques);
- To provide for the health and safety of residents and visitors (by regulating land that has a high water table or is subject to flooding or avalanches, providing community services, using sanitary sewer connections where built, and encouraging access to aesthetic and recreational areas and other techniques);
- To encourage private investment in the development of recreational and ancillary facilities (by providing an ample supply of development land and promoting winter and summer recreational resources through municipal cooperation with the province and Chamber of Commerce); and
- To minimize the cost of the community services by controlling sprawl and encouraging compact development and staging of and payments for servicing.

The plan further stated (Resort Municipality of Whistler 1976, 2):

> . . . recreation is recognized as the Resort Municipality of Whistler's prime resource . . . the Community Plan should provide for the best use of this resource for the most people at the least cost. Costs here include social, environmental and dollar costs to both the local community and the province.

An important concept of the community plan was to develop a compact integrated town or village center to unify the sprawling development throughout the valley. There was considerable resistance to the recommendations of the community plan by local landowners and developers, which resulted in many public hearings and some changes to the plan with most investors allowed to develop some land in the proposed town site as a compensatory measure for the land use controls to be established elsewhere in the area.

The Whistler garbage dump site was selected for the town center because of its central location in the valley and in the area that offered a panoramic view of

Whistler and Blackcomb Mountains. Being near the ski slopes provided the opportunity of concentrating major traffic for greater efficiency in the development of a road network. Also, the site was relatively level and in public ownership. The village center site plan was announced in 1978, and Whistler Village Land Company was incorporated as a wholly-owned subsidiary of the Resort Municipality to develop and regulate the site (this company experienced some delays and financial problems and was later replaced by a new crown corporation). The objective of the site planning was to create a sense of community through a unique, attractive, closely knit, pedestrian-oriented village center with peripheral parking. More ski lifts were developed and both mountains were first in operation during the 1979–80 skiing season. In 1983 the golf course opened, and in 1985, the Whistler Conference Center was opened.

As the private sector tourism organization, the Whistler Resort Association (WRA), comprised of owners, agents of owners, or occupants of resort land, was organized in 1979. All enterprises in the village and other designated resort lands are required by law to join the association. The primary function of the WRA is to market Whistler as a year-round international resort area. It also provides an accommodation reservation service and information center. In 1981, the municipality contracted a consulting firm to prepare an outdoor recreation master plan, which is a conceptual framework for year-round outdoor recreation, and a parks referendum was held and passed to obtain funding for recreation development. With this funding, implementation of the recreational amenities was nearly completed in the late 1980s.

The role and importance of planning in Whistler is stated in the municipality literature (Resort Municipality of Whistler 1989) as follows:

> The Official Community Plan articulates the policies and objectives outlining the kind of resort and community Whistler aspires to. The Plan summarizes and coordinates all major Municipal policies and initiatives in guiding and regulating development, providing services, offering a high quality resort experience and maintaining a high quality of life in the community.

The plan is updated about every five years with the updating process an intensive one, based on research, analysis, and active community involvement. The original plan was revised in 1982, and the revision contained the policy objectives as follows (Urban Programme Planners 1982):

- To provide for an adequate supply of year-round recreation accomodation that is varied in terms of its location, type, and price;
- To provide for an adequate supply of affordable housing for permanent residents and employees;
- To provide for a transportation system for the efficient movement of people and goods within the Resort Municipality of Whistler and between the Municipality and other parts of province;
- To provide municipal servicing of the population in a cost-effective manner;

- To encourage the development of commercial and light industrial establishments in order to provide goods and services;
- To protect and preserve the natural environment of the Resort Municipality of Whistler;
- To discourage development from occurring on lands subject to hazardous conditions; and
- To enhance the recreational potential of the Resort Municipality of Whistler.

This plan was again updated and revised in 1988.

There was continuing conflict during the 1980s between tourism and logging interests, with the community concerned about the environmental and visual impact of logging operations and forestry companies wishing to retain the economic benefits of this activity. This issue remains a controversial one.

The Whistler resort has largely succeeded in becoming a high quality year-round destination while at the same time providing a highly livable community for its residents. A definite sense of resort community identity and an interesting village environment have been created through imaginative and sound planning and strong development controls, with emphasis on maintaining the environmental quality of both the community and the entire recreation area. Although the winter skiing season is still the dominate one, summer activities and tourist visits have greatly increased during the 1980s with the conference center attracting many groups and other summer activities being popular.

The resort and community are planned for expansion. The permanent population is expected to grow from the present 2,400 to about 7,000 by the year 2000, with skier (winter season) visits projected to be well over two million and summer visits to be about 455,000 by then. The village center is programmed to expand, and more accommodation and residential units will be developed. Access for most visitors is by road, but the airport at Pemberton, 35 kilometers north of Whistler, is upgrading its facilities and operations.

References

Belt, Collins and Associates. 1989. *Master Plan—Mauna Lani Resort.* Hololulu.

Coltman, Michael M. 1989. *Introduction to Travel and Tourism: An International Approach.* New York: Van Nostrand Reinhold.

Hawkins, Ann Elizabeth, 1987. *A Carrying Capacity Model for Resort Planning and Management with an Application to Whistler, Canada.* Unpublished thesis. Burnaby, British Columbia: Simon Frazer University.

Pacific Consultants K.K. 1973. *The Nusa Dua Area Development Plan.* Tokyo.

Planning Department, Resort Municipality of Whistler. 1989. *Whistler Resort Profile.* Whistler.

Resort Municipality of Whistler. 1976. *Official Community Plan.* Whistler.

SCETO. 1970. *Bali Tourism Plan.* Paris.

Sno-engineering Inc. 1975. *Ski Resort Potential–Squamish–Pemberton Valley Corridor.* Littleton, New Hampshire.

Urban Programme Planners. 1982. *Official Community Plan.* Whistler.

Planning Urban and Other Forms of Tourism

Planning Approach

Urban and other forms of tourism, including special interest, adventure, alternative, water transport based, transportation-oriented, residential, and others were described in Chapter 7. The approach to planning these depends very much on the forms of tourism involved, but some general approaches are applicable. A basic consideration is the relationship to the national and regional policy and plan, which will have identified the appropriate forms of tourism to be developed and established some parameters or guidelines for their detailed planning. In the absence of national or regional policy and planning, then the regional framework will still need to be researched and decisions made on the relevant relationships (for example, whether an urban area serves as a tourism gateway to the region and base for organizing tours to other parts of the region, as well as providing its own tourism resources to attract and serve tourists staying there).

The planning procedure for urban and other forms of tourism is generally the same as for resort planning:

- Assessment of the tourism product and market;
- Selection of any specific development sites required;
- Conceptual planning and prefeasibility analysis to determine if the development concept is likely to be economically viable and not generate any serious environmental or sociocultural impacts;
- Environmental and carrying capacity analysis and community relationships;
- Detailed analysis of regional relationships;
- Determination of facility, land use, and infrastructure requirements;

- Plan formulation, including outline planning of alternatives, evaluation of these, and final plan selection and refinement with phasing of development;
- Environmental and sociocultural impact assessment;
- Economic and financial feasibility analysis; and
- Preparation of the implementation program with, if applicable, staging of development.

Much of the success of many of these forms of tourism depends on effective organization as well as development of physical facilities.

Community participation in the planning process and plan implementation is especially important because the planning for urban tourism and often for some of the other forms takes place in existing developed areas where people are living and development patterns are already well established. For some forms of alternative and special interest tourism, sociocultural and environmental considerations are particularly sensitive, and involvement of the local residents in planning and implementation is essential to make certain that the tourism developed brings benefits to the residents and is not disruptive to the society. Community participation can be organized through appointment of a special project committee and coordination with local government agencies, community organizations and their spokesmen, private sector tourism organizations, and, in some cases, local religious leaders.

Urban Tourism Planning

Tourism may be very important in towns and cities, and, in terms of tourist arrivals, extent of accommodation and visits to attraction features, may exceed the use of designated tourist resorts. In addition to serving as gateways and staging areas to a region or country, cities such as London, Paris, New York, San Francisco, Tokyo, Bangkok, New Delhi, and Nairobi offer a wide range of attractions in themselves, including museums, parks, theaters, historic places, significant modern buildings, shopping, dining, entertainment, and the overall urban ambience and cityscape views. Towns, especially those with important historic or other special features, also may attract many tourists. The historic towns, for example, of Toledo, Segovia, and Avila near Madrid are major attractions for tourists visiting central Spain.

The characteristics of urban tourism and its planning have been studied less than resort and outdoor recreation development (Pearce 1987), but some recent studies have been made, for example by Jansen-Verbeke (1988), and there is sufficient understanding to provide a basis for planning.

Special Problems of Urban Tourism Planning

Planning for tourism development in towns and cities typically presents special problems, such as competing demands for development of certain prime sites for hotels, offices, retail or residential uses, traffic congestion in central areas, which may be exacerbated by tourism development, and over-use of primary tourist attractions and perhaps their degradation by intensive use. For example, British domestic tourists visiting London have complained about the congestion at Westminster Abbey and the Tower of London during the peak foreign tourist season, with the situation compounded in that these places are, respectively, a house of worship and a security vault. Because central city areas and many urban attractions, such as historic sites, museums, and major theaters, are already in place, planning must be accomplished with these as given fixed points. This planning situation is further complicated by the fact that most urban attractions are located in already congested city centers, and that is where most tourists wish to stay in order to see as much as possible in short time periods.

At the same time, urban tourism, in addition to its basic economic benefits of generating income and employment, can be an important technique for helping support urban facilities and services such as theaters and museums, helping to justify and paying for historic preservation and infrastructure improvements and, in some cases, can be a vital force for inner-city redevelopment and revitalization. For example, St. Katherine's Dock redevelopment on the Thames riverfront in London and much of the waterfront and festival market place redevelopment currently underway in American cities depend in large part on the support of the tourism sector. More generally, tourism can play an important role in the economic strategies of many older cities undergoing a transition from a manufacturing and goods-handling economy to a service economy. The USA has accumulated much experience in this field, and European cities are increasingly using this approach (Hall 1987). Smaller city, town, and even village revitalization can be accomplished through development of tourism if these places offer some special features of interest.

However, as referred to previously, tourism should not be seen as a panacea for inner-city redevelopment and small town revitalization. Not all places have the resources for tourism, nor would there likely be sufficient numbers of tourists to visit all these places if they did have some attracting power; resources could be wasted on trying to meet excessive competition. Also, the extent of use of these facilities by residents will be an important factor in their economic justification. Each situation must be individually evaluated. As is the case with the national and regional level of development planning, urban development should be based on a diversified economy to the greatest extent possible, and not create an over-reliance on tourism.

Planning Procedure

If at all possible, the urban tourism plan should be prepared as part of the urban comprehensive plan or central area redevelopment plan to achieve maximum integration of tourism development and logical resolution of any conflicting land uses. If the urban tourism plan is prepared separately, then integration into the overall urban fabric, including the transportation system, should, of course, still be an utmost consideration. The planning procedure for planning urban tourism requires first a survey, land use mapping, and evaluation of the primary and secondary tourist attractions, a market analysis and establishment of market targets related to the attractions and any regional relationships (establishing the objectives of tourism development that may be interrelated with overall urban development objectives), and consideration of whether improvements are required to the existing attractions and what new attractions such as a convention center, museum or expanded shopping, dining, and entertainment facilities are required to achieve the objectives and attract the targeted markets. In deciding the development objectives, an important factor is consideration of maintaining the well-being of the urban residents so that, in the process of receiving benefits from tourism, they are not also overwhelmed by it and do not experience a serious reduction in the quality of urban services and livability of their urban environment.

An important element of the market analysis in many cities will be the business and convention/conference related markets, which may comprise a significant share of the total tourist market. Business travelers use many of the same facilities as holiday tourists in urban areas and also make use of many of the same attractions, not only dining and entertainment, but also visiting museums and historic places. However, business travelers in addition require some special facilities such as business centers in hotels and efficient communication services. The use demand analysis of many attraction features and other tourist facilities and services must consider use by local residents, which often is substantial. The regional relationships of whether the city is a gateway and staging area to the country or region and if there are day tour possibilities to attractions outside the urban area must be considered in the market analysis.

The existing tourist accommodation and other tourist facilities and services are surveyed and evaluated with the requirements for additional accommodation and other facilities and services calculated based on the market analysis. Some of the existing accommodation may need to be upgraded and, in some places, there are opportunities for renovation of historic hotels, which, in addition to providing acceptable accommodation, can be attractions in themselves. The infrastructure must be surveyed and analyzed to determine whether it is presently adequate and can handle increased usage required for tourism. Especially critical is evaluation of the transportation system, including public transportation by type, cost, convenience, and safety, and its network for serving tourist accommodation, other facilities, and attraction areas.

Also important to evaluate is the overall environmental character and quality of the urban or town environment including:
- Its visual quality of architectural style and character;
- Extent of parks, open space, and landscaping;
- Views and vistas offered;
- Extent of traffic and pedestrian congestion;
- Cleanliness of the environment and extent of littering;
- Any serious problems of air, water, and noise pollution;

- Any difficult climatic patterns, such as extremely cold winters or very hot summers; and
- The extent and type of crime and the general level of public safety.

The possibilities of tourists walking within the central area and from their hotels to the attractions features should be particularly reviewed because many tourists prefer walking in order to have direct experience with the urban ambience.

Based on survey and analysis of these factors, the major opportunities and constraints for tourism development can be identified and, where relevant, mapped. Opportunities might include, for example, possibilities for historic preservation of individual buildings or whole urban districts that in addition to being attractions may have potential for recycling for urban and tourism uses, sites for new hotels, renovation of some existing hotels, sites for a convention center, redevelopment and opening up of a waterfront area for tourism uses, development of sidewalk cafes, maintenance of scenic views, development or improvement of parks, expansion of dining and entertainment facilities or enhancement of an entertainment district, development or redevelopment of an interesting shopping complex, improvement of museums, development of an urban walking/public transportation trail system, and improvement of street landscaping.

Constraints to be overcome, mitigated, or planned around might include, for example:

- A high level of traffic congestion;
- Limited public transport;
- Few existing hotels and limited sites available for new hotel and other tourist facility development;
- Limited attraction features or need for improvement of existing attractions;
- Language barriers between residents and tourist markets;
- High crime rate;
- Difficult climatic conditions or high level of air pollution at certain periods;
- Architecturally uninteresting urban character;
- Obstruction of views by inappropriate site development; and
- Lack of information about tourist facilities and attractions.

In some cases of an established and already interesting city, the major opportunity for new or expanded tourism may be to recognize, enhance, carefully manage, and market what exists without becoming involved in major changes or expensive investment. This approach has been applied successfully, for example, in some European cities, including Zurich, Switzerland and Endinburgh, Scotland, where emphasis has been placed on balancing residents urban livability with tourism's economic benefits (Owen 1989). In other cases, major efforts and investments will be necessary, and often these can be combined with general redevelopment efforts to improve and revitalize city centers, urban waterfronts, or development of cultural/theater centers, providing facilities and services for residents as well as tourists and often including facilities for both business and holiday tourists.

The medium-size city of San Diego, California has adopted this multi-purpose approach of maintaining and revitalizing its downtown to achieve both tourism and general urban development objectives. Already occupying a very attractive waterfront location but possessing rather obsolete development patterns, major projects based on an integrated redevelopment plan were undertaken during the 1980s. These projects included development of:

- A major convention center;
- A large visually striking outdoor-oriented shopping center (Horton Plaza);
- An interesting architecturally themed specialty shopping and restaurant complex on the waterfront (Seaport Village);
- Several new hotels and renovation of some historic hotels;
- The Gas Lamp historic district;
- Large exhibit halls on the waterfront;
- A maritime museum of historic ships' exhibit with visitors allowed on-board;
- New residential and officer complexes;
- A public transportation system;
- Good access from the regional highway system and ample parking areas; and
- Other features.

This redevelopment is planned to continue during the 1990s and, in addition to new building development, is expected to encourage recycling of existing buildings and districts to contemporary commercial and visitor-oriented functions. The downtown area also is conveniently accessible to other historic, cultural, and recreational attractions in the metropolitan region.

Some Planning Principles

Although it is difficult to generalize principles for urban tourism planning, some basic considerations to be made in preparing the tourism plan include the following:

- Location of hotels and other accommodation in conveniently accessible areas with attractive, safe surroundings, and near to at least some attraction features, shopping, dining, and entertainment facility areas.
- Related to the above, clustering accommodation, some attraction features, and other tourist facilities and services within walking distance or conveniently accessible by public transportation to one another.
- Provision of a wide range of types and price ranges of accommodation and other tourist facilities and services within the framework of the types of market targets.
- Provision of good public transportation that connects the various accommodation and facility areas and attractions, or availability of reliable taxi services.
- Pedestrianization, to the extent possible, of the tourism areas to allow for and encourage walking with a well-developed sidewalk system, walkways through parks, and pedestrianization of shopping areas by closing off streets and providing these areas with landscaping and street furniture. Development of an "urban trail" system that visitors can follow through interesting parts of the city and connecting the attraction features. However, pedestrianization is not an automatic cure for central city problems and

needs to be carefully investigated in order to determine its optimum patterns before implementation.

- Where necessary, improvement of the city appearance with landscaping, interesting architectural styles, a park system, and opening up views.
- Taking advantage of waterfront areas by locating interesting types of shopping facilities, plazas, and walkways along the waterfront oriented to water views, or taking similar advantage of other interesting environmental features.
- Encouragement of good urban design by controlling height limits to maintain view planes and corridors, providing plazas and sitting areas, and so forth.
- Conservation of historic buildings and districts through historic preservation regulations and incentives, with complete preservation and small museum development of very important buildings and, for other buildings, exterior preservation with renovation of their interiors for modern functions, some of which are tourism-oriented. Total historic district preservation is preferable to individual building preservation in that the historic urban character is retained; however, new building development may sometimes be allowed if it is in the same historic or a compatible neutral style.
- Improvement of tourist attractions where needed and control of visitor flows to prevent congestion or environmental degradation of the attractions (this subject is addressed in Chapter 10).
- If central city congestion (exceeding the carrying capacity) is a problem, encouragement of development of some accommodation in the city periphery and at the airport (to serve certain tourist markets) in order to relieve the pressure on the central city, and decentralization of tourism to other parts of the region (this is not always easy to accomplish if the major central city attractions are unique). Development of more than one accommodation and related facilities tourism area in the city will distribute tourism development more widely.
- In addition to good transportation services, ensure provision of adequate water supply, sewage, and solid waste disposal so that infrastructure systems are not overloaded, leading to environmental problems.
- Provision of good information services to tourists about what to do and see and the availability of tourist facilities, and of multi-lingual capabilities in tourism enterprises where necessary. Development of a visitor information center in a strategic location is often important; in intensively used tourism areas and streets, tourist information booths located on street corners and properly identified information officers strolling along the streets are useful techniques to assist tourists.
- In high crime areas, attempt to control the crime in tourism areas (as well as elsewhere) with sufficient police security, and inform tourists about how to avoid becoming crime victims by taking protective measures and staying away from crime areas in general or at certain times. Make certain that adequate medical facilities services are available to tourists, including through information about these in hotels.
- Plan tourism development so that it also directly benefits and can be used by

residents, does not preempt residents' enjoyment of their urban environment, and reinforces residents' sense of well-being about their city.

An important aspect of successful urban tourism is effective organization and management of tourist flows and tourist facilities by both the public and private sectors, as well as continuous monitoring of tourism activities.

Importance of Good Urban Design

Some of the most successful tourism towns and cities are those that possess and maintain an overall attractive and sometimes dramatic urban character combined with specific attractions or gateway and staging area functions. The basic site of the city, such as on an ocean, lake, or riverfront or on hills, helps create an attractive and interesting setting. But equally important is how well development has been integrated into the site and enhances it or, in the case of less interesting flat land sites, how effectively the development creates its own distinctive urban environment. If the basic urban design has been done well and establishes the city character, such as the Italian Renaissance cities of Florence and Venice and the towns of Siena and Verona, the challenge is to maintain that character through application of strict zoning and development standards. In modern cities (and sometimes historic cities) where there is much pressure for more intensive development, urban design studies and regulations are essential.

San Francisco, known for its striking urban setting on hills and waterfronts, has been progressive in adopting regulations based on detailed urban design studies that control the heights and bulks of buildings and maintain view planes and corridors in the city so that the natural site character is not lost, development is not so intensive as to create undue congestion, and views of the hills and water areas are retained. This city's urban design policy also emphasizes conserving the traditional relationships between buildings and streets and developing downtown streetscapes at a human scale that are interesting for pedestrians in terms of activities and architectural forms. San Francisco has also opened up portions of its waterfront with tourism-related retail and entertainment complexes such as Ghiradeli Square, a nineteenth century converted and renovated chocolate factory that was the prototype of these waterfront redevelopment complexes. Toronto, Canada applies very strict controls on maintenance of views that are considered to be public amenities for both residents and visitors. Urban design is done primarily to provide a more livable and interesting environment for residents, but it also is an important element of successful urban tourism planning, and tourism can help justify application of design measures.

Planning of Historic Towns

Much of the same procedure and considerations that apply to general urban tourism planning are also applicable to historic towns, such as those referred to in

Sana'a, Yemen Arab Republic—This historic area of the capital city of Sana'a offers a unique Middle Eastern traditional urban form of 'high-rise' architecturally-ornamented buildings and labyrinthine street patterns, which is being conserved with international assistance as an important manifestation of the Yemini cultural heritage. This environment combined with market, craft, and residential activities also provides a highly interesting setting for urban tourism in this newly developing tourist destination, with tourism helping to justify the historic conservation program.

Spain and Italy, as well as many others in Europe and some in the Americas, the Middle East, and Asia, and historic centers of large cities. However, the problems are often greater and the solutions more difficult. Because many of these historic places were built on hill tops for defensive purposes (not for scenic views), such as some Medieval villages in Europe and the historic towns of Yemen in the Middle East, access to the sites may be quite restricted. Within the towns, the street patterns, laid out for a different type and scale of transportation, are often narrow and convoluted with no allowance made for automobile and bus parking and are not adaptable to contemporary transportation needs. Other infrastructure of electric power, water supply, and sewage disposal may be obsolete. If not controlled, traffic congestion and environmental pollution can be serious in these places, with tourism activities further exacerbating the problems. If the towns are still economically dynamic, there can be much pressure to replace the historic buildings with incompatible modern ones.

Historic preservation will be further examined in Chapter 10, but in terms of urban tourism planning, it is important to consider preservation of the historic urban fabric and character, with application of development controls and management policies to make optimum use of existing tourist facilities and development in general. Organization and control of visitor flows and sometimes the overall total numbers of tourists may be necessary to reduce congestion levels. Legal regulations on historic preservation are essential to preserve the historic character of these places, with no new building development allowed and incentives offered to restore existing buildings and renovate interiors for modern functions, or requiring that any new development be in a compatible scale and architectural style with the historic character.

In Old San Juan, Puerto Rico, a large historic city center and now a major tourist attraction area as well as a still-functioning urban district, strict historic building preservation controls are applied, with public and private restoration efforts having been underway for several years, but new development is permitted if architecturally compatible. This approach has been aesthetically successful and helps maintain the commercial and residential viability of the area. In Spain, which allowed much unplanned and uncontrolled tourism development during its earlier years of rapid tourism growth, has in recent years made progress in preserving some of its historic towns by requiring major modern development be located outside the old town walls, with the historic town centers largely preserved, but with compatible development of hotels and other tourist facilities allowed. Some historic buildings can be renovated for use as tourist facilities and shops while major tourism development such as large hotels can be developed outside the historic area, but with good access to it.

Because of their obsolete street patterns, control and management of traffic is particularly important in historic towns. In addition to congestion, vehicles of the combustion engine type generate air pollution, which can greatly corrode stone buildings and sculpture and degrade the historic value of these towns. Complete pedestrianization of the historic districts is often the best solution and is ideal for sight-seeing tourists in a small-scale urban environment, although it is necessary to allow service vehicles into the historic districts at certain times, such as early mornings when there is not much pedestrian traffic, in order to serve commercial establishments. Provision of parking areas for automobiles and tour buses adjacent to the pedestrian precincts is necessary, and use of nonpolluting shuttle bus service within the historic districts may be appropriate in some places. Traffic can also be somewhat controlled and its danger to pedestrians reduced through establishment of one-way street systems. Unfortunately, these traffic control measures have not yet been applied as frequently as they should have, often because of resistance by local land owners and shop managers who fear that their property values and business operations will be affected. There is need for more study and experimentation with innovative approaches to traffic control and organization of visitor flows in historic towns.

Socioeconomically, a problem can be created in historic towns and in general in the development of urban tourism when buildings are converted to tourism and other modern uses that increases their property values to the extent that some residents cannot afford to continue living there nor traditional shopkeepers able to maintain their profit margins. In the absence of property price and rent controls, which are often difficult to effect, alternative housing and commercial facilities will need to be provided for these residents and shopkeepers, preferably developed in the same community so that social relationships can be maintained but in a lower cost location.

Planning for Special Interest, Adventure, and Alternative Forms of Tourism

As described in Chapter 7, special interest tourism refers to tourist activities oriented to specific aspects of attractions related to specialized interests of particular tourist market segments. In terms of market demand, it is one of the fast-growing types of tourism, and it can be developed in areas that may have few major attraction features or limited infrastructure not allowing for major tourism development in the near future. Also, in places that for various reasons do not wish to develop large-scale tourism, special interest tourism provides the opportunity to receive some tourism benefits, without major investment being required, and to attract those tourists who have a particular interest in and consequently respect for aspects of the local culture and environment. Related to special interest is adventure tourism whereby the tourists engage in physically and personally challenging and sometimes dangerous activities.

As previously referred to, alternative tourism is a categorical term applied to forms of tourism, typically small-scale, that are designed not to generate negative environmental or sociocultural impacts and bring the tourists in close contact with residents and the environment as a learning experience. An aim of alternative tourism is often to bring the benefits of this sector directly to the local residents. Forms of alternative tourism include village, farm or agro-tourism, and eco-tourism. However, as emphasized previously, the approach taken in this book is that all forms of tourism should be planned to be environmentally and socially sensitive, achieving sustainable development and bringing benefits to local communities.

Special interest, adventure, and alternative tourism may all co-exist with other forms of tourism in the same country or region, albeit usually in different areas.

Some Special Interest Tourism Planning Considerations

Identification of the possibilities for development of special interest tourism requires evaluation of the natural and cultural features of an area that are unusual, unique, or particularly well developed, can be appreciated by tourists without generating environmental or social problems, and for which there are existing or potential tourist markets. The scope for developing special interest tourism is very broad. The bird or insect life of an area may offer possibilities for ornithological or butterfly tours. A variety of types of volcanic activity may provide the basis for geological tours. A system of nature parks and reserves may be the basis for

Machu Picchu, Peru—This important Incan archaeological complex appeals to both general sight-seeing tourists and special interest tourists who are visiting the pre-Columbian sites of western South America. Because of the remote and often mountainous locations of such sites in this region, visitor access and use patterns must be carefully organized and controlled.

wildlife and botanical tours. A network of archaeological sites may appeal to amateur archaeologists. Local traditional production of handwoven textiles may have potential for organizing textile tours with stops at villages to observe the spinning, dyeing, and weaving process. An area rich in a variety of distinctive architectural styles may offer a basis for architectural tours. Important historic routes such as the Silk Roads in Asia, the Crusaders routes in Europe and the Middle East, the Viking routes in Northern Europe, the salt roads in North Africa, and the Lewis and Clark Expedition trail in North America can be retraced by interested tourists. Literary tours can be organized based on visiting homes of famous authors and poets, as have been organized in Britain and New England, USA. Because the scope of special interest tourism is so broad, the experience of other areas that have developed this form of tourism can often offer some guidelines and ideas for the area being planned.

A principal consideration in developing special interest tourism is organization, development of modest tourist and transportation facilities where needed, and selective marketing. Organization requires careful programming of itineraries, usually for tour groups but also for independent tourists, with prearrangements made at stopping points and provision of knowledgeable guides with foreign language capability where necessary. Special interest tourists already know their subject in general but want to learn more about it and expect well-informed guide services. Observing safety measures while traveling may be an important factor for some types of special interest tourism. In some cases, opportunities for the tourists to not only observe but also participate in the special interest activity may require arrangement. Existing accommodation and some other tourist facilities and services and transportation may already be available for use by special interest tourists, or if it is necessary to develop these, they can often be modest in scale and cost.

Marketing should be selective and is not necessarily expensive, but does require specific knowledge of marketing sources such as special interest tour operators and, for more general marketing, the information media of specialized types of magazines and organizational newsletters. Most special interest groups are organized into clubs or associations that produce their own publications, or else there are commercial periodicals oriented to subjects of specialized interests. As one example of many, the magazine, *Archaeology*, popular in the USA, contains information on the many archaeological tours being organized each year throughout the world.

A particular planning consideration of special interest as well as general interest tourism is that the attraction feature, whether natural or cultural, is not degraded by tourism use, and often controls will need to be established on the number of tourists involved and the distribution of tourist flows, and education of both tourists and local residents to respect the environment and one another.

For organizing special interest tourism related to professional interests of tourists, such as doctors, lawyers, teachers, architects, and engineers, tours can be organized in the area for these tourists to visit the facilities related to their professions, meet their professional counterparts, and observe examples of the local professional outputs. The local professionals also learn from their visitors, and long-term exchange of information may result from the contacts made.

More generally, for tourists who want to learn more about the local society and meet residents, home visit programs can be organized, such as has been done in Japan, whereby tourists can arrange through a central agency such as the tourism office to visit private homes for an evening. The local families who wish to be included on the home visit program indicate their interest to the agency, which maintains a list of these families in its program.

Planning for Adventure Tourism

As is the case with special interest tourism, many types of adventure tourism are becoming increasingly popular, reflecting the trend towards tourists wanting to participate in activities. By definition, adventure tourism involves a certain element of danger, whether real or perceived, which adds to the challenge presented to the tourists. Other physically demanding sports such as hang gliding, ski diving, and parasailing may be an aspect of adventure tourism if some travel has been involved for the participants to reach their activity destinations.

Adventure tourism can take place in both more and less developed areas, but typically relates to less developed, sometimes remote places and is outdoors-oriented. As is the case with special interest tourism, adventure tourism requires specialized types of attractions but not always major specific attractions and can be suitable for less developed tourism areas with otherwise limited attractions or lack of facilities, services, and infrastructure, and for places that do not want to develop large-scale or mass tourism. Some types of adventure tourism, such as safaris, big-game hunting and fishing, and mountain climbing can be of high value with tourists paying substantial amounts to engage in these activities. More generally, adventure tourism can bring benefits to remote and often low income areas if it is organized to employ local people and purchase some goods locally.

The national or regional plan will have indicated whether certain forms of adventure tourism have potential in an area, are environmentally and socially suitable, and are marketable. In the absence of a national or regional plan, these factors can be assessed through survey and analysis of the attraction features and related markets, and evaluation can be made of possible impacts if certain forms of adventure tourism are developed. Specialists, such as on trekking and mountain climbing, game fishing, cave exploration, and white water boating, should be employed to assess these specialized forms of tourism.

Each type of adventure tourism will have its own facility and service requirements (for example, trails that may be preexisting and night stopovers for trekking and hiking, trails and camping sites for safaris, access points and base camps for mountain climbing, riverfront terminal points for river rafting and boating, and lodges or camps for hunting and fishing). Efficient organization and provision of services can be the key to the success of adventure tourism. Especially important for most of these activities, except for conventional forms of hunting and fishing in Europe and North America, are expert guide services and often support staffs such as porters. Availability of supplies is necessary, and any specialized equipment required must either be brought by the tourists or locally available. Game fishing, for example, requires specialized types of boats and fishing equipment, as well as qualified boat captains/guides. Observance of safety measures can be an important consideration, with medical services and sometimes emergency evacuation equipment provided. For example, in mountain climbing and trekking areas, helicopter service must be available for evacuation of ill or injured tourists and their support staff in remote areas.

One of the essential considerations in planning for development or expansion of adventure tourism is the environmental and sometimes social impacts of the tourist activities, as well as determination of the conservation measures that must be applied both to conserve the tourism resources and control impacts affecting the local society and the environment in general. Basic to planning adventure tourism is establishing carrying capacities, because many of these types of resources cannot withstand excessive use without degradation and even destruction, and adventure tourists themselves usually will not tolerate a high level of congestion, which depreciates their touristic experience. For some types of adventure tourism, congestion may also increase the real element of danger presented to the tourists and their local support staff.

An example of the need for and application of environmental controls is in the Himalayan region of Central Asia, especially in Nepal but also in some other countries of the region, where trekking and mountain climbing are increasingly popular tourist activities. Nepal has experienced serious environmental problems from trekkers and mountaineers who have left large amounts of litter and garbage along the mountain trails and at campsites. Tourists and their porters also cut trees for fuel, which aggravated the already severe erosion resulting from residents' removal of the forest cover. In response to these problems, the Nepalese government has adopted and published mountaineering, trekking, and river rafting regulations to be observed by tourists (Nepal Ministry of Tourism 1988). Biodegradable garbage must be buried and other litter carried back out of the mountains for proper disposal, and the trekkers and mountaineers must carry portable fuel (usually kerosene) with all tree cutting prohibited. Mountain climbing expeditions must obtain permits for the places they wish to climb and make reservations in advance (there is a long waiting list for Mt. Everest expeditions), with the number of expeditions underway at the same place during one season strictly controlled. As another control measure, trekkers and river rafting teams must obtain permits for their activities.

The Nepalese government with some international volunteer assistance has organized an on-going clean-up campaign for the trails, including the Everest Trail. The mountain villagers in these areas receive tourism benefits from providing staff and some supplies to the tourists and have learned from experience not to allow their traditional sense of hospitality to be abused by tourists. The regulations specify the minimum payments to be made to guides and porters so that they receive equitable wages. As a regional planning measure to reduce the pressure of tourist use on the presently developed tourism areas of Kathmandu Valley and Pokhara and to decentralize tourism more, Nepal is systematically planning and developing new tourist facility areas and places for trekking and mountaineering elsewhere in the country. Although mountain tourism is less developed in India, Pakistan, and Bhutan, those countries have adopted similar approaches to controlling development and use of their fragile mountain environments.

For hunting and fishing tourism, controls must be established on the amount of game taken based on the extent of the resource and its capability of renewal. In Mongolia, where limited but high value hunting is allowed for both the more and less common large animals, the government has established a sustainable population level for each species based on its habitat requirements and other factors, takes a census each year of the animals, and allows only the number of permits for taking game that will not reduce the sustainable population levels. In Africa, where there is much justifiable concern world-wide about maintenance of animal populations as part of the continent's and world's environmental heritage, most of the East African countries prohibit any sport hunting (except by cameras), while some countries in southern Africa, with larger game resources, permit highly controlled sport hunting to cull the animal populations to their sustainable levels. This hunting provides a significant source of tourism income.

Where hunting is allowed, those areas must be separated from places where game viewing, photography, and general recreation take place for obvious safety reasons, with the concept of visitor use zoning applied to the park and conservation areas.

Planning for Village Tourism

As a structured form of tourism, village tourism refers to tourists staying in or near a village, often traditional villages in remote areas, learning about the village and local cultural way of life and customs, and often participating in some village activities. The villagers build, own, and manage the tourist facilities and services and thereby receive direct benefits from tourism. The best known example of planned and programmed village tourism is that developed in the Lower Casamance region of Senegal (Saglio 1979). This project was aimed at exposing tourists to traditional village life, providing for spontaneous interaction between the tourists and residents, dispelling tourists' often erroneous preconceptions about the local environment and culture, and encouraging a sense of cultural pride on the part of residents. The model called for simple lodgings to be built, using traditional materials, methods, and styles, by the villagers and to be owned and managed by them. These lodgings were located along tour routes on the river system, away from established tourists' routes, with tourists traveling by traditional canoes. With this type of accommodation, the contrast between the quality of tourists' and residents' facilities was lessened and the investment costs small. Management of the lodgings by the villagers was organized through cooperatives. Local cuisine was served to the tourists. Part of the project objective was also to provide employment for young people to reduce the trend towards their migration to urban areas.

To avoid tourist saturation of the area, the tourist camps were located in villages with at least 1,000 inhabitants and accommodation limited to 20 to 30 beds in each camp. Expansion was in the form of developing new camps in different locations and not increasing the size of existing camps. Technical assistance was provided to plan and initiate the project, but it was planned in close coordination with the villagers. Although there were delays in implementation, the initial camps developed in the late 1970s were successful, and the project has expanded substantially throughout the region since then. Socioeconomic impacts are still being monitored.

Village tourism has also taken place elsewhere on a more spontaneous basis. In a Dayak village on the Mahakam river in East Kalimantan (in the Indonesian part of Borneo), a traditional "long house" has been developed for tourist accommodation, with villagers managing the accommodation and providing meals and traditional entertainment; tourist access is by river boat. On the Darien River in Panama, tourists travel by boat and stay in Kuna Indian homes, eat local foods, and participate in traditional activities. For horse riding tours through central Viti

Levu, the largest island in Fiji in the South Pacific, tourist night stopover facilities have been developed at various villages.

The development of 'bed and breakfast' accommodation in private homes in Britain and, more recently, in the USA and Canada, provide an opportunity for tourists to stay in local homes, meet residents, and walk about in a village environment. Bed and breakfast establishments are now also being developed in towns and cities and, in North America, can be as expensive as good quality hotels, but some tourists prefer the more homelike character of these places. This type of accommodation also brings economic benefits directly to local resident entrepreneurs, supplementing or being the primary source of household income. The historic inns in Britain, elsewhere in Europe, and the USA and Canada, many of which are being renovated and becoming popular with tourists, also are a form of village tourism.

Village tourism development, especially in remote, traditional areas, requires realistic feasibility analysis, modeling based on the local situation, careful selection of sites and planning of facilities in close coordination with the villagers, cooperation of the villagers among themselves in development and management, and selective marketing. The villages must decide themselves whether they want to develop tourism, and the villagers should be directly involved in the planning, development, and management process and not have these decisions imposed on them. It is the type of tourism that can provide the framework for mutual understanding between tourists and residents, bring benefits directly to villagers, and spread tourism's economic benefits more widely in an area, but socioeconomic and environmental impacts must be continuously monitored and any necessary adjustments made to the program.

Planning Farm and Rural Tourism

Farm tourism refers to working farms that supplement their income with some form of tourism business, most commonly from accommodation by renting extra guest rooms in the farm house to tourists or converting a separate farm building to accommodation units. Also, providing camping facilities, operating a farmhouse restaurant, selling farm products, and leasing fishing rights on a farm creek are forms of farm tourism. This type of tourism is developed for its economic benefits of supplementing farm income with little investment required and represents a successful symbiotic relationship for areas where neither farming nor tourism could be independently justified. It also provides the opportunity for urban families to experience and better understand agricultural activities through exposure and actual participation in them. In some cases, the opportunity for the farm families and especially the wives and children to meet other people is considered an important social benefit. In areas where farming cannot by itself survive, the farm life-style and attractive agricultural landscapes can be maintained through the controlled development of tourism.

Farm tourism is particularly well developed in Austria, especially in the western mountainous part of the country, and is also common in Britain and other European countries. It recently has commenced developing in the USA and Canada. Other countries, such as Greece, are investigating the feasibility for developing farm tourism in their mountainous areas as a means of providing much needed employment and income in those areas.

As indicated by Murphy (1985), the location of farm tourism appears to be influenced by three factors: the level of income provided by farming and the need for a supplementary income source; the presence of tourism resources; and the accessibility to major tourist generating regions. Farm tourism is often developed for economic reasons in marginal farming areas, such as uplands, that also offer scenic views and the potential for horse riding, fishing, hunting, and hiking as important attractions and activities for the tourists.

In addition to temperate climate agricultural areas where farm tourism has been developed, there would seem to be opportunities elsewhere for agro-tourism, such as in tropical plantations with tourists staying on the plantation and learning about its operations. Being typically large sized and sometimes in scenic areas (for example, tea plantations in hilly environments and palm plantations in coastal locations), these environments also offer potential for recreational activities. Agro tourism also applies to ranches. Fishing village tourism, with tourists staying in fishermen's houses and participating in fishing activities, should be feasible in some places and provide supplementary income to the fishing families.

In terms of planning, the regional tourism development strategy analysis will determine whether there is need and potential for encouragement of farm or agro-tourism and, based on location criteria, identify areas suitable for development of it. Farmers can be informed of this potential, and those who want to participate can be given some technical and financial assistance, if that is needed, for development of accommodation and other tourist facilities. Compilation of information on the farm accommodation and activities available and promotional marketing can be done by the regional government tourism office.

Other Forms of Alternative Tourism

As mentioned in Chapter 7, other forms of alternative tourism include walking and bicycling tours with tourists staying in hostels, private homes or bed and breakfast establishments, meeting local people and learning about the society and environment, nature eco-tourism of hiking and non-motorized boating in natural areas with local guides to explain the environmental characteristics, urban eco-tourism with tourists learning about the urban society and environment, and volunteer individuals and organizations traveling to an area and assisting in the development of community projects while, at the same time, learning about the community. These forms of tourism are not unique, but emphasize the contact with society and nature and, if planned properly, have little impact on the local culture and environment. Planning for such tourism is primarily one of organization, including provision of informed guide services. Based on its excellent national parks, Costa Rica, for example, is successfully developing eco-tourism.

Planning for Other Forms of Tourism

Other forms of tourism include water transportation based, transportation-oriented, residential, camping and caravaning, youth tourism, and those related to ethnic and nostalgic travel and religious pilgrimages. Each of these requires special planning considerations in their development and, because each is a specialized form of tourism, only some general considerations can be referred to here.

Water Transport Based Tourism

As explained in Chapter 7, cruise ship travel of all types is an expanding form of tourism and already well developed in the Caribbean, North American West Coast region, Mediterranean, Pacific Islands and is developing elsewhere. Cruises are not uncommon in Southeast Asia and the Indian Ocean, and there are even cruises now going to the Antarctic. In addition to providing economic benefits to the ship owners and cruise operators and employment for crew members who may represent many different national and cultural backgrounds, cruise shore stops bring some benefits to an area, from passenger expenditures on land tours, eating in local restaurants, local entertainment, and purchase of local handicrafts and specialty and duty-free items. Duty-free shopping has been particularly developed at some stopping points as both an attraction for tourists and an important source of local income. In tourism planning, cruise ship stops can also be used as a technique for starting tourism in remote areas that do not yet have the facilities, services, and infrastructure for developing land based tourism, or for places that do not wish to develop land based tourism.

For developing cruise ship tourism, an area needs to have some attractions as a basis for local tours, which may include urban attractions and shopping (cruise ships usually put in at port towns or cities), some features to visit outside the city, restaurants for lunch, and transportation facilities and services of taxis and tour buses with guides. The port itself needs a docking facility adjacent to sufficiently deep water for the types of cruise ships stopping or an off-shore, preferably protected anchorage of sufficient depth for anchoring the ship, which will then use small boats for ferrying passengers to and from shore. Efficient on-shore organization for tours is important, and customs and immigration facilitation must be provided for foreign passengers.

In remote areas, imagination is sometimes required to provide for cruise ship stopovers. In the South Pacific Island of Niue, a seldom experienced visit by a large cruise ship was handled by organizing local school buses to provide ground tour transportation, and adult and student groups were organized to provide traditional entertainment at the bus tour stopping points. In an isolated southern island of Vanuatu, where a cruise ship stops regularly, the local village organizes a traditional feast and entertainment, a walking tour of the village, and sale of handicrafts. For organizing these on-shore activities, the cruise ship operator pays a flat fee to the village government, which it uses to improve community facilities, thus bringing community-wide benefits from the cruise stops.

For the frequent cruise stops in Suva, Fiji, the passengers are greeted by the government police band as they disembark, buses are waiting to take groups on prearranged land tours, and a tourist information booth is set up on the cruise ship dock to provide information to those passengers not taking the organized cruises. In Suva, one small district of the city within walking distance of the cruise ship dock is occupied by duty-free shops catering to cruise passengers as well as other tourists, and a handicraft market place is established nearby. These retail activities provide a major source of tourist income to local entrepreneurs.

Cruise ship tourism also has carrying capacity limitations that must be considered. One aspect is the capacity of the docking and disembarkation facilities, and another is the capacity of the port town or city to cope with large shiploads of tourists. Some smaller Caribbean port towns are questioning whether they can conveniently handle a large number of passenger tourists at one time, especially when more than one cruise ship is in port on the same day, without generating too much pedestrian congestion and unduly disturbing residents' use of their shopping district and other urban facilities. In such situations, an approach that can be applied is to limit the type and number of ships allowed to stop over with coordination of ship schedules so that only a maximum acceptable level of passengers is in town at any given time. A consideration in this type of control is allowing those types of ships to stop that carry passengers who bring the greatest local benefits, that is, higher spending tourists. In very fragile environments such as the Antarctic, environmental controls must be strictly applied to cruise ship tours.

Riverine and canal tourism, which was referred to in Chapter 7, is already developed in some areas and has much potential for expansion in places with suitable rivers and canals and related shore stops. This type of tourism can also be used as a technique to commence tourism in remote, undeveloped areas. The facilities required are primarily boats equipped with sleeping cabins and kitchen facilities and shoreside docking points, with adequate access available to and from the cruising area. As is the case with cruise ship tourism, the docking points can be linked with on-shore excursion arrangements and, where needed, stores for provision of supplies.

Yachting tourism, referring to medium- and long-distance boat travel, is already well developed in the Mediterranean and Caribbean and is developing in other regions, such as the Pacific Islands, which offer scenic and interesting destinations and stopover points. Yachts require protected anchorages, preferably but not necessarily with piers, boat slips, and on-shore facilities for purchasing supplies and fuel and making boat repairs. It is an advantage if the port town also offers some dining, entertainment, and touring attractions. An example of a recently developed yacht port in a newly developing yachting region is at Vava'u in the northern islands of Tonga in the South Pacific. Tonga is generally well positioned in a central location in the South Pacific and Vava'u possesses an anchorage that is well protected from the hurricanes that frequent the region, a very scenic small island/water environment for local cruising and recreation, as well as on-shore facilities of stores for purchase of supplies and fuel, a boat repair facility, some restaurants and bars, and a interesting island setting for short land tours. In addition to long-distance owner-operated yachts, a charter yachting operation has commenced in Vava'u, whereby small yachting groups fly in, rent a yacht for one or two weeks of sailing, and then return to the port and fly home.

Transportation-Oriented Tourism

Road touring facilities are an important form of tourism in North America, Europe, Australia, New Zealand, and other places that have high levels of automobile ownership and are becoming more common in other countries. India, for example, is developing roadside facilities primarily for domestic tourists traveling by automobile and bus, and some Southeast Asian countries are developing road touring facility complexes. Road touring facilities include accommodation of motels or hotels, restaurants, convenience shopping, fuel service stations, and sometimes entertainment and recreation facilities. In the USA, these facilities are unfortunately often not planned in an integrated manner, and highways on city peripheries are commonly characterized by lines of motels and restaurants each with its own large, lighted, sometimes flashing advertising sign. In other places along highways, especially in rural areas, integrated and well-designed roadside travel centers have been developed. The characteristics of the tourism area being planned will greatly determine the type and extent of road touring facilities required. Locationally, these facilities need to be alongside or near the highway for convenient access by the tourists and to reduce through-traffic flows in areas off the highways. Proximity to a major intersection or interchange on limited access highways is an advantage to reduce access points required to the highway and serve different directions of traffic.

As indicated, planning an integrated complex of accommodation, service stations, restaurants, and shops provides a more interesting and convenient stopover for tourists, concentrates off-highway traffic and parking in just a few locations, and offers a more attractive type of development for the benefit of the residents' environment. An integrated center can also provide specialized touring facilities such as a tourist information office and some entertainment and recreation facilities, especially for children. In more isolated, less heavily traveled areas, a minimum level of roadside commercial facilities are required, such as a small motel and combined service station and shop that also offers information to tourists. In addition to commercial stopping points, roadside stops with toilet and picnicking facilities and rest areas, often with tourist information available, are commonly developed by a government agency for the convenience of tourists.

Hotels associated with large airports and sometimes physically part of the terminal building or connected to it are required for transit passengers and are now also being used somewhat for business meetings. In tourism planning, assessment should be made of the need for airport-related hotels and accessible sites allocated for this development in suitable nearby locations. Hotels are also often developed near major bus and train stations in urban areas for the convenience of travelers.

Residential Tourism

As described in Chapter 7, residential tourism refers to second homes used for vacation purposes by the owners or, in some cases, retirement homes purchased or leased by retirees originating from a different area. These homes may be simple cabins, bungalows, houses, villas, townhouses, or apartments and often a combination of these types in one development. Vacation and retirement homes and entire integrated vacation-oriented and retirement communities are particularly common in the USA, including Hawaii, Canada, the Caribbean, Europe and the Mediterranean region, and Japan and are commencing to be developed elsewhere. Residential tourism development tends to be located in scenic upland or mountain areas, seaside locations, and places with mild climates and are often oriented to some form of recreation facilities. They may also be developed in places with historically and architecturally interesting environments. Some vacation homes may eventually become the retirement homes for their owners.

Residential tourism can bring direct benefits of income generation for an area through initial purchase or leasing of the property, payment of property taxes and user fees that support local services and may well be in excess of the cost of services provided (especially for education), and local purchases of food, clothing, and other consumer items. This source of income tends to be dependable year after year because the vacationers have purchased or leased, on a long-term basis, their property, and the retirees, of course, live there most of the time. Because vacation and retirement homes are typically developed in rural and small community areas and the vacationers and retirees are usually from larger cities, this type of tourism can help redistribute income from urban to rural and small town areas. Also, these newcomers may be more concerned about the environmental quality and historic character of the area (because those are features that attracted them there) than long-term residents, and consequently help support local conservation programs.

Residential tourism may also create problems, depending on where and how it is developed. There may some loss of the local identity of communities with the influx of outsiders, including those who have the time and money to run for local elected political positions and start influencing local government decisions. Local property values and taxes may increase if there is considerable purchase by outsiders that may result in long-term residents and their children not being able to afford local property. Negative environmental impacts may be generated if infrastructure for the new homes is not properly developed and land for development is taken from conservation areas such as national forests.

These advantages and disadvantages must be considered in planning for the appropriate scale and type of vacation and retirement home areas. Poorly planned and unregulated development of residential tourism generates considerable negative environmental impact (Gartner 1987). Small scale development may often be more suitable than large scale in some places for both social and environmental reasons. At any scale, the integrated planning approach should be used so that this new development is well served with infrastructure and community facilities and services and attractively sited and designed. The usual residential planning layout principles and standards apply to the planning of residential tourism areas but with special consideration given to including recreation facilities. In some places, a holiday village planning approach will be the most suitable in order to provide a relatively compact configuration that does not consume too much land and is efficient to serve with infrastructure. In areas of high conservation value, utmost consideration must be given to not removing too much of the conservation area from public use or degrading its conservation value and careful environmental integration of the development so that overall scenic and natural qualities are maintained.

Camping and Caravan Facilities

Camping and caravan or recreational vehicle (RV) tourism is very popular in many places and often combined with other forms of tourism such as trekking and hiking in scenic areas and general sight-seeing or touring activities. From the planning standpoint, the two main considerations are the location of camping and caravan parks and the layouts and provision of infrastructure and services in the parks. Also, in some places with limited road development and especially narrow road widths, the movement of larger caravans, whether trailers being pulled by automobiles or trucks or that are self-contained single-unit vehicles, may be a factor in generating road congestion and dangerous traffic situations. It may be necessary to prohibit caravans of over a certain size in areas of restricted road development.

Locational criteria of camping and caravan parks, outside of nature and historic park and conservation areas where their location is determined as part of the overall park facility planning, include:

- Accessibility from a main highway or road;
- Possessing an attractive environment with some existing landscaping or potential for landscaping;
- Not preempting areas more important for other uses or of high conservation value;
- Availability of infrastructure or feasibility of providing infrastructure, especially of water supply, sewage disposal, and often electric power; and
- Availability of land at a reasonable cost.

Layout and development should be based on integrated site planning and design, with provision made for adequate access into the park and vehicular parking where needed, some landscape buffering around each camping or caravan site, centrally located toilet and shower facilities in camping parks, sewage and electric power hookups in caravan parks, and often some recreational and retail service facilities. Adequate water supply and sewage disposal are essential. Effective park management and maintenance are important, whether publicly or privately developed.

Ethnic, Nostalgic, Religious, and Youth Tourism

In some places, ethnic and nostalgic tourism, described in Chapter 4, of tourists visiting their ancestral or own original homelands and places with personal historic associations is important. Sometimes, these types of tourists stay with friends and relatives, or else use tourist facilities and services already available but, in other places, additional facilities will need to be developed. The location and type of such facilities will depend very much on the type and extent of tourist markets involved and where they visit.

Places of important religious pilgrimages may require substantial development of tourist facilities and services and planning of these also depends on the local situation, and to what extent the local religious organizations provide some visitor facilities. Planning for religious pilgrimages can require major efforts and expenditures such as has been done to receive the Moslem pilgrims in Saudi Arabia, which involved developing large-scale receiving and transit facilities at the Jedda Airport as well as facilities in and near Mecca and Medina. At some of the religious sites in India, hundreds and even thousands of hotel rooms of all types are required. Proper organization of the flow of pilgrim traffic at the religious sites is essential.

An important consideration in planning of ethnic, nostalgic, and religious tourism is that, although the primary motivations for travel relate to ethnic, nostalgic, and religious factors, many of these tourists also want to engage in general sight-seeing and perhaps recreation and other holiday pursuits in the areas they are visiting. The possibility of developing other attractions and activities should be reviewed and planned for in these areas in order to increase visitor length of stay, expenditures, and satisfaction levels.

Youth tourism requires organization of transportation and development of youth hostels or other types of inexpensive, often group-oriented accommodation. Youth hostels are located at or near the destination attraction feature, such as a park, recreation area, or archaeological or historic site, or in urban areas and require convenient access, often including public type transportation. Although a basic and often dormitory type of accommodation, youth hostels should maintain acceptable hygienic and safety standards. Informal budget accommodation aimed at the youth market has been developed by the private sector in some places, and provision must be made that these also meet basic hygienic and safety standards. Organizational youth camps such as for the Boy and Girl Scouts should be planned in an integrated manner and include recreation and other facilities as well as accommodation.

Case Studies

The two case studies presented relate to special interest and village tourism planning. The national tourism plan for Bhutan reflects that country's policy for strictly controlled, high value special interest and adventure tourism based on the inherent natural and cultural resources of the country. The village tourism development study for some islands in eastern Indonesia demonstrate a systematic and carefully programmed approach to developing village tourism in close coordination with the villagers involved.

Tourism Planning and Development in Bhutan

Tourism in Bhutan is an example of highly controlled special interest and adventure-oriented high value tourism based on a planned and staged approach with much involvement of the government and religious leaders in the tourism planning and management process. Located in the eastern Himalaya Mountains, the Kingdom of Bhutan offers the attractions to tourists of spectacular mountain scenery and strongly traditional Buddhist cultural patterns, including the distinctively Bhutanese architectural styles of monasteries, palaces, shops, and homes. Bordering India on the south are foothills with subtropical wildlife and vegetation. The population of the country is about 1.5 million, most of which is agricultural, with only 5 percent living in urban areas. Nomadism is still practiced by certain groups in the higher elevations. Although the official per capita income figure is low by international standards, many Bhutanese live a relatively secure and comfortable subsistence life-style that is not, to a great extent, integrated into the modern cash economy.

Tourism in Bhutan started after the Royal Coronation of the present king in 1974, when it was realized that the hotels developed for that event could be utilized for tourists. The objectives of tourism at the time of its introduction were to:

- Generate revenue, especially foreign exchange;
- Publicize the culture and traditions of the country to the outside world; and
- Play an active role in the country's socioeconomic development.

However, the government was aware that the unrestricted flow of tourists could lead to sociocultural and environmental problems, and it applied a strict policy of controlling tourism development. Until the mid-1980s, the maximum number of international holiday tourist arrivals, excluding Indians, was maintained at 2,000 annually, but, in 1986, 2,500 arrivals were targeted. Actual arrivals were 1,900 in 1984, 1,896 in 1985, 2,405 in 1986, and about 2,500 annually in 1987–89, plus an estimated 1,500 Indians and others coming for business, government, and official mission purposes. Average length of stay of tourists was 9.3 nights in 1988. All non-Indian holiday tourists must come on prearranged, all-inclusive package tours, and no individual tourists are permitted entry into the country. Minimum daily expenditures per tourist have been established (these have been increased throughout the years and in 1990 were about US$200 per day, depending on the season and type of tour). These controls are exercised through entry visa procedures and arrangements with overseas tour operators.

The primary tourist markets of Bhutan are the USA, Japan, the Federal Republic of Germany, and other countries of Western Europe. Approximately 80 percent of the tourists come on cultural tours and most of the remainder for trekking tours (including cultural treks to visit monasteries). A very limited number of mountain climbing expeditions are allowed. Most tourism takes place in the western region of the country, which includes the international airport at Paro, the road access point from India, and the capital city of Thimpu. Part of the central region was opened to tourists in 1984.

A tourism development plan was completed for the country in 1984 and, after long debate by the government, adopted in 1986 (UNDP and WTO 1986). Three types of of tourism zones are identified in the plan:
• Himalayan zone for mountaineering and high altitude trekking;
• Central zone for cultural tours, including trekking; and
• Southern foothills zone for wildlife tourism in conjunction with Indian winter tourism.

The government intends to continue the policy of controlled tourism development, gradually opening up new areas as infrastructure is developed. The overriding aim is to ensure that the type and rate of growth of tourism does not damage the natural environment and cultural heritage. In fact, the tourism plan views controlled tourism as an important vehicle for conserving and enhancing the cultural assets of the country.

In the tourism plan, growth targets for tourist arrivals were set at 3,000 for 1990 and 5,600 for 1995 under the preferred strategy. The National Seventh Five-Year Development Plan for 1992–96, which was being prepared in 1990, further specifies the arrivals as follows:

Year	Foreign Tourists	Neighboring Tourists*
1992	4,000	1,000
1993	4,500	1,500
1994	5,000	2,000
1995	5,500	2,500
1996	6,000	3,000

* mostly from India

The tourism strategy is to focus development around tourism service centers in the main potential areas, linked by tourist routes. Eight such centers are recommended for the long-term period in the western, central, eastern, and southern regions of the country. The development strategy identifies three time phases:

- Short-term (1986–90)—continuation of the process of improving standards of tourist facilities and services with high utilization of existing infrastructure in the presently opened areas in the western and central regions.
- Medium-term (1991–95)—expansion of tourism in the central region with development of some new facilities and infrastructure, and starting cultural safari tourism in the eastern region.
- Long-term (post-1995)—further expansion of tourism development in the western and central regions, gradual extension of development in the eastern region, and development of wildlife tourism in the southern region.

Figures 9.1 show the short, medium, and long-term tour facilities recommended by development period in the Bhutan tourism plan.

The plan recognized that, for marketing purposes, an identifiable image needed to be developed for Bhutan based on the country's cultural heritage as a living tradition in an independent Himalayan kingdom. The plan reinforces the already established policy of the government that the architectural design of any new development, including tourist facilities, must utilize traditional design motifs and building materials to the greatest extent possible. This policy has been followed, and recently developed hotels and other buildings, especially in the rapidly growing capital of Thimpu, maintain the traditional architectural character

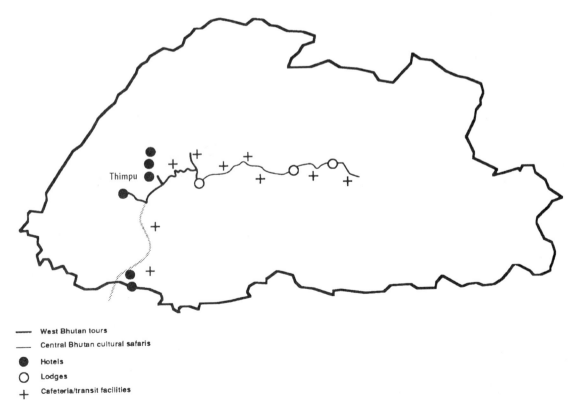

——— West Bhutan tours

——— Central Bhutan cultural safaris

● Hotels

○ Lodges

+ Cafeteria/transit facilities

Figure 9.1A. Tourism Development Plan for Bhutan—Short-term Tour Facilities.

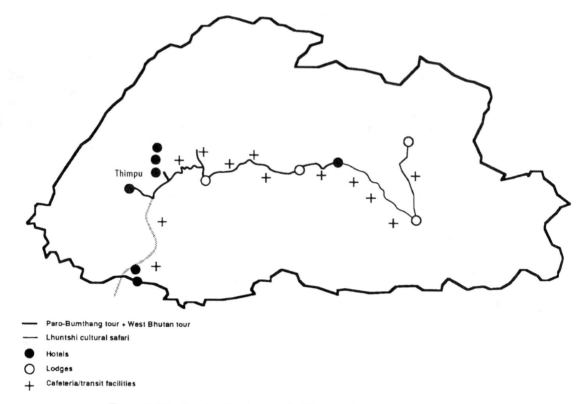

Figure 9.1B. Tourism Development for Bhutan—Medium-term Tour Facilities.

and blend in well with older development and the natural environment. Adequate sewage disposal systems for hotels are also required, and electric power is provided from the national grid in the more developed areas and on-site generators in other areas.

In the early 1980s, the Bhutan Tourism Corporation (BTC) was established to manage the operational side of tourism, including most of the hotels; there are also some privately owned and managed hotels. Recognizing the need for training persons to work in tourism as a totally new activity in Bhutan, a hotel and catering school has been developed in Thimpu with the assistance of international agencies. Also, several tourism officials have received short- and long-term overseas training in various aspects of tourism and hotel management.

With the adoption of the tourism plan in 1986, the Bhutan government issued an instruction to formulate an action plan to be integrated into the sixth national development plan and expressed a desire to accelerate the growth of tourism and its economic benefits, while still safeguarding the Bhutanese way of life and traditions, with a target of 5,000 foreign tourist arrivals annually for 1989 and 1990 to be set. However, the political climate for tourism changed, and some Buddhist religious leaders, who continue to exert considerable influence on na-

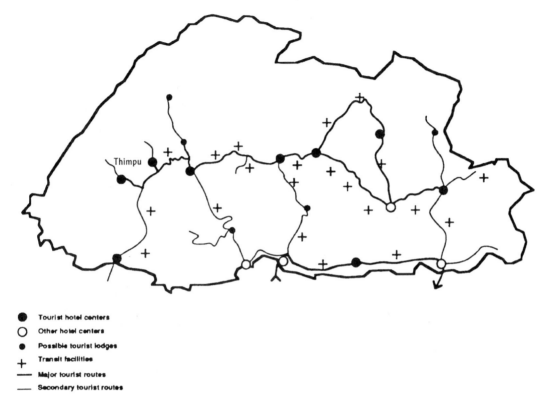

Tourist hotel centers
Other hotel centers
Possible tourist lodges
Transit facilities
Major tourist routes
Secondary tourist routes

Figure 9.1C.   Tourism Development Plan for Bhutan—Long-term Tour Facilities.

tional policy, objected to certain forms of tourist activities, particularly those that involve tourists visiting important religious places.

In July 1987, a special commission on tourism reported to the National Assembly that tourism may have an adverse moral impact on young people if they observe tourists' behavior that might be interpreted as belittling the mystical power of the country's religion. This resulted in a Royal Command to the BTC to designate certain monasteries and temples that tourists are prohibited to visit, effective in 1988 (Brown 1988). The situation in 1990 seems to be more satisfactory to the various parties concerned and, as indicated previously, the preliminary five-year plan for 1992–96 is targeting the numbers of tourist arrivals very much in line with the tourism plan's initial recommendations.

Village Tourism Program in Nusa Tenggara, Indonesia

The village tourism program in the two provinces of Nusa Tenggara Barat and Nusa Tenggara Timur in the eastern part of Indonesia was prepared in the mid-1980s (UNDP & WTO 1987) as part of an implementation project of the Nusa

Tenggara tourism development plan previously prepared (UNDP & WTO 1981). Nusa Tenggara is comprised of several larger and many smaller islands with a diversity of different cultural groups and related traditions, customs, belief systems, economic activities, architectural styles, and crafts. The region possesses considerable scenic beauty of mountains, valleys, and coastlines, good beaches and marine areas, and some unusual wildlife. Outside of the towns, traditional life-styles still largely prevail, although these are changing rapidly because of the general economic development and improved communications taking place. The type of tourism proposed for development in the region was a combination of general interest sight-seeing, beach resort and marine activities, and culturally- and environmentally-oriented special interest tourism based on such features as traditional life-styles, architectural styles, hand-woven textiles and other crafts, wildlife (particularly the unique Komodo Dragon—a large monitor lizard), controlled hunting, and nature trail hiking.

The principal objectives of the village tourism program were to bring the economic benefits of employment and income from tourism more directly to village residents while, at the same time, satisfying the tourism experience desires of certain tourist market segments who wish to understand in some depth the cultures and environments of the region. Other benefits to the villagers would be development of technical and managerial skills that could be transferred to other economic activities, maintenance and revitalization of certain aspects of the traditional cultural patterns of building styles, handicrafts and art forms such as dance in their authentic manner, and reinforcement of a sense of pride by the villagers in their traditions, which otherwise might be rejected or lost in the face of general socioeconomic development. Within the regional context, village tourism was seen as providing additional attractions, activities, and infrastructure for tourists, expanding the tourist markets and increasing tourists' average length of stay, and being complementary to the more conventional beach and marine tourism underway in the region.

The concept of the program was the development of small-scale tourist facilities and services in or near villages, with these facilities and services owned and operated by the villagers as cooperatives or individually, depending on the local social system. This tourism development could be based either on the inherent traditional cultural features of the village or nearby natural attraction features, with the village developed as a service center for tourists visiting those nearby places. A basic approach that was applied throughout the project was for the planning team to coordinate closely with the local government agencies involved and the villagers themselves. Only villages that indicated that they were interested in participating in the program were considered for inclusion in it.

The program was organized for six villages to be selected for initial development as a pilot project. Based on this initial development, the program would be refined and more villages would be included in later phases of the project. This pilot project was viewed as a prototype not only for the Nusa Tenggara region but also for other regions in Indonesia. Thirty-six villages throughout the region were identified as having the potential to participate in the program. These were field surveyed, researched, and evaluated according to certain criteria as to their suitability. Figure 9.2 reproduces the evaluation carried out for some of these villages as an example of the selection criteria and approach applied. Based on this evaluation, 13 of the 36 villages were short-listed. These were further evaluated and discussed with the government, and 6 were selected for the pilot program, with 3 of these offering inherent traditional village attractions and 3 to serve as service centers for nearby attractions such as mountain hiking and visiting unusual scenic natural features.

Village tourism programs were prepared for each of the six villages by the project team, based on specific objectives formulated in consultation with the villagers. These programs were presented to the respective provincial and local governments for comment, finalized through further discussions with the village leaders, and then approved by them. For the cultural villages, the programs emphasized the development of cultural features such as village tours of traditional activities and architectural styles, music and dance performances, and handicraft demonstrations, as well as providing certain basic services for visitors, such as accommodation and meals. For the service center villages, accommodation (including campgrounds in some places), small restaurants, tour guide services, equipment rental, sales of supplies for hiking and camping, and other facilities and services would be provided. Physical land use plans and facility designs were prepared for all the villages with emphasis given to use of traditional architectural styles and local building materials in any new or remodeled facilities.

Emphasis was placed on the development of village organizations that would be responsible for coordination of the implementation and administration of the programs as well as serve as local forums for discussion of the progress and any problems to be solved in implementation and administration. Various types of education and training of villagers to effectively manage and operate the facilities and services were emphasized, and a training program was organized. The program prepared for each village included a specific development budget based on estimated costs of the physical facilities, infrastructure, the education and training required, and any other costs involved. Program implementation schedules were prepared, and the agencies or parties responsible for each aspect of implementation were identified.

Each of the village programs was examined with respect to the likely economic costs and benefits, that is, feasibility analysis. This included consideration of tourist arrivals, tourist spending, employment generation, gross and net operating profits, distribution of profits, and net tourism revenues remaining in the village after payment for 'imported' goods and services. It was determined that the programs would have varying economic impacts on the villages, ranging from limited supplementation of individual income and local government revenues to expansion and diversification of the local economies through significant revenue generation and creation of employment opportunities.

Long-term development objectives, referring to a period of approximately 15 years, were set forth as guidelines for future development in and around the villages, which included overall village development as well as tourism development. This initial programing for village tourism was followed through with additional studies further specifying regional relationships and local planning. Some

| Location | | Site Specific Factors | | | | | | | Regional Factors | | | |
Village	Region	Cultural Activities	Natural Environment Activities	Site Features	Surroundings	Accessibility	Special Consideration	Preliminary Rating	Priority (Phase)	Importance to Regional Tourism	Final Rating	Preliminary Selection
SUKARARE	LOMBOK	◐	○	○	○	◐	◐	○	●	◐	◐	
RAMBITAN	LOMBOK	◐	○	●	◐	●	◐	◐	●	●	●	·
KUTA	LOMBOK	○	●	○	●	●	◐	◐	●	◐	◐	·
SEMBALUN LAWANG	LOMBOK	◐	●	◐	●	◐	◐	◐	●	●	●	·
SEMBALUN BUMBUNG	LOMBOK	◐	●	○	●	◐	◐	◐	●	◐	◐	
SENARU	LOMBOK	○	●	●	●	◐	○	◐	●	○	●	·
BATU KOQ	LOMBOK	○	●	◐	◐	●	◐	◐	●	◐	●	
PEMENANG	LOMBOK	○	◐	○	○	◐	◐	◐	●	○	◐	
SENGGIGI	LOMBOK	○	●	○	○	◐	○	◐	●	◐	◐	·
BATU TERING	SUMBAWA BARAT	○	○	○	○	○	◐	○	○	◐	○	
SEMAMUNG	SUMBAWA BARAT	●	○	○	◐	◐	◐	◐	○	○	○	
POTO	SUMBAWA BARAT	●	○	◐	○	○	◐	○	○	◐	○	
MBAWA	SUMBAWA BARAT	○	○	●	●	○	◐	◐	●	◐	◐	·
MARIA	SUMBAWA BARAT	◐	◐	◐	◐	●	◐	◐	●	○	◐	

Degree Of Interest For Tourism

● HIGH
◐ MODERATE
○ LOW

Figure 9.2.   Rating of Villages—Nusa Tenggara Barat.

budget was allocated by the government, and technical assistance was provided by both the local government agencies involved and the original project team that commenced implementation of the project, with the villagers much involved in the construction of facilities.

References

Brown, Graham. 1990. "South Asia Tourism Development." *Tourism Management.* 9(3): 240-245.

Gartner, William C. 1987. "Environmental Impacts of Recreational Home Developments." *Annals of Tourism Research.* 14(1): 38-57.

Hall, Peter. 1987. "Urban Development and the Future of Tourism." *Tourism Management.* 8(2): 129-130.

Jansen-Verbeke, Myriam. 1988. *Leisure, Recreation and Tourism in Inner Cities.* Amsterdam: Netherlands Geographical Studies. No. 58.

Murphy, Peter E. 1985. *Tourism: A Community Approach.* New York: Methuen.

Nepal Ministry of Tourism. 1988. *Some Regulations Relating to Mountain Tourism in Nepal.* Kathmandu: His Majesty's Government.

Owen, Charles. 1989. "Maximizing Tourism Potential: A Tale of Four Cities." *Tourism Management.* 10(4): 272-274.

Pearce, Douglas. 1987. *Tourism Today: A Geographical Analysis.* Harlow, England: Longman Group.

Saglio, Christian. 1979. "Tourism for Discovery: A Project in Lower Casamance, Senegal." *Tourism: Passport to Development?* 321-335. Emanuel de Kadt, editor. New York: Oxford University Press.

United Nations Development Programme and World Tourism Organization. 1981. *Tourism Development Plan for Nusa Tenggara, Indonesia.* Madrid: World Tourism Organization.

———1986. *Tourism Development Master Plan for Bhutan.* Madrid: World Tourism Organization.

———1987. *Village Tourism Development Programme for Nusa Tenggara, Indonesia.* Madrid: World Tourism Organization.

10

Planning Tourist Attractions

Planning Approach

One of the important benefits of tourism, in its best form, is that it can be a significant vehicle for achieving conservation of the environmental and cultural heritage of an area that, without tourism, might not be financially feasible or politically acceptable to accomplish. Tourism can economically justify and help pay for conservation of important features of the natural, archaeological, and historic environment that are susceptible to degradation or complete loss, and maintenance of aspects of cultural traditions, arts, and crafts that otherwise might die out (and already have almost disappeared in some places). The use of tourism as a technique to achieve conservation is applicable everywhere but is especially important in less developed countries that do not have the economic resources to meet both conservation and general socioeconomic objectives. Also, many types of attractions, if properly developed, can be an important means of educating both domestic and foreign tourists about the environment, history, and culture of an area, as well as provide places for recreation and enjoyment.

As described in Chapter 4, tourist attractions include natural, cultural, and special features and related tourist activities. At the national and regional planning levels, existing and potential attractions are surveyed and evaluated, as related to tourist markets, with a determination made as to those that have primary importance or attracting power and those that are secondary and complementary to the primary features. Basic planning principles at that level are provision of adequate access to and clustering of attractions for efficiency in providing infrastructure and convenience of visiting by tourists. Attractions development can be staged at the national and regional planning level with different attractions developed in coordination with tourist facility development and, for large attractions, staged within themselves as market demand warrants and resources are available.

It is common practice in a national or regional plan to include prototypical plans for development of specific priority attractions in order to demonstrate appropriate planning and design principles for these features and to provide a basis for near-future development of them.

At the community planning level, suitable detailed planning and development of attractions is essential for the success of tourism and to ensure that the development and use of attractions will not result in environmental or sociocultural problems and that the attraction resources are permanently sustained. Attractions planning as used here includes conservation of the attraction features as well as planning for development of visitor facilities and use that optimizes the visitor enjoyment and appreciation of the attractions. The approach is a combination of physical planning for visitor facilities as well as conservation, where needed, of the attraction features and careful organization and management of visitor use of the features. Attractions are viewed as resources, either natural or cultural or often a combination of these in one place, that require careful planning and continuing management to maintain their sustainability. The continuing management process may require adjustments to be made to the initial facilities and management plan. Even special types of attractions such as theme parks, casinos, convention and sports facilities, and some special events become resources that require careful management for continued use and viability although they are more replaceable than natural and cultural resources.

Because of the danger of congestion and overuse of major attractions, a problem already confronting some features, organization and control of visitor use and flows is a basic consideration in much attractions planning. Such places as Yosemite National Park in California, Venice in Italy, and the Tower of London in the U.K. have been experiencing congestion problems for several years. Even in less developed tourism countries, such as at the Ming Tombs and Great Wall access point near Beijing, China, congestion at certain times is very evident. This problem will become more acute as both domestic and international tourism grows throughout the world. Therefore, establishing carrying capacities of attractions and applying techniques to organize visitor flows and control overuse may be an overriding factor in attractions planning and management. Approaches to mitigate these problems are being developed, including imaginative visitor flow management techniques, regional policies of decentralization of tourism, and ways to reduce the seasonality factor, although for major unique places, these problems probably cannot be completely resolved without establishing absolute controls on the extent of visitor use.

Much attractions planning, such as for nature parks, historic sites, and theme parks, are specialized disciplines with highly developed techniques applied based on experience and experimentation of the specialist planners involved and also may overlap planning for objectives other than just tourism. This book does not pretend to present all the techniques and principles applied in those fields. Rather, it suggests some basic approaches and principles that tourism planners should be aware of in their coordination with the specialist attraction planners. An important consideration that must be made throughout the attractions planning process is reconciliation of conservation and visitor use or tourism objec-

Historic Devon House (top) and river rafting (bottom) in Jamaica—As examples of imaginative attractions development, the restored Devon House in Kingston, representing the nineteenth century Jamaican architectural style, has been furnished in period furniture and is the museum centerpiece of a complex of craft shops and restaurants and other features including annual craft fairs. River rafting on a variety of Jamaica's rivers has been developed as a popular attraction for tourists that is not environmentally disruptive and provides an additional activity to the country's primary attraction of beach tourism. (Courtesy of the Jamaica Tourist Board)

tives that need not necessarily be in conflict with one another if there is effective planning and continuous management, including coordination between the tourism and other involved government agencies and with the private sector.

Planning and Managing Natural Attraction Resources

Planning and managing natural attraction features involves establishing a basic policy and planning approach, understanding the planning process and techniques, applying planning principles, and effecting continuous management of the resources.

Policy and Planning Approach

The planning and management of natural as well as cultural attraction resources should be based on national or regional policy such as a national or state parks policy, or in the absence of such policy, the planning team must assume what would be a suitable policy for the area. If there is no adopted policy, it may be appropriate for the project team to recommend in the tourism plan an appropriate policy and establishment of a parks and conservation system for consideration by the area government in preparing and adopting a suitable policy and plan for parks and conservation.

The recently revised policy of Parks Canada is a good example of a policy approach that was adopted for both natural and historic sites of national significance based on many years experience with previous policies and actual development of parks (Parks Canada 1982). The main purpose of the revised policy was to provide an integrated and comprehensive statement of broad principles to serve as a guide for future initiatives and for more detailed policy statements on specific areas, set within the context of overall program objectives. A further purpose of the integrated policy is to provide other agencies and the public with a consolidated statement of objectives for the program as a whole and for individual activities within it.. Policies were established for: 1) the overall Parks Canada program—the objectives and broad common principles underlying existing and future activities; 2) policy for each of the current activities; and 3) policy direction for the new initiatives of Canadian landmarks, Canadian heritage rivers, and heritage buildings.

The basic approach for planning of natural tourist attractions such as national parks is application of the environmental planning approach, which, as previously explained, emphasizes conservation of the natural environment as well as designing visitor facilities and organizing visitor use that fit well into the environment and do not degrade it. This can also be expressed as achieving a balance between optimum enjoyment and appreciation of the environment by visitors without degradation of the environment by tourism and maintaining the conservation objectives. The park or conservation plan is often termed a management plan because the planning concept is that of continuous management of the natural resource so that it serves both conservation and tourism objectives.

Planning Process and Techniques

The process of planning natural attractions is generally as follows:
- Determination of the development and conservation objectives within the framework of the parks and conservation policy;
- Environmental/ecological analysis, including any special surveys required such as of the wildlife, flora, and ecological systems, with identification of special environmental areas to be preserved, such as wildlife habitats;
- Establishment of visitor carrying capacities, based on various assumptions of types of visitor use;
- Projection of visitor demand by type of use, such as day tours, hiking, and camping and, if necessary, reconciliation made with the carrying capacity analysis to arrive at optimum visitor use levels;
- Determination of the types of visitor facilities needed and facility space requirements;
- Formulation of the plan, including preparation and evaluation of outline plans based on the plan's objectives and environmental impacts, and finalization of the selected plan with any staging of development indicated;
- Preparation of a visitor use organization and flow patterns plan where appropriate;
- Final environmental impact analysis; and
- Implementation of the plan and continuous management of the resource and its visitor use.

The planning technique normally applied is that of designating zones for the various different use and conservation areas. These zones may include strict conservation zones for flora, fauna, or ecological system preservation in which only scientists and park staff are permitted, and remote wilderness areas where only backpacker hiking tourists are permitted. There are also general use nature zones where visitors may drive or walk to observe the flora, fauna, and scenery. Various visitor facilities zones allow for campgrounds, visitor center and visitor recreation facilities, accommodation, and services. The zones are based on the intensity of visitor use allowed and are derived from the environmental analysis and especially the location of the important ecological areas. The use zones are then connected with a circulation network of access points, roads, and walking and riding trails. Conservation of the natural features takes precedence over visitor use.

Planning Principles

It has been found that the best principle for development of visitor facilities is to concentrate the major facilities in one area as an integrated well-designed complex. The facility complex, often called the visitor center, typically includes the reception/lounge area, an information counter (often combined with the reception area), a shop or shops selling books and other items related to the park features, a snack bar or restaurant (or both), an exhibit area or small museum about the park, perhaps a small lecture and audio-visual presentation hall, an emergency medical service, toilets, and related landscaping and parking for cars and tour buses. The park management office may be located here or elsewhere. The visitor center is usually situated on the access road near the park entrance or in the place where visitors commence their exploration of the park as the first stop that visitors make. The architectural style of the center should be compatible with the natural environment and be well integrated into it. Natural type buildings materials such as stone and wood are always preferable.

In some cases of isolated parks, visitor accommodation may be integrated into the visitor complex. This accommodation may include a range of different types and price levels of hotels and cottages, campgrounds, and possibly caravan parks. In other cases, accommodation is available in a nearby town or resort or situated just outside the park entrance. Because of increasing congestion and concern about environmental pollution within some parks, the trend is towards location of major accommodation outside of the park and therefore is considered in the regional planning of the area, but campgrounds might still be suitably located inside the park in a facility use area. In some places with large-scale environments, carefully planned resort hotels can be developed within the park, such as has been done in some of the East African game parks.

An example of integration of park facilities into a large single complex is Uluru National Park in central Australia. The major features of the park are Ayers Rock, a striking monolithic form jutting above the desert plain, and Mt. Olga, a tight cluster of domed hills, valleys, and clefts, located some 20 miles from Ayers Rock. An Aboriginal tribe once lived in the area, and Ayers Rock has significant Aboriginal associations. The park facility center development was completed and opened in the mid-1980s but was based on the concepts of a plan prepared in 1969 (Belt, Collins & Associates 1969) and slightly modified over the intervening years with detailed environmental impact studies conducted during that period. Located within the park between the two major features but some distance away from both of them and away from the line of sight between the features, the integrated visitor complex includes various types of accommodation, visitor information services, and commercial, recreation, and other facilities and services for tourists in an attractively designed environment. No other accommodation or major facilities are allowed in or near the park and previous motels near the base of Ayers Rock were removed. Visitors take day tours to the park features, including the possibility of climbing the Rock, and signs are place along trails to identify and explain aspects of the features and their Aboriginal use and mystical associations. Efforts were made to incorporate Aboriginal people into the park development and operations.

Based on the zoning plan of the park, which indicates the extent of use allowed in the various areas, other park facilities are planned and designed. These may include vehicular roads, hiking and riding trails, scenic viewpoints, shelters, picnicking areas, toilets, waste receptacles, campgrounds, information and directional signs, and small interpretive exhibits. The design of these facilities should also be compatible with and integrated into the environment by using natural building materials. Strict environmental controls should be applied to the development of any visitor and park management facilities, including provision of an adequate potable water supply, sanitary disposal of sewage and solid waste, and proper maintenance of park vehicles to control air pollution.

The type of access allowed into and through the park will depend entirely on the local situation. In some cases, private cars may be allowed into certain areas where there are parking lots; in other cases, only park-operated vehicles are allowed; or only walking or horse/donkey/mule riding are permitted. In some of the national parks in Sri Lanka, for example, visitors' vehicles must remain at the entrance, and visitors tour the park in park-operated safari type vehicles with qualified guides.

Beach and marine environments require special planning considerations. Major facilities at beach parks should be set back from the beach area, behind the vegetation line, with the main facilities planned as an integrated complex. Often an approach used to control conflicting uses of the water area is zoning for different types of uses, such as separate zones for swimming, boating, water skiing, and body, board, and wind surfing. Strict conservation controls must be applied to the use of underwater environments, such as prohibition of taking coral, fish, and live shells, control of the use of boat anchors (special types of permanent anchoring devices have been developed which do not result in destruction of coral), and control of underwater littering. Ecologically important underwater areas should be designated as marine parks or reserves with very strict use controls applied. As an interesting educational approach, marine parks can be developed with underwater trail systems to be followed by snorkelers and scuba divers, with the different species of plant and animal life identified with underwater markers, but still with controls on damaging the environment, as has been done in the Virgin Islands National Park in the Caribbean.

Management of Park Use

Proper management of park or conservation area use is a key factor in successful park management. A basic consideration, as mentioned, is not allowing the carrying capacity of the park in general and of ecologically sensitive areas in particular to be exceeded—not always an easy task. Even excessive walking in areas of important vegetation may generate environmental damage through compaction and erosion of the soil (Edington and Edington 1986), or uncontrolled viewing of wild game may disturb the animals' normal living patterns (Mathieson and Wall 1982). Carrying capacity levels can be maintained through various techniques such as distributing visitors more evenly throughout the park and to other less used parks, trying to encourage even seasonal distribution of visitor use, and prohibiting visitors to visit certain sensitive areas of the park except by special permit or prohibiting visits during certain seasons when wildlife is especially vulnerable.

Sufficient and accurate information in the form of guide books, brochures, signs, exhibits, and other material and presentations by park rangers should be provided to the visitors about the characteristics and interesting features of the park, while informing them about the control measures that must be observed, with explanation as to why the regulations are necessary. These measures might include ones related to visitors staying on the trails, camping only in designated areas, not littering the landscaping (with litter receptacles or other means of disposal provided), not feeding or going close to certain animals, controlled use of fire, prohibition of graffiti and defacement of park features, and prohibition of tree cutting and removal of flora and fauna specimens.

Continuous monitoring of the impact of visitor use of the park or conservation area and of visitors' attitudes and satisfaction levels should be undertaken, so that any environmental problems arising from tourism can be controlled and, at the same time, visitors can find their nature experience interesting, enjoyable, and educational.

In order to properly manage a nature park or reserve, an adequate number of trained personnel is essential. Although there is some cost involved in properly developing and maintaining visitor facilities in the park, at least some of this cost can be recovered through park user fees, profits from retail sales in the visitor center, and franchises for the operation of restaurants, shops, and sometimes hotels. More generally, the government should consider the overall economic benefits generated by the park as an attraction for tourism development in the area, and allocate a sufficient budget from its general fund for maintaining this important natural resource.

Regional Management Approach

On a more general regional level, the importance of managing natural tourism resources is evidenced by the approach applied to the Mt. Fuji area in Japan (Bosselman 1978). The highest mountain in Japan, Mt. Fuji itself is a very important attraction to the Japanese for both religious and recreational reasons, with climbing the mountain a goal of many of the country's citizens. Associated with the mountain are many lakes and forested areas offering much recreational potential. The Mt. Fuji area is relatively near to the large domestic tourist markets of the Tokyo metropolitan region and is easily accessible from Japan's other major urban places. In the 1960s and 1970s, the Mt. Fuji area was attracting many tourists and experiencing rapid uncontrolled development of hotels and other tourist facilities, second homes, golf courses, and highways (but otherwise limited infrastructure), all leading to serious land use and environmental problems and general degradation of the area, as well as complaints from local long-term residents. In an effort to apply better controls on tourism development, part of this area was included in the Fuji-Hakone-Izu National Park. The designation of "national park" in Japan does not imply outright acquisition of land but rather more control over its use, as is the case in the U.K. The Mt. Fuji park area includes substantial lands in national forests and other land owned by prefectures and local governments (also mostly forest lands), with about one-fourth in private ownership. Under the umbrella of the national park status, it was possible to channel some central government funding to the area and to apply more stringent land use controls, especially through the national Environmental Protection Agency, although local governments still maintain some control.

For those areas in the Mt. Fuji park that have Environmental Agency controls, five different zones were applied:

1. Special protection areas for wilderness preservation;
2. A conservation district in which individual homes might be permitted for farmers or other residents, but no second home or hotel development is allowed;
3. A general use district that permits most types of second homes and recreational development subject to site planning standards but does not allow clear-cutting of trees;
4. A zone similar to the general use district except that clear-cutting is permitted; and
5. An ordinary zone in which land use regulation is left to the local government except that developers must give notice to the environmental agency a month before proceeding with development, which provides the agency with some time for negotiation with the developer to modify his proposal if deemed necessary.

Although not a perfect means of rationalizing land use in a conservation and recreation area, the approach applied in the Mt. Fuji area offers some opportunity for controls that has application in many other already partially developed tourism areas in the world.

Specialized Nature Facilities

Zoos, including the safari park type, botanical gardens, aquariums, marineland type parks, and natural history museums, can be important complementary features to nature tourism. Many of these are developed for local residents, but the major ones, as mentioned in Chapter 4, attract both domestic and international tourists. They are usually located in or near major urban areas, and some draw upon large metropolitan populations as well as long-distance tourists. In addition to being attractions for their intrinsic content, they are increasingly performing an important function in conserving natural resources through maintenance and breeding of endangered species and educational programs related to conservation. The planning of such facilities in an area should consider any improvements needed to existing facilities, including to their conservation and educational functions and the need for any new facilities as attractions for residents and tourists. Recently applied techniques for animal display emphasize either reproducing their natural habitats to the extent feasible in zoo environments or developing an existing natural environment in the area as a safari type park with the animals wandering freely and the visitors viewing them from vehicles.

Planning and Managing Cultural Attraction Resources

The planning and managing of cultural attraction resources is similar to that of natural resources:
- Establishment of a policy basis for planning and management;
- Use of the environmental (for built attraction features) and cultural (for other types of attractions) conservation approach with a balance maintained between conservation and visitor use;
- Application of the planning process, techniques, and principles where relevant;
- Organization of visitor use; and
- Continuous management of the resources.

Because some types of cultural attraction resources relate to living cultures, sociocultural impact can be a particularly important consideration. As is the case with natural resources, the educational and aesthetic values of cultural attractions are a major aspect of their successful presentation to tourists.

Unfortunately, the pattern has been that many aspects of traditional cultures can virtually disappear during the early stages of modern development, with little sense of loss by the society because of its eagerness for economic progress. Later, people begin to realize that they have lost their unique character and try to revive aspects of their traditions, such as language, music, dance, crafts, architecture, festivals, and some customs. This revitalization of traditions can sometimes be accomplished. It is obviously better, when possible, to carefully manage the cultural resources before they have become lost, integrating them into modern development.

An important prerequisite for the management of cultural resources is research into their historical development, characteristics, cultural and religious significance, and authentic form (realizing that the form may have evolved and changed through time). Without understanding the background of the resources, it is not possible to establish the basis for their conservation and presentation to tourists.

Planning of Archaeological and Historic Sites

Archaeological sites include remains of single monuments and entire urban, town, or village complexes or portions of them, and may be underwater as well as on land. These remains may be virtually intact structures or only foundations and often include artifacts of daily living, trade goods, and various forms of arts and crafts of the archaeological period. As mentioned previously, archaeological sites are not all from ancient periods, but can be relatively recent as evidenced by the work now being done in industrial archaeology of the late eighteenth and nineteenth centuries. Archaeological techniques and research, especially with the application of recently developed technology, have undergone much progress in recent years with the understanding of previous cultures being greatly expanded, and this field will continue providing interesting places for tourists to visit throughout the world.

Historic sites and areas range from "historic spatial modules" (Fitch 1982) of entire historic towns and villages to historic rooms in art museums. Currently, the most active module of preservation is that of historic districts in urban places, of which there are many examples in the world. Historic and architectural preservation also does not necessarily represent only very old historical periods. For example, there is now much interest and actual preservation taking place of the Art Deco building style, popular in the 1930s, in places such as Miami, Florida in the USA, of the Art Nouveau style of the early twentieth century in Europe and North America, and examples of individual works of important twentieth architects in various places. Outdoor architectural museums of groups of traditional or historic buildings, of which Skansen located near Stockholm, Sweden is an early model, have also been developed in several places of the world.

Traditionally, archaeological and historic conservation focused on outstanding examples of buildings and ruins that usually had been designed for civic and religious use or as wealthy persons' houses because these were the structures that were well constructed with permanent materials and survived through the centuries. Common persons' houses and many commercial buildings, being not as well built, deteriorated and disappeared or were replaced by more recent development in urban areas. Thus, a rather elitist perception of the past was portrayed to visitors. Now, there is more emphasis placed on attempting to understand, through research and excavation, the living environments and life-styles of ordinary people of the past, and to present and interpret these in an interesting manner in order to convey a more complete historical picture. This approach also is not restricted to the distant past but can portray, for example, the typical life-style of a nineteenth century industrial worker or coal miner or what daily life was like in a typical village or urban environment of that period. Historic sites include places of important historical events, such as battlefields or sites where discoverers and explorers landed, even if there are no historic buildings represented.

The process for planning archaeological and historic attraction sites is the same as that applied to natural resources except, of course, that the survey and analysis is of the archaeological or historic feature with determination of the conservation needs. The survey and analysis may involve archaeological or historical research and perhaps some site excavation. Establishing visitor carrying capacities is essential. Sociocultural as well as environmental impact analysis is important if there are residents living in the site area, such as in urban historic districts.

In planning the site and its environs, the major consideration is conservation of the principal archaeological or historic features. This may take the form of applying preservation techniques such as restoration and maintenance of buildings or preservation of the site as it is. The government agencies or foundations involved in archaeological and historic conservation in the area will have decided the type of measures to be applied.

The type and extent of visitor facilities and services are determined based on projected visitor use. The zoning approach of designating various conservation use intensity areas is applied. Typically, the facilities should be concentrated in one or a few areas and integrated into a visitor center complex. This complex should be located at or near the main entrance to the site and be easily accessible to the cultural feature but not impinging upon it. Usually, a natural area should be maintained around the feature (or, in an urban area, low intensity uses maintained around the area), so that it can be fully appreciated. In historic districts, it is common to locate tourist facilities and related commercial enterprises in the less important historic buildings that have had interior renovation with the building facades preserved and restored. These provide an interesting environment for tourists and can help pay for the the buildings' preservation.

A visitor use plan should be prepared that indicates the logical access and exit points and flow of visitors through the site. It may be necessary to prohibit direct access to very fragile features but only allow views of them, and to control the total number of visitors at the site at any one time if there is danger of excessive congestion or site deterioration. Signs can be utilized to explain the background and major characteristics of the site. Brochures can also be available to explain the site in more detail. At many sites, well-trained and sometimes multi-lingual guides should be available. Tourists should be informed of any control measures that they should observe, such as not littering or smoking.

Imaginative approaches are now being applied to achieve effective and interesting presentations of cultural heritage sites through the use of live animators or technical means such as dioramas with mannequins and historical artifacts to explain and demonstrate or re-create historical scenes and activities. Even the typical noises and odors of the historical period or event can be reproduced to give a greater sense of authenticity to the scene. Participatory involvement of tourists in the historic environment is also a common approach. This has been organized, for example, in nineteenth century Welsh coal mining towns in the U.K. where tourists don miners' garb and descend into a formerly used mine shaft. A more standard technique that has been successfully used for several years and is still effective for large outdoor sites is sound and light shows, which narrate and illuminate the site's features and relate important events that took place there. Also a common approach is to use a site as a stage setting for performances of drama, dance, music, and historical epics that relate to the historical period or culture represented by the site.

Continuous monitoring must be maintained of the visitor satisfaction levels and sociocultural and environmental impacts of the facility development and visitor use, with any adjustments that are needed made to facilities and services.

Management of Arts and Handicrafts

Arts (used in this section to refer to the visual arts, such as painting and sculpture, and not to the performing arts reviewed in the next section) and handicrafts are an important attraction for tourists. Their sales can be a significant source of income for residents, and they represent an important aspect of the cultural heritage of an area. A basic concept in the management of arts and handicrafts is that they be authentic, at least in terms of utilizing local traditional skills, techniques, motifs, and materials. An approach usually applied is that designs can be modified to suit tourist market demand if the authenticity of skills, techniques, motifs, and materials is maintained. However, purists will maintain that completely original types of items and their design must be retained to make the handicraft authentic. Each area must make its own decision on this issue. Souvenirs, which do not represent authentic handicrafts of the area, may also be produced (or imported) and sold to tourists, providing employment and income to the area, but these should be differentiated from the true handicrafts.

To ensure authenticity of arts and handicrafts, an effective technique used by governments in some tourism areas is to establish minimum quality standards for local handicrafts, inspect all handicrafts submitted to them for approval, and identify those items that meet the standards with some type of stamp of certification. The tourists are informed of the procedure and so will know whether they are purchasing authentic items. These items can be priced at a higher level than noncertified ones, thus giving artisans and shopkeepers the incentive to make authentic crafts available.

There may be various problems associated with maintaining acceptable quality standards and fair pricing for arts and handicrafts and ensuring that the handicraft producers receive their equitable share of the purchase price of the items. An approach that can used to overcome these problems is one that has been applied for some years in India and elsewhere. The government (in the case of India, the various state governments) establishes its own handicraft centers, which maintain minimum quality standards, pay the producers an equitable price, and set a fair sales pricing structure. The tourists are informed about these centers, which are an attraction in themselves to visit, where they can observe the quality and pricing, learn about the crafts, and purchase some if they want. Private handicraft shops must usually meet the standards established by the government centers in order to remain competitive.

Arts and handicraft-making demonstrations by the artists and craft persons can be an interesting and educational experience for tourists and may induce them to make purchases that they would not have otherwise made. Demonstrations can be done in government centers or private factories and shops or both.

In some areas, special programs may be required to train local artisans in production techniques of good quality and authentically designed arts and crafts. If some craft skills and designs have been largely lost, not an uncommon situation, research may be required to determine their original forms, materials, and crafting techniques. This program may include development of new item designs and even new crafts if traditional designs are not adaptable or crafts were never highly developed in the area, but these should still reflect some uniqueness to the area and utilize local materials and skills. Also, there is often the need for establishing marketing techniques and outlets that have not yet been developed for the area.

An example of a programmed approach to improving the handicrafts of a country is in Fiji in the South Pacific. Some years ago, many of the traditional handicrafts, mostly utilitarian and ceremonial items of high quality workmanship and interesting design, were no longer being produced, and skills and designs had been forgotten. Through international assistance, original designs were researched in the national museum and elsewhere, several of the most interesting items selected, local artisans trained to produce these items using local materials, and a well-located sales outlet established. The authentic crafts are now popular with tourists, an aspect of the Fijian cultural heritage has been revived, and a group of artisans and related personnel are being supported by the handicraft production and sales. Also, souvenir type items are still available to tourists.

A recent study in the Caribbean (Holder 1989) concluded that tourism has stimulated dying interest and activity in several areas of the visual and performing arts and crafts, and has provided markets for these, especially handicrafts, which could never have been sustained by local demand. However, the study indicated that only a small amount of human and financial resources are currently being allocated to the crafts sector, and there is much potential to increase foreign revenue and other economic benefits if greater handicraft production could be encouraged. The study recommended that the Caribbean governments must devise a craft development policy that takes account of the various areas needing assistance such as education and skills training, marketing, supply of raw materials, sources of finance, and reinforcing linkages with other economic sectors. Because of the large market for arts and crafts offered by tourism, as well as direct export, there is much potential in many tourism areas for improvement and expansion of good quality arts and crafts.

Management of Other Cultural Resources

Various other types of cultural resources require management both for achieving tourist appreciation of them and to conserve the resources involved. The major types of other cultural resources are described in the following sections.

Performing Arts

The management of cultural resources such as dance, music, and drama must be tailored to each specific situation. For performing arts in a modern setting, the main considerations are development of suitable theaters or halls in convenient locations and organization and training of the performing groups. Because these arts are developed primarily for residents' enjoyment with tourists providing supplementary, although often substantial, support, planning of these facilities and organization of the performing groups are the responsibilities of the residents and their governments. These facilities are typically an aspect of urban tourism planning, although they may also be developed in small town or rural settings.

For traditional dance, music, and drama unique to distinct cultural groups and often an important type of attraction in cultural tourism, a decision must often be made as to whether the performances are more effectively presented to visitors in their original setting, usually a village or town environment, a hotel performance stage, a separate performance hall, or a combination of these in one destination area. The traditional village setting imparts a greater sense of interest and authenticity to the performance and may bring more direct benefits to the villagers, but also may be disruptive to normal village activities. In any case, adequate access, parking, and performing stage facilities are required so that the performances do not generate undue congestion. The authenticity and quality of performances should be maintained, even if somewhat adapted for tourists' schedules and understanding.

For traditional performances, special training programs may be required, as was described for the visual arts and handicrafts, of local people in their traditional performing arts, such as through as dance and music school or cultural institute. If some of these traditional arts are being lost, research into their original forms may be necessary. A commonly-used approach for research and training of traditional art forms (including the visual arts and handicrafts) is to develop a multi-purpose cultural center or institute where many of these activities can take place in one location. Visitor facilities can be included for performances and exhibits, with tourism helping to financially support the institute. A cultural institute can also include replicas of traditional architectural styles and building forms.

Special Cultural Events

Special cultural events such as religious carnivals, art fairs, and dance, music, drama, or general cultural festivals can be significant attractions for residents and tourists, and can be an important technique for reviving and focusing interest on the preservation of the local cultural expressions that otherwise might be forgotten. If special cultural events already exist, then tourism needs to be organized to take advantage of these without generating any serious problems such as congestion or violation of religious codes. Sometimes, the special event will need to be further developed or improved and promoted. If no special cultural events exist in an area, it may be possible to organize one based on some unique aspects of the culture, such an annual arts, music, or cultural festival.

Traditional Cultural Patterns

Traditional cultural patterns of life-styles, belief systems, customs, ceremonies, dress, and economic activities comprise an important component of cultural tourism as an attraction that can also educate tourists and bring economic benefits to an area, but they are the most difficult to portray to tourists in an authentic manner without the danger of some disruption to the local communities. Places of traditional cultural patterns are typically associated with less developed countries and regions, but are also an attraction in more developed countries, such as the Amish communities in the eastern USA, which attract many tourists, and isolated mountain villages in Europe that are developing tourism.

The extent of impact by tourism on the community will vary greatly from one place to another depending very much on community attitudes and on how the contact with tourists is handled. Assuming the traditional communities wish to have some tourism, and many do, the question arises of how to maintain the authenticity of their exposure to tourists without some artificiality involved. This topic of "staged authenticity" has been raised and researched by various persons (for example, Cohen 1989), with no conclusive answers provided.

Exposure to traditional life-styles and activities is most effective if it takes place in the original, authentic settings such as traditional villages, although this is not always possible. If tours are organized to the villages, visitor use must be carefully organized with knowledgeable guides, explanation to tourists of local customs and protocol, control of where the tourists can go (at least not into private houses except by prearrangement), and what can be photographed. Visits should be allowed only during certain time periods. Much of the success of this approach depends also on controlling the number of tourists in each group and the number of groups allowed each week. Another approach is the one described in Chapter 9, where small-scale, locally styled and managed accommodation is allowed in or near the village.

If it is decided that no tourists should visit authentic traditional villages or rural areas or if it is not feasible for them to make these visits, a common approach is to develop model villages, farms, or other types of replicas as authentic reconstructions, which can also include demonstrations of traditional activities. These are, of course, artificial environments, but they can still educate tourists about the traditional life of the region or country in an interesting manner. One of the best known and most successful examples of this type of approach is the Polynesian Cultural Center on Oahu in Hawaii. This large center includes authentic reconstructions of houses and buildings representing several of the Pacific Island cultures with demonstrations of traditional handicrafts, activities, dance, and music organized within each of the cultural groups of buildings. There is a central performance stage for evening Polynesian shows, and the center is well provided with visitor facilities of restaurants and rest areas. The center is operated by the Church of Jesus Christ of Latter-day Saints (the Mormons), with the center revenues going to support the adjacent Mormon college, whose students from the various island cultures work in the center, thus giving it an additional sense of authenticity. Other examples of model cultural presentations are Fiji's Orchid Island, Thailand in Miniature near Bangkok, Korea's Folk Village, and Mini-Indonesia near Jakarta.

Korean Folk Village, Republic of Korea—Located south of Seoul, this replicated village exhibits traditional architectural styles and furnishings of buildings, ceremonies, folk dances, and craft activities. It is an example of historic and cultural modeling, which has been successfully used in various places in the world. (Courtesy of the Republic of Korea tourism office)

Economic Activities

Both traditional and modern economic activities, such as touring farms and plantations, fishing and fish breeding operations, factories of all types, and large dams are of interest to many tourists. These activities typically do not require any major special facilities but only overall organization, competent guide services, availability of brochures, and perhaps some special parking areas and refreshment and toilet facilities.

Museums

Museums perform an essential role in cultural management and education through artifact preservation and educational exhibits and programs for residents of the area, as well as domestic and international tourists. Culturally-oriented museums include those on the visual arts, history, ethnography, crafts, and many specialized areas. Many tourists make an effort to visit the museums in the area they are touring and, as a form of special interest tourism, special museum tours are organized for a country or several countries. In addition to major museums are small site museums located at archaeological, historical, and natural sites that help in explaining the feature to visitors.

In the detailed planning of tourist attractions of an area, recommendations should be made on improvements needed to existing museums to make them interesting and educational for tourists, and on any new types of museums needed and their locations. Determination of improvements required should be made within the framework of basic facilities such as space availability and lighting and also contemporary museum management approaches. In contrast to the traditional museum approach of only displaying art works or artifacts, the present museum approach is to, through imaginative exhibits, explain themes such as the historical evolution of an area, the development of certain art styles, and the cultural patterns and typical daily life of societies, to re-create street scenes, and many other subjects. For cultural tourists, these types of exhibits are especially interesting in helping them understand an area. Good museums also have continuing educational programs, including "hands-on" participatory activities and special short-term exhibits designed primarily for residents but also of interest to tourists when they are in the area. Museums attracting international tourists usually require multi-lingual labeling and guide services or multi-lingual portable cassette players for visitors to rent.

Cuisine

The local cuisine reflects the history and culture of an area and can be an attraction for many tourists. In addition to providing good quality food for tourists, efforts should be made to promote any dishes unique to the area—most tourists enjoy at least trying the local cuisine. Wider use of local cuisine also brings the economic benefit of utilizing locally produced food items and local skills. In some areas, the cuisine needs to be adapted for tourists' tastes but can still retain its unique character and use of local ingredients.

Antiques and Important Cultural Artifacts

Legal provision should be made to prohibit the export of important antiques and cultural artifacts so that these remain in the country for residents to appreciate as part of their cultural heritage. These artifacts, if available for public viewing, also help tourists to understand the culture of an area. In addition to antique value, some items have religious significance, such as certain types of West African wood carvings, American Northwest Indian totems, and Buddhist images in some Asian countries. Most countries have adopted antique export control legislation, but sometimes enforcement of these laws is not fully effective, especially in the face of international illicit demand. For example, smuggling of important pre-Columbian artifacts out of Mexico and other Latin American countries is a major problem even though laws exist prohibiting export of such items. A decision needs to be made on which items contribute to the cultural heritage of an area and which items can be exported. Indonesia, for example, prohibits the export of indigenous antiques but allows the export of antiques that originated in other cultures such as antique Chinese ceramics. Tourists should be informed of the local antique export laws and which agency to consult if in doubt about particular items.

An approach that can be used to discourage casual tourist purchase and removal of antiques (not professional smuggling of important items) is to have good reproductions available and so labeled for sale to tourists and, for antique craft items such as wood carvings and textiles, attempt to revive the craft to produce items as authentic as the antique originals. Through this approach, local employment and income are provided, traditional skills are revived, and tourists' needs can be satisfied.

Planning Considerations for Special Types of Attractions

Special types of attractions not related to the natural or cultural resources of an area include theme parks, major sports facilities, conference and convention centers, gambling casinos, and others. The detailed planning of these are specialized fields for which qualified and experienced planners and designers are available. However, some general considerations for their planning are described here.

Theme Parks

As explained in Chapter 4, theme parks have become very popular in the USA and are being developed in other countries. A theme park is an extensive, usually commercial leisure park that may extend over tens or hundreds of hectares and normally includes several theme areas of indoor and outdoor presentations or displays, activities, and amusements with animation, plus well-developed catering, retail, and visitor services. Themes may be historical, geographical/environmental, social, technological or futuristic, and other types that stimulate, educate, and entertain the visitors. Substantial infrastructure and often accommodation and other tourist facilities are required.

If existing, the national or regional tourism plan will have identified whether a theme park is appropriate for an area and, if so, what type and size is suitable. In the absence of regional planning, a special feasibility study for a proposed park, which examines the market potential, determines the appropriate type, size, and location of the park, and analyzes its costs, revenues, and financial feasibility, is necessary. An accessible, large, and undeveloped site is required for the park itself, and often adjacent undeveloped land is also needed for development of related facilities such as accommodation and other tourist facilities and perhaps for employee housing communities. The infrastructure of road, rail, or air access and provision for water supply, electric power, sewage and solid waste disposal, and telecommunications must be examined. After development, sophisticated marketing, a high level of management, and good quality physical maintenance of the facilities are essential.

Theme park planning must be coordinated with planning of the region in which the park is located so that lands outside but near the park are developed in an integrated manner with land use controls applied. Large theme parks can generate considerable development in their regions that, if not regulated, can result in land use and environmental problems.

Convention Facilities Planning

Convention and conference tourism has been rapidly expanding, and convention centers are often considered in the development of urban tourism and resorts. In addition to attracting tourists in general, conventions and other types of conferences and meetings can often be scheduled during the otherwise low tourist arrival periods and help counter seasonality problems that affect many tourism areas. However, as referred to previously, convention tourism is highly competitive with many places already having developed convention centers, and the scheduling of conventions is rather unpredictable. Convention centers do not generate much direct employment in themselves, and such centers may not be financially self-sustaining. Rather the center stimulates benefits to other tourist facilities and services and the area in general, which may well justify the center's development. It is essential that a market and financial feasibility analysis be carefully conducted before a decision is made on whether to make the investment in a convention center and the type and size of center that is most suitable.

For location of major convention centers, Murphy (1985) emphasizes the importance of a location in a gateway city that has major national and international airline connections to participants' generating areas around the world. He identifies several site location criteria within the city, consisting of:

- Availability of a large building site of at least a half or full city block;
- Central location and accessibility to good quality hotels and an inter-city transportation terminal for domestic delegates;
- Close to major shopping and entertainment districts, the prime location being in a downtown or regional business district;
- Availability of parking spaces on-site or nearby for persons driving to the conferences; and
- Proximity to recreation facilities and attractive surroundings as delegates want to maintain their exercise routines and the cities want to encourage sight-seeing within the city and environs.

Also important is the location of the convention city in a region or country that offers the opportunities for interesting pre- and post-conference tours of attractions further away from the city. Because spouses often travel with delegates to conferences, the availability of shopping, entertainment, and touring services is especially important.

For small conferences and meetings, location of meeting facilities in smaller cities, or often in resorts and resort towns if they have good access and some recreation, dining, and entertainment facilities, is appropriate and may be desired by the conference organizers to provide a quieter environment for the meetings. Most larger hotels develop their own meeting facilities for small gatherings, and some hotels maintain substantial in-house conference facilities. The hotel meeting facilities also serve an important function in some areas of providing suitable space for local use, such as seminars and training courses and non-meeting activities such as weddings and receptions.

Other Types of Facilities

Major sports facility centers are often initially planned for an international event such as the Olympic, Commonwealth, Asian, or African Games, with one of the benefits being the development of facilities that can be used on a permanent basis. These are typically planned as integrated complexes and may include some accommodation for the athletes. Planning requirements include a large site with good access, as well as the availability of tourist accommodation and other facilities and services within a reasonable distance (and often linked to the sports complex by some form of public transportation).

Major national or international fairs and expositions, which may be undertaken primarily for reasons of regional or national prestige, as are major sports events, also provide building complexes, infrastructure, and even exhibits that can be used on a permanent basis. As is the case with sport facilities, the requirements of a large site, integrated planning, and very good access to and within the metropolitan area and nearby tourist accommodation and other facilities and services apply to the planning of fairs and expositions. In some metropolitan areas, development of these complexes can provide the opportunity for redevelopment of obsolete urban districts, which offers additional incentive for organizing the events. At the same time, major fairs and sports events can be very disruptive to community activities and may not necessarily be profit-making in themselves. Cities must carefully weigh the advantages and disadvantages of undertaking major events such as these.

Gambling casinos are usually developed within hotel or resort environments or urban districts that offer a variety of activities and services for the tourists. In developing countries or areas with lower income levels and sometimes traditional values, a consideration in the development of gambling tourism that may influence the location of casinos is whether residents will be allowed to use the facilities and, if so, under what conditions are they allowed access. Major race tracks such as for horse, car, and dog racing also require substantial amounts of land, excellent access, and parking and be within reasonable distance of tourist accommodation and other facilities and services.

Golf courses, tennis courts, and other types of recreation facilities for tourists are, as described in Chapter 8, usually developed in conjunction with resorts and are planned according to internationally accepted standards. Science and technology museums or centers may be of sufficient importance, such as the Air and Space Museum in Washington, DC and the Science and Technology Center in Singapore, to attract tourists who are visiting the area. There are other types of special facilities (for example, scenic cable cars systems extending up mountain sides and over valleys for scenic views) that are popular secondary attractions in some places. Cable cars allow for widespread tourist use and access to scenic areas for persons who otherwise could not make the ascent on foot, and the cable car ride itself is an interesting experience. The environmental impact of developing these systems should be carefully evaluated, especially in areas that have high conservation value.

Some Special Considerations for Visitor Use

As emphasized in previous sections, in addition to planning physical facilities, planning efficient visitor use without generating serious environmental or social problems is essential. The major objectives in visitor use planning are that:

- Visitors have ample opportunity to enjoy, appreciate, and understand the attraction features;
- Visitor use does not reach a level that results in excessive congestion that depreciates visitor enjoyment of the feature and leads to irritation of the visitors;
- Visitor use does not result in environmental degradation of the feature, whether related to the natural or cultural environment; and
- Residents of the area are not preempted from visiting and enjoying their own attractions.

Because some attraction features around the world are already reaching or have exceeded their saturation levels, various techniques are being employed to mitigate problems of visitor overuse, and these should be considered in tourist attraction planning and management.

A basic approach that has already been referred to in this book is one involving regional policies of decentralization of tourism in order to relieve tourist use pressures in certain areas and distribute use more evenly throughout a country or region. This approach, which usually requires investment in development of attractions, facilities, services, and infrastructure and in marketing, also helps distribute the benefits of tourism more widely. London has experienced an intensive level of tourist use during its high tourism season for several years, and the U.K. has attempted to decentralize tourism outside the London area with some but not complete success. As mentioned, Nepal is opening new tourism centers as well as trekking and mountaineering areas in part to relieve tourist pressures on Kathmandu Valley and Pokhara. In the USA, the relatively recent development of national recreation areas near metropolitan regions may help relieve use demands on more distant national parks.

In some areas, as mentioned, the approach has been to strictly control tourism from its beginning so that it will not result in impact problems from tourism overuse or development. Bhutan has adopted very controlled, high value special interest tourism, and the Galapagos Islands limit the number of visitors. The various alternative tourism approaches previously described are aimed, in part, at limiting impacts through small-scale types of tourism development.

Another technique is selective marketing with lesser known but similar types of attractions being emphasized in marketing programs, and the overused, better known features not overtly marketed. This approach has been applied in the U.K. to redirect tourist flows from well-known and overused historic castles and homes to lesser known but equally interesting ones, as well as to promote the prehistoric site at Avebury in place of the famous but excessively visited Stonehenge (Thorburn 1986). Also, because overuse is usually seasonal, marketing techniques can be applied to reduce seasonality and more evenly distribute tourist use throughout the year.

Where serious congestion and especially environmental degradation of the attractions are resulting from visitor overuse, stringent measures need to be applied. One of these approaches is to close off the feature at certain times or even permanently. For example, in the Great Barrier Reef Marine Park in Australia, 4 of the 14 reef islands in the park are closed to public access between October and March each year to prevent disturbance to nesting birds and turtles. During this period there is also a ban on overflying by aircraft at altitudes below 1,000 feet. Another island is closed at all times to public access, with the aim of protecting its biological systems from any kind of alteration resulting from human use (Edington and Edington 1986).

Another approach in cases where intensive visitor use may irreparably damage fragile features is to construct replicas of the feature, perhaps on a nearby site so that the overall setting is the same, that tourists can visit and then close off the original site except for maintenance and research purposes. This approach was applied to the famous prehistoric cave paintings of Lascaux in France, which were being damaged by intensive visitor use (including raising of the humidity levels in the caves), through the development nearby of an accurately reproduced cave environment and paintings; this replica is very popular with tourists. The original is saved, but tourists can still appreciate an important expression of their cultural heritage. If the immediate site is being damaged, an approach that has been used to prohibit direct on-site access but allow viewing from a distance such as has been done at Stonehenge and the Parthenon in Athens for several years.

Other approaches being experimented with include establishing maximum levels of visitors allowed at any given time. This approach was tried in Venice during the summer of 1987, when the city government passed a law establishing a maximum of 50,000 tourists permitted into the city at any one time. It was possible to enforce this regulation because of the controlled access points into the city and through coordination of tour group schedules. In campgrounds, for example, use can be controlled by not allowing more than a maximum number of campers at one time through a permit and reservation system, such as is applied at Yosemite National Park in California. Controlled admission policies may need to become an increasingly applied form of maintaining acceptable levels of visitor use, but, where possible, alternative attractions, activities, and facilities should be provided to the tourists.

Admission pricing policies can also be applied, with high admission fees charged at specific features such as museums and zoos in order to discourage the casual visitors. If pricing policies are applied aimed particularly at foreign tourists, provision should be made for ensuring that residents have reasonable access. Often a technique employed is to charge higher admission prices to foreign tourists and low prices or free admission to residents such as is practiced at major public museums in Spain and at archaeological sites in Sri Lanka. In many places, discounted admission prices are given to students and senior citizens.

For effective organization of visitor use at a site, various techniques can be employed. Colonial Williamsburg, Virginia, a restored colonial town of the eighteenth century that makes use of animation and demonstrations, is one of the first and still best examples of historical restoration and cultural heritage site development in the USA. Undertaken by a non-profit foundation established in the mid-1920s, the site encompasses about 170 acres with some one hundred buildings restored, and restoration of others still underway. Attendance in recent years has exceeded one million annually (Lundberg 1985) and visitor use organization has been well developed. Techniques employed to cope with the increasing number of visitors while still providing an interesting touristic experience include:

- Audio-visual briefing in a large information center located on the periphery of the historic area near the car park with regulated flows of visitors through the center;
- Banning of private cars in the historic area and use of non-polluting shuttle buses to convey visitors who do not wish to walk from place to place;
- Restriction on group bus tours to lessen peak congestion periods;
- Live entertainment provided for visitors waiting to enter buildings (so that they do not become bored and irritable); and
- Continuing expansion of the historic area, which will distribute visitors more widely.

Handling large numbers of visitors at major attractions or events often implies visitor queuing (waiting in line). In recent years, the psychology of queuing is being investigated with the results indicating that queues engender a loss of personal control and overestimation of time spent in waiting along with boredom and discomfort for many visitors. Realizing that queues are often inevitable, techniques can be applied to make them more acceptable to tourists such as using new queue shapes and forms, devising in-queue mental activities and entertainment, physically incorporating queues into the exhibit space, and giving greater attention to physical comfort and service facilities for those waiting in queues (Pearce 1989).

Case Studies

Four different types of case studies are presented on planning for visitor facilities and use at conservation sites and conservation management approaches. The National Archaeological Park plan for Borobudur in central Java applies the concept of use zoning. The development plan for Fatehpur Sikri in northern India utilizes sound principles of proper relationships of visitor facilities to the monument and compatible facility design. The visitor use plan for Bandelier National Monument in the southwestern USA controls vehicular access and uses imaginative interpretation techniques. The conservation program to control wildlife poaching in Zambia applies a successful community involvement approach. Related to these case studies, a case study in Chapter 12 presents the visitor facility redevelopment plan for Crater Lake National Park.

Borobudur National Archaeological Park

Borobudur, a large late eighth century Buddhist monument located in central Java near Yogyakarta, Indonesia, is one of the most impressive and important archaeological sites in Southeast Asia. From the early 1970s to the early 1980s, major reconstruction works were undertaken by the Indonesian government, with UNESCO and other international assistance, to stop the water-related damage that was deteriorating the monument and, through provision of a suitable drainage system, preserve the monument indefinitely. During the mid to late 1970s, archaeological park plans were prepared for Borobudur and Prambanan, another important monument in the Yogyakarta area (JICA 1979). These park plans were formulated within the framework of regional tourism plans previously prepared for all of Java and central Java.

The background research for the planning project included surveying the several historic places in central Java, reviewing the traditional Buddhist planning theories of the period of Borobudur, and studying the relationship of the monuments to Yogyakarta, the gateway city and tourism center of the central Java region and the two monuments being planned, and an important tourist destination in its own right. The park plan formulation gave much consideration to the importance of the monuments in the tourism and educational process, their impact on the local communities, and the need for continuing research and preservation of other archaeological sites in the area.

Total visitor numbers to the Borobudur park were projected (2.8 million in 1988 and 3.6 million in 1993) with annual seasonal, weekly, and daily visitor fluctuations calculated. For planning purposes, maximum visitor capacities were determined for peak daily and hourly periods, and the types of domestic and foreign visitors determined. Visitor facility needs were calculated based on the projected park usage and the conservation facilities required. The land use planning approach was that of establishing zones for various types and intensities of land use around the monument. Five zones were established, as depicted in Figure 10.1, and defined generally as follows:

- Zone 1—area for protection of the immediate environment of the monument with no development allowed except for landscaping.
- Zone 2—area for development of facilities for visitor use, park operation and archaeological conservation activities.
- Zone 3—area, including the access road and smaller monuments, within which land uses are strictly controlled to be compatible with the park concept.
- Zone 4—area for maintenance of the historical scenery.
- Zone 5—area for undertaking archaeological surveys and protection of unexcavated archaeological sites.

The total zoning area encompassed about 115 square kilometers with Zones 1 and 2 comprising approximately 132 hectares. Visitor and conservation facilities designated for Zone 2 included: theme facilities of an archaeological museum and conservation center; operation facilities of the park office, information center, ticket booth, visitor entrance plaza, parking area, maintenance shops, and security booths; and service facilities of restaurants, souvenir shops, public toilets, and shelters.

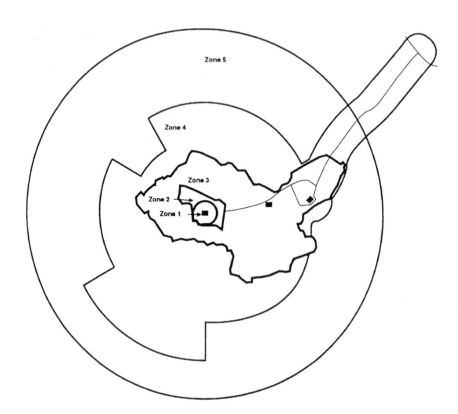

Figure 10.1. Borobudur National Archaeological Park Zoning Plan.

A land acquisition and facility development program and construction schedule were prepared and cost estimates calculated, and the plan included detailed layout and design of the park facilities and road and utility systems. Recommendations were made on the park operational structure and visitor organization, land use control guidelines, and a development frame and improvement program for the nearby villages. An evaluation was made of the panoramic scenery and streetscapes of the area, and guidelines were presented for safeguarding the historic scenery, including the respective government roles and participation of the local residents. Based on the marketing study and other factors, a financial feasibility analysis was prepared and economic impacts were calculated. Project development commenced in the early 1980s and continued through the mid-1980s. An important component of the implementation program involved relocation of some residents further away from the monument in order to effect the zoning plan.

The Fatehpur Sikri Development Plan

Located near Agra in north-central India, Fatehpur Sikri was constructed as a city and palace complex by the Mughul emperor Akbar in the sixteenth century, served as a capital city during much of Akbar's reign, and then was abandoned when the capital was moved to Agra. Built of local red sandstone and remarkably well preserved, the site occupies about 1,000 acres enclosed by a fort wall. A large mosque associated with the monument complex is still being used for religious purposes and also attracts visitors. This monument complex is one of the most important archaeological sites in India and represents a significant phase of the Mughul history of the country. Near to the site are three large existing villages.

The plan prepared for this monument in the mid-1980s applied an integrated planning approach giving consideration to conservation of the monument, and development of visitor facilities, including accommodation and ways in which the nearby villages could benefit from tourism development (India Department of Tourism, no date). The table of contents from the plan report indicates the planning approach used as follows:

- Introduction—the background; Fatehpur Sikri today; the monuments; the three villages; the plan and its scope; an integrated approach.
- Problems and potentials—problems; potential for development.
- Archaeological appraisal—general disposition; buildings constructed before Akbar; the wall and the gateways; the core complex; the peripheral buildings; other monuments; summary.
- The integrated approach—potential of land areas; conservation of monuments; criteria for landscape development; criteria for development of land; movement patterns and linkages; tourist facilities.
- Land use plan—conservation; the settlements; agricultural land; landscape areas.

- Redevelopment—Rang Mahal complex; Stone's Cutters' Mosque; public bath of Buland Darwaza; Nagar Haveli; main bazaar (Fatehpur).
- Traffic circulation and facilities—the main road; the monuments; tourist facilities.
- Management and development control—open space; new buildings; bazaars; finishing and harmony; height of constructions.
- Environmental graphics.
- Crafts.
- Summary of recommendations.

The integrated development plan included a land use plan for the general area, indicating interrelationships of the monument area, visitor facilities complex, the three villages, and the transportation network; a plan for the monument complex with recommendations for conservation improvements needed; and a plan for the tourist facilities complex with detailed layout and design of this complex. The facilities site selection criteria were established in the plan formulation as:

- Easily accessible from any of the main roads in the area;
- Offers a commanding view of the archaeological complex in profile;
- Inconspicuous when viewed from the monument; and
- Not too near the monument but within a conveniently accessible distance.

As shown in Figure 10.2, the tourist facility complex is located relatively near to but is not impinging on the archaeological site and has good access to the main road and the monument entrance.

The facilities complex was laid out according to the Islamic concept of "Charbagh," which refers to four gardens, reflecting the Mughal style of the monument. The complex is divided into four quadrants, two are for hotel guest rooms, one is the entrance area, and the fourth is open with a small ruin as its focal point. For landscaping the site, the principle applied was to create a simple landscape that would not compete with the existing historical environment and would complement the the essentially simple character of the tourist facility buildings. Mughal principles of garden design in contemporary idiom were recommended for the monument conservation area and roads and footpaths.

The plan included a recommended information and directional sign system and sign graphics techniques, including use of interesting symbols that would be recognized by tourists of various language backgrounds. Recommendations were made on tourist information material that should be available. Local crafts were investigated, and the potential identified for their further development as an attraction for tourists and source of income for village residents. The infrastructure required was described, and an implementation program specified, including actions that should be taken on monument and environmental conservation, as well as cost estimates calculated by development program period. Implementation of the plan commenced in the late 1980s, and a portion of the tourist facilities complex has been opened.

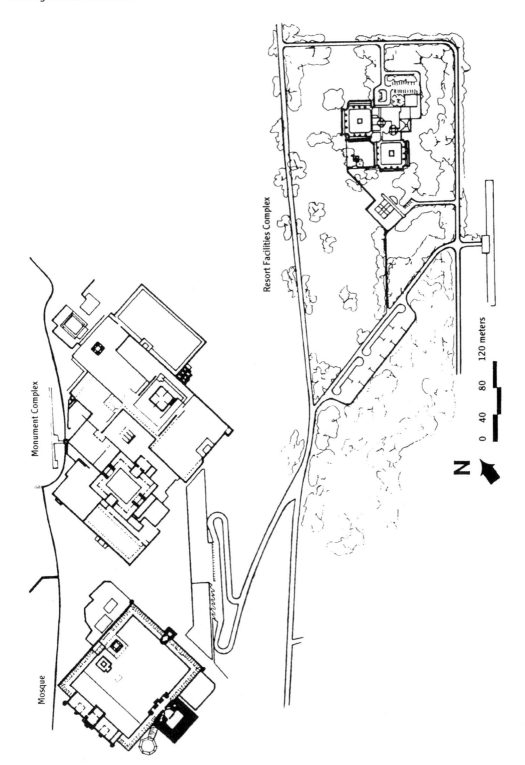

Mosque

Monument Complex

Resort Facilities Complex

N

0   40   80   120 meters

Figure 10.2. Fatehpur Sikri Development Plan.

Visitor Organization at Bandelier National Monument

Located near Santa Fe, New Mexico in the the southwestern USA, Bandelier National Monument covers nearly 50 square miles and is administered by the National Park Service. The most accessible features of the monument are archaeological ruins in Frijoles Canyon, a deep gorge that is an oasis in the dry country of New Mexico. Cliff dwellings of the Anasazi culture extend along the base of the northern wall of the canyon for about two miles. The houses of masonry were irregularly terraced, from one to three stories high, with many cave rooms gouged out from the cliff face. These were built and occupied starting in the twelfth century and extending to the early sixteenth century and then abandoned. The Park Service development of this site is a good example of the contemporary approach to visitor use.

As shown in Figure 10.3 (NPS no date); a parking area and visitor center are located at the entrance to the site. The center contains museum exhibits, visitor information services and material, an audio-visual room, a

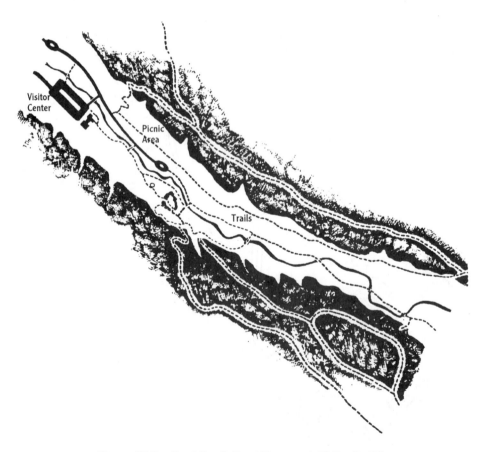

Figure 10.3. Bandelier National Monument—Visitor Facilities.

retail shop, and toilet facilities. Slide programs are presented in the visitor center to provide orientation to and interpretation of the area. The main Frijoles Canyon ruins are reached by a loop trail laid out to exhibit a complete sampling of the ruins with the circuit walk taking about one hour. Self-guided walking tours can be taken and, during the summer months, members of the ranger staff conduct guided walks and give nightly talks at the campfire circle on the archaeology, ethnology, and natural history of the region. For self-guided walks, a number key system with a tour guide booklet is used. Important sites along the trail are identified with number signs, and the booklet describes each of these sites according the numbering system. Descriptive signs along the trail explain the geology and natural history of the area. No private vehicles are allowed into this area.

Near the monument entrance station, a campground has been developed with tent spaces, tables, fireplaces, water taps, and toilets. Elsewhere in the monument, there is a campground designed for organized group camping that requires advance reservation. Overnight accommodation is available for visitors to the monument in nearby towns. Most of Bandelier National Monument is designated as a wilderness area where use is strictly controlled. An extensive trail system extends throughout this rugged and scenic wilderness area to various specific natural and archaeological features. Hikers and campers using these trails must obtain permits for back-country trips, and should use portable stoves for cooking, bring out all trash, and be careful with sanitation. Suggested trail hikes range from 45 minutes to 2 days or longer if several trails are taken.

Visitors are reminded that all objects in the monument area—Indian artifacts, wild flowers, trees, and rocks—must be left in place and undisturbed. It is illegal to remove or damage these, and high fines are imposed under the Archaeological Resources Protection Act on persons removing artifacts.

Wildlife Management in Zambia

Located in southern Africa, Zambia's tourism resources are based on wildlife and other natural resources such as Victoria Falls and places of historic and archaeological importance, but wildlife viewing and controlled hunting are the primary attractions for tourists. However, the wildlife population was declining rapidly. For example, in the Luangwa Valley, the number of elephants decreased from an estimated 100,000 to 30,000 due mainly to illegal poaching. The Zambian government, through the Ministry of Tourism, realized the importance of wildlife to tourism and introduced imaginative community-oriented programs to protect wildlife and involve local residents in conservation and tourism (Zambia Ministry of Tourism 1989). In order to curb poaching, a conservation strategy, titled the Administrative Management Design for Game Management (ADMADE), was introduced in the Lupande Game Management Area of the South Luangwa National

Park, a very important conservation area for elephants, black rhinoceros, and other wildlife, in the 1980s.

The objectives of ADMADE were to provide:

- An effective network of buffer zones for the national parks;
- A self-sustained management program that will protect the long-term interest of wildlife conservation;
- An improved and sustainable basis for supporting local community projects;
- A closer working relationship between national parks and village communities on wildlife affairs; and
- A protected wildlife estate that sustains foreign exchange earnings for the country.

ADMADE provides a direct and effective way of implementing and managing wildlife programs. The village communities in wildlife areas become actively involved in wildlife management based on an approach of wildlife revenues being shared between the national parks and wildlife services management budget and the village requirements for development of community facilities and services. This program of revenue sharing offers the major advantage in that it creates a vested interest and protective attitude among local residents toward the wildlife in their areas. The Ministry of Tourism realized that, given the insufficient funding for wildlife conservation, local social resistance to poaching is the cheapest and most effective way to combat it.

The ADMADE program has been so successful that the village communities are now greatly involved in anti-poaching activities, and regard the wildlife in their areas as an important source of community development, with health clinics, schools, and potable water supply systems already having been developed. Village wildlife scouts are trained to voluntarily carry out anti-poaching patrols, greatly supplementing the number of fully paid wildlife scouts, of which there were only 500 at the end of 1988.

For the purposes of wildlife management and to facilitate the implementation of management decisions, wildlife management units and authorities are established under the chairmanship of the district governor. The functions of the authority are to:

- Monitor both legal and illegal take-offs of wildlife resources;
- Determine sustained yield animal quotas for various forms of management, including safari hunting, culling, resident hunting, capture for export, and stocking depleted areas;
- Liaise with the National Park and Wildlife Service on the issuance of hunting licenses;
- Ensure that 40 percent of the revenue generated from the exploitation of wildlife resources is committed to the management costs of the wildlife resources within the management unit;
- Ensure that 35 percent of the revenues earned from the units is provided to the local village communities in areas where such revenues were generated;
- Prepare a work plan for the unit;
- Enforce the National Parks and Wildlife Act;

- Act as a planning body for formulating new wildlife policies and appropriate management activities; and
- Coordinate and implement policy governing wildlife management.

Because of the success of the ADMADE program, similar programs applying the same management concepts have been initiated and have proven successful elsewhere, including the wetlands project located in the Kafue and Bangweulu Flats. Applying the same village involvement approach, the project has reduced poaching, with the villagers now coordinating with the government and taking anti-poaching initiatives.

Another effective type of program has been the Luangwa Integrated Resource Development Project (LIRDP), covering the same conservation area. This is a multi-purpose project that involves wildlife management, agriculture, forestry, fisheries, and water resources. The objectives of LIRDP are to:

- Improve the standard of living of the people in the project area through sustainable use of the full range of the area's natural resources;
- Cover the cost of administration of LIRDP; and
- Without prejudice to the above objectives, provide revenues and other benefits at the national level.

These objectives were derived from a set of policy decisions taken at the national level as follows:

- The programs of government departments concerned with land use and marketing should be coordinated at the local level to produce a land use program compatible with the particular socioeconomic and ecological conditions in the area.
- The activities of nongovernmental organizations in the area, including aid agencies, research agencies, wildlife utilization companies, and the tourism industry, should be coordinated with the land use programs at the local level.
- A mechanism should be developed for ensuring local inputs into decision making with respect to land use planning and the use of revenue and other benefits derived from the area's natural resources.
- Revenue derived from the use of natural resources in the area should be returned to the area for reinvestment in the local economy.

The concept of LIRDP is to increase the productivity and revenue-earning potential of the natural resources in the area and to redistribute the benefits in favor of the people living in the area, who have in the past paid the greatest price for wildlife conservation in terms of alienated land, lost opportunity of resource use, and danger to life and livelihood. The project provides the people with the incentive to make sustainable use of natural resources and discourages illegal take-offs of wildlife.

All these programs were initiated to fully involve the local communities in tourism development in their areas. One conclusion of the program was that, in order to develop tourism in an area, the local people must participate in it and receive some of the benefits of tourism. Through these types of programs, the local people are understanding the important role that tourism and conservation performs in their own well-being.

References

Belt, Collins & Associates, et al. 1969. *Ayers Rock—Mt. Olga National Park Development Plan.* Honolulu, Hawaii.

Bosselman, Fred P. 1978. *In the Wake of the Tourist: Managing Special Places in Eight Countries.* Washington, DC: The Conservation Foundation.

Cohen, Erik. 1989. "Primitive and Remote: Hill Tribe Trekking in Thailand." *Annals of Tourism Research.* 16(1): 30–61.

Edington, John M. and M. Ann Edington. 1986. *Ecology, Recreation and Tourism.* Cambridge: Cambridge University Press.

Fitch, James Marston. 1982. *Historic Conservation: Curatorial Management of the Built World.* New York: McGraw-Hill.

Holder, Jean. 1989. "Tourism and the Future of Caribbean Handicraft." *Tourism Management.* 10(4): 310–314.

India Department of Tourism and National Institute of Design. No date. *Fatehpur Sikri: Integrated Development Plan.* New Delhi: Government of India.

Japan International Cooperation Agency. July 1979. *Borobudur and Prambanan National Archaeological Parks—Final Report.* Tokyo.

Lundberg, Donald E. 1985. *The Tourist Business.* New York: Van Nostrand Reinhold.

Mathieson, Alister and Geoffrey Wall. 1982. *Tourism: Economic, Physical and Social Impacts.* Harlow, England: Longman.

Murphy, Peter E. 1985. *Tourism: A Community Approach.* New York: Methuen.

National Park Service (USA). No date. *Bandelier National Monument, New Mexico.*

Parks Canada. 1982. *Parks Canada Policy.* Hull, Quebec, Canada.

Pearce, Philip L. 1989. "Towards the Better Management of Tourist Queues." *Tourism Management.* 10(4): 279–284.

Thorburn, Andrew. 1986. "Marketing Cultural Heritage." *Travel & Tourism Analyst.* December 1986: 39–48.

Zambia Ministry of Tourism. 1989. *Tourism Development and Planning: A Case Study of the Lupande Game Management Area.* Unpublished paper. Lusaka.

11

Development and Design Standards

Importance of Establishing Standards

Development and design standards for tourist facilities such as resorts, hotels, and visitor facilities at attraction features relate to building location, size, and other characteristics, interrelationships with the natural environment, architecture, landscaping, engineering, and quality levels. These standards determine to a large extent the physical character of facilities and their immediate environment. Establishing facility standards is an essential aspect of developing tourism because they influence both the satisfaction level of tourists and the overall quality and character of the environment for residents. Many of these standards determine the extent to which the tourism development is integrated into the environment and does not generate environmental problems.

Development and design standards should be set forth generally in the national or regional plan and more specifically in the resort, urban, or other tourism-related land use plan. They should be determined before detailed facility planning and design takes place because they establish the parameters of this detailed level of planning and design. Many of these standards are incorporated into zoning regulations and design guidelines so that they have a legal basis for application and maintain continuity of a particular development approach in the area.

Development and design standards will vary appreciably from one place to another depending on the specific development concept adopted and the local environmental situation. These standards establish only the physical framework of detailed planning and design, within which there should be considerable flexibility allowed to the planner/architect/designer to apply creativity and imagina-

303

tion. However, there are some generally accepted development and design principles and types of standards that should be considered and applied in virtually all planning situations. If suitable standards have not been adopted by the local government or the public or private corporation responsible for the development, there is no guarantee that the resulting tourist facility development will be appropriate from either the tourism marketing or environmental quality standpoints. Establishing and applying minimum standards does not ensure outstanding facility development, which depends on the talents of the designers involved, but it does usually result in at least acceptable quality development and prevention of any serious environmental problems.

Site planning, formulation of development standards, architecture, landscape architecture, and engineering are, of course, specialized fields, and no attempt is made to present all aspects of these disciplines as applied to tourism in this chapter. Rather, the approach used here is to point out some basic considerations that the general reader should be aware of and to provide some technical basis for working with the specialists involved. The bibliography lists various references on planning and designing tourist facilities that readers can pursue on specific subjects if they wish further information.

Some Site Planning Considerations

Site planning refers to the specific location (or siting) of buildings and related development forms on the land and considers the functions of the buildings, their physical interrelationships, and the characteristics of the natural environmental setting. Site planning also includes location of roads, parking areas, landscaped and open space areas, footpaths, and recreational facilities, all of which are integrated with the building locations. As is the case at the more general levels of planning, application of the environmental approach to site planning is essential so that the development is well integrated into the natural environment, and environmental problems are not generated. Thus, detailed survey and analysis of the environmental characteristics of the site is one of the first steps in the site planning process, along with determination of the specific types, functions, and sizes of buildings and other development forms that are being planned. This section reviews some of the basic considerations that must be made in site planning of tourist facilities.

Avoiding Environmental Hazards

One of the important considerations in site planning is that buildings or other major structures are not located and designed in such a manner that environmental hazards may result. Particularly hazardous areas are steep hillsides with unstable soil conditions or low-lying places subject to flooding. Improper cut and fill and building design on steep slopes can lead to land slippage and property damage, while minimizing cut and fill and using appropriate building design combined with other techniques can create a safer environmental situation.

As emphasized in Chapter 8 and elsewhere, very steep hillsides (usually over 20 percent) should not be developed at all and, in fact, these places can be used as attractive landscaped and open space features in a resort or urban environment. If development is considered desirable in sloping areas, developers should analyze soils and geological characteristics to determine the best engineering design approach to utilize, install proper drainage so that soils do not become water saturated, leading to land slippage, and plant landscaping to prevent erosion and hold the soil in place. Any landfill should be carefully compacted and retaining walls well built.

In low-lying areas, if considered developable, a proper drainage system must be constructed and any land fill well compacted to prevent uneven settling of the soil. For development near the shoreline in low-lying areas, a common environmental situation in beach hotel development, consideration must be given to whether the buildings will be threatened by high waves coming onshore during a storm or tsunami (tidal or seismic wave). In such situations, if development is considered generally feasible, it may be necessary to set the buildings well back from the shoreline or construct them on raised landfill or platforms. In earthquake-prone areas, special consideration must be given to analyzing soil conditions with respect to their susceptibility to land slippage and settling during an earthquake, and to structural engineering of buildings and structures to be sure they are earthquake resistant. Most earthquake-prone areas have adopted earthquake-resistant types of building construction regulations.

Building Relationships

The grouping of buildings, such as accommodation and their relationships to amenity and recreational facilities, is an important concern of site planning. The type of grouping depends on the density and character of development desired as related to the natural environment. Figure 11.1 illustrates different approaches to the site planning of single units, from low density, single, street-oriented units to cluster groups, all with offstreet parking. Figure 11.2 shows attached units, ranging from a row configuration to cluster groups and higher density courtyard and linear arrangements of block buildings. Parking can either be centralized, which is usually preferable or, for motels, related to each unit.

For larger-scale developments, parking is centralized near to but not encroaching on the hotel entrance and visually screened by landscaping or an elevation difference. The hotel central facility complex of the lobby, reception desk, main restaurant, shops, and recreation facilities should be within relatively close walking distance of all guest rooms or, in a large low density complex, some form of transportation, such as small electric carts, provided.

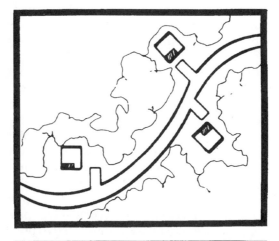

Solitary Units
Buildings contained by the
landscape and very private

Linear Layout
Buildings closer together,
encouraging social interaction
among guests

Cluster Layout
Buildings group-oriented,
encouraging social activities
among guests

Figure 11.1. Single Unit Layouts.

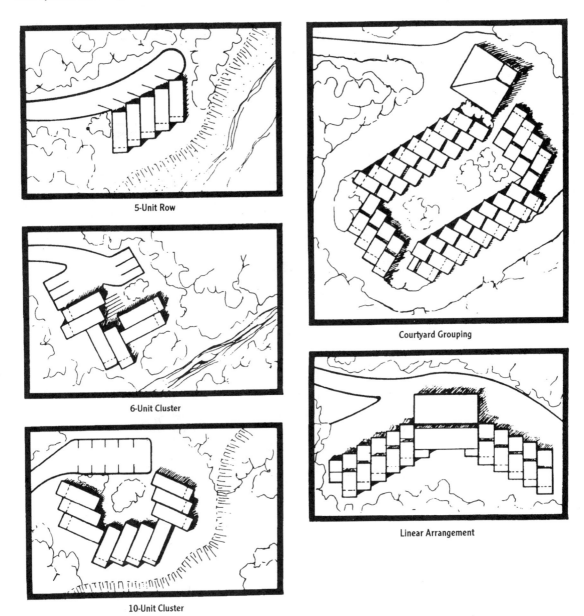

5-Unit Row

6-Unit Cluster

10-Unit Cluster

Courtyard Grouping

Linear Arrangement

Figure 11.2.   Cluster Groupings.

Maintaining Views

Another important consideration, especially in resort planning, is maintenance of views or at least view corridors toward the amenity feature, such as a beach, of the site and its setting. Figure 11.3 illustrates alternative approaches to providing views in a low-rise type development, including the concept of staggering rows

Case 1 Seafront cottage units all in a line

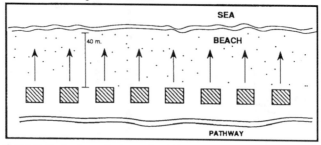

Case 2 Seafront cottage units staggered and offset

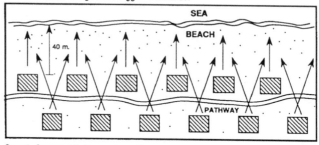

Case 3 Cottage units in a garden setting

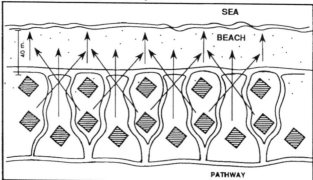

Case 4 Row units in a garden setting

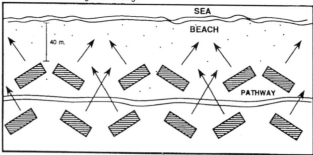

Figure 11.3. Relationship to Amenity.

of buildings so that each one has some visual contact with the beach. Also, the location, heights, and orientation of buildings should be controlled so that view planes of distant features such as mountains or the sea are maintained. Figure 11.4 depicts an example of view plane analysis of urban environments for which the objective is to maintain views of hill, water, and cityscape features from selected points through control of building heights.

On hilly sites, a major environmental consideration is often how best to design accommodation on a hillside overlooking an amenity feature such as a beach-marine view or mountain scenery. In a natural setting, it is important to integrate the buildings into the environment as well as provide views. Often the mistake is made of developing high-rise buildings on hilltops or hillsides, which offers good views from the buildings but also destroys the natural appearance of the hills. A much better approach is to design low-rise buildings stepped down the hillside, as illustrated in Figure 11.5. These buildings are well integrated into the natural environment, provide the opportunity for more extensive use of landscaping, and still have good view outlooks.

Site Development Standards

Related to site planning are development standards, which are applicable in tourist facility planning as well as to general development, especially in town, urban, and environmentally sensitive areas, in order to ensure a functional, safe, and attractive environment for both residents and visitors.

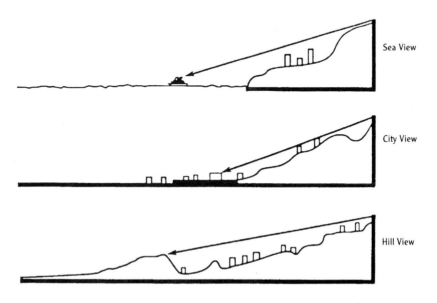

Figure 11.4. View Plane Analysis.

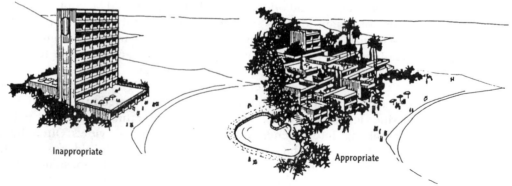

Figure 11.5. Hillside Development.

Types of Development Standards

There are several types of specific standards that are applicable to the controlled development of tourist facilities. These standards typically include the following:

- Density of development;
- Heights of buildings;
- Setbacks of buildings from amenity features, shorelines, roads, lot lines, and other buildings;
- Ratio of the building floor area to the site area;
- Coverage of the site by buildings and other structures;
- Parking requirements ; and
- Other requirements, such as for landscaping and open space, public access to amenity features, signs, and utility lines.

Establishing Development Standards

The exact requirements for each type of standard will vary depending on the intended character of the tourism development and the environmental situation, although there is a generally accepted range of requirements for each of the various types of development. For a medium or large size tourism area, it is common practice to adopt different standards for the different types of designated tourism development areas such as beach and mountain resorts and urban places, depending on the character of tourism desired in the various places and the particular characteristics of their environments. These standards are explained in the following sections.

Unit Densities

In tourism, density refers to the number of accommodation units per acre or hectare, which determines to a great extent the overall character of the development. Very low density of 5 to 10 units per acre (12 to 25 units per hectare) implies either individual cottage units or attached units with much open space and landscaping; a low to medium density of 10 to 30 units per acre (25 to 75 units per hectare) usually requires two-story block buildings or higher buildings with much open space and landscaping; and a higher density of 30 to 60 units per acre (75 to 150 units per hectare) typically requires buildings of about four stories if adequate open space and landscaping are provided. Urban resorts and hotels, of course, are often of much higher density, with medium and high-rise buildings and limited open space. Hotel densities in Waikiki in Hawaii and Miami Beach in Florida go up to 300 units per acre. Allowable densities are indicated by stating the maximum number of units per acre or hectare.

Building Heights

The maximum allowable heights of buildings greatly influence the character of tourism development because of the obvious visibility of higher buildings, and is an especially important consideration in resorts where many tourists want an environmental change from their metropolitan homes and nearby residents do not wish to urbanize their landscapes. If a very natural site appearance is desired, the buildings would be limited to one or two stories (the American definition of the ground floor being the first story is used here) combined with generous open space and landscaping. If the natural environment is to remain dominant but a higher density or more compact development is wanted, a four-story maximum height may be established (this height is still usually below the tops of tall trees). Taller buildings will create a more urban character of development, although, if combined with ample open space and landscaping, higher buildings can be acceptable in a resort environment. Buildings of more than two stories will usually require elevators, which entails additional cost for installation and maintenance—an important factor to consider when developing hotels in remote places.

Buildings height regulations are usually indicated in feet or meters, which can be related to the number of stories (for example, 15 meters will allow four stories), but also takes into account controlling the height of roofs or other structures that may be developed in the tourism environment. For example, it is not uncommon for the hotel lobby roof to be designed as a high structure to provide an architectural feature, but this may exceed the desired maximum height of buildings in the development. Figure 11.6 shows how building heights are measured.

Case 1—Building on sloping grade

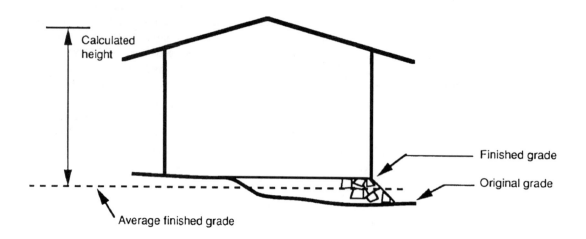

Case 2—Building with permitted intrusion above height limit

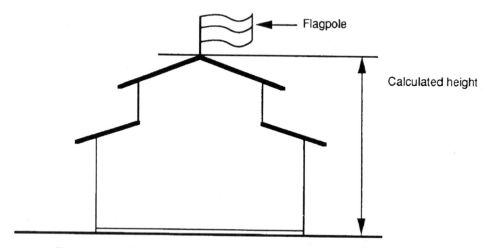

Figure 11.6. Examples of Maximum Building Height Determination.

Building Setbacks

The setbacks, or minimum distances required, of main buildings from amenity features, shorelines, roads, the site or lot boundaries, and other buildings are important to maintain a sense of openness and sufficient space for landscaping, privacy of building occupants, and in some cases for safety reasons. Adequate setbacks from beaches and shorelines are particularly necessary for several reasons:

- Protection of buildings from damage that may result from beach erosion and high waves;
- Maintenance of a natural appearance along the shoreline;
- Allowance of adequate space inland from the shoreline for public access and recreational use by tourists and residents; and
- Provision of privacy for the guests using accommodation or residents living near the beach, in the case of residential tourism.

Shoreline setback requirements vary appreciably but generally should be about 30 to 50 meters (about 100 to 165 feet) where feasible. In some areas, the setback should be greater than 50 meters, depending on the local environmental characteristics of coastal and other considerations, and, in other places, it is less. In Hawaii, for example, the shoreline setback is only 40 feet (about 12 meters), while in India, it is 500 meters generally and 200 meters in certain designated coastal tourism areas such as Goa and Orissa. In small island resort environments, the setback may need to be less because of limited land area. This can be acceptable if there are no environmental hazards and vegetation is planted near the beach for visual screening and erosion control.

Figure 11.7 depicts how building setbacks are measured from the mean (average) high tide and vegetation lines, the usual reference points for setback measurements in coastal areas. This figure also illustrates establishment of a marine zone within which water uses are controlled. Building setbacks from other buildings in a cottage hotel development are shown in Figure 11.8, which in this case are measured between the patio areas of the cottages, which are the places of concern for the sake of privacy and not between the nearest walls, as is usually the case, but is not as relevant in many configurations of development. Building setbacks from adjacent roads and the site lot lines are important to maintain a sense of privacy and an attractive setting for the building complex. It also provides a buffer from undesirable noises and views generated by the roads or adjacent land uses.

Setback requirements from roads, other buildings, and site boundaries will vary appreciably depending on the local situation. Within setback areas, including shoreline setbacks, it is common practice to allow small temporary structures, such as shelters and some types of recreation facilities.

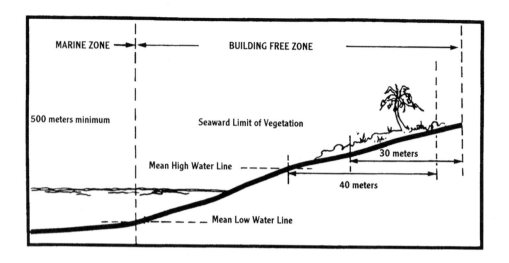

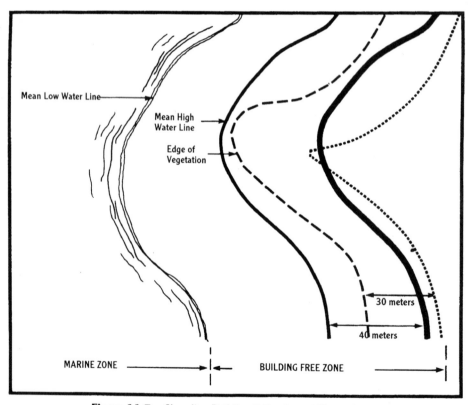

Figure 11.7. Shoreline Building Setbacks and Marine Zone.

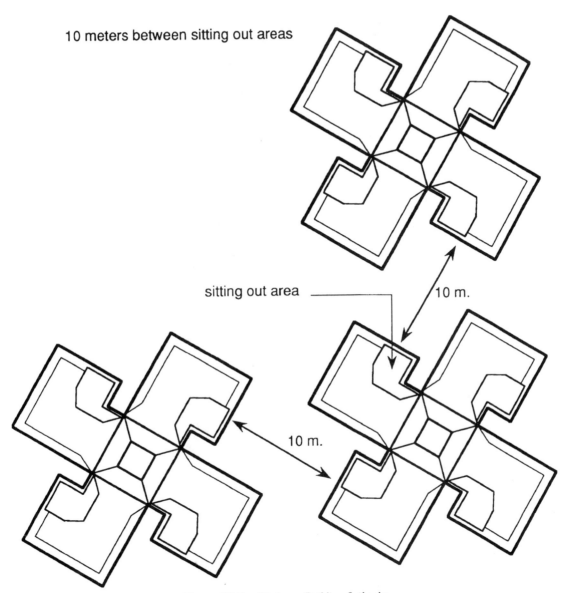

10 meters between sitting out areas

sitting out area

10 m.

10 m.

Figure 11.8. Minimum Building Setbacks.

Floor Area Ratio

Floor Area Ratio (FAR) is also a measurement of the intensity of development, and refers to the ratio between the total floor area of all stories of all the buildings and the total site area. The FAR is calculated by dividing the gross floor area by the area of the site and is expressed as a percentage. Figure 11.9 shows an example of the FAR as related to unit density and site coverage. The FAR standard varies appreciably, depending on the type of development.

Case 1—Single-story building

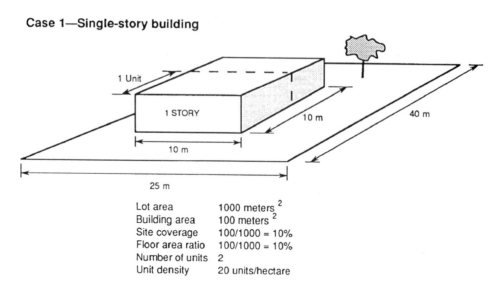

Lot area   1000 meters ^{2}
Building area   100 meters ^{2}
Site coverage   100/1000 = 10%
Floor area ratio 100/1000 = 10%
Number of units   2
Unit density   20 units/hectare

Case 2—Two-story building

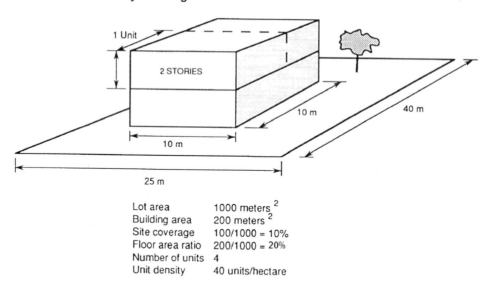

Lot area   1000 meters ^{2}
Building area   200 meters ^{2}
Site coverage   100/1000 = 10%
Floor area ratio 200/1000 = 20%
Number of units   4
Unit density   40 units/hectare

Figure 11.9. Examples of Unit Density, Site Coverage, and Floor Area Ratio Calculations.

Site Coverage

The site coverage by buildings and structures, also indicated as a percentage, is an important control on the amount of landscaped area and open space in the development. In a low to medium density resort, the site coverage by buildings should be limited to about 25 percent, to allow for sufficient open space and generous landscaping.

Offstreet Parking

Provision should be made for sufficient offstreet parking to handle all vehicles likely to be stopping at the resort, including for employees and at peak period use, so that streets are not congested with parked vehicles. Special provision of larger spaces may need to be made for parking of tour buses. The specific requirments for offstreet parking will vary greatly, depending on the type and location of development. Motels serving domestic tourists will, for example, require more parking spaces than international hotels catering to foreign guest arriving by airplane, bus, or train. However, even in the latter case, consideration will need to be given to whether many of these tourists will be renting cars for their use. Use by residents of tourist facilities such as hotel restaurants will also need to be considered in determining parking needs.

In some newly developing tourism areas it may be difficult to precisely project parking requirements, and, in fact, these requirements may change over time, resulting from, for example, greater use of rental cars by tourists or increasing affluence of residents, leading to greater local car ownership and use of tourist facilities. In these situations, provision can be made for possible future parking needs by allowing for parking expansion areas in appropriate locations, but initially landscaping these as part of the hotel open space until such time as they may be needed. In this manner, an excessively large area is not sterilized by parking lot development, but sufficient parking space will be available for possible future use. Parking areas of any type should be well landscaped and fit into the overall environment of the development.

Landscaping

In addition to the site coverage requirement, it is common to also require that a minimum amount of landscaping be developed (including any natural vegetation on the site) and that landscaping be provided in otherwise unattractive spaces, including large parking areas, alongside roadways, and around utility buildings and structures in order to screen them from view (some design concepts of landscaping are examined in a subsequent section of this chapter). The minimum landscaping requirement is also expressed as a percentage of total site area.

Public Access

As emphasized in Chapter 8, adequate public access should be provided to amenity features and public facilities, such as beaches and cultural centers, in tourism areas. In a beach resort development, for example, public access corridors to the beach are essential so that residents can use their own amenities. These should also be accessible to tourists staying in other places. In addition to incorporating public access in resort land use plans, this can more generally be required by regulation, such as there being public access points to a suitable section of a shoreline at regular distances apart (for example, approximately every thousand meters) in a developed area that may have residential and commercial as well as tourism development.

Sign Controls

Large, unattractive, and inappropriately located signs can greatly detract from the appearance of any area, including tourism areas. In most types of tourism areas, sign control standards should be established with respect to their type, location, size, materials used, and lighting. Often, an approach applied is to not allow any outdoor advertising signs in tourism areas, but only well-designed identification and directional signs constructed of materials that are compatible with the environment and can be discretely lighted at night. The exception to this standard is in some distinctive urban districts such as Times Square in New York, the Ginza in Tokyo, and main streets in Las Vegas, where bright, flashing advertising signs add a desired glitzy character to the urban scene.

Underground Utility Lines

Overhead electric and telephone lines and their supporting poles are unattractive elements and disturb views in any environment, including tourism areas. Although very high voltage electric lines are difficult to place underground, the lower voltage distribution lines can be economically undergrounded. This should be required in resorts and other tourism areas, as well as in developed places in general. Placing utility lines underground is initially more expensive but, because of lower maintenance costs, may be no more costly over the long term than overhead lines. In areas prone to occasional high winds that can topple utility poles and lines (or trees over the lines), undergrounding offers additional safety and maintenance advantages.

Design Considerations

Architectural, landscaping, and engineering design standards must be decided for tourism areas, as described in the following sections.

Architectural Design

Architectural design standards for hotels and other tourist facilities must be more flexible than development standards to allow for the creativity of the architect. However, when a certain design character is desired in an area or development site, which is usually the case in tourism areas, basic guidelines should be established and provided to the architects for their use in the design process. These guidelines are also used by the approving authority in its review of the proposed

Visitor center (top) and the lodge central facility (bottom) in Zion National Park, Utah, USA—The park visitor center includes museum exhibits, an auditorium for lectures and audio-visual presentations, a book shop, a rear viewing terrace, and other facilities, and its design utilizes local type building stone. The park lodge, restored to its original style, utilizes local type building stone, employs a suitable architectural style for this area, and is well integrated into the natural environment of its site.

facility design. Some basic types of guideline considerations are described below. Not included here are standards on tourist facility layouts, room sizes, length of corridors, and other standards, which are available in reference books on these subjects.

Local Styles and Motifs

If there are distinctive local, traditional, or historic architectural styles already developed in the area, these should be incorporated into tourist facility designs to the greatest extent possible so that these facilities fit into the local environment, reinforce the architectural character of the area, and impart a distinct sense of place to the facility development. In some cases, there is a problem of completely transferring the local style because of differences in scale and function, but usually some local motifs can be utilized. Local motifs, including handicrafted materials, can also be incorporated into the interior decor of the facilities. If no local styles prevail, sometimes a neutral international but environmentally-oriented style is appropriate, rather than importing a style from elsewhere that is not related to the area.

Roof Lines

The design of roofs (flat, pitched, overhang, etc.) is an especially critical design element because in low buildings roof lines are very visible and greatly influence the character and appearance of the structures. Roof lines should reflect the local architectural style and be consistent with the characteristics of the natural environment.

Use of Local Building Materials

To the greatest extent possible, local building materials should be utilized, especially if they relate to the local architectural style, as is often the case with wood, brick, or stone construction. Also, use of local building materials may be less expensive than imported materials and provides employment and income for residents of the area. Exceptions to this standard are where use of traditional local materials, even though attractive and functional, may create environmental problems. For example, in some tropical islands, coral blocks removed from the island reefs were a popular building material traditionally, but this should now be prohibited because of environmental damage caused to the reef, as also should lime plaster material made from the burning of coral, which still is commonly practiced in some island communities. As another example, wood shake roofs used in many places of the world are now causing concern because of the fire hazard that they present. Generally, use of reflecting surfaces such as shiny metal roofs and bright colors should be prohibited so that the buildings are not obtrusive in their environments. Also, metal roofs can generate very hot building interiors in high temperatures environments, leading to increased demand for air conditioning.

Environmental Relationships

Building design should relate to the natural environment. For example, in tropical and subtropical areas, buildings should incorporate indoor-outdoor relationships through use of open-sided lobbies, verandas, patios, and courtyard gardens. In hotter climates, designing for natural ventilation may preclude the need for air conditioning during much of the year, while in colder climates, orientation of buildings to the maximum sun exposure will reduce heating requirements. Building design should also take advantage of any views from the site, as explained previously.

Landscaping Design

Generous and suitable landscaping is an essential element in creating an attractive and interesting resort and tourist facility environment and also serves important functional purposes. Even in urban environments, exterior and interior landscaping can help create a desired character of the facility. Landscape architecture is concerned with the relationship and appearance of the total environment, with particular reference to plants and landscaping features such as water bodies, footpaths, and outdoor furniture and lighting. Good landscaping attempts to provide unity and cohesion in the local environment and a sensitive balance between man-made features and the natural elements.

More specifically, landscaping in tourism areas involves the effective use of plant materials and other features for such purposes, according to certain principles as:

- Creating an attractive setting conducive to relaxation and recreation.
- Screening objectionable views and providing privacy.
- Providing vegetative buffers to absorb unpleasant sounds, smells, and dust.
- Arranging plants to provide relief from intense sun glare and rain, as well as to reduce surface temperatures.
- Minimizing the effects of high winds, particularly along coastal areas, yet still allowing for the flow of gentle breezes.
- Organizing the plant material to complement a landform, to enhance a building line or facade, to gradually unfold an attractive vista or to frame a major entrance area. In some cases, the plants themselves can be used to provide focal points and major visual features.
- Situating plants in strategic places where they can be best appreciated. Many plants are more attractive if planted in mass and seen from a distance whereas others must be seen at close range to be fully appreciated.
- Arranging and massing trees and shrubs, particularly native flowering species, to provide dramatic color and textural variation.
- Introducing tourists to new species and varieties of plants, especially from the local area.

These and other principles are illustrated in Figure 11.10. Landscaping can

Moderate Air Temperature

Bank Edging

Direct Air Movement

Provide Rain Shelter

Prevent Erosion

Guiding Elements

Reduction of Road Noise

Visual Boundaries

Beautification Elements

TYPES OF TREES

Round

Horizontal

Broad

Conical

Vertical

Figure 11.10. Landscape Planting Functions.

also be used to screen and ameliorate poor building design or inappropriate use of building materials, not an uncommon situation in tourism as well as other development areas.

Where available, local indigenous plant material should be utilized in landscaping because local plants grow well in their own environment and reinforce the natural vegetative character of the site. However, certain imported exotic plants that do well in the local environment may also be appropriate. Any existing major plants and especially mature trees on the site should be saved and incorporated into the final landscaping as was emphasized in Chapter 8. Plant material that is easy and inexpensive to maintain and conserves resources should be used (for example, not using plants which require large amounts of water in an arid climate). Water features such as creeks, canals, ponds, and small waterfalls can offer very interesting accents and visual focal points in a landscaped area, but these should be carefully designed for ease of maintenance and conservation of water such as recirculating the water used in ornamental fountains and waterfalls.

Footpaths are an important element of landscaping hotel, resort, and visitor facility sites. In addition to serving their pedestrian function, footpaths should be attractive, safe, and practical to use, as well as be designed to offer interesting views. Outdoor furniture (benches, tables, etc.), shelters, and kiosks are often important to include when landscaping tourist facilities; these should be suitably designed reflecting the building design, properly located, and well constructed.

Night lighting in landscaped areas is important for both functional reasons of safety and security and for aesthetic appreciation of buildings and landscaping. Lighting is used at entrances, access drives, and parking lots, along footpaths, in recreational areas, to illuminate interesting building and landscape features, for information signs, and in service yards. Except in service and high security areas, the most suitable type of lighting is typically indirect and not too bright (for example, use of low shaded lights along a footpath that light the pathway but do not shine in the walkers' eyes).

Designing for the Handicapped

More emphasis is now being placed on designing for the handicapped, including the physically disabled, sensory impaired, slower moving elderly people, and the mentally ill and retarded. This design approach is also being extended to tourists who are handicapped. Barrier-free design should be applied to tourist transportation facilities and attractions, with techniques applied such as:

- Developing hard, relatively smooth, wide walkway paving surfaces;
- Curbs with ramped cuts at intersections;
- Ramped access with automatic door openings or through bars at entrances to buildings, such as museums; and
- Restrooms, drinking fountains, and public telephones designed for use by persons in wheelchairs.

Many airports are already equipped to handle handicapped persons. In attraction areas, vehicular traffic should be well separated from pedestrian ways for safety reasons in general and especially for the safety of the handicapped. At attraction features, presentation techniques should include those that can be appreciated by the sensory impaired and retarded, with special programs organized where relevant.

Engineering Design

Engineering design standards should be established to ensure that at least minimum infrastructure and construction requirements are met in tourism development areas. In less developed countries or regions where these standards have not yet been adopted or exist but are considered unsuitable, international standards or those of a more developed country can be adapted and applied. The basic types of engineering standards are reviewed in the following sections.

Roads

Various categories of roads are established for the tourism area based on projected traffic usage, as well as respective road widths and related drainageways, walkways, and landscaping requirements determined. Cross-sections of these various types of roadways are drawn, and construction and materials specifications are written.

Drainage

In addition to the drainage associated with roads, the specifications for other types of drainageways, such as for various sizes of culverts and canals, are established.

Water Supply

Water supply quality standards are established based on either local standards, if they are acceptable, or on international standards such as those set by the World Health Organization. The source of water supply will, of course, depend on local conditions, but standards should be established for the amount of water required for various types of tourism development, the quality level of the water, water pressure to be maintained, and the specifications of the distribution system. Water supply standards should include provision for fire protection and water conservation techniques, as explained in Chapter 5.

Electric Power

The source of electric power will also vary from place to place, but standards can be established for the amount of power to be available based on projected demand, reliability of supply, consistency of voltage, and the specifications for installation of the distribution system. Any possibilities for utilizing energy conservation techniques such as solar heating should be applied, as explained in Chapter 5.

Sewage Disposal

The type of sewage disposal system will depend on the scale of development and local conditions, and may range from the use of septic tanks to large integrated sewage collection and treatment systems. Standards should be established with respect to the degree of treatment required—primary, secondary, or tertiary—and the disposal technique of effluent, based on preventing any pollution. As emphasized previously, investigation should be made of the potential for recycling sewage effluent, especially in water deficient areas, for use as landscaping irrigation water or even potable use.

Solid Waste Disposal

The type of solid waste disposal will also vary, depending on the local situation, but standards should be established to ensure that there is proper disposal and that the techniques of disposal, such as incineration or landfill, will not generate any pollution problems. Recycling of solid waste should be required to the greatest extent possible.

Telecommunications

International standards exist that can be applied to the development of telephone, telegraph where needed, telex, radio-telephone, and other means of telecommunications.

Boat Piers and Marinas

Often associated with tourism development, boat piers and marinas should have sound engineering standards applied to ensure their proper construction and maintenance, including avoiding any environmental problems. International planning, design, and engineering standards are available for boat piers and marinas, but these must be adapted to each local situation.

Building Construction Standards

Standards and specifications for the construction of tourist facility buildings and other structures are essential. Usually, these are already existing in the area as building codes but should be reviewed to ensure that they are suitable, including review for public safety and fire protection. For example, use of automatic sprinkler systems are now commonly required in hotels.

Sanitation and Public Health Standards

Maintaining minimum sanitation and hygiene standards is also essential in tourism development, especially for restaurants, bars, and toilet/bathing facilities. Usually sanitation standards, in the form of a public health code, exist in the tourism area but should be reviewed to make certain that they are adequate. Public health standards also relate to room size, ventilation, and fenestration requirements.

Other Types of Engineering Design Standards

Other types of engineering design considerations for tourism include, for example, ski lift equipment, cable car systems, and theme park machinery, which require specific standards, especially as related to safety factors.

Tourist Facility Quality Standards

Tourist facility quality standards, including the quality level of services as well as facilities, are usually established at the national or regional levels, but if not, they need to be considered at the community development level. These types of standards are particularly applicable to accommodation, restaurants, and tour and travel services.

Accommodation and Restaurants

Minimum standards should be established for hotels and other types of accommodation, based, for example, on the size of rooms, provision of ancillary facilities, and other factors, such as public health and sanitation standards. A hotel licensing procedure should be applied to ensure that the accommodation meets these minimum standards, with unlicensed enterprises not being allowed to operate. This licensing may differentiate hotels from other types of accommodation, such as guest houses and youth hostels. The licensing procedure should stipulate that periodic, usually annual, inspections be carried out to ensure that the minimum standards are continuing to be met, with warnings given to establishments that do not meet all standards and the licenses withdrawn if the standards are not met within a certain period of time after the warning has been given. The exception to the warning system approach would be cases where public health is endangered and the license must be withdrawn immediately until the problems are remedied.

A hotel classification system is commonly utilized to differentiate the various quality levels of accommodation establishments. These systems apply a long list of different facility and service factors to determine the ratings. As explained in Chapter 5, hotel classification systems are usually based on one- to five-star ratings, with the five-star category representing luxury hotels with a full range of facilities and services, and one star being the basic level accommodation that still meets the minimum standards. Room rates are typically but not always related closely to the classification categories. A separate classification may be applied to non-hotel types of accommodation such as guest houses.

A hotel classification system is very useful to give tour operators and tourists a specific idea of the quality levels of accommodation available in an area and, in some cases, provides hoteliers with an incentive to upgrade their establishments, where this is desirable and feasible. The disadvantage of such a system is that it is difficult to neatly categorize all types of accommodation. For example, a very high quality but small hotel may receive a low rating because of its limited number of rooms, even though its quality level of facilities and services warrants a higher rating and a high room tariff. A hotel classification system needs to be carefully and objectively administered with periodic reinspections made of hotels to determine if they should remain in the same category or be shifted to a higher or lower one.

Standards are more difficult to apply to independent restaurants beyond the minimum level of public health, sanitation, and safety standards necessary to obtain a license. In some countries, restaurants are rated using a star (or sometimes a fork symbol), with this rating typically done by a private organization, such as Michelin in Europe. In some countries or regions where most local restaurants are considered to be unsatisfactory for average tourist use, the tourism office has applied a system of designating the acceptable establishments as officially approved tourist restaurants. These restaurants are then identified as being approved on their signs and in guide books.

Tour and Travel Operations

Tour and travel agencies must also meet minimum standards of maintaining qualified staffs and being financially responsible. A licensing procedure should be applied to ensure that minimum standards are met. Often, bonding or some other form of financial guarantee is required to make certain that the agency has sufficient financial resources and will not suddenly become bankrupt, leaving tourists stranded, as has happened on occasion. Tour agency quality standards should include that any tour buses, cars, and other vehicles that they operate are in efficient and safe condition, and that vehicle drivers are properly licensed.

Some countries, such as the Federal Republic of Germany, have adopted consumer protection legislation for tourists, which requires that tour and travel agencies accurately describe the tours that they are selling and clearly state the tour pricing. This legislation resulted from past experience of some tour operators misrepresenting their product and being financially irresponsible, justifiably leading to tourist dissatisfaction and complaints.

Tour guides should be properly trained and licensed, based on their having passed an examination given by the tourism office, to ensure that they are minimally qualified to function as guides. In some places where unlicensed and unqualified guides are common, tourists should be informed about this problem and licensed guides are available and can be identified by a badge or other means.

Application of Standards

Development standards can be adopted as part of the tourism area's general zoning regulations or applied specifically to a particular development for which a tourism land use plan has been prepared, with their administration being the responsibility of the area's planning and zoning agency. Often a set of regulations that specifies the various land use zones and the development standards or minimum requirements within each zone are adopted, particularly for a large resort or other type of tourism development area.

Architectural and landscaping guidelines are usually applied through a design review committee or board that includes design professionals in its membership. This body has the responsibility for reviewing all tourism development proposals with respect to meeting the design guidelines and requiring any revision necessary before the final design approval is granted. This committee or board may also be given the right to review proposals with respect to meeting the zoning regulations and development standards. In some places, basic architectural and landscaping design standards may be required by regulation. Engineering design standards, such as for water and power, are typically administered by the public works and other government agencies.

Hotel and restaurant licensing and classification systems and tour, travel agency, and tour guide licensing are usually administered by the tourism office of the country, region, or local area. Application of sanitation and public health requirements are normally administered by the public health department.

The government procedure for receiving, reviewing, and taking action on tourism development proposals should be thorough to ensure that all standards are met, but also must be as efficient as possible so that the developers and their planning and design staff are not forced to spend an excessive amount of time and money on the review and approval process. It is important that all the standards be available to the developers in advance of their planning and design activities.

Quality control standards can be established, at least at the minimum level, by government regulations. However, quality control is the basic responsibility of tourism enterprises for their own benefit and productivity through maintaining a satisfied tourist clientele. A study on quality control of tourism products and services by the WTO concluded, that (WTO 1988, 30):

> . . . the tourism enterprise or organization must move from simply monitoring quality to managing quality on the basis of a quality policy. This process must be developed within the staff.

Quality control must serve first to correct problems identified as such and systematically to seek improvements for reasons of competitiveness or good economic social health. Quality policy is therefore everyone's business and must be oriented toward at least four objectives:

- Improving the quality of products and services
- Improving productivity
- Improving the quality of life in the workplace
- Improving the organization and methods of work

It is therefore at all levels of the enterprise and with respect to all of its functions that the state of mind of quality should be instilled through management commitment, quality training for all staff, including executives and management, and a capacity for expression and problem-solving at staff level; the quality process is a process of accepting responsibility . . .

Case Studies

Two case studies are presented to demonstrate the application of development and design standards. The fishing lodge plan for Zanzibar illustrates both an environmentally-oriented layout and a suitable local architectural style. The Wachusett Mountain ski resort in the northeastern USA represents functional site planning and use of progressive energy-saving techniques.

Sport Fishing Hotel Plan in Zanzibar

Case studies in Chapters 3 and 7 described the background of the Zanzibar Tourism Development Plan (UNDP and WTO 1983), which includes both Zanzibar and Pemba Islands. This project was a comprehensive one, including both the regional tourism policy and structure plan, as well as detailed planning and design for selected priority development projects. For the detailed planning and design, an initial step was to survey the existing traditional architectural styles of the islands. It was determined that the two prevailing styles are the Arab and Swahili styles, which were then researched. These styles, including use of local building materials, formed the basis for design of the various priority development projects.

One of the projects selected was a proposed fishing and diving hotel or small resort on Pemba Island. The site was selected in the regional plan because of its accessibility by both land and boat from the Pemba's main town and local airport, as well as its situation on a suitable boat anchorage, providing access to excellent big game fishing waters off the Tanzanian coast and nearby marine areas for diving. The site was undeveloped and available for future development. The hotel was designed to be a small-scale, medium-quality, relatively simple but comfortable resort with the high standard fishing facilities typically desired by sport fishermen who will pay a substantial cost to engage in their avocation, as well as diving activities. Development was to take place in phases.

The specifications for the hotel were determined as follows:

- Reception and restaurant facilities:
    1. Reception/lobby building of approximately 100 square meters; and
    2. Restaurant/bar/kitchen building of approximately 150 square meters.
- Recreation facilities:
    1. Beach bar and changing/shower room;
    2. Storerooms for fishing and diving equipment of approximately 100 square meters;
    3. Pier of appropriate design; and
    4. Two boats for fishing and one for diving.
- Type and size of cottages—twenty cottages of approximately 45 to 50 square meters, each with individual bathrooms and natural ventilation.
- Bedroom furniture:
    1. Two single beds;
    2. Writing table;
    3. Two chairs;
    4. Reading lamp; and
    5. Local artwork.
- Sitting room furniture:
    1. Couch;
    2. Two chairs;
    3. Coffee and end tables;
    4. Lamps; and
    5. Local artwork.
- Bathrooms:
    1. Three-fixture with hot and cold water, bathtub, and shower; and
    2. Other appropriate fixtures.
- Floor coverings in rooms—tile or hardwood with throw rugs.
- Wall coverings—low maintenance paint.

As shown on the site plan and profile in Figure 11.11, the hotel is comprised of separate units laid out around a central facility complex of the reception/lobby, restaurant, and equipment stores. The restaurant/bar is oriented to views of the water and nearby islands. All the units have footpath access with extensive landscaping to provide privacy. The units are set back from the shoreline but near to it. The plan includes a swimming beach and beach bar for relaxation when the guests are not fishing or diving. The pier is located on the protected side of the site peninsula. This first phase of the resort shown on the plan is situated on the point of the peninsula where the best location for a pier and moorings is found and to take advantage of the splendid views of the bay area. Later phases would be developed further up the peninsula toward a nearby beach but still sufficiently close to the central facilities.

The accommodation units and central facilities are designed in the Swahili

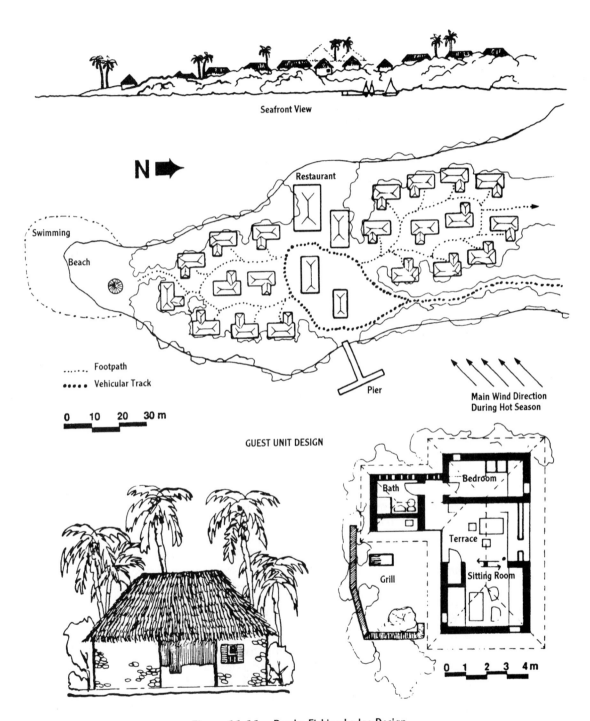

Seafront View

N ➡

Restaurant

Swimming

Beach

.... Footpath
●●●● Vehicular Track

0   10   20   30 m

Pier

Main Wind Direction
During Hot Season

GUEST UNIT DESIGN

Bath

Bedroom

Terrace

Grill

Sitting Room

0   1   2   3   4 m

Figure 11.11. Pemba Fishing Lodge Design.

style, as shown in Figure 11.11, which is appropriate for this small-scale, low-profile development, and utilizes local building materials. As shown on the ground floor plan of the units, they are somewhat self-contained, providing, in addition to the bedroom, a sitting room, terrace, and outdoor grill area where fish caught can be cooked for guests. These hotel specifications and hotel site planning and design concepts will provide a specific guide to the architect preparing the final hotel plan and design.

Wachusett Mountain Ski Resort

The resort development at Wachusett Mountain, located in central Massachusetts in the northeastern USA, represents an environmentally sensitive and appropriately designed type of resort that utilizes some innovative energy-saving techniques (Urban Land Institute, 1984). In contrast to the large Whistler resort described in Chapter 8, Wachusett Mountain resort is much smaller and does not include accommodation, but it is also designed for year-round use. Occupying about 450 acres, Wachusett has ski trails of about 1,000 feet in vertical elevation difference, three chair lifts and one surface tow with a legal limitation of less than 2,000 skiers at one time because it is located in a state reservation. It also has some 12 miles of cross-country trails. At 2,006 feet in elevation, Wachusett Mountain is the highest mountain in central Massachusetts, and its peak affords a panoramic view of that part of the state. The area is in the 1,955-acre Wachusett Mountain State Reservation, which supports an abundance of wildlife and vegetation and attracts sight-seeing tourists throughout the year.

Situated 52 miles from Boston and 61 miles from Providence, Rhode Island, the resort has a large day and after-work trip population area of several million persons, and it especially attracts persons who do not want to take longer trips to more distant ski areas. In the late 1980s, the area was attracting about 340,000 skier visits during good years, plus off-season visitors.

The area was opened to skiing in 1933, when skiers drove to the top of the mountain and skied down. In 1961, the state installed two T-bars and six years later voted to move Wachusett and other reservations to state control, to be administered under the Massachusetts Department of Natural Resources. The state operated the ski area during the 1967–68 season, but this was not successful. The Wachusett Mountain Associates was established and has managed the facility privately since then. In 1981, this company prepared plans for expansion, including new ski trails, the three chair lifts, and a new lodge for development over a two-year period. The first stage of the plan was rapidly implemented to be open for the 1982–83 winter season, and the project was finished during the following year.

From the site planning standpoint, the new lodge was located to provide convenient access on the logical route taken by skiers from the parking lot to the slopes. Distances between the lodge and ski lifts were a critical factor. If they were too great, skiers would be caused discomfort by walking long distances on skis to and from the lodge. If they were too close, the areas surrounding the lodge could become congested with the crossing of lift-line and lodge traffic, detracting from effective circulation in the area. The distance determined to be optimum was siting the lodge approximately 100 to 150 feet from each of the three chair lifts.

As illustrated in Figure 11.12, the lodge was designed to be energy efficient

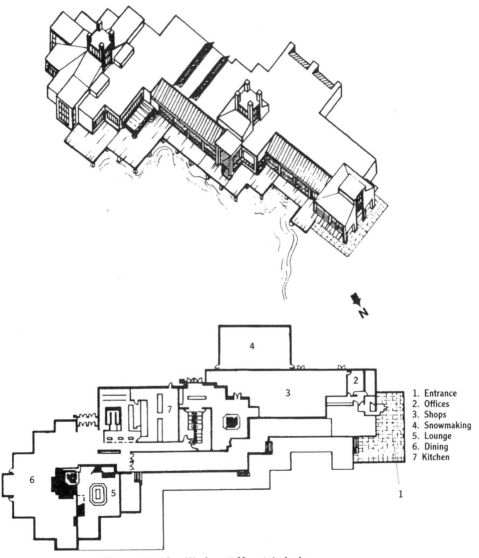

1. Entrance
2. Offices
3. Shops
4. Snowmaking
5. Lounge
6. Dining
7 Kitchen

Figure 11.12. Wachusett Mountain Lodge.

with the south of the building facing the slope, containing expanses of glass that allow in considerable solar heat and light, as well as an unobstructed view of the slopes. On another side facing a pond, a large wooden deck extends the entire length with a glass canopy overhead that lets in the sunlight. Adequate air circulation and natural lighting come partly through primarily glass chimneys that protrude from the building's roof. These are designed to exhaust hot summer air from the building and to allow fresh air circulation, thus reducing the dependence on air conditioning, while the glass allows natural light to enter. Waste heat from the snowmaking equipment heats the building. A small pond next to the lodge supplies water for the snowmaking process, and the building was designed to take advantage of the aesthetic qualities of the pond. The snowmaking equipment is incorporated into the side of the lodge, and the heat produced travels through ducts that release it directly into the building with the unneeded heat flowing outdoors. The amount of heat generated by the equipment produces about five times that required for the building, providing ample heating throughout the winter season.

Interior design and finishing materials were selected to be multi-purpose, to be able to handle the rough use given it by ski boots and equipment and by families with children, and to be a familiar environment for the skiers, while still being suitable for more refined summer dining facilities. Materials were carefully selected that had been tested for heavy use but that also had the visual and textural qualities desired. A rustic theme was chosen, utilizing wood and stone finishes, copper hoods over the fireplaces, and goat's hair carpet, providing a comfortable yet quality character.

The lodge facilities were also designed to be family-oriented and for all-season use. An area that serves as a nursery in the winter converts to an art gallery in the summer, and the bar is visually separated from the dining room. There is a teen center with an ice cream parlor and video games, and bus service provides access to the area for children below driving age. During off-ski seasons, the area attracts conferences and other groups that come to the mountain for hiking, scenic views, and the colorful autumn foliage. Then the lodge converts a portion of its interior into a high quality restaurant, and the sporting goods store adapts its merchandise to a different clientele.

There are five minor watersheds in the reservation, which includes the ski area. Lake Wachusett, which receives the watersheds' runoff, is a major source of water supply for a nearby town. There was considerable concern about potential contamination of the lake by erosive runoff from the new ski trails not yet sufficiently revegetated and possible discharges from the lodge. In order to preclude this potential pollution problem, the developer constructed a water diversion system at a substantial cost.

References

United National Development Programme and World Tourism Organization. 1983. *Zanzibar Tourism Development Plan*. Madrid: World Tourism Organization.

Urban Land Institute. 1984. *Project Reference File—Wachusett Mountain Ski Area*. Vol. 14, No. 20. Washington, DC.

World Tourism Organization. 1988. *Quality Control of Tourism Products and Services*. Madrid: World Tourism Organization.

Part Four

Environmental and Socioeconomic Considerations

Part Four examines the environmental and socioeconomic impacts to be considered in planning for tourism development. As repeatedly emphasized, the approach of this book is that tourism is a socioeconomic sector and should be planned in an integrated manner aimed at sustainable development of the natural and cultural resources of tourism. Therefore, the environmental and sociocultural conservation approach, within the framework of achieving economic benefits, must be applied throughout the planning process. However, it is organizationally useful in this part to specifically review environmental and socioeconomic impacts, and how negative impacts can be prevented or at least mitigated and positive ones reinforced. The first chapter of this part examines considerations of the physical environment and the second chapter looks at sociocultural and economic factors.

During the 1960s and much of the 1970s, tourism was developed primarily based only on economic objectives, with limited regard in many areas for environmental and sociocultural impacts. Because of the negative impacts (much of which are still evident) resulting from that earlier development, concern in the 1980s focused on prevention and control of environmental and sociocultural impacts, along with achieving economic objectives. Fortunately, it is being realized that the two are intertwined, with long-term economic benefits being dependent, in large part, on sustained use of tourism resources. Although still being researched, much has been learned in recent years about prevention and control of impacts, and a reasonably sound basis is now available for planning of sustainable tourism development, but implementation is a continuing challenge.

12

Environmental Impacts

Relationship Between Tourism and the Environment

In its broadest definition, environment comprises all the natural and cultural surroundings of people. As used in this chapter, environment refers to the physical environment, which includes natural and built components. The natural environment is what exists in nature—climate and weather, the land and its soils and topography, geology, water features, flora, fauna, and ecological systems. The built environment is comprised of man-made physical features, mainly all types of buildings, other structures, and infrastructure development, as well as archaeological and historic sites. In comprehensive environmental impact analysis, sociocultural and economic factors of the environment are also considered and, in fact, it is often difficult and undesirable to try to separate the socioeconomic and physical components of the environment. However, separate examination of these components is usually made, as is done here, for the sake of organizational convenience.

The close relationship of tourism and the environment and the fact that this relationship is recognized by international agencies was emphasized in Chapter 2. The three aspects of the tourism-environment relationship are:

- Many features of the physical environment are attractions for tourists.
- Tourist facilities and infrastructure constitute one aspect of the built environment.
- Tourism development and tourist use of an area generate environmental impacts.

Exacerbating the potential problems of the environmental impacts of tourism is that it is often developed in environmentally fragile and vulnerable environments, such as on small islands, in coastal, marine, mountainous, and alpine areas, in certain arid lands, and at archaeological and historical sites, because these types of places offer important resources or attractions for tourists. The types and extent of environmental impact as well as socioeconomic impacts also relate closely to the type and intensity of tourism development that is undertaken. Early attention was drawn to the importance of considering the environmental impacts of tourism by various authors, including Dasman, Milton and Freeman (1973), Cohen (1978), Bosselman (1978), OECD (1980), Pigram (1980), and Travis (1982). In the 1980s, much more attention was directed to this subject.

An example of the recognition being given to the importance of environmental protection in sustained tourism development is in the Caribbean region, where tourism is a major and essential element of economic development. One of the goals of the Caribbean Tourism Organization (formerly Caribbean Tourism Research and Development Center) is to maximize the 'health' of the Caribbean environment. The organization's ideas on the Caribbean environment from a tourism perspective are summarized by Holder (1988, 119) as follows:

- The environment is tourism's resource. It is our environment, or rather the experience or enjoyment of it, that the tourism industry promotes and sells.
- A proper understanding of tourism and commitment to a lasting and healthy tourism is possibly the best method of ensuring the preservation of the Caribbean environment.
- Tourism is critical to the economic survival of the Caribbean.
- The long-term commitment to tourism required to ensure the careful planning necessary for minimizing negative environmental effects was absent in the early stages of Caribbean tourism development.
- It is necessary that we thoroughly assess the costs and benefits of tourism development in Caribbean states. Successful remedial action will however require a vastly changed attitude to tourism itself.
- Because of Caribbean economic realities and increasing dependency on tourism, the region has no option but to devise sophisticated systems of management, education, research and monitoring with respect to its environmental resources.

This book has emphasized the importance of applying the environmental approach to tourism planning (which is of course applicable to the planning for any type of development) that is aimed at preventing environmental problems from arising in the first place. This approach is obviously much preferable to that of trying to remedy problems after they arise, which can be an expensive and sometimes ineffective procedure. The environmental approach requires detailed research and understanding of environmental characteristics and use of various techniques and principles, as described in previous chapters. An essential technique is the establishment of carrying capacities, as described in Chapter 6. In the Caribbean example, Holder (1988) also points out the importance of tourism development not exceeding carrying capacities, especially in small island environments. However, as has been indicated, it is often difficult to determine the precise standards to be applied in carrying capacity analysis, thus making the application of this technique somewhat argumentative although still an essential one for establishing development level guidelines. Other approaches, such as applying integrated planning strategies where resource use is balanced among various sectors (of which one is

Hiking in the Swiss Alps—The natural environment offers many opportunities for participatory activities, of which hiking or trekking is one of the most popular. If carefully organized and controlled, hiking does not result in any substantial disruption to the natural environment and can be an interesting recreational and educational experience for touirists. (Courtesy of the Swiss National Tourist Office)

tourism), adopting policies to reduce extreme seasonality of tourism use, and carefully organizing and controlling visitor use of tourist attractions are also important to incorporate into the planning process, as has been emphasized in this book.

Even though the environmental planning approach is used, it is still essential that specific environmental assessment be made of tourism projects, as well as the environment in general, to ensure that no problems are being generated and that the environmental management of tourist facilities and resources is effective on a permanent basis. In order to competently apply the environmental approach and to assess environmental impacts, it is necessary to understand the specific types of impacts and various ways in which these can be prevented or lessened, as are described in this chapter.

There are three types of related environmental concerns in developing tourism. One is the prevention or control of environmental impacts generated by the tourism development itself, including tourist use of areas, and remedying problems if they do arise. The second related concern is the need for continuous management of the environmental resources for tourism, which was addressed in Chapter 10 on planning for tourist attractions. The third is maintenance and, where necessary, improvement of the overall environmental quality of the tourism areas for the benefit of both tourism and residents.

Types of Environmental Impacts

Tourism can generate either positive or negative environmental impacts, or no appreciable impacts, depending on how its development is planned and managed. The most commonly accepted types of impacts are reviewed in the following sections. There may be additional or more specific impacts in particular tourism development areas.

Positive Impacts

Tourism, if well planned and controlled, can help maintain and improve the environment in various ways.

Conservation of Important Natural Areas

As has been previously emphasized, tourism can help justify and pay for conservation of important natural areas and development of parks and reserves, including the establishment of national and regional parks because they are attractions for tourists. Without tourism, these natural areas might be developed for other uses or allowed to ecologically deteriorate, with a consequent loss of environmental heritage. This factor can be an especially important benefit in countries that have limited resources for nature conservation. In East Africa, for example, the great emphasis being placed on wildlife conservation that must include the animals' habitats is mostly justified from the countries' perspectives by the economic benefits derived from tourism for which wildlife is a major attraction. As pointed out by Burnett (1989, 254), ". . . recreation among Africans is strongly social . . . and places little emphasis on self-actualization and self-realization. Consequently, the kind of individualized achievement that Westerners associate with park recreation is little valued by Africans. The African approach to recreation considerably reduces any tendency to view national parks as recreation resources." Without tourism, there would be little justification from the local viewpoint for this type of conservation.

Marine conservation, especially of reef areas, is receiving much attention in some places because these are important attractions for tourism (Salm 1985) and furthermore protect beaches (also a major type of tourism resource) from erosion. As habitats for sea life, reefs are additionally important in maintaining certain types of fisheries. The damage and destruction of reef areas is becoming serious in some places, as has been referred to previously.

Conservation of Archaeological and Historic Sites and Architectural Character

Tourism provides the incentive and helps pay for the conservation of archaeological and historic sites (as attractions for tourists) that might otherwise be allowed to deteriorate or disappear, thus resulting in the loss of the cultural heritage of areas. The substantial amount of historic preservation taking place in Europe, North America, and elsewhere provides important tourist attractions, with tourism helping pay for this effort. In South and Southeast Asia, much of the archaeological and historic preservation taking place can be economically justified in these lower income countries because they provide attractions for tourists, and in some cases, such as Sri Lanka, admission fees paid by tourists are used directly for archaeological research and conservation.

Improvement of Environmental Quality

Tourism can help provide the incentive for 'cleaning up' the overall environment through control of air, water, and noise pollution, littering, and other environmental problems, and for improving environmental aesthetics through landscaping programs, appropriate building design, sign controls, and better building maintenance. In the Mediterranean region, there is much justifiable concern being expressed about the pollution of the Mediterranean Sea because it is affecting tourism and recreational use of the region, and programs are being commenced to control pollution sources of this water body.

Enhancement of the Environment

Although a more subjective benefit, development of well-designed tourist facilities (for example, attractive, landscaped hotels) may enhance rural or urban landscapes that are otherwise dull and uninteresting.

Improvement of Infrastructure

An economic as well as environmental benefit, local infrastructure of airports, roads, water, sewage, and solid waste disposal systems and telecommunications can be improved through the development of tourism, which uses and helps pay for the infrastructure, thus leading to an overall reduction of pollution problems and an enhancement of the environmental quality of areas. Water resource management may also be improved through development of tourism because of its demands for additional water supplies.

Increasing Environmental Awareness

In places where residents have limited interest in and concern about the natural environment and its conservation, observing tourists' interest in nature and realizing the importance of conservation to the economic success of tourism can encourage local awareness in this subject.

Negative Impacts

The various types of negative or undesirable environmental impacts that can be generated by tourism development if it is not carefully planned, developed, and managed include those listed below. Not all these impacts would likely take place in one area because the types of impacts often depend on the kind of tourism development and the specific environmental characteristics of the tourism area. The scale of tourism development in relation to the carrying capacity of the environment greatly influences the extent of environmental impact. Many of the types of impacts considered here can result from various types of development, and most are not unique to tourism.

Water Pollution

If a proper sewage disposal system has not been installed for hotels, resorts, and other tourist facilities, there may be pollution of ground water from the sewage, or if a sewage outfall has been constructed into a nearby river, lake, or coastal sea water and the sewage has not been adequately treated, the effluent will pollute that water area. This is not an uncommon situation in beach resort areas where the hotel has constructed an outfall into the adjacent water area that may also be used by tourists for swimming. Surface water pollution in rivers, lakes, and sea waters can also result from recreational and tourist transportation motor boats spilling oil and gas and cleaning their bilges into the water, especially in enclosed harbors and places where natural water circulation is slow.

Air Pollution

Tourism is generally considered a 'clean industry,' but air pollution from tourism development can result from excessive use of internal combustion vehicles (cars, buses, and motorcycles) used by and for tourists in particular areas, especially at major tourist attraction sites that are accessible only by road. Often compounding this problem are improperly maintained exhaust systems of the vehicles. Also, pollution in the form of dust and dirt in the air may be generated from open, devegetated areas if the tourism development is not properly planned, developed, and landscaped or is in an interim state of construction.

Noise Pollution

Noise generated by a concentration of tourists, tourist road and off-road RVs such as dune buggies and snowmobiles, airplanes, motor boats, and sometimes certain types of tourist attractions such as amusement parks or car/motorcycle race tracks may reach uncomfortable and irritating levels for nearby residents and other tourists. Very loud noise can result in ear damage and psychological stress.

Visual Pollution

Visual pollution may result from several sources:
- Poorly-designed hotels and other tourist facility buildings that are not compatible with the local architectural style and scale or well integrated into the natural environment;
- Use of unsuitable building materials on external surfaces;
- Badly planned layout of tourist facilities;
- Inadequate or inappropriate landscaping;
- Use of large and ugly advertising signs;
- Overhead utility (electric and telephone) lines and poles;
- Obstruction of scenic views by development; and
- Poor maintenance of buildings and landscaping.
  As indicated below, littering of the landscape also results in visual pollution.

Waste Disposal Problems

Littering of debris on the landscape is a common problem in tourism areas because of the large number of people using the area and the kinds of activities, such as picnicking, that they engage in. Improper disposal of solid waste from hotels, restaurants, and resorts can generate both litter and environmental health problems from vermin, disease, and pollution as well as being unattractive.

Ecological Disruption

Several types of ecological problems can result from uncontrolled tourism development and use. Overuse of fragile natural environments by tourists can lead to ecological damage (for example, killing or stunting the growth of vegetation in parks and conservation areas by many tourists walking through them and compacting the soil around the vegetation, trees being cut by hikers and campers for use as fuel to make campfires, and erosion resulting from overuse of hiking and riding trails in steep-sloped areas). For example, Edwards (1987) records the damaging effect on the local plant community resulting from the trampling of horses used for recreational horse riding in certain coastal areas of England and Wales. Deforestation of ski slopes may lead to erosion, landslides, and avalanches. Animal behavioral patterns can be disturbed by uncontrolled photography and feeding of them, and their habitats can be disrupted or reduced by excessive encroachment of tourism development into them. Also, road development may interfere with normal animal migration patterns. Cave ecologies may be changed by excessive visiting of tourists and use of lighting systems, which leads to increased temperatures, and can be damaged by tourist breaking and collecting pieces of cave formations. Fragile desert ecosystems in the Southwestern USA are being disturbed by use of off-road RVs. Snowmobiles can disrupt animals' winter season behavioral patterns.

The coastal and marine environment is particularly vulnerable to overuse and unsuitable development. Excessive collection or, for endangered species, any collection of live sea shells, coral, turtle shells, and other such items by tourists, or by local persons for sale to tourists as souvenirs, can deplete those species. Breaking of coral by boat and ship anchors has become a major problem in some areas, and killing of coral by sedimentation and pollutants resulting from onshore development, whether by tourism-related or general development, has become a problem in such places as Florida. Inappropriate design and location of groins, piers, and similar structures into the coastal waters may change local beach formation processes, leading to erosion and deposition. Uncontrolled filling of mangrove swamps by development destroys an important habitat for sea life and disturbs natural water circulation patterns. Excessive use of or development on sand dunes can lead to their erosion and loss of dune wildlife habitat. Uncontrolled viewing by tourists can disrupt turtle nesting activities on beaches.

Environmental Hazards

Poor land use planning, siting, and engineering design of tourist facilities, as well as any type of development, can generate erosion, landslides, flooding, and other problems. For example, there is increasing alarm in the Alpine regions of Europe that deforestation programs, largely undertaken to service winter sports tourism, are a major cause of mud slides, floods, and avalanches. In one instance, a series of mud slides and floods in North and South Tyrol during three weeks in July 1987, left more than 60 persons dead, 7,000 homeless, and 50 towns, villages, and holiday centers wrecked (Romeril 1989). As was experienced in the Tyrolian region, poor design and environmental disruption may result in the destruction of or damage to tourist facilities themselves by earthquakes, high winds, flooding, land slippage, and avalanches. There are examples in the Pacific Islands of hotels that were built too close to the shoreline and are being undermined by erosion or have been damaged by high waves during storms. In some cases, good planning may not prevent damage by environmental disasters but may greatly reduce the extent of it.

Damage to Archaeological and Historic Sites

Overuse or misuse of environmentally fragile archaeological and historic sites can lead to the damage of these features through excessive wear, increased humidity, vibration, vandalism, graffiti writing, and so forth, of which examples were given in Chapter 10.

Land Use Problems

If not well developed according to sound land use planning principles, tourism development can result in land use problems. Tourist facilities may preempt land that is more valuable for other types of land uses, such as agriculture and parks, or that should remain under strict conservation control. Facilities may take the form of 'ribbon' or linear commercial development, which is inefficient to serve with infrastructure, generates dangerous traffic conditions, and can be visually ugly. Vacation home development can lead to problems of urban sprawl. Hotels may be constructed too close to beaches or other attraction features, thus detracting from those features. Without integrated land use and infrastructure planning, the infrastructure may become overloaded, leading to traffic congestion and insufficient water supply and sewage disposal systems.

Environmental Quality

Maintaining a high level of overall environmental quality is important for the success of most types of tourism areas. As previously referred to, tourists are becoming increasingly sophisticated and demanding in their requirements for a high level of quality in their touring and destination environments, and will often pay a premium to experience an attractive, clean, and pollution-free environment (realizing that some outstanding attraction features in any type of environmental setting will attract tourists). A high level of environmental quality is, of course, just as important for residents living in the area as it is for tourists visiting it. Consideration of overall environmental quality includes not only control of the environmental impacts from tourism development but also minimizing all types of environmental problems in tourism areas. Therefore, as emphasized in Chapter 3, the environmental quality of tourism areas should be evaluated according to the factors listed in that chapter as part of the initial surveys of the tourism area. That survey will have indicated any environmental quality problems that should be addressed in the tourism plan, with recommendations made to mitigate existing problems and prevent future ones through the application of the environmental policies and impact control measures described in the next section. Many of these apply to general as well as tourism development.

Environmental Policies and Impact Control Measures

There are various environmental policies and more specific impact control measures that can be applied to achieve environmentally integrated tourism development that does not generate negative environmental impacts but reinforces positive ones and, where needed, improves the overall environmental quality of tourism areas. Many of these have been referred to previously as part of the environmental planning process but are repeated here to form a comprehensive summary.

Environmental Policies

Some general environmentally-related policies have wide application in the planning of tourism, although they are not necessarily applicable to all areas. A basic policy and theme of the approach used in this book is developing tourism in a carefully planned and controlled manner, not exceeding carrying capacities, and, where warranted, establishing an absolute upper limit on development, such as has been done in Bhutan and the Seychelles, at least for certain time periods. Another basic approach is to use tourism as a technique for environmental conservation and maintenance of overall environmental quality, often through environmental resource-based types of tourism development. Also important, especially in newly developing tourism areas, is to maintain a moderate rate of tourism growth in order to allow sufficient time to properly plan and develop the area and to monitor and control environmental impacts. As will be emphasized in the next chapter, a moderate rate of growth also gives residents time to adapt to and learn how to participate in tourism development.

A physical planning technique that has been emphasized is to concentrate tourist facilities in certain areas, often in the form of integrated resorts, in order to allow for the efficient provision of infrastructure (thus reducing the possibility of pollution), provide the opportunity for integrated land use planning and application of development controls, and contain any negative environmental as well as sociocultural impacts that might arise. The concentration approach is especially applicable in larger-scale mass tourism areas. Within the framework of the concept of facility concentration, staging of development is important for efficient provision of infrastructure, and so that when one area or tourist attraction feature starts to become saturated, new areas can be developed. This approach also helps to to better distribute tourist use throughout the country or region and not overload one or a few places.

In many cases, saturation levels and overloading of the environment and infrastructure occurs only during seasonal peak tourist use periods. As was explained in Chapter 9, various techniques should be applied to reduce seasonality to the greatest extent possible, both at the national or regional levels, through applying strategies of developing seasonally different types of tourism throughout the year, and (at specific places) through offering a variety of tourist activities taking place at different seasons, seasonal discounts, off-season marketing programs, staggering of domestic tourist vacation periods, and other approaches. Through highly controlled development, such as establishing a maximum number of accommodation rooms, even peak season use need not exceed saturation levels. Selective marketing techniques can also be used to attract environmentally-oriented tourists who respect the environment and are conservation-minded in using it.

If larger-scale tourism is expected to generate environmental (or sociocultural) problems, consideration should be given to other forms of tourism development, such as 'quality,' special interest, adventure or 'alternative' tourism. Quality tourism implies highly controlled development and selective marketing, attracting affluent tourists with high expenditure patterns so that economic benefits are generated without a large number of tourists visiting the areas. Special interest and adventure forms of tourism typically require limited facility development and are based on the inherent resources of areas. They are selectively marketed and attract tourists who have particular interests in and respect for these resources. Types of alternative tourism such as village, farm or rural, and ecotourism, if well planned and controlled, involve limited numbers of tourists and facility development, which result in little environmental impact. Water-based tourism (cruise ship, river boat, and yachting travel) also has limited environmental impacts if properly controlled.

In order to protect fragile archaeological and historic sites from excessive visitor use, the concept of modelling (that is, building a replica of the feature for visitors to appreciate and preserving the original feature for scientific use only) can be applied, as explained in Chapter 10. For example, the Viking settlement at L'Anse aux Meadows in northern Newfoundland could have been destroyed by tourists walking through the archaeological pits if a reconstructed village that includes an interpretive center about the Viking activities in North America had not been developed for tourists to visit, with public access to the original site prohibited (Smith 1989).

Environmental Impact Control Measures

Specific environmental impact control measures that are applied during the planning process to prevent environmental problems or that can be applied as remedial techniques to lessen or eliminate existing problems and are also important in maintaining or improving overall environmental quality are listed below:

- Installation of water supply and sewage disposal systems for hotels and other tourist facilities that meet local standards, if they are of sufficiently high level, or internationally accepted standards in order to prevent pollution problems. These systems should utilize conservation techniques where feasible.
- Development of electric power systems that, in addition to providing adequate and reliable power, utilize conservation techniques.
- Use of proper solid waste disposal techniques with recycling of waste products to the greatest extent feasible.

- Construction of adequate drainage systems to prevent flooding during rainy periods and standing water that may cause health problems.
- Development of adequate road and other transportation systems in order to prevent traffic congestion, and maximizing use of mass transit and pedestrian systems.
- Provision of open space and parks and generous use of suitable landscaping on hotel and resorts sites, at tourist attraction features, in urban areas, and along shorelines, roads, and walkways.
- Application of land use zoning regulations with suitable development standards and good site planning principles in tourism areas, including standards such as adequate setback of buildings from shorelines, attraction features, and roads, and maximum densities and building heights. Recreational use zoning must also be applied to water areas.
- Careful management of visitor flows and, where necessary, application of visitor use controls at natural and cultural tourist attractions to avoid congestion and environmental deterioration of these places.
- Application of suitable architectural design standards and use of building materials for all structures in tourism areas so that they are architecturally and environmentally compatible, and make use of energy conservation design techniques.
- Prevention of linear commercial development along roads and shorelines through effective land use planning and zoning.
- Application of appropriate design standards to and control of the location and size of signs, with information (not advertising) signs allowed.
- Requirement for undergrounding of utility lines in tourism areas and careful siting and landscape screening of utility stations.
- Control of littering through tourist and general public education and placement of litter receptacles. Legal prohibition of littering is commonly enacted, with fines imposed on litterers.
- Proper maintenance of tourist vehicles (buses, taxis, rental cars, boats, etc.) so that they do not generate an undue amount of air and noise pollution, and use of nonpolluting vehicles, such as electric carts or shuttle buses in resorts.
- Establishment of controls on ship bilge cleaning operations and dumping of garbage and litter into any water areas.
- Control or prohibition on use of motorized boats in environmentally sensitive water areas in order to prevent water and noise pollution.
- Establishment of controls on:
  1. Collection of live sea shells, coral, turtle shells, and ornamental fish by tourists and by local persons for sale to tourists as souvenirs;
  2. Spear fishing;
  3. Mining of beach sand and coral formations for construction purposes;
  4. Use of boat anchors in coral-bottom bays and harbors;
  5. Collection of scarce species of plants and animals by tourists or for sale to tourists;
  6. Cutting of trees for use as firewood in camping and trekking areas; and
  7. Feeding of wild animals.

8. Any other tourist use controls necessary to prevent environmental problems in tourism areas should be applied.

- Requirement for proper design of boat piers and marinas so that they do not lead to erosion or other problems.
- Organization of proper building, park, and landscaping maintenance programs for public areas, and encouragement of good maintenance in private development.
- Maintenance of environmental health and safety standards for both residents and tourists, especially to control environmentally-derived diseases and high accident rates resulting from traffic congestion, fires, and other hazards.
- Proper site planning, design, and engineering of hotels and other tourist facilities to minimize damage from environmental hazards such as earthquakes, tsunamis, high winds, high rainfall and flooding, land erosion, and landslides.

With respect to visitor use controls that inevitably must be established, it important to inform tourists not only about the controls but also about why they exist so that tourists understand the reasons for controls. A useful if sometimes unpleasant technique is to show tourists illustrations of what has happened in places where use controls were not applied. Residents also must often be informed about environmental management so that they will appreciate the reasons for controls being established.

On some tourism development sites, tourist facility development will unavoidably disrupt the natural ecosystem balance. It may be decided that this is justified in order to implement the development for other reasons. In such situations, the plan should recommend ways to establish a new ecological balance and stability in order to prevent future environmental problems resulting from the development.

Despite the best planning and controls, some environmental problems may arise. Continuous monitoring of environmental impacts must be maintained, with any necessary remedial measures taken. Even with the accumulation of considerable understanding about environmental impacts, it is very difficult for a development and management plan to anticipate all the types or extent of impacts that may occur.

Environmental Impact Assessment

Many countries and regions have adopted environmental protection legislation, and the Environmental Impact Assessment (EIA) procedure is being increasingly applied throughout the world to all types of development, including tourism projects, to ensure that any negative environmental impacts are analyzed and minimized. Even though a sound environmental planning approach has been applied to prepare the tourism project plan, the EIA is still important to make certain that no serious impacts will result from the development.

Club Mediterranée Resort in the Republic of Maldives—Each of the more than 60 resorts in the Maldives occupies an entire island, with strict design and environmental controls applied so that environmental degradation is minimized and the islands retain most of their natural appearance.

EIA Approach

With the increasing concern about the environmental impacts of development, the EIA procedure has been formulated to assess the impacts of proposed development projects, including tourism projects. EIAs are designed to follow a particular format and are required to be submitted to the government for its review as part of the project approval procedure. The precise format of EIAs will vary from one place to another, but typically it includes social and economic factors, as well as impacts on the physical environment. The EIA procedure is a very useful technique to ensure that environmental impacts of proposed projects have been taken into consideration and preventive actions taken, and provides the basis for making any necessary adjustments to the plans. Also, if developers know that an EIA must be made, they are more likely to use the environmental planning approach to avoid having to later modify their plans.

For countries and regions that do not have the legal machinery requiring formal EIA procedures, the tourism or planning office can establish its own checklist for assessing proposed tourism projects and undertake the assessment themselves in conjunction with the capabilities available in other relevant government agencies. In the absence of EIA legislation, every attempt should still be made by the government tourism and planning offices to evaluate impacts of proposed projects.

The approach to evaluation of environmental as well as sociocultural impacts being widely utilized now is to view them as costs and benefits, even though they are more difficult to quantify than economic costs and benefits. An evaluation can then be made of the total economic, environmental, and sociocultural costs and benefits of tourism plans and projects to arrive at a meaning-ful total assessment.

EIA Model

A basic model for environmental impact assessment is presented here to provide a guideline, but each area should adapt this to its particular requirements. This model does not include economic and sociocultural factors, reviewed in the next chapter, which can be added for a comprehensive assessment. First, an environmental impact checklist is prepared, such as follows:

- Air pollution;
- Surface water pollution, including rivers, streams, lakes, ponds, and coastal waters;
- Ground water pollution;
- Pollution of domestic water supply;
- Noise pollution, in general and at peak periods;
- Solid waste disposal problems;
- Water drainage and flooding problems;
- Damage or destruction of flora and fauna;
- Ecological disruption and damage, including both land and water areas, wet-lands, and plant and animal habitats in general;
- Land use and circulation problems within the project area;
- Land use and circulation problems generated by the project in nearby areas;
- Pedestrian and vehicular congestion in general and at peak periods;
- Landscape aesthetic problems (building design, landscaping, signs, etc.);
- Environmental health problems, such as malaria and cholera;
- Damage to historic, archaeological, and other cultural sites;
- Damage to specific important and attractive environmental features, such as large trees, hilltops, and unusual geological formations;
- Generation of erosion, landslides, and similar problems; and
- Likelihood of damage to the project from natural environmental hazards, such as earthquakes, volcanic eruptions, hurricanes.

Each factor is then evaluated in terms of possible types and extent of impact. A useful technique is to prepare an evaluation matrix, such as the one shown in Figure 12.1, which summarizes and synthesizes the impacts so that a com-prehensive evaluation can be made of all the factors. Definition of each level of impact (for example, none, minor, moderate, and serious) will need to be made so that the evaluation is systematic. For some factors, such as air and water pollu-tion, quantitative data may be available. For other factors, such as landscape aes-thetics, qualitative evaluation must be made. This same matrix technique can be used for evaluating the overall environmental quality of tourism areas.

354

Type of Impact	Evaluation of Impact				
	No Impact	Minor Impact	Moderate Impact	Serious Impact	Comments
Air Quality					
Surface Water Quality					
Groundwater Quality					
Road Traffic					
Noise Levels					
Solid Waste Disposal System					
Archaeological & Historic Sites					
Visual Amenity					
Natural Vegetation					
Wild Animal Life -Ground Animals -Birds & Insects					

Note:
This list of types of impacts is only a sampling. There may be additional or different factors in an actual environmental analysis.

Figure 12.1. Sample Evaluation Matrix for Environmental Impact.

Case Studies

Two case studies are presented on applying environmental impact controls and assessment. The Rim Village plan for Crater Lake National Park in the western USA reflects an environmental planning approach to redeveloping an existing badly developed visitor facility area and includes a systematic environmental impact assessment. Tourism development in the Maldives in the Indian Ocean represents a sound environmental approach applied at both the national/regional and resort planning levels to control the negative impacts of tourism development in a small island and marine environment.

The Crater Lake National Park Rim Village Development Plan

This study is an example of an enviornmental plan and assessment prepared for a visitor facility area that is intended to remedy an existing environmentally undesirable development in a national park setting. Located in the state of Oregon in the western USA, Crater Lake National Park has been long established as a poplular destination for visitors. Except for campground areas, most of the visitor facilities are situated near the lake crater's edge in an area called the Rim Village. Many of the Rim Village facilities had been developed between 1910 and 1925, but there was no coherent organization to the village layout, and negative impacts from vehicles and pedestrians became substantial. Although somewhat improved in the 1930s, increasing visitation led to the expansion of parking areas and day use buildings and conversion of the campground to a picnic area. By 1984, there were over 30 separate structures, many of them beyond economic repair, and a network of walkways and extensive parking in the village near the crater rim. On peak days, 1,000 to 1,500 vehicles move through the village, and pedestrians at the crater rim are greatly disturbed by the view, sound, and smell of vehicular traffic. Park facilities are limited, scattered, and not appropriately designed for their functions. The historic 80-room Crater Lake Lodge, open during the summer, does not meet present-day standards and requires removal or rehabilitation.

The general management plan prepared for the park in 1977 contained proposals for improvement of the park environment and visitor services but left the question of accomodation in the park open to the future decision. In 1984, public meetings were held on a draft concept plan and environmental assessment for the redevelopment of the Mazama campground/Rim Village corridor, with various alternatives presented. These were accepted except for the concern expressed about preservation of the historic lodge, which was to be restudied for its possible rehabilitation and feasibility of year-round use. Most elements of the 1984 plan were approved, including restoration of a pedestrian environment in the village by relocating the linear parking area, development of an interpretive center, and connection of the Rim Village facilities to the Munson Valley sewage treatment plant.

In 1987, new alternatives were presented for public comment, all of which included the basic concept of the Rim Village remaining as the focal point for overnight lodging, day use visitor facilities, and interpretation. A major objective of all alternatives was the restoration of the rim area to a more natural, leisurely, pedestrian-oriented environment, but various alternatives were considered for accommodation. At the public hearings, it was clear that the public consensus was for the present lodge to be preserved and used for lodging and that there should be year-round availability of accommodation and improved food services. The sentiment was that Crater Lake should play a stronger role in tourism in the area through providing year-round lodging while preserving the existing lodge's historic qualities.

Figure 12.2 shows the development concept plan for the Rim Village (National Park Service 1988). Most development along the rim edge will be relocated, with congestion and vehicular traffic adjacent to the rim reduced. The rim area will become a more natural setting for summer and winter visitors. The key element in the development concept is relocation of the parking areas away from the rim. The entire area of the rim now occupied by parking areas will be returned to pedestrian use or be restored to more natutal conditions. The redevelopment of the rim walkways and landscape rehabilitation will be based on a study of the historic landscape of the 1930s, re-creating the leisurely environment of that era. The landscape will be designed to handle large numbers of people with meandering walkways, seating, and gathering areas.

The existing scattered structures will be removed and visitor facilities will be concentrated in a new activity center as an integrated complex incorporating interpretation functions, day use visitor and dining facilities, and 60 guest rooms designed for year-round use, and will be located in an already disturbed area. Architectural quidelines for this center are based on an historical rustic theme already established elsewhere in the park, including the use of native materials, complementary color schemes, suitable scale, and siting that harmonize with the natural environment. Public rooms will incorporate regional arts and crafts and rustic detailing. The design intent is to create a new facility that in time will become as much of a park landmark as the nearby historic lodge is perceived to be. As shown in the plan drawing, the historic Crater lake Lodge will be fully rehabilitated for continued use as a summer lodge and dining faclilty. A new access road will facilitate removal of existing lodge traffic from the rim area.

An environmental impact assessment was prepared for the proposed plan with the conclusion that the redevelopment will not have a significant effect on the environment. The major types of impacts evaluated are summarized with respect to the village rim area as follows:

- Crater Lake ecosystem—Protection of Crater Lake will be enhanced with the reduced potential of pollutants from wastewater, automobiles, and snow plowing entering the lake ecosystem.
- Natural environment—The developed area will be reduced from 32 to 12 acres, allowing for the restoration of about 20 acres to more natural conditions, although localized impacts from occasional visitor use will continue in these restored areas. Redesign of the village will concentrate most use in areas de-

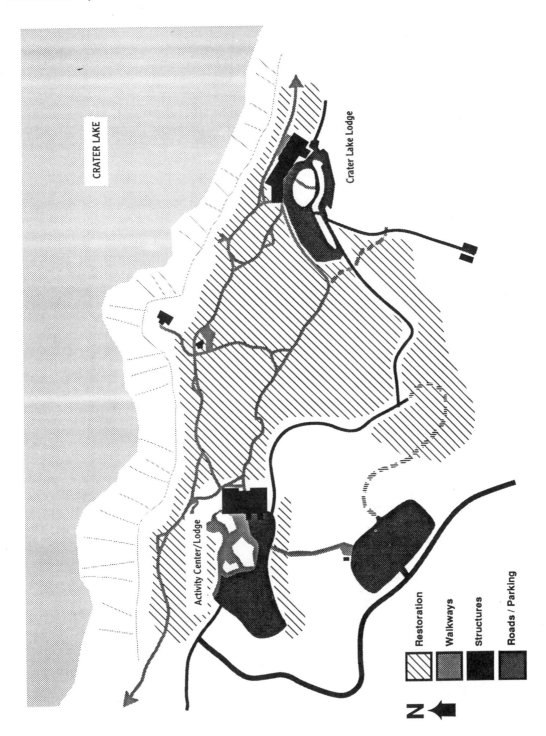

Figure 12.2. Crater Lake National Park Development Concept Plan—Rim Village.

signed to handle heavy use. Development will be mostly in currently or previously disturbed areas, requiring little disturbance of existing vegetation, although new and improved access roads may require the removal of some mature mountain hemlocks. The plan will not affect any known endangered or threatened species, nor will water sources and wetlands be adversely affected. The development is not located within the 100-year or 500-year floodplain. Restoring 20 acres to more natural conditions will provide some additional wildlife habitat. The expansion of accommodation and employees will increase water consumption and sewage treatment requirements, but water supplies are adequate and the existing sewage treatment facilities in Munson Valley were originally designed for future expansion. Air quality will improve in the Rim Village with the reduction of vehicle movement by eliminating 6,000 feet of roads and parking strips and developing central parking areas.

- Cultural environment—The rehabilitation of Crater Lake Lodge and its continued use for lodging will have a long-term beneficial effect in maintaining that historic building. The removal or relocation of an historic comfort station will be decided before implementation of the plan. No impact will occur to known archaeological resources, and a site-specific archaeological survey will be conducted and clearance obtained prior to any construction.
- Socioeconomic environment—The regional and local economy and state tourism will benefit from the plan. There will be no closure of visitor services during the plan implementation. Construction activities will benefit the local economy over the short term. Upon completion, the year-round operation and increased lodging capacity will benefit the regional and local economy through increased employment, sales tax revenues, and expenditures by the concessioner for supplies and services.

Public hearings were held on the development plan and environmental impact assessment and written comments accepted, with strong support for the plan as shown. On the basis of the environmental assessment and the public and agency comments, the National Park Service determined that this proposal is not one that requires a formal environmental impact statement. Preliminary cost estimates and phasing were prepared for plan implementation, which is expected to take place during the 1990s decade and beyond.

Tourism in the Maldives

The Republic of Maldives represents one of the most successful examples of planning and developing environmentally controlled and regionally staged small-island tourism in the world. Located south of India in the Indian Ocean and spread over a north-south distance of about 800 kilometers, the Maldives archipelago is comprised of 26 atolls containing approximately 1,190 low-lying islands, of which some 200 are inhabited. The total population of the country is slightly less than 200,000, with about 50,000 living in the capital city of Male. The country is Islamic, and religious values and customs are strictly maintained. With very limited natural resources and a somewhat isolated location, the economy is based primarily on fisheries, in recent years on tourism, and to a lesser extent on shipping operations.

The primary tourist attractions of these islands are the warm, sunny climate, scenic island beauty, and activities related to the extensive beach and marine environment. Snorkeling and scuba diving is especially popular and well developed. Tourism commenced in 1972, when two resorts were opened and 1,092 tourists visited the islands, and has grown rapidly since then to reach 158,500 arrivals in 1989 (Republic of Maldives Ministry of Tourism 1989). The primary tourist markets are Western European countries, especially the Federal Republic of Germany, Italy, and the United Kingdom. Japan is also becoming an important market country. In 1989, the average length of stay of tourists was 9.2 days. There is considerable seasonality of tourism, with the high arrival period taking place from December to March and the low period being May and June. International tourism receipts have exceeded payments received for all other exports during the 1980s and was more than U.S. $60 million in 1988. However, there is also a high import content of goods used in tourism and net foreign exchange earned is less than that figure (Sathiendrakumar and Tisdell 1989). In 1988, tourism contributed 17.4 percent to the gross national product. At the end of 1989, there was a capacity of 7,720 tourist beds in about 60 resorts and hotels.

The physical configuration of tourism is a highly unusual one in the Maldives. The resorts, which vary in size from 6 to more than 150 rooms, each occupy a separate island and are totally self-contained. These resort islands are accessible only by boat from the international airport (also on its own island) and Male which totally occupies another island. Most of the resorts have, by policy, been located on uninhabited islands, in order to reduce any possible sociocultural impacts. Each resort must provide its own infrastructure of electric power, water supply, sewage and solid waste disposal, and other services, and also housing and community services for its employees. The families of the employees remain on their home islands, often some distance away. Most of the resorts are developed in Kaafu (Male) Atoll where the capital city and international airport are situated, with a lesser number located on nearby Alifu (Ari) Atoll. There are a few resorts on other atolls, including one on Seenu (Addu) Atoll in the far south where there is a large former military airport.

The Department of Tourism (now a ministry) was organized in 1978 and, during the 1980s, has been very active in guiding the growth of tourism and applying strict development and operating standards on new and existing resorts. This ministry has the power to close substandard resorts if, after imposing fines, operating standards have not been improved. One of its important functions is to formulate and implement environmental protection policies and regulations. The coral island and reef ecosystem is extremely fragile, and the government recognizes that both fishing and tourism are dependent upon its preservation. The ministry also coordinates closely with the private tourism sector and regularly holds meetings with the resort owners and managers, tour operators, and specialists such as the diving instructors.

A long-range tourism development plan was prepared for the Maldives in

1983 (Dangroup International 1983) and some but not all of its recommendations were considered feasible for implementation. The present government policy is to continue expanding tourism for its economic benefits, but in a systematic manner of staged development from Kaafu Atoll and with strict environmental controls applied. Because Kaafu Atoll is reaching its saturation level of development, including one of the resort islands being taken over by the government for the urban expansion of Male, the policy is for major new tourism development to take place in Alifu Atoll. Several islands there have been designated for resort use. During this development stage, no new resorts will be allowed elsewhere in the country except perhaps for some expansion in Addu Atoll, if needed, because of its accessibility to the existing airport there. The long-range plan identified other tourism zones and service centers for future development in the country.

In 1988, the government approved plans for 16 new resorts in Alifu Atoll. Some of these were constructed and opened by 1990. These resorts are still within reasonable travel time by fast boat from the international airport. The feasibility of establishing hydrofoil and seaplane service is also being investigated with experimental operations underway in 1990. Additionally, the government policy is to encourage upgrading of existing resorts to higher standards, including environmental standards where needed in order to maintain the viability and competitiveness of these resorts and, in certain cases, aim for a somewhat higher quality level of tourist markets. Some of this upgrading was accomplished in the late 1980s.

As a basis for deciding the number of rooms and resort facility development allowed on each resort island, the government has established carrying capacity standards based on several factors (Republic of Maldives Ministry of Tourism no date):

- Control of tree cutting so that the natural appearance and facade of the island is maintained, with no building height allowed to appear above the tree tops;
- The maximum area to be utilized by buildings is 20 percent, with two-story buildings allowed to conserve land area if there is sufficient vegetation to conceal these buildings from view, and with equal space left free on the island for every building developed on the lagoon; and
- In order to preserve the tourists' perception or image of the beach orientation of tourism in the Maldives, all guest rooms should be facing the beach, with a minimum of five meters of linear beach available in front of each room, and 68 percent of the total length of beach on the island shall be utilized for guest room frontage, 20 percent for general resort facility frontage, and the remaining 12 percent left as open space.

The exact capacity of each resort island will be decided after reviewing the proposed resort layout and determining how well the plan meets the above guidelines and fits into the overall environment. All the islands designated for resort development are owned by the government. The resort developer receives a long-term lease for the development, paying an annual land rent that is calculated individually for each island.

For environmental protection, the government applies various measures, including:

- Architectural control of resort buildings so that they are well integrated into the island environment, take advantage of the tropical climate and use local building materials, such as thatch roofs, to the greatest extent possible. However, the use of coral stone for building is now strictly controlled to prevent environmental damage to the coral reefs.

- Controls on the heights of buildings (no more than two stories), setbacks of buildings from the shoreline (minimum of five meters), and suitable landscaping to complement the natural vegetation that, as mentioned, must be preserved.
- Design of boat piers (which are necessary for access to the resorts) in such a manner (on pilings with free flow of water under the piers) that they do not result in beach erosion or deposition.
- Requirement for adequate potable water supply, usually a combination of restricted use of the limited groundwater, roof catchment, and desalination.
- Requirement for proper sewage disposal systems that do not pollute the groundwater or adjacent ocean and lagoon waters.
- Requirement for proper solid waste disposal systems, utilizing controlled incineration, compaction, and disposal in deep water areas. Empty cans must be compressed and plastic materials cannot be thrown into the sea.
- Encouragement given to undergrounding utility lines, with installation of overhead lines discouraged.
- Application of controls on collection of coral, seashells, and certain types of fish, with no live coral collection or spear fishing allowed.

There are plans to establish marine conservation areas where controls would be even more stringent.

In order to respect the local Islamic codes and customs, nude bathing is prohibited, with fines imposed on both the bather and resort management if this regulation is violated, and the locally accepted dress code must be observed by tourists when they visit Male or the island villages. Gratifyingly, these regulations have been respected by tourists, with very few exceptions. Maldivian resort employees are not allowed to handle alcoholic beverages in the resorts (most bartenders are from Sri Lanka) and Maldivian visitors to the resorts are prohibited from entering the bars or other places where liquor is sold, except for business purposes. Importation of pork is controlled and may only be imported by permit to be consumed in the resorts, with any pork dishes served so labeled. Boat cruises for tourists can only be conducted in designated atolls where tourist facilities are available. However, tour groups are taken to certain traditional villages for sight-seeing and to purchase local handicrafts made in those villages.

To ensure that Maldivians and especially the urban residents in Male have sufficient recreation facilities, an island in the Kaafu Atoll near Male has been designated and developed as a recreation park and is popular with Maldivians. A similar island park is planned for Alifu Atoll for the residents there. The land area of these island parks is limited, and therefore they can be visited by tourists only on days when there is little demand for use by residents. Preference is given to Maldivians for employment in resorts, and work permits for expatriate employees are allowed only for bartenders and others who have special skills not available locally.

Because most fruits and vegetable must be imported for resort use, one resort has taken the initiative in developing a hydroponic farm, which has been economically successful in supplementing the supply of certain imported vegetables. A chicken farm has been established to provide some locally produced poultry, and the locally caught fish and other sea food are used extensively in the tourists' menus. Beef and pork must be imported.

The Ministry of Tourism has implemented a public education program to educate Maldivians about tourism, emphasizing the economic importance of this sector and raising the environmental conscience of those involved in tourism. This program is conducted in the public school system and on the radio, the islands' primary communications medium, although local television is also available. Traditionally not attuned to structured regular employment, more Maldivians are being attracted to work in tourism, a policy considered essential by the government to reduce the traditionally high unemployment factor, increase income levels, and decrease the amount of foreign employment. For the safety of tourists engaged in marine sports, the government applies strict safety controls on such activities as wind surfing and diving, including requiring that resorts employ internationally qualified diving instructors.

Training persons to work in tourism is being emphasized, and a hotel and catering training school, assisted by the United Nations Development Programme, World Tourism Organization, and European Economic Community, was opened in Male in 1987 and is successfully operating, with plans for expansion. Also, several of the government tourism staff have taken internationally sponsored tourism-related overseas training courses and university programs, including on the topics of tourism planning and the environmental aspects of developing tourism.

With respect to the future of tourism, the government wishes to continue monitoring the environmental impacts to ensure that there are no problems. An important consideration in deciding on future expansion of this sector will be the availability of sufficient labor supply (with this country's relatively small population) to work in tourism as well as maintain sufficient manpower for the proper functioning of other economic activities, especially fisheries.

References

Burnett, G. Wesley and Richard Conover. 1989. "The Efficacy of Africa's National Parks: An Evaluation of Julius Nyere's Arusha Manifesto of 1961." *Society and Natural Resources.* Vol 2: 251–260.

Bosselman, Fred P. ed. 1978. *In the Wake of the Tourist: Managing Special Places in Eight Countries.* Washington, DC: The Conservation Foundation.

Cohen, Eric. 1978. "Impact of Tourism on the Physical Environment." *Annals of Tourism Research.* 5(2): 215–237.

Dangroup International. 1983. *Tourism Development—Republic of Maldives.* Copenhagen.

Dasman, Raymond F., John P. Milton and Peter H. Freeman. 1973. *Ecological Principles for Economic Development.* New York: John Wiley & Sons.

Edwards, Jonathan R. 1987. "The U.K. Heritage Coast: An Assessment of the Ecological Impacts of Tourism." *Annals of Tourism Research.* 14(1): 71-87.

Holder, Jean S. 1988. "Pattern and Impact of Tourism on the Environment in the Caribbean." *Tourism Management.* 9(2): 119-127

National Park Service (United States Department of the Interior). 1988. *Crater Lake National Park Development Concept Plan.* Denver: Denver Service Center.

Organization For Economic Co-operation and Development. 1980. *The Impact of Tourism on the Environment.* Paris.

Pigram, J. J. 1980. "Environmental Implications of Tourism Development." *Annals of Tourism Research.* 7(4): 554-583.

Republic of Maldives Ministry of Tourism. No date. *Carrying Capacity for Islands to Be Developed as Tourist Resorts.* Male.

——. 1989. *Annual Statistical Report of Tourism in the Maldives.* Male.

Romeril, Michael. 1989. "Tourism and the Environment—Accord or Discord?" *Tourism Management.* 10(3): 204-208.

Salm, R. V. 1985. "Integrating Marine Conservation and Tourism." *International Journal of Environmental Studies.* Vol. 25: 229-238.

Sathiendrakumar, Rajasundram and Clem Tisdell. 1989. "Tourism and the Economic Development of the Maldives." *Annals of Tourism Research.* 16 (2): 254-269.

Smith, Valene L. 2nd ed. 1989. *Hosts and Guests: The Anthropology of Tourism.* Philadelphia: University of Pennsylvania Press.

Travis, Anthony S. 1982. "Managing the Environmental and Cultural Impacts of Tourism and Leisure Development." *Tourism Management.* 3 (4): 256-262.

13

Socioeconomic Impacts

Approach to Evaluating Socioeconomic Impacts

Because of their close interrelationships, sociocultural and economic impacts are examined together in this chapter. Both of these areas are rather specialized. A tourism economist is usually included on the planning team, and increasingly a tourism or development sociologist or anthropologist is also a requisite team member on some types of planning studies. This chapter provides an overview of the complicated subject of socioeconomic impacts and encourages that an analytical approach be applied in evaluating these impacts, existing or potential, which can then provide a basis for determining appropriate policies and measures to prevent or remedy negative impacts and reinforce positive ones.

As part of the investigation of socioeconomic impacts, attitudinal surveys of residents, business surveys of tourism enterprises, and surveys of tourist characteristics, attitudes, and expenditure patterns are an important means of obtaining information on socioeconomic impacts in already developing tourism areas, although these must be carefully analyzed by the planning team in order to be useful. In any tourism area, continuous monitoring of socioeconomic impacts is essential to determine how effectively policies and strategies are functioning and to detect and try to remedy any problems before they become serious.

Perspective on Socioeconomic Impacts

The socioeconomic impacts of tourism have made this field a rather controversial one in recent years, especially where tourism development have been rapid and largely unplanned and uncontrolled, with the result that there have been adverse sociocultural as well as environmental impacts. Often, the economic benefits were problematical or at least less substantial than they could have been with better planning. However, the approach used in this book is that significant economic benefits can accrue from tourism and negative sociocultural impacts minimized through carefully planned and managed development. As is the case with environmental impacts, the type and extent of sociocultural and economic impacts depends very much on the type and intensity of tourism development and on the sociocultural and economic characteristics of the tourism area and, as emphasized, how tourism is planned, developed, and managed.

However, even with the best policies, plans, and implementation programs, it should be recognized that all types of new development, including tourism, bring change and certain types of impacts and that change is not necessarily undesirable but can help maintain the vitality of societies. In any type of area, tourism is usually only one of the agents of socioeconomic change, albeit a very visible one. Change is also brought about by the development of other economic sectors, such as manufacturing or mining, improvement of schools and other community facilities, exposure to the popular media of radio, television, newspapers, and magazines, returning residents who have traveled outside the area and bring new ideas and challenges to local values and life-styles, and other factors. Often, tourism is used as a convenient scapegoat for all undesirable changes that may be taking place in an area whereas, in fact, tourism may be only one element of a complicated pattern of development.

Tourism can and does bring about socioeconomic changes and is usually deliberately developed to generate economic benefits and through them social betterment. Therefore, it is important to understand the specific types of impacts and the policies and specific measures that can be used to cope with the impacts, whether positive or negative. Because each area is socioeconomically unique and each type of tourism has its own characteristics, it is dangerous to over-generalize about the types and extent of impacts and ways to handle them. The approach used here is to present the various types of impacts and the alternative ways to respond to them. The planner, based on specific study of the tourism area in cooperation with political leaders and community residents, must evaluate which of these or possibly others may have application to the local situation.

Host and Guest Relationships

Before examining specific types of impacts, it is important to understand the basis for these impacts taking place. The terminology of 'hosts and guests,' popularized in the tourism anthropology book of that name (Smith 1989), is now a generally accepted expression for the dichotomy of the residents of a tourism area and the tourists visiting the area. Some types of socioeconomic impacts are the normal changes and stresses resulting from any kind of economic development, even when the residents and tourists are of the same cultural backgrounds and socioeconomic levels, as is often the case with domestic tourism. Other impacts result from socioeconomic differences between residents and tourists of either the same or different cultural backgrounds. The respective levels of social, economic, and political development of the residents and tourists can be a critical factor.

A third type of impact can result from substantial cultural differences between residents and tourists. These differences may relate to basic value and logic systems, religious beliefs, traditions, customs, life-styles, behavioral patterns, dress codes, sense of time budgeting, attitude toward strangers, and many other factors. Differences in languages between tourists and residents can create frustrating situations and sometimes lead to misunderstandings. Even within particular countries and societies, there are often considerable socioeconomic and cultural differences among regions and especially between urban and village/rural areas, with urban dwellers having adopted more modern values and life-styles, while village and rural people may still be very traditional.

Compounding the complexity of resident–tourist relationships is the situation that often there are various different cultural and socioeconomic levels represented among the tourists visiting the areas (that is, several tourist cultures), and there may also be different cultural backgrounds and socioeconomic levels represented among the residents (that is, several host cultures), all of which may come into contact with one another. With the substantial migration of peoples from their home countries to other societies taking place today, a tourist destination may contain various ethnic groups, as well as the main culture of the society. Thus, in many tourism areas, cultural impacts cannot be viewed in terms of single host and tourist cultures. Also, as referred to by Jafari (1987), an observation generally made is that the 'tourists' culture' is somewhat different than their home culture, with tourists feeling emancipated from their ordinary cultural bounds and adopting the symbols and behavioral patterns of a non-ordinary life-style. Tourists have fewer social constraints and typically feel less inhibited when traveling than they do in their home cultures, with some tourists seeking experiences that would not be socially accepted in their own cultures.

As indicated by de Kadt (1979), tourist–resident encounters occur in three main contexts: where the tourist is purchasing some good or service from the host, where the tourist and host find themselves side by side (for example, on a beach or at a nightclub), and where the two parties come face to face with the object of exchanging information or ideas. The first two are quantitatively the most common, although the third type is where cross-cultural or international understanding is increased. However, sociocultural impacts can result from any type of encounter between residents and tourists. As pointed out by Mathieson and Wall (1982), tourists and residents interact within a network of goals and expectations, with the tourists being mobile, relaxed, free-spending, and enjoying their leisure, while the residents are relatively stationary and, if employed in tourism, spend a large part of their time catering to tourists.

In referring to a UNESCO study (1976), Mathieson and Wall (1982) indicated that, under conditions of mass tourism, tourist–resident relationships are characterized by their transitory nature, temporal and spatial constraints, lack of spontaneity, and unequal and unbalanced experience. Tourists usually spend only a limited amount of time in one place, although some tourists may return to their same favorite vacation area regularly. In sightseeing type of tourism, tourists want to see as much as possible in a short time. Relationships are usually on a structured and often commercial basis. Also, as pointed out above, tourists have a different attitude and expectation of experience than do the residents.

Dogan (1989) makes the point that as tourism develops in an area, a previously homogeneous community, characterized by a common response to tourism, becomes diversified with groups exhibiting different responses to touristic developments. These responses may range from resistance, retreatism, and maintaining boundaries between themselves and tourists to revitalization of traditional culture and adoption of the tourists' culture.

Types of Socioeconomic Impacts

There can be both positive and negative economic and sociocultural impacts resulting from tourism, depending on the type and intensity of tourism developed, as well as the characteristics of the host society. Whether impacts are considered positive or negative depends, in part, on objective criteria, such as income earned, but are also subject to the perceptions of the host community, with different community groups having varying reactions to their tourism development, often with no consensus reached by the total community. Socioeconomic impacts are identified and organized here based on the general acceptance of which ones are respectively positive and negative, and are applicable, except where noted, to both domestic and international tourism.

Positive Impacts

Positive types of economic and sociocultural impacts include those explained in the following sections.

Economic Benefits

Direct economic benefits include provision of employment, income, and (for international tourism) foreign exchange, which lead to improved living standards of the local community and overall national and regional economic development. In economically depressed areas, the employment and income provided by tourism, especially to young people, may help stem out migration from those areas. Increased government revenues, through various types of taxation on tourism that can be used to develop community and infrastructure facilities and services and assist in general economic development are also a direct economic benefit. These direct and the indirect economic benefits are usually the primary reasons for developing tourism in an area.

Tourists attending the Miring ceremony in Sarawak (top) and woodcarving of handicraft items (bottom) in Malaysia—Carefully organized participation by tourists in village activities, such as traditional ceremonies, is a technique of tourists learning about local customs, brings the economic benefits of tourism directly to villagers, and develops a sense of pride by villagers in their cultural heritage. Quality controlled handicraft production provides an attraction for tourists, especially if they can view demonstrations of craftsmanship, helps maintain traditional craft skills, and is an important source of income for local artisans and foreign exchange for the country. (Courtesy of the Malaysian tourism office)

An important indirect economic benefit of tourism is that it serves as a catalyst for the development or expansion of other economic sectors, such as agriculture, fisheries, construction, certain types of manufacturing, and handicrafts, through their supplying the goods and services used in tourism. Another indirect socioeconomic benefit is improvements made to transportation and other infrastructure facilities and services for tourism that also serve general national, regional, and community needs. Although dependent very much on local economic and cultural development policy, tourism may be seen by the host country or region as being advantageous in teaching technical and managerial skills to segments of its population, some of which can be transferred to other sectors and, more generally, encouraging people to adopt regular employment habits and work for the things they want. Tourism can employ a large percentage of women and, in some traditional societies, may provide an opportunity for emancipation of women through training and employment.

Conservation of Cultural Heritage

Tourism can be a major stimulus for conservation of important elements of the cultural heritage of an area because their conservation can be justified, in part or whole, by tourism as tourist attractions. These elements include:

- Conservation of archaeological and historic sites and interesting architectural styles as emphasized in Chapter 12 on environmental impacts.
- Conservation and sometimes revitalization of traditional arts, handicrafts, dance, music, drama, customs and ceremonies, dress, and certain aspects of traditional life-styles. For example, Mathieson and Wall (1982) document the positive effects that tourism has had on the revitalization of traditional arts and crafts, including development of new forms utilizing local skills and materials of the southwestern USA Indians (Navajo, Pueblo, and other groups) and Canadian Inuit (Eskimos) in eastern Canada.
- Financial assistance for the maintenance of museums, theaters, and other cultural facilities and activities and for supporting the organization of special cultural festivals and events because they are important attractions for tourists as well as being used by residents. Admission fees paid by tourists at some major museums in the world, for example, provide substantial revenues to maintain those institutions, and theater tickets purchased by tourists at important urban theaters help support those facilities.

Renewal of Cultural Pride

A sense of pride by residents in their culture can be reinforced or even renewed when they observe tourists appreciating it. This is especially true of some traditional cultures that are undergoing change as a result of general economic development and are losing their sense of cultural self-confidence. For example, Esman's study (1984) concludes that tourism has helped the Cajun group of Louisiana, USA, retain a strong sense of separate identity and ethnic pride by reinforcing the differences between the Cajuns and outsiders, even though some of the traditional cultural patterns have been lost. In multi-cultural countries, regional tourism can help maintain the cultural identity of minority cultural groups that otherwise might be submerged by the nation's dominant culture, including the political recognition that the minority culture is an important one to retain.

Cross-Cultural Exchange

Tourism can promote cross-cultural exchange of tourists and residents learning more about one another's cultures, resulting in greater mutual understanding and respect, or at least tolerance of different value systems and traditions through understanding their cultural basis. Although this point has been debated because of the typically superficial contact between tourists and residents, Mings (1988) concluded that tourism in Barbados probably did improve international understanding or, at least, there was little evidence to indicate international tourism is obstructing mutual understanding. In a multi-ethnic country or region such as India, Indonesia, or Yugoslavia, domestic tourism can ideally help achieve cross-cultural understanding and build a sense of national unity among diverse groups of people. This is often stated as an important objective of developing domestic tourism in newly developing, culturally diverse countries.

Negative Impacts

If not well planned and controlled, tourism may generate negative impacts or reduce the effectiveness of positive ones, including those addressed in the following sections.

Loss of Potential Economic Benefits

Loss of potential economic benefits to the local area can occur and local resentment can sometimes be generated if many tourist facilities are owned and managed by outsiders. Also, local elites can be created if tourist facilities and services are owned and managed by only a few local persons or families, with most of the community receiving minimal benefits. However, there may be few alternatives to outside ownership during the initial stages of development if local capital is very limited. Potential foreign exchange earnings are reduced when imported goods and services are utilized in tourism, although, in some places such as small island economies, there is no alternative to having a relatively high import of tourism, with the net foreign exchange and income earned still considered well worth the investment in tourism.

Economic and Employment Distortions

Economic distortions can take place geographically if tourism is concentrated in only one or a few areas of a country or region, without corresponding development in the other places. Resentment by residents in the undeveloped areas may ensue from this situation. Even within the tourism areas, there may be resentment of persons earning relatively good incomes in tourism by those who are unemployed or have lower income jobs. Employment distortions may be created if tourism attracts too many employees from other economic sectors, such as agriculture and fisheries, because of its higher wages and perhaps more desirable working conditions, if there is not an overall surplus of workers available. Inflation of local prices of land and certain goods and services may take place, placing a financial hardship on residents because of the demands of tourism.

Resentment and conflict may arise within families if tourism provides new and higher wage employment for certain family members, especially women and young people, than the heads of households receive in traditional activities such as agriculture and fishing. There may be resentment by residents if migrant workers are brought in to work in tourism, especially if they stay on after they are no longer needed, and cultural conflicts may arise between residents and migrant workers if they are of different cultural backgrounds. If expatriate managers and technical staff are employed in tourism, often at much higher wages than the local scale, there may be resentment by local, lesser-skilled workers, in addition to the loss of potential economic benefits as referred to in the previous section.

There may be resentment by residents of the perceived or actual higher affluence levels and more leisure time of tourists, especially if there are substantial socioeconomic differences between residents and tourists. Sometimes there is lack of understanding by residents that most tourists will have worked hard for much of the year to save sufficient money to take their vacations, with the residents being exposed to them only when they are at leisure and spending money freely.

Overcrowding and Loss of Amenities for Residents

If there is overcrowding of amenity features, shopping, and community facilities and congestion of transportation systems by tourists, residents cannot conveniently use them and will become irritated and resentful of tourism. Domestic tourists may also become resentful of international tourists if their own attractions are congested by foreigners. If local features such as beaches are closed off to the local population and maintained for the exclusive use of tourists, residents lose access to their own amenities and can become hostile towards tourism. This situation is exacerbated if physical barriers, such as fences built alongside or across beaches, are imposed between residents and tourists.

Cultural Impacts

Overcommercialization and loss of authenticity of traditional arts and crafts, customs, and ceremonies can result if these are over-modified to suit tourist demands (for example, important traditional dance and music performances, some of which may have religious significance, being greatly shortened and changed to fit tourists' tastes and schedules, and traditional high quality handicrafts being mass produced to provide tourist souvenirs). This situation often results from the insensitivity or lack of understanding of the 'cultural brokers' of tour operators or handicraft organizers, whether foreign or local, who are not concerned about cultural integrity or authenticity.

In extreme cases, there may be loss of cultural character, self-respect, and overall social identity because of submergence of the local society by the outside cultural patterns of seemingly more affluent and successful tourists. Deterioration of cultural monuments and loss of cultural artifacts may result from uncontrolled tourist use and misuse by tourists, as explained in Chapter 12.

The demonstration effect of tourists from different cultural and socioeconomic backgrounds on residents and especially on young people may take place. This effect involves residents observing and imitating the behavioral, dress, and life-style patterns of tourists, without understanding their cultural basis and sometimes not being able to financially afford to adopt the tourists' life-style. Because the demonstration effect particularly affects more impressionable younger people, it may drive a wedge and create conflicts between different generations in a community.

Misunderstandings and conflicts can arise between residents and tourists because of differences in languages, customs, religious values, and behavioral patterns (for example: in some societies, handshaking is the common form of greeting while bowing is the custom in other societies; in some societies, foot and finger pointing is considered very impolite, while it is accepted in other places; in churches, wearing of shoes is the norm, while in mosques, shoes must be removed before entering; in many societies, consumption of alcoholic beverages is prevalent, while in others, it is prohibited or discouraged). Violations of local dress codes by tourists may be resented by residents and even lead to conflicts if strong religious values are being transgressed.

The question that sometimes arises with respect to cultural impacts is whether international tourism can be developed in countries with vastly different religious values than those of the historically predominant Western types of tourist markets (although the types of markets are changing rapidly as brought out in Chapter 1). As pointed out by Din (1989), in the case of Islam for example, while certain regulations prohibit prostitution, gambling, and the consumption of alcoholic beverages, religion does not necessarily exert any significant influence on the operation of tourist-related activities if appropriate measures are adopted. Malaysia, Indonesia, the Maldives, and the northern and western African Islamic countries already attract significant numbers of tourists, and other Islamic countries have the potential for developing or further expanding tourism.

On balance, the negative cultural impacts seem to be outweighed by the positive ones if cultural evolution is accepted as a desired objective. De Kadt (1979: 14–15) summarizes the cultural impacts of tourism as presented in a joint UNESCO–World Bank Seminar on the Social and Cultural Impacts of Tourism, as follows:

In the area of arts, crafts, and cultural manifestations . . . the effects of tourism are also mixed. The frequent charge that tourism contributes to a degeneration in this field appears, however, to be an exaggeration. Even though curio production, "airport art," and performances of fake folklore are of course stimulated by tourist demand, the seminar papers and discussion brought to light that frequently arts, crafts, and local culture have been revitalized as a direct result of tourism. A transformation of traditional forms often accompanies this development but does not necessarily lead to degeneration. To be authentic, arts and crafts must be rooted both in historical tradition and in present-day life; true authenticity cannot be achieved by conservation alone, since that leads to stultification.

Social Problems

Problems of drugs, alcoholism, crime, and prostitution may be exacerbated by tourism, although tourism is seldom the basic cause of such problems as pointed out, with respect to prostitution, by Pearce (1989) in his review of the literature on this subject. Some countries in Asia have become identified with sex tours among certain market groups. This has been of concern to some tourism officials of those countries because of the undesirable image portrayed in promoting general interest tourist markets, as well as the effects on the prostitutes themselves, although this attitude varies appreciably depending on the cultural value systems involved. With respect to the relationship between crime and tourism, Mathieson and Wall (1982) in their review of the literature conclude that it appears that tourism contributes to crime, especially on a seasonal basis. This occurs through the generation of friction between the host population and tourists and the fact that the target for criminals is expanded and situations are created where gains from crime may be high and the likelihood of detection small.

Socioeconomic Policies and Impact Control Measures

There are some generally accepted socioeconomic policies and impact control measures that are being applied with some successful results in various places in the world, relative to preventing future or mitigating existing negative socioeconomic impacts and reinforcing the positive ones. As emphasized, each tourism area situation is unique, and an approach that is effective in one area is not necessarily appropriate in another, nor are all the techniques necessarily applicable in a particular area. In larger countries and regions, different approaches may be suitable in different places.

General Socioeconomic Policies

For both socioeconomic and environmental reasons, it is important to develop tourism in a gradual manner so that local residents have sufficient time to adapt to, understand, and participate in it and so the government can properly plan, organize, and monitor tourism development as it proceeds. This also provides the time to apply a community development approach, which is an essential fundamental policy, especially at the local level of development (community involvement in general urban and regional planning has been commonly practiced for many years). Residents and their spokesmen should be involved in the decision-making process of planning and developing tourism so that they have a role in determining the future of this sector in their community (including development objectives and appropriate forms of tourism), understand what are the benefits and problems of tourism, and how they can participate in and control its development and benefits. In the process of community involvement, techniques can be evolved by which those residents who want can participate in the development of tourism can receive its benefits. Through community involvement and understanding of tourism, residents will more likely support it in the future, than if tourism policies and plans are imposed on them from the outside, whether by government or the private sector. Community involvement can be effected, for example, through organizing tourism advisory committees or boards and holding open meetings with residents and community groups.

A form and scale of tourism development that is appropriate for the local environment and society should be planned and maintained. In some areas, small-scale and dispersed development may be the most appropriate, while in other places, large-scale mass tourism may be quite acceptable, or a combination of different forms in a country or region may be suitable. The concept of social carrying capacity, which has been proposed by, for example, D'Amore as explained by Murphy (1985) is important to include in the overall carrying capacity study as was described in Chapter 6. Social carrying standards relate to such factors as establishing thresholds on congestion levels generated by tourism, providing convenient access to amenity features by residents, and, more generally, determining their tolerance level of tourism. If the social carrying capacity or tolerance level is exceeded, not only will residents be irritated and resentful, but they will also not present a hospitable and friendly face to tourists, which will result in tourist dissatisfaction. Part of the concept of an appropriate scale of tourism relates to integrating tourism into the total economy and developing other economic sectors so that there is a balanced economy and employment structure. However, in places of limited economic resources, there may be no choice but to develop tourism as the dominant sector, and other approaches can be applied to mitigate possible sociocultural impacts.

In order to use tourism as a technique of cultural conservation and revitalization, it should be based to the greatest extent possible on the cultural resources of an area. By policy, tourism can be deliberately used to help justify and financially support the preservation of archaeological and historic sites, conservation and even expansion of traditional dance, music, drama, arts, and handicrafts unique to the area, development of museums and cultural centers, and organization of cultural events.

Economically, a basic policy is to integrate tourism, at whatever level and scale of development, into the national, regional, and local economies through such techniques as establishing strong cross-sectoral linkages with other economic sectors, maximizing local employment in tourism, and encouraging local management and ownership of tourist facilities and services to the greatest extent possible.

At the national and regional levels, regional distribution policies can be applied so that no one area becomes too congested with tourists, residents can conveniently use their own amenity features and community facilities and services, and income from tourism is more evenly distributed. In some situations, application of the enclave approach of concentrating tourist facilities only in certain areas may be appropriate in order to contain any impacts of tourism, as well as providing the other advantages of concentration previously described.

With respect to the impact of tourism and modern development in general on more traditional societies, experiences indicate that many traditional societies want to adopt the more desirable and beneficial aspects of 'modern' development, which makes their lives more secure, comfortable and often more interesting, open, and democratic. In many cases, they want to drop certain of their traditions, such as dowry and bride price, perceived as being restrictive or otherwise undesirable. But, at the same time, they still wish to retain other distinctive characteristics of their society and a sense of separate ethnic identity. The cultural conservation approach that seems to be effective in many such societies is that of cultural selectivity and adaptation within the framework of maintaining the unique character of the society. Often, if the philosophical or religious values (and their related ceremonies and rituals) of the society are maintained along with its distinctive art and craft forms and manifestations of its cultural and historical heritage, this provides a basis for maintaining the society's cultural identity. However, other societies or usually certain elements of the societies wish to retain virtually all aspects of their traditions along with having some modern economic development. This can create conflicts that are not easily resolved.

Socioeconomic Impact Control Measures

Some specific measures that can be applied to lessen negative impacts and reinforce positive ones include the following:

- Maintain the authenticity of local dance, music, and drama performances and of arts and handicrafts, even though these may be adapted and expanded, based on traditional skills, through establishing quality controls and organizing training programs. Also, conserve archaeological and historic sites, as explained in Chapter 10.
- Provide financial incentives, training, and other techniques for local owner-

ship, management, and operation of hotels and other tourist facilities and services so that residents can participate in and receive direct economic benefits from tourism, as will be further explained in a later section of this chapter.

- Make certain that residents have convenient access to tourist attractions, facilities, and services, including reducing admission fees for residents if appropriate. Also, make sure that amenity features have public access and are not preempted by tourism development, such as by providing public access to beaches in tourism areas. More generally, an adequate system of public parks and recreation areas should be developed, primarily designed for use by residents, but that are also open to tourists, so that community residents have adequate amenity features available to them.

- Apply visitor use organization and control measures to prevent overcrowding of tourist attractions, as explained in Chapter 10.

- If most residents cannot afford to use the existing commercial tourist facilities, provide special inexpensive or subsidized accommodation and recreation facilities for exclusive or priority use by domestic tourists. Low-cost hostels can be provided for domestic youth travelers. Discounts on transportation facilities can be made available to domestic tourists, or at least to domestic tour groups and student travelers.

- Educate residents about the concept, benefits, and problems of tourism and the current development policies and plans for tourism in the area and about the customs, behavioral patterns, and value systems of tourists coming to the area from different cultural backgrounds. Inform tourists about local customs, dress, and behavior codes and other social characteristics. In educating residents about tourism, the popular media of radio, television, newspapers and magazines, and even village meetings in some areas can be utilized. Public awareness programs on tourism should be carefully organized and tailored to local needs. To inform tourists, many tourism areas now produce a brochure of information about local customs and 'do's and don'ts' for tourists so that they are aware of what is socially acceptable, including the local policy on tipping, which often presents tourists with confusing situations and misunderstandings with local employees.

- Design hotels and other tourist facilities to reflect local architectural styles so that these facilities are not physically alien to residents, give a unique sense of place to tourists as explained in Chapter 11, and reinforce and in some places help revive distinctive local architectural styles.

- Through techniques of selective marketing and controlling the types of tourist attractions, activities, and facilities provided, encourage the kinds of tourists who will appreciate and respect the local cultural traditions.

- Train local residents to work effectively in all levels of tourism in order to, in addition to enhancing local economic benefits, reduce the possible number of migrant workers to the area, thus lessening any resident–migrant worker conflicts and preclude misunderstandings with tourists, resulting from poor quality service and cultural differences. Language training is often an important element of employee training.

- Apply strict control on drugs, crime, and prostitution (if prostitution is considered to be improper by local standards). Tourists can be required to leave the country if they are involved in these problems or be locally prosecuted and punished for serious offenses. Additional police protection may be necessary in tourism areas if crime is a problem.

Sociocultural Programming

The national, regional, or community tourism office must take the lead role in identifying socioeconomic impacts and applying policies and measures to minimize the costs and optimize the benefits, although it may utilize technical capabilities from other organizations. In some areas, especially in more traditional societies where tourism is commencing development, an integrated sociocultural program can be organized to provide a structured approach to these activities. Obviously, this program must be based on research of the specific characteristics of the tourism area's society and the type and scale of tourism being planned.

Figure 13.1 shows a model sociocultural program organizational structure that can be adapted to specific situations. As shown in the chart, the support factors for the program are technical capability, facilities and equipment, and funding. Typically, the organizations that are involved in the coordination and implementation of the program are community organizations, relevant government agencies, and often any religious organizations that exist in the area. One of the important outputs of the program is education, both community education about tourism (sometimes called public awareness programs) and tourist education about the local society and cultural traditions. The other type of output is cultural conservation, which may include techniques and programs for conservation and often presentations to tourists relative to dance and music, arts and handicrafts, special cultural events and annual festivals, archaeological, historic, and architectural preservation (in some areas, entire traditional villages should be preserved), and establishment of museums and cultural centers. Such sociocultural programs may be long term or continuous, but the program focus should be modified as the needs change.

Economic Enhancement Programming

There are various approaches that can be applied to optimize the economic benefits of tourism to the country, region, and local community. In the national and regional plan, the policies are established to ensure that economic benefits are enhanced even though some of them are applied at the local level. In the absence of national and regional planning, the local community can often adopt and apply appropriate policies and strategies. In the initial tourism development of an area, application of these measures can be commenced, realizing that considerable time may be required to fully implement them, depending on the local situation and especially on the general level of economic development of the area. Where

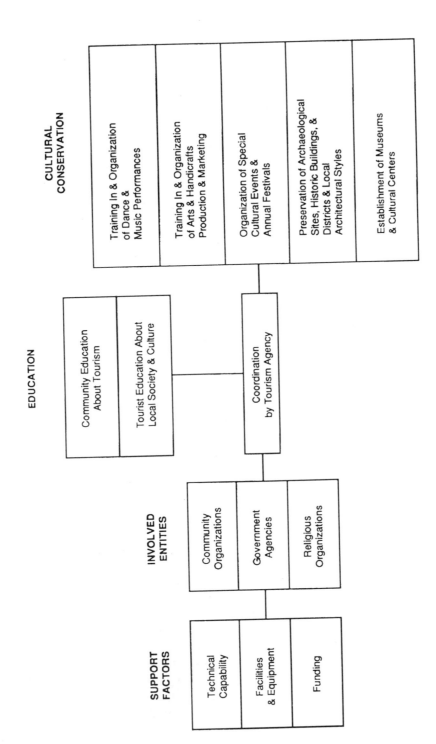

Figure 13.1. Model Sociocultural Program Organizational Structure.

tourism development is already underway but not yet mature, the economic impact analysis will indicate whether there are opportunities to increase benefits through implementation of various strategies. Some of the common approaches to enhance economic benefits and maximize local participation in the benefits are explained in the following sections.

Strengthening Economic Cross-Sectoral Linkages

Basic to the enhancement of economic benefits is making optimum use of goods and services produced within the country, region, and community as inputs to tourism, that is, increasing the local value added to tourism. This reduces the leakage factor of money spent (often valuable foreign exchange at the national level) to purchase imported goods and services. In some areas, such as resource-limited island economies, it may be necessary to import a considerable amount of items used in tourism. This situation is justifiable because tourism still brings substantial benefits that otherwise would not exist. However, opportunities for import substitution and increasing tourist expenditures should be explored in any environment.

Cross-sectoral linkages between tourism and agriculture and fisheries can often be strengthened through improving local production of food items—vegetables, fruits, diary products, meat, poultry, fish, and other seafood—used in tourist restaurants. It may be necessary to modify existing or develop new types of food items for the tourist market in terms of variety and quality. Production and marketing must be integrated to ensure that a reliable supply of the items is available when and where needed. In some places, where suitable soils are limited or the climate is not suitable, hydroponic farming can be economically viable compared to the cost of imported food items or aquaculture techniques used to increase seafood production. As has been referred to previously, there may also be scope to include more of the local cuisine, based on locally produced food items on the tourist menu. It should not necessarily be assumed that tourists only want to eat food to which they are accustomed, even though it may have to be imported.

Other opportunities for using locally produced goods exist in the incorporation of local building materials in the construction of tourist facilities and in the manufacture of furnishings and supplies for hotels and other facilities. Facilities and furnishings should be designed to make use of local materials if they are available and suitable. For example, locally made furniture, ceramics and dishware, and textiles can be designed for hotel rooms, lobbies, and restaurants, which in fact may make these places more interesting for tourists if local styles are incorporated. Tour buses and other tourist transportation can perhaps be manufactured or at least assembled locally. Expanding handicraft production is also a technique that can be used to increase local input of materials as well as labor in tourism, as has been referred to previously. Local handicrafts can be used as decor in hotels and other tourist facilities.

Many of these local goods and services developed or improved for tourism are also often marketable to residents and may have potential for direct export, thus further improving the economy and, at the national level, increasing foreign exchange earnings.

Ownership of Tourist Facilities and Services

Obviously, complete local ownership of hotels and other tourist facilities and services such as restaurants and tour and travel agencies will maximize retention of profits from the capital investment made, as well as give the local population more control over tourism development and operation. But if local capital resources are limited, which is often the case in newly developing tourism areas, or if some of the available capital is needed for other economic sectors, it may be necessary to allow outside capitalization and, in some cases, even encourage this in order to get tourism started so that it can generate the needed income and employment.

Joint venture ownership of a combination of outside and local capital is a commonly used technique to capitalize projects so that at least some local capital is utilized. Often, joint venture is required to have a minimum of 51 percent local input so that local control of the project is ensured. Techniques for promoting local control can include requiring that, over time, the local investment input in a joint venture project is increased gradually as local capital becomes more available. Sometimes, the value of the land on which tourism projects are located, if locally owned, can be used as part of the local contribution to the capitalization. Various forms of subsidies or loans can be made available to local persons or companies to acquire equity ownership in tourist facilities.

To encourage the spreading of equity ownership among the general local population so that it does not concentrate in the hands of local elites or outsiders, whether elsewhere in the country or foreigners, various techniques can be employed. Hotel or resort corporations can be set up with public sale of shares, perhaps with first priority for purchase given to the local population, with the profits being distributed as dividends to the shareowners. Another technique is organization of condominium type accommodation units, whether part of a hotel or self-catering apartments, townhouses, and villas, which can be individually sold to local persons or families with modest resources. The units can still be under common property management in order to benefit from management expertise and marketing activities but with the individual owners receiving their share of the profits. In some areas, development of locally owned small-scale hotels, guest houses, and restaurants can be encouraged through loans and even technical and managerial assistance provided to local entrepreneurs.

Local Employment

Maximizing employment of local (as opposed to foreign or other national or regional) personnel in tourist facilities and services enhances local economic benefits because, in addition to the benefit of generating local employment, the workers wages and salaries will remain in the local economy. Expatriate workers will spend some of their wages locally but typically will send a substantial percentage to their home countries or regions. In some cases, such as the Middle Eastern Gulf Coast countries, foreign workers are essential to provide both the numbers of workers and skills required, although even some of those countries are adopting policies of training local persons to assume jobs now held by foreigners. In other cases, foreign employees, especially at the managerial and highly skilled levels, are required initially because local capabilities have not yet been developed, despite the local need for jobs.

Where outside employment in tourism is considered to be a problem for either social or economic reasons, or anticipated to become one in newly developing tourism areas, policies must often be adopted that give priority for employment to persons from the local area. However, these policies must go together with implementation of training programs to ensure that local persons possess the technical, managerial, and social skills to effectively work in tourism. This approach requires considerable time and investment for the proper training to be implemented but is usually worth the effort involved. In some cases, lower level jobs are occupied by local persons, but higher level technical and managerial positions are held by outsiders. Private sector management may prefer this situation. In such cases, it may be necessary for the government to adopt policies that the foreign employees be phased out over a period of time and replaced with local employees, often requiring that management provide appropriate training and experience for local persons to assume the higher level positions. This is, of course, desirable but must be done within the framework of maintaining the quality level of the establishments.

Local Management of Tourist Facilities and Services

In-country or local management of hotels and other tourist facilities, whether or not locally owned and employing local persons, results in a greater amount of the profits being retained in the country and greater local control over tourism. Management fees of foreign operators typically are sent overseas. However, foreign management, especially by a large international hotel chain, brings the benefits of both competent management skills and an international marketing network and name recognition as well as integrated reservation services. Some tourists, for example, want to stay only in well-known international chain hotels wherever they travel. Each situation must be specifically evaluated as to the relative advantages and disadvantages of utilizing international management companies. Many countries have both locally and internationally managed large-scale hotels and therefore optimize the respective advantages and disadvantages. If international chain hotels are allowed to operate in a country or region, the management contracts should be carefully negotiated to be fair to both the local and international parties involved.

Local Tour and Travel Services

International tour and travel operators serve an essential function in organizing and promoting tours to an area, but sometimes they may also control local tour operations, especially if the local agency operations are not well developed. This results in the loss of potential income and employment from the economy, as well as limiting local control of tourist activities. Usually, it is desirable to develop the local inbound tour operations capability to handle this function, and in some cases, the government may need to establish a regulation that inbound tour services be handled only by local operators. This approach may also require that suitable training programs be organized for local tour operators.

Shopping

Shopping for handicrafts, souvenirs, specialty and duty-free items, and general consumer goods is an important activity for many tourists and can constitute a major component of tourist expenditures and source of tourist income. One way to encourage higher expenditures by tourists is to provide a greater variety of goods for tourists to purchase within the framework of maintaining the quality integrity of handicrafts and specialty items. However, any major investment in expansion of shopping facilities should be based on a careful feasibility analysis, and effective merchandising techniques applied.

Expansion of Tourist Activities

In addition to shopping, a common technique to increase tourist expenditures and often their length of stay is to expand the variety of tourist activities available. Tourist attractions can be added, including natural, cultural, and special types of attractions, and additional tours can be organized to new places in the area. Tourism product improvement and diversification is becoming an important aspect of expanding or upgrading tourism in already developed tourism areas. In an effort to diversify the tourism product by developing new tourist attractions and activities and opening up new tourism areas, it is important not to neglect maintaining and, where necessary, improving the existing tourism product in order to retain its viability and appeal to tourists. Expansion of tourist activities should also be based on careful market and economic feasibility analysis, to ensure that the investment will be justified.

If deemed necessary, a specific program can be prepared and integrated into the area's overall economic development program that will provide a structured approach to apply economic enhancement techniques. Integrated economic programming may be especially needed for establishing stronger cross-sectoral linkages, which can be a complicated process.

Measuring Economic Costs and Benefits

The macro level means of economic measurement of costs and benefits and micro level of project feasibility analysis constitute important components of tourism planning and are utilized as major criteria, along with environmental and sociocultural factors, by which to evaluate the alternative plans as well as the final one in the planning process. The basic input for preparing economic analysis is tourist expenditures, which will, of course, vary greatly depending on the type of tourist markets and forms of tourism development. In a partially developed tourism area, visitor expenditure surveys are conducted to determine the amount and distribution of tourism spending. If little or no tourism exists in the planning area, then expenditures can be projected based on various assumptions, including tourist spending patterns in similar destination areas. In Hawaii, for example, the distribution of expenditures was reported by the Hawaii Visitors Bureau in 1978 (Lundberg 1985) to be:

- Lodging—32.3 percent;
- Food and beverage—27.2 percent;
- Transportation—11.7 percent;
- Clothing—9.3 percent;
- Gifts and souvenirs—9.7 percent;
- All other—5.0 percent; and
- Entertainment—4.8 percent.

As a relatively mature destination area, this distribution of spending in Hawaii is not likely to have changed greatly since the late 1970s, although the amount will have, of course, increased.

Economic impact and project feasibility analysis is a specialized subject beyond the scope of the book, but the basic considerations are presented here so that the tourism planner is aware of these in his coordination with the tourism economist.

Types of Economic Impact Measurements

The economic impacts of tourism are determined by the tourism economist utilizing various types of measurement, as briefly described in the follow sections.

Contribution to Gross National or Gross Regional Product (GNP or GRP)

If possible to segregate as a separate sector, the contribution of tourism in numerical and percentage terms to the GNP or GRP can be calculated, as is done for manufacturing or agriculture. Related to this factor is the calculation of the income earned from tourism. Unfortunately, tourism is seldom shown as a separate sector but is included in services, transportation, and other sectors in national or regional accounts. Consequently, best estimates must be made, often based on the income generated by tourism. Tourism can be an important component of the economy, ranging up to 5 and 10 percent of the total GNP or GRP for both domestic and international tourism in some large countries or regions, and can be much more important in smaller countries with well-developed tourism sectors and especially some island tourist destinations.

Contribution to Foreign Exchange Earnings

The gross foreign exchange (or for regional economies, income from outside the area) can be calculated from the foreign tourist expenditure patterns. But it is essential to determine the import content of tourism (that is, the cost of imported goods and services used in tourism), to derive the net foreign exchange earned. There are several types of imported goods and services:

- Goods such as food items and hotel supplies;
- Commissions paid to travel agents and tour operators whose businesses are located outside the area;
- Advertising and promotion expenditures paid to businesses outside the area and the operating costs of national or regional tourism promotion offices outside the area;
- Lease rent, such as on hotel properties, paid to absentee owners;
- Interest and profits paid to outside property investors and stockholders;
- Management fees paid to transnational management companies;
- Expatriation of wages and salaries made by foreigners working in tourism; and
- Tourists' use of credit cards and travelers checks that do not benefit local banks.

Import costs are also often associated with materials and equipment used in the initial construction of hotels, other tourist facilities, and infrastructure and their continuing maintenance. Potential foreign exchange earnings are reduced when governments exempt customs duties or taxes on foreign-owned companies as investment incentives.

The leakage factor tends to be higher in smaller countries and regions with limited economies or in larger countries whose economies are not highly integrated, as well as in newly developing tourism destinations where many construction and other materials used in tourism must be imported. Often, incentives are offered to attract investment in tourism, and are lower in well-developed or well-integrated economies. Some of the less-developed Caribbean, Pacific, and Indian Ocean island countries are heavily reliant on imports, and their net foreign exchange earnings range only up to 50 percent. The better developed island countries retain up to 70 percent of foreign exchange, while countries with relatively well-developed manufacturing sectors and integrated economies have higher net foreign exchange earnings. For example, India, although a less-developed country in terms of per capita income, has well-developed manufacturing and agricultural sectors, as well as mostly Indian-owned and managed hotels, and its import content for tourism is only about 5 percent. Countries such as Kenya,

Greece, and Yugoslavia have somewhat less but still substantial retention of foreign exchange earnings.

As mentioned previously, for places of limited resources, tourism still brings much needed economic benefits even though the import content of tourism goods and services is high, and some of these imports still generate employment such as goods handling services.

Employment Generation

The local employment generated by tourism is measured based on direct or primary and indirect or secondary jobs. Direct employment is that which is involved in tourism enterprises, such as hotels, restaurants, retail shops, and tour operations. Indirect employment is the jobs generated in the supplying sectors, such as agriculture, fisheries, and manufacturing. Also, the induced employment of additional persons supported by the spending of income by the direct and indirect employees is sometimes calculated. Employment generated by construction of tourist facilities and related infrastructure should also be considered, even though this may be temporary. In some tourism areas, the seasonality of employment should be noted in the calculation.

Employment ratios are usually calculated based on the average number of employees per hotel room or other types of accommodation unit. Depending on the kind of accommodation, the type and extent of other tourist facilities, and the services and general employment productivity in the area, the direct employment ratio can vary from .5 to 2.0 employees per room. In good quality hotels in the Asia-Pacific region, where a high level of service is provided, for example, the employee/room ratio is about 1.5, although, it is lower than that in Hawaii, where both wages and productivity are high. The employment ratio in lesser quality and self-catering types of accommodation is lower than this figure. Indirect employment is often about equal to or somewhat higher than direct employment, depending on the extent of integration of the economy.

Employment is sometimes measured in economic terms, with respect to how much investment is required to produce one job or the employment-output ratio, that is, the number of workers employed divided by the contribution of tourism to the national income. Although tourism is often portrayed as a labor intensive activity, the typically high cost of constructing good quality accommodation and related infrastructure now presumes substantial capital investment being made for each job generated, although the non-hotel job generation must still be considered. Lower quality accommodation costs less but also generates fewer employees per room. Employment can also be measured in terms of how much tourist income is needed to create one new job in the local economy.

Multiplier Effect

The term multiplier is used to describe the total effect, both direct and secondary, that an external source of income has on an economy. In tourism the multiplier is usually applied to encompass the direct and secondary effects of tourist expenditures on the economy, although it can be applied to employment or other variables. Based on tourist expenditures, the multiplier effect refers to the number of rounds of spending with regards to the initial expenditures within the local economy or the ways in which tourist spending filters through the economy, thus indicating the extent of impact on local income, employment, and other economic sectors, as graphically shown in Figure 13.2. As set forth by Lundberg (1985), the multiplier effect is expressed in formula form as:

$$TIM = \frac{1 - TPI}{MPS + MPI}$$

TIM = Tourism Income Multiplier, or factor by which tourist expenditures should be multiplied to determine the tourist income generated by these expenditures

1 = Tourist expenditure

TPI = Tourists' Propensity to Import, or buy imported goods and services that do not create income for the area

MPS = Marginal Propensity to Save, or residents' decision not to spend some of their tourist income

MPI = Marginal Propensity to Import, or the residents' decision to buy imported goods or spend money abroad

The size of the multiplier in tourism depends in large part on how well developed the supplying sectors are and how closely linked they are to tourism. When tourism's primary activities purchase their goods and services mostly from the local economy, the multiplier is higher than if many imported goods and services are used. The multiplier is typically higher for tourism than it is for manufacturing because tourism is usually more labor intensive, which provides more employee income for local spending. Also, the goods and services produced in tourism are 'consumed' by tourists locally and not shipped out as is the case with many manufactured products. Because tourism often involves many relatively small businesses, tourist spending filters rapidly and more widely through the society. The multiplier effect ranges from less than one for small island economies to more than two for large, highly integrated economies. The multiplier should be calculated carefully and not give a misleading result.

Contribution to Government Revenues

Another measure of economic impact and often an influencing factor on deciding tourism development policy is its direct contribution to government revenues, which can be substantial. Potential revenues include hotel and other user or expenditure taxes, airport departure taxes, customs duties on imported goods used in tourism, income taxes on tourism enterprises and persons working in tourism, and property taxes on tourism establishments. The extent and types of sources are, of course, determined by the government and are especially flexible relative to the direct tourist taxes, such as a hotel or tourist expenditure tax, which ranges in various countries from as low as 3 to as high as 15 percent.

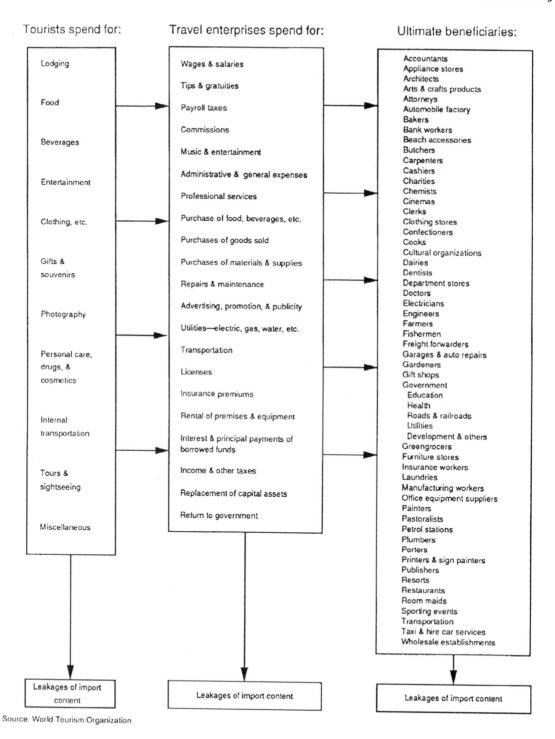

Figure 13.2. Multiplier Effect—How Tourism Spending Flows into the Economy.

Although a potentially important and legitimate source of revenue, there is the danger of applying too high a hotel or expenditure tax, which can be both irritating to tourists and increase their travel costs to the extent that it may be a deterrent to visiting the area, especially if they feel that they are not receiving commensurate government services. A frequent complaint of tourism officials is that the hotel tax goes into general use government funds and is not, at least in part, reserved for improvement and further development or promotion of the tourism sector. Sometimes, a special earmarked hotel tax is applied, most commonly for local training of employees in tourism.

Input-output analysis is now widely used to examine economic impact (Fletcher 1989) if the basic tables have been prepared for the country or region. This technique makes it easier to accurately calculate the economic impact of tourism and provide a basis for enhancing tourism economic benefits, although this approach has some limitations.

To arrive at a balanced understanding of the economic impacts of tourism, all the means of measurement should be calculated.

Cost-Benefit Analysis

Cost-benefit analysis of proposed tourism development can be conducted generally at the macro national and regional levels and should be more specifically calculated along with feasibility analysis at the project level, such as for hotels and resorts. Cost-benefit analysis is a technique used to determine how much benefit the economic sector will produce in terms of foreign exchange, employment, income, and government revenues, related to the costs of development. It can be used to compare the relative costs and benefits and most productive use of investment resources in different sectors. In tourism economic cost-benefit analysis, the various measurements described in the previous sections determine the benefits. Although less quantifiable, calculation of tourism economic benefits should include the catalytic effect on other economic sectors and the overall stimulus that tourism gives for economic and human resource development. The costs to be calculated include the basic infrastructure necessary for tourism, transportation systems and equipment, accommodation of all types, restaurants, a proportionate share of developing and maintaining cultural institutions (such as museums), exhibition and convention centers, attractions development, tourist-oriented retail enterprises, and other types of tourist facilities. The additional costs imposed by tourism on public services such as medical facilities and services and public service costs for any migrant employment in tourism should be considered.

As emphasized previously, economic costs and benefits must be combined with sociocultural and environmental costs and benefits to arrive at an overall evaluation of the net costs and benefits of tourism to an area. It may be that the type of tourism that brings the greatest economic benefits also results in serious environmental or social costs and is not justified, whereas a tourism plan and program that balances economic, environmental, and sociocultural factors is the optimum one. For an individual project, cost-benefit analysis, which considers total costs and benefits to the area of the project, should be differentiated from financial feasibility analysis of only the project itself. A particular project such as a hotel or resort may, for example, be financially feasible to the developer but incur net costs at the area level if factors such as infrastructure development as well as area-wide environmental and social costs are considered.

A feasibility study is detailed systematic analysis of all aspects of a particular project in order to determine its financial, marketing, environmental, and social feasibility. A feasibility study is not designed to justify the viability of a project but objectively determine whether it will likely be viable and, if so, to what extent it will be viable. However, if the result of the study is positive, this is still no guarantee that the project will be successful because the future is unpredictable and some of the assumptions made in the study, no matter how carefully analyzed, may not prevail in the future. The two traditional main elements of a project feasibility study are market feasibility and financial feasibility, with a third element of environmental and sociocultural feasibility now recognized as essential. The feasibility study must establish the rate of return on investment, which the investor can compare to rates of return on alternative investment of his resources.

Case Studies

Two case studies are presented on socioeconomic considerations. One is the socioeconomic programming for tourism in Bali, which was carried out over a period of several years. The second is the sociocultural policy and program proposed for Zanzibar. Both these case studies are a follow-through of the tourism planning analysis and recommendations presented for these areas in previous case studies, in order to demonstrate the integrated approach applied to tourism development in these places.

Socioeconomic Programming in Bali

A case study in Chapter 6 presented the regional tourism plan analysis for Bali, and a case study in Chapter 8 described the planning of the large resort of Nusa Dua, whose location was selected in the regional plan analysis. Although Bali already had considerable tourism development in other areas, part of the concept of developing this resort was containment of much of the new tourism development in one area, that is, the enclave approach, which would somewhat contain any impacts of tourism as well as provide the opportunity for integrated planning and provision of high quality infrastructure thus precluding environmental impacts.

As part of the integrated approach to tourism development in Bali, various programs were also undertaken by the central and regional governments on socioeconomic aspects during the mid to late 1970s and continuing into the 1980s. Some of these programs were assisted by the World Bank project involved in Nusa Dua, and others were solely the responsibility of the governments involved. These represent some model approaches that have application elsewhere, especially in more traditional societies. Also, some environmental quality approaches to development are reviewed here as part of the overall program.

Bali has about 2.5 million people living in a dense, mostly village settlement pattern, with some undeveloped higher mountain areas, although the urban places are expanding rapidly. The economy is primarily agricultural, based especially on irrigated rice cultivation, with some limited small-scale industry and, in recent years, a substantial amount of tourism. With the rapid growth of population and limited resources, other than agriculture, tourism is viewed as an essential component of the economy that provides employment and income. By the late 1980s, Bali was attracting over one-half of the more than one million total international tourists annually visiting Indonesia, plus a substantial number of domestic tourists from other parts of the country.

The island's attractions for tourists are scenic beauty, beaches, and particularly its culture, which is based on the Balinese form of Hinduism, incorporating some pre-Hindu beliefs and practices and having developed independently since its derivation from India many centuries ago. The culture is an exceedingly rich and varied one with numerous temples, many religious rituals and ceremonies, distinctive music, dance and drama, and highly developed visual arts and handicrafts of several styles of painting, wood and mask carving, gold and silver working, stone carving, textile and basket weaving, and other forms. Balinese village patterns, architectural styles of temples, houses, former palaces, and other buildings, and village activities are very interesting attractions for many tourists. The traditional dance, music, drama, and shadow puppetry are performed frequently as part of normal village life. Although most tourists stay in beach-oriented resort areas, with some staying in small-scale accommodation in towns elsewhere, they spend much of their time touring the island by bus, taxi, or rental car, motorbike, and bicycle, providing considerable direct contact between the Balinese and tourists outside of the tourism establishments.

The Balinese culture, including the effects of tourism on the culture and society have been studied by various researchers over the years (for example, McKean 1989), with the general conclusion that the culture is exceedingly strong, resilient, adaptable, and in many ways sophisticated, and can effectively absorb and integrate tourism. In fact, tourism has been a major force in reinforcing the culture, its arts and crafts, and a sense of pride by the Balinese in their unique culture. Because of its importance to tourism development and foreign exchange earnings at the national level, this sector has also probably given the island society greater recognition in central government policy and planning of this large and diverse country. However, not all traditional cultures are as basically strong and adaptable as the Balinese, and it should not be assumed that the large amount of tourism experienced in Bali could be as effectively absorbed in some other cultures. In any case, as tourism is expanded in Bali for its much needed economic benefits, its sociocultural and economic impacts should continue to be monitored, and its future expansion carefully planned.

Bali possesses several types of traditional cooperative societies, some that are general purpose village and 'neighborhood' organizations and others that are for special purpose functions. Aspects of the tourism programs were carried out through these traditional organizational structures in coordination with regional government agencies. Technical assistance was provided by government officials, with some initial assistance from foreign advisers and funding provided through government sources and World Bank assistance. The specific approaches applied in Bali are described in the following sections under the categories of sociocultural, economic, and planning and design.

Sociocultural Program

Several approaches were applied in controlling possible negative sociocultural impacts and ensuring positive ones relative to the development of the Nusa Dua resort. This resort is situated in what was in the 1970s a highly traditional, isolated, and low income area, with a village located adjacent to the resort and other villages in the vicinity. The Nusa Dua Beach was being used by fishermen from the nearby village. With the upcoming resort development, the concerns were that the fishermen would be preempted from their fishing activity, and the village would not benefit from the resort development in an orderly manner. In order to maintain the fishermen's livelihood, those places on the beach used by the fishermen for launching and storing their boats were reserved for that purpose, and access was provided through the resort to the boat storage areas. In fact, the fishing activities have proven to be of considerable interest to the tourists staying in the resort. Also, as mentioned in a previous case study, pedestrian access corridors were provided through the resort for general public access to the beach and a walkway developed along the shoreline with the hotels set well back from the beach to allow for ample public use of the beach.

To integrate the village into resort activities, meetings were held with the village leaders to explain tourism in general and the specific resort development being planned so that they would understand this new activity and how they could benefit from it. During the initial stage of the resort development, the social impact on the village was systematically monitored to make certain that no serious problems were being generated, and the villagers were given the opportunity to work on the construction of the project. To provide the opportunity for permanent employment of villagers in the resort, priority for training (and later employment) in hotel, catering, and tour operations in the hotel and tourism training school developed in the resort was given to young persons living in the village. Because of their limited schooling, this required organizing special remedial courses for them so that they could then qualify to enroll in the regular courses. Financial assistance was provided to the students so they could participate in these courses. This program was very successful, and many of the villagers are now working in the resort.

In order that the village would receive some direct environmental and social benefits, the resort corporation provided basic infrastructure to the village and nearby areas, including road improvements, piped water supply, and electric power supply, none of which existed previously. Community facilities were also upgraded. The village was connected to and benefited from the new resort access road that connected the resort and village area to the airport and capital city of Denpasar. Although the resort is relatively self-contained in terms of facilities, the village also developed small restaurants and handicraft shops that are visited by the tourists, thus bringing more economic benefits to the village. However, land use controls were applied to prevent ribbon type shop development along the access road.

Elsewhere in the areas of Bali that are visited by tourists on sightseeing, shopping, and performance tours, part of the sociocultural program was to educate villagers in those areas about tourism and how they could benefit from it, through meetings held with the villagers over a long-term period. For those who wished to participate directly in tourism, advice was given on how they could establish small businesses or otherwise work in tourism.

Sponsored directly by the regional government, an annual cultural festival was organized for presenting on a competitive basis, dance, music, drama, arts, and crafts from throughout Bali. This was developed for the purpose of maintaining a high quality level of arts and crafts and to expose Balinese, and especially urban dwellers, more to their own culture. The festivals are very popular, attracting many Balinese and tourists who are on the island at festival times. A well-designed, large, open-air performance theater and exhibit area, which is part of a cultural center complex, is used for these annual festivals. A regional Balinese music and dance training center has been in operation for some time, although less formal training still takes place in some of the villages, and maintains the quality standard for traditional dance forms.

Although not part of an organized program, the impact of tourism on local arts and crafts should be noted. Bali has always been known for its high quality arts and crafts, some styles of which developed as a result of European influence during the 1930s and later, but are still distinctively Balinese in character. In response to tourism demands, arts and crafts have greatly expanded, providing a livelihood for many people. Some lower quality type items are now being produced for sale to tourists, but substantial amounts of high quality arts and crafts are also still being created and sold. Balinese artisans make the distinction between the different quality levels of art and use the income from the lower quality items to help support continued creation of the higher quality ones, including experimentation with new forms and designs.

For presentation of dance performances, a significant element of Balinese life and an important attraction for tourists, several approaches have evolved as being successful. Some performances are organized on a regular basis in villages, with tourists coming to attend the performances. The village setting is an authentic and interesting one for the dances and does not require the dancers traveling elsewhere. Other performances are held regularly in specially designed and centrally located performing stages and theaters within the tourism areas where the tourist accommodation is concentrated. Tourists attend these performances much in the same manner as they would attend performances at theaters in their home countries. Both the tourists and performers must travel to these performance theaters. Still other performances are held on specially designed stages within the resort and hotel complexes. These are quite attractive settings, designed with some traditional architectural character, but lack the natural charm of the village environments. Some criticism has been directed at the reproduction of temple settings for secular performances in these tourism environments. Performances with religious significance have been slightly modified for tourist presentations so that religious values are not compromised.

In order to inform the general public about tourism, a regular weekly radio program on tourism and its current activities is presented by the regional tourism office. In addition to general tourist literature about the Balinese culture and environment, special requirements concerning tourist dress and behavior are included in the literature and sign-posted at relevant places. On beaches, signs specify that nude bathing is prohibited and that suitable beach attire must be worn; in public offices, illustrated signs indicate what is considered proper clothing to be worn in public places; at temples, a popular type of attraction for tourists, signs are posted about proper dress being worn inside the temples and when, under certain conditions, persons are not allowed to enter the temples. Tourists are welcome to visit temples, and donations for temple maintenance are accepted. Tourists are also welcome to attend temple and other special ceremonies such as cremations but, at very important and crowded religious ceremonies, foreigners may be prohibited from entering the inner temple grounds although they can visit the outer temple areas. Attendance by tourists at ceremonies is usually no problem, but occasionally a tourist will violate behavioral and common courtesy codes, especially to obtain better vantage points for photography.

Economic Program

Various programs were aimed at enhancing and spreading more widely the economic benefits of tourism. To develop stronger linkages between agriculture and tourism, the program was to improve the variety, quality, and reliability of the supply of locally produced food items for the tourist hotels and restaurants. An experimental farm was first established to improve the quality and variety of fruits, vegetables, and poultry products and then advice given to farmers on how to produce these in larger quantities. An important aspect of this program was marketing—organizing a reliable and adequate supply of the items when and where the tourism enterprises needed them.

A problem facing many tourism areas, including Bali, is the proliferation of uncontrolled itinerant vendors, vending stalls, and small shops and restaurants. There is need for these activities to serve tourists and they provide much needed local employment and income, but they can also be visually unattractive, generate pollution problems, and create a nuisance and irritation to both tourists and residents. In order to organize this large 'informal' tourism sector, which was particularly a problem in the beach areas, the Bali government applied the approach of developing simple but well-designed and integrated beach markets that contain spaces for rent at low cost to local vendors, who install small shops and restaurants.

The beach markets were located at convenient places for tourists and were well set back from the beach but near enough to be seen and easily approached from it. When the beach markets were established, the itinerant vendors and scattered vending stalls were prohibited to operate because they then had alternative places for business. Most of the beach markets were economically successful for the entrepreneurs and also became social gathering places for residents and tourists. Tourist markets of a similar type were developed in some villages. Other tourism areas have adopted this same approach.

Bali attracts a wide socioeconomic range of tourists. In addition to large resort hotels and medium-size cottage accommodation, the policy of the Bali government has for many years been to allow establishment of guest houses (called homestays in Bali), where rooms in private homes are available for rent to tourists at a very reasonable cost. Some of these homestays have evolved into inns and small cottage hotels. This type of accommodation, which is found in many of the tourism areas of Bali, provides direct employment and income, including any operational profits made to local residents, as well as interesting, inexpensive places for tourists to stay. It also provides an opportunity for residents and tourists to have convenient social contact. These homestays and cottage hotels fit well into the small-scale environments typical of Bali, although they need to be controlled with respect to location and provision of adequate access, water supply, and other infrastructure. Residents are also involved in the ownership and management of many other small-scale tourism enterprises such as restaurants and handicraft shops.

Land Use and Design Controls

Related to both cultural and environmental considerations, the policy in Bali is to plan and design tourist facility development so that its location is somewhat controlled and architectural styles used reflect the traditional Balinese styles and characteristics of the natural environment. For all the sight-seeing or excursion roads on the island, land use plans and zoning regulations were prepared, specifying where development of tourist facilities and village expansion areas could take place and where open space, view planes, and preservation of high quality agricultural lands would be maintained. This was especially important because of the tendency for entrepreneurs to build shops outside the villages alongside roads in agricultural areas, creating a ribbon development situation, obstructing open space views, and removing agricultural land from production. Encouragement is given to applying traditional architectural design to tourist facilities, and no major facilities of unsuitable design will be approved by the government, although most developers will use local design motifs in any case because of their attractive appearance and appeal to tourists. A maximum building height limit of 15 meters has been applied to all types of development, including tourist facilities in Bali for many years, and only one hotel from a previous era exceeds that height limit. As referred to in Chapter 8, strict land use and design controls were applied in the Nusa Dua resort development.

Village Beautification Program

A technique applied in Bali and elsewhere is to encourage improvement and maintenance of the environmental quality of villages through organization of annual village beautification contests. Each year, a date is announced for the inspection of all the villages on the island, with respect to their attractiveness, cleanliness, and community improvements. The best villages are selected and publicly awarded with much local publicity. This approach gives incentive for villages to improve their appearance, which benefits the villages, develops a sense of community pride by the villagers, and improves the overall environmental quality of Bali, making the island a more interesting and attractive home for Balinese, as well as a desired destination for tourists.

Sociocultural Programming for Tourism in Zanzibar

Case studies in Chapters 3 and 7 presented the background, organization, and tourism development policy of the regional tourism development plan for Zanzibar (UNDP and WTO 1983). Zanzibar possesses a distinctive Swahili culture that has evolved during the past few hundred years from a combination of East African and southern Arabian influences. The Stone Town portion of Zanzibar city represents the largest and most interesting of the Arab (Omani) style urban settlements in East Africa. Zanzibar is commencing to develop tourism for its much needed economic benefits, but it also wishes to preserve the islands' cultural heritage, not generate social problems from tourism, and use this sector as a means for achieving cultural conservation.

In the plan, considerable emphasis was given to the sociocultural as well as environmental effects of tourism development. The plan report reviewed the importance of sociocultural evaluation for tourism and the sociocultural characteristics of the Zanzibar society, including its cultural evolution and social attitudes. The plan evaluation concluded that, at present, tourism has not led to many sociocultural problems because of the strong sense of social traditions and identity that resists indiscriminate sociocultural penetration. The Zanzibar government policy, which controls types of foreign sociocultural influences, has thus far limited the number of tourists coming to the islands. Also, most of those who do visit are seriously interested in Zanzibar's history, culture, and society.

The plan indicated that, despite minimum impacts from tourism at the present time, several actions need to be taken, as tourism expands, to avoid any negative impacts, maintain a satisfactory tourist-resident relationship, and use tourism as a technique of cultural conservation. In the area of cultural considerations, the plan's recommendations were as follows (UNDP and WTO 1983, 179–181):

- Cultural policy on tourism. There is need for the Ministry of Culture in consultation with the Ministry of Natural Resources and Tourism to prepare a policy on the relationship between culture and tourism including:
  1. A statement on Zanzibar culture which identifies the characteristics of the Zanzibar culture
  2. Proper relationship (set of standards) between the Zanzibar culture and tourism, which will be a barometer for measuring positive and negative cultural interactions
- Maintenance of historical sites
  1. Preservation and some restoration of historical sites should be done for the benefit of both residents and tourists. Preservation recommendations are made in . . .
  2. More direct contribution by tourism to preservation . . . can be done by charging a small admission fee to foreign tourists visiting these places and by establishing commercial operations such as cafes and souvenir shops on some of the sites
  3. Closer cooperation between the Tourism Department and the Ministry of Culture on the question of preservation and its cost
  4. Use of specialized technical assistance on preservation of historic places.

- Traditional music and dance
  1. Since some of the traditional dances (ngoma) are in the process of disappearing, strong action should be taken to preserve them. This can be done by creating a troupe made up of interested people who would learn all types of traditional dances and perform them regularly. This music should be recorded and the tapes preserved.
  2. A cultural center should be established where these traditional dances, Taarab and other cultural activities can be performed on a regular basis for both Zanzibaris and tourists.
- Handicrafts
  1. There is need for the government to control the quality of handicrafts. This can be done through provision of quality materials and incentives which should be given first to those who produce articles of high quality, and training of craftsmen generally.
  2. The government should encourage cooperative activities in handicrafts by offering credit to the artisans and helping to provide market outlets for their products.

With respect to social impacts, the plan made the following conclusions and recommendations:

- Up to now there are no serious social problems in Zanzibar as a result of tourism.

- The government policy requiring decency (dress and behavior) on the part of tourists and of preventing prostitution should continue.
- The government should not allow indiscriminate entry of tourists in Zanzibar. Mass tourism should be discouraged.
- In establishing beach resort hotels, several policies should be applied:
  1. The hotels should not be established too near existing villages to avoid disrupting village life.
  2. Local people should be given priority for employment in the hotels and assisted in providing agricultural and fish products to the hotels. Steps should be be taken to prevent unwarranted migration from other parts of Zanzibar to the villages near hotels.
  3. Steps should be taken to raise the socioeconomic level of the people living near the hotels in order to reduce the gap between them and the tourists. This can be done by introducing adult education classes and helping them to improve their economic activities such as agriculture and fishing.
  4. Whenever there is need to move people in order to establish hotels, ample compensation must be paid and assistance provided in resettlement. Because compensation in money may be misused by the recipients, the government should pay some of the compensation in kind.

The plan recommended various educational approaches of residents and tourists as follows:

- In the promotional literature of Zanzibar, there is need for a more detailed description of the sociocultural characteristics of the Zanzibar society and this type of information should be available to tourists when they arrive in Zanzibar.
- The general public in Zanzibar should be educated more about tourism according to the public education program recommended . . .
- People dealing directly with tourists, especially hotel workers and tourism officials, should receive training to prepare them better for encounters with tourists.

The public education program on tourism proposed elsewhere in the plan report recommended that the public media of television, radio, and newspaper be utilized for public awareness programs and that meetings be held between tourism officials and villagers living near proposed resort areas about tourism and its development program. The plan recommended that tourism be introduced as part of general studies programs at schools, with special lectures arranged by tourism officials, student visits made to inspect hotels, and information given to students about career opportunities in tourism and how to prepare for entry into this field.

The public awareness program was recommended to include the following topics:

- Concept of tourism;
- Explanation of the tourism development plan and program for Zanzibar;
- Main tourist generating countries;
- Profiles of different tourist groups;
- Tourism's contribution to economic development;

- Misconceptions regarding tourists as being special, rich, difficult to please, and so on;
- Desire of tourists to record their holiday experience by means of souvenirs, handicrafts, and photographs;
- Establishment of friendships and understanding of local customs, culture, religions, and food dishes;
- Characteristics of different socioeconomic groups of tourists;
- Desire of tourists to investigate village and domestic life-styles;
- Tourists' clothing and attire during the holiday period;
- Language barriers;
- Tipping and rewards; and
- Dealing with infringements and invasion of privacy.

References

Din, Kadin H. 1989. "Islam and Tourism: Patterns, Issues, and Options." *Annals of Tourism Research.* 16(4): 542–563.

Dogan, Hasan Zafer. 1989. "Forms of Adjustment: Sociocultural Impacts of Tourism." *Annals of Tourism Research.* 16(2): 216–236.

Esman, Marjorie R. 1984. "Tourism as Ethnic Preservation: The Cajuns of Louisiana." *Annals of Tourism Research.* 11(3): 451–467.

Fletcher, John E. 1989. "Input-Output Analysis and Tourism Impact Studies." *Annals of Tourism Research.* 16(4): 514–529.

Jafari, Jafar. 1987. "Tourism Models: The Sociocultural Aspects." *Tourism Management.* 8(2): 151–159.

de Kadt, Emanuel. ed. 1979. *Tourism: Passport to Development?* New York: Oxford University Press.

Lundberg, Donald E. 1985. *The Tourist Business.* New York: Van Nostrand Reinhold.

Mathieson, Alister and Geoffrey Wall. 1982. *Tourism: Economic, Physical and Social Impacts.* Harlow, England: Longman Group Ltd.

McKean, Philip Frick. 1989. "Towards a Theoretical Analysis of Tourism: Economic Dualism and Cultural Involution in Bali." *Hosts and Guests: The Anthropology of Tourism.* 120–138. Valene L. Smith, editor. New York: Oxford University Press.

Mings, R. C. 1988. "Assessing the Contribution of Tourism to International Understanding." *Journal of Travel Research.*

Murphy, Peter E. 1985. *Tourism: A Community Approach.* New York: Methuen. Longman Group Ltd.

Pearce, Douglas. 2nd ed. 1989. *Tourist Development.* Harlow, England: Long-
    man Group Ltd.

Smith, Valene L. ed. 2nd ed. 1989. *Hosts and Guests: The Anthropology of Tour-
    ism.* Philadelphia: University of Pennsylvania Press.

United Nations Development Programme and World Tourism Organization.
    1983. *Zanzibar Tourism Development Plan.* Madrid: World Tourism Orga-
    nization.

UNESCO. 1976. "The Effects of Tourism on Sociocultural Values." *Annals of
    Tourism Research.* 4: 74–105.

Part Five

Institutional Elements and Plan Implementation

Achieving integrated planning and successful tourism development depends as much on effective institutional factors and techniques of implementation as they do on appropriate policy, physical planning, and impact analysis and controls. Part Five first examines tourism manpower planning, public and private sector organizational structures, legislation and regulations, investment policies as necessary institutional elements to be analyzed, and recommendations formulated. This part then reviews techniques of implementation, including the concept of development programming, the importance of applying zoning, facility, and service regulations, the need for careful tour programming, and the process of project planning and development. Effective market planning and promotion programming as related to the tourism product is an essential aspect of implementation. The importance of continuous monitoring with plan and program adjustments made as necessary is emphasized as an essential component of the successful management of tourism.

Although implementation should take place according to a logical and sequential process, the point is made that successful implementation is, in the final analysis, dependent on political and community commitment to the concept of planned and controlled development of tourism and on strong leadership in applying the techniques of implementation. As in other parts of this book, some case studies are presented on approaches that have been applied to certain institutional elements and implementation techniques.

14

Planning the Institutional Elements of Tourism

Tourism Manpower Planning

Manpower planning is applying a systematic approach to ensure that the right people are in the right job at the right time. This is especially important in tourism, which is a type of service activity, depending in large part for its success on human resources and the quality of personnel working in tourism. Previously rather neglected, development of manpower is now receiving more attention as an essential input to the tourism development and management process. Tourism manpower planning is a specialized activity to be done by a manpower planning and training specialist, but the tourism planner should be aware of the basic techniques used, as are reviewed here.

In some areas, comprehensive manpower planning studies for all types of jobs in the economy, including tourism, will have already been prepared, but this will need to be reviewed with any necessary modifications made, based on the tourism plan, or the manpower planning component of the tourism planning project can be incorporated into any comprehensive manpower study that may exist. Although ideally prepared as one component of an integrated tourism planning project, it is common for tourism manpower planning studies to be prepared independently of any tourism planning project, especially as research for development or expansion of a hotel, catering, and tourism training institution or for preparation of a tourism education and training program.

Approach to Manpower Planning

Manpower planning in tourism should be approached systematically for all types and levels of tourism-related personnel, including national, regional, and community government tourism management administrations, accommodation and catering management and operations, tour and travel management and operations, and related tourist facility and service operations, such as for public and private tourist attractions and road, air, and water transportation operations if their manpower planning is not already being handled by other organizations. This planning takes into account both the types of jobs to be filled and the numbers of people and their requisite training to fill these jobs.

Manpower planning involves the four steps of:

- Evaluating the present utilization of manpower in tourism and identifying any existing problems and needs;
- Projecting the future manpower needed by the number of personnel required in each category of employment and determining the qualifications for each category of job;
- Evaluating the human resources available in the future; and
- Formulating the education and training program required to provide the requisite qualified manpower.

Each of these steps is described in the following sections.

Evaluation of Present Manpower and Training

The first step is to conduct a survey of existing manpower working in tourism. In a complete study, the survey of present employment in tourism should be done for all public and private enterprises involved in this sector. But, if the tourism sector is already quite large, a sampling approach may need to be used. A decision will need to be made on what activities comprise the tourism sector—certainly hotels, tour and travel operations (including tour guides), tourist-oriented restaurants, tourist-oriented shopping facilities, government tourism offices and boards, and perhaps related activities such as tourist transportation services that are not part of tour and travel agencies, public and private tourist attraction operations (nature parks, archaeological and historic places, theme parks, certain types of sports and recreation facilities, entertainers, and so forth).

The survey of present employment should include job classifications, number of employees, and their characteristics (age-sex profile, education level, national origin, and so forth), with any particular problems and needs identified, such as insufficient training and deficient qualifications for the positions held or high turnover. Prevailing attitudes of employees toward their work should be rated. The survey should identify the seasonality factor of employment if that exists. The survey should also obtain information from which employment ratios can be derived, particularly the number of employees per hotel room by type of accommodation, which is very useful for projecting future employment needs.

A survey and evaluation should be made of any existing training programs that are provided by tourism enterprises, the status of any existing tourism education and training institutions, such as hotel schools, and special training programs that may be sponsored by the government or other agencies. This will be important information for input into the later stage of determining education and training institutional development and programs required.

Projecting Future Manpower Needs

If prepared as part of an integrated tourism planning project, future manpower needs are projected to the same horizon year as the tourism plan, often with intermediate projection periods, usually for five-year intervals. The basis for making manpower projections at the national or regional levels is the projection of tourist arrivals and accommodation by number and type and of other tourist facilities and services required, along with considerations of the types of tourism being planned. At the hotel and resort planning levels, the projection can be more precisely made based on the specific type and extent of facilities and services being planned.

As explained in Chapter 13, for gross employment projections, a common technique is to establish a ratio of the number of jobs per accommodation unit to include the direct employment in hotels and other tourist facilities and services. Then a ratio can be applied for the indirect employment in tourism if that figure is also needed, but this type of employment usually falls into manpower planning for other economic sectors. As explained, higher quality hotels will require more employment per room than do lower quality accommodation, where less service is provided and the types of jobs will be somewhat different, with higher quality hotels requiring more specialized positions than lower quality establishments. The survey of existing employment will have indicated present job ratios, which can be adjusted for the future type of tourism, or, if there is little existing tourism development, ratios from similar types of tourism areas elsewhere can be used.

In addition to the type and quality level of accommodation, the type of tourism will influence other employment needs. For example, sight-seeing tourism requires more tour guides and drivers than does beach tourism, but beach and marine tourism requires specialized jobs such as lifeguards, diver guides, and sports fishing operators and guides. With respect to government personnel required in tourism, the employment needs will depend upon the type and extent of government involvement in the tourism sector and the recommended organizational structures for tourism, which are reviewed in a subsequent section of this chapter.

When the general types of jobs are determined, a job classification system based on the specific types of work and skill levels can be formulated for all aspects of tourism. The projection of manpower needs can then be made by job classification, based on the future type and extent of tourism development and on international formulas that have been established for distribution of types of jobs. The classification system should be comprehensive and will include at least the major categories of hotel and catering, tour and travel operations, and tourism management and tourist information services, with the specific jobs and number of persons required listed under each of these categories. Also, as mentioned, there may be more specialized classifications depending on the type of tourism, such as arts and handicrafts production, retail and duty free shops, entertainment and recreation, and nature park and historic site maintenance and visitor operations.

If tourism already exists in the area, then present employees are indicated by job classification, including any vacant positions. Account must be taken of the employment turnover or attrition factor, that is, the number of persons who leave their jobs and the tourism sector for whatever reasons and create vacant positions that must be filled with new trained personnel. In some cases, the turnover factor may be quite high, especially at the lower skill levels, requiring a rather large number of new personnel to keep the sector functioning properly.

Figure 14.1 presents a model manpower planning table that is not complete but gives an idea of the approach used. Some positions, such as accountants, that are essentially the same in the different operations can be consolidated to arrive at total needs for that classification. Manpower planning tables also may indicate skill levels of positions, typically the four categories of managerial skills, supervisory and higher level technical skills, middle level skills, and basic skills.

Human Resources Evaluation

An evaluation should be conducted of the general human resources available at present and in the future in order to determine if there is or will be sufficient basic manpower to be trained in tourism. Population projections can be analyzed to determine future total manpower resources available. This human resources evaluation should consider in particular the number of young persons who will be available for employment and their likely basic education levels, as well as the distribution between males and females. In a large country or region, the location of manpower availability should be considered, although some mobility of labor is always possible. The evaluation of human resources available for tourism should, of course, be conducted within the context of total manpower planning for the area and the manpower needs projected for other economic sectors.

The human resources evaluation should take into account any special sociocultural considerations (for example, the attitude of people toward working in tourism, especially in hotel and catering employment) and whether there are any religious or social restraints on women working in tourism and on either women or men taking certain types of positions in tourism. If these considerations are expected to present constraints on availability of manpower, there may be need for public education to change attitudes or special techniques applied to accommodate the constraints.

Most areas need to have the employment provided by tourism. This is one reason for developing this sector, but in some places there may not be a sufficient

Job Classification	Existing Employment	Vacant Positions	Projection of New Positions		Attrition Factor	Total Manpower Needs
			1995	2000		
HOTEL AND CATERING **Administration** Manager Assistant Manager Marketing Manager Chief Accountant Assistant Accountant Secretary Typist **Reception/Front Office** Front Office Manager Receptionist Assistant Receptionist Reservation Clerk Cashier Switchboard Operator Head Porter Porter **Housekeeping and Laundry** Executive Housekeeper Assistant Housekeeper Room Maid Head Linenkeeper Head of Laundry Service Laundry Worker **Restaurant and Bar** Restaurant Manager Head Bartender Assistant Restaurant Manager Head Waiter Waiter Barman Assistant Waiter Cashier **Kitchen** Executive Chef Assistant Chef Cook Cook Assistant **Maintenance** Building Maintenance Engineer Gardener Watchman Cleaner *Note: Specialized personnel may be* *required, such as hairdresser,* *entertainer, recreation leader, etc.* **TOUR AND TRAVEL OPERATIONS** Agency Manager Head of Ticketing Head of Tour Programs Sales Manager Ticketing Clerk Tour Leader Tour Guide Cashier Driver **TOURISM MANAGEMENT** Director of Tourism Chief of Marketing Chief of Planning and Development Marketing and Promotion Specialist Public Relations Officer Tourism Planning Specialist Tourism Statistician Tourist Facility Standard Specialist Tourism Training Specialist Tourist Information Service Clerk						

Figure 14.1. Model Manpower Planning Table.

present or future labor supply to satisfy all the job requirements included in tourism. As referred to in Chapter 13, a decision must then be taken on whether to allow migration of workers into the area and, if so, a determination made on how many will be needed and what job qualifications will be required.

Formulation of Education and Training Programs

Formulating the education and training program requires that first a job description and employee qualifications be written for each of the job classifications. Then, determination should be made of the type of training required to provide the necessary qualifications. For many jobs, experience will, of course, also be needed. The job description should be specific in terms of skills required, often including language capability and the level of responsibility involved. If tourism already exists in the area, the employment survey will have indicated what additional training is needed of present employees, which may be substantial if there is need to upgrade tourism. This must be considered along with the training of new personnel. The additional training may be both of a remedial type to bring some personnel up to an acceptable standard, as well as training for promotion to higher skill or supervisory/managerial levels.

The manpower needs projection by job classification and number, the job descriptions and qualifications required, and the additional training needed for present tourism employees provide the basis for determining the education and training requirements in terms of type of training and number of persons to be trained now and in the future. The type of training needed must include general tourism knowledge, specific skills, and (for higher level employees) supervisory and managerial techniques and approaches. In some cases of less developed areas where the backgrounds of trainees are limited, basic knowledge of hygiene, reading, writing, and mathematics must also be incorporated into the tourism training program or else given as special remedial courses before the tourism training is undertaken.

In addition to the essential skills required, motivation to do good work is necessary and, in many types of tourism jobs, a positive attitude toward serving tourists (often including foreigners). Public relations and communications skills are also essential. For example, in a study to determine which skills are most in need of development and that should be targeted for training in all aspects of tourism in Hawaii, the skills that were ranked the highest by both employees and employers were human relations, communications, and courtesy (Sheldon and Gee 1987). These social skills need to be considered in selecting candidates for training in tourism and also included in tourism training programs. Because of cultural differences that typically prevail between employees and tourists in less developed and traditional types of tourism areas, social skills training can be particularly important in those places and should include sociocultural and expectation profiles of the major tourist markets, with, of course, any necessary language training.

Various types of education and training should be considered in a comprehensive education and training plan. Often combined into a single plan or program to satisfy the various needs, these types of education and training include the following:

- On-the-job training provided in the places of employment, such as hotels and restaurants. For low skill level employees, on-the-job training may be sufficient, without the need for formal training.
- Short courses on various aspects of tourism, designed either on new subjects or for upgrading existing skills. Short courses may be given in the place of employment, in a local training institution, elsewhere in the country, or in foreign countries. They may be offered by an institution on a regular basis or organized for a specific group of participants on a particular subject on a one-time basis.
- Formal, regular vocational programs of one-half, one, two, or three years, usually in a hotel and tourism training institution or department of a multi-program vocational school.
- Regular university type diploma, bachelor's and master's degree programs (usually three to six years in duration) in hotel, tourism, or transportation management.
- Study tours, which include visiting places that offer examples of tourism development and operations, such as resorts, hotels, and tourist attractions, and meeting with tourism officials and administrators from different places.
- Tailor-made programs, which may include a combination of some academic courses, study tours, and on-the-job attachments. For developing countries, these are often arranged as overseas programs.
- Correspondence courses, which are available on all aspects of hotel, catering, tour operations, and tourism management.

It is common practice for employees in tourism, especially hotel, catering, and tour and travel operations, to work for some time after their initial training and then return to school to take short courses or regular programs to expand their skills and knowledge, including supervision and management techniques. Personnel in tourism management often take short courses, such as on current tourism planning, marketing, and research methodology, after their initial education in order to keep abreast of the field. Education and training should be viewed as a continuous process for the benefit of both the employees and the tourism sector, and programs should be oriented accordingly.

Hotel and tourism training institutions can be either government or privately operated. Many larger countries have both public and private institutions in order to meet the varied demands by students and the tourism sector. Where local institutions do not exist, arrangements are often made for overseas training by either the government or private sector. Establishment of a hotel, catering, and tourism training institution is a major project, requiring considerable financial investment and expertise. It is not uncommon for the government and private sector, especially hotels and tour and travel operations, to jointly fund a training school in order to meet the financial requirements. Increasingly, as tourism develops and becomes recognized as an important activity and profession, universities are establishing hotel and tourism departments oriented at the operations and management levels. Formulation of training programs should also take into account training carried out by individual hotel companies, as described in the next section.

Tourism occupations have historically been perceived as having rather low professional status. For this reason, tourism is not always seen as offering the most attractive occupations in both more and less developed countries. In her study on professionalism in tourism in Hawaii, Sheldon found that the accommodation and transportation sectors of tourism were considered to be the most professional and food service the least professional. She concluded that (Sheldon 1989, 502) "Formal education programs (two-year, four-year, and graduate programs) are one of the keys to developing competent and professional employees, and thereby raising the status of employment in the tourism industry." She indicated that educational institutions are also responsible for developing the knowledge upon which the professions are based. Therefore, these institutions should be strongly supported. Sheldon additionally recommended the up-grading of seasonal, part-time, and low-paid jobs to more rewarding and prestigious positions, and developing a code of ethics for those fields of tourism that do not yet have such codes, as well as clearly defining the career path of each field, which will help to attract and keep good quality employees.

Corporate Manpower Planning

The tourism manpower planning explained previously is done at the national, regional, and sometimes community levels for all the tourism personnel needs. Large hotels and hotel chains also perform manpower planning for their own specific needs, including projecting their employment requirements by job classification, and they often operate their own training programs. These may be only on-the-job type training or may include sponsorship of employees to take special short courses or regular programs elsewhere. Some hotel chains, such as the Oberoi chain based in India, operate their own high quality training schools. Although this type of private sector training may be quite competent and fill an important training need, the disadvantage from the overall sectoral point of view is that the training may be highly specialized in the particular approaches and techniques of the company involved and may not be completely transferable to the entire sector. From the hotels' point of view, their employees are trained in a manner that is most suitable to the company's practices.

Monitoring and Updating the Manpower Plan

As is the case with any aspect of tourism, the manpower plan needs to be monitored to make certain that it is fulfilling its objectives, with any necessary modifications being made as time passes. Tourism trends may change, requiring a somewhat different mix of employment and type of training; the human resource base may develop differently than expected; or tourism may expand at a faster or slower rate than projected, which requires adjustments to the intake of students in the training program and the scale of the program. A formal review, including surveys of employment in tourism and, if necessary, revision of the manpower plan, should be undertaken about every five years.

Training methodology and content should also be kept up-to-date (for example, on subjects of new computerization techniques in hotel, airline, and tour and travel operations, emergence of new trends in tourism, and current tourism planning, marketing, and research methodology).

Organizational Structures for Tourism

Organizational structures for tourism management includes public and private sector types of organizations at the regional, national, and international levels and sometimes at the urban and community level in tourism areas.

Importance of Tourism Organizations

In order to plan, develop, market, coordinate, and manage tourism in a country or region, effective organizational structures are essential. However, the types of government or public sector structures and the extent of their involvement in tourism must be adapted to the particular needs and ideological and political structure of the country and the type and extent of tourism development. As indicated in Chapter 7, an important type of policy decision is what the extent of government involvement in tourism will be. A basic premise of this book is that the government, whether at the national, regional, or local levels or a combination of these, should assume the overall responsibility for tourism management with respect to development policy and planning, setting and maintaining facility and service standards, some aspects of marketing, and increasingly the environmental quality of tourism areas. Otherwise, integrated, planned, and controlled tourism would not necessarily be achieved, nor would tourism be responsive to the area's and society's needs.

However, it is only in recent years, with the rapid development of tourism in many places, that some areas have adopted policies of relatively strong government involvement in tourism. In the more open market economies of Western Europe and North America, national government involvement has been particularly slow to evolve, with some exceptions such as Spain, Portugal, and France, although other European governments are becoming more involved as they recognize the increasing importance of tourism to their economies. In Eastern Europe, Yugoslavia has become a major tourist destination, based on government development of this sector. In the USA, the national government passed the National Tourism Policy Act and created the United States Travel and Tourism Administration (USTTA) in 1982, although this agency has limited funding compared to many other countries. However, in the USA, some of the state and city governments are actively involved in tourism planning and marketing, and all levels of government provide important attractions for tourists, particularly in the form of parks and historic preservation. In less developed countries that still have rather weak private sectors, the government typically must play a strong role in tourism development, including marketing and making capital investments or offering investment incentives in order to encourage the commencement of tourism. In socialist countries, governments are greatly involved in the development, operation, and marketing of tourism, although this situation is in the process of changing during the late 1980s and early 1990s, with privatization policies being adopted.

In determining the most suitable types of organizational structures, each area must be specifically evaluated as to what its particular needs and objectives in developing tourism are and which would be the most effective organizational approach to satisfy the objectives, within the context of the overall government structure. Because tourism is a complicated, multi-sectoral activity, achieving coordination among the government agencies involved in the various aspects of tourism and between the government and private sector enterprises is a major consideration. As will be explained, private sector organizations can be important in the coordinated development and operation of tourism, and their most appropriate organizational structures must also be determined.

Public Organizational Models

Various public type organizational models or a combination of these for different functions can be considered in determining the most suitable public organizational structures. These range from a greater to lesser degree of direct government involvement in tourism, as follows:

- A separate government ministry with responsibility for all aspects of tourism management.
- A government ministry (or cabinet level department) with a mixed portfolio, part of which is responsible for all aspects of tourism.
- A separate or mixed portfolio government ministry that is responsible for policy, planning, and establishing and administering facility and service standards and licensing requirements and procedures. It often does some development and research, with marketing and perhaps some development and research being done by a non-statutory or statutory board or tourism development corporation.
- A non-statutory board appointed by the government that has no legal powers and is therefore subordinate to a government department and is responsible for all or certain aspects of tourism.
- A statutory board that is established by law, comprises an autonomous legal entity, and is responsible for all or certain aspects of tourism.
- A tourism development corporation that is a separate legal entity funded by

Tuen Ng, the Dragon Boat Festival in Hong Kong—Festivals of all types are important attractions for tourists and reflect the cultural heritage of residents. However, they require careful organization to be successful, and some tourism offices include a specific organizational function for festivals and special events. (Courtesy of the Hong Kong Tourist Association and taken by Ray Cranbourne)

government or a combination of public and private sector funding. It is responsible for all tourism development and related matters or for development of particular tourism projects, such as resorts or tourist attraction features or particular types of tourist facilities and services in an area, such as hotels or tour and travel services.

A separate government ministry for tourism is justified when tourism has become (or is expected and desired to become) an important sector of the economy. Establishment of a separate ministry of tourism also gives this sector additional political status and public image importance and hence perhaps greater recognition and funding. When tourism is combined with other functions in a mixed portfolio ministry, difficult questions arise as to what the optimum combination is to achieve effective development and management of tourism. In some cases, tourism may be best combined with transport and communications because of their close relationship, or with trade and commerce if the economic development aspect of tourism is being emphasized, or with culture or parks and conservation if that relationship is important.

On allocation of organizational activities, often the most effective approach is to place the tourism policy, planning, research, facility standards, and licensing and education and training functions in a government ministry because, as emphasized, those are the logical government functions to achieve integrated, planned, and controlled development and management of tourism. The responsibility for marketing and marketing research and perhaps some development functions can be given to a statutory board. An autonomous board is typically more flexible and can be more responsive to market trends than can a government agency. A statutory board can include government as well as private sector representation with board members appointed by the government minister of tourism so that the board still reflects the government policy on tourism. The statutory board can be funded solely by the government or jointly by the government and the private tourism sector. The financial accounts of statutory boards should be reviewed periodically by the government auditing office to make certain that their often large budgets (for marketing) are being properly utilized.

For development of specific tourism projects that are sponsored by the government, establishment of an autonomous development corporation is often the most effective organizational technique. This corporation can be responsible for more than one project, depending on the local situation. A public corporation approach is especially useful for implementing large integrated projects, such as resorts where they cannot be developed easily by the private sector, even though the project is expected to eventually be profit-making and the private sector may develop and operate the commercial facilities in the project. In some areas with well-developed private sectors, large projects are undertaken entirely by private corporations, but with strict government controls on land use zoning, development standards, and environmental controls and approval required of the overall project plan before construction can commence.

Because coordination among government agencies and between the public and private sectors is so essential for the effective development and management of tourism, a tourism board or committee often needs to be organized. This body should include representation from the various government agencies involved in aspects of tourism, the private tourism sector, and any other institutions or groups concerned with tourism. Whether advisory or vested with decision-making authority, this body serves a very useful purpose of providing the opportunity for mutual discussion and reaching an agreement on matters relevant to the smooth and coordinated management of tourism. It can coordinate on matters such as immigration and customs procedures, transportation development and operation, other infrastructure development, tourist facility licensing requirements, park development and environmental protection, and cultural activities, including archaeological and historic conservation.

For large-scale projects, various types and levels of public and private sector organizations may need to be involved, as was the case with development of the Langudoc-Roussillon project, which encompasses 180 kilometers of the western section of the French Mediterranean coast. As described by Pearce (1989), this major tourism development project, which was commenced in the early 1960s, required the clearly defined and coordinated division of responsibility among various agencies because no one organization had the resources or competence to undertake everything required, but the success of the project depended on all facets of development being carefully coordinated. The roles of the central, regional, and local authorities and the private sector were defined from the outset of the project, with the central agencies responsible for preparing the overall development plan, acquiring the land, and undertaking major infrastructure works. A specially appointed 'mission,' with representation of various involved agencies and a small technical team, coordinated the overall development. The regional governments provided some finance for the infrastructure and participated in the development of some new resorts through the creation of four mixed public-private funded companies. After the planning and development of the infrastructure, the private sector entered the development process to construct various forms of accommodation and other tourist facilities. Considerable international investment was made in the project.

NTA Organization

The organizational structure of the National Tourism Administration (NTA) or regional tourism agency, or non-statutory or statutory board, or a combination of these, can take various forms depending on the particular functions and size of the agency. However, some general guidelines can be set forth for a prototypical organizational structure. First, the functions of the NTA need to be decided. These are usually:

- Policy;
- Planning;
- Perhaps some development and facility operation;
- Coordination;
- Statistics;

- Research;
- Marketing and tourist information services;
- Coordination of education and training;
- Establishing and administering tourist facility standards and licensing requirements and procedures;
- Administrative functions; and
- Perhaps some specialized functions, such as organization of special events.

Planning and development are closely interrelated, as are marketing and information services and statistics and research. In a medium-size organization, the typical organizational chart could be as shown in Figure 14.2. The number of subsections will depend on the size of the organization. As indicated previously, the marketing and information services department could be organized as a statutory board, and, if there is a substantial development function, that function can be organized under a development corporation.

If international tourism is important in the area, a decision will need to be made on whether to maintain overseas offices in the market origin countries or region and, if so, where these are best located. If the cost of maintaining overseas offices is not justified, consideration can be given to making use of the facilities and services of existing embassies or consulates or of contracting a private firm in the market country to carry out promotional activities on a fee basis.

Staffing of the NTA will, of course, depend very much on the functional needs and resources available. If staffing is limited, some staff members may need to handle more than one function. It is essential that the staff be properly trained to effectively fulfill their functions, especially in the areas of tourism planning, development and facility standards, marketing and information services, and statistics and research.

Financing Public Tourism Organizations

Financing of the government tourism office or statutory board activities is usually directly from government funding. Any operational activities of the tourism office, such as managing hotels, restaurants, or duty free shops, may also provide profits that can help fund the office, although the advantages and disadvantages of involvement of government in profit-making operational activities must be carefully weighed. If there is a type of tourism tax, such as a hotel or tourist expenditure tax in the area, a logical source of funding can be allocation of all or part of this tax to the tourism office budget or for special purposes such as marketing. As mentioned previously, this allocation of the tourism tax may be resisted by the government because it wants these tax revenues for general use, but such an allocation should be considered, especially in newly developing or rapidly expanding tourism areas, as a source of funding for further development.

For financing tourism promotional programs, the government typically provides the funding for overall promotion, while the private sector finances promotion of its particular products. However, an effective means for increasing gov-

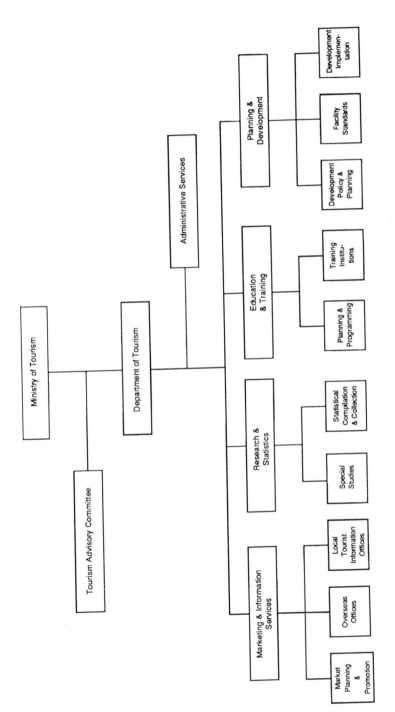

Figure 14.2. Typical NTA Organization Chart.

ernment promotional budgets and achieving more coordinated promotion between the the public and private sectors is joint promotion in terms of pooling financial resources and preparing coordinated programs. The private sector can still conduct its own promotion of specific projects after allocating some of its promotion budget to a joint promotion program. For these combined promotion activities, often a joint promotion board is organized, which agrees to contribute funding to the tourism office or statutory board, with the right to participate in determining the type of promotion program and its budget.

Private Sector Tourism Organizations

Tourism-related private sector organizations serve several important purposes:
- Providing a forum for discussing and resolving common problems of tourism enterprises;
- Making coordinated recommendations to the government tourism office for improvements in the tourism sector;
- Providing representation on tourism boards and committees;
- Conducting research and training that is relevant to the private sector; and
- Sponsoring special events.

Private sector organizations are typically organized by type of enterprises, such as hotels, restaurants, tour and travel agencies, and sometimes retail or duty-free shops. Normally, they are organized separately, such as a hotel association, but may be combined (for example, as a hotel and restaurant association). In a few small countries or regions, all the tourism-related enterprises may be combined in one association. Even if organized as separate associations, they need to coordinate, perhaps through a committee, on issues that involve the entire tourism sector. Sometimes, the local chamber of commerce plays an active private sector tourism role. Financing of private tourism-related organizations is through dues paid by the member tourism enterprises, often based on a sliding scale, depending on the relative sizes of the enterprises.

At the community level of tourism development, tourism councils or committees can be organized to advise and work with the local government on tourism development. These groups have representation from the private sector tourism enterprises, the general business community, and spokesmen of various types of local organizations, including cultural and environmental groups, in order to obtain a cross-section of community opinion.

International Tourism Organizations

The various global and regional organizations related to tourism, such as the WTO and its regional commissions and the PATA were reviewed in Chapter 2. These organizations currently perform various important roles and it is expected that their activities and influence will expand in the future. It is being generally recognized that countries can benefit from tourism more through international and regional cooperation in activities such as joint marketing, tour programming, complementary facility and attraction development, and application of compatible facility and service standards than if each area pursues it own interests on a completely competitive basis. Regional cooperation can be especially beneficial to smaller countries that have limited resources for developing tourism and may not be well known among the international tourist markets. Often, a staff member of the NTA is designated to be responsible for maintaining relationships with international organizations and representing the government at international tourism meetings.

Tourism-Related Legislation

An important role of the government is to enact and administer legislation and regulations on tourism. Tourism and related legislation provide the legal basis for the development, management, and operation of tourism. Relevant laws and regulations are reviewed and evaluated as part of the comprehensive tourism planning process or, if not existing, their absence noted, with any new or revised legislation prepared. Many countries have adopted tourism-related legislation tailored to their particular needs, and various models are available, for example, from the WTO.

Tourism Legislation

Directly related tourism legislation includes the basic tourism law, which sets forth the policy of developing tourism and establishes the NTA, regional, or urban tourism organizational structure, functions, and sources of funding. Various specific regulations relate to the standards and licensing requirements and procedures for hotels, restaurants, tour and travel agencies, often tour guides, and perhaps a hotel classification system, as well as tourist protection requirements. These regulations must be carefully prepared based on the understanding of the needs of the country, and the mechanisms and staff capabilities must be available to apply the regulations on a continuing basis.

Related Laws and Regulations

Other types of legislation and regulations that have general application to the area and are related to certain aspects of successful tourism should be investigated and may need to be drafted or revised. In the area of physical planning, there may be need for basic planning legislation if it does not yet exist, and especially need for zoning regulations that include accommodation and other tourist facility land use controls. The basic development controls that are essential to achieve the desired type of development and help maintain the environmental quality of an area (examined in Chapter 11) are usually included in zoning regulations. Construction building codes should also be examined to make certain that they are suitable for tourist facility development.

Also needed for general as well as tourism development is environmental protection legislation to ensure that environmental quality standards are maintained. As indicated in Chapter 12, such legislation usually requires that an environmental impact assessment (EIA) be made for any major type of development, including tourist facilities, so that no serious negative physical or sociocultural impacts result from development. Sometimes, a consideration in development of tourist facilities is the acquisition of land for hotels and resorts. If the local land tenure patterns are difficult, special regulations and procedures may need to be applied to make the land available at a fair price to both the present owners and tourism developers.

Public health, sanitation, safety, and fire codes, facility operating and liquor licenses, liability laws relating to guests and their belongings, labor, and taxation legislation all relate to development and operation of tourist facilities. Regulations related to transportation facilities and services such as control of fares, licensing of carriers, safety requirements, and routes also affect the operation of tourism.

In areas developing tourism based on scenic areas, nature parks, and archaeological and historic places, legislation on parks and conservation is very important to maintain these features. These places need to be legally designated and planned, with the plans implemented based in part on application of relevant regulations.

Not related to developing the tourism area but, rather, to the market origin countries is the increasingly common consumer protection legislation, which is designed to protect the tourist consumer from being taken advantage of by unscrupulous or mismanaged tourism enterprise operators.

Tourism Investment Incentives

Substantial investment of financial resources is required in developing tourism, especially for accommodation and other tourist facilities and services, transportation facilities and other infrastructure, and often for tourist attractions or visitor facilities at attraction features. Also, tourism manpower development may require considerable investment, as does marketing and some other institutional elements. This section specifically reviews policy approaches for investment in tourist facilities and related infrastructure, and, where needed, financial incentives to attract private investment. In highly socialized economies, all investment is made by the government, often through public corporations, but in mixed and capitalist-oriented economies, private sector investment is necessary. That is the focus of the review here.

Investment Policies

The survey and analysis steps of the planning process on investment policies will determine the present investment policies of the tourism area for mobilization of the capital necessary for all types of development, including tourism. The availability of capital for investment, whether international or local or a combination of these, must also be examined. The tourism development plan and program recommendations and economic analysis will indicate the magnitude of capital investment required and the type of investment needed, such as for development of infrastructure, hotels, resorts, and tourist attractions.

In some places with highly developed economies, there may be sufficient financial resources available in the public and private sectors for the investment required, and the need will be only for financial programming in the public sector, as well as allowing the private sector to mobilize its own capital resources. However, in many places, there are constraints on the availability of capital, and efforts will need to be directed towards finding financial resources. In any situation, an investment policy must be defined.

A basic consideration and decision that needs to be made by the government is the source of financing infrastructure development for tourism. As previously emphasized, the tourism plan should make maximum use of existing infrastructure. Any new or improved infrastructure should be multi-purpose to the greatest extent possible, serving general community needs as well as tourism. However, substantial investment may still be needed to improve the existing and, where needed, develop new infrastructure for tourism. For major infrastructure development or improvements, such as for airports, main roads, and often for water supply, electric power, sewage and solid waste disposal systems, the government usually must make the investment required, at least up to the boundaries of the development sites. This may be viewed as an incentive to attract private investment to the area. User fees may eventually repay all or of part of the initial investment or at least the operational costs, especially of utility systems such as water supply.

For isolated hotels and resorts, the common practice is for the government to develop the major infrastructure, including up to the boundaries of the development site. The on-site infrastructure costs are typically financed by the developer who recovers his investment through revenues generated by the hotel or resort. As indicated in the next section, the government may directly or through a public corporation develop the on-site infrastructure as an incentive to attract private investment to the site, but it can eventually recover some or all of this cost.

For public type tourist attractions such as national parks and major archaeological and historic sites, the government typically makes the investment to manage conservation of these places and develop visitor facilities and services. Some of this cost can be recovered through admission fees and revenues from franchising the commercial operations such as restaurants, retail sales outlets, and sometimes accommodation to private entrepreneurs. Wholly commercial attraction features such as theme parks and casinos are usually totally privately financed but, in some areas, may be financed and developed by a public corporation.

For development of commercial tourist facilities of hotels, resorts, tourist restaurants, tour and travel operations, and so forth, the investment policy will depend on the availability of capital resources and the capability of attracting the resources for this investment. It may be that some investment capital is available locally, but there are competing demands and alternative investment opportunities for the available capital. If, as referred to in Chapter 13, there is insufficient local capital, then consideration must be given to attracting outside capital, and a decision must be made whether total outside capitalization is allowed or if joint venture will be required so that some local control of the property is retained. Outside capitalization, of course, results in the loss from the local area of some of the investment profits and interest payments on any loans involved.

If there is difficulty in attracting either the limited local financing or outside capital, then provision of incentives to attract the investment required can be considered. From the policy standpoint, the question of whether to provide incentives and the types and extent of incentives must be examined carefully with respect to the costs of lost revenue, resulting from the incentives being offered relative to the benefits gained from the development and to what extent any incentives are really needed. Before implementing an incentive policy, Mill and Morrison (1985, 237) state that a destination should first:

1. Examine the performance of other countries' schemes in the light of their resources and development objectives;
2. Research the actual needs of investors;
3. Design codes of investment concessions related to specific development objectives, with precise requirements of the investors (such as in terms of job creation); and
4. Establish targets of achievement and periodically monitor and assess the level of realization of such targets.

Wanhill (1986) maintains that a high operating leverage is a major source of financial risk and that grants to reduce initial capital costs are more effective in reducing risks and that, except for guaranteed investment security, most incentives are unnecessary. He concludes that the primary type of incentive should be the capital grant or its equivalent in the provision of facilities.

If incentives are provided, they should not be greater than is absolutely necessary to attract the desired investment and should be provided only as long as needed based on prevailing circumstances. As these change, the incentives should be adjusted or dropped accordingly. Sometimes, the tourism area will offer incentives in excess of those needed or maintain the incentives longer than required and consequently will lose potential revenue. Any incentives offered should be periodically reviewed to decide if they are still necessary or if they should be adjusted or dropped.

Types of Investment Incentives

If it has been determined that investment incentives are required, then the types of incentives or a combination of incentives are decided upon. The various types of incentives include the following:

- Provision of land at moderate or no cost at suitable sites to develop hotels, resorts, or other tourist facilities. In some areas where land acquisition by the private sector is difficult, just the assembly of land by the government for suitable development sites is sufficient incentive.
- Provision of off-site infrastructure at no cost to the developer. This is commonly provided, in any case.
- Provision of all or part of the on-site infrastructure, for which the cost may be eventually recovered through user fees or lease rent of the hotel and other commercial sites on a long-term basis. This is a common approach when a public corporation develops the site.
- Complete or partial exemption from customs duties on imported items used in the initial development and perhaps operation and maintenance of tourist facilities and services, such as materials, machinery, and equipment required for hotels and restaurants, and transportation vehicles, such as tour buses, cars, and tourist boats. The specific items and amounts of exemption allowed are listed in the incentives legislation.
- Complete or partial exemption from company income taxes on profits made from the facilities for a specified number of years, that is, a tax holiday.
- Reduction of company taxation by means of favorable depreciation allowances on investment, turnover taxes, and so on.
- Complete or partial exemption from property taxes for a specified number of years.
- Provision of loans up to a certain percentage of investment cost at regular or low interest rates for tourist facility development, or guarantee by the government for loans made by private financial institutions. Loans can also be provided for the working or opertional capital initially needed by enterprises.
- Provision of grants for development of tourist facilities up to a certain percentage of investment costs or, for hotels, based on the number of accommodation units.
- Allowance of foreign exchange credits from foreign sources for allocation to investment in tourist facilities.
- Provision of subsidies on interest payments of loans for the initial years of operating hotels and other tourist facilities (this initial period of operation is when revenues and profits are typically low).
- Allowance for extended periods of grace on repayment schedules of loans made for the investment required in order to allow for the initial period of low profitability.
- Unrestricted repatriation of all or part of invested capital, profits, dividends, and interest subject to specified tax provisions.
- Provision of grants for staff training programs.
- Guarantees against nationalization or appropriation of the investment.

It is important that the incentive provided be only for approved projects that conform to the development plan and program and are suitably designed. The project plans should be reviewed and approved before the incentives are granted. The incentives may also be restricted to the types of facilities and locations for which the government wishes to encourage development (for example, higher quality hotels, cottage hotels, or accommodation in certain areas, often newly developing tourism areas). Certain aspects of tourism may be selectively encouraged through incentives, such as local tour operations by offering incentives for purchase of transportation vehicles, or boating/yachting tourism by providing incentives for development of marina and harbor facilities. Incentives may also be applicable to the expansion of existing hotels and other facilities, as well as totally new development.

Although not a direct incentive, a technique that is sometimes used to open up new tourism areas or a resort project is for the government or development corporation to invest in and construct the first hotel as the 'pioneer' developer. This hotel will commence the development to start attracting tourists and, if successful, then private developers will have the confidence to invest in other hotels either with or without investment incentives being offered, depending on the local circumstances.

In situations where incentives are not required and the profitability of tourism development is obviously assured, the government may require that the developers make payments for their proportionate share of the costs of government development of the basic off-site infrastructure. Even other costs, such as any social or environmental costs resulting from the development, can be required to be paid by the developer (for example, buying land and planting forest cover elsewhere to replace that which was removed for tourism development and resettlement costs of persons dislocated by the development).

Case Studies

Two case studies are presented, one on national tourism legislation and the other on tourist facility investment incentives. The tourism law for Iceland is very progressive in several ways, including on environmental and social considerations. The investment incentives adopted in Portugal are also progressive in that they are tailored to achieve certain specific development objectives.

Law on Organization of Tourism in Iceland

The law on organization of tourism in Iceland (National Tourist Board of Iceland 1976), which establishes the National Tourist Board and other tourism regulations, is interesting in several respects. Several of the important points included in this law have application in other countries. In Article 1, the law identifies domestic and foreign tourism "as an important aspect of the Icelandic economy and social life in respect of economic benefits and protection of the environment." This statement recognizes both the major types of tourism and the fact that social and environmental, as well as economic, objectives are important.

Article 4 specifies that three members of the National Tourist Board shall be appointed by the Minister of Communications without being nominated and that the remainder shall be appointed by the minister on the basis of nominations by the following parties, each of whom nominates one member:

- The Association of Group Travelers
- The Federation of Icelandic Travel Agencies
- The Union of Icelandic Travel Guides
- Licensed Bus Owners' Association
- The Tourist Association of Iceland
- Icelandic Airlines Ltd.
- The Nature Preservation Council
- Union of Local Authorities in Iceland
- The Icelandic Hotel and Restaurant Association
- Airlines other than Icelandic Airlines Ltd.

This widespread representation of the government, all the tourism-related associations, all the airlines, the Nature Preservation Council, and local authorities provides the opportunity for close coordination of the major entities involved in developing tourism.

Article 7 specifies the responsibilities of the National Tourist Board as follows:

- Organizing and planning tourist services in Iceland;
- Providing information about Iceland;
- Participating in international cooperation in the field of tourism;
- Supporting individual tourist organizations and their activities;
- Organizing study and training programs for tourist guides in accordance with special regulations on this subject;
- Initiating various types of service and information activities for tourists;
- Cooperating with the Nature Preservation Council and other interested organizations in ensuring that the environment, landscape, nature, and matters of cultural value are not disturbed or despoiled by the activities covered by this law;
- Initiating measures for improving the environment and making places frequented by tourists more attractive, and ensuring that they be used in a clean and hygienic manner;
- Investigating the fairness of complaints with respect to poor service to tourists;
- Preparing for and managing conferences on tourism, which shall be held no more seldom than every other year; and
- Completing other tasks that are entrusted to the Tourist Board by the provision of this law or by means of other directives.

As indicated, the responsibilities are wide-ranging, including (again) emphasis on the natural and cultural environment.

In Article 8, provision is made for a source of funding that comes directly from tourist expenditures on duty-free goods (10 percent of its total annual sales) for: 1) provision of information services by the Tourist Board; 2) appropriation to the Tourist Fund to provide financial aid; and 3) financial grants to private and public concerns for the purpose of establishing or improving services for tourists at much frequented locations. This approach guarantees that some funding will be available and reflects the principle that the tourism sector should directly pay, at least in part, for its management and expansion.

Chapter III of the law establishes a government travel agency that includes, among other activities, as specified in Article 11, operation of summer hotels on the premises of boarding schools in accordance with agreements reached with the management of these schools, but not creating undesirable competition with other hotels operating in the same areas throughout the year. This is good multiuse of facilities for seasonal activities, especially for young travelers, and as stipulated, does not compete with commercial hotels.

Chapter IV is the travel agency law that requires licensing of travel agencies (Article 16) and licensing conditions (Article 17), including possessing an experienced staff, and a stipulation in Article 18 that the agency must have a minimum financial bank guarantee for possible future court settlements and emergency use. These requirements for travel agencies to maintain qualified staff and be financially responsible are now being commonly applied.

As specified in Chapter V of the law, a tourist fund was established to be used to provide development incentives in the form of capital loans made for construction of hotels, restaurants, and other tourist facility projects, as well as outright grants of up to 30 percent of construction cost for accommodation that is operated throughout the year (Article 24). In addition to funding from duty-free sales as referred in Article 8, the tourist fund is financed by appropriations from the treasury and from operational revenues of the fund (Article 25). Article 30 stipulates that certain student boarding facilities can be required to be designed for summer accommodation, reinforcing the multi-use potential referred to Article 11.

Article 35 authorizes that group tour operators may be required to obtain insurance to cover the cost for search and rescue operations that may be necessary (hiking in isolated areas is a popular tourist activity in Iceland) and that specially trained guides may be required to be employed. These are important considerations in a tourism area where there is some physical danger associated with tourist activities.

In order to ensure that certain tourist attractions be properly preserved and improved, Article 36 authorizes that the user (admission) fees collected at the attractions be utilized for preservation and improvement of visitor facilities. This is an increasingly common approach to fund such improvements, based on the principle that users should pay for the amenities that they visit and enjoy.

Financial Incentives for Investment in Tourist Facilities in Portugal

The financial incentive schemes for investment in tourist facilities in Portugal (Ministry of Finance and Planning and Ministry of Trade and Tourism 1980) was enacted to supplement existing financial aid schemes in order to encourage development of large-scale projects that meet certain requirements. The preamble to the law points out that tourism is a very important component of the country's economy due to its positive impact on the balance of payments (foreign exchange earnings) and the amount of employment directly and indirectly generated in the tourism sector and related activities. The two types of financial incentives provided are: 1) subsidies for interest payments on loans; and 2) extended periods of grace of loan repayment periods. The law is a good example of a suitable approach toward offering incentives in several respects.

As indicated in Article 3, only projects " . . . which will provide a significant contribution to the economic and social development of the country may be entitled to special benefits to be established on a case-by-case basis . . ." This stipulation results in only very worthwhile and productive projects, and not any development proposals, being entitled to the incentives.

Assessment of project productivity must be made systematically, as set forth in Article 5, as follows:

- Investment projects shall be assessed according to their economic productivity and this shall be determined by calculating the investment/output ratio. There will be a premium for any export content in the project and penalty for any import content.
- Project rating (P) shall be the sum of two numbers, one having a variable value depending upon the project's productivity calculated in accordance with the provisions of the preceding paragraph and the other having a constant value corresponding to the project's touristic utility.
- The method of calculating project rating (P) in accordance with the provision of the preceding paragraphs shall be defined in an order to be issued jointly by the Ministry of Finance and Planning and the Ministry of Trade and Tourism.

This approach provides an objective basis for determining the level of subsidies, which is more cost-effective and beneficial to the country than offering the same subsidies to all eligible projects.

Article 6 stipulates that the project rating established will be the basis for determining the amount of subsidy on interest payments, granted along with the Bank of Portugal's basic discount rate and the proportion of developer's capital invested in the project. This article further indicates that "The subsidized rates shall be available for a period of five years for investment in hotels or in other such establishments providing accommodation or for a period of three years for investment in catering establishments or for the period required to carry out the project whenever this is lower than the established period." This provision allows the subsidies to be in effect for the typically initial low profit period of facility operation.

As stipulated in Article 7, the initial level of subsidy granted is based on the project's provisional rating of estimated productivity. Then the project's definitive productivity is assessed after three years of operation for hotels and two years for restaurants. If the definitive rating is different than the provisional one, the subsidy is adjusted accordingly. This checking of the actual productivity rating ensures that the subsidy granted is the proper one for the project.

Article 11 stipulates that the maximum period of loans is 20 years with the maximum grace period being 5 years, and that the loans should be granted only for projects that contribute to the overall tourism sector policy. These stipulations, although rather general, ensure that only suitable and productive projects are eligible for loans and that there are maximum loan and grace periods so that the loan assistance is not abused or wasted.

References

Mill, Robert Christie and Alastair Morrison. 1985. *The Tourism System: An Introductory Text.* Englewood Cliffs, New Jersey: Prentice Hall.

Ministry of Finance and Planning and Ministry of Trade and Tourism of Portugal. 1980. *Financial Incentive Schemes for Investment in Tourism Facilities.* Lisbon.

National Tourist Board of Iceland. 1976. *Law on the Organization of Tourism.* Reykjavik.

Pearce, Douglas. 2nd ed. 1989. *Tourist Development.* Harlow, England: Longman Group.

Sheldon, Pauline J. 1989. "Professionalism in Tourism and Hospitality." *Annals of Tourism Research.* 16(4): 492–503.

Sheldon, Pauline J. and Chuck Y. Gee. 1987. "Training Needs Assessment in the Travel Industry." *Annals of Tourism Research.* 14(2): 173–182.

Wanhill, Stephen R. C. 1986. "Which Investment Incentives for Tourism?" *Tourism Management.* 7(1): 2–7.

15

Tourism Plan Implementation

Approach to Implementation

As emphasized throughout this book, the tourism plan must be prepared in such a manner that it is realistic to implement. The implementation approaches and techniques should be considered throughout the planning process. The plan should also contain a specific section on implementation, with the techniques and procedures clearly set forth so that the users of the plan understand the approach to implementation and have clear guidelines on the techniques and procedures to be followed. In more developed areas that have a substantial history of planning and where planning mechanisms are already in place, implementation techniques are better understood and may be easier to apply but, in less developed and new tourism areas, implementation is often not as easily accomplished. Because of tourism's complicated and multi-sectoral character, tourism plan implementation can be especially challenging to achieve in a coordinated manner.

As with any type of development planning, implementation must take into account political considerations without greatly compromising the plan's objectives. Plan implementation is in large part a political process because governance is involved in achieving implementation. In many places, one of the best approaches to convince political representatives about the need for effective plan implementation is to demonstrate the long-term economic benefits of good planning and controlled development. Increasingly, these representatives are also becoming aware of the need for controlling undesirable environmental and sociocultural impacts through the planning process.

Inherent in the political considerations of the plan being adopted and implemented, especially at the local level, is community understanding and support of the plan through their having participated in its preparation and knowing that they will receive benefits, not problems, from tourism. Additionally, during the implementation of the plan, the community should be kept informed of the approach and status of implementation through community awareness programs. In the final analysis, the success of implementation will depend on political determination and commitment to the concept of planned and controlled tourism, the community support of this approach, and strong political leadership that is backed up by competent technical advice.

In examining implementation here, the respective roles and importance of coordination of the public and private sectors are reviewed first, and then the specific techniques for implementing the physical plan, project development and other recommendations are described. An overview of market planning and promotion is included here because of their close relationship to implementation. Some of the special considerations that must be made are indicated. Finally, the formal process of plan implementation and monitoring are specified and the importance of monitoring is emphasized.

Roles and Coordination of the Public and Private Sectors

As explained in Chapter 7, determining the respective roles of the public and private sectors in the development of tourism is a basic policy decision. As elaborated in Chapter 14, the role of government needs to be a strong one with respect to deciding policy and planning, setting and administering facility standards, and in other areas such as education and training. Government's role in implementation is also a critical one relative to several functions:

- Programming development;
- Adopting and administering tourism-related legislation and regulations;
- Developing major infrastructure;
- Developing public type tourist attractions such as nature parks, conserving archaeological and historic sites, developing and maintaining museums and cultural centers and organizing special events; and
- Carrying out some marketing of tourism for the area.

However, as has been mentioned previously, some of the cost of developing and maintaining infrastructure and tourist attractions can be recovered by collecting user fees. Beyond those functions, the respective roles of government and the private sector will vary, depending on the circumstances of the area and its economic and political ideology.

In a capitalist or mixed economy, development of tourist facilities and services such as hotels and other accommodation, tour and travel agencies, commercial type tourist attractions and activities, and local infrastructure is usually the responsibility of the private sector, or in some areas, of public corporations. The government still applies regulations to the private sector development and, if necessary, offers investment incentives to the private sector. Certain 'social' types of facilities such as low-cost accommodation for domestic tourists, youth hostels, and campgrounds may be developed by the government or private non-profit organizations. As has been indicated, the government sometimes functions as a pioneer in developing hotels and other facilities and services in new tourism areas until the private sector is induced to make investments in the area. There are, however, exceptions to this, where government-owned corporations will develop and operate a single hotel or chain of hotels that are profitable and can compete with facilities of private corporations.

The respective roles of the public and private sectors may change through time, depending on changing circumstances, although the government should maintain the basic policy, planning, and implementation functions indicated above. Initially, when tourism areas are commencing development, the government may need to take more of a lead role, including investment in commercial facilities and services. Later, when tourism is better established and proven to be successful, the private sector can take the primary investment role. It is important to recognize changing circumstances and adapt the policies accordingly.

Whatever the mix of public and private sector involvement in tourism, coordination among the various agencies and levels of government, between government and the private sector, and among private sector enterprises is an essential element of successful implementation. There needs to be coordination among national, regional, metropolitan, and local levels of government on policy and planning and in developing infrastructure, among the various different government agencies involved in aspects of tourism at each level, and between the public and private sectors at each level. The private sector tourism enterprises need to coordinate among themselves. As explained in Chapter 14, various organizational structures can be put in place to effect this coordination, including community participation in coordination, particularly at the local levels.

Implementation of Physical Plans, Projects, and Programs

Several techniques are applied to implement the physical plans—the national and regional structure plans, urban tourism plans, and resort and tourist attractions plans—and other recommendations, as described in the following sections.

Development Staging and Programming at the National and Regional Levels

An essential technique to achieve systematic and efficient implementation is staging and programming development. Development staging is included as an element of the national and regional or more detailed facility or attraction land use plan, as explained in previous chapters on those topics. Staging at the national and regional levels indicates when and where development, including infrastructure, should logically be commenced and carried out in the various tourism areas or continued by increments in those areas. Determination of staging depends on such factors as market growth, location and accessibility of the various areas and their relationship to tourist attractions development, programming of major general purpose infrastructure such as airports and roads, and the availability of financing. Environmental and sociocultural considerations and specific area needs for economic development may also influence staging. Staging is usually indicated as first, second, and later stages and related to time periods, often in five-year increments.

The first stage development (or action) program is often prepared as part of the initial tourism planning project or shortly after the plan has been adopted, and is then updated and revised periodically. At the national and regional levels, the development program specifies all types of development needed, usually on an annual basis, and the estimated cost of each project, at least of the public sector type projects, in the program. The development program should include both public and private sector type projects and the infrastructure, as well as superstructure, required so that development is integrated. The plan may also have identified special studies, such as on handicraft improvements or more detailed planning for a national park, to be undertaken. The cost of preparing these studies and plans should also be included in the development program.

An action program is more inclusive than a project development program and, in addition to physical development projects, also includes other actions necessary to implement the plan on a staged basis. Examples of the other actions would be adopting certain legislation and regulations, effecting organizational changes, and implementing sociocultural and training programs. The action program approach is being increasingly used because it is more comprehensive and gives the government specific guidelines and timing objectives for taking all the actions required for implementation.

Figure 15.1 shows a model action program for a large region, which includes both public and private sector type projects and other actions required, categorized by type, such as tourist facilities, tourist attractions, special projects, infrastructure, further studies and detailed planning, and actions require on institutional elements. An actual action program would also include cost estimates where relevant and the agencies and parties responsible for each project or action. Indication of responsible parties lets everyone know who is responsible and assigns accountability, which can be monitored.

Zoning and Facility Regulations

Zoning regulations demarcate specific areas for different types of land uses and the development standards to be applied within each land use zone as a means of controlling land uses according to the plan and ensuring that the standards are followed. These zones include various types of commercial, residential, industrial, agricultural, parks and conservation, and perhaps other types of land uses. In tourism areas, tourism-related land uses are included in zoning regulations (for example, mixed-use resort; low, medium, and high density hotels; and tourism commercial zones). The parks, open space, and

MODEL NATIONAL/REGIONAL TOURISM ACTION PROGRAM

PROJECT/ACTION	1991	1992	1993	1994	1995
Tourist Facilities					
Urban hotel expansion	Planning & design	Construct	Open		
New urban hotel	Planning & design	Construct	Construct	Open	
Beach hotel 1	Planning & design	Construct	Construct	Open	
Beach hotel 2		Planning & design	Construct	Construct	Open
Beach hotel 3					Planning & design
Mountain lodge			Planning & design	Construct	Open
Tour agency 1	Organize	Open			
Tour agency 2				Organize	Open
Tour stopover & restaurant 1	Planning & design	Construct	Open		
Tour stopover & restaurant 2			Planning & design	Construct	Open
Tourist information center	Planning & design	Construct	Open		
Duty-free shop	Planning & design	Construct	Open		Expand
Tourist Attractions					
National Park 1	Overall planning	Facilities design	Construct facilities	Open	
National Park 2				Overall planning	Facilities design
Beach–Marine Park	Planning & design	Construct facilities	Open		Expand facilities
Historic site 1	Planning & design	Restoration works	Construct facilities	Open	
Historic site 2				Planning & design	Restoration works
Archaeological site		Planning & design	Conservation works	Construct facilities	Open

Figure 15.1. Model National/Regional Tourism Action Program.

PROJECT/ACTION	1991	1992	1993	1994	1995
Tourist Attractions (cont.)					
Cultural center		Planning & design	Construct	Construct	Open
Museum expansion			Design	Construct	Open
Infrastructure					
Airport expansion	Planning	Construct	Construct	Open	
Beach area roads	Planning	Construct	Construct	Open	
Mountain roads		Planning	Construct	Construct	Open
Beach area water & electricity supply	Planning	Construct	Construct	Open	
Mountain area water & electricity supply			Planning	Construct	Open
Other Projects & Actions					
Tourism law & regulations	Review & adopt				
Investment incentives	Review & adopt				
NTA office & tourism promotion board	Establish	Initial staff training		Expand	
Sociocultural program	Organize	Commence	Continue	Continue	Continue
Economic program	Organize	Commence	Continue	Continue	Continue
Village tourism project	Planning	Organize	Commence		
Tourism training center	Planning	Construct	Open		Expand
Subregional planning of new tourism area				Planning	Adopt plan

Note: This simplified model action program is assumed to be based on a recently prepared tourism plan for a country or region that has very limited existing tourism development but wants to expand fairly rapidly. This five-year program includes preparatory activities for the next five-year program as indicated by the activities of planning for a third beach hotel, a second national park, a second historic site, and subregional planning for a new tourism area. Each major project identified would have its own detailed development program.

Figure 15.1. Continued.

conservation zones are often geographically related to the tourism use zones. As was explained in Chapter 11, the tourist facility development standards, such as densities of accommodation units, building heights, building setbacks, floor area ratios, site coverage, and parking requirements, are incorporated into the zoning regulations under the appropriate land use zone. Some of these standards, such as building height limits and setbacks, are also applicable to all types of development in the area.

At the national and regional levels, zoning, if it exists at all, is general and usually identifies the major types of land uses, such as urban, agriculture, and conservation, and may include a tourism zone that designates the areas where tourism development such as resorts is suitable. The state of Hawaii, for example, has adopted regional level land use zones, including a tourism development zone for all of its islands. At the local urban and community level, the detailed zoning regulations, as indicated above, are applied within each tourism-related zone and its development standards specified. Zoning regulations are enforceable by law and require that all proposed projects be submitted for review and approval, according to the regulations, to the appropriate government agencies, before construction can be started.

In the absence of comprehensive zoning maps and regulations in tourism areas, regulations on the location, type, and standards for tourism development can be separately adopted and applied in the same manner as zoning regulations, including that all proposed tourism projects be submitted to the government for its review. Alternatively, the tourism plan showing the locations and standards for tourism development, if adopted, can be used as a guideline for reviewing proposed tourism projects.

The physical planning department (sometimes called the urban and regional or town and country planning department) should be directly involved in the establishment and administration of zoning regulations applicable to tourism development, in cooperation with the tourism agency. The planning department is the government's expert agency on any type of physical development matters. Other agencies that should usually be involved in reviewing tourism development proposals include the public works and transportation planning agency, the environmental protection agency (an environmental impact assessment may be required), and sometimes others depending on the local government organization.

As referred in Chapter 11, tourist facility design guidelines, such as on architectural styles and landscaping, are administered by a separate design review board or committee or directly by the planning department. Engineering standards are typically administered by the public works department.

The standards formulated for licensing hotels, restaurants, tour and travel services, and other tourist facilities and services, and the hotel classification system (if it is recommended), are adopted by the government and usually administered by the tourism department. Other applicable standards, such as on hygiene and sanitation, are administered by the relevant agencies.

Tour Programming

As important aspect of implementation for sight-seeing tourism is effective tour programming based on the plan. In addition to being an important tourist activity, well-designed and imaginative tour programs can provide various benefits to the country or region, including:

- Spreading the economic benefits more widely geographically and throughout society by developing tourist facilities and services such as restaurants and shops along the tour routes, which will encourage tourist spending at those stopover points;
- Providing additional employment and income, both directly and indirectly, through the local facilities and services required to operate tour programs; and
- Expanding the tourist markets and extending the average length of stay of tourists by providing a variety of interesting tours.

Tour programs should be designed based on the national or regional structure plan, which has identified the logical tour routes as related to the location of tourist accommodation and attraction and market considerations of the type and extent of tourists expected to visit the area. In the absence of a national or regional plan, consideration of the location of accommodation and attractions, the expected tourist markets, and the transportation network can provide the basis for tour programming. As indicated in Chapter 7, development of loop tour routes, which avoids backtracking, is preferable in order to provide a more interesting experience for tourists and to spread the economic benefits of tours more widely. In national, regional, or urban tourism plans and regional relationships components of resort plans, it is useful to include prototypical tour programs that provide the framework and guidelines for preparing the specific programs in the future and are useful in calculating tourist length of stay and other plan factors. Various types of tour programs should be considered, often ranging from half-day to those lasting several days or a few weeks, perhaps utilizing different means of transportation and oriented to different tourist market groups and interests.

Tours can include general sight-seeing, countryside viewing, visits to museums, archaeological and historic places, nature parks, stopovers for performances and shopping, and other types of places, depending on the attractions available. Special interest as well as general tours can be considered. A several day tour may include visiting all the major attractions in a country or region. Tours may include road and rail travel, sea and river cruises, air tours (airplane and helicopter), safari and trekking/hiking/walking tours, or a combination of these. Tours within a country may well be related to tours that tourists are taking of other countries on their trip, including on the same special interest themes for all the places visited.

In addition to efficient programming in terms of scheduling and costing, having knowledgeable tour guides available is essential for the success of tours, particularly for special interest tours where tourists are expecting an in-depth understanding of what they are visiting.

Parks, Conservation, and Cultural Activities Programs

Because scenic areas, nature parks, conservation areas, and archaeological and historic sites comprise such significant types of tourist attractions in many areas developing tourism, as well as being important for their value as environmental and cultural heritage sites for residents' appreciation, parks and conservation often warrant special emphasis in the tourism implementation program. If there are no national or regional parks and conservation plan or historic preservation program in effect, then these will be important considerations in tourism development planning and programming, or, if such plans do exist, they and the tourism program need to be carefully coordinated.

Nature, archaeological, and historic parks and conservation areas should be legally designated, with detailed management plans prepared and implemented for them. For important sites, international assistance, such as from UNESCO, may be available for their planning and management. More generally, the tourism agency will need to support the appropriate agencies in their parks and conservation programs so that the attractions are properly planned and managed.

Cultural facilities and activities, such as music, dance and drama theaters, performing groups, cultural festivals, the production, presentation, and sales of visual arts and crafts, and the interpretation of traditional villages and their life-styles, should be included in the implementation program if they are not the responsibility of other agencies. If other agencies *are* involved, their activities should be coordinated with and supported by the tourism department.

Other Programs

Other programs such as those for employee education and training, public awareness, and economic enhancement need to be further specified if necessary, and implemented with funding provided and suitable organizational structures established. These other programs may be carried out by various government agencies and the private sector but should be carefully coordinated with the tourism department.

Project Planning and Development

For implementing specific development projects, such as hotels and resorts, detailed planning and feasibility analysis are necessary. The first step is site selection and prefeasibility analysis to determine the general character and scale of development and its likely viability. If this has not been carried out as part of the national and regional plan, then it will need to be done as a separate study but within the context of regional tourism policy and structural relationships. The next step is detailed land use planning and feasibility analysis, including market and economic/financial feasibility to determine the specific type and extent of development and confirm that it is feasible with an acceptable rate of return, as explained in Chapter 13. During this phase of the study, there must be feedback between the planning and feasibility analysis to arrive at the optimum plan that generates economic benefits to the area, achieves an acceptable financial rate of return, and does not generate any serious environmental or sociocultural impact

Hiking to view the Vatnajökull Icecap glacier in Iceland—This country has a carefully regulated tourism sector based in large part on cross-country trekking and scenic viewing. (Courtesy of the Iceland Tourist Board and taken by Johan Hendrik Piepgrass)

problems. Based on the land use plan, site planning, architectural, landscaping, and engineering design can be undertaken with application of suitable design standards, as explained in Chapter 11. At this point, a specific environmental impact assessment should be carried out with any necessary modifications made based on the results of the EIA.

Then, project funding is obtained (funding sources will usually have been investigated during the planning and feasibility analysis activities), and the project is implemented (often in stages for large projects) and managed over the long term. The planning and feasibility analysis required for priority projects identified in the national and regional development program should be specified as a first component of the project and the time and budget required to accomplish this planning and analysis allocated in the program. If it is a public sector type project, such as visitor facilities at an attraction site, the planning and feasibility analysis costs will become borne by the public sector, but if it is a private sector type project such as a hotel or resort, these costs will usually be assumed by the private company involved. However, the government may pay for the initial prefeasibility study costs of commercial projects in order to identify suitable projects and provide incentives for the private sector to become involved.

Project planning and development is a specialized subject, but, in general terms, the process can be sequentially described as follows:

- Step 1—Project identification: This is preferably done as part of the overall tourism development plan and program for the area.
- Step 2—Project screening: This involves conceptual planning and prefeasibility analysis.
- Step 3—Project planning and feasibility: This involves detailed planning and design, market, and economic/feasibility analysis, and the EIA.
- Step 4—Project funding: This includes finding the source of funding, may require project promotion and provision of incentives, and the mobilization of funds.
- Step 5—Project implementation: This is the actual physical development of the project and related activities such as recruitment and perhaps training of employees to work in the project.
- Step 6—Project management: This is management of the project on a continuous basis, including promotion to the tourist markets.

Another step may be interposed between steps 3 and 4 or 4 and 5 if there is a need to establish a special form of project organizational structure, such as a development corporation.

Throughout the project, whether publicly or privately funded, close coordination should be maintained with the local community to make certain that they agree with and understand the project concept and development plan and program and have the opportunity to participate in the benefits of the project. Ideally, the community will have been involved in the initial consideration and identification of the project. As referred to in Chapter 7, on resort selection criteria, if the community does not agree with the project, it will not be approved, or its configuration may be changed to suit community desires and needs. Public meetings should be organized to discuss the project. In many places that have established legal planning mechanisms, public hearings on proposed development projects are required to be held.

Project implementation is a complicated process, especially for large projects such as resorts with several hotels and a variety of other facilities, and requires careful programming. Critical path organization techniques should be applied to achieve efficient coordination of project activities. Figure 15.2 shows a model implementation program for a hypothetical large-scale resort project in outline format, realizing that an actual project would also include more detailed activities. Projects seldom follow their prearranged schedules exactly, and adjustments must be made as the project proceeds. However, without this type of program to be used as a guide, implementation would be much less efficient and there would not be a framework for monitoring the work activities.

MODEL RESORT COMPLEX DEVELOPMENT PROGRAM

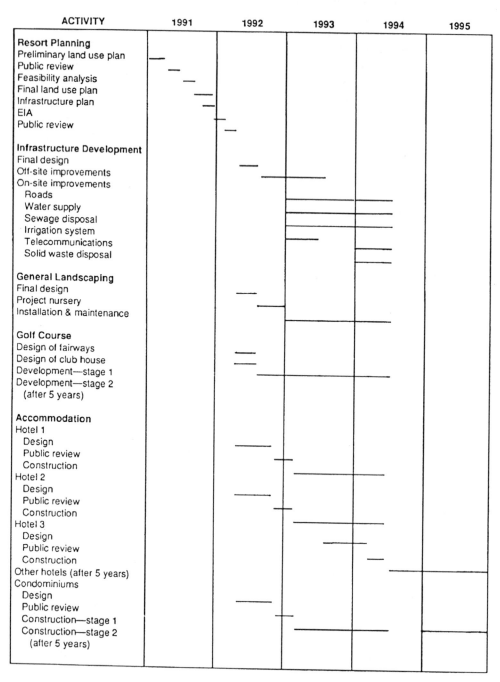

Figure 15.2. Model Resort Complex Development Program.

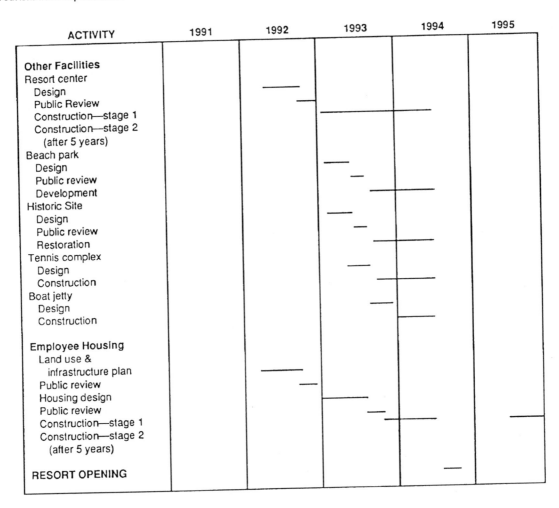

ACTIVITY	1991	1992	1993	1994	1995
Other Facilities					
Resort center					
Design		—			
Public Review		—			
Construction—stage 1			—		
Construction—stage 2					
(after 5 years)					
Beach park					
Design			—		
Public review			—		
Development			—		
Historic Site					
Design			—		
Public review			—		
Restoration			—		
Tennis complex					
Design			—		
Construction			—		
Boat jetty					
Design			—		
Construction			—		
Employee Housing					
Land use &					
infrastructure plan		—			
Public review		—			
Housing design			—		
Public review			—		
Construction—stage 1			—		
Construction—stage 2					
(after 5 years)					
RESORT OPENING				—	

Note: This simplified development program assumes that the site has already been selected, the prefeasibility analysis conducted, and the land acquired, or that the developer has an option for purchase of the land pending the results of the public review of the preliminary land use plan, with the acquisition taking place during the first year of the program. The design phase, which is indicated for the facility components, includes site planning and design of on-site infrastructure, buildings, and landscaping. Construction includes site preparation, on-site infrastructure and landscaping development, and construction of buildings. As indicated, this program is for the first stage of development, to be followed during the next five-year period with a second stage. Typically, temporary infrastructure is developed to commence construction of facilities so that the final infrastructure does not need to be completed before facility construction starts. This scheduling does not allow for the additional time often required for negotiations with hotel developers and assumes a rapid public review process, which, in fact, often requires more time, especially to prepare revisions to be made to the plans as a result of the public review.

Figure 15.2. Continued.

Market Planning

Marketing of tourism for an area is essential in order to inform prospective tourists about what the area has to offer, as well as persuade them to visit it. Market planning is a specialized discipline that is the subject of entire books, but the tourism planner should be aware of the basic approaches in tourism marketing as it relates to development of the tourism product and overall implementation of the tourism plan, as well as to the continuing management of tourism. From the national and regional tourism standpoint, market planning deals with the techniques of how to attract the targeted types and numbers of tourists to the country or region. The first step is formulating the marketing objectives and strategy, which then provides the basis for preparing the tourism promotion program.

Marketing Objectives and Strategy

In a comprehensive and integrated planning approach, as presented in this book, the marketing objectives will be represented by the market targets of the types and numbers of tourists to be attracted as established in the market analysis. These will have been established for the long-term period of the plan and for periodic intervals, usually five-year periods. The marketing strategy is then formulated based on the objectives of market targets, keeping in mind the recommended tourism development policy and plan, including the staging of development and tourism product being offered.

The marketing strategy sets forth the most effective approach to be applied to achieve the objectives (for example, the types of promotional techniques to be used; the timing or priority scheduling of promotional efforts to certain countries or regions or specific types of tourist markets; the image and reality of the area to be conveyed; any particular obstacles to be overcome, such as recent political instability or natural disasters; and relationship of the marketing to certain major development projects, such as a resort or significant attraction feature). Any contingencies that may arise, such as a closed market source possibly becoming available, are considered in the strategy so that it has flexibility. An important consideration that would have been made in establishing the market targets that carry over to the marketing strategy is selective marketing to certain groups that, for example, will have inherent respect for and be conscious of environmental and cultural conservation if this is of priority concern in the tourism policy or exhibit high expenditure patterns and demand high quality facilities and services (the so-called quality market). The marketing strategy can include both domestic and international tourist markets.

Consideration will need to be given to whether and in which countries or other regions promotion offices can be justified. This may require a feasibility analysis of the relative costs and benefits of supporting such offices. The strategy also addresses whether the promotion should be primarily directed to tour operators (if the tour group types of markets are aimed for), the tourist consumers (if independent travelers are desired and anticipated to be an important market), or a combination of these. Special interest tourism will require a different strategy than general relaxation, recreation, and sight-seeing tourism. The sources of funding for marketing and the respective roles of the public and private sectors in participation and cooperation on marketing efforts should be addressed.

The marketing strategy should be related to both the longer and shorter-term objectives so that the foundation is laid to achieve the longer-term objectives but with the shorter-term ones planned more specifically. For example, during the shorter-term, it may be more cost-effective to direct promotional efforts at a few selected markets; while on the longer-term, the activities can be expanded to a larger number of potential markets. The marketing strategy should be reviewed fairly often and modified if necessary, based on changing circumstances in the tourist markets, any changes taking place in provision of the tourism product in the area, and general market trends, but still within the framework of the overall tourism development policy.

Promotion Program

Based on the marketing strategy and knowledge of marketing distribution channels and the various techniques available, the specific promotion program is prepared. This program is usually designed for a three- to five-year period and specifies by year the types of promotion to be undertaken and their estimated costs. Continuing costs, such as for maintenance of local information services and overseas promotion offices, can be included in the promotion program. The types of promotional techniques to be considered are diverse but include the following:

- Preparing collateral material such as brochures, posters, postcards, maps, travel agent manuals, and information leaflets and distribution of these to the tourist consumers and travel trade. The types and numbers of collateral material to be produced by year and their distribution channels must be decided upon.
- Preparing audio-visual presentation material such as slide, film, and video shows for use in seminars and other types of presentations. Video cassettes are now a common form of audio-visual medium.
- Advertising in consumer-oriented newspapers and magazines, with specification of the type or name of the periodical (advertising costs vary greatly among newspapers and magazines, depending on their circulation and quality).
- Advertising in travel trade publications aimed at tour operators and other trade organizations.
- Advertising on radio and television, with specification of which ones (television commercials can be very expensive in many of the market countries).
- Attendance, including setting up exhibit booths, at annual tourism trade fairs such as the International Tourism Exchange in Berlin (ITB) and World Travel Mart in London (in 1989, ITB, the largest travel promotion forum in the world, attracted more than 2,500 exhibitions representing the public and private sec-

tors of some 140 countries and territories). The number of tourism trade fairs is increasing rapidly throughout the world, and a decision must be made as to which ones to attend.

- Special promotional trips to certain market countries and areas to conduct sales seminars for travel agencies. These seminars may be conducted by the overseas promotion offices if they exist.
- Inviting and hosting visits by tour operators and travel writers and photographers (this should be done discriminatingly so that unqualified persons wanting free travel do not take advantage of this opportunity).
- Preparing and publishing tourist guide and general information books of the area if they are not available commercially (these can be sold and the publication costs recovered).

Promotion of convention tourism requires specialized techniques and knowledge. If convention tourism is important or is desired to be significant in an area, a special convention bureau or convention department of the NTA is usually organized. Promotional activities should be closely coordinated between the public and private sectors, and the opportunities for joint promotion and funding should be explored, as was indicated in Chapter 14.

Tourist Information Services

An important function of marketing is provision of information services to tourists before and after they arrive at their destinations. In some newly developing tourism areas, a common complaint from tourists is the lack of information about the areas. Most tourists wish to know about the facilities, services, and attractions available, and many are interested in some general background information about the history, geography, culture, and other characteristics of the areas. Tourist information material is also useful to inform tourists about any local customs that they should observe, any local security problems to be aware of, local policies and expectations on tipping, where to obtain medical services, and location of embassies, consulates, religious institutions, and so forth. Tourist information offices should be established in convenient locations in the tourism area and staffed by knowledgeable personnel who have the requisite language capabilities. An often successful approach is development of a visitor information center that contains some exhibits and perhaps offers audio-visual presentations in addition to tourist information material of brochures, maps, transportation schedules, and guide and general background books (which can be for sale).

It is important that the information given to tourists be accurate, up-to-date, and not misleading. If there are problems in reaching and touring certain places, these should be explained to the tourists so that they know what to expect, as well as informing them about the desirable aspects of the places. If tourists are misinformed or given the wrong impressions, they are more likely to be dissatisfied than if told forthrightly about any problems so that they can anticipate them. The approach can be taken that, despite some problems, such as irregular transportation schedules or mediocre accommodation, the destination is still well worth the effort to visit.

Some Other Considerations

Some of the other considerations in implementing tourism development are tourist health, travel facilitation, and the importance of maintaining tourist facilities and infrastructure and adopting any new technologies in tourism. Also important is consideration of any special organizational approaches that will facilitate development.

Tourist Health

With both the increasing travel, and especially long-haul travel, of more people and the development of new destinations throughout the world, tourist health is justifiably receiving more attention in recent years. When tourists travel to environments very different than their own, they are exposed to new bacteria, viruses, and parasites. Some destinations are not able to maintain the high levels of local hygiene and sanitation standards to which many tourist are accustomed. If tourists experience health problems as a result of their traveling, it presents obvious problems for the tourists themselves and depreciates the attractive power and reputation of the destination areas to other tourists. Some diseases that tourists can contract while traveling, such as food poisoning, malaria, hepatitis B, typhoid, cholera, certain types of dysentery, and AIDS, can be particularly devastating. As emphasized in the tourism literature by Petty (1989) and Dawood (1989), the travel trade should inform tourists about any medical risks that they may encounter and emphasize that proper precautions be taken, such as obtaining proper immunization prior to traveling and adapting their behavioral patterns to the health situation of their destination.

It is just as important that destination areas make every effort to improve their infrastructure to prevent environmentally derived types of diseases (although in some places this may by feasible only in the immediate tourism environment) attempt to control the transmission of communicable diseases, and inform tourists about any particularly serious health hazards so that they take precautions accordingly. In his research on the problems of AIDS in tourism areas, one of the conclusions reached by Cohen (1988) was that the best policy for the government to adopt was one of openness about the problem, giving attention to protecting public health. This approach informs the tourists and residents about the situation so they can take precautions, establishes a sense of credibility and responsibility towards tourists, and provides the basis for taking measures to mitigate the problem.

International Travel Facilitation

Travel facilitation is used here particularly in reference to facilities, services, requirements, and procedures for international tourists arriving at and departing from their destinations at the tourist gateway transportation points, which, for long-haul travel, often are international airports. As mentioned previously, these are the gateways and 'front doors' of countries, as well as the first impression of a destination for tourists, which sets the stage for their experience in the countries. Often neglected in the past as not being of great importance, more attention is now being given in many countries to make these facilitation procedures as efficient and pleasant as possible, while still maintaining the legal requirements necessary. In the planning and developing of tourism, the present travel document requirements, facilities, and procedures of travel facilitation should be examined for any opportunities of improvements that can be made, including the public relations approach used by officials involved. It is now common, for example, to organize classes for customs and immigration officials to educate them about the importance of tourism, as well as how to handle tourists in a friendly and efficient manner. At the same time, tourists should be informed through brochures and signs about any legal requirements and urged to act in an honest manner.

Within the airport, information services should be available for tourists and transportation should be effectively organized, with fair pricing structures and frequent schedules to the tourists' destinations. Money exchange services should be available and conducted efficiently. Because of the waiting often required, airports should have comfortable lounges, food and beverage services, and retail shopping available.

Maintenance of Facilities and Infrastructure and Use of New Technologies

Just as important as the initial development of tourist facilities and infrastructure is the proper continuing maintenance of them as part of the management of tourism. If initially well developed, but not well maintained and allowed to deteriorate, the original investment in facilities and infrastructure is wasted. Subsequently, tourists and the travel trade will soon learn about the problems, and the destination will lose its good reputation. Furthermore, remedial action taken after deterioration can be expensive. Therefore, development programs and budgeting schedules of both the public and private sectors should include sufficient funding for adequate maintenance. More generally (as has been emphasized previously), in the process of developing new facilities and attractions in an area, the older ones should not be neglected in order to retain their viability and continue contributing to the expansion and diversification of tourism.

New technologies are constantly evolving in tourism, especially in the use of computerization and communications in providing tourism services. Both the government and private sector tourism personnel should be educated about these new techniques and the appropriate equipment installed. Because of the greater efficiency offered by new technologies and in order to improve services provided to tourists, investment in current technologies can be well justified.

Special Organizational Approaches

Special organizational and financial approaches are sometimes a very useful technique for accomplishing improvements in tourism development that otherwise are not feasible to implement within the established institutional systems. These approaches can be oriented particularly to achieving public–private sector cooperation on complicated projects and serving as a catalyst for accomplishing broader tourism development objectives. An example of such an approach is Tourism Action Plan, Ltd. (TAP) in Jamaica. TAP was established in February, 1988 as a joint public–private sector company with the following objectives (TAP 1990):

- To identify and prioritize the areas with potential for enhancing Jamaica's tourism product and to plan, develop and implement all initiatives so as to help ensure and improve Jamaica's competitiveness as a tourism destination.
- To stimulate investment in tourism and related sectors and foster the participation of public and private enterprise in the development of the industry.
- To seek to ensure at all times the best practicable reconciliation of aesthetic, cultural, architectural, economic and environmental considerations, all of which must be taken into account in securing commitment and cooperation from all parties concerned in any specific project.
- To liaise and cooperate with all other entities, both public and private, in furthering the development of above-stated objectives.

The private sector is the beneficiary owner of 75 percent of the allocated shares of the company, while the public sector owns 25 percent. The program was initiated by the government with an international grant from the United States Agency for International Development (USAID) and local contributions.

TAP has played an important role in rationalizing the sometimes aggressive vending of retail items to tourists (the anti-harassment program) and establishing and operating tourist information booths in several tourism towns. A major program of TAP is Operation Facelift, which is aimed at improving the tourism and commercial centers in various resort areas and towns of the country. These integrated programs include improvements to sidewalks, landscaping, building facades, markets, street vending areas, parks and community facilities, roads and parking areas, and water supply and sewage treatment systems. Historic restoration is also part of TAP programs. Each target area is specifically evaluated with respect to the improvements required, and plans and programs are tailored to these needs. Incentive grants may be given for private sector improvements. Close working relationships are established and maintained among the various government agencies involved in the project areas and with the private sector organizations, especially the Chambers of Commerce and the Jamaica Hotel and Tourist Association.

Implementation and Monitoring Process

The previous sections of this chapter dealt with some major considerations and techniques of implementation. The formal implementation and monitoring actions required for the tourism plan and the importance of and approach to monitoring plan implementation and tourism in general are reviewed here.

Implementation Sequence of Actions

The sequence of actions required for implementing the national and regional plan, which are also applicable to the community level of tourism planning, is shown on the right side of Figure 3.1 in Chapter 3 and is described in the following sections.

Plan Review

Close coordination with the relevant government agencies, private sector representatives, and other concerned parties, such as community organizations, should have been maintained throughout the planning process. In addition, as explained in Chapter 2, a formal body, such as a project steering committee or the tourism board if one exists, will have provided guidance and advice to the planning team and reviewed the draft plan reports. Thus, the final plan will already represent the input and feedback from the public and private sectors and other organizations. However, the final plan should still be formally reviewed by the governing body to make certain that there is agreement on the plan, as well as an understanding of it. If there is an established legal planning procedure, this review may take the form of a public hearing with participation by the general public or their spokesmen. If the plan is well understood and accepted, it is much more likely to receive support for its implementation. In some places, an effective approach for the final plan review, along with dialogue and education about tourism in general, is to hold a seminar, including government officials, private sector representatives, and community spokesmen, on the plan and future of tourism in the area, prior to plan adoption.

Plan Adoption

After review of the plan document and agreement on its recommendations, the plan should be legally adopted as the official guideline for tourism development in the area. Although the plan can still be used without being adopted, it will not have the force of law and will be easier to deviate from. As is the case with any plan, the legal mechanism for adoption should include provision for modification to the plan when justified, but only through legal procedure.

Adoption of Legislation and Regulations

The legislation and various types of regulations that are prepared for implementing aspects of the plan and managing the continuing operation of tourism need to be legally adopted. Some regulations, such as those for land use zoning and development standards, may be either adopted separately or incorporated into existing regulations if they exist.

Integration into Public and Private Sector Development Policies, Plans, and Programs

After adoption, the relevant aspects of the plan should be integrated into other related plans of the area that may exist, such as national, regional, and urban development policies and plans, park, recreation, and conservation plans, transportation and any other relevant infrastructure plans, and agricultural and fisheries programs. This integration will give greater assurance that those aspects of the tourism plan will be implemented by the concerned sector in an integrated manner.

Many countries in the world use the procedure of preparing and adopting national or regional development plans or programs for approximate five-year periods. If this is the case in the tourism planning area, it is especially important to incorporate the tourism development or action program (also usually prepared for five years) into the country's or region's overall development program. Often, the tourism action program can form the tourism sector component of the overall development program. Because most countries' development plans constitute specific guidelines for development planning, programming, and budgeting, it is crucial to integrate the tourism development program into it.

Private sector companies and public development corporations may also have tourism-related development programs. The tourism sector programs should be integrated into these. For example, a hotel development or management company may have a program for developing new hotels in the area and should be aware of the national or regional tourism development program, including that for infrastructure development, and conform to it.

Development Funding and Project Implementation

Project funding may be by either the public or private sector, with local or international financing, but usually with government funding of major infrastructure and most tourist attractions and private funding of commercial facilities and services. A previous section of this chapter explained the project planning, funding, and development procedure. In preparing the development program, possible sources of funding should have been anticipated so that this funding is available when needed.

Continuous Monitoring of Tourism

An essential part of plan implementation and sound management of tourism is the continuous monitoring of the progress of the development program, the specific economic, environmental, and sociocultural impacts of tourism, and, more generally, how effectively the tourism development objectives and policies are being realized. Monitoring the results of the marketing strategy and promotion program is also important to determine how well the market targets are being achieved.

Adjustments to the Plan and Program

The monitoring will have determined whether tourism is 'on track' or whether adjustments need to be made to certain components of the plan or implementation schedule in order to achieve the development objectives. For example, it may have been determined that certain types of accommodation are in demand by the tourist markets and should be developed in larger numbers or that certain tourist attractions are becoming congested and other attractions should be developed or different tour itineraries organized. If certain development projects are falling behind schedule, their implementation will need to be accelerated.

Periodic Formal Plan Review and Revision

The tourism plan or certain components of the plan may become outdated after several years because of changing circumstances. This is especially true in the rapidly developing world of tourism. Therefore, the tourism plan should be formally reviewed about every five years and any necessary revisions made. The plan revision should be as carefully prepared as was the original plan, but the revised plan may still include many of the original planning objectives, policies, principles, and recommendations because they remain valid over a long-term period, unless there has been a major shift in political ideology and overall development policy. Often, the plan revision is needed mostly for evaluating changing market trends, considering new types of tourism products, future expansion (beyond the original plan period) of tourism or its need for control in the case of destinations reaching maturity and saturation, and preparing a new short-term development program.

Importance of Monitoring

Monitoring the progress of the development program and specific project developments is too often neglected because of the effort and some cost involved. However, monitoring should be considered an integral part of the planning process in order to evaluate the effectiveness of the program, detect any problems or delays that may arise before they become serious, and adopt measures to put the program back on track. Monitoring should be undertaken on a formal, structured basis with economic, environmental, and sociocultural impact and other types of surveys conducted and total program evaluation carried out. The results should be analyzed and reported. A common data base should be established so that the results can be compared over a long period of time. At the local level, these surveys should include interviews and meetings with residents of the tourism area to ascertain their response to and participation in tourism, as well as surveys of tourists' attitudes toward their touristic experiences in the area.

In addition to program evaluation and impact surveys, monitoring should be applied to evaluate whether the overall tourism development policy, plan, and program are the most effective ones to achieve the development objectives. If certain approaches are determined to be deficient, adjustments can be made. Effective tourism planning and development requires some experimentation with different approaches to decide which are the most appropriate for the area. Planning should be viewed as a continuous process striving to achieve integrated development and sustainable use of tourism resources.

Case Studies

Two case studies are presented on implementation approaches. Both are a follow-through of plans that were previously presented as case studies, in order to demonstrate continuity of the planning process in particular areas. The tourism marketing plan for Malta exemplifies the importance of the relationship of market planning and product improvement in order to achieve the overall tourism development objectives and policies. The sample schedule of development activities for Zanzibar illustrates the application of model project development programming to a specific area.

Tourism Marketing Plan and Product Improvement Program for Malta

Various case studies in previous chapters presented certain aspects of the Tourism Development Plan for the Maltese Islands (Howarth and Howarth

1989), including the strategic policy plan for the islands in Chapter 7. As explained, the major objective of the plan was to improve and diversify the tourism product and shift the tourist markets to be more diversified and of a higher quality, within the framework of continuing to expand tourism as a major economic sector of the country. The plan made the basic point that the tourism product and tourist market development must be closely related and, in order to shift the markets as desired, the tourism product must also be modified accordingly.

As shown in Figure 15.3, the marketing plan approach reflects the relationship between the tourism product and the tourist market. Leading from the national long-term objectives of increasing income and employment from tourism is the marketing strategy that comprises the three elements of: 1) market diversification; 2) quality improvement; 3) and lengthening the season (of tourist arrivals). Based on this long-term strategy, the policies section of the diagram indicates the policies recommended for 1990-95 for marketing and related product improvements. From the policies are derived the action plans for 1990-95.

The plan report further specifies a diversified product development program as follows:

- Implement the tourism area upgrading schemes (1990-92).
- Promote hotel and facilities upgrading with an incentive package (1990-92).
- Encourage the development of high quality hotels and other facilities related to specific target markets (1990-92).
- Promote the development of leisure facilities, including:
    1. Yachting marina at Manoel Island;
    2. Marsa golf course upgrading;
    3. Tennis complexes;
    4. Underwater national park;
    5. Indoor sports and recreation complexes;
    6. Entertainment facilities, theaters, open air festivals, and so on;
    7. Flexible shopping hours and extensive duty-free shopping facilities;
    8. Improve basic infrastructure of roads, sewage disposal, electric power, and communications and finish development work on infrastructure of existing resorts;
    9. Improvements to the quality and availability of entertainment and tourist attractions;
    10. Implement the cultural heritage properties plan; and
    11. Plan and develop a theme light and laser harbor spectacular, as already proposed.

The plan recognizes that sufficient time will be required to achieve the shifting of markets and the product improvements needed, but that, by 1995, the desired changes will be well underway. The longer-term plan envisages the Maltese Islands as a quality, 'good value-for-money' destination, appealing to the middle to higher income market groups.

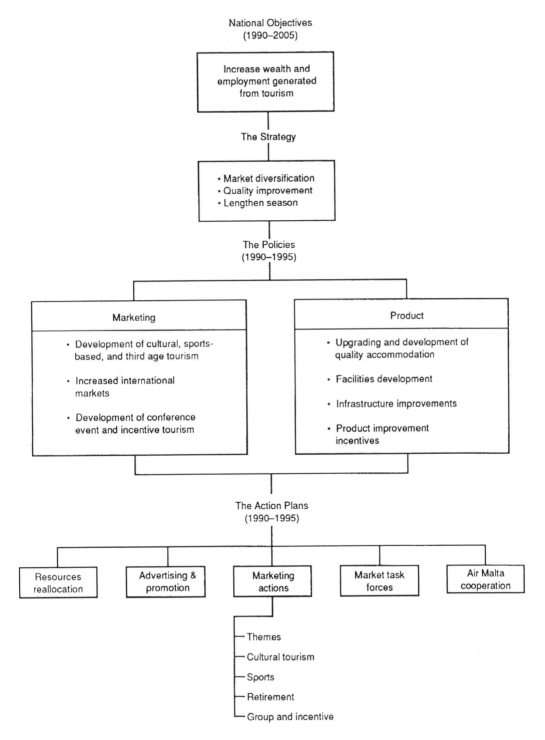

Figure 15.3. Maltese Islands Tourism Development Plan—Marketing Plan Overview.

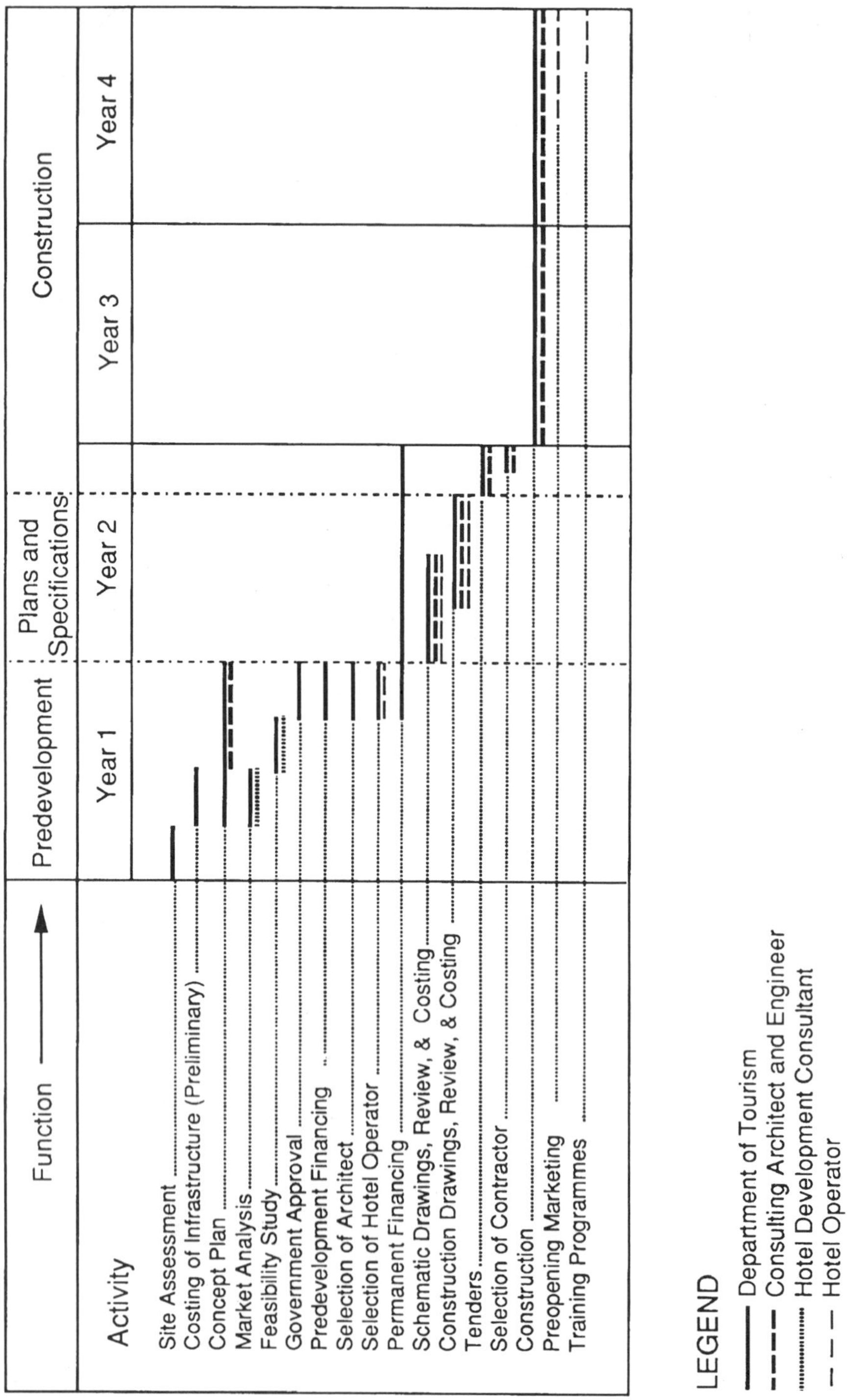

Function ➝	Predevelopment	Plans and Specifications	Construction	
Activity	Year 1	Year 2	Year 3	Year 4
Site Assessment				
Costing of Infrastructure (Preliminary)				
Concept Plan				
Market Analysis				
Feasibility Study				
Government Approval				
Predevelopment Financing				
Selection of Architect				
Selection of Hotel Operator				
Permanent Financing				
Schematic Drawings, Review, & Costing				
Construction Drawings, Review, & Costing				
Tenders				
Selection of Contractor				
Construction				
Preopening Marketing				
Training Programmes				

LEGEND

——— Department of Tourism
– – – Consulting Architect and Engineer
·········· Hotel Development Consultant
– – – Hotel Operator

Figure 15.4. Zanzibar Tourism Development Plan—Sample Schedule of Development Activities.

Sample Schedule of Project Development Activities in Zanzibar

Various case studies presented in previous chapters explained the background and development policy of the Zanzibar Tourism Development Plan (UNDP and WTO 1983). In the development program section of the plan, a sample schedule of the development activities required for specific project implementation, such as for hotel or resort, was set forth as a guide for the government to use in organizing and reviewing such projects. This schedule (shown in Figure 15.4) is a model of activities. The actual schedule timing would be somewhat different, depending on the type and size of the project, as well as other considerations. As indicated on the chart, the activities are divided into the three major sequential categories of: 1) predevelopment; 2) plans and specifications; and 3) construction.

This example assumes the active involvement of the Department of Tourism in project development, but this function could also be carried out by a public or private development corporation. However, the Department of Tourism, in coordination with the planning department, should still take a strong advisory and review role. The party responsible for providing infrastructure to and within the site would need to be decided upon, depending on the infrastructure development policies of the government. The site selection may have been made in the regional plan, but, if not, that would be the first step in the sequence of activities. This chart shows a relatively short training program period for employees who will be working in the development after it is opened, and a longer training period might be needed, depending on actual training needs.

The chart indicates the responsible parties for each of the activities. Various types of consultants typically play a major technical role in the development process because the government or development corporation usually does not have this expertise or time available. However, the government agencies involved in reviewing the project plans should possess the technical capabilities to properly review and comment on the plans and program.

References

Cohen, Erik. 1988. "Tourism and AIDS in Thailand." *Annals of Tourism Research.* 15(4): 467–486.

Dawood, Richard. 1989. "Tourists' Health—Could the Travel Industry Do More?" *Tourism Management.* 10(4): 285–287.

Howarth and Howarth, Inc. 1989. *Maltese Islands Tourism Development Plan.* London.

Petty, Richard. 1989. "Health Limits to Tourism Development." *Tourism Management.* 10(3): 209–212.

Tourism Action Plan, Ltd. 1990. *Objectives.* Kingston, Jamaica: Tourism Action Plan, Ltd.

United Nations Development Programme and World Tourism Organization. 1983. *Zanzibar Tourism Development Plan.* Madrid: World Tourism Organization.

Appendixes

An Action Strategy for Sustainable Tourism Development

Following is a reproduction of the draft of *An Action Strategy for Sustainable Development,* prepared by the Tourism Stream Action Strategy Committee of the Globe '90 conference on sustainable development held in Vancouver, Canada in March 1990.

Acknowledgements

Globe '90 was an international conference designed to promote environmentally sustainable development and business opportunities for the environment industry. The tourism stream of the conference brought together 42 representatives of the tourism industry, government international agencies, and non-government organizations to discuss the challenges of achieving sustainable tourism development.

This paper is a result of much deliberation by a group of international experts from the fields of industry, academia, and government whose expertise represents tourism, environment, economic analysis, and policy formulation and whose background experiences are from diverse countries of the world.

This action strategy presents specific actions to be taken by governments, the tourism industry, nongovernment organizations, and tourists. Many individuals and organizations contributed to the preparation of the action strategy. Their contributions are gratefully acknowledged. The action strategy also builds on work undertaken at workshops on sustainable tourism development in Waterloo and Malta in January and March 1990, respectively.

The Context

Globally, tourism continues to grow at a dramatic rate. This trend is expected to continue into the foreseeable future, and with it comes conflicts between tourist activity and the environment. Without significant change toward more sustainable forms of development, it is quite probable that severe damage to the cultural and natural environment will accelerate. Faced with this situation, the tourism stream delegates to Globe '90 suggested the need for implementing sustainable tourism development actions and policies.

Public opinion focuses more than ever before on the importance of environmental and health related factors in influencing life-style choices. These opinions are being reflected in activities encouraging those business ventures that enhance the environment, as well as preference for products and services that are environment-friendly. As these trends develop, there will be a growing interest in creating tourism products and services that are similarly oriented toward sustainable development.

Introduction

Tourism and its role in sustainable development are currently the subject of much concern. A number of studies and conferences have examined the scope and implications of "green" approaches to tourism. It seems clear that sustainability holds considerable promise as a vehicle for addressing the problems of mass tourism as well as supporting "alternative tourism" and "ecotourism." Equally there is a need to move beyond definition and toward action.

The environment is tourism's base. Tourism shapes and affects the environment. A widely acknowledged problem is the extent to which ill-conceived and poorly planned tourism development can erode the very qualities of the natural and human environment that attract visitors. Recognition of this problem is required at the national and regional levels. Particular attention must be paid to the local level where impacts and concerns are most apparent.

The concept of sustainable development explicitly recognizes interdependencies that exist among environmental and economic issues and policies.

Sustainable development is aimed at protecting and enhancing the environment, meeting basic human needs, promoting current and intergenerational equity, and improving the quality of life of all peoples.

The real challenges for the tourism industry and sustainable development must be met now. Nationally and internationally we require a vision of balanced development that establishes a working partnership among tourism and other sectors.

New mechanisms for coexistence must be developed through an integrated planning process that gives equal weight to tourism and other economic development initiatives. Tourism development requires the active exercise of ecological and social responsibility at the international, national and local levels.

The goals of sustainable tourism are:

1. To develop greater awareness and understanding of the significant contributions that tourism can make to the environment and the economy;
2. To promote equity in development;
3. To improve the quality of life of the host community;
4. To provide a high quality of experience for the visitor; and
5. To maintain the quality of the environment on which the foregoing objectives depend.

1. Definitions

The definition of sustainable tourism development is elusive. It is a relatively recent concept whose definition will undoubtedly continue to evolve over the next decade. However, a number of notions have been advanced in the Bruntland report on *Our Common Future* that contribute to a definition. Sustainable tourism development can be thought of as meeting the needs of present tourists and host regions while protecting and enhancing opportunity for the future.

Sustainable tourism development is envisaged as leading to management of all resources in such a way that we can fulfill economic, social, and aesthetic needs while maintaining cultural integrity, essential ecological processes, biological diversity and life support systems.

2. Implications for Policy

a. The introduction of the idea of sustainable development is shifting the focus away from the traditional "growth versus development" argument. The focus is increasingly on opportunities for employment, income and improved local well-being while ensuring that all development decisions reflect the full value of the natural and cultural environment.
b. Tourism development involving any loss of existing natural or cultural wealth or environmental capital will increasingly indicate how future generations will be compensated. The loss of natural and cultural assets can no longer simply be substituted for by capital wealth created by new development.

c. Tourism, as an industry, can enhance environmental quality and at the same time create jobs. This provides a positive relationship between tourism and the environment. While some tourism salaries may not be as high as other sectors, tourism jobs do provide for longer-term development opportunities where other industries are not sustainable.

d. Economic growth must be adequately measured. It must include the real cost of protection and recycling not only in the present but also the future when these costs will be much higher. When tourism is compared to other industry sectors in this way, its image will greatly improve.

e. Sustainable tourism development must provide for intergenerational equity. To be fair to future generations of tourists and the travel industry we must leave them a resource base no less than we have inherited. Each generation of tourism developers, planners and operators is obliged to look after the generations that follow.

f. Sustainable tourism development must avoid all actions that are *irreversible*. Some natural and cultural resources can be replaced. But old-growth forests, wildlife species and similar features, once lost, can never be enjoyed by future generations. As well, ancient monuments, historic urban areas, and distinct landscapes are irreplaceable.

g. Development which causes major changes in the environment usually has a greater impact on the poor than the rich. In the cases of relatively poor or developing regions the preservation of sustainable livelihoods must be taken into account. This is a concern where there is dependence upon fish stocks, wildlife, water supply, and other resources upon which tourism can have an impact.

h. Development in one region or country clearly can have positive or negative effects on other regions or countries. Therefore countries should work together to ensure that tourism is integrated into the overall planning and management of the environment. Cooperation in establishing and attaining economic, social and environmental goals in regard to tourism is necessary.

i. In situations where the resource base has been seriously degraded, mitigation and rehabilitation actions must be undertaken to reflect the concept of sustainable tourism development.

j. Sustainable tourism development involves promoting appropriate uses and activities that draw from and reinforce landscape character, sense of place, community identify and site opportunity.

k. Sustainable tourism development must be given policy definition and direction for each country, region and locality where it is to occur. This must be done in the light of environmental, social and economic conditions and requirements that exist there.

l. Sustainable tourism development requires guidelines for levels and types of acceptable growth but does not preclude new facilities and experiences.

m. Sustainable tourism development means promoting working partnerships among the network of actors and linking scientific research and public consultation to decision-making.

n. Sustainable tourism development involves the establishment of education and training programs to improve public understanding and enhance business and professional skills.

o. Sustainable tourism development involves making hard political choices based on complex social, economic and environmental trade-offs in a more extended time and space context than that traditionally used in decision-making.

3. Implementation

3.1 Role of Governments in Promoting Sustainable Tourism Development

Governments should:

1. Undertake area and sector specific research into the environmental, cultural and economic effects of tourism.
2. Support the development of tourism economic models to help define appropriate levels and types of economic activities for natural and urban areas.
3. Assist and support lower levels of governments to develop their own tourism development strategies in conjunction with conservation strategies.
4. Develop standards and regulations for environmental and cultural impact assessments, monitoring and auditing of existing and proposed tourism developments.
5. Apply sectoral and/or regional environmental accounting systems for the tourism industry.
6. Design and implement public consultation techniques and processes in order to involve all stakeholders in making tourism-related decisions.
7. Develop and implement new economic indicators which define national well-being in the sustainable development sense. These indicators, such as those for "sustainable income," must incorporate environmental and resource services and resource depletion.
8. Design and implement educational and awareness programs which will sensitize people to the issues of sustainable tourism development.
9. Develop adequate tools and techniques to analyze the effect of tourism development projects on heritage sites and ancient monuments as an integral part of cultural and environmental impact assessment.
10. Develop design and construction standards which will ensure that tourism

development projects are sympathetic with local culture and natural environments.

11. Ensure that carrying capacities of tourism destinations reflect sustainable levels of development and are monitored and adjusted appropriately.
12. Enforce regulations for illegal trade in historic objects and crafts; unofficial archaeological research; the prevention of erosion of aesthetic values and desecration of sacred sites.
13. Regulate and control tourism in environmentally and culturally sensitive areas.
14. Include tourism in land use planning.
15. Create tourism advisory boards that involve all stakeholders (the public, indigenous populations, industry, NGOs, etc.).
16. Ensure that all government departments involved in tourism are briefed on the concept of sustainable development. The respective Ministers (e.g., Environment, Natural Resources, etc.) should collaborate to achieve sustainable tourism development.
17. Ensure that tourism interests are represented at major caucus planning meetings that affect the environment and economy.
18. Ensure that national and local tourism development agreements stress a policy of sustainable tourism development.

3.2 Role of Non-government Organizations in Promoting Sustainable Tourism Development

Non-government organizations (NGOs) represent and protect the interests of the public. They also have access to local information, expertise and labor.

1. NGOs should be part of sustainable tourism advisory boards at all levels of government and/or industry and offer input into sustainable tourism planning and development. This would include assessment of regional as well as site-specific development plans and the appropriate mix and location of different land use designations.
2. NGOs should continue to seek local support for appropriate sustainable tourism development as well as opposition to inappropriate tourism development. They should also support the protection of an adequate sustainable tourism resource base.
3. NGOs should promote the use of local residents to assist in sustainable tourism research and data collection.
4. NGOs should offer to other agencies information on locally innovated sustainable tourism products and proposals, including the use of locally appropriate technologies.
5. NGOs should become more involved in public education concerning:
   a. the economic importance of sustainable tourism development;

    b.   the need for a secure resource base (particularly natural landscapes);

    c.   sustainable tourism development projects; and

    d.   appropriate behavior related to sustainable tourism on the part of government, industry and tourists.

6. NGOs should be encouraged to identify and communicate to the appropriate agencies those issues related to sustainable tourism as well as solutions to these problems. This includes monitoring:

    a.   impacts of sustainable tourism on the local culture and environment;

    b.   equity participation in local sustainable tourism developments;

    c.   impacts of other sectors of the economy on sustainable tourism; and

    d.   government and industry commitments to sustainable tourism.

3.3 Role of the Tourism Industry in Promoting Sustainable Tourism Development

The private sector is responsible for delivering products and services to the tourist. In this regard it is imperative that the industry support sustainable development through the following actions:

1. *Protecting the Biosphere*, for example, by minimizing and eliminating pollution which causes environmental damage (e.g. use of herbicides on golf courses, artificial snow-making on ski hills) and by supporting parks and reserves at key sites.

2. *Sustaining the Use of Resources*, for example, by ensuring sustainable use of land, water, forests in tourism activities.

3. *Reducing and Disposing of Wastes*, for example, by recycling, reusing, and reducing wherever possible and by having high standards for sewage treatment and waste disposal.

4. *Adopting Energy Efficiency Practices*, for example, by maximizing when possible the use of solar power, wind power, etc.

5. *Minimizing Environmental Risks*, for example, by minimizing environmental and health risks (e.g. avoid hazardous locations such as near malarial swamps, favored wildlife areas, unique features, ancient sites).

6. *Undertaking Green Marketing*, for example, by promoting "soft" tourism that minimizes adverse environmental and cultural impacts (e.g. nature tourism) as well as informing tourists of the impacts of their presence.

7. *Mitigating Damage*, for example, by replacing or restoring degraded environments and compensating for local adverse effects.

8. *Providing Complete and Credible Information to Tourists*, for example, by disclosing hazardous locations.

9. *Incorporating Environmental Values in Management of Operations*, for example, by ensuring environmental representation at the executive level on board or management groups.

10. *Conducting Regular Environmental Audits*, for example, by conducting

independent assessments of environmental performance of the entire business operations (e.g. monitor water quality, carrying capacity, energy consumption, environmental aesthetics, sewage, etc.).

3.4 Role of the Individual Tourist in Promoting Sustainable Tourism Development

As the ultimate user of the environment, it is important that tourists undertake activities which support sustainable tourism development. In this regard, their behavior should be focused on:

1. Choosing an operator which has the reputation of being ethical and environmentally responsible.
2. Learning about and respecting the human and natural heritage of the host communities, including the geography, history, customs and current local concerns.
3. Traveling in a culturally and environmentally sensitive manner, refraining from inappropriate behavior which negatively affects the host community or degrades the local natural environment.
4. Refraining from purchasing or using those products, services and transportation which endanger the local ecology and culture.
5. Practicing minimal-impact travel and following environmental regulations in natural and cultural heritage areas.
6. Supporting resource conservation activities that require assistance in the host countries.

3.5 Role of International Organizations in Promoting Sustainable Tourism Development

The Globe '90 Conference delegates wanted immediate action to ensure better dialogue at the regional and local level.

In recognition of the influence that international organizations have on the distribution of information and motivating actions, it is suggested that all organizations interested in tourism should undertake the following:

a. Develop and disseminate applicable information among their members, particularly with respect to:
    — a sustainable tourism awareness program;
    — a framework for integrated community planning; and
    — a Code of Ethics.
b. Establish stronger links with other international organizations that are involved in sustainable tourism development.

c. Accelerate efforts to protect the world's cultural and natural heritage through international legal instruments such as the World Heritage Convention.

Note: The final section of the document deals with its distribution to international agencies and other concerned parties.

B

Model Terms of Reference for Preparation of a National Tourism Development Plan

This model terms of reference (TOR) is for a hypothetical integrated national tourism planning project. For actual use, this TOR would need to be adapted to the particular planning needs and characteristics of the country. The TOR is designed for a comprehensive planning study, including the major elements of:

- National tourism development policy and plan;
- First-stage regional tourism plans;
- First-stage tourism development action program;
- Conceptual land use plan, design, and prefeasibility analysis for a priority resort development project; and
- Conceptual land use plans, designs, and prefeasibility analyses for development of visitor facilities, each at a natural attraction feature and an archaeological or historic site.

By providing this comprehensive and integrated planning approach, the country will have the planning basis for immediately commencing (or expanding) tourism development in a controlled manner. In many cases, it is preferable to include the successively more detailed levels of planning in one project in order to maintain a compatible approach to the first stage of all levels of development within the framework of the overall long-term policy and structure plan. The conceptual land use plans serve as the basis for specific planning of the resort and tourist attractions involved and also are a model for planning of other similar development sites. As indicated in the TOR, there may be need for the project to recommend additional special studies, such as for a specific feasibility analysis for the development of a tourism training school.

A complete TOR would also include the team members' positions and time inputs required, coordination arrangements with the government (such as establishing a project steering committee), and, where relevant, local community involvement in the planning process, the project budget, equipment, and logistical support necessary to carry out the project and the project work program. In a project of this type, counterpart team members are often appointed from the government staff to work with the project team in order for them to learn about tourism planning principles and techniques and specifically to understand the reasons for the various plan recommendations being made so that they can later be more effectively involved in plan implementation. Projects of this type may also include provision for formal training of government staff in tourism planning and marketing, as well as other specialized areas of tourism management. The model TOR is set forth in the following sections.

General Development Objective

Provide increased foreign exchange earnings, income, employment, and stimulus to other economic sectors through the controlled development of international and domestic tourism, which maintains sustainable use of tourism resources, assists in conservation of the country's environmental and cultural heritage, and leads to greater international and national understanding of the country's variegated environments and cultures.

Special Considerations

1. Tourism will be planned for controlled development so that it does not generate any serious environmental or sociocultural problems and is used as a means of environmental and cultural conservation.
2. Tourism development will be tailored to the specific characteristics and needs of each area of the country, with maximum participation of community residents in the development process and tourism benefits accruing, to the greatest extent possible, to the local communities.
3. Tourism development will be integrated into the overall development plans and patterns of the country, with strong linkages established to other economic sectors, leading to a balanced economy to the greatest extent possible.
4. In addition to providing recreation and leisure travel pursuits, domestic tourism will be used as a means to redistribute national income, especially from urban and more affluent to rural and less developed areas, and to encourage greater mutual understanding by citizens of the different areas

and societies of the country, leading toward a greater sense of national unity. Approaches will be applied to socioeconomically broaden domestic travel.

Specific Objectives, Outputs, and Activities

Objective 1

Provide the framework and guidelines for long-range comprehensive tourism development through preparation of a comprehensive 15-year national tourism development policy and plan for both domestic and international tourism. The plan components are specified in the following outputs with identification of the activities required to prepare each component.

Output 1

Tourism development objectives considering economic, environmental, and sociocultural factors.

Activities

1. Review of present government objectives for overall development and, if existing, for tourism development. This review will include document research and meetings with relevant government officials and other parties.
2. Formulation of the objectives in a preliminary manner to be later refined, if necessary, based on the findings and conclusions of the surveys, analyses, and plan preparation.

Output 2

General survey and analysis of the environmental, historical, sociocultural, economic, resource, land use, and other relevant characteristics of the country, and of present development policies and plans.

Activities

1. Field surveys and document research of the general environmental characteristics of climate, topography, hydrography, flora, fauna, ecological systems, development hazards, present land use, settlement and land tenure patterns, important natural resource areas, and other relevant characteristics of the physical environment.
2. Field surveys and document research of the historical influences and sociocultural and economic patterns of the country, including population size,

characteristics, and distribution, social organization and cultural traditions, and economic development and employment patterns.
3. Review of present development policies and plans, including physical and
socioeconomic plans.
4. Survey and evaluation of the environmental quality level of the country
and particularly in any existing and possible future tourism areas, including air, water, and noise pollution levels, environmental cleanliness, and
attractiveness of the built environment.

Output 3

Inventory and evaluation of the existing and potential tourist attractions and activities.

Activities

1. Field surveys and document research of existing and potential tourist attractions and related activities, including areas of natural scenic beauty,
unusual and interesting fauna and flora, desirable climatic areas, places offering land- and water-based recreation potential, archaeological and historic sites, interesting cultural traditions, arts and handicrafts, festivals and
special events, cuisine and any other features that would be of interest to
international and domestic tourists.
2. Survey of any special type attraction features that may exist and review of
the need for and feasibility of developing special features such as convention centers and theme parks.
3. Evaluation of the existing and potential tourist attractions and related activities, including identifying primary and secondary attractions and formulating recommendations on ways in which the attractions should be
conserved, improved, and developed for visitor use (this evaluation will
be done in conjunction with the market analysis).

Output 4

Characteristics and evaluation of transportation access to and within the country,
and of other infrastructure for present and future tourism development.

Activities

1. Field surveys, document research, and evaluation of the existing and already planned future international access to the country of both facilities
and services, including, for example, of air access, the origin, frequency,
and capacities of air flights, and the capability of the airport facilities to effectively handle tourist flows.
2. Field surveys, document research, and evaluation of the present and already planned future internal transportation system to serve tourism, in-

cluding the road, rail, water, and domestic air service network and services, with particular reference to existing and possible future tourism development areas.

3. Field surveys, document research, and evaluation of the present and already planned future other types of infrastructure for tourism, including water supply, electric power, sewage and solid waste disposal, drainage, and telecommunications, with particular reference to existing and possible future tourism development areas.

4. Identification of specific problems and constraints of transportation and other infrastructure that will need to be resolved for the development of tourism.

Output 5

Inventory and evaluation of the existing and already planned accommodation and other tourist facilities and services.

Activities

1. Field surveys and document research of the existing and already planned future hotels and other types of tourist accommodation, inventory of their characteristics, and determination of recent room occupancy levels.

2. Field surveys and document research of existing and already planned future other types of tourist facilities and services of tour and travel agencies and services, tourist restaurants, medical facilities and services, banking and money exchange, entry and exit facilitation requirements and procedures, especially of immigration and customs, retail shopping and personal services, public safety, postal services, tourist information facilities and services, and any other necessary tourist facilities and services.

3. Evaluation of the suitability of accommodation and other tourist facilities and services to serve tourism now and in the future, with identification of any particular problems to be resolved.

Output 6

Analysis of the present and future international and domestic tourist markets, and establishment of market targets and related accommodation and other tourist facility and service needs.

Activities

1. Data collection and analysis of the present number and characteristics of international and domestic tourist arrivals to and within the country.

2. Organization and conducting of a sample survey of international and domestic tourists to obtain further information on their characteristics, in-

cluding expenditure patterns, and on their attitudes toward tourist attractions, accommodation, and other facilities and services.

3. Survey (on a selective basis), and evaluation of information obtained from tour operators in the major existing and potential international tourist market countries in order to determine their and their clients' perception of the country as a destination and any particular problems that they may have experienced in organizing tours for the country; and survey and evaluation of information from any national tour operators who handle domestic tourists.

4. Determination of the types and extent of international tourist markets that can be attracted to the country and are suitable markets consistent with the objectives of tourism development, giving consideration to the types of tourist attractions and activities, accommodation, and other facilities and services available now and in the future, travel distance and cost to get to the country, and the relative attractiveness of competing destinations.

5. Determination of the type and extent of domestic tourist markets that can be developed, and their destinations in the country.

6. Determination of market targets by five-year periods of the plan for international tourist arrivals and domestic tourist movements by numbers and characteristics, including average length of stay, giving consideration to the integrated environmental, sociocultural, and carrying capacity analysis.

7. Projection of the type and number of accommodation units required and of other tourist facilities and services needed, based on the market targets, giving due consideration to the existing tourist facilities and services.

Output 8

Integrated environmental, sociocultural, and economic analysis and determination of the general tourist carrying capacity of the country and its major tourism areas.

Activities

1. Integrated analysis of the environmental, sociocultural, and economic characteristics, tourist attractions and activities, transportation and other infrastructure systems, and existing tourism development patterns.

2. Determination of the general tourist carrying capacity of the country, based on considerations of the carrying capacities of existing and potential tourism development areas, major tourist attractions and activities, overall environmental and sociocultural limits to absorb tourism, and any long-term infrastructure constraints, with feedback to the market analysis and establishment of market targets.

3. Identification of the major opportunities and constraints for tourism development during the short-, medium-, and long-term periods.

Output 8

International and domestic tourism development policy, giving consideration to balanced economic, environmental, and sociocultural factors.

Activities

1. Review of the objectives for developing tourism, the overall development policy of the country, the existing and potential tourist attractions and activities, the market analysis and targets, and the integrated analysis of environmental, economic, and sociocultural factors, including national and regional carrying capacities and the major opportunities and constraints on development.
2. Formulation of a set of policy statements on the most appropriate types and extent of tourism development and any special considerations that should be applied in developing tourism such as economic, environmental, and sociocultural factors. These will be formulated first as alternative policies for impact evaluation and reviewed by the government (and project steering committee) and then determined in final form.

Output 9

National tourism development structure plan, including major tourist attractions and activity areas, tourism development regions, and the transportation access and linkages.

Activities

1. Review of the integrated analysis of the economic, environmental, and sociocultural characteristics, tourist attractions and activities, transportation access to and within the country, other infrastructure and carrying capacities for tourism regions and the entire country, and the market analysis and targets and projections of tourist facility needs.
2. Review of the international and domestic tourism development policies formulated in Output 8.
3. Formulation of alternative conceptual structure plans and evaluation of these with respect to meeting the plan's objectives, optimization of economic benefits and minimization of environmental and sociocultural impacts for review by the government, and decision on the best alternative, with feedback and any necessary modifications made to the development objectives, market targets, and tourist facility needs.
4. Preparation of the final structure plan, indicating the international access points and any improvements required to the access facilities and services to the country, the tourism development regions or zones, their primary and secondary tourist attractions, the type and extent of accommodation and other tourist facilities and services required nationally and by region,

and the internal transportation linkages and any improvements required to internal transportation facilities and services.

5. Specification of the staging of development by region or parts of regions for approximate five-year periods, based on the market analysis, accessibility, logical expansion patterns of development and any other criteria including the policies and projects in the government's overall development program.

6. Formulation of various logical tour routes, connecting the access points of the country with the tourism development regions and major tourist attractions.

Note: If organizationally more convenient, transportation can be made a separate section of the plan report because of its importance.

Output 10

Recommendations on improvements required to present tourist facilities and services and related infrastructure.

Activities

1. Review of the evaluation of presently developed tourist facilities and services and tourism infrastructure as related to the desired tourist markets.

2. Formulation of recommendations for any improvements required to present facilities and services and related infrastructure to adequately serve the desired present tourist markets.

Note: This output is included only if there is some present tourism development that requires improvements to meet present market demands and environmental or other standards recommended in the plan.

Output 11

Regional tourism policy and structure plans for the first-stage development regions.

Activities

1. Review of national tourism development policy and the structure plan recommendations for these regions, including the type and level of tourism development.

2. Formulation of the tourism development objectives of the regions, including economic, environmental, and social factors.

3. Conducting of any detailed surveys and analyses of the regions required, in addition to those prepared for national plan.

4. Formulation of the regional tourism development policies, considering

both national and regional development objectives, the surveys and analyses, and regional economic, environmental, and sociocultural factors.

5. Formulation of regional tourism development structure plans, including access points to the regions, the primary and secondary tourist attractions, the type, location, and approximate size of tourism development areas (such as resort sites), the internal transportation network and other infrastructure considerations, and regional tour patterns. These plans will first be prepared in outline alternative form with evaluation of impacts for review by the government, and then prepared in final form.

6. Specification of any recommendations needed relative to economic, environmental, and sociocultural factors and any regional level institutional elements.

Note: Urban tourism planning for first stage development could also be prepared, if needed, along with the first stage regional plans.

Output 12

Economic analysis of the present and projected future level of tourism development, and ways to enhance economic benefits.

Activities

1. Preparation of an economic impact analysis of the present and projected future levels of tourism development, including tourist expenditure patterns, and the economic measures of tourism's contribution to the GNP, gross and net foreign exchange earnings and identification of sources of foreign exchange leakages, direct and indirect employment by number and type, multiplier effect, contribution to government revenues, and any other economic measures.

2. Analysis of the overall economic costs and benefits of tourism development as proposed in the plan.

3. Specification of ways in which the economic benefits of tourism can be enhanced (for example, through greater production of local goods and services used in tourism).

Output 13

Environmental impact evaluation of tourism and ways to reduce and prevent negative impacts and reinforce positive ones, realizing that the overall planning approach will allow for environmental protection and sustainable development.

Activities

1. Systematic assessment of the types and extent of positive and negative environmental impacts of any present tourism development and of the possible impacts of the projected future development.
2. Formulation of recommendations on specific ways to reduce any present and prevent any future negative impacts and reinforce positive ones.
3. Review of the present conservation objectives, policies, and programs underway in the country, and formulation of recommendations on any modifications needed to these with respect to tourism development and, more generally, how tourism can be used as a means to achieve environmental conservation.
4. Specification of approaches in which optimum visitor use can be made of conservation areas, including national parks, nature reserves, and archaeological and historic sites, without generating environmental problems, and the types of visitor controls that should be applied at these places.
5. Formulation of ways in which the environmental quality of tourism areas and the country in general can be improved.

Output 14

Sociocultural impact evaluation of tourism and ways to reduce and prevent negative impacts and reinforce positive ones (realizing that sociocultural factors will have been considered throughout the planning process).

Activities

1. Systematic evaluation of the types and extent of positive and negative sociocultural impacts of present tourism development and of the possible impacts of the projected future level of development.
2. Formulation of recommendations on specific ways to reduce any present and prevent any future negative impacts and reinforce positive ones, including preparation of a sociocultural program if needed and, more generally, how tourism can be used as a means of cultural conservation and maintenance.
3. Specification of a public education program on tourism, including in the school system, and of ways to educate tourists about local cultural values, traditions, and customs.

Output 15

Tourist facility development and design standards to be applied to development of accommodation and other tourist facilities.

Activities

1. Review and evaluation of any existing development standards and formu-

lation of any necessary modifications to these and any new standards required. These standards include: density of development (for example, maximum number of accommodation units per acre or hectare); maximum building heights; minimum setbacks of buildings from the shoreline, roads, site boundaries, and other buildings; maximum site area coverage by buildings; floor area ratios; minimum site area for open space and landscaping; vehicular parking requirements; and sign controls. Appropriate graphic illustrations of development standards will be prepared.

2. Review of the traditional architectural styles and building materials, review of environmental influences on design, review and evaluation of any existing architectural design standards, and formulation of suitable architectural design guidelines, including architectural motifs and use of local building materials to the greatest extent possible, based on considerations of traditional local styles, appropriate contemporary styles, and local environmental characteristics. Appropriate graphic illustrations of architectural concepts will be prepared.

3. Review of the indigenous and well-adapted exotic landscaping plants available, review and evaluation of any existing landscaping design standards, and formulation of suitable landscaping design guidelines, including types of plants and landscaping principles, giving consideration to the natural environmental conditions, use of local plant material, and low maintenance requirements of the landscaping. Appropriate graphic illustrations of landscaping concepts will be prepared.

4. Review of existing engineering standards for roads, water supply, sewage and solid waste disposal, and telecommunications, and formulation of suitable engineering standards, including any acceptable existing, modified existing, or new standards for resort, hotel, and other tourist facility development. Appropriate graphic illustrations will be prepared.

5. Provision of the relevant input of tourist facility development and design standards to Output 20, on legislation and regulations.

Output 16

Accommodation and other tourist facility quality standards.

Activities

1. Review and evaluation of any present standards for licensing and classifying hotels and other accommodation, and of other tourist facilities and services such as tour and travel operations including tour guides and tourist restaurants.

2. Formulation of any modifications necessary to present standards and any new standards required. If a hotel classification system is recommended, the terms of reference should be written for preparing such a system.

3. Provision of the necessary input to Output 20 on legislation and regulations.

Output 17

Manpower planning study and education and training program for tourism.

Activities

1. Survey and analysis of the present number and type of employees in the tourism public and private sectors and evaluation of any existing training needs to upgrade the present employees (this information may be available or may require a special survey of hotel, catering, and other tourism establishments and the government tourism office), and survey and evaluation of any existing public or private tourism education and training institutions and programs.
2. Projection of the type and number of tourism employees, by job classification and skill level, which will be required based on the projected level of tourism development (done in coordination with the tourism economist team member preparing the employment input analysis of tourism).
3. Evaluation of the human resources available to work in tourism, including reviewing any existing manpower planning studies for the country, and identification of any possible problems in the requisite manpower being available.
4. Formulation of the education and training policy and program necessary to prepare the required type and number of personnel to effectively work in tourism, including any upgrading training needed of present employees. If it appears that a tourism training institution should be developed or upgraded, terms of reference will be written for conducting a specific feasibility study of establishing such an institution as a separate project.

Output 18

Recommended public and private organizational structures for tourism, including for effective coordination of the tourism sector.

Activities

1. Review of the present organizational structures for tourism, including the government department of tourism, any tourism boards, and coordinating or advisory bodies and private sector tourism organizations.
2. Formulation of recommendations on the most effective government organizational structure for tourism, including the location of tourism in the overall government organization and preparation of an organizational chart and description of the functions of the NTA and any related boards, and identification of the staffing requirements of the NTA.
3. Formulation of recommendations on the most effective organizational approach to achieve coordination among government agencies and between the public and private sectors on all aspects of tourism development and management, including implementation of the tourism plan.

4. Formulation of the most effective organizational structures for the private enterprises involved in tourism, including hotels, restaurants, tour and travel agencies, tour guides, retail shops and handicraft artisans.
5. Provision of the necessary input to Output 20 on legislation and regulations.

Output 19

Any investment incentives required to encourage private sector investment in the development of tourist facilities and services.

Activities

1. Review and evaluation of financial resources and any existing investment incentives for tourism development or development in general, including tourism.
2. Formulation of any modifications necessary to existing incentives and any new incentives required, and provision of input on preparation of regulations on these incentives to Output 20.

Output 20

Legislation and regulations for tourism development, including for the establishment and functions of the NTA, tour and travel agencies, accommodation and other tourist facility standards, investment incentives, and zoning.

Activities

1. Review of any existing legislation and regulations relative to tourism and the tourism plan implementation, and of the general legal system of the country.
2. Formulation of any necessary modifications to existing legislation and any new legislation and regulations required for tourism. These will be prepared in draft form, with the final legal drafting done by the government.

Output 21

An integrated tourism data system designed for continuous operation.

Activities

1. Review and evaluation of the present data system for tourism, including tourist arrivals and characteristics and accommodation characteristics and occupancy rates. The current Embarkation/Disembarkation (ED) card used by the country will be reviewed and revised if necessary.
2. Formulation of ways in which the data system can be improved, including collection, compilation, analysis, and reporting procedures, or, if there is no

existing system, establishment of a new system and suitable data sources. Computer technology will be applied for maintenance of this system.

Output 22

Identification of the various techniques for implementation of the tourism plans.

Activities

1. Review of the possible techniques of implementing the tourism plans that have not been specified in the other outputs, such as legislation and regulations.
2. Formulation of the most effective approaches and techniques for plan implementation.

Output 23

Draft and final national tourism development plan reports.

Activities

1. Preparation of the draft and draft final reports for review and comments by the government and other concerned parties.
2. Preparation of the final report with suitable explanatory text and graphic illustrations of photographs, maps, charts, and so forth, in an attractive format, with a separate summary report.

Objective 2

Provide the framework for implementation of the first stage of the development plan through preparation of a five-year tourism development action and related programs, to be integrated into the overall national development program.

Output 1

Five-year tourism development action program.

Activities

1. Selection, in consultation with the government, of the priority physical development projects, including infrastructure projects necessary for first-stage development of the national and regional plans, with general development cost estimates. Any existing overall national development plan or program will be reviewed for compatibility with the tourism projects selected, and any necessary reconciliations made.

2. Determination of other actions required, such as adoption of legislation and regulations and implementation of organizational recommendations, for first-stage development.
3. Preparation of the consolidated tourism action program (with projects and actions indicated by year) for the five-year period and designed to be integrated into the overall national development plan or program.

Output 2

Tourism marketing strategy and promotion program.

Activities

1. Formulation of the tourism marketing strategy, based on the tourism development policy and plan and its market analysis and targets.
2. Preparation of a specific tourist promotion program, with budgetary cost estimates, for the next three- to five-year period, specifying by year the promotion techniques and their estimated costs, including production of promotional collateral material and audio-visual presentations, advertising, attendance at trade fairs, and hosting of visiting tour operators, travel writers, and photographers, with consideration given to establishing promotion offices in other countries.

Output 3

Prototypical tour programs within the country and the region that includes the country.

Activities

1. Review of the tourism plan recommendations on type and location of tourist attractions and tourism development areas and the tour routes, and of regional touring relationships with nearby countries.
2. Formulation of prototypical tour programs of various types and lengths, including both internal and regional programs.

Output 4

Draft and final development action program and related reports.

Activities

1. Preparation of the draft program and any related reports for review by the government and other concerned parties.
2. Preparation of the final reports, with appropriate text and charts.

Objective 3

Provide the planning basis for development of three priority tourism development projects, including one resort and visitor facilities at two tourist attraction features, one nature park, and one archaeological or historic site. These plans will also serve as models for the planning of other similar development projects.

Output 1

Conceptual plan and prefeasibility analysis for a medium-size tourist resort.

Activities

1. Selection of the resort and its site from the tourism development program and in consultation with the government, and review of the recommendations for the type and size of the resort in the national and regional tourism plans.
2. Environmental analysis of the site and nearby areas, including natural characteristics and any existing land use, settlement, and sociocultural patterns, and determination of the site's carrying capacity.
3. Determination of the type and extent of tourist facility and other land use requirements, including accommodation, retail commercial, cultural and recreation facilities, park, conservation and landscape areas, and transportation network, giving consideration to the recommendations on type and extent of development for this area in the national and regional plans, any additional market analysis required, and the opportunities and constraints offered by the site itself.
4. Formulation of the plan showing the access to the site and its regional relationships, the various land use areas, internal transportation system, and conceptual layout (site plan) of buildings and other facilities, and park, recreation, open space, and landscaped areas. The sources and any special considerations of other types of infrastructure will be indicated.
5. Formulation of development standards, architectural and landscaping design concepts and guidelines for the tourist facilities, and engineering design standards for the project.
6. Preparation of a general environmental impact assessment of the proposed plan, including natural, sociocultural, and economic considerations (the final environmental impact assessment will be made of the final detailed plan to be prepared later).
7. Preparation of a prefeasibility analysis of the project, including projected costs and revenues and rate of return and market considerations.
8. Preparation of a preliminary development program for the project, including for detailed planning, design, and engineering, with recommendations on the most suitable organizational structure and financing for the project finalization, implementation, and operation.

Output 2

Conceptual plans for visitor facilities and use and conservation measures for a natural tourist attraction, such as a national park, and a major archaeological or historic site.

Activities

1. Selection of the sites from the development program and in consultation with the government.
2. Environmental analysis of the sites and nearby areas, including any existing land use, settlement, and sociocultural patterns, and determination of the sites' visitor carrying capacities.
3. Projection of the number of visitors to the sites and determination of the types and extent of visitor facilities required and conservation measures needed, giving consideration to the recommendations for these sites in the national and regional plans and the environmental analyses of the sites.
4. Formulation of the plans showing the access to the sites, location of various visitor facilities, the internal circulation system, and other infrastructure required, conservation areas and any special considerations that need to be made, and a conceptual layout (site plan) of buildings, parking, other facilities, and landscaped areas.
5. Formulation of development standards, architectural and landscaping design concepts and guidelines, and engineering design standards for the visitor facilities.
6. Formulation of visitor use plans and guidelines for efficient visitor movement on the sites.
7. Preparation of general environmental impact assessments of the project plans (the final environmental impact assessments will be made of the final detailed plans, to be prepared later).
8. Preparation of prefeasibilty analyses of the site plans, including costs and revenues, realizing that the projects may not be intended as profit making in themselves.
9. Preparation of preliminary development programs for the projects, including for detailed planning, design, and engineering, with recommendations on the most suitable organizational structure and financing for finalization, implementation, and operation of the projects.

Output 3

Draft and final plan reports.

Activities

1. Preparation of the draft plan reports for review by the government and other concerned parties, including the local communities.

2. Preparation of the final reports in an attractive format, with suitable explanatory text and graphic illustrations.

Note: The local communities in the resort and tourist attraction areas should be involved throughout the planning process.

C

Contents of the Zanzibar Tourism Development Plan Report

Chapter

1 **Introduction**
   Scope of Project
   Study Team and Methodology
   Tourism Development Objectives
   Acknowledgements

2 **Environment for Tourism**
   Location
   Natural Environment
      Topography, Hydrography and Vegetation
      Climate
   Historical Influences
      Early History
      Recent History
   Socio-Economic Influences
      Population and Settlement Patterns
      Economic Conditions in Tanzania
      Economic Conditions in Zanzibar
      Economic Factors Affecting Tourism
   Government Structure

3   **Tourist Attractions**
                Cultural Attractions
                        General Cultural Features
                        Cultural Centre
                        Historic Places
                        Museums
                        Arts and Handicrafts
                        Duty Free Shopping
                Natural Attractions
                        Beaches and Water Environment
                        Nature Conservation Areas
                        Scenic and Agricultural Landscapes
                Parks and Recreation Facilities

4   **Transportation**
                International Access
                        Air Traffic Patterns in Africa
                        Existing Air Service to Tanzania
                        Flight Capacity
                        Air Fares
                        Evaluation of International Air Access
                        Cruise Ships
                Domestic Air Transportation
                        Recent Development
                        Aircraft
                        Airports
                        Flight Capacity and Reliability
                        Air Fares and Route Economics
                        Reservations, Ticketing and Ground Handling
                        Air Traffic Planning
                        Improvements Needed
                Airport Facilitation
                        Entrance Visa Requirements
                        Clearance of Passengers and Baggage
                Domestic Sea and Land Transportation
                        Sea Ferries
                        Road Network
                Foreign Currency Requirements

5   **Tourist Facilities and Services**
                Accommodation
                        Existing and Proposed Accommodation
                        Required Improvements to Existing Hotels
                        Standards of Hotel Operations
                Other Tourist Facilities and Services
                        Tourist Information Services

Restaurants and Bars
Cuisine
Evening Entertainment
Shopping, Personal Services and Money Exchange
Postal Services
Health and Public Safety
Infrastructure
Water Supply
Electric Power and Telecommunications
Sewage and Solid Waste Disposal

6   **Market Analysis**
World and Regional Tourism
World Tourism
Regional Tourist Flows
Tourism in Tanzania
Background and Tourist Arrivals
Factors Affecting Tourism
Travel Status
Mode of Travel
Origin of Tourists
Other Visitor Characteristics
Seasonality
Domestic Tourism
Impact on Tourism to Zanzibar
Other Markets in East Africa
Economic Importance of Tourism In Kenya
Origin of Kenya Tourists
Kenya Travel Characteristics
Potential of Kenya Market for Zanzibar
Other Markets
Current Status of Tourism in Zanzibar
Visitor Characteristics
Factors Affecting Travel to Zanzibar
Future Prospects
Distribution of Future Demand
Market Targets
Preconditions for Achieving Targets
Bases for Market Targets
Determination of Market Targets

7   **Tourism Policy and Structure Plan**
Tourism Development Policy
Tourism Structure Plan
Development Area Criteria
Zanzibar Town Development Area

                 Bwejuu Beach Development Area
                 Mangapwani Beach Development Area
                 Longer-term Development Areas in Zanzibar Island
                 Chake Chake Development Area
                 Verani Development Area
                 Longer-term Development Areas in Pemba

8   **Tour Programming**
          Current Tour Programme Characteristics
               Operational Problems
               Tours Currently Offered
               Pricing Policies
          Recommended Tour Programmes
               Basic and Special Interest Tours
               Tours with Long-term Potential
          Marketing of Tour Programmes

9   **Development Guidelines**
          Traditional Building Styles
               Arab Style
               Swahili Style
          Shangani Tourist District Design Concepts
               Visual Images
               Proposed Tourism Development
               Shangani Hotel
               Old Fort/Cultural Centre
               Tippu Tip House Museum and Restaurant
          Hotel and Resort Design Concepts
               Bwejuu Beach Hotel
               Chanju Island Holiday Village
               Bwawani Hotel Renovation
               Pemba Sport Fishing Hotel
               Pemba Hotels' Renovations
          General Development Standards
               Building Setbacks and Heights
               Open Space, Landscaping and Parking
               Architectural Design, Interior Decoration and Furnishings

10   **Environmental Quality**
          Elements of Environmental Quality
          Environmental Quality in Zanzibar
          Environmental Principles for Tourism Development
               Development Principles
               Need for Environmental Monitoring

11   **Socio-Cultural Considerations**
          Importance of Socio-Cultural Evaluation
          Socio-Cultural Characteristics of Zanzibar
               Cultural Evolution
               Social Attitudes

Cultural Impact of Tourism in Zanzibar
Conservation of Historic Places
Revitalization of Music and Dance
Cultural Development Policy and Programme
Improvement of Handicrafts
Limited Cultural Impact
Social Impact of Tourism in Zanzibar
Extent of Social Impact
Considerations for Beach Resort Development
Socio-Psychological Aspects
Conclusions and Recommendations

12   **Manpower Needs and Training Programme**
Evaluation of Current Needs
Hotel Sector
Tourism Sector
Current Employment Characteristics
Existing Education and Training Institutions
Current Manpower and Training Needs
Projected Manpower Needs
Recommended Training Programme
Immediate Training Programme—Hotel Sector
Training Methods and Facilities
Sector Responsibility for Training
Training Cost Estimates
Organization for Training
Public Education Programme

13   **Marketing Plan**
Institutional Framework
Marketing Considerations
Market Review
Market Research
Review of the Tourism Product
Market Image
Marketing Objectives and Strategy
Marketing Programme
Mobilization
Basic Marketing
Advanced Marketing
Kenya Market
Costs of the Marketing Programme

14   **Development Programme**
Programme Schedule
Improvements to Tourist Attractions
Hotel Development Programme
Beach Rest Houses and Budget Hotels
Parks and Recreation Areas

The Development Process
Role of the Department of Tourism
Development Activities
Institutional Impediments to Development

15   **Economic Considerations**
Benefits of Tourism
Types of Benefits
Projection of Foreign Exchange Earnings
The Multiplier Effect
Employment
Shadow Prices
Related Economic Activities

16   **Prefeasibility Analysis**
Hotel Prefeasibility Analysis
Investment Programme
Estimates of Hotel Financial Results
Analysis of Results
Recommendations for Development
Existing Financial Reporting
Sources of Financing Tourism Development

17   **Organization for Tourism**
Organization of Hotels and Related Facilities
Department of Tourism Organization
Ministerial Location
Recommended Reorganization
Zanzibar Friendship Bureau
Recommended Reorganization
Staffing, Facilities and Financing
Tourism Coordinating Committee

18   **Plan Implementation**
Adoption of Tourism Policy, Plan and Programme
Improvements to Facilities and Services
Monitoring Programme
Special Projects Needed
Tourism Advisory Project
Fellowships and Study Tours Project
Archaeological Site Preservation Project
Handicraft Development Project

Appendixes
A   Designated Historic Sites in Zanzibar
B   Projected Manpower Needs by Year, Position and Level
C   Development Cost Format for Proposed Hotels
D   Cost Estimates for First Stage Projects

Selected Bibliography

Ashworth, Gregory and Brian Goodall. ed. 1990. *Marketing Tourism Places*. London: Routledge.

Ashworth, G.J. and J. Turnbridge. 1990. *The Tourist-Historic City*. London: Pinter Publishers.

Bosselman, Fred P. ed. 1978. *In the Wake of the Tourist: Managing Special Places in Eight Countries*. Washington, DC: The Conservation Foundation.

Burkart, A. J. and S. Medlick. 2nd ed. 1981. *Tourism: Past, Present and Future*. London: Heinemann.

Canadian Government Office of Tourism. 1979. *Planning Seasonal Tourist Accommodation: Four Design Alternatives*. Ottawa.

Chibb, Som Nath. 1989. *Essays on Tourism*. New Delhi: Cross Section Publications.

Coltman, Michael M. 1989. *Introduction to Travel and Tourism: An International Approach*. New York: Van Nostrand Reinhold.

Coltman, Michael M. 1989. *Tourism Marketing*. New York: Van Nostrand Reinhold.

Dasman, Raymond F., John P. Milton, and Peter H. Freeman. 1973. *Ecological Principles for Economic Development*. New York: John Wiley & Sons.

Davern, Jeanne M. ed. 1976. *Places for People: Hotels, Motels, Restaurants, Bars, Clubs, Community Recreation Facilities, Camps, Parks, Plazas, and Playgrounds*. New York: McGraw Hill.

Davidoff, Philip, Doris Davidoff, and Douglas Eyre. 1988. *Tourism Geography*. Elmsford, NY: National Publishers.

De Kadt, Emanuel. ed. 1979. *Tourism: Passport to Development?* New York: Oxford University Press.

Dorward, Sherry. 1990. *Design for Mountain Communities: A Landscape and Architectural Guide.* New York: Van Nostrand Reinhold.

Doswell, Roger and Paul R. Gamble. 1979. *Marketing and Planning Hotels and Tourism Projects.* London: Hutchinson & Co.

Economic Commission for Europe. 1988. *Spatial Planning for Recreation and Tourism in the Countries of the EEC Region.* New York: United Nations.

Edgell, David L., Jr. 1990. *International Tourism Policy.* New York: Van Nostrand Reinhold.

Edgell, David L., Sr. 1990. *Charting a Course for International Tourism in the Nineties.* Washington, DC: U.S. Department of Commerce.

Edington, John M. and M. Ann Edington. 1986. *Ecology, Recreation and Tourism.* Cambridge, England: University of Cambridge Press.

Enggass, Peter M. 1988. *Tourism and the Travel Industry: An Information Sourcebook.* New York: Oryx Press.

Feifer, Maxine. 1985. *Going Places: The Ways of the Tourist from Imperial Rome to the Present Day.* London: Macmillan.

Fitch, James Marston. 1982. *Historic Preservation: Curatorial Management of the Built World.* New York: McGraw Hill.

Fussel, Paul. ed. 1987. *The Norton Book of Travel.* New York: W.W. Norton & Company.

Gearing, Charles E., William W. Swart, and Turgut Var. 1976. *Planning for Tourism Development.* New York: Praeger.

Gee, Chuck Y., James C. Makens, and Dexter J. L. Choy. 2nd ed. 1989. *The Travel Industry.* New York: Van Nostrand Reinhold.

Getz, Donald. 1990. *Festivals, Special Events and Tourism.* New York: Van Nostrand Reinhold.

Goldsmith, Edward, Peter Bunyard, Nicholas Hildyard, and Patrick McCully. 1990. *Imperiled Planet: Restoring Our Endangered Ecosystems.* Cambridge, Mass.: MIT Press.

Gorman, Michael, Frank Height, Mary V. Mullin, and W. H. Walsh, ed. 1977. *Design for Tourism.* Elmsford, New York: Pergamon Press.

Graburn, Nelson H. H. ed. 1976. *Ethnic and Tourist Arts: Cultural Expressions from the Fourth World.* Berkeley: University of California Press.

Gunn, Clare A. 2nd ed. 1988. *Tourism Planning.* New York: Taylor & Francis.

——. 2nd ed. 1988. *Vacationscape: Designing Tourist Regions.* New York: Van Nostrand Reinhold.

Hawkins, Donald, Elwood Shafer, and James Rovelstad. 1980. *Tourism Planning and Development Issues.* Washington, DC: George Washington University.

Hedman, Richard and Andrew Jaszewski. 1984. *Fundamentals of Urban Design.* Chicago: Planners Press, American Planning Association.

Hindley, Geoffrey. 1983. *Tourist, Travellers and Pilgrims.* London: Hutchinson.

Hudman, Lloyd E. and Donald E. Hawkins. 1989. *Tourism in Contemporary Society: An Introductory Text.* Englewood Cliffs, New Jersey: Prentice Hall.

Johnson, Ronald W. and Michael G. Schene. 1987. *Cultural Resources Management.* Malabar, Florida: Robert E. Krieger Publishing Co.

Kaiser, Charles Jr. and Larry E. Helber. 1978. *Tourism Planning and Development.* Boston: CBI.

King, Brian and Geoff Hyde. 1989. *Tourism Marketing in Australia.* Melbourne: Hospitality Press.

Krippendorf, Jost. 1987. *The Holiday Makers: Understanding the Impact of Leisure and Travel.* Oxford: Heinemann.

Laventhol & Howarth. 1984. *Hotel/Motel Development.* Washington, DC: Urban Land Institute.

Lawson, Fred. 1976. *Hotels, Motels and Condominiums: Design, Planning and Maintenance.* London: Architectural Press.

——. 1981. *Conference, Convention and Exhibition Facilities: A Handbook of Planning, Design and Management.* London: Architectural Press.

Lawson, Fred and Manuel Baud-Bovy. 1977. *Tourism and Recreation: A Handbook of Physical Planning.* Boston: CBI.

Lea, John. 1988. *Tourism and Development in the Third World.* New York: Routledge, Chapman and Hall.

Lundberg, Donald E. 6th ed. 1990. *The Tourist Business.* New York: Van Nostrand Reinhold.

Lynch, Kevin. 3rd ed. 1984. *Site Planning.* Cambridge, Mass.: MIT Press.

McHarg, Ian L. 1969. *Design with Nature.* Garden City, New York: The Natural History Press.

McIntosh, Robert W. and Charles R. Goeldner. 6th ed. 1990. *Tourism: Principles, Practices, Philosophies.* New York: John Wiley & Sons.

Mathieson, Alister and Geoffrey Wall. 1982. *Tourism: Economic, Physical and Social Impacts.* Harlow, England: Longman Group.

Mayo, Edward J. Jr. and Lance P. Jarvis. 1981. *The Psychology of Leisure Travel.* Boston: CBI.

Middleton, Victor T. C. 1988. *Marketing in Travel & Tourism.* Oxford, England: Heinemann.

Mill, Robert Christie. 1990. *Tourism: The International Business.* Englewood Cliffs, New Jersey: Prentice Hall.

Mill, Robert Christie and Alastair M. Morrison. 1985. *The Tourism System: An Introductory Text.* Englewood Cliffs, New Jersey: Prentice Hall.

Morrison, Alastair M. 1989. *Hospitality and Travel Marketing.* London: Chapman & Hall.

Murphy, Peter E. 1985. *Tourism: A Community Approach.* New York: Methuen.

Norwich, John Julius. 1985. *A Taste for Travel.* New York: Alfred A. Knopf.

Organization for Economic Co-operation and Development. 1980. *The Impact of Tourism on the Environment.* Paris.

Organization of American States. 1987. *The Optimum Size and Nature of New Hotel Development in the Caribbean.* Washington, DC.

Pearce, Douglas. 1987. *Tourism Today: A Geographical Analysis.* Harlow, England: Longman Group.

——. 2nd ed. 1989. *Tourist Development.* Harlow, England: Longman Group.

Pearce, Philip L. 1982. *The Social Psychology of Tourist Behaviour.* Elmsford, New York: Pergamon Press.

Petersen, David C. 1989. *Convention Centers, Stadiums and Arenas.* Washington, DC: Urban Land Institute.

Ritchie, R.R.B. and C.R. Goeldner, ed. 1987. *Travel, Tourism and Hospitality Research: A Handbook for Managers and Researchers.* New York: John Wiley & Sons.

Richter, Linda K. 1989. *The Politics of Tourism in Asia.* Honolulu: University of Hawaii Press.

Rubenstein, Harvey M. 3rd ed. 1987. *Guide to Site and Environmental Planning.* New York: John Wiley & Sons.

Rutes, Walter A. and Richard H. Penner. 1985. *Hotel Planning and Design.* New York: Watson-Guptill Publications.

Sassa, Alberto. 1983. *Elements of Tourism Economics.* Rome: Catal.

Singh, Tej Vir, H. Leo Theuns, and Frank M. Go. ed. 1989. *Towards Appropriate Tourism: The Case of Developing Countries.* Frankfurt um Mein: Peter Lang.

Simonds, John Ormsbee. 2nd ed. 1986. *Earthscape: A Manual of Environmental Planning and Design.* New York: Van Nostrand Reinhold.

Smith, Douglas. 1978. *Hotel and Restaurant Design.* New York: Van Nostrand Reinhold.

Smith, Stephen L. J. 1989. *Tourism Analysis: A Handbook.* Harlow, England: Longman Group.

Smith, Valene L. ed. 2nd ed. 1989. *Hosts and Guests: The Anthropology of Tourism.* Philadelphia: University of Pennsylvania Press.

Torre, I. Azeo. 1989. *Waterfront Development.* New York: Van Nostrand Reinhold.

Turner, Louis and John Ash. 1975. *The Golden Hordes.* London: Constable.

U.S. National Park Service (United States Department of the Interior). 1988. *Management Policies.* Washington, DC: U.S. Government Printing Office.

Uzzell, David. 1989. *Heritage Interpretation. Vols. I and II.* London: Pinter Printers.

Wahab, Salah. 1975. *Tourism Management.* London: Tourism International Press.

Walker, Theodore D. 1987. *Design for Parks and Recreational Spaces.* New York: Van Nostrand Reinhold.

Williams, Allan M. and Gareth Shaw. 2nd ed. 1990. *Tourism and Economic Development: Western European Experience.* London: Pinter Publishers.

Witt, Stephen F. and Luiz Moutinho. 1989. *Tourism Marketing and Management Handbook.* Hemel Hempstead, U.K.: Prentice Hall International.

World Tourism Organization. 1977. *Integrated Planning.* Madrid.

——. 1981. *Social and Cultural Impacts of Tourist Movements.* Madrid.

——. 1981. *Tourism Multipliers Explained.* Madrid.

——. 1983 *Concept and Production Innovations of the Tourism Product.* Madrid.

——. 1983. *New Concepts of Tourism's Role in Modern Society: Possible Development Models.* Madrid.

——. 1983. *Risks of Saturation or Tourist Carrying Capacity Overload in Holiday Destinations.* Madrid.

——. 1983. *Study of Tourism's Contribution to Protecting the Environment.* Madrid.

——. 1985. *Methodology for the Establishment and Implementation of Tourism Master Plans at Both the Domestic and Regional Levels. . . .* Madrid.

——. 1985. *The Security and Legal Protection of the Tourist.* Madrid.

——. 1985. *The Role of Transnational Tourism Enterprises in the Development of Tourism.* Madrid.

——. 1985. *The State's Role in Protecting and Promoting Culture as a Factor of Tourism Development. . . .* Madrid.

——. 1985. *The State's Role in Encouraging the Development of New Destinations and Ensuring Balanced Distribution of Tourist Flows . . . .* Madrid.

——. 1985. *Financial and Budgetary Control of Tourism Development Projects.* Madrid.

——. 1988. *Quality Control of Tourism Products and Services.* Madrid.

——. 1988. *Guidelines for the Transfer of New Technologies in the Field of Tourism.* Madrid.

——. 1989. *Carrying Capacity in Mountain and Alpine Regions.* (Draft). Madrid.

World Tourism Organization and United Nations Environment Programme. 1983. *Workshop on Environmental Aspects of Tourism.* Madrid.

Young, John. 1990. *Sustaining the Earth*. Cambridge, Mass: Harvard University Press.

Young, George. 1973. *Tourism: Blessing or Blight?* Harmondsworth, England: Penguin.

Index

Accommodations, 38, 111–115
   automobile travelers, 113
   case example, Cyprus, 127–130
   classification system for, 115, 326–327
   condominium ownership, 115
   holiday villages, 113–114
   hotel classification system, 326–327
   hotels, 112–113
   miscellaneous types of, 113
   projections for, 135–137
   self-catering units, 114–115
   standards, 326–327
   time-sharing, 115
Adoption of plan, 449
Adventure tourism, 163–164
   case example, Bhutan, 259–263
   planning for, 247–250
Age-sex profiles, 59
Air pollution, as environmental impact, 344
Air travel, early tourism and, 8, 9
Alexander the Great, 4
Alexandria, 4
Aloha Week, 85
Alternative tourism
   examples of, 166–167
   forms of, 245, 252
   planning for, 252–253
   use of term, 166
Ancient times, travel in, 3–4
Antiques/artifacts, planning/managing resources, 286–287
Archaeological sites, 80–82
   damage as environmental impact, 347
   examples of, 80–82
   modelling, 349
   planning/managing resources, 278–280
   preservation of, 349
   recent developments, 82

Architectural design. See Design standards
Art galleries, as cultural attraction, 85
Arts/handicrafts
   as cultural attraction, 83
   planning/managing resources, 281–282
Aruba, 88
Ashrams, 113
Atlantic City, 88, 200
Attractions
   case studies
      Burma, 95–98
      Fiji, 103–106
      Malta, 98–99
      Mongolia, 99–103
   clustering of development, 181–182
   convention/conference tourism, 87–88
   cost factors, 92–93
   cuisine as, 90
   cultural attractions, 80–85
   entertainment, 89
   ethnic tourism, 91
   evaluation of, 94–95
   gambling casinos, 88–89
   health tourism, 80
   hotels/resorts as, 90
   natural attractions, 77–80
   nostalgic tourism, 91
   religious pilgrimages, 91
   safety/public health considerations, 92
   shopping, 86–87
   special events, 88
   sports, 89–90
   survey of, 93–94
   theme parks, 86
   transportation as, 90
   types for attention in planning, 76–77
Attractions planning
   case examples

Attractions planning (cont'd.)
    Bandelier National Monument, 298–299
    Borobudur National Archaeological
      Park, 293–295
    Fatehpur Sikri, 295–297
    Zambia, 299–310
  convention facilities planning, 288–289
  cultural attractions planning, 278–287
  fair/exposition planning, 289
  gambling casinos, 289
  international events planning, 289
  natural attractions planning, 272–278
  special attractions, 290
  special factors for visitor use, 290–292
  theme park planning, 287–288
Automobile travelers, accommodations for, 113
Avebury, 291

Baden Baden, 88
Bali
  resort area selection analysis, 152–154
  socioeconomic programming, 390–396
Balikbayans program, 91
Bandelier National Monument, visitor organization,
    298–299
Banking services, evaluation of, 118
Beaches
  carrying capacity, 149–150
  as natural attraction, 78
Bed and breakfast establishments, 113, 251
Bhutan, 291
Borobudur National Archaeological Park, planning for,
    293–295
Brighton, 200
Buddha's Trail, 91
Buffer zone, around resort, 213
Building heights, standards for, 311
Building setbacks, standards for, 313
Burma
  survey/evaluation of attractions, 95–98
  tourism development plan, 185–187

Camping, 113, 167–168
Cancun, 200
Capital, availability of, tourism planning and, 64
Caravan tourism, 113, 168
  planning for, 257–258
Caribbean Tourism Organization, 340
Carlsbad Caverns, 79
Carnival, 85
Carrying capacities, 144–151
  capacity standards, 149–150
  case example, Goa, 157–159
  definition of, 144
  measurement criteria, 145–148
  resort planning and, 207–208
  and seasonality, 147
China, road networks, 4
Circuses, traveling, 86

Climate
  as natural attraction, 77–79
  survey of, 56
Club Mediterrane, 114
Club Robinson, 114
Coastal/marine areas, survey of, 57
Colonial Williamsburg, 82, 292
Commercial travel, 3–4
Community involvement, in planning, 27, 29, 236
Community services, evaluation of, 124
Computers, planning aids, 27
Condominiums
  ownership, 115
  time-sharing, 115
Conservation
  as environmental impact, 342–343
  use of term, 31
Conservation areas
  implementation of plan and, 436–437
  management of, 275–276
  as natural attraction, 79–80
Construction, standards, 325
Consumer protection regulations, 420
Contemporary trends, tourism related, 12–15
Convention tourism
  planning/managing resources, 288–289
  promotion program, 444
Cook, Thomas, 8
Corporate level, manpower planning, 410
Cost-benefit analysis, measure of economic impact,
    389–390
Costs of travel, tourism and, 92–93
Crater Lake National Park, environmental impact
    assessment, 355–358
Critical path techniques, 439
Cruise ships, 88
  forms of tourism, 164
  market survey, 109–110
  tourism planning, 253–254
Crusaders routes, 246
Cuisine
  as attraction, 90–91
  planning/managing resources, 286
  unusual, 117
Cultural attraction resource planning, 278–287
  antiques/artifacts, 286–287
  archeological sites, 278–280
  arts/handicrafts, 281–282
  cuisine, 286
  cultural events, 283
  economic activities, 285
  historic sites, 278–280
  museums, 285–286
  performing arts, 282–283
  traditional culture patterns, 283–284
Cultural attractions
  archaeological sites, 80–82
  arts/handicrafts as, 83
  cultural patterns as, 82–83
  economic activities as, 83
  festivals as, 85

historic sites, 80–82
residents as, 85
urban areas as, 83–84
Cultural events
implementation of plan and, 437
planning/managing resources, 283
Cultural impacts, of tourism, 370–371, 372–374
Cultural patterns
planning/managing resources, 283–284
survey of, 59
Cultural pride, conservation of and tourism, 370–371
Cycling tourism, 166
Cyprus, accommodation analysis, 127–130

Dayak village, 250
Design standards
architectural design, 318, 320
environmental relationships, 321
local building materials, use of, 320
local styles/motifs, 320
roof lines, 320
Diet resorts, 80
Disneyland, 86
Disney World, 86
Domestic tourist, definition of, 21
Draft final report, 44
Draft report, 44
Drainage
evaluation of, 124
standards, 324
Duty-free goods, 87

Ecological disruption
as environmental impact, 345–346
types of, 345–346
Ecological systems, survey of, 57
Economic activities
as cultural attraction, 83
planning/managing resources, 285
Economic development, diversity in, 30
Economic enhancement programming
cross-sectoral linkages, strengthening, 380–381
expansion of tourist activities, 383
local employment, 381–382
local management, 382
local tour/travel services, 383
ownership of tourist facilities, 381
shopping, 383
Economic impact, tourism, 10–11, 368, 370, 371
Economic impact measures
contribution to foreign exchange earnings, 385–386
contribution to government revenues, 387, 389
contribution to gross national (regional) product, 384–385
cost-benefit analysis, 389–390
employment generation, 386
multiplier effect, 386–387
Economic patterns, 142
survey of, 60

Educational profiles, 59
Electric power
evaluation of, 122
standards, 324–325
Embarkation/disembarkation immigration cards, 109
Employee services, evaluation of, 124
Employment, local, 381–382
Employment distortions, tourism and, 372
Employment generation, measure of economic impact, 386
Employment profiles, 59
Engineering design standards
building construction standards, 325
drainage, 324
electric power, 324–325
marinas/piers, 325
public health standards, 326
roads, 324
solid waste disposal, 325
telecommunications, 325
water supply, 324
Entertainment, as attraction, 89
Entry/exit facilitation, evaluation of, 119
Environmental analysis, resort planning and, 205–208
Environmental features, as natural attraction, 79
Environmental hazards
avoiding, 304–305
as environmental impact, 346
types of, 346
Environmental impact assessment
approach to, 352
case examples
Crater Lake National Park, 355–358
Maldives, 358–362
evaluation matrix, 354
legal requirements, 420
model for, 353
Environmental impacts
air pollution, 344
conservation of archeological/historic sites, 343
conservation of natural areas, 342–343
control measures, 349–351
damage to archeological/historic sites, 347
ecological disruption, 345–346
enhancement of environment, 343
environmental hazards, 346
improvement of environmental quality, 343
infrastructure improvements, 343–344
noise pollution, 345
visual pollution, 345
waste disposal problem, 345
water pollutions, 344
Environmental planning
sustainable development approach, 32–34
tourism planning, 32–34
Environmental policies, applications of, 348–349
Environmental quality
factors in, 61
improvement as environmental impact, 343
maintenance of, 347
survey of, 60–61

Environmental relationships, building design and, 321
Ethnic tourism, 91
    planning for, 258
European Economic Community, 18
Everest Trail, 249
Excursionists, 109
    compared to tourists, 19
Exemptions, as incentives, 423
Expansion, of existing resorts, 218–219
Experimental Prototype Community of Tomorrow
    (EPCOT), 86

Facilities/services survey, 111–119
    accommodations, 111–115
    eating/drinking outlets, 116–117
    entry/exit facilitation procedures, 119
    general approach, 111
    medical facilities, 118
    money exchange facilities, 118
    personal services, 117
    postal services, 119
    public safety, 118
    shopping, 117
    tourist information, 117
    tour/travel operations, 116
Facilities, 38
    design, 37–38
    local ownership of, 381
    projections for, 137–138
    site planning, 37
    standards
        accommodations, 326–327
        restaurants, 326–327
        tour/travel operations, 327–328
Fairs/expositions, planning/managing resources, 289
Farm tourism, planning for, 251–252
Fatehpur Sikri, planning for, 295–297
Feasibility analysis, 437
Festivals, as cultural attraction, 85
Fiji, 251, 254, 282
    survey/evaluation of attractions, 103–106
    tourism planning process, 69–71
Final report, 44
Financing
    planning/development and, 438
    resort planning, 216–217
    tourism project, 45
Fishing tourism, 89–90, 167, 249
Floating accommodations, 113
Floor area ratio, standards for, 315
Flora/fauna, as natural attraction, 78–79
Florence, 242
FONATUR, 200
Foreign exchange earnings, measure of economic impact,
    385–386

Galapagos Islands, 145, 291
Gambling casinos
    as attractions, 88–89

planning/managing resources, 289
Gateway area concept, 180–181
Geographic survey, 55–58
    climate, 56
    coastal/marine areas, 57
    ecological systems, 57
    geology, 57
    location of region, 56
    natural resource areas, 57–58
    topography, 56
    vegetation, 57
    wildlife, 57
Geology, survey of, 57
Goa, carrying capacity, 157–159
Government
    financing of infrastructure development, 421
    funding of tourism organization, 416
    implementation of plan and, 430
    ministry, tourism development, 412, 413
    revenues as measure of economic impact, 387, 389
    role in tourism policy, 171–172
    tourism planning and, 62–63
Grand Tour, The (Nugent), 6
Great Barrier Reef Marine Park, 291
Gross national (regional) product, measure of economic
    impact, 384–385
Growth rate, control of, 173
Guest houses, 113

Hague Declaration on Tourism, 33
Handicapped, design for, 323–324
Hawaii, 17
Health tourism
    diet resorts, 80
    spa resorts, 80
Health of tourists, 445
    diseases contracted while traveling, 445
    prevention of problems, 445
    See also Public health
Historic associations, examples of locations for, 91–92
Historic routes, 246
Historic sites, 80–82
    damage as environmental impact, 347
    examples of, 80–82
    forms of, 279
    planning/managing resources, 278–280
    recent developments, 82
    towns, planning, 242–245
History of area, in tourism planning, 58
History of tourism, 3–12
    ancient times, 3–4
    eighteenth century, 6–8
    Grand Tour, 6
    Middle Ages, 4–5
    nineteenth century, 8
    Renaissance, 5–6
    road networks and, 4
    twentieth century, 8
Holiday villages, 113–114
Host/guest relationship, 366–368

Hotels
  as attraction, 90
  classification system, 115, 326-327
  types of, 112-113
Houseboats, 113
Human resources evaluation, in manpower planning, 406
Hungary, thermal spa locational analysis, 154-157
Hunting tourism, 89-90, 249-250

Iceland, legislation on organization of tourism, 424-426
Implementation of plan
  adjustments to plan, 450
  adoption of plan, 449
  approach to, 429-430
  coordination of public/private sectors, 430-431
  funding, 450
  governmental role in, 430
  integration into public/private sector, 449
  monitoring of tourism, 450
  parks/conservation areas/cultural programs, 436-437
  periodic review of plan, 450
  plan review, 448
  project planning/development, 437-439
  staging/programming at national/regional levels, 431-432
  tour programming, 435-436
  zoning/facility regulations, 432-435
Improvements, to existing resorts, 218-219
Incentives. See Investment incentives
Inception report, 44
Industrial Revolution, 6
Information services. See Tourist information services
Infrastructure, 39, 177
  community services, 124
  cost analysis, 141
  demand analysis, 141
  drainage, 124
  electric power, 122
  employee services, 124
  government financing of, 421
  importance of, 119
  improvement as environmental impact, 343-344
  new technologies and, 446-447
  overload, avoiding, 184
  projections for, 140-141
  sewage disposal, 123
  solid waste disposal, 123
  surveys of, 119-124
  telecommunications, 123-124
  use of term, 119
  water supply, 121-122
Institutional elements, 39
Institutional-related survey
  capital, availability of, 64
  governmental structures, 62-63
  investment policies, 64
  legislation/regulations, 64
  political ideologies, 63
  present policies/plans for development, 62
  tourism programs, 64-65

tourism structures, 63
Integrated analysis
  economic patterns, 142
  factors in, 177
  physical elements, 142
  sociocultural analysis, 142-143
Integrated resorts, 162
International events, 63
International level, tourism planning, 34-35
International tourism organizations, 418-419
International Union for Conservation of Nature and Natural Resources, 79
Inter-Parliamentary Conference on Tourism, 33
Investment incentives
  adjustment of, 422
  case example, Portugal, 427-428
  nature of project and, 424
  pioneer development and, 424
  types of, 423
Investment policies, 421-422
  financing of infrastructure and, 421
  government and, 421-422
  pre-implementation requirements, 422
  tourism planning and, 64

Joint Declaration of the World Tourism Organization, 32

Kyongju, 200-201

Land area requirement, 176
Land availability, 178
Landscaping
  design standards, 321-323
  planting functions, 322
  standards for, 317
Land tenure, survey of, 60
Land use
  patterns, survey of, 60
  planning, 37
  requirements, resort planning and, 208-211
Langudoc-Roussillon, 415
L'Anse aux Meadows, 349
Lascaux cave paintings, 291
Las Vegas, 88
Legislation, 64
  case examples, Iceland, 424-426
  directly related tourism legislation, 419
  related laws/regulations, 419-420
Lewis and Clark expedition trail, 246
Local building materials, use of, 320
Local styles/motifs, 320
Location of region, survey of, 56

Machu Picchu, 145
Maldives, environmental impact assessment, 358-362
Malta
  environmental analysis, 151-152

Malta (cont'd.)
   marketing plan, 451-454
   survey/evaluation of attractions, 98-99
   tourism planning process, 67-69
   tourism development plan, 187-188
Mammouth Cave, 79
Manila Declaration of the World Tourism Organization, 32
Manpower planning
   corporate level, 410
   education/training, 408-410
   evaluation of present manpower, 404-405
   human resources evaluation, 406
   importance of, 403
   monitoring/updating manpower plan, 410-411
   planning table, 407
   projection of future needs, 405-406
Mardi Gras, 85
Marinas/piers
   as natural attraction, 78
   standards, 325
Marine conservation, 343, 346
Market analysis
   necessity of, 132
   projection techniques, 133-134
   time factors, 134
Marketing
   case example, Malta, 451-454
   objectives/strategy, formulation of, 442-443
   promotion program, 443-444
   tourist information services, 444-445
Matrix evaluation technique, in planning analysis, 95
Mauna Lani, Hawaii, resort planning, 225-228
Mayan Road, 34-35
Medical facilities, evaluation of, 118
Middle Ages
   religious pilgrimages, 5
   travel in, 4-5
Modelling, archeological sites, 349
Monaco, 88
Money exchange services, evaluation of, 118
Mongolia
   survey/evaluation of attractions, 99-103
   transportation analysis, 125-127
Monitoring
   of development plan, 451
   of tourism, 450
   in tourism planning process, 54-55
Motor lodges/motor hotels, 113, 167
Mountain climbing, 249
Mountain tourism, 168-169
Mount Fuji, 276-277
Multiplier effect
   formula for, 387
   measure of economic impact, 386-387
Museums
   as cultural attraction, 85
   planning/managing resources, 285-286, 290

National planning
   case examples

     Burma, 185-187
     Malta, 187-188
     Northern Ireland, 192-196
     Zanzibar, 188-192
   clustering of attractions development, 181-182
   gateway area concept, 180-181
   infrastructure aspects, 184
   seasonality, 184-185
   staging of development, 185
   tourism planning, 35
   tourism regions, establishment of, 182-183
Nationals resident abroad, 21
National Tourism Administration, 415-416
   functions of, 415-416
   staffing of, 416
National Tourism Policy Act, 411
Natural attractions
   beaches, 78
   climate, 77-78
   conservation areas, 79-80
   environmental features, 79
   flora/fauna, 78-79
   marine areas, 78
   scenic beauty, 78
Natural resource areas, survey of, 57-58
Natural resource attraction planning, 272-278
   park use, management of, 275-276
   planning approach, 272-273
   principles in, 273-275
   process/techniques, 273
   regional management approach, 276-277
   specialized nature facilities, 277-278
Nature tourism, 167
Nepal, 29, 249
New Caledonia, 88
Niue, 253
Noise pollution, as environmental impact, 345
Northern Ireland, tourism development plan, 192-196
Nugent, Thomas, 6
Nusa Dua, Bali, resort planning, 220-225
Nusa Tenggara, Indonesia, tourism planning process,
   65-67

Objectives
   in tourism planning, 51-52, 174, 176
Olympics, 4, 88
On-the-job training, 409
Operation Facelift, 447
Opportunities/constraints, identification of, 143-144
Organizational structures. See Tourism organizations
Overcrowding, tourism and, 372

Panama, 250
Parking, offstreet, standards for, 317
Parks
   as natural attraction, 79-80, 437
   See also Conservation areas
Parks Canada policy, 272
Pedestrianization, urban tourism, 240

Pensions, 113
Pera Hera, 85
Performing arts, planning/managing resources, 282-283
Personal services, evaluation of, 117
Physical planning department, zoning and, 435
Pioneer development, investment incentives, 424
Planning, general, 25-28
    basic process in, 28
    community involvement, 27, 29
    flexible approach, 26-27
    integrated approach, 27
    master plan, 26
    systems approach, 27, 29
    types of planning activities, 25-26
    See also Tourism planning
Political ideologies, tourism planning and, 63
Political stability, tourism and, 92
Polynesian Cultural Center, 284
Population characteristics, survey of, 59
Portugal, investment incentives, 427-428
Postal services, evaluation of, 119
Prater, 86
Prefeasibility assessment, 40
Private sector
    coordination with public sector, 430-431
    funding of tourism products, 416, 418
    tourism organizations, 418
Projection techniques, market analysis, 133-134
Project planning/development, 437-439
    coordination and, 439
    feasibility analysis, 437
    funding, 438
    site selection, 437
    steps in, 439
Project Tiger, 79
Promotion program, 443-444
    convention tourism, 444
    types of activities in, 443-444
Public access, standards for, 317-318
Public corporation, tourism development, 414
Public health
    standards, 326
    tourism and, 92
Public safety
    evaluation of, 118
    urban tourism, 241
Public sector, coordination with private sector, 430-431
Public tourism organizations, 412, 414-415
    autonomous development corporation, 414
    board/committee, 414-415
    forms of, 412, 414
    large scale projects and, 415
    most effective approach to, 414
    National Tourism Administration, 415-416
Pyramids, 4

Railway, early tourism and, 7-8
Receptive services, 38
Recommendations, in tourism planning process, 54
Recreational vehicles, 113, 168

Recreation facilities
    as attraction, 89-90
    planning/managing resources, 290
Reef conservation, 343, 346
Regional level
    development of tourism regions, 182-183
    regional management, natural resource attractions,
        276-277
    regional relationships, resort planning and, 205
    tourism planning, 35-36
Regulations
    tourism planning and, 64
    zoning, 435
    See also Legislation
Religious pilgrimages, 5
    examples of locations for, 91
    planning for, 258
Renaissance, travel in, 5-6
Reno, 88
Reports
    draft final report, 44
    draft reports, 44
    final report, 44
    inception reports, 44
    learning from other reports, 55
    in tourism planning process, 55
    tourism project, 43-44
Residential tourism
    benefits/problems to area, 256-257
    forms of, 165-166
    planning for, 256-257
Residents, as cultural attraction, 85
Resort-based tourism
    as attraction, 90
    integrated resorts, 162
    retreat resorts, 163
    town resorts, 162
Resort Municipality of Whistler, resort planning, 228-233
Resort planning
    basic principles, 212-214
    case examples
        Mauna Lani, Hawaii, 225-228
        Nusa Dua, Bali, 220-225
        Resort Municipality of Whistler, 228-233
    facility/land use/infrastructure requirements, 208-211
    financial plan, 216-217
    general approach, 199-200, 201-205
    improvements to existing resorts, 218-219
    plan formulation, steps in, 214-216
    regional relationships, 205
    site environmental analysis, 205-208
    team approach, 204
    time aspects, 203
Restaurants
    evaluation of, 116-117
    standards, 326-327
Retreat resorts, 163
Review of plan, 448
Revision of plan, 450
River boat tourism, 165
    planning for, 254

Road networks
    Chinese, 4
    Roman, 4
Roads, standards, 324
Rome, ancient, 4
Roof lines, 320
Rural tourism, 166

Safari tourism, 168
Safety of area, tourism and, 92
Salt roads, 246
San Diego, 239
San Diego Zoo, 79
San Francisco, 242
San Juan, historic district, 244
Scenic beauty, as natural attraction, 78
Seaside resorts
    ancient, 4
    eighteenth/nineteenth centuries, 6-7
Seasonality
    and carrying capacities, 147
    reduction of, 184-185
Second homes. See Residential tourism
Self-catering units, 114-115
Senegal, 250
Sewage disposal, evaluation of, 123
Shopping
    as attraction, 86-87
    duty-free goods, 87
    encouraging higher expenditures, 383
    evaluation of facilities, 117
    examples of stores, 87
Siena, 242
Signs, control of, 318
Silk roads, 246
Site coverage, standards for, 316
Site development standards, 309-318
    building heights, 311
    building setbacks, 313
    establishment of, 310
    floor area ratio, 315
    landscaping, 317
    offstreet parking, 317
    public access, 317-318
    sign controls, 318
    site coverage, 316
    types of, 310
    underground utility lines, 318
    unit densities, 311
Site planning factors
    building relationships, 305
    environmental hazards, avoiding, 304-305
    views, maintaining, 307-309
Six Flags parks, 86
Smuggling, arts/artifacts, 286-287
Social problems, tourism and, 374
Social tourism, 169
Sociocultural analysis, 142
Sociocultural programming, 378
    case example, Zanzibar, 396-399

Sociocultural surveys
    cultural patterns, 59
    population characteristics, 59
Socioeconomic impacts
    conservation of cultural heritage, 370
    control measures, 376-378
    cross-cultural exchange, 371
    cultural impacts, 372-374
    economic/employment distortions, 372
    economic impacts, 368, 370, 371
    host/guest relationship and, 366-368
    overcrowding, 372
    renewal of cultural pride, 370-371
    social problems, 374
Socioeconomic policies, general policies, 375-376
Socioeconomic programming, case example, Bali, 390-396
Solid waste disposal
    evaluation of, 123
    standards, 325
Spa resorts, 80
Special events, as attraction, 88
Special interest tourism, 163-164
    case example, Bhutan, 259-263
    planning for, 245-247
Sports events, as attraction, 88
Sports facilities, as attraction, 89-90
Sports tourism, planning/managing resources, 289
Sri Lanka, tourism planning process, 72-73
Staged authenticity, 284
Staging
    on national/regional level, 431-432
    steps in, 432
Standards
    application of, 328-329
    case examples
        Wachusett ski resort, 332-334
        Zanzibar sport fishing hotel plan, 329-332
    design standards, 318-326
    importance of, 303-304
    site development standards, 309-318
    tourist facility standards, 326-328
Statutory board, tourism development, 412, 413
St. Katherine's Dock, 237
Study tours, tourism training, 409
Subregional level, tourism planning, 36-37
Surveys
    analysis/synthesis of information, 53
    of attractions, 93-95
    economic survey, 60
    environmental quality survey, 60-61
    facilities/services, 111-119
    geographic survey, 55-58
    infrastructure surveys, 119-124
    institutional-related surveys, 62-65
    land use surveys, 60
    process of conducting, 52
    sociocultural survey, 59
    special surveys, 53
    See also specific types of surveys
Sustainable tourism development, 32-34

Action Strategy plan, 459-467
Systems approach, to planning, 27, 29

Team members, tourism project, 41-42
Telecommunications
    evaluation of, 123-124
    standards, 325
Terms of reference
    model for national development plan, 469-486
    tourism project, 40-41
Theme, resort planning and, 212
Theme parks
    development of, 86
    examples of, 86
    nature of, 86
    planning/managing resources, 287-288
Time-sharing, 115
Tivoli Gardens, 86
Tonga, 254-255
Topography, survey of, 56
Tourism
    components of system, 22
    contemporary trends, 12-15
    economic impact, 10-11
    history of, 3-12
    new products, 14
    problems related to, 15-16
    purpose of, 15
    reasons for, 16-17
    statistical information related to, 9-11
Tourism Action Plan, Ltd., 447
Tourism Bill of Rights and Tourist Code, 32-33
Tourism development
    components of, 38-40
    facility design, 37-38
    facility site planning, 37
    land use planning, 37
    special studies, 38
Tourism organizations
    case example, Tourism Action Plan, Ltd., 447
    financing of, 416, 418
    importance of, 411-412
    international tourism organizations, 418-419
    National Tourism Administration, 415-416
    private sector organizations, 418
    public organizational models, 412, 414-415
Tourism planning
    alternative plans, 178
    elements in approach to, 29-30
    environmental planning, 32-34
    finalizing plans, 180
    importance of, 15-17
    on international level, 34-35
    on national level, 35
    preparation of plans, 17-18
    reference material related to, 31
    on regional level, 35-36
    special aspects of, 30-31
    on subregional level, 36-37
    terminology related to, 31

Tourism planning process
    analysis/synthesis of information, 53
    case studies
        Fiji, 69-71
        Malta, 67-69
        Nusa Tenggara,Indonesia, 65-67
        Sri Lanka, 72-73
    goals/objectives in, 51-52
    implementation/monitoring, 54-55
    institutional elements, survey of, 62-65
    outline of planning report, 55
    plan formulation, 53-54, 174-180
    recommendations, 54
    study preparation, 49, 51
    surveys, 52-53, 55-61
Tourism plans
    international agencies and, 18
    preparation of, 17-18
Tourism policy
    approach to formulation of, 170
    on extent of tourism development, 173
    on growth rate of tourism, 173
    location/staging of development, 173-174
    reasons for development of, 172
    role of government, 171-172
    sustainable development and, 172
    on type of tourism for development, 173
Tourism project
    coordination of, 42
    funding, 45
    prefeasibility assessment, 40
    project work program, 43
    reports, 43-44
    team members, 41-42
    terms of reference, 40-41
Tourist
    arrivals/characteristics, 107-109
    definition of, 18-21
    domestic tourist, 21
    compared to excursionists, 19
Tourist information services, 444-445
    accuracy of information and, 444-445
    evaluation of, 117
    importance of, 444
Tourist markets
    cruise ship tourists, 109-110
    tourism trends, 110-111
    tourist arrivals/characteristics, 107-109
    tour operators, 110
    travel patterns, 110
Tour operators, market survey, 110
Tour programming, 435-436
    benefits to region, 436
    design of, 436
    types of tours, 436
Tour/travel operations
    activities of, 116
    local operations, 383
    standards, 327-328
Town resorts, 162
Trade and Convention Center, 87

Training
  formulation of programs, 408-410
  importance of, 410
  training institutions, 409
  types of approaches to, 409
Transportation, 38-39, 177
  case example, Mongolia, 125-127
  evaluation of, 120-121
  planning of, 184
  projections for, 138-140
  unique, as attraction, 90
Transportation-oriented tourism, 167
  planning for, 255-256
Travel facilitation
  improvement of, 446
  meaning of, 446
Travel patterns, market survey, 110
Trekking tourism, 168
Trends, market survey, 110-111
Trip, definition of, 21

Uluru National Park, 274
Unit densities, standards for, 311
United Nations Conference on International Travel and
      Tourism, 18-19
United Nations Development Programme, 18, 65
United Nations Educational, Scientific and Cultural
      Organization, 82
United Nations Environment Programme, 32
United States Agency for International Development, 447
United States Travel and Tourism Administration, 411
Urban areas, as cultural attraction, 83-84
Urban tourism, 163, 167
  constraints to overcome, 239
  good urban design, importance of, 242
  historic towns, 242-245
  planning for, 37
  planning principles, 240-242
  planning procedure, 237-240
  special problems, 236-237
Urban trail system, 240
Utility lines, underground, standards for, 318

Vanuatu, 254
Vava'u, 254-255
Vegetation, survey of, 57
Venice, 242, 291
Verona, 242

Views, site planning factors, 307-309
Viking routes, 246
Viking Village, 82
Village tourism, 166
  case example, Nusa Tenggara, Indonesia, 263-267
  planning for, 250-251
Virgin Islands National Park, 275
Visitor use planning, factors in, 290-292
Visual pollution, as environmental impact, 345

Wachusett ski resort, standards, 332-334
Waikiki, 200
Waste disposal problems, as environmental impact, 345
Water pollution, as environmental impact, 344
Water supply
  evaluation of, 121-122
  standards, 324
Water transport tourism
  cruise ship tourism, 164
  planning for, 253-255
  river boat tourism, 165
  yachting tourism, 165
Wild Animal Park, 79
Wildlife, survey of, 57
Wonderland, 86
Work program, tourism project, 43
World War II battlegrounds, 91

Yachting tourism, 165
  planning for, 254-255
Yellowstone National Park, 76
Yemen, 243
Yosemite National Park, 292
Youth hostels, 113, 258
Youth tourism, 168
  planning for, 258-259

Zambia, wildlife management, 299-310
Zanzibar
  sociocultural programming, 396-399
  sport fishing hotel plan, standards, 329-332
  tourism development plan, 188-192, 487-492
Zoning, 432, 434-435
  areas related to, 432, 434-435
  enforcement, 435
  at national/regional level, 435
  physical planning department and, 435